T0183828

Lecture Notes in Computer Science 11647

Commenced Publication in 1973
Founding and Former Series Editors:
Gerhard Goos, Juris Hartmanis, and Jan van Leeuwen

Editorial Board Members

Piotrek Hofman · Michał Skrzypczak (Eds.)

Developments in Language Theory

23rd International Conference, DLT 2019
Warsaw, Poland, August 5–9, 2019
Proceedings

 Springer

Editors
Piotrek Hofman
University of Warsaw
Warsaw, Poland

Michał Skrzypczak
University of Warsaw
Warsaw, Poland

ISSN 0302-9743   ISSN 1611-3349   (electronic)
Lecture Notes in Computer Science
ISBN 978-3-030-24885-7   ISBN 978-3-030-24886-4   (eBook)
https://doi.org/10.1007/978-3-030-24886-4

LNCS Sublibrary: SL1 – Theoretical Computer Science and General Issues

This Springer imprint is published by the registered company Springer Nature Switzerland AG
The registered company address is: Gewerbestrasse 11, 6330 Cham, Switzerland

Preface

This volume of *Lecture Notes in Computer Science* contains the papers presented at the 23rd International Conference on Developments in Language Theory (DLT 2019) organized by the faculty of Mathematics, Informatics and Mechanics at University of Warsaw in Poland, during August 5–9, 2019.

The DLT conference series is one of the major international conference series in language theory and related areas. Since it was started by G. Rozenberg and A. Salomaa in Turku (1993), it travelled around the world visiting different locations: Magdeburg (1995), Thessaloniki (1997), Aachen (1999), Vienna (2001), Kyoto (2002), Szeged (2003), Auckland (2004), Palermo (2005), Santa Barbara (2006), Turku (2007), Kyoto (2008), Stuttgart (2009), London (2010), Milan (2011), Taipei (2012), Marne-la-Vallée (2013), Ekaterinburg (2014), Liverpool (2015), Montréal (2016), Liège (2017), and Tokyo (2018). In 2019 for the first time it took place in Poland.

The series of International Conference on Developments in Language Theory (DLT) provides a forum for presenting current developments in formal languages and automata. Its scope is very general and includes, among others, the following topics and areas: combinatorial and algebraic properties of words and languages; grammars, acceptors, and transducers for strings, trees, graphs, arrays; algebraic theories for automata and languages; codes; efficient text algorithms; symbolic dynamics; decision problems; relationships to complexity theory and logic; picture description and analysis; polyominoes and bidimensional patterns; cryptography; concurrency; cellular automata; bio-inspired computing; and quantum computing.

There were 33 abstract submissions, among which three were withdrawn, from 20 countries: Belarus, Belgium, Canada, China, Czech Republic, Finland, France, Germany, India, Italy, Japan, Portugal, Russia, Singapore, Slovakia, South Korea, Taiwan, UAE, UK, and USA. Each of the 30 submissions was reviewed by at least three reviewers and thoroughly discussed by Program Committee (PC). The committee decided to accept 20 papers for publication and oral presentation. The volume also includes papers of three invited talks given at the conference.

We warmly thank all the invited speakers and all authors of the submitted papers for making DLT 2019 successful. As the PC chairs, we would like to express our cordial gratitude to the members of the PC and the external reviewers for reviewing the papers, participating in the selection process, and helping to maintain the high standard of the DLT conferences. We appreciate the help of the EasyChair conference system for facilitating our work of organizing DLT 2019 very much. We would like to thank the editorial staff of Springer, in particular Saravanan Gnanaprakasam, Alfred Hofmann, Anna Kramer, and Erika Siebert-Cole, for their guidance and help during the process of publishing this volume.

We also would like to thank Ewelina Sołtan, and all the members of the research support unit at the Faculty of Mathematics, Informatics, and Mechanics at the University of Warsaw for their support. Last but not the least, we are grateful to

Organizing Committee members: Grzegorz Fabiański, Kamila Łyczek, Vincent Michielini, Radosław Piórkowski, and Janusz Schmude. DLT 2019 was financially supported by University of Warsaw, we would like to express our sincere gratitude for their philanthropic support.

We are all looking forward to DLT 2020 at that will be held during May 11–15, 2020, at University of South Florida, Tampa FL, USA.

June 2019   Piotr Hofman
                                                                                 Michał Skrzypczak

Organization

Steering Committee

Marie-Pierre Béal	University of Paris-Est Marne-la-Vallée, France
Mikołaj Bojańczyk	University of Warsaw, Poland
Cristian S. Calude	The University of Auckland, New Zealand
Volker Diekert	University of Stuttgart, Germany
Yo-Sub Han	Yonsei University, Seoul, Republic of Korea
Juraj Hromkovic	Swiss Federal Institute of Technology in Zurich, Switzerland
Oscar H. Ibarra	University of California, Santa Barbara, USA
Nataša Jonoska	University of South Florida, USA
Juhani Karhumäki	University of Turku, Finland
Martin Kutrib	University of Giessen, Germany
Giovanni Pighizzini	University of Milan, Italy
Michel Rigo	University of Liège, Belgium
Antonio Restivo	University of Palermo, Italy
Wojciech Rytter	University of Warsaw, Poland
Kai Salomaa	Queen's University at Kingston, Ontario, Canada
Shinnosuke Seki	University of Electro-Communications, Tokyo, Japan
Mikhail Volkov	Ural Federal University, Ekaterinburg, Russia
Takashi Yokomori	Waseda University, Tokyo, Japan

Program Committee

Jacques Duparc	University of Lausanne, Switzerland
Pierre Ganty	IMDEA Research, Spain and Université de Bruxelles, Belgium
Paweł Gawrychowski	University of Wrocław, Poland
Tero Harju	University of Turku, Finland
Kenji Hashimoto	Nagoya University, Japan
Piotrek Hofman (Co-chair)	University of Warsaw, Poland
Tomohiro I.	Kyushu Institute of Technology, Japan
Denis Kuperberg	École normale superieure de Lyon, France
Christof Löding	RWTH Aachen University, Germany
Amaldev Manuel	Indian Institute of Technology Goa, India
Thomas Place	Université de Bordeaux, France
Svetlana Puzynina	Sobolev Institute of Mathematics, Russia
Karin Quaas	Leipzig University, Germany
Cristian Riveros	Pontifical Catholic University of Chile, Chile
Krishna S.	Indian Institute of Technology, Bombay, India
Philippe Schnoebelen	Laboratoire Spécification et Vérification, France
Marinella Sciortino	University of Palermo, Italy

Michał Skrzypczak (Chair)	University of Warsaw, Poland
Mikhail Volkov	Ural Federal University, Russia
James Worrell	University of Oxford, UK
Georg Zetzsche	Max Planck Institute for Software Systems, Germany

Organizing Committee

Grzegorz Fabiański	Support
Piotrek Hofman	Co-chair
Kamila Łyczek	Graphic Designer
Vincent Michielini	Support
Radosław Piórkowski	Webmaster
Janusz Schmude	Brochure Editor
Michał Skrzypczak	Chair

Additional Reviewers

Bartłomiej Dudek
Ramanathan Thinniyam
Abhisekh Sankaran
Sarah Winter
Elise Vandomme
Irène Marcovici
Martin Sulzmann
Olga Parshina
Mahsa Shirmohammadi
Mikhail Berlinkov
Matthias Niewerth
Simone Rinaldi
Christian Choffrut
Ulrich Ultes-Nitsche
Zhimin Sun
Carton Olivier
Benjamin Hellouin de Menibus
Arseny Shur
Alessandro De Luca
Andrea Frosini
Vladimir Gusev
Pablo Rotondo
Laurent Doyen

Lucas Martinelli Tabajara
Marek Szykuła
Simon Iosti
Benedikt Bollig
A. V. Sreejith
Stefan Göller
Aleksi Saarela
Kenny Zhuo Ming Lu
Flavio Dalessandro
Anup Basil Mathew
Natalie Schluter
Dmitry Chistikov
Eryk Kopczynski
Dmitry Ananichev
Yasunori Ishihara
Cyril Nicaud
Moses Ganardi
Sylvain Lombardy
Olivier Carton
Markus L. Schmid
Giuseppa Castiglione
Dominik Köppl

Contents

Invited Papers

Inherent Size Blowup in ω-Automata

Udi Boker[⊠]

Interdisciplinary Center (IDC) Herzliya, Herzliya, Israel
udiboker@gmail.com

Abstract. We clarify the succinctness of the different ω-automata types and the size blowup involved in boolean operations on them. We argue that there are good reasons for the classic acceptance conditions, while there is also place for additional acceptance conditions, especially in the deterministic setting; Boolean operations on deterministic automata with the classic acceptance conditions involve an exponential size blowup, which can be avoided by using stronger acceptance conditions. In particular, we analyze the combination of hyper-Rabin and hyper-Streett automata, which we call *hyper-dual*, and show that in the deterministic setting it allows for exponential succinctness compared to the classic types, boolean operations on it only involve a quadratic size blowup, and its nonemptiness, universality, and containment checks are in PTIME.

Keywords: ω-automata · Size blowup · Acceptance conditions

1 Introduction

Automata on infinite words, often called ω-automata, were introduced in the 1960s in the course of solving decision problems in logic, and since the 1980s they play a key role in formal verification of reactive systems. Unlike automata on finite words, these automata have various acceptance conditions (types), the most classic of which are weak, Büchi, co-Büchi, parity, Rabin, Streett, and Muller.

There are good reasons for having multiple acceptance conditions in ω-automata: each is closely connected to some other formalisms and logics, and has its advantages and disadvantages with respect to succinctness and to the complexity of resolving decision problems on it (see [6]).

There is a massive literature on the translations between the different automata types, accumulated along the past 55 years, and continuing to these days. (See, for example, [4,8,14,17,25,27,32–34,36,37,41].) Having "only" seven classic types, where each can be deterministic or nondeterministic, we have 175 possible non-self translations between them, which has become difficult to follow. Moreover, it turns out that there is inconsistency in the literature results concerning the size of automata—Some only consider the number of states, some

This work was supported by the Israel Science Foundation grant 1373/16.

P. Hofman and M. Skrzypczak (Eds.): DLT 2019, LNCS 11647, pp. 3–17, 2019.
https://doi.org/10.1007/978-3-030-24886-4_1

also take into account the index (namely, the size of the acceptance condition), while ignoring the alphabet size, and some do consider the alphabet size, but ignore the index.

To make an order with all of these results, we maintain a website [3] that provides information and references for each of the possible translations. The high-level tables of the size blowup and of the state blowup involved in the translations are given in Table 1.

There are many works on the complementation of nondeterministic ω-automata (see [38] for a survey until 2007, after which there are yet many new results), while very few on boolean operations on deterministic ω-automata. This is possibly because nondeterministic automata are exponentially more succinct than deterministic ones and are adequate for model checking. However, in recent years there is a vast progress in synthesis and in probabilistic model checking, which require deterministic or almost deterministic automata, such as limit-deterministic [39] or good-for-games automata [7,9,21].

In [6], we completed the picture of the size blowup involved in boolean operations on the classic ω-automata types, as summarized in Table 2. Observe that all of the classic ω-regular-complete automata types, namely parity, Rabin, Streett, and Muller, admit in the deterministic setting an exponential size blowup on boolean operations, even on the positive ones of union and intersection.

Indeed, the problem with boolean operations on classic deterministic automata and the current interest in the deterministic setting, may explain the emergence of new, or renewed, automata types in the past seven years. Among these are "Emerson-Lei" (EL), which was presented in 1985 [18], and was recently "rediscovered" within the "Hanoi" format [1], "generalized-Rabin" [24], and "generalized-Streett" [2]. The EL condition allows for an arbitrary boolean formula over sets of states that are visited finitely or infinitely often, generalized-Rabin extends the Rabin pairs into lists, and generalized-Streett analogously extends Streett pairs.

While boolean operations on EL automata are obviously simple, it is known that its nonemptiness check is NP-complete [18] and its universality check is EXPSPACE-complete [20].

We analyzed in [6] additional non-classic acceptance conditions, and showed that there is no inherent reason for having an exponential size blowup in positive boolean operations on deterministic ω-regular-complete automata that admit a PTIME nonemptiness check: We observed that generalized-Rabin is a special case of a disjunction of Streett conditions, which was already considered in 1985 under the name "canonical form" [18], and which we dubbed "hyper-Rabin". We showed that it may be exponentially more succinct than the classic types, it allows for union and intersection with only a quadratic size blowup, and its nonemptiness check is in PTIME (see Tables 2 and 3). Indeed, there seem to also be practical benefits for generalized-Rabin automata [13,19,24], which may possibly be extended to the more general hyper-Rabin condition.

We further analyze in Sect. 5 the possibility of deterministic ω-regular-complete automata that admit PTIME algorithms for nonemptiness, universality, and containment checks, and for which all boolean operations, including complementation, only involve a quadratic size blowup. We show that it is indeed possible with an approach that upfront seems to only bring redundancy—maintaining a pair of equivalent automata, one with the hyper-Rabin condition and one with its dual (hyper-Streett) condition. We call such a pair a *hyper-dual* automaton. Observe that in the deterministic setting, it is the same as a pair of hyper-Rabin automata, one for a language L and one for its complement $\overline{L}$.

One may wonder what benefit can we have from a deterministic hyper-dual automaton, having inner automata for both L and $\overline{L}$, rather than having an automaton only for L, and complementing it when necessary. We list below some of the benefits:

– A deterministic hyper-dual automaton, despite having a pair of inner automata for both L and $\overline{L}$, is at most twice the size of classic automata, such as Rabin and Streett, and may be exponentially more succinct than them. (Propositions 2 and 7).
– The approach of maintaining an automaton and its complement obviously allows for "free" complementation, yet it might have a price in union and intersection. For example, a pair of equivalent deterministic automata, one with the Rabin condition and one with its dual (Streett) condition, would have an exponential size blowup on both union and intersection. The hyper-dual combination is strong enough to prevent this price, and not too strong for preserving decision problems in PTIME.
– In some scenarios, an automaton is generated iteratively, starting with a basic one, and enlarging it with consecutive boolean operations. In such scenarios, a hyper-dual automaton may have a big advantage—its initial generation is not more difficult than of Rabin or Streett automata, and each boolean operation only involves up to a quadratic size blowup, while preserving the ability to check nonemptiness, universality, and containment in PTIME.
– Compared to complementing a hyper-Rabin automaton on demand:

  • In theory, a deterministic hyper-Rabin automaton can always be complemented into a hyper-Streett automaton that is not bigger than the corresponding hyper-dual automaton. Yet, the complementation procedure is exponential, and does not guarantee the smallest possible hyper-Streett automaton. Hence, having in a hyper-dual automaton a small hyper-Streett automaton in addition to the hyper-Rabin automaton provides a significant potential advantage.
  • In iterative generations, complementation need not be made over and over again, size optimizations would take into account both the hyper-Rabin and hyper-Streett conditions, and progress is guaranteed to be homogenous with no heavy steps in the middle.
  • When expressing some property with only a hyper-Rabin automaton in mind, it might be that we generate a small initial automaton whose complementation would involve an exponential size blowup. Targeting hyper-dual automata, we may limit ourselves to properties that can be expressed with small hyper-dual automata, which then guarantees easy boolean operations.

2 ω-Automata and Their Acceptance Conditions

A *nondeterministic automaton* is a tuple $\mathcal{A} = \langle \Sigma, Q, \delta, \iota, \alpha \rangle$, where Σ is the input alphabet, Q is a finite set of states, $\delta : Q \times \Sigma \to 2^Q$ is a transition function, $\iota \subseteq Q$ is a set of initial states, and α is an acceptance condition. If $|\iota| = 1$ and for every $q \in Q$ and $\sigma \in \Sigma$, we have $|\delta(q, \sigma)| \leq 1$, we say that $\mathcal{A}$ is *deterministic*.

A *run* $r = r(0), r(1), \cdots$ of $\mathcal{A}$ on an infinite word $w = w(0) \cdot w(1) \cdots \in \Sigma^\omega$ is an infinite sequence of states such that $r(0) \in \iota$, and for every $i \geq 0$, we have $r(i+1) \in \delta(r(i), w(i))$. An automaton accepts a word if it has an accepting run on it (as defined below, according to the acceptance condition). The language of $\mathcal{A}$, denoted by $L(\mathcal{A})$, is the set of words that $\mathcal{A}$ accepts. We also say that $\mathcal{A}$ *recognizes* the language $L(\mathcal{A})$. Two automata, $\mathcal{A}$ and $\mathcal{A}'$, are *equivalent* iff $L(\mathcal{A}) = L(\mathcal{A}')$.

Acceptance is defined with respect to the set *inf(r)* of states that the run r visits infinitely often. Formally, $inf(r) = \{q \in Q \mid$ for infinitely many $i \in \mathbb{N}$, we have $r(i) = q\}$.

We start with describing the most classic acceptance conditions, after which we will describe some additional ones.

- *Büchi*, where $\alpha \subseteq Q$, and r is accepting iff $inf(r) \cap \alpha \neq \emptyset$.
- *co-Büchi*, where $\alpha \subseteq Q$, and r is accepting iff $inf(r) \cap \alpha = \emptyset$.
- *weak* is a special case of the Büchi condition, where every strongly connected component of the automaton is either contained in α or disjoint to α.
- *parity*, where $\alpha = \{S_1, S_2, \ldots, S_{2k}\}$ with $S_1 \subset S_2 \subset \cdots \subset S_{2k} = Q$, and r is accepting iff the minimal i for which $inf(r) \cap S_i \neq \emptyset$ is even.
- *Rabin*, where $\alpha = \{\langle B_1, G_1 \rangle, \langle B_2, G_2 \rangle, \ldots, \langle B_k, G_k \rangle\}$, with $B_i, G_i \subseteq Q$ and r is accepting iff for some $i \in [1..k]$, we have $inf(r) \cap B_i = \emptyset$ and $inf(r) \cap G_i \neq \emptyset$.
- *Streett*, where $\alpha = \{\langle B_1, G_1 \rangle, \langle B_2, G_2 \rangle, \ldots, \langle B_k, G_k \rangle\}$, with $B_i, G_i \subseteq Q$ and r is accepting iff for all $i \in [1..k]$, we have $inf(r) \cap B_i = \emptyset$ or $inf(r) \cap G_i \neq \emptyset$.
- *Muller*, where $\alpha = \{\alpha_1, \alpha_2, \ldots, \alpha_k\}$, with $\alpha_i \subseteq Q$ and r is accepting iff for some $i \in [1..k]$, we have $inf(r) = \alpha_i$.

Notice that Büchi and co-Büchi are special cases of the parity condition, which is in turn a special case of both the Rabin and Streett conditions.

Two additional types that are in common usage are:

- *very weak (linear)* is a special case of the Büchi (and weak) condition, where all cycles are of size one (self loops).
- *generalized Büchi*, where $\alpha = \{\alpha_1, \alpha_2, \ldots, \alpha_k\}$, with $\alpha_i \subseteq Q$ and r is accepting iff for every $i \in [1..k]$, we have $inf(r) \cap \alpha_i \neq \emptyset$.

A general way of describing an acceptance condition was given by Emerson and Lei in 1985 [18]: For a set S of states, we define that *Inf(S)* holds in a run r if $S \cap inf(r) \neq \emptyset$ and *Fin(S)* holds otherwise. Then,

- *Emerson-Lei* is an arbitrary boolean formula over *Fin* and *Inf* of sets of states. (A positive boolean formula is enough, as $\neg Fin(S) = Inf(S)$.)

Using the Emerson-Lei notation, we define below some additional types that were defined (or renewed) in recent years.

- *Generalized-Rabin:* $\bigvee_{i=1}^{n} Fin(B_i) \wedge Inf(G_{i_1}) \wedge Inf(G_{i_2}) \wedge \ldots \wedge Inf(G_{i_{k_i}})$.
- *Generalized-Streett:* $\bigwedge_{i=1}^{n} Inf(G_i) \vee Fin(B_{i_1}) \vee Fin(B_{i_2}) \vee \ldots \vee Fin(B_{i_{k_i}})$.
- *Hyper-Rabin:* $\bigvee_{i=1}^{n} \bigwedge_{j=1}^{m} Fin(B_{i,j}) \vee Inf(G_{i,j})$.
- *Hyper-Streett:* $\bigwedge_{i=1}^{n} \bigvee_{j=1}^{m} Fin(B_{i,j}) \wedge Inf(G_{i,j})$.

Another related type is *circuit* [22], which further shortens Emerson-Lei, by representing the acceptance formula as a boolean circuit. In Sect. 5, we also consider the combination of hyper-Rabin and hyper-Streett automata, which we call *hyper-dual*. Very-weak, weak, and co-Büchi automata, as well as deterministic Büchi automata, are less expressive than the other automata types, which recognize all ω-regular languages.

The *index* of an automaton is the length of the boolean formula describing its acceptance condition. For the more standard types, this definition coincides with the standard definition of index: The number of sets in the generalized-Büchi, parity, and Muller conditions, the number of pairs in the Rabin and Streett conditions, and 1 in the very-weak, weak, co-Büchi, and Büchi conditions.

The *size* of an automaton is the maximum size of its elements; that is, it is the maximum of the alphabet size, the number of states, the number of transitions, and the index.

3   Succinctness

Size Versus Number of States. Out of the four elements that constitute the size of an automaton, the number of states and the index are the dominant ones.

Considering the alphabet, the common practice is to provide the upper bounds for arbitrary alphabets and to seek lower bounds with fixed alphabets. For example, [28] strengthen the lower bound of [30] by moving to a fixed alphabet, and [41] starts with automata over a rich alphabet and then moves to a fixed alphabet. It turns out that this approach works well for all relevant translations, eliminating the influence of the alphabet. As for the number of transitions, they are bounded by the size of the alphabet times quadratically the number of states, and the transition blowup tends to go hand in hand with the state blowup.

Considering the number of states and index, one cannot get the full picture by studying their blowup separately, as they are interconnected, and sometimes have a trade-off between them. For example, one can translate a Streett automaton to a Rabin automaton with an exponential state blowup and no index blowup [14] as well as with only a quadratic state blowup and an exponential index blowup [5]. Therefore, there is only a quadratic inevitable state blowup and no inevitable index blowup. Yet, there is an exponential inevitable size blowup [5].

The high-level tables of the size blowup and of the state blowup involved in the translations of automata with classic acceptance conditions are given in Table 1. The size blowup relates to an automaton of size n, and the state blowup to an automaton with n states (and index as large as desired).

Table 1. Size blowup and state blowup involved in automata translations [3].

Size Blowup To / From	Deterministic							Nondeterministic						
	W	C	B	P	R	S	M	W	C	B	P	R	S	M
Det. W	·							·						
C		·							·	$\Theta(n)$				
B			·	$\Theta(n)$						·				
P				·			$2^{\Theta(n)}$			$\Theta(n^2)$	·			$2^{\Theta(n)}$
R		$2^{\Theta(n)}$			·	$\Theta(2^{n\log n})$			$O(n^2)\ \Omega(n)$		$O(n^2)\ \Omega(n)$	·	$O(n^2)\ \Omega(n)$	
S			$2^{\Theta(n)}$			·			$\Theta(n)$		$2^{\Theta(n)}$		·	
M	$O(n^2)\ \Omega(n)$	?		$O(2^{n\log n})\ 2^{\Omega(n)}$			·	$O(n^2)\ \Omega(n)$		$\Theta(n^3)$		$\Theta(n^2)$		·
Non-Det. W	·							·						
C		$2^{\Theta(n)}$							·	$\Theta(n)$				
B				$2^{\Theta(n\log n)}$		$*^1$				·				$2^{\Theta(n)}$
P						$2^{2^{\Omega(n)}}$			$\Theta(n^2)$	·			
R			$*^2$	$2^{\Theta(n^2\log n)}$			$2^{\Theta(n)}$			$O(n^2)\ \Omega(n)$	·	$O(n^2)\ \Omega(n)$	
S						·						·	
M			$*^3$	$2^{O(n^3\log n)}\ 2^{\Omega(n\log n)}$						$\Theta(n^3)$		$\Theta(n^2)$	·

State Blowup To / From	Deterministic							Nondeterministic						
	W	C	B	P	R	S	M	W	C	B	P	R	S	M
Det. W	·							·						
C		·	$\Theta(n)$						·	$\Theta(n)$				
B			·							·				
P				·						$\Theta(n^2)$	·			
R		$2^{\Theta(n)}$			·	$\Theta(2^{n\log n})$	·		$\Theta(n)$		$2^{\Theta(n)}$	·		
S			$2^{\Theta(n)}$									$\Theta(n^2)$	·	
M						·							·
Non-Det. W	·							·						
C		$2^{\Theta(n)}$							·	$\Theta(n)$				
B				$2^{\Theta(n\log n)}$						·				
P									$\Theta(n^2)$	·			
R			?	$2^{2^{\Theta(n)}}$			$2^{\Theta(n)}$				·		
S			$*^4$	?	$*^5$	?	$*^4$				$\Theta(n^2)$	·	
M			?	$2^{2^{\Theta(n)}}$									·

$*^1$: Upper bounds between $2^{2^{O(n)}}$ and $2^{2^{O(n^3\log n)}}$ $*^2$: To DBW: $2^{\Omega(n\log n)}$
$*^3$: Lower bound to DBW: $2^{\Omega(n)}$ $*^4$: $2^{O(n^2\log n)}$ and $2^{\Omega(n\log n)}$ $*^5$: $2^{\Theta(n^2\log n)}$

The capital letters stand for the type names: Weak, Co-Büchi, Büchi, etc. A question mark in the tables stands for an exponential gap between the currently known lower and upper bounds. The size blowup involved in the translations of the stronger acceptance conditions, as discussed in Sect. 5, is given in Table 4.

Inevitable: Succinctness + Complementation $\geq$ Double-Exp. Aside from the translations between specific automata types, one may wonder what might be the succinctness of an arbitrary, possibly yet unknown, automaton type. It turns out that there is an inherent tradeoff between the succinctness of an automaton and the size blowup involved in its complementation—It is shown in [35] that there is a family of ω-regular languages $\{L_n\}_{n\geq 1}$, such that for every n, there is an Emerson-Lei automaton of size n for L_n, while every ω-automaton for $\overline{L_n}$ has at least 2^{2^n} states.

Hence, for an automaton of some type T whose complementation only involves a single-exponential size blowup, there must also be at least a single-exponential size blowup in translating arbitrary ω-automata into T-automata. Analogously, if we aim for a single-exponential blowup in determinization, and no blowup in the complementation of deterministic automata, there must be at least a double-exponential size blowup in translating arbitrary automata into deterministic T-automata.

In this sense, the classic types, except for Muller, provide a reasonable trade-off between their succinctness and the size blowup involved in their determinization and complementation, having all of these measures singly exponential.

Proposition 1 ([6]). *For every $n \in \mathbb{N}$ and nondeterministic ω-automaton of size n, there is an equivalent nondeterministic Büchi automaton of size in $2^{O(n)}$ and an equivalent deterministic parity automaton of size in $2^{2^{O(n)}}$.*

4 Boolean Operations and Decision Problems

In the nondeterministic setting, boolean operations on the classic automata types, except for Muller, roughly involve an asymptotically optimal size blowup: linear for union, quadratic for intersection, and singly exponential for complementation. These blowups are inevitable already in automata over finite words. In the deterministic setting, however, the picture is different, having an exponential size blowup on union or intersection for all of the classic ω-regular-complete types. In this setting, the stronger acceptance conditions, as elaborated on in Sect. 5, match the inevitable blowups, having only quadratic size blowup. The size blowup involved in boolean operations is summarized in Table 2.

Seeking small size blowup on boolean operations is only one side of the equation—one should consider it in conjunction with the succinctness of the automaton type and the complexity of the nonemptiness and universality problems. The EL acceptance condition, for example, is very flexible and there is a small size blowup in boolean operations on deterministic EL automata, however at the cost of a high complexity of the decision problems.

Table 2. The size blowup involved in boolean operations.

Operations Size Blowup	On Deterministic Automata			On Nondeterministic Automata		
	Union	Intersect.	Complement.	Union	Intersect.	Complement.
Weak	Quadratic		No blowup	Linear	Quad.	$2^{\Theta(n)}$ [31] (if possible)
Co-Büchi			No blowup [25] (if possible)			
Büchi						$2^{\Theta(n \log n)}$ [11,30,33]
Parity	Exponential [6,29]		No blowup		Quad. - Quartic	
Rabin	Quad. [6]	Exp. [6]	Exp. [28]		Quad. [6]	$2^{\Theta(n^2 \log n)}$ [10,12,26]
Streett	Exp. [6]	Quad. [6]				
Muller	Exp. [6]		Exp. [33]		Exp. [6]	Double-Exp. [6]
Hyper-Rabin	Quadratic Prop. 3, [6]		Exp. [6]	Linear	Quad. Prop. 4, [6]	Exp. [6]
Hyper-Streett						Double-Exp. [6]
Hyper-dual			No blowup			Exp. Prop. 4
Emerson-Lei						Double-Exp. [6]

The best possible complexity for the nonemptiness problem is NLOGSPACE and linear time, taking its lower bound from the reachability problem. It is indeed achieved with Büchi automata. For the stronger classic acceptance conditions, except for Streett, it remains in NLOGSPACE, while exceeding the linear time, and for Streett it is PTIME-complete. The further stronger conditions either remain in PTIME, as Hyper-Rabin and Hyper-dual, or become NP-complete, as hyper-Streett and Emerson-Lei.

The best possible complexity for the universality problem on nondeterministic automata is PSPACE-complete, taking its lower bound from automata on finite words. It is achieved for all the classic types, as well as for the hyper-Rabin and hyper-dual types. A possible way to perform the universality check of an automaton $\mathcal{A}$ of these types is the following: translate $\mathcal{A}$ to a Streett automaton $\mathcal{B}$ with only a polynomial size blowup, then complement $\mathcal{B}$ to a Büchi automaton $\mathcal{C}$ on the fly, having a potential exponential space, and check the nonemptiness of $\mathcal{C}$ in logarithmic space, yielding a PSPACE algorithm in the size of $\mathcal{A}$ [33].

The complexity of the nonemptiness and universality problems (of nondeterministic automata) is summarized in Table 3.

Table 3. The complexity of the nonemptiness and universality checks of nondeterministic automata. The complexity is w.r.t. the automaton size n, and if specified, w.r.t. m states and index k.

Checks of Nondeterministic	Nonemptiness	Universality
Weak	Linear time, NL-complete [16,40]	PSPACE-comp. [33]
Co-Büchi		
Büchi		
Parity	$O(m \log k)$ time, NL-comp. [18,23]	
Rabin	$O(mk)$ time, NL-comp. [40]	
Streett	PTIME-comp. [18]	
Muller	NL-comp. [15]	
Hyper-Rabin	PTIME-comp. [18]	PSPACE-comp. [18]
Hyper-Streett	NP-complete [6]	EXPSPACE-comp. [20]
Hyper-dual	PTIME-comp. Prop. 8	PSPACE-comp. Prop. 8
Emerson-Lei	NP-complete [18]	EXPSPACE-comp. [33]

Table 4. The size blowup involved in translations between hyper-Rabin/Streett automata. The translations to and from generalized-Rabin/Streett automata have the same blowup. All results are from [6].

Translations Size Blowup From	To	Deterministic		Nondeterministic	
		H-Rabin	H-Streett	H-Rabin	H-Streett
Det.	Hyper-Rabin	·	Exp.	·	$O(n^2)$
	Hyper-Streett	Exp.	·	Exp.	·
Non-Det.	Hyper-Rabin	Exp.		·	$O(n^2)$
	Hyper-Streett	Double-Exp.		Exp.	·

5 Hyper-dual

We look in this section into a new automaton type that consists of two equivalent inner automata, one with the hyper-Rabin condition and one with the hyper-Streett condition. In the deterministic setting, it is the same as having two hyper-Rabin automata, one for the requested language and one for its complement.

Despite the first impression that it only brings redundancy, it seems to have an interesting potential in the deterministic setting—It allows for all boolean operations with only a quadratic state blowup, and for polynomial-time algorithms of the decision problems of emptiness, universality, and automata comparison. (A further discussion of its benefits is given at the end of the Introduction.)

Construction. Constructing a hyper-dual automaton is not more difficult than constructing any classic automaton—having an automaton $\mathcal{A}$ with the Rabin or Streett condition, a pair $(\mathcal{A}, \mathcal{A})$ is a proper hyper-dual automaton.

Proposition 2. *The Rabin and Streett acceptance conditions are special cases of both the hyper-Rabin and the hyper-Streett conditions.*

Proof. Observe that the Streett condition is the hyper-Rabin condition with a single disjunct, while the Rabin condition is a hyper-Rabin condition, in which every disjunct consists of two elements $Fin(B) \vee Inf(\emptyset)$ and $Fin(Q) \vee Inf(G)$, where Q is the entire set of states in the automaton, and $B, G \subseteq Q$.

As for hyper-Streett, the claim follows from the duality to hyper-Rabin.

Boolean Operations. Further generating deterministic hyper-dual automata by boolean operations is easy, involving only a quadratic size blowup—The complement of a deterministic hyper-dual automaton $\mathcal{C} = (\mathcal{A}, \mathcal{B})$ is $\overline{\mathcal{C}} = (\overline{\mathcal{B}}, \overline{\mathcal{A}})$, while the union and intersection of deterministic hyper-dual automata $\mathcal{C}' = (\mathcal{A}', \mathcal{B}')$ and $\mathcal{C}'' = (\mathcal{A}'', \mathcal{B}'')$ is $\mathcal{C} = (\mathcal{A}' \cup \mathcal{A}'', \mathcal{B}' \cup \mathcal{B}'')$ and $\mathcal{C} = (\mathcal{A}' \cap \mathcal{A}'', \mathcal{B}' \cap \mathcal{B}'')$, respectively, involving a quadratic size blowup (Table 2).

Proposition 3. *Complementation of a deterministic hyper-dual automaton involves no size blowup, and the union and intersection of two deterministic hyper-dual automata involve a quadratic size blowup.*

In the nondeterministic setting, it is almost similar to handling only hyper-Rabin automata, for a simple reason—translating a nondeterministic hyper-Rabin automaton into an equivalent hyper-Streett automaton only involves a quadratic size blowup (Table 4).

Proposition 4. *Complementation of a nondeterministic hyper-dual automaton involves a singly-exponential size blowup, and the union and intersection of two nondeterministic hyper-dual automata involve a quadratic size blowup.*

Properness Check. Constructing a hyper-dual automaton from a classic automaton and boolean operations guarantees its properness. Checking whether an arbitrary pair of hyper-Rabin and hyper-Streett automata is a proper hyper-dual automaton might not be too interesting and it is also coNP-complete for deterministic automata and EXPSPACE-complete for nondeterministic automata.

Proposition 5. *Given a pair $\mathcal{C} = (\mathcal{A}, \mathcal{B})$ of a deterministic hyper-Rabin automaton $\mathcal{A}$ and a deterministic hyper-Streett automaton $\mathcal{B}$, the problem of deciding whether $\mathcal{C}$ is a proper hyper-dual automaton is coNP-complete.*

Proof. For the upper bound, we should validate that $L(\mathcal{A}) = L(\mathcal{B})$. This is the case iff $L(\mathcal{A}) \subseteq L(\mathcal{B})$ and $L(\mathcal{B}) \subseteq L(\mathcal{A})$, which is the case iff $L(\mathcal{A}) \cap \overline{L(\mathcal{B})} = \emptyset$ and $L(\mathcal{B}) \cap \overline{L(\mathcal{A})} = \emptyset$.

Observe that $\overline{L(\mathcal{B})} = L(\overline{\mathcal{B}})$, and that $\overline{\mathcal{B}}$ is a hyper-Rabin automaton. Thus, checking whether $L(\mathcal{A}) \subseteq L(\mathcal{B})$ is in PTIME: constructing $\mathcal{A} \cap \overline{\mathcal{B}}$ is possible in quadratic time (Table 2), and its emptiness check in PTIME (Table 3).

As for checking whether $L(\mathcal{B}) \subseteq L(\mathcal{A})$, observe that $\overline{L(\mathcal{A})} = L(\overline{\mathcal{A}})$, and that $\overline{\mathcal{A}}$ is a hyper-Streett automaton. Thus, the check is in co-NP: constructing $\mathcal{B} \cap \overline{\mathcal{A}}$ is possible in quadratic time (Table 2), and its nonemptiness check in NP (Table 3).

For the lower bound, consider a pair $\mathcal{C}$ in which $\mathcal{A}$ is an empty automaton. Then $\mathcal{C}$ is proper iff $\mathcal{B}$ is empty, and the nonemptiness check of a DHSW is NP-complete (Table 3).

Proposition 6. *Given a pair $\mathcal{C} = (\mathcal{A}, \mathcal{B})$ of a nondeterministic hyper-Rabin automaton $\mathcal{A}$ and a nondeterministic hyper-Streett automaton $\mathcal{B}$, the problem of deciding whether $\mathcal{C}$ is a proper hyper-dual automaton is EXPSPACE-complete.*

Proof. For the upper bound, we can translate $\mathcal{A}$ and $\mathcal{B}$ to Büchi automata, having an exponential size blowup (Proposition 1), and then check the equivalence of the two Büchi automata in PSPACE.

For the lower bound, consider a pair $\mathcal{C}$ in which $\mathcal{A}$ is an automaton recognizing Σ^ω. Then $\mathcal{C}$ is proper iff $\mathcal{B}$ is universal, and the universality check of a hyper-Streett automaton is EXPSPACE-complete (Table 3).

Succinctness. Comparing hyper-dual automata to the classic types, there is no size blowup in the translation of Rabin and Streett automata to a hyper-dual automaton (Proposition 2), while there is an exponential size blowup in the other direction when considering deterministic automata—for the translation to a Rabin automaton, we have the lower bound of deterministic Streett to Rabin, by considering two copies of the Streett automaton as a hyper-dual automaton, and analogously to the translation to Streett (Table 1).

Proposition 7. *There is a $2^{\omega(n \log n)}$ size blowup in the translation of deterministic hyper-dual automaton to deterministic Rabin and Streett automata.*

An upper bound for translating a deterministic hyper-dual automaton to deterministic Rabin and Streett automata involves a $2^{O(n^4 \log n)}$ size blowup: We can consider a hyper-Rabin automaton of size n with n disjuncts in its acceptance condition as the union of n deterministic Streett automata of size n, which can then be viewed as a single nondeterministic Streett automaton of size n^2. A Streett automaton of size m can be translated to deterministic Rabin and Streett automata of size $2^{O(m^2 \log m)}$ (Table 1), providing a total size blowup of $2^{O(n^4 \log n)}$.

In the nondeterministic setting there is an exponential blowup in the translation to a Rabin automaton, due to the lower bound in the translation of a nondeterministic Streett automaton to a nondeterministic Rabin automaton (Table 1), while the translation to a Streett automaton only involves a quadratic size blowup, as a hyper-Rabin automaton with n disjuncts can be viewed as the union of n Streett automata.

Usage and Decision Procedures. Equipped with both a hyper-Rabin automaton and a hyper-Streett automaton, we can "enjoy both worlds", by choosing which of them to use for each task. As a result, using them for synthesis, model-checking probabilistic automata, or game solving is not more difficult than using a hyper-Rabin or hyper-Streett automaton, and all decision problems in the deterministic setting have polynomial-time algorithms. In the nondeterministic setting, the decision problems are roughly as for hyper-Streett automata due to the quadratic translation of hyper-Rabin to hyper-Streett.

Proposition 8. *Nonemptiness and universality checks of a deterministic hyper-dual automaton, as well as the containment and equivalence problems of two deterministic hyper-dual automata, are in PTIME.*

Proof. Consider a hyper-dual automaton $\mathcal{C} = (\mathcal{A}, \mathcal{B})$. Then $\mathcal{C}$ is empty iff $\mathcal{A}$ is, and it is universal iff $\overline{\mathcal{B}}$ is empty, which reduces to checking the (non-)emptiness of hyper-Rabin automata, which is in PTIME (Table 3).

Consider two hyper-dual automata $\mathcal{C}' = (\mathcal{A}', \mathcal{B}')$ and $\mathcal{C}'' = (\mathcal{A}'', \mathcal{B}'')$. Then $L(\mathcal{C}') \subseteq L(\mathcal{C}'')$ iff $L(\mathcal{A}') \cap \overline{L(\mathcal{B}'')} = \emptyset$. Observe that $\overline{L(\mathcal{B}'')} = L(\overline{\mathcal{B}''})$, and that $\overline{\mathcal{B}''}$ is a hyper-Rabin automaton. Thus, checking whether $L(\mathcal{A}') \subseteq L(\mathcal{B}'')$ is in PTIME: constructing $\mathcal{A}' \cap \overline{\mathcal{B}''}$ is possible in quadratic time (Table 2), and its emptiness check in PTIME (Table 3).

For checking whether $L(\mathcal{C}'') \subseteq L(\mathcal{C}')$, we can analogously consider $\mathcal{A}'' \cap \overline{\mathcal{B}'}$. $\square$

6   Conclusions

Automata on infinite words enjoy a variety of acceptance conditions, which are indeed necessary due to the richness of ω-regular languages and their connection to various kinds of other formalisms and logics. In the deterministic setting, which has recently become very relevant, it seems that there is still place for new acceptance conditions. In particular, when the automata are to be involved in positive boolean operations, one may consider the hyper-Rabin condition, and when complementations are also in place, one may consider the hyper-dual type.

References

1. Babiak, T., et al.: The Hanoi omega-automata format. In: Kroening, D., Păsăreanu, C.S. (eds.) CAV 2015. LNCS, vol. 9206, pp. 479–486. Springer, Cham (2015). https://doi.org/10.1007/978-3-319-21690-4_31
2. Blahoudek, F.: Translation of an LTL fragment to deterministic Rabin and Streett automata. Master's thesis, Masarykova Univerzita (2012)
3. Boker, U.: Word-automata translations (2010). http://www.faculty.idc.ac.il/udiboker/automata
4. Boker, U.: On the (in)succinctness of muller automata. In: CSL, pp. 12:1–12:16 (2017)
5. Boker, U.: Rabin vs. Streett automata. In: FSTTCS, pp. 17:1–17:15 (2017)
6. Boker, U.: Why these automata types? In: Proceedings of LPAR, pp. 143–163 (2018)
7. Boker, U., Kuperberg, D., Kupferman, O., Skrzypczak, M.: Nondeterminism in the presence of a diverse or unknown future. In: Fomin, F.V., Freivalds, R., Kwiatkowska, M., Peleg, D. (eds.) ICALP 2013. LNCS, vol. 7966, pp. 89–100. Springer, Heidelberg (2013). https://doi.org/10.1007/978-3-642-39212-2_11
8. Boker, U., Kupferman, O.: Translating to co-Büchi made tight, unified, and useful. ACM Trans. Comput. Log. **13**(4), 29:1–29:29 (2012)
9. Boker, U., Kupferman, O., Skrzypczak, M.: How deterministic are good-for-games automata? In: Proceedings of FSTTCS, pp. 18:1–18:14 (2017)
10. Cai, Y., Zhang, T.: A tight lower bound for Streett complementation. In: Proceedings of FSTTCS, pp. 339–350 (2011)
11. Cai, Y., Zhang, T.: Tight upper bounds for Streett and parity complementation. In: Proceedings of CSL, pp. 112–128 (2011)
12. Cai, Y., Zhang, T., Luo, H.: An improved lower bound for the complementation of Rabin automata. In: Proceedings of LICS, pp. 167–176 (2009)
13. Chatterjee, K., Gaiser, A., Křetínský, J.: Automata with generalized rabin pairs for probabilistic model checking and LTL synthesis. In: Sharygina, N., Veith, H. (eds.) CAV 2013. LNCS, vol. 8044, pp. 559–575. Springer, Heidelberg (2013). https://doi.org/10.1007/978-3-642-39799-8_37
14. Choueka, Y.: Theories of automata on ω-tapes: a simplified approach. J. Comput. Syst. Sci. **8**, 117–141 (1974)
15. Clarke, E.M., Browne, I.A., Kurshan, R.P.: A unified approach for showing language containment and equivalence between various types of ω-automata. In: Arnold, A. (ed.) CAAP 1990. LNCS, vol. 431, pp. 103–116. Springer, Heidelberg (1990). https://doi.org/10.1007/3-540-52590-4_43
16. Clarke, E.M., Emerson, E.A., Sistla, A.P.: Automatic verification of finite-state concurrent systems using temporal logic specifications. ACM Trans. Program. Lang. Syst. **8**(2), 244–263 (1986)
17. Colcombet, T., Zdanowski, K.: A tight lower bound for determinization of transition labeled Büchi automata. In: Albers, S., Marchetti-Spaccamela, A., Matias, Y., Nikoletseas, S., Thomas, W. (eds.) ICALP 2009. LNCS, vol. 5556, pp. 151–162. Springer, Heidelberg (2009). https://doi.org/10.1007/978-3-642-02930-1_13
18. Emerson, E.A., Lei, C.-L.: Modalities for model checking: branching time logic strikes back. Sci. Comput. Program. **8**, 275–306 (1987)
19. Esparza, J., Křetínský, J., Sickert, S.: From LTL to deterministic automata: a safraless compositional approach. Form. Methods Syst. Des. **49**(3), 219–271 (2016)

20. Filiot, E., Gentilini, R., Raskin, J.F.: Rational synthesis under imperfect information. In: Proceedings of LICS, pp. 422–431 (2018)
21. Henzinger, T.A., Piterman, N.: Solving games without determinization. In: Ésik, Z. (ed.) CSL 2006. LNCS, vol. 4207, pp. 395–410. Springer, Heidelberg (2006). https://doi.org/10.1007/11874683_26
22. Hunter, P., Dawar, A.: Complexity bounds for regular games. In: Jędrzejowicz, J., Szepietowski, A. (eds.) MFCS 2005. LNCS, vol. 3618, pp. 495–506. Springer, Heidelberg (2005). https://doi.org/10.1007/11549345_43
23. King, V., Kupferman, O., Vardi, M.Y.: On the complexity of parity word automata. In: Honsell, F., Miculan, M. (eds.) FoSSaCS 2001. LNCS, vol. 2030, pp. 276–286. Springer, Heidelberg (2001). https://doi.org/10.1007/3-540-45315-6_18
24. Křetínský, J., Esparza, J.: Deterministic automata for the (F,G)-fragment of LTL. In: Madhusudan, P., Seshia, S.A. (eds.) CAV 2012. LNCS, vol. 7358, pp. 7–22. Springer, Heidelberg (2012). https://doi.org/10.1007/978-3-642-31424-7_7
25. Kupferman, O., Morgenstern, G., Murano, A.: Typeness for ω-regular automata. In: Wang, F. (ed.) ATVA 2004. LNCS, vol. 3299, pp. 324–338. Springer, Heidelberg (2004). https://doi.org/10.1007/978-3-540-30476-0_27
26. Kupferman, O., Vardi, M.Y.: Complementation constructions for nondeterministic automata on infinite words. In: Halbwachs, N., Zuck, L.D. (eds.) TACAS 2005. LNCS, vol. 3440, pp. 206–221. Springer, Heidelberg (2005). https://doi.org/10.1007/978-3-540-31980-1_14
27. Liu, W., Wang, J.: A tighter analysis of Piterman's Büchi determinization. Inf. Process. Lett. **109**(16), 941–945 (2009)
28. Löding, C.: Optimal bounds for transformations of ω-automata. In: Rangan, C.P., Raman, V., Ramanujam, R. (eds.) FSTTCS 1999. LNCS, vol. 1738, pp. 97–109. Springer, Heidelberg (1999). https://doi.org/10.1007/3-540-46691-6_8
29. Löding, C., Yue, H.: Memory bounds for winning strategies in infinite games (2008, unpublished)
30. Michel, M.: Complementation is more difficult with automata on infinite words. CNET, Paris (1988)
31. Miyano, S., Hayashi, T.: Alternating finite automata on ω-words. Theor. Comput. Sci. **32**, 321–330 (1984)
32. Piterman, N.: From nondeterministic Büchi and Streett automata to deterministic parity automata. Log. Methods Comput. Sci. **3**(3), 5 (2007)
33. Safra, S.: Complexity of automata on infinite objects. Ph.D. thesis, Weizmann Institute of Science (1989)
34. Safra, S.: Exponential determinization for ω-automata with strong-fairness acceptance condition. In: Proceedings of 24th ACM Symposium on Theory of Computing (1992)
35. Safra, S., Vardi, M.Y.: On ω-automata and temporal logic. In: Proceedings of 21st ACM Symposium on Theory of Computing, pp. 127–137 (1989)
36. Schewe, S.: Büchi complementation made tight. In: Proceedings of 26th Symposium on Theoretical Aspects of Computer Science, volume 3 of LIPIcs, pp. 661–672 (2009)
37. Schewe, S., Varghese, T.: Determinising parity automata. In: Csuhaj-Varjú, E., Dietzfelbinger, M., Ésik, Z. (eds.) MFCS 2014. LNCS, vol. 8634, pp. 486–498. Springer, Heidelberg (2014). https://doi.org/10.1007/978-3-662-44522-8_41
38. Vardi, M.: The Büchi complementation saga. In: Proceedings of STACS, pp. 12–22 (2007)
39. Vardi, M.Y.: Automatic verification of probabilistic concurrent finite-state programs. In: Proceedings of FOCS, pp. 327–338 (1985)

40. Vardi, M.Y., Wolper, P.: Reasoning about infinite computations. Inf. Comput. **115**(1), 1–37 (1994)
41. Yan, Q.: Lower bounds for complementation of ω-automata via the full automata technique. In: Bugliesi, M., Preneel, B., Sassone, V., Wegener, I. (eds.) ICALP 2006. LNCS, vol. 4052, pp. 589–600. Springer, Heidelberg (2006). https://doi.org/10.1007/11787006_50

Deciding Context Unification
(with Regular Constraints)

Artur Jeż[✉]

University of Wrocław, Wrocław, Poland
aje@cs.uni.wroc.pl

Abstract. Given a ranked alphabet, context are terms with a single occurrence of a special symbol • (outside of the alphabet), which represents a missing subterm. One can naturally build equations over contexts: the context variables are treated as symbols of arity one and a substitution S assigns to each such a variable a context $S(X)$. A substitution S is extended to terms with context variables in a natural way: $S(X(t))$ is a context $S(X)$ in which the unique occurrence of • is replaced with $S(t)$. For historical reasons, the satisfiability of context equations is usually referred to as *context unification*.

Context unification generalizes word equations and first-order term unification (which are decidable) and is subsumed by second order unification (which is undecidable) and its decidability status remained open for almost two decades. In this paper I will sketch a PSPACE algorithm for this problem. The idea is to apply simple compression rules (replacing pairs of neighbouring function symbols) to the solution of the context equation; to this end we appropriately modify the equation (without the knowledge of the actual solution) so that compressing the solution can be simulated by compressing parts of the equation. When the compression operations are appropriately chosen, then the size of the instance is polynomial during the whole algorithm, thus giving a PSPACE-upper bound. The best known lower bounds are as for word equations, i.e. NP. The method can be extended to the scenario in which tree-regular constraints for the variables are present, in which case the problem is EXPTIME-complete.

1 Introduction

Context unification is a generalization of word equations to terms. In the word equations problem we are given an alphabet Σ and a set of variables $\mathcal{X}$. Then, given an equation of the form $u = v$, where both u, v are words over the letters and variables, we ask about the existence of a substitution of variables by words over the alphabet that turns this formal equation into a true equality (of words over the alphabet). The first algorithm for this problem was given by Makanin [18]; the currently best algorithms for this problem utilize different (and simpler) approach and work in PSPACE [11,22], the best known lower bound is NP, and it follows easily from, say, the NP-hardness of integer programming.

© Springer Nature Switzerland AG 2019
P. Hofman and M. Skrzypczak (Eds.): DLT 2019, LNCS 11647, pp. 18–40, 2019.
https://doi.org/10.1007/978-3-030-24886-4_2

We view terms as rooted, ordered (meaning that the children of a node are ordered using a usual left-to-right order) trees, usually denoted with letters t or s. Nodes are labelled with elements from a ranked alphabet Σ, i.e. each letter $a \in \Sigma$ has a fixed arity $\mathrm{ar}(f)$; those elements are usually called *letters*. A tree is *well-formed* if a node labelled with f has exactly $\mathrm{ar}(f)$ children; we consider only well-formed trees, which can be equivalently seen as *ground terms* over Σ. We will also use term notation to denote the trees in text, for example, $f(c, c')$ denotes the tree with root labelled with f and two children, first (left) labelled with c and the second (right) with c'; those children are leaves.

When generalizing the word equations from words to terms, one first needs to decide, what a variable can represent. If a variable can only represent a well-formed term, then we arrive at a standard first-order unification problem, which can be solved in linear time; so this does not even generalize the word equations. Thus the variables are allowed to take arguments, i.e. they define trees with missing subtrees. Formally, we extend the alphabet with parameter symbols $\bullet_1, \bullet_2, \ldots$ of arity 0. If a term t uses $\bullet_1, \bullet_2, \ldots, \bullet_i$ then $t(t_1, \ldots, t_i)$, where $t_1, \ldots, t_i$ do not use parameters, is t in which $\bullet_j$ is replaced with t_j. Thus the variables are ranked: X takes $\mathrm{ar}(X)$ arguments and the substitution for it has to use $\bullet_1, \bullet_2, \ldots, \bullet_{ar(X)}$. For instance, an equation $f(X(c), X(c)) = X(f(c, c))$ has a solution $X = \bullet$. Under this substitution both sides evaluate to $f(c, c)$. There are other solutions, for instance $X = f(\bullet, \bullet)$, which evaluates both sides to $f(f(c, c), f(c, c))$; in general, solution that evaluates both sides to full binary tree of arbitrary height is easy to construct. When no further restrictions are given, this problem is the second order unification and is undecidable [9].

In context unification we require that each $\bullet_j$ is used exactly once. For instance, the aforementioned equation $f(X(c), X(c)) = X(f(c, c))$ as an instance of context unification has exactly one solution: $X = \bullet$, other solution are excluded by the restriction that $\bullet$ is used exactly once. It is easy to see that the case of many argument NP-reduces to the case with only one argument, and we deal with only this case further on. Context unification was introduced by Comon [1,2], who also coined the name, and independently by Schmidt-Schauß [24]. It found usage in analysis of rewrite systems with membership constraints [1,2], analysis of natural language [20,21], distributive unification [25] and bi-rewriting systems [13].

Context unification is both subsumed by second order unification (which is undecidable) and subsumes word equations (which are decidable). Furthermore, other natural problems between those two usually trivially reduce to word equations or are undecidable. Thus, in a sense, context unification is the only such problem, whose decidability remains open. This is one of the reasons why it gained considerable attention in the term rewriting community [23] and no wonder that there was a large body of work focused on context unification and several partial results were obtained [2,6–8,12,15,17,26,28,29]. Note that in most cases the corresponding variants of the general second order unification remain undecidable, which supported the conjecture that context unification is decidable.

Context unification was shown to be equivalent to 'equality up to constraint' problem [20] (which is a common generalisation of equality constraints, subtree constraints and one-step rewriting constraints). In fact one-step rewriting constraints, which is a problem extensively studied on its own, are equivalent to stratified context unification [21]. It is known that the first-order theory of one-step rewriting constraints is undecidable [19, 32, 33]. For whole context unification, already the $\forall \exists^8$-equational theory is Π_1^0-hard [34].

Some fragments of second order unification are known to reduce to context unification: the *bounded second order unification* assumes that the number of occurrences of the argument of the second-order variable in the substitution term is bounded by a constant; note that it *can be zero* and this is the crucial difference with context unification; cf. monadic second order unification, which can be seen as a similar variant of word equations, and is known to be NP-complete [14]. This fragment on one hand easily reduces to context unification and on the other hand it is known to be decidable [27]; in fact its generalisation to higher-order unification is decidable as well [30] and it is known that bounded second order unification is NP-complete [15].

The context unification can be also extended by allowing some additional constraints on variables, a natural one allows the usage of the *tree-regular constraints*, i.e. for any variable we require that its substitution comes from a certain regular set of trees. It is known that such an extension is equivalent to the linear second order unification [16], defined by Levy [12]: in essence, the linear second order unification allows bounding variables on different levels of the function, which makes direct translations to context unification infeasible, however, usage of regular constraints gives enough expressive power to encode such more complex bounding. Note, that the reductions are not polynomial and the equivalence is stated only on the decidability level.

The usage of regular constraints is very popular in case of word equations, in particular it is used in generalisations of the algorithm for word equation to the group case and essentially all known algorithms for word equations problem can be generalised to word equations with regular constraints [3, 4, 31].

Results

The decidability status of context unification remained unknown for almost two decades. In this paper I present a proof that context unification can be solved in **PSPACE**, using a generalization of an algorithm for word equations; see [10] for a full version.

The idea is to apply simple compression rules (replacing pairs of neighbouring function symbols) to the solution of the context equation; to this end we appropriately modify the equation (without the knowledge of the actual solution) so that compressing the solution can be simulated by compressing parts of the equation. It is shown that if the compression operations are appropriately chosen, then the size of the instance is polynomial during the whole algorithm, thus giving a **PSPACE**-upper bound. The best known lower bounds are the same for word equations, i.e. context unification is **NP**-hard. The method can be extended to the scenario in which tree-regular for the variables are present, in which case the problem is EXPTIME-complete.

This idea, known under the name of recompression, was used before for word equations [11], simplifying the existing proof of containment in PSPACE. Furthermore, applications of compression to fragments of context unification were known before [6,8,15,30] and the presented algorithm extends this method to terms in full generality. In this way solving word equations using recompression [11] generalises to solving context unification. This in some sense fulfils the original plan of extending the algorithms for word equations to context unification.

2 Definitions

2.1 Trees

As said before, we are given a ranked alphabet Σ, i.e. there is an arity function $\text{ar} : \Sigma \to \mathbb{N}$, and we deal with rooted (there is a designated root), ordered (there is a fixed linear order on children of each node) Σ-labelled trees. We say that a tree is well-formed when a node labelled with $a \in \Sigma$ has $\text{ar}(a)$ children. We also view such trees as terms, then a tree is well-built if seen as a term it is well-built.

2.2 Patterns

We want to replace fragments of a tree with new nodes, those fragments are not necessarily well-formed. Thus we want to define 'trees with holes', where holes represent missing arguments. Let $\mathbb{Y} = \{\bullet, \bullet_1, \bullet_2, \ldots\}$ be an infinite set of symbols of arity 0, we think of each of them as a place of a missing argument; its elements are collectively called *parameters*. A *pattern* is a tree over an alphabet $\Sigma \cup \mathbb{Y}$, such that each parameter occurs at most once in it. The usual convention is that the used parameters are $\bullet_1, \bullet_2, \ldots, \bullet_k$, or $\bullet$, when there is only 1 parameter; moreover, we usually assume that the order (according to preorder traversal of the pattern) of occurrences of the parameters in the pattern is $\bullet_1, \bullet_2, \ldots, \bullet_k$. We often refer to *parameter nodes* and *non-parameter nodes* to refer to nodes labelled with parameters and non-parameters, respectively. A pattern using r parameters is called r-pattern. A pattern p *occurs* (at a node v) in a tree t if p can be obtained by taking a subtree t' of t rooted at v and replacing some of subtrees of t' by appropriate parameters. This is also called an *occurrence* of p in t. A pattern p is a subpattern of t if p occurs in t.

In a more classic terminology, 1-patterns are also called contexts, hence the name "context unification".

Given a tree t, its r-subpattern p occurrence and an r-pattern p' we can naturally replace p with p': we delete the part of t corresponding to p with removed parameters and plug p' with removed parameters instead and reattach all the subtrees in the same order; as the number of parameters is the same, this is well-defined. We can perform several replacements at the same time, as long as occurrences of replaced patterns do not share non-parameter nodes. In this terminology, our algorithm will replace occurrences of subpatterns of t in t.

We focus on some specific patterns: A *chain* is a pattern that consists only of unary nodes plus one parameter node. Chains that have two nodes that are labelled with different letters, i.e. of the form $a(b(\bullet))$ for $a \neq b$, are called *pairs*; chains whose all unary nodes are labelled with the same letter a, i.e. of the form $a(a(\ldots(a(\bullet)\ldots)))$, are called *$a$-chains*. A chain t' that is a subpattern of t is a *chain subpattern* of t, an occurrence of an a-chain subpattern $a(a(\ldots(a(\bullet)\ldots)))$ is *maximal* if it cannot be extended (in t) by a nor up nor down. A pattern of a form $f(\bullet_1, \bullet_2, \ldots, \bullet_{i-1}, c, \bullet_i, \ldots, \bullet_{\mathrm{ar}(f)-1})$ is denoted as (f, i, c).

We treat chains as strings and write them in the string notation (in particular, we drop the parameters) and 'concatenate' them, that is, for two chains $s_a = a_1(a_2(\ldots a_k(\bullet)\ldots))$ and $s_b = b_1(b_2(\ldots b_\ell(\bullet)\ldots))$ we write them as $s_a = a_1 a_2 \cdots a_k$ and $s_b = b_1 b_2 \cdots b_\ell$ and their concatenation $s_a s_b = a_1 a_2 \cdots a_k b_1 b_2 \cdots b_\ell$ denotes the chain $a_1(a_2(\ldots a_k(b_1(b_2(\ldots b_\ell(\bullet)\ldots)))\ldots))$. In this convention ab denotes a pair and a^ℓ denotes an a-chain. We use those conventions also for 1-patterns and also for 1-patterns followed by a single term, i.e. for 1-patterns $p_1, \ldots, p_k$ and a term t the $p_1 p_2 \cdots p_k t$ denotes the term $p_1(p_2(\ldots p_k(t)\ldots))$.

2.3 Context Unification: Formal Statement

By $\mathcal{V}$ we denote an infinite set of context variables $X, Y, Z, \ldots$. We also use individual term variables $x, y, z, \ldots$ taken from $\mathcal{X}$. When we do not want to distinguish between a context variable or term variable, we call it a *variable* and denote it by a small Greek letter, like $\alpha, \beta, \gamma, \ldots$.

Definition 1. *The* terms over Σ, $\mathcal{X}$, $\mathcal{V}$ *are ground terms with alphabet* $\Sigma \cup \mathcal{X} \cup \mathcal{V}$ *in which we extend the arity function* ar *to* $\mathcal{X} \cup \mathcal{V}$ *by* $\mathrm{ar}(X) = 1$ *and* $\mathrm{ar}(x) = 0$ *for each* $X \in \mathcal{V}$ *and* $x \in \mathcal{X}$. *A context equation* is an equation of the form $u = v$ *where both* u *and* v *are terms over* $\Sigma \cup \mathcal{X} \cup \mathcal{V}$.

We are interested in the solutions of the context equations, i.e. substitutions that replace term variables with ground terms and context variables with 1-patterns, such that a formal equality $u = v$ is turned into a valid equality of ground terms. More formally:

Definition 2. *A* substitution *is a mapping S that assigns a 1-pattern $S(X)$ to each context variable $X \in \mathcal{V}$ and a ground term $S(x)$ to each variable $x \in \mathcal{X}$. The mapping S is naturally extended to arbitrary terms as follows:*

- $S(a) := a$ *for each constant* $a \in \Sigma$;
- $S(f(t_1, \ldots, t_n)) := f(S(t_1), \ldots, S(t_m))$ *for an m-ary* $f \in \Sigma$;
- $S(X(t)) := S(X)(S(t))$ *for* $X \in \mathcal{V}$.

A substitution S is a solution *of the context equation $u = v$ if $S(u) = S(v)$. The size of a solution S of an equation $u = v$ is $|S(u)|$, which is simply the total* *number of nodes in* $S(u)$. *A solution is* size-minimal, *if for every other solution* S' *it holds that* $|S(u)| \leq |S'(u)|$. *A solution* S *is* non-empty *if* $S(X)$ *is not a parameter for each* $X \in \mathcal{X}$ *from the context equation* $u = v$.

For a ground term $S(u)$ and an occurrence of a letter a in it we say that this occurrence *comes from* u if it was obtained as $S(a)$ in Definition 2 and that it comes from α if it was obtained from $S(\alpha)$ in Definition 2.

Example 1. Consider an alphabet $\Sigma = \{f, c, c'\}$ with $\text{ar}(f) = 2$ and $\text{ar}(c) = \text{ar}(c') = 0$ and an equation $X(c) = Y(c')$ over it. It has a solution (which is easily seen to be size-minimal) $S(X) = f(\bullet, c')$ and $S(Y) = f(c, \bullet)$; under this substitution this equation evaluates to $S(X(c)) = S(Y(c')) = f(c, c')$.

3   Local Compression of Trees

3.1   Compression Operations

We perform three types of *subpattern compression* on a tree t:

a-**chain compression.** For a unary letter a and every $\ell > 1$ we replace each occurrence of a maximal a-chain subpattern a^ℓ by a new unary letter a_ℓ.

ab **compression.** For two different unary letters a and b we replace each occurrence of a subpattern ab with a new unary letter c.

(f, i, c) **compression.** For a constant c and letter f of arity $\text{ar}(f) = m \geq i \geq 1$, we replace each occurrence of subpattern (f, i, c), i.e. $f(\bullet_1, \bullet_2, \ldots, \bullet_{i-1}, c, \bullet_i, \ldots, \bullet_{m-1})$, with subpattern $f'(\bullet_1, \bullet_2, \ldots, \bullet_{i-1}, \bullet_i, \ldots, \bullet_{m-1})$, where f' is a fresh letter of arity $m - 1$ (intuitively: the constant c on i-th place is 'absorbed' by its father labelled with f).

These operations are collectively called *subpattern compressions*. When we want to specify the type but not the actual subpattern compressed, we use the names *chain compression, pair compression* and *leaf compression*. These operations are also called $\mathsf{TreePattComp}(ab, t)$, $\mathsf{TreePattComp}(a, t)$ and $\mathsf{TreePattComp}((f, i, c), t)$, or simply $\mathsf{TreePattComp}(p, t)$ for a pattern $p \in \{a, ab, (f, i, c)\}$.

The a-chain compression and ab compression are direct translations of the operations used in the recompression-based algorithm for word equations [11]. On the other hand, the leaf compression is a new operation that is designed specifically to deal with trees.

3.2   Compression of Non-crossing Patterns

Consider a context equation $u = v$ and its solution S. Suppose that we want to perform the ab compression on $S(u)$ and $S(v)$, i.e. we want to replace each occurrence of a subpattern ab with a fresh unary letter c. Such replacement is easy, when the occurrence of ab subpattern comes from the letters in the equation or from $S(\alpha)$ for some variable α: in the former case we modify the equation by replacing the occurrences of ab with c, in the latter the modification is done implicitly (i.e. we replace the occurrences of fab in $S(\alpha)$ with c). The problematic part is with the ab subpattern that is of neither of those forms, as they 'cross' between $S(\alpha)$ and some letter outside $S(\alpha)$. This is formalised in the below definition, the intuition and definition is similar also for a-chains and (f, i, c) patterns.

Definition 3. *For an equation $u = v$ and a substitution S we say that an occurrence of a subpattern p in $S(u)$ (or $S(v)$) is*

explicit with respect to S: *if all non-parameter letters in this occurrence come from explicit letters in $u = v$;*
implicit with respect to S: *if all non-parameter letters in this occurrence come from $S(\alpha)$ for a single occurrence of a variable α;*
crossing with respect to S: *otherwise.*

We say that ab is a crossing pair *(a has a crossing chain; (f, i, c) is a crossing father-leaf subpattern) with respect to S if it has at least one crossing occurrence (there is a crossing occurrence of an a^ℓ chain; has at least one crossing occurrence) with respect to S. Otherwise ab (a, (f, i, c)) is a* non-crossing pair *(has no crossing chain; is a* non-crossing father-leaf subpattern*) with respect to S.*

To make the notions more uniform, we will also say that $p \in \{ab, a, (f, i, c)\}$ is a crossing/non-crossing subpattern, meaning that ab is a crossing/noncrossing pair, a has crossing chain/has no crossing chains and (f, i, c) is a crossing/non-crossing father-leaf subpattern.

When ab is non-crossing with respect to a solution S, we can simulate the TreePattComp$(ab, S(u))$ on $u = v$ simply by performing the ab compression on the explicit letters in the equation, we refer to this operation as PattCompNCr$(ab, 'u = v')$. Then occurrences of ab that come from explicit letters are compressed, the ones that come from $S(\alpha)$ are compressed by changing the solution and there are no other possibilities. The same applies also to compression of a-chains and (f, i, c)-compression.

As we discuss correctness of nondeterministic procedures, in the following we will say that a nondeterministic procedure is *sound*, if given a non-satisfiable context equation it cannot transform it to a satisfiable equation, regardless of the nondeterministic choices.

Lemma 1. PattCompNCr *is sound.*

Let $u = v$ has a solution S and let $p \in \{ab, a, (f, i, c)\}$ be a noncrossing subpattern. Then the returned equation $u' = v'$ has a solution S' (over an alphabet expanded by letters introduced during the subpattern compression) such that $S'(u') = $ TreePattComp$(p, S(u))$.

Example 2. Consider the following context equation over the alphabet $\{a, b, c, c', f\}$, with $\mathrm{ar}(a) = \mathrm{ar}(b) = 1$, $\mathrm{ar}(c) = \mathrm{ar}(c') = 0$ and $\mathrm{ar}(f) = 2$:

$$bXaXc = baa(f(aYc', bb(f(c, c')))),$$

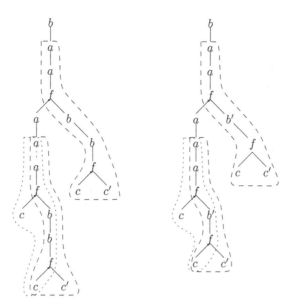

Fig. 1. An illustration to Example 2. The Figure presents the tree obtained at both sides under the substitution, the values substitutions for variables are depicted: in dashed line for X and dotted for Y. On the right the tree after the compression of bb is depicted.

see also Fig. 1. It is easy to see that there is a unique solution $S(X) = aa(f(\bullet, bb(f(c, c'))))$ and $S(Y) = aa(f(c, bb(f(c, \bullet))))$.

The subpattern ba has a crossing occurrence on the left-hand side, as a is the first letter of $S(X)$ and bX is a subpattern. Subpattern bb has only noncrossing occurrences, some of them explicit and some implicit. Subpatterns $(f, 2, c'), (f, 1, c), a^3$ are also crossing.

Compressing b subpattern leads to an equation

$$bXaXc = baa(f(baYc', b'(f(c, c')))).$$

Then the solution is $S'(X) = aa(f(b\bullet, b'(f(c, c'))))$ and $S'(Y) = aa(f(bc, b'(f(c, \bullet))))$.

4 Uncrossing

In general, one cannot assume that an arbitrary pair ab, a-chain or (f, i, c) subpattern is non-crossing. However, for a fixed subpattern p and a solution S we can modify the instance so that this p becomes non-crossing with respect to a solution S' (that corresponds to S of the original equation). This modification is the cornerstone of our main algorithm, as it allows subpattern compression to be performed directly on the equation, regardless of how the solution actually looks like.

4.1 Uncrossing a Pair

We begin with showing how to turn a crossing pair ab into a non-crossing one. As a first step, we characterise crossing pairs in a more operational manner: for a non-empty substitution S, a variable α and a context variable X by a *first letter* of $S(\alpha)$ we denote the topmost-letter in $S(\alpha)$, by the *last letter* of $S(X)$ we denote the function symbol that is the father of '•' in $S(X)$. Then ab is crossing with respect to S if and only if one of the following conditions holds for some variable α and context variable X:

(CP1) $a\alpha$ occurs in $u = v$ and b is the first letter of $S(\alpha)$ *or*
(CP2) Xb occurs in $u = v$ and a is the last letter of $S(X)$ *or*
(CP3) $X\alpha$ occurs in $u = v$, a is the last letter of $S(X)$ and b the first letter of $S(\alpha)$.

In each of (CP1–CP3) it is easy to modify the instance so that ab is no longer a crossing pair:

Ad (CP1): We *pop up* the letter b: we replace α with $b\alpha$. In this way we also modify the solution $S(\alpha)$ from bt to t. If the new substitution for α is empty (which can happen only when α is a context variable), we remove α from the equation.

Ad (CP2): We *pop down* the letter a: we replace each occurrence of X with Xa. In this way we implicitly modify the solution $S(X)$ from sa to s. If the new substitution for X is empty, we remove X from the equation.

Ad (CP3): this is a combination of the two cases above, in which we need to pop-down from X and pop-up from α.

The whole uncrossing procedure can be even simplified: for each context variable X we guess its last letter and it if is a, then we pop it down. Similarly, for each variable α we guess its first letter and if it is b then we pop it up. If at any point a context some variable becomes empty then we remove its occurrences. We call the whole procedure Uncross $(ab, \text{'}u = v\text{'})$ and its details are in the pseudocode in Algorithm 1.

If $u = v$ has a solution S then for appropriate non-deterministic choices Uncross$(ab, \text{'}u = v\text{'})$ returns an equation $u' = v'$ that has a solution S' such that ab is non-crossing with respect to S' and $S'(u') = S(u)$.

Lemma 2. *Let $a \neq b$ be two different unary letters. Then* Uncross$(ab, \text{'}u = v\text{'})$ *is sound and if $u = v$ has a non-empty solution S (over an alphabet Σ) then for appropriate non-deterministic choices the returned equation $u' = v'$ has a non-empty solution S' (over the same alphabet Σ) such that $S'(u') = S(u)$ and ab is a non-crossing pair with respect to S'.*

Example 3. Continuing Example 2, recall that ba is a crossing subpattern in

$$bXaXc = baa(f(aYc', bb(f(c, c')))) ,$$

Algorithm 1. Uncross(ab, '$u = v$')

1: **for** $X \in \mathcal{V}$ **do**
2:    **if** the last letter of $S(X)$ is a **then**   ▷ Guess
3:        replace each occurrence of X in $u = v$ by Xa
4:                            ▷ Implicitly change $S(X) = sa$ to $S(X) = s$
5:        **if** $S(X)$ is empty **then**   ▷ Guess
6:            remove X from $u = v$: replace each Xs in the equation by s
7: **for** $\alpha \in \mathcal{V} \cup \mathcal{X}$ **do**
8:    **if** the first letter of $S(\alpha)$ is b **then**   ▷ Guess
9:        replace each occurrence of α in $u = v$ by $b\alpha$
10:                           ▷ Implicitly change $S(\alpha) = bs$ to $S(\alpha) = s$
11:      **if** $S(\alpha)$ is empty **then**   ▷ Guess; applies only to context variables
12:          remove α from $u = v$: replace each αs in the equation by s

---

where the alphabet is $\{a, b, c, c', f\}$, with $\mathrm{ar}(a) = \mathrm{ar}(b) = 1$, $\mathrm{ar}(c) = \mathrm{ar}(c') = 0$ and $\mathrm{ar}(f) = 2$ and $S(X) = a(a(f(\bullet, b(b(f(c, c'))))))$ and $S(Y) = a(a(f(c, b(b(f(c, \bullet))))))$. We pop a up from X, obtaining

$$baXbaaXbc = baa(f(aYc', bb(f(c, c')))),$$

the solution is $S'(X) = a(f(\bullet, bb(f(c, c'))))$ and $S'(Y) = S(Y)$. It is easy to verify that ba is no longer crossing.

4.2   Uncrossing Chains

Suppose that some unary letter a has a crossing chain with respect to a non-empty solution S. As in the case of pairs, it is easy to see that a has a crossing chain with respect to S if and only if one of the following holds for variable α and context variable X (note that those conditions are in fact (CP1–CP3) for $a = b$):

(CC1) $a\alpha$ occurs in $u = v$ and the first letter of $S(\alpha)$ is a;
(CC2) Xa occurs in $u = v$ and a is the last letter of $S(X)$;
(CC3) $X\alpha$ occurs in $u = v$ and a is the last letter of $S(X)$ as well as the first letter of $S(\alpha)$.

The cases (CC1) and (CC2) are symmetric while (CC3) is a composition of (CC1) and (CC2). So suppose that (CC2) holds. Then we can replace each occurrence of X in the equation $u = v$ with Xa (implicitly changing the solution $S(X) = ta$ to $S(X) = t$), but it can still happen that a is the last letter of $S(X)$. So we keep popping down a until the last letter of $S(X)$ is not a, in other words we replace X with Xa^r, where $S(X) = ta^r$ and the last letter of t is not a. Then a and X can no longer satisfy condition (CC2), as the last letter of $S'(X)$ is different than a. A symmetric action and analysis apply to (CC1), and (CC3) follows by applying the popping down for X and popping up for α. To simplify the arguments, for a ground term or 1-pattern t we say that a^ℓ is the a-prefix of

t if $t = a^\ell t'$ and the first letter of t' is not a (t' may be empty). Similarly, for a 1-pattern t we say that a^r is the a-*suffix* of t if $t = t'a^r$ and the last letter of t' is not a (in particular, t' may be empty).

We call this procedure Uncross $(a, 'u = v')$, its formal details are given in Algorithm 2.

Algorithm 2. Uncross $(a, 'u = v')$ Uncrossing all a-chains

1: **for** $\alpha \in \mathcal{V} \cup \mathcal{X}$ **do**
2:      **if** a is the first letter of $S(\alpha)$ **then**   ▷ Guess
3:          guess $\ell \geq 1$ ▷ a^ℓ is the a-prefix of $S(\alpha)$
4:          replace each α in $u = v$ by $a^\ell \alpha$ ▷ implicitly change $S(\alpha) = a^\ell t$ to $S(\alpha) = t$
5:          **if** $S(\alpha)$ is empty **then**   ▷ Guess; applies only to context variables
6:              remove α from $u = v$: replace each $\alpha(t)$ in the equation by t

7: **for** $X \in \mathcal{V}$ **do**
8:      **if** a is the last letter of $S(X)$ **then**   ▷ Guess
9:          guess $r \geq 1$ ▷ a^r is the a-suffix of $S(X)$
10:          replace each X in $u = v$ by Xa^r ▷ implicitly change $S(X) = ta^r$ to
      $S(X) = t$
11:          **if** $S(X)$ is empty **then**   ▷ Guess
12:              remove X from $u = v$: replace each $X(t)$ by t

---

Lemma 3. Uncross$(a, 'u = v')$ *is sound and if $u = v$ has a non-empty solution S (over an alphabet Σ) then for appropriate non-deterministic choices the returned equation $u' = v'$ has a non-empty solution S' (over the same alphabet Σ) such that $S'(u') = S(u)$ and a has no crossing chains with respect to S'.*

Example 4. Continuing Example 2:

$$bXaXc = baa(f(aYc', bb(f(c, c')))),$$

where the alphabet is $\{a, b, c, c', f\}$, with $\mathrm{ar}(a) = \mathrm{ar}(b) = 1, \mathrm{ar}(c) = \mathrm{ar}(c') = 0$ and $\mathrm{ar}(f) = 2$ and $S(X) = aa(f(\bullet, bb(f(c, c'))))$ and $S(Y) = aa(f(c, bb(f(c, \bullet))))$.

There are crossing a chains, because aY is a subpattern and a is the first letter of $S(Y)$. We pop the a-prefixes from X, Y, there are no a-suffixes. The instance is now

$$baaXaaaXc = baa(f(aaaYc', bb(f(c, c')))),$$

where $S'(X) = f(\bullet, bb(f(c, c')))$ and $S'(Y) = f(c, bb(f(\bullet, c)))$. It is easy to verify that a has no crossing chains.

4.3 Uncrossing Father-Leaf Subpattern

We now show how to uncross a father-leaf subpattern (f, i, c). It is easy to observe that father-leaf subpattern (f, i, c) is crossing (with respect to a non-empty S) if and only if one of the following holds for some context variable X and term variable y:

(CFL 1) f with an i-th son y occurs in $u = v$ and $S(y) = c$;

(CFL 2) Xc occurs in $u = v$ and the last letter of $S(X)$ is f and $\bullet$ is its i-th child;

(CFL 3) Xy occurs in $u = v$, $S(y) = c$ and f is the last letter of $S(X)$ and $\bullet$ is its i-th child.

We want to 'pop-up' c and 'pop-down' f. Popping up c is easy (we replace y with c); popping-down f is more complex. Let us first present the intuition:

- In (CFL1) we *pop up* the letter c from y, which in this case means that we replace each occurrence of y in the equation with $c = S(y)$. Since y is no longer in the context equation, we can restrict the solution so that it does not assign any value to y.
- In (CFL2) we *pop down* the letter f: let $S(X) = sf(t_1, \ldots, t_{i-1}, \bullet, t_i, \ldots, t_{m-1})$, where s is a 1-pattern and each t_i is a ground term and $\mathrm{ar}(f) = m$. Then we replace each X with $Xf(x_1, x_2, \ldots, x_{i-1}, \bullet, x_i, \ldots, x_{m-1})$, where $x_1, \ldots, x_{m-1}$ are fresh term variables. In this way we implicitly modify the solution $S(X) = s(f(t_1, t_2, \ldots, t_{i-1}, \bullet, t_i, \ldots, t_{m-1}))$ to $S'(X) = s$ and add $S'(x_j) = t_j$ for $j = 1, \ldots, m - 1$. If $S'(X)$ is empty, we remove X from the equation.
- The third case (CFL3) is a combination of (CFL1)–(CFL2), in which we need to pop-down from X and pop up from y.

We call this procedure $\mathsf{Uncross}((f, i, c), 'u = v')$, its formal description is given in Algorithm 3.

Algorithm 3. $\mathsf{Uncross}((f, i, c), 'u = v')$

1: **for** $x \in \mathcal{X}$ **do**
2:     **if** $S(x) = c$ **then**   ▷ Guess
3:        replace each x in $u = v$ by c ▷ S is no longer defined on x
4: **let** $m \leftarrow \mathrm{ar}(f)$
5: **for** $X \in \mathcal{V}$ **do**
6:     **if** f is the last letter of $S(X)$, $\bullet$ is its i-th child and Xc is a subpattern in $u = v$
      then   ▷ Guess
7:        replace each X in $u = v$ by $X(f(x_1, x_2, \ldots, x_{i-1}, \bullet, x_i, \ldots, x_{m1}-))$
          ▷ Implicitly change $S(X) = sf(t_1, t_2, \ldots, t_{i-1}, \bullet, t_i, \ldots, t_{m-1})$ to $S(X) = s$
          ▷ Add new variables $x_1, \ldots, x_{m-1}$ to $\mathcal{X}$ and extend S by setting $S(x_j) = t_j$
8:        **if** $S(X)$ is empty **then**   ▷ Guess
9:           remove X from the equation: replace each $X(t)$ in the equation by t
10: **for** new variables $x \in \mathcal{X}$ **do**
11:     **if** $S(x) = c$ **then**   ▷ Guess
12:        replace each x in $u = v$ by c ▷ S is no longer defined on x

---

Lemma 4. *Let* $\mathrm{ar}(f) \geq i \geq 1$ *and* $\mathrm{ar}(c) = 0$, *then* $\mathsf{Uncross}((f, i, c), 'u = v')$ *is sound and if* $u = v$ *has a non-empty solution* S *(over an alphabet* Σ*) then for* *appropriate non-deterministic choices the returned equation $u' = v'$ has a non-empty solution S' (over the same alphabet Σ) such that $S'(u') = S(u)$ and there is no crossing father-leaf subpattern (f, i, c) with respect to S'.*

Example 5. Continuing Example 2, the equations

$$bXaXc = baa(f(aYc', bb(f(c, c'))))$$

where the alphabet is $\{a, b, c, c', f\}$, with $\mathrm{ar}(a) = \mathrm{ar}(b) = 1$, $\mathrm{ar}(c) = \mathrm{ar}(c') = 0$ and $\mathrm{ar}(f) = 2$, has a solution $S(X) = aa(f(\bullet, bb(f(c, c'))))$ and $S(Y) = aa(f(c, bb(f(c, \bullet))))$. A subpattern $(f, 2, c')$ is crossing, as Yc' is a subpattern, the last letter of Y is f and the hole $\bullet$ is the second child of this f We uncross it by popping down from Y: The instance is now

$$bXaXc = baa(f(aY(f(y, c')), bb(f(c, c'))))$$

where $S'(X) = S(X)$, $S'(Y) = f(c, b(b(\bullet)))$ and $S(y) = c$. It is easy to see that $(f, 2, c')$ is now noncrossing.

5   The Algorithm

In its main part, ContextEqSatSimp iterates the following operation: it nondeterministically chooses to perform one of the compressions: ab compression, a-chain compression or (f, i, c) compression, where a, b, c, f are some letters of appropriate arity. It then nondeterministically choose, whether this pattern is crossing or not. If so, it performs the appropriate uncrossing. Then it performs the subpattern compression for p and adds the new letter (or letters, for chains compression) to Σ. We call one iteration of main loop of ContextEqSatSimp a *phase*.

Algorithm 4. ContextEqSatSimp('$u = v$', Σ) Checking the satisfiability of a context equation $u = v$

1: **while** $|u| > 1$ or $|v| > 1$ **do**
2:     choose p from $\{a, ab, (f, i, c)\}$ to compress, $a, b, c, f \in \Sigma$
3:     **if** p is crossing **then**   ▷ Guess
4:         Uncross(p, '$u = v$')
5:     PattCompNCr(a, '$u = v$')
6:     add letters representing compressed subpatterns to Σ
7: Solve the problem naively   ▷ With sides of size 1, the problem is trivial

---

The extended algorithm ContextEqSat works in the same way, except that at the beginning of each iteration it removes from the alphabet the letters that are neither from the original alphabet neither are present in the current context equation. It is easy to show that such removal does not change the satisfiability of the given equation.

Theorem 1. ContextEqSatSimp *and* ContextEqSat *store an equation of length* $\mathcal{O}(n^2k^2)$, *where n is the size of the input equation and k the maximal arity of symbols from the input alphabet. They non-deterministically solve context equations, in the sense that:*

- *if the input equation is not-satisfiable then they never return 'YES';*
- *if the input equation is satisfiable then for some nondeterministic choices in* $\mathcal{O}(n^3k^3 \log N)$ *phases they return 'YES', where N is the size of size-minimal solution.*

As a corollary we get an upper bound on the computational complexity of context unification.

Theorem 2. *Context unification is in* PSPACE.

6 Space Bounds

While the soundness of the algorithm follows from soundness of its subprocedures, the space bounds, and so the termination, remains to be shown.

6.1 General Bounds

First, we recall that the following known bound on the size of the a-chains for size-minimal solutions. This ensures that we can compress the chains in polynomial space.

Lemma 5 (Exponent of periodicity bound [28]). *Let S be a size-minimal solution of a context equation $u = v$ (for an alphabet Σ). Suppose that $S(X)$ (or $S(x)$) can be written as $ta^m t'$, where t, t' are 1-patterns (or t' is a ground term, respectively) and a is a unary letter. Then $m = 2^{\mathcal{O}(|u|+|v|)}$.*

Now we bound the number of variables occurrences during the algorithm. Note that this bound works for all nondeterministic choices.

Lemma 6. *The number of occurrences of context variables during* ContextEqSat *is at most n. The number of occurrences of term variables is at most nk.*

The bound for context variables is obvious, as we never introduce new ones. For term variables observe that during the (f, i, c) uncrossing we introduce new term variables, by popping them from context variables. However, it can be shown that when we pop new term variables from X, all term variables previously introduced by X have been removed. This yields the bound.

As a next step, we estimate the number of different crossing subpatterns. This follows by a simple argument that such a pattern can be associated with a top or bottom letter in a variable.

Lemma 7. *For an equation $u = v$ during* ContextEqSat *and its solution S the number of different crossing subpatterns of the form $a, ab, (f, i, c)$ is at most $n(k+1)$.*

We can also limit the number of new letters introduced during the uncrossing. Again, this follows a simple calculation.

Lemma 8. *Uncrossing and compression of a subpattern introduces at most $n(k+1)$ letters to the equation.*

6.2 Strategy

The strategy of choosing nondeterministic choices is easy: if there is a noncrossing pattern, then we compress it, as this decreases both the size of the equation and of the minimal solution.

If there is none, then we choose a pattern, whose compression makes equation smallest possible (after this one compression). As there are only $n(k+1)$ such candidates, see Lemma 7, one of them will appear roughly $(|u|+|v|)/n(k+1)$ many times. Its compression removes $(|u|+|v|)/2n(k+1)$ letters and introduces at most $n(k+1)$ many letters, see Lemma 8. This shows that we never exceed the quadratic bound on $|u|+|v|$ given in Theorem 1.

If we additionally make choices so as to minimize the size of the solution, then we can guarantee to terminate after the number of steps depending on $\log N$ (and not N), so as claimed in Theorem 1.

7 Detailed Example

We now run the algorithm on Example 2, see also the Fig. 2. Recall the equation:

$$bXaXc = ba(a(f(aYc', b(b(f(c, c'))))))),$$

where the alphabet is $\Sigma = \{a, b, c, c', f\}$, with $\mathrm{ar}(a) = \mathrm{ar}(b) = 1$, $\mathrm{ar}(c) = \mathrm{ar}(c') = 0$ and $\mathrm{ar}(f) = 2$ and $S(X) = a(a(f(\bullet, b(b(f(c, c')))))))$ and $S(Y) = a(a(f(c, b(b(f(c, \bullet))))))))$. There is no need to preprocess the alphabet.

As b has no crossing chains, so we compress it, obtaining

$$bXaXc = baa(f(aYc', b'(f(c, c')))),$$

where the alphabet is $\Sigma \cup \{b'\}$, with $\mathrm{ar}(b') = 1$ and the solution and $S(X) = aa(f(\bullet, b'(f(c, c'))))$ and $S(Y) = aa(f(c, b'(f(c, \bullet))))$. Now every potential subpattern for compression is crossing. We choose $(f, 1, c)$ for compression and uncross it. To this end we pop f down from X. Note, that according to the algorithm, f is not popped down from Y, even though f is its last letter, it does not take part in any crossing occurrence of a subpattern $(f, 1, c)$. The instance is now

$$bX(f(aXf(c, x), x)) = baa(f(aYc', b'(f(c, c')))),$$

with a solution $S(X) = aa$, $S(Y) = aa(f(c, b'(f(c, \bullet))))$ and $S(x) = b'(f(c, c'))$. We compress $(f, 1, c)$, obtaining

$$bX(f(aXf'x, x)) = baa(f(aYc', b'f'c')),$$

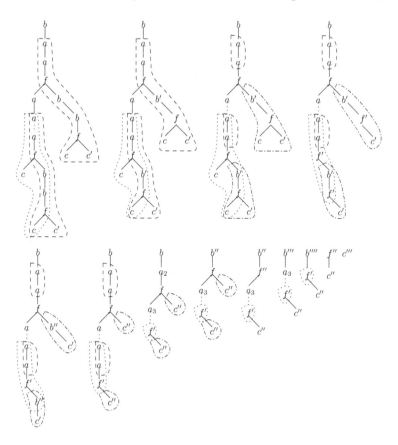

Fig. 2. An illustration of running the algorithm on the instance from Example 2. The Figure presents the term obtained at both sides under the substitution, the values substitutions for variables are depicted: in dashed line for X and dotted for Y, later also dash-dotted for x. The changes are according to the consecutive actions described in the section: b chains compression, uncrossing $(f, 1, c)$, compression of $(f, 1, c)$, compression of $b' f'$, uncrossing and compression of $(b'', 1, c')$, uncrossing a-chains and compression of a chains, compression of ba_2, uncrossing and compression of $(f, 2, c'')$, compression of $b'' f''$, compression of $b''' a_3$, uncrossing and compression of $b'''' f'$ and finally compression of $(f'', 1, c'')$.

with a solution $S(X) = aa$, $S(Y) = aaf'b'f'$, $S(x) = b'f'c'$, here f' is of arity $\mathrm{ar}(f') = 1$ is added to the alphabet, which is now $\Sigma \cup \{b', f'\}$. Note that there is a new term variable x. Now $b'f'$ is noncrossing, so we compress it (into b'' of arity 1), obtaining

$$bX(f(aXf'x, x)) = baa(f(aYc', b''c')),$$

with a solution $S(X) = aa$, $S(Y) = aaf'b''$ and $S(x) = b''c'$. The b' is no longer used, so it is removed from the alphabet, which is now $\Sigma \cup \{b'', f'\}$ We choose to compress $b''c'$, as a $(b, 1, c')$ subpattern, we first uncross it by popping f down from Y and then we compress into a new constant c'', the b'' can be removed. So the alphabet is now $\Sigma \cup \{f', c''\}$ and the equation is

$$bX(f(aXf'x, x)) = baa(f(aYc'', c'')),$$

with a solution $S(X) = aa$, $S(Y) = aaf'$ and $S(x) = c''$.

Now we uncross and compress a-blocks: in uncrossing we replace X with a^2 and pop-up a^2 from Y. Afterwards we replace a^2 with a_2 and a^3 with a_3. The alphabet is now $\Sigma \cup \{f', c'', a_2, a_3\}$ and the equation is

$$ba_2(f(a_3f'x, x)) = ba_2(f(a_3Yc'', c'')),$$

with a solution $S(Y) = f'$ and $S(x) = c''$.

Now we compress the noncrossing ba_2 into b'' (note that we reuse the letter b''), a_2 is removed from the alphabet, which is now $\Sigma \cup \{b'', f', c'', a_3\}$ and the equation is

$$b''(f(a_3f'x, x)) = b''(f(a_3Yc'', c'')),$$

with a solution $S(Y) = f'$ and $S(x) = c''$. Now we choose to compress $(f, 2, c'')$, so we pop up c'' from x (thus removing it). After the compression, the alphabet is $\Sigma \cup \{b'', f', f'', c'', a_3\}$ and the equation is $b''f''a_3f'c'' = b''f''a_3Yc''$, with a solution $S(Y) = f'$.

We compress noncrossing $b''f''$, obtaining the alphabet $\Sigma \cup \{b''', f', c'', a_3\}$ and the equation is $b'''a_3f'c'' = b'''a_3Yc''$, with a solution $S(Y) = f'$. We now compress $b'''a_3$, which is noncrossing, yielding an equation $b''''f'c'' = b''''Yc''$, with a solution $S(Y) = f'$ over an alphabet $\Sigma \cup \{b'''', f', c''\}$.

Now we uncross $b''''f'$, by replacing Y with f' and compress it, obtaining a trivial equation $f''c'' = f''c''$ over an alphabet $\Sigma \cup \{f'', c''\}$, for which we perform the final compression $(f'', 1, c'')$, yielding an equation $c''' = c'''$.

8 Regular Constraints

We now consider the problem of context unification with regular constraints. In this setting, the input contains (some description of) regular tree languages $L_1, \ldots, L_\ell$ of ground terms and/or 1-patterns over the input alphabet Σ. Those automata are used for enriching the equation with additional constraints of the form $\alpha \in L_i$, meaning that the substitution for the variable α should be from language L_i. Naturally, those languages have to be specified in some way, we choose one, see Sect. 8.2, but other natural descriptions are equivalent, see discussion at the end of that section.

Context unification with regular constraints was investigated mostly because *linear second order unification* [12] and context unification with regular constraints reduce to each other [16]; note that those reductions are not polynomial-time, so cannot be used directly to claim the computational complexity of linear second order unification. On the other hand, adding constraints to unification is interesting and important on its own.

To generalise ContextEqSat to this setting, we assign to each letter in the alphabet its transition function; such transition functions can be generalised to patterns, so in particular to substitutions for variables; transition vectors and vectors of such transitions are defined in Sect. 8.1 and we explain how to use them to define constraints for context unification in Sect. 8.2. When we compress a certain subpattern into one letter, we compose those transition functions. When we pop letters from variables we assign to the variable a new transition function, so that the composition of transition function of popped letters and the new transition function for a variable is equal to the old transition function for a variable.

However, several simplifications do not work in this setting. This is for a reason: it is known that the non-emptiness problem for intersection of (deterministic) finite tree automata is EXPTIME-complete [5] and we can easily encode this problem within context unification with regular constraints, so we cannot hope to extend our algorithm to this setting without affecting the computational complexity.

To resolve this problem, we *extend* the input alphabet by adding to it one letter f_Δ for every possible vector of transition functions Δ (we limit the allowed arities, though, to the maximal arity of letters in the input alphabet). We do not store this alphabet explicitly, instead we use an (EXPTIME) oracle to decide, whether a letter belongs to the alphabet or not. It is easy to see that a context equation is equisatisfiable over its input alphabet and over such an extended alphabet. Later on, for any equation, we consider its solution over an alphabet consisting of the extended alphabet and letters present in the equation.

Ultimately, for algorithms ContextEqSatRegSimp and ContextEqSatReg which are generalisations of ContextEqSatSimp and ContextEqSat to scenarios with regular constraints, respectively, we want to show the following theorem.

Theorem 3. ContextEqSatRegSimp *and* ContextEqSatReg *keep an equation of size* $\mathcal{O}(n^2 k^2)$. *Given an unsatisfiable context equation with regular constraints they never return 'YES'. Given a satisfiable one with a minimal-size solution of size* N *they return 'YES' after* $\mathcal{O}(n^2 k^2 \log N)$ *compression steps, for appropriate non-deterministic choices.*

ContextEqSatReg *uses an oracle for the intersection of tree-regular languages, which can always be implemented in* EXPTIME. *Except for that, it runs in* PSPACE.

As a corollary, we get an EXPTIME bound on the satisfiability of context unification with regular constraints.

Corollary 1. *Context unification with regular constraints is* EXPTIME-*complete.*

8.1 Tree Automata

A tree automaton is defined as a triple $(\Sigma, Q, \delta_{f\,f \in \Sigma})$, where Σ is a ranked alphabet, Q is a set of states and each δ_f is a transition relation (sometimes called *transition function* for historical reasons) of a letter from Σ.

To be more precise, when $\mathrm{ar}(f) = r$ then $\delta_f \subseteq Q^r \times Q$. The meaning of the transition functions is that we consider labelling of ground terms with states (such labellings are usually called *runs*) such that a node labelled with f whose children are assigned states $(q_1, q_2, \ldots, q_r)$ can be assigned any state q such that $(q_1, q_2, \ldots, q_r, q) \in \delta_f$. Thus we think of δ_f as a nondeterministic transition function, and by $\delta_f(q_1, q_2, \ldots, q_{\mathrm{ar}(f)})$ we denote the set of states $\{q : (q_1, q_2, \ldots, q_{\mathrm{ar}(f)}, q) \in \delta_f\}$.

We can treat a letter f as a pattern with a unique non-parameter node f; in this way we can define δ_p for arbitrary patterns: given an r-pattern p the tuple $(q_1, q_2, \ldots, q_{\mathrm{ar}(f)}, q)$ is in δ_p if and only if there is a run for p in which nodes $\bullet_1, \bullet_2, \ldots, \bullet_{\mathrm{ar}(f)}$ are labelled with $q_1, q_2, \ldots, q_{\mathrm{ar}(f)}$ and the root of p is labelled with q. Note that this implicitly gives a rule of composing transition functions; such composition is associative in case of 1-patterns.

Concerning the notation, we will explicitly compose only transition functions for patterns that occur during the subpattern compression. Thus for unary patterns $p_1, p_2, \ldots, p_\ell$ by $\delta_{p_1} \delta_{p_2} \ldots \delta_{p_\ell}$ we denote the transition function of the pattern $p_1 p_2 \ldots p_\ell$ and when $p_1 = p_2 = \cdots = p_\ell$ then we denote this function by $(\delta_{p_1})^\ell$. Similarly, for an r-ary pattern f and ground terms $t_1, t_2, \ldots, t_m$ by $\delta_f[\bullet_{i_1}/\delta_{t_1}, \bullet_{i_2}/\delta_{t_2}, \ldots, \bullet_{i_m}/\delta_{t_m}]$ we denote the transition function of a pattern obtained by replacing $\bullet_{i_1}, \bullet_{i_2}, \ldots, \bullet_{i_m}$ by $t_1, t_2, \ldots, t_m$, respectively. Note, that it could be that $m < r$, i.e. not all parameters of a pattern f are substituted by ground terms.

For a fixed sequence of automata $A_1, A_2, \ldots, A_\ell$ (and it is fixed for a fixed instance of context unification with regular constraints) with transition functions $\{\delta_f^1\}_{f \in \Sigma}, \{\delta_f^2\}_{f \in \Sigma}, \ldots, \{\delta_f^\ell\}_{f \in \Sigma}$ by Δ_p we denote the tuple of transition functions $(\delta_p^1, \delta_p^2, \ldots, \delta_p^\ell)$ for a pattern p; this is a *vector of transitions* of this pattern. Note that this is a vector of sets. We denote vectors of transitions by $\Delta, \Delta_1, \ldots$ and consider them even without underlying patterns, and refer to r-vector of transitions, when this is a vector of transitions of an r-ary pattern.

We extend the composition of transition functions and its notation to vectors of transitions in a natural way, i.e. we perform the appropriate operation coordinate-wise on each transition function.

8.2   Context Unification with Regular Constraints

Now we are ready to define the problem of context unification with regular constraints. As an input we are given a finite alphabet Σ, finite automata $A_1, A_2, \ldots, A_\ell$ over Σ (with state sets $Q_1, Q_2, \ldots, Q_\ell$ and transition functions $\{\delta_f^1\}_{f \in \Sigma}, \{\delta_f^2\}_{f \in \Sigma}, \ldots, \{\delta_f^\ell\}_{f \in \Sigma}$), a context equation $u = v$ and a set of constraints on the vectors of transitions for variables u in total. To be more precise, those constraints are:

term variable constraints: we are given 0-vectors of transitions Δ_x for some variables $x \in \mathcal{X}$;

equations constraints: similarly, we are given 0-vector of transition Δ_u;

context variable constraints: we are given 1-vectors of transitions Δ_X for some context variables $X \in \mathcal{V}$.

The meaning of the constraints is clear: we ask, whether there is a substitution S, such that $S(u) = S(v)$, $\Delta_{S(u)} = \Delta_u$ and $\Delta_{S(\alpha)} = \Delta_\alpha$ for each variable α.

8.3   Modifications of ContextEqSat

We now explain the modifications of ContextEqSatSimp to ContextEqSatRegSimp, i.e. consider the algorithm that enriches the alphabet with every letter that it created.

Compression. When a subpattern p is compressed into f, we calculate its vector of transitions and set $\Delta_f \leftarrow \Delta_p$.

Popping Letters. When popping letters, we guess the new vectors of transitions for the variable, so that the composition of vectors of transitions (in the appropriate order) of the popped letter and variable is the same as it used to be; this applies also to popping of term variables during the uncrossing of leaf-pair. For instance, when we replace X with $X(f(x_1, \bullet_2, x_3))$ then we guess new transitions $\Delta'_X, \Delta_{x_1}, \Delta_{x_3}$, such that $\Delta_X = \Delta'_X(\Delta_f[\bullet_1/\Delta_{x_1}, \bullet_3/\Delta_{x_3}])$; we add $\Delta_{x_1}, \Delta_{x_3}$ to sets constraints and update Δ_X to Δ'_X. When we remove a context variable X, we need to ensure that its transition function Δ_X is the same as $\Delta(\bullet)$, i.e. it is an identity; similarly, when we replace x with c we need to validate that $\Delta_x = \Delta_c$.

Ending. When the whole equation is reduced to a single equation $c = c$, we check whether the transition function for c is the same as for the whole equation, i.e. $\Delta_u = \Delta_c$. If so, we accept, if not, we reject.

Satisfiability. Whenever we claim that an equation is satisfiable (so, it has some solution S), we need to additionally assert that the transition for a variable (and the whole equation) is as in the constraints kept by the instance, that is, $\Delta_{S(\alpha)} = \Delta_\alpha$ for each variable α and $\Delta_{S(u)} = \Delta_u$.

Subprocedures. Lemma 1 holds in the new setting, to this end it is enough to recall that during compression the new letter has the same transition function as the pattern it replaced and for popping, we always guess the popped letters and the new constraints of variables so that the composition of their vectors of transitions is equal to the vector of transitions of the variable before the popping.

The discussion above shows the proof of Theorem 3 in case of ContextEqSatRegSimp. The only remaining problem is that the alphabet used by ContextEqSatRegSimp grows and the size of transition vectors of the involved letters can be even exponential. However, careful inspection shows that one can define appropriate subclass of all vectors of transitions, called *reachable*. They are of polynomial size and can be composed in polynomial time; moreover, each letter that occurs during ContextEqSatReg has a reachable vector of transition and vice versa—each reachable vector of transitions can be realised by tree or a pattern over the input alphabet. Lastly, one can check in EXPTIME, whether a vector of transitions is reachable. This ends the analysis for Theorem 3.

9 Open Questions

Computational complexity. The exact computational complexity of context unification remains unknown: the presented algorithm shows containment in PSPACE and the best known lower bound is NP, by a trivial reduction of Integer Programming. Perhaps the additional structure of terms allows showing a stronger lower bound?

Size of minimal solutions. Extension of the given proof shows that the size of the smallest solution of a context unification is of at most doubly exponential size. At the same time, we know no solution which is super-exponential, so the same as in the case of word equations. An exponential upper bound would imply containment in NP, a counterexample would somehow suggest that PSPACE *is* the computational complexity of the problem.

Unary second order unification. The decidability status of subproblem of second order unification, in which each second order has arity 1, remains unknown. The presented approach does not generalize to this case and at the same time the existing proof of undecidability essentially requires second-order variables of rank 2.

One context variable. Context unification with one context variable is known to be in NP [6] and some of its fragments are in P [7,8]. It remains an open question, whether the whole problem is in P.

References

1. Comon, H.: Completion of rewrite systems with membership constraints. Part I: deduction rules. J. Symb. Comput. **25**(4), 397–419 (1998). https://doi.org/10.1006/jsco.1997.0185
2. Comon, H.: Completion of rewrite systems with membership constraints. Part II: constraint solving. J. Symb. Comput. **25**(4), 421–453 (1998). https://doi.org/10.1006/jsco.1997.0186
3. Diekert, V., Gutiérrez, C., Hagenah, C.: The existential theory of equations with rational constraints in free groups is PSPACE-complete. Inf. Comput. **202**(2), 105–140 (2005). https://doi.org/10.1016/j.ic.2005.04.002
4. Diekert, V., Jeż, A., Plandowski, W.: Finding all solutions of equations in free groups and monoids with involution. Inf. Comput. **251**, 263–286 (2016). https://doi.org/10.1016/j.ic.2016.09.009
5. Frühwirth, T.W., Shapiro, E.Y., Vardi, M.Y., Yardeni, E.: Logic programs as types for logic programs. In: LICS, pp. 300–309. IEEE Computer Society (1991). https://doi.org/10.1109/LICS.1991.151654
6. Gascón, A., Godoy, G., Schmidt-Schauß, M., Tiwari, A.: Context unification with one context variable. J. Symb. Comput. **45**(2), 173–193 (2010). https://doi.org/10.1016/j.jsc.2008.10.005
7. Gascón, A., Schmidt-Schauß, M., Tiwari, A.: Two-restricted one context unification is in polynomial time. In: Kreutzer, S. (ed.) CSL. LIPIcs, vol. 41, pp. 405–422. Schloss Dagstuhl–Leibniz-Zentrum fuer Informatik (2015). https://doi.org/10.4230/LIPIcs.CSL.2015.405

8. Gascón, A., Tiwari, A., Schmidt-Schauß, M.: One context unification problems solvable in polynomial time. In: LICS, pp. 499–510. IEEE (2015). https://doi.org/10.1109/LICS.2015.53

9. Goldfarb, W.D.: The undecidability of the second-order unification problem. Theor. Comput. Sci. **13**, 225–230 (1981). https://doi.org/10.1016/0304-3975(81)90040-2

10. Jeż, A.: Context unification is in PSPACE. In: Esparza, J., Fraigniaud, P., Husfeldt, T., Koutsoupias, E. (eds.) ICALP 2014. LNCS, vol. 8573, pp. 244–255. Springer, Heidelberg (2014). https://doi.org/10.1007/978-3-662-43951-7_21. Full version http://arxiv.org/abs/1310.4367

11. Jeż, A.: Recompression: a simple and powerful technique for word equations. J. ACM **63**(1), 4:1 (2016). https://doi.org/10.1145/2743014

12. Levy, J.: Linear second-order unification. In: Ganzinger, H. (ed.) RTA 1996. LNCS, vol. 1103, pp. 332–346. Springer, Heidelberg (1996). https://doi.org/10.1007/3-540-61464-8_63

13. Levy, J., Agustí-Cullell, J.: Bi-rewrite systems. J. Symb. Comput. **22**(3), 279–314 (1996). https://doi.org/10.1006/jsco.1996.0053

14. Levy, J., Schmidt-Schauß, M., Villaret, M.: The complexity of monadic second-order unification. SIAM J. Comput. **38**(3), 1113–1140 (2008). https://doi.org/10.1137/050645403

15. Levy, J., Schmidt-Schauß, M., Villaret, M.: On the complexity of bounded second-order unification and stratified context unification. Log. J. IGPL **19**(6), 763–789 (2011). https://doi.org/10.1093/jigpal/jzq010

16. Levy, J., Villaret, M.: Linear second-order unification and context unification with tree-regular constraints. In: Bachmair, L. (ed.) RTA 2000. LNCS, vol. 1833, pp. 156–171. Springer, Heidelberg (2000). https://doi.org/10.1007/10721975_11

17. Levy, J., Villaret, M.: Currying second-order unification problems. In: Tison, S. (ed.) RTA 2002. LNCS, vol. 2378, pp. 326–339. Springer, Heidelberg (2002). https://doi.org/10.1007/3-540-45610-4_23

18. Makanin, G.: The problem of solvability of equations in a free semigroup. Matematicheskii Sbornik **2**(103), 147–236 (1977). (in Russian)

19. Marcinkowski, J.: Undecidability of the first order theory of one-step right ground rewriting. In: Comon, H. (ed.) RTA 1997. LNCS, vol. 1232, pp. 241–253. Springer, Heidelberg (1997). https://doi.org/10.1007/3-540-62950-5_75

20. Niehren, J., Pinkal, M., Ruhrberg, P.: On equality up-to constraints over finite trees, context unification, and one-step rewriting. In: McCune, W. (ed.) CADE 1997. LNCS, vol. 1249, pp. 34–48. Springer, Heidelberg (1997). https://doi.org/10.1007/3-540-63104-6_4

21. Niehren, J., Pinkal, M., Ruhrberg, P.: A uniform approach to underspecification and parallelism. In: Cohen, P.R., Wahlster, W. (eds.) ACL, pp. 410–417. Morgan Kaufmann Publishers/ACL (1997). https://doi.org/10.3115/979617.979670

22. Plandowski, W.: Satisfiability of word equations with constants is in PSPACE. J. ACM **51**(3), 483–496 (2004). https://doi.org/10.1145/990308.990312

23. RTA Problem List: Problem 90 (1990). http://rtaloop.mancoosi.univ-paris-diderot.fr/problems/90.html

24. Schmidt-Schauß, M.: Unification of stratified second-order terms. Internal Report 12/94, Johann-Wolfgang-Goethe-Universität (1994)

25. Schmidt-Schauß, M.: A decision algorithm for distributive unification. Theor. Comput. Sci. **208**(1–2), 111–148 (1998). https://doi.org/10.1016/S0304-3975(98)00081-4

26. Schmidt-Schauß, M.: A decision algorithm for stratified context unification. J. Log. Comput. **12**(6), 929–953 (2002). https://doi.org/10.1093/logcom/12.6.929

27. Schmidt-Schauß, M.: Decidability of bounded second order unification. Inf. Comput. **188**(2), 143–178 (2004). https://doi.org/10.1016/j.ic.2003.08.002

28. Schmidt-Schauß, M., Schulz, K.U.: On the exponent of periodicity of minimal solutions of context equations. In: Nipkow, T. (ed.) RTA 1998. LNCS, vol. 1379, pp. 61–75. Springer, Heidelberg (1998). https://doi.org/10.1007/BFb0052361

29. Schmidt-Schauß, M., Schulz, K.U.: Solvability of context equations with two context variables is decidable. J. Symb. Comput. **33**(1), 77–122 (2002). https://doi.org/10.1006/jsco.2001.0438

30. Schmidt-Schauß, M., Schulz, K.U.: Decidability of bounded higher-order unification. J. Symb. Comput. **40**(2), 905–954 (2005). https://doi.org/10.1016/j.jsc.2005.01.005

31. Schulz, K.U.: Makanin's algorithm for word equations-two improvements and a generalization. In: Schulz, K.U. (ed.) IWWERT 1990. LNCS, vol. 572, pp. 85–150. Springer, Heidelberg (1992). https://doi.org/10.1007/3-540-55124-7_4

32. Treinen, R.: The first-order theory of linear one-step rewriting is undecidable. Theor. Comput. Sci. **208**(1–2), 179–190 (1998). https://doi.org/10.1016/S0304-3975(98)00083-8

33. Vorobyov, S.: The first-order theory of one step rewriting in linear Noetherian systems is undecidable. In: Comon, H. (ed.) RTA 1997. LNCS, vol. 1232, pp. 254–268. Springer, Heidelberg (1997). https://doi.org/10.1007/3-540-62950-5_76

34. Vorobyov, S.: $\forall\exists$*-Equational theory of context unification is Π_1^0-hard. In: Brim, L., Gruska, J., Zlatuška, J. (eds.) MFCS 1998. LNCS, vol. 1450, pp. 597–606. Springer, Heidelberg (1998). https://doi.org/10.1007/BFb0055810

Single-Stranded Architectures for Computing

Shinnosuke Seki[1,2(✉)]

[1] University of Electro-Communiactions, 1-5-1, Chofugaoka, Chofu,
Tokyo 1828585, Japan
s.seki@uec.ac.jp
[2] École Normale Supériéure de Lyon, 46 allée d'Italie, 69007 Lyon, France

Abstract. RNA is a chain of ribonucleotides of four kinds (denoted respectively by the letters A, C, G, U). While being synthesized sequentially from its template DNA (transcription), it folds upon itself into intricate higher-dimensional structures in such a way that the free energy is minimized, that is, the more hydrogen bonds between ribonucletoides or larger entropy a structure has, the more likely it is chosen, and furthermore the minimization is done locally. This phenomenon is called cotranscriptional folding (CF). It has turned out to play significant roles in *in-vivo* computation throughout experiments and recently proven even programmable artificially so as to self-assemble a specific RNA rectangular tile structure *in vitro*. The next step is to program a computation onto DNA in such a way that the computation can be "called" by cotranscriptional folding. In this novel paradigm of computation, what programmers could do is only twofold: designing a template DNA and setting environmental parameters. Oritatami is an introductory "toy" model to this paradigm of computation. In this model, programmars are also allowed to employ an arbitrarily large finite alphabet Σ as well as an arbitrarily complex rule set for binding over $\Sigma \times \Sigma$. We shall present known architectures of computing in the oritatami model from a simple half-adder to Turing machine along with several programming techniques of use, with hope that they will inspire *in-vivo* architectures of CF-driven self-assemblable computers, which could be even heritable.

1 Introduction

An organism is encoded on its single-stranded DNA. Its data and functions are "called" via *transcription*, in which a temporal copy of a factor of DNA is synthesized using ribonucleotides of four kinds ($\Sigma_{\mathrm{RNA}} = \{A, C, G, U\}$), and *translation*, in which the resulting RNA strand is decoded into a chain of amino acids, that is, protein. DNA, RNA, and protein are all chemically-oriented. The life of organisms can be regarded as a massive dynamical network of such molecular

This work is in part supported by the JST Program to Disseminate Tenure Tracking System, MEXT, Japan, No. 6F36 and JSPS KAKENHI Grant-in-Aid for Challenging Research (Exploratory) No. 18K19779, both to S.S.

P. Hofman and M. Skrzypczak (Eds.): DLT 2019, LNCS 11647, pp. 41–56, 2019.
https://doi.org/10.1007/978-3-030-24886-4_3

"words" and interactions driven by intermolecular forces among their compositional units, that is, nucleotides, ribonucleotides, and amino acids (see, e.g., [4,12] for further reading of molecular biology).

The last several decades have seen breathtaking growth and developments in the technology of programming such molecular networks for computation. The developments were launched by the successful demonstration of DNA computer to solve a 7-node instance of Hamiltonian path problem by Adleman [1], which we shall explain in the next paragraph, and have been driven by significant proof-of-concept multi-stranded architectures for computing including Winfree's tile assembly model (TAM) [43], toehold mediated strand displacement (TMSD), and DNA origami by Rothemund [37]. TAM is a dynamical variant of Wang tiling [41]. By TAM, Winfree founded the theory of algorithmic molecular self-assembly by agglomeration of DNA tiles via their programmable interactive sites (see [11] for a thorough review). TMSD was utilized for the first time for a computational purpose by Yurke et al. in order to let a DNA "fuel" strand open and close DNA tweezers [44], though it was known as branch migration since 70s. It has then been leveraged as various physical and logical computational mechanisms (see [19] and references therein). DNA origami provides a methodology to fold a template circular DNA strand by short DNA strands which can be programmed to "staple" two specific sites of the template together into various shapes. It has become a ubiquitous methodology in molecular self-assembly. For example, DNA origami provides a scaffold that accommodates other molecular architectures such as TMSD; Jonoska and Seeman thus endowed DNA origami-made tiles with signal-passing mechanisms to turn on/off their interactive sites [28].

The Adleman's DNA computer provides an introductory example to various concepts of significance for molecular architectures for computing. (DNA) nucleotides ($\Sigma_{\mathrm{DNA}} = \{\mathtt{A}, \mathtt{C}, \mathtt{G}, \mathtt{T}\}$) tend to form hydrogen bonds according to the Watson-Crick complementarity $\mathtt{A}$–$\mathtt{T}$ and $\mathtt{C}$–$\mathtt{G}$[1], which is extended to the antimorphic involution θ that satisfies $\theta(\mathtt{A}) = \mathtt{T}$, $\theta(\mathtt{C}) = \mathtt{G}$, $\theta(\mathtt{G}) = \mathtt{C}$, and $\theta(\mathtt{T}) = \mathtt{A}$ in order to capture hybridization among DNA strands. A DNA strand w and its Watson-Crick complement strand $\theta(w)$ thus form a completely double-stranded DNA. In the Adleman's DNA computer, a node x is encoded as a DNA strand $p_x s_x$ for some strands p_x, s_x of length 10 and the directed edge from x to y is encoded as $\theta(s_x p_y) = \theta(p_y)\theta(s_x)$. This edge strand hybridizes with the strand for x as well as with the strand for y to result in the following structure of length 40:

$$\overrightarrow{p_x \quad s_x} \ \overrightarrow{p_y \quad s_y}$$
$$\overleftarrow{({}^x s)\theta({}^R d)\theta}$$

According to a Hamiltonian path of a given instance, edge strands can thus concatenate node strands one after another and yield a structure of length 140. These node strands and edge strands are designed so carefully as not to hybridize between strands or within one strand in any undesirable manner.

---

[1] Other pairs also occur in nature but much less probably.

Fig. 1. Self-assembly of an RNA rectangular tile by cotranscriptional folding [18]. While being synthesized (transcribed) by RNA polymerase, the resulting RNA strand (transcript) is getting folded into the specific rectangular tile highly probably.

Hairpin-freeness and more general structure-freeness of (sets of) words were thus motivated (see, e.g., [6,27,29,30] and references therein). A *hairpin* is formed by combining x and $\theta(x)$ of a factor $xy\theta(x)$ into a stem and leaving y as a loop. For an intermolecular hybridization, its multiple reactants must encounter first. In contrast, a hairpin finds its interactive sites on one strand and hence forms fast; with complementary factors x and $\theta(x)$, a strand immediately folds into a hairpin and may get inert, though of course some multi-stranded architectures for computing rather leverage hairpins for their sake (see, e.g., [38]).

Single-stranded architectures for computing are, in principle, a network of intramolecular hybridizations if external control is ignored. Hairpins therefore serve them as a primary driver. Whiplash PCR by Hagiya et al. [20,39] is an architecture of a DNA strand that makes a transition from a state to another by hybridizing its 3'-end w_p, which encodes the current state p, to the substrand $\theta(w_p w_q)$ (forming a hairpin), extending the 3'-end enzymatically along $\theta(w_q)$ via DNA polymerase, and deforming the hairpin; the resulting DNA strand ends rather with w_q, that is, the system has thus transitioned to the state q. Komiya et al. demonstrated that their Whiplash PCR can make 8 transitions continuously at around 80 °C [31]. Indeed, high thermal stability of DNA precludes the hairpin deformation at room temperatures. DNA-made architectures are most often driven by thermodynamic control. Rose et al. [36] eliminated the need of thermal cycling from Whiplash PCR by incorporating TMSD.

RNA strands serve more naturally as a single-stranded architecture for computing *in vivo*. Their isothermal reactivity even at room temperatures certainly makes them more suitable than DNA for *in-vivo* computation. Computability of RNA is exploited considerably in nature, often in collaboration with proteins, as represented prominently by ribosome. This high reactivity has thwarted researchers' attempts to put RNA under control to a satisfactory extent so far. Nevertheless, RNA is enhancing its presence in molecular engineering as an alternative of DNA (see, e.g., [2,3,15,26,40]) mainly because an RNA strand can be synthesized enzymatically from its DNA template, which can be synthesized commercially at a reasonable cost nowadays. These two features are ingeniously combined in nature into a single-stranded computational engine called *cotranscriptional folding*. The RNA synthetic process is called *transcription* (see Fig. 1), in which an RNA polymerase enzyme attaches to a double-stranded DNA (colored in gray), scans its template strand[2] nucleotide by nucleotide from 3'-end to 5'-end in order to extend an RNA strand called *transcript* (blue) according to the lossless mapping A → U, C → G, G → C, and T → A. While being synthesized thus sequentially, the transcript folds upon itself into intricate structures kinetically, that is, being governed by forces among nucleotides and by likelihood. This is the *cotranscriptional folding*. A riboswitch, which is a segment of a (single-stranded) messenger RNA, regulates expression of a gene by folding cotranscriptionally into one structure with a hairpin called terminator stem in the absence of NaF or into another structure without the terminator stem in its existence [42]. Significant roles of cotranscriptional folding in nature like this have been discovered one after another (see, e.g., [33,35] and references therein). Researchers have been challenging to tame cotranscriptional folding for biotechnological applications. In 2014, Geary, Rothemund, and Andersen successfully "programmed" an artificial rectangular tile into a DNA strand in such a manner that, as illustrated in Fig. 1, the corresponding transcript folds cotranscriptionally into the programmed tile highly probably [18]. An instance of the DNA program can be reused to yield multiple copies of the tile, which further self-assemble into the honey-comb structure. The whole architecture is named RNA origami. Its first step, self-assembly by cotranscriptional folding, is much less understood than the second, which is accounted by the well-established theory of DNA algorithmic tile self-assembly ([11] provides a thorough review of this theory, for example).

Theoretical study of algorithmic self-assembly by cotranscriptional folding has been initiated by the proposal of a computational model called *oritatami* in the conference version of [17]. Oritatami does not aim at predicting RNA cotranscriptional folding in nature. It rather aims at providing a right angle to study the novel computational paradigm inspired by cotranscriptional folding, so-called *co-synthetic stepwise optimization*. In that paper [17], Geary et al. demonstrated that one can count in oritatami! This pioneering work of them was followed by successful reports of programming computational tasks in oritatami such as tautology check [24], bit-string bifurcation [32], and simulation of nondeterministic finite automata (NFA) [23,32]. In particular, the study by Masuda, Seki, and Ubukata in [32] initiated another line of research, that is, self-assembly of shapes by cotranscriptional folding. Demaine et al. [9] and Han and Kim [21] independently developed this line further for the self-assembly of general shapes. Throughout progression of studies as such, the oritatami model has proven itself to be a proper platform to study other key drivers of computation by cotranscriptional folding including modularization, memorization without random access memory (RAM), steric hindrance, and so on, in spite of its substantial abstraction. As a first milestone of oritatami research, all of these key drivers were successfully interlocked together to simulate a universal Turing machine with just polynomial overhead [16]. The resulting transcript should be the first single-stranded architecture for universal computation.

---

[2] The other strand is sometimes called *coding strand* because its sequence is equivalent to the product RNA transcript.

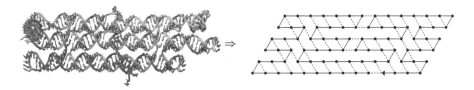

Fig. 2. Abstraction of a design of RNA rectangular tile that is self-assembled by RNA origami [18] as a directed path over the triangular lattice with pairings. The idea and artwork were provided by Cody Geary.

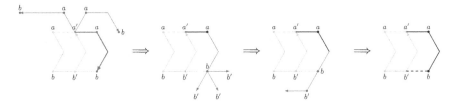

Fig. 3. Folding of a glider motif by a delay-3 deterministic oritatami system. The parts of the conformation colored in red, black, and blue are the seed, the prefix of transcript stabilized already, and the nascent suffix (of length 3), respectively. (Color figure online)

2   Single-Stranded Architectures for Computing in Oritatami

Let us first introduce the oritatami model briefly; for complete descriptions, see [17]. Terminologies from graph theory are used; for them, see [10]. Oritatami systems run on the 2-dimensional triangular lattice. As shown in Fig. 2, the covalent backbone of a single-stranded RNA structure is modeled as a directed path P over the lattice whose vertices are labeled with an element of Σ, a finite set of types of abstract molecules (called *beads*), and hydrogen bonds of the structure are modeled as a set of edges H that is pairwise-disjoint from the set of paths in P; the structure thus abstracted is called a *conformation*. An oritatami system Ξ is a 6-tuple $(\Sigma, \sigma, w, R, \delta, \alpha)$, which folds a word $w \in \Sigma^*$ (transcript) cotranscriptionally upon an initial conformation σ (seed) according to a set of (symmetric) rules $R \subseteq \Sigma \times \Sigma$ that specifies which types of beads are allowed to form a hydrogen bond once they get next to each other. The other two parameters δ and α shall be explained shortly.

Dynamics and Glider. A computation by the oritatami system Ξ is a sequence of conformations $C_0 = \sigma, C_1, C_2, \ldots$ such that C_i is obtained by elongating the directed backbone path of C_{i-1} by the i-th bead (letter) of w so as to maximize the number of hydrogen bonds. The dynamics of oritatami system should be explained best by an example. Figure 3 illustrates a directional oritatami motif called *glider*, where a seed is colored in red. Let $\Sigma = \{a, b, a', b', \bullet\}$, a transcript w be a repetition of $a \bullet bb' \bullet a'$, and the rule set R be $\{(a, a'), (b, b')\}$, that is,

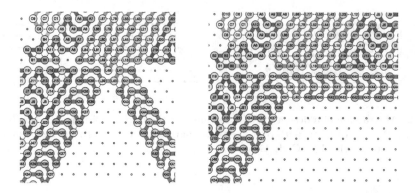

Fig. 4. Steric hindrance: one smallest-possible bump, formed by the chain L47–L48–L49, causes a drastic change in the conformation that this probe glider module takes after the collision. (Color figure online)

•-beads are inert. The *delay* parameter δ governs how many beads ahead should be taken into account at the stabilization of a bead. In this example, $\delta = 3$. By the fragment of the first δ beads $a \bullet b$, the system elongates the seed in all possible ways to test how many hydrogen bonds the resulting temporal conformation can form; note that the hydrogen bond between a c-bead and a d-bead necessitates that $(c, d) \in R$, these beads be located at unit distance, and they are not bonded covalently, that is, not contiguous in w. There are three possible elongations of the seed by $a \bullet b$ in Fig. 3. Since • is inert and there is no sufficiently close a'-bead around so as for the a-bead to form a hydrogen bond with, the stabilization is governed by the b-bead, which can form a hydrogen bond only if the fragment is folded as illustrated bold. Accordingly, the first bead, a, is stabilized to the east of its predecessor, and then the next (4th) b'-bead is transcribed. This b'-bead just transcribed cannot override the previous "decision" because with the sole b-bead around it is bonded covalently. The next •-bead is inert with respect to R so that it cannot override the previous decision either by definition. This dynamics is called *oblivious*. In [17], another kind of dynamics called *hasty* was studied, which does not question previous decisions.

Can we save bead types further? What if a' is replaced by a and the rule (a, a') is modified to the self-interaction (a, a)? The resulting system will stabilize the very first a-bead at two different positions nondeterministically. This nondeterminism can be, however, prevented by setting another *arity* parameter α to 1, which bounds the number of hydrogen bonds per bead from above. The arity is *maximum* if it is equal to 6, the degree of the triangular grid graph. Saving bead types is computationally hard in general [22] while some specific kinds of rules such as self-interaction [25] can be removed in polynomial time.

The glider is the most versatile oritatami motif discovered so far. First of all, it enables oritatami systems to fold into a directional structure of arbitrary length. It also serves as a "wire" to propagate 1-bit of information arbitrarily far [24], which helps to keep functional modules far enough not to interfere.

The Turing-universal oritatami system in [16] leverages gliders even as a probe to read out a letter of current binary word (over 0 and 1) of a simulated cyclic tag system, which is a RAM-free binary string rewriting system proposed by Cook [8]. See Fig. 4; a probe glider colored in purple is launched from southwest so as to hit a region where a letter (0 or 1) is encoded geometrically by a bump or its absence, and the collision redirects the glider either southeastwards or eastwards.

Nondeterminism. Oritatami systems may encounter nondeterminism in a position where a bead is stabilized, as briefly observed above, or in a way a bead forms hydrogen bonds. The tautology checker [24] and NFA simulator [23] utilize the position-wise nondeterminism. The bond-wise nondeterminism takes place only if arity is small enough for a bead to use up its binding capability; for instance, if arity is 1, a bead immediately gets inert after it forms a bond. This type of nondeterminism never arises if arity is maximum, i.e., equal to the degree of triangular grid graph because under the current optimization criterion to maximize the number of bonds, it is not beneficial to give up a bond whenever possible geometrically. Oritatami systems have been barely studied at any arity but the maximum; let alone this kind of nondeterminism.

2.1   A Single-Stranded Architecture for Counting in Binary

The first oritatami system Ξ_{bc} implemented odd bit-width binary counter under the hasty dynamics at delay 4 [17]. It employs 60 bead types $\{0, 1, \ldots, 59\}$ and its transcript is a repetition of 0-1-2- $\cdots$ -58-59; with such a periodic transcript, an oritatami system is said to be *cyclic* because transcription from a circular DNA template likely yields a periodic transcript [14]. *Modularization* proves itself to be quite fundamental also for oritatami design. The period of the transcript is semantically divided into four factors called *modules* A:0-1- $\cdots$ -11, B:12-13- $\cdots$ -29, C:30-31- $\cdots$ -41, and D:42-43- $\cdots$ -59, and the rule set R of Ξ_{bc} is designed in such a way that Modules A and C function as a half-adder and the interleaving B and D build a scaffold on which the half-adders are interlocked properly in order for the output and carry-out of a half-adder to be propagated to other half-adders.

   Increment from 0 to 1 by Ξ_{bc} is illustrated in stages in Fig. 5. Its seed encodes the initial count 0 with 3-bits in binary as a sequence of bead types in the following format: 30-39-40-41 to Module A and 0-9-10-11 to C for input bit 0. The transcript folds macroscopically into one zig ($\leftarrow$) and zag ($\rightarrow$) to increment the count by 1. The folding pathway of Ξ_{bc} is designed to guarantee that Module A encounters in a zig only four environments specified by whether the input from above is

$$30\text{-}39\text{-}40\text{-}41 \text{ (input 0)} \quad \text{or} \quad 30\text{-}35\text{-}36\text{-}41 \text{ (input 1)} \tag{1}$$

and whether it starts folding just below the input (top) or away by distance 3 (bottom). In these environments, Module A folds deterministically into the respective conformations in the upper row of Fig. 6, or we should say that the

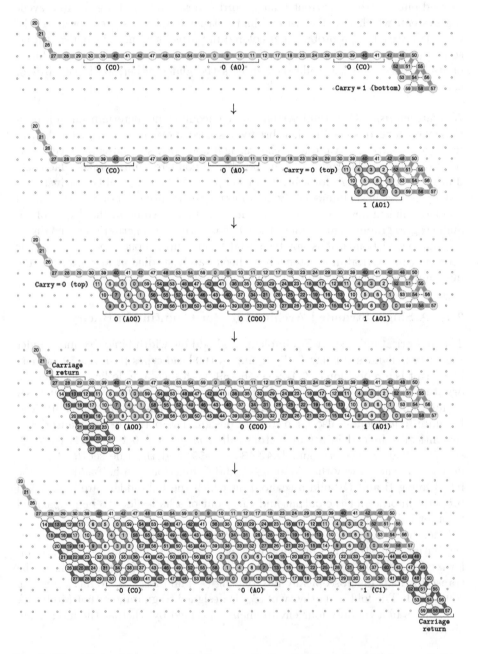

Fig. 5. The oritatami binary counter increments its value from 0, which is encoded on its seed, to 1 through one zigzag. (Color figure online)

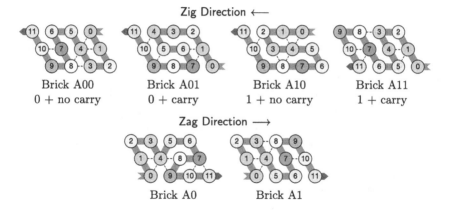

Fig. 6. All the six bricks of Module A.

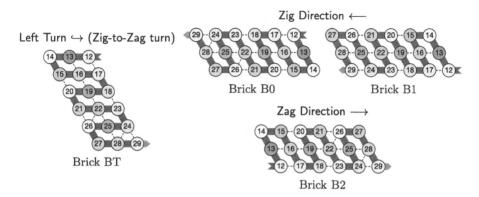

Fig. 7. All the four bricks of Module B: B0 and B1 for zig, B2 for zag, and BT for zig-to-zag turn.

rule set R is designed to have Module A behave so. Such conformations folded in an expected environment are called *bricks* as the whole folding is built upon them. Module A ends folding at the bottom (with carry-out) only when it started at the bottom (with carry-in) and read input 1 from above. The interleaving Module B ends at the same height as it started so that the carry-out from the Module A is fed into the next Module C properly. Module B utilizes the two bricks to propagate this carry (see Fig. 7), which also plays a role of spacing Modules A and C sufficiently to prevent their interference. At the end of the zig, Module B encounters a signal of carriage-return 27-28-29 encoded on the seed and folds into the brick BT for zig-to-zag turn. Note that this brick exposes the signal below to trigger the next zig-to-zag turn. Module C behaves exactly in the same manner as A mod 30. In contrast, Module D is not such a mod-30 variant of B. It is rather responsible for right carriage returns. Bit-width being odd and the introduction of Module D eliminate the need for one module to take responsibility for both turns. Observe also that due to the odd bit-width and alternation of A and C, two instances of A never get adjacent even vertically or neither do C's. Being placed side-by-side, instances of A would interfere quite likely inter-modularily via rules that are supposed to work intra-modularily, that is, to fold an instance into bricks. One programming principle of oritatami systems is to design a macroscopic folding pathway in which any two instances of every module are spaced at least $\delta + 1$ away, which is the radius of the *event horizon* of delay-δ oritatami systems. Duplicating a module using pairwise-distinct bead types is quite useful for this purpose though at the cost of bead types.

The zag formats the count for the sake of succeeding zig. Observe that the bricks A00, A01, A10, A11 encode output 0 in two ways and 1 in other two ways. Using two bricks of C which correspond to A0 and A1 in Fig. 6, a zag reformats these outputs 0 and 1 according to the input format (1) for Module A in a zig.

2.2   Arithmetic Overflow and Infinite Binary Counter.

This counter $\varXi_{bc}$ can count up to $2^m - 1$ but not any further since it is not capable of handling arithmetic overflow, where m is the width in bits of the count encoded on the seed (in the example run, $m = 3$). Precisely speaking, given $2^m - 1$ in binary, a zig would end at the bottom (with carry), but as shown in Fig. 7, Module B is not designed to read carriage-return from distance 3 away. Endowing Module B with the ability to widen width in bits of the count would convert $\varXi_{bc}$ to an infinite counter, which is significant in the theory of molecular self-assembly (see, e.g., [7]). It should be important to widen by 2 bits at one time so that the width in bits is kept odd.

2.3   Applications of the Binary Counter

By definition, the oritatami system is not equipped with finite state control unlike the finite automaton (FA) or Turing machine. The cyclic tag system (CTS) was chosen as a model to be simulated due to its freeness from random access memory in order to prove the Turing-universality of oritatami systems [16]. The binary counter demonstrated two basic ways of information storage and propagation in oritatami, that is, as a sequence of bead types and as a way to enter a region where a receiver is to fold. This counter actually provides a medium to store and propagate even multiple-bit of information arbitrary far; imagine if the zag-to-zig turn brick of D is modified so as to start the next zig rather at the top (no carry), then the next zigzag retains the current value instead of incrementing it. Despite of its weakness as a memory (for example, it cannot even decrement), it found an intriguing application in the self-assembly of shapes by cotranscriptional folding.

After being modified so as to operate under the oblivious dynamics, the binary counter was embedded into another oritatami system as a component (higher-level concept of module) by Masuda, Seki, and Ubukata towards the self-assembly of Heighway dragon fractal by cotranscriptional folding [32]. This fractal is an alias of the well-known paper-folding sequence, over {L, R} of left

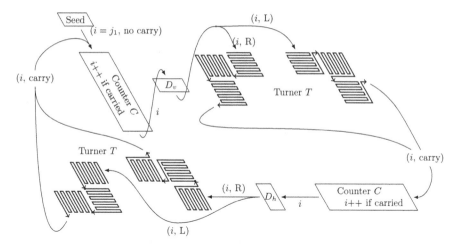

Fig. 8. Component automaton for the Heighway dragon oritatami system [32]. Transitions are labeled with the information propagated.

and right turns. It is an *automatic sequence* (see [5]) and hence admits a DFA that outputs its i-th letter, being fed with the binary representation of i from its least significant bit. Such a DFA for paper-folding sequence A_{pfs} consists of 4 states and is cycle-free. In order to produce Heighway dragon, it hence suffices to count in binary, to simulate A_{pfs}, and to make a turn according to the simulation while remembering the current count i. In principle, A_{pfs} could be simulated by the Turing-universal oritatami CTS simulator, but the resulting component would be literally too large and roughly-faced to be embedded into another system and its usage of 542 bead types cannot be ignored, either. Masuda et al. developed a custom-made simulator of A_{pfs} quite simply by exploiting its cycle-freeness. This component, denoted by D, does not lose the input count i but rather propagates it. Another newly-developed component T consists of three instances of a rhombus-shaped sub-component, which bifurcates[3] the binary representation of current count i and lets the output of the previous A_{pfs} guide the transcript so as to read the bifurcated count leftward or rightward. Transcribing the modified counter, say C, D, T in this order repeatedly[4] interlocks these components properly as illustrated in the component automaton in Fig. 8 into a finite portion of Heighway dragon fractal.

Can we program an oritatami system to self-assemble the actual infinite Heighway dragon? Assume that an infinite counter is given, which is nontrivial but seems feasible as stated in Sect. 2.2. However, it seems challenging for it to

---

[3] It actually does trifurcate a binary string. The output frontward is just not needed in their system.

[4] In fact, the period is twice as long as this because the component D for vertical segments of the dragon must be distinguished from D for horizontal segments for some technical reason; see [32].

reside with other components on a periodic transcript. Periodicity of a transcript is the only one way known so far to make an infinite oritatami system to be describable in a finite mean. Once a counter component C is arithmetically overflown and width in bit is expanded, the succeeding D and T components must also get expanded, that is, their sequences are lengthened. A solution is to program all the functions as C, D, and T into one sequence of bead types, but then how can a system call an appropriate function when needed? It might be also the case that Heighway dragon cannot be self-assembled by any oritatami system. If so, how can we prove the impossibility?

3   Towards Algorithmic Programming of Oritatami Systems

Modularization is one of the most fundamental programming techniques. In addition to its conventional benefits such as reusability of modules, modularization has automatized oritatami programming to a considerable extent at least at the modular level. Consider the following rule design problem (RDP):

Input: a transcript $w = 1\text{-}2\text{-}\cdots\text{-}n$, a set of k pairs of an environment which is free from any bead $1, 2, \ldots, n$ and a folding path of length n, delay δ, and arity α;

Output: a rule set R such that at delay δ and arity α, the transcript w folds deterministically along the j-th folding path in the j-th environment for all $1 \leq j \leq k$.

This problem is NP-hard in k, the number of pairs of an environment and a target folding path [17] but linear in n, the length of transcript. Geary et al. have proposed an algorithm to solve this problem whose time complexity is exponential only in k and δ [17]. The delay δ has been bounded by 4 in literature so far. It might be just beyond ability of human programmers to take an exponentially increasing number of conformations in δ into account at every bead stabilization. Hence, the upper bound on k serves as a significant criterion to evaluate a modularization. The binary counter bounds k by 6 (see Figs. 6 and 7), that is, it was modularized properly according to this criterion. All of its four modules A, B, C, and D were programmed by this algorithm indeed.

This fixed-parameter-tractable (FPT) algorithm runs in linear time in n, but it is still important to bound n by a small constant, that is, to downsize modules. As long as they are small, the increase in the size of Σ to ensure that their transcript and environments do not share any bead type remains moderate or may even be cancelled by the modules' reusability. It is indispensable for the transcript not to reuse a bead type or borrow a bead type from environments for the efficiency of this algorithm. In fact, if the transcript is rather designed by an adversary using even a bead type from environments, then the resulting rule set design problem becomes NP-hard in n even when $k = 1$ [34].

3.1 Programmability of Modules: Self-standing Shape and Steric Hindrance

Gliders have proven itself to be quite programmable thanks to its small number of intramodular bonds (just one per three beads) and its intermodular-binding-independency (self-standing property). Modules of non-self-standing shape tend to be less programmable than those of self-standing shape due to their computationally-meaningless bonds. Compare it with structural modules B and D (colored in red in Fig. 5). They do bind to the module above even in the absence of logical need to do so except for carriage return in order merely to be shaped into a parallelogram. Freeing them from binding intermodularily would require heavy hardcording with much more intramodular bonds and severely impair their programmability. Recall that these parallelogram-shaped modules were designed to operate under the hasty dynamics. Oritatami systems seem less governable under the oblivious dynamics, which has received a greater deal of attention. Modules of self-standing shape have thus gained the significance further.

Programmers should proactively save bonds also from information propagation. In this respect, entering a receiver's region from different positions is superior to explicitly encoding as a sequence of bead types. This geometric encoding utilizes *steric hindrance*. For example, when an instance of Module A of the binary counter starts folding with no carry-in, the module "just" above geometrically precludes many stable conformations that the nascent transcript fragment could take without anything above; on the other hand, being carried-in, some bead of the module above might be too far (at least $\delta + 2$ points away) for the nascent fragment to interact. A sender also can take advantage of steric hindrance as illustrated in Fig. 4. The CTS simulator [16] encodes 0 as a unit triangular bump and 1 as its absence (flat surface). When it is read, a glider is launched towards the position where the letter is thus encoded geometrically. Unlike Module A, this glider collides with this position always in an identical manner, but the bump geometrically prevents this glider from changing its direction obtusely and makes the glider choose the second most stable conformation that rather redirects the glider acutely.

3.2 Towards Algorithmic Design of Folding Pathways

The FPT algorithm requires folding paths to be followed by a module transcript given as input. An entirely different problem thus arises of how to design such paths. This design task is yet to be done algorithmically, but at the modular level, it might be solvable at worst by brute force as long as modules are sufficiently small. Above the modular level, programmers encounter global folding pathway design problem and the astronomical number of global folding pathways stands in their hope of fully automatizing the design of oritatami architectures. The global folding pathway design also involves intrinsic issues to decide where modules should be deployed on the plane and how they should be traversed unicursally without crossing itself, and desirably these issues are addressed in a way to result in a periodic transcript with shortest period possible. Furthermore, global folding pathway should be designed so as to avoid "functional hotspots" and rather to scatter functions along the whole transcript as much as possible. The CTS simulator demonstrates novel techniques for this purpose and also confines relatively functionally-hot spots geometrically to prevent interference.

The Heighway dragon is unicursally traversable so that the global folding pathway illustrated in the component automaton in Fig. 8 has been obtained rather quite naturally. In general, however, this global folding pathway problem is quite challenging, being illustrated even experimentally in the corresponding design process of the RNA origami single-stranded architecture [18]. The zigzag global folding pathway of the binary counter is the most frequently-used so far.

4   Conclusions

Oritatami is a novel computational model of co-synthetic stepwise local optimization, which is a computational paradigm created by RNA cotranscriptional folding. In this paper, we have introduced existing oritatami architectures for computing briefly and raised several research directions. The Turing universality [16] is not the final objective of the study of computability of oritatami at all. In fact, organisms do not seem to require such a strong computational power to support their life. Almost nothing is known about the non-Turing universality of oritatami. Demaine et al. proved that at delay 1 and arity 1, deterministic oritatami systems can produce conformations of size at most 9 m starting from a seed of size m, and hence, the class of such oritatami systems is not Turing universal [9]. Some partial results of the non-Turing universality are recently proved on oritatami systems with unary transcript [13]. Can we characterize a subclass of oritatami systems that is strictly weaker than the Turing machine?

Acknowledgements. This paper mainly summarizes the author's collaboration with Cody Geary, Pierre-Étienne Meunier, and Nicolas Schabanel. Artworks in Figs. 1 and 2 are by Geary and those in Figs. 4, 5, 6, and 7 are by Schabanel. The author would like to take this opportunity to express his sincere gratitude towards them.

References

1. Adleman, L.: Molecular computation of solutions to combinatorial problems. Science **266**, 1021–1024 (1994)
2. Afonin, K.A., et al.: In vitro assembly of cubic RNA-based scaffolds designed in silico. Nat. Nanotechnol. **5**(9), 676–682 (2010)
3. Afonin, K.A., Kireeva, M., Grabow, W.W., Kashiev, M., Jaeger, L., Shapiro, B.A.: Co-transcriptional assembly of chemically modified RNA nanoparticples functionalized with siRNAs. Nano Lett. **12**(10), 5192–5195 (2012)
4. Alberts, B., et al.: Molecular Biology of the Cell, 6th edn. Garland Science, New York (2014)
5. Allouche, J.P., Shallit, J.: Automatic Sequences: Theory, Applications, Generalizations. Cambridge University Press, Cambridge (2003)

6. Arita, M., Kobayashi, S.: DNA sequence design using templates. New Gener. Comput. **20**(3), 263–277 (2002). https://doi.org/10.1007/BF03037360
7. Bryans, N., Chiniforooshan, E., Doty, D., Kari, L., Seki, S.: The power of nondeterminism in self-assembly. Theor. Comput. **9**, 1–29 (2013)
8. Cook, M.: Universality in elementary cellular automata. Complex Syst. **15**, 1–40 (2004)
9. Demaine, E.D., et al.: Know when to fold 'em: self-assembly of shapes by folding in oritatami. In: Doty, D., Dietz, H. (eds.) DNA 2018. LNCS, vol. 11145, pp. 19–36. Springer, Cham (2018). https://doi.org/10.1007/978-3-030-00030-1_2
10. Diestel, R.: Graph Theory, 4th edn. Springer, Heidelberg (2010)
11. Doty, D.: Theory of algorithmic self-assembly. Commun. ACM **55**(12), 78–88 (2012)
12. Elliott, D., Ladomery, M.: Molecular Biology of RNA, 2nd edn. Oxford University Press, Oxford (2016)
13. Fazekas, S.Z., Maruyama, K., Morita, R., Seki, S.: On the power of oritatami cotranscriptional folding with unary bead sequence. In: Gopal, T.V., Watada, J. (eds.) TAMC 2019. LNCS, vol. 11436, pp. 188–207. Springer, Cham (2019). https://doi.org/10.1007/978-3-030-14812-6_12
14. Geary, C.W., Andersen, E.S.: Design principles for single-stranded RNA origami structures. In: Murata, S., Kobayashi, S. (eds.) DNA 2014. LNCS, vol. 8727, pp. 1–19. Springer, Cham (2014). https://doi.org/10.1007/978-3-319-11295-4_1
15. Geary, C., Chworos, A., Verzemnieks, E., Voss, N.R., Jaeger, L.: Composing RNA nanostructures from a syntax of RNA structural modules. Nano Lett. **17**, 7095–7101 (2017)
16. Geary, C., Meunier, P.E., Schabanel, N., Seki, S.: Proving the Turing universality of oritatami cotranscriptional folding. In: Proceedings of the ISAAC 2018. LIPIcs, vol. 123, pp. 23:1–23:13 (2018)
17. Geary, C., Meunier, P.E., Schabanel, N., Seki, S.: Oritatami: a computational model for molecular co-transcriptional folding. Int. J. Mol. Sci. **20**, 2259 (2019). Its Conference Version was Published in Proceedings of the MFCS 2016
18. Geary, C., Rothemund, P.W.K., Andersen, E.S.: A single-stranded architecture for cotranscriptional folding of RNA nanostructures. Science **345**, 799–804 (2014)
19. Guo, Y., et al.: Recent advances in molecular machines based on toehold-mediated strand displacement reaction. Quant. Biol. **5**(1), 25–41 (2017). https://doi.org/10.1007/s40484-017-0097-2
20. Hagiya, M., Arita, M., Kiga, D., Sakamoto, K., Yokoyama, S.: Towards parallel evaluation and learning of boolean μ-formulas with molecules. In: Proceedings of the DNA3. DIMACS Series in Discrete Mathematics and Theoretical Computer Science, vol. 48, pp. 57–72 (1999)
21. Han, Y.-S., Kim, H.: Construction of geometric structure by oritatami system. In: Doty, D., Dietz, H. (eds.) DNA 2018. LNCS, vol. 11145, pp. 173–188. Springer, Cham (2018). https://doi.org/10.1007/978-3-030-00030-1_11
22. Han, Y.S., Kim, H.: Ruleset optimization on isomorphic oritatami systems. Theor. Comput. Sci. **575**, 90–101 (2019)
23. Han, Y.S., Kim, H., Masuda, Y., Seki, S.: A general architecture of oritatami systems for simulating arbitrary finite automata. In: Proceedings of the CIAA2019. LNCS, Springer (2019, in press)
24. Han, Y.S., Kim, H., Ota, M., Seki, S.: Nondeterministic seedless oritatami systems and hardness of testing their equivalence. Nat. Comput. **17**(1), 67–79 (2018). https://doi.org/10.1007/s11047-017-9661-y

25. Han, Y.S., Kim, H., Rogers, T.A., Seki, S.: Self-attraction removal from oritatami systems. Int. J. Found. Comput. Sci. (2019, in press)

26. Jepsen, M.D.E., et al.: Development of a genetically encodable FRET system using fluorescent RNA aptamers. Nat. Commun. **9**, 18 (2018)

27. Jonoska, N., Mahalingam, K.: Languages of DNA based code words. In: Chen, J., Reif, J. (eds.) DNA 2003. LNCS, vol. 2943, pp. 61–73. Springer, Heidelberg (2004). https://doi.org/10.1007/978-3-540-24628-2_8

28. Jonoska, N., Seeman, N.C.: Molecular ping-pong game of life on a two-dimensional DNA origami array. Philos. Trans. Roy. Soc. A Math. Phys. Eng. Sci. **373**(2046) (2015)

29. Kari, L., Konstantinidis, S., Sosík, P., Thierrin, G.: On hairpin-free words and languages. In: De Felice, C., Restivo, A. (eds.) DLT 2005. LNCS, vol. 3572, pp. 296–307. Springer, Heidelberg (2005). https://doi.org/10.1007/11505877_26

30. Kari, L., Seki, S.: On pseudoknot-bordered words and their properties. J. Comput. Syst. Sci. **75**(2), 113–121 (2009)

31. Komiya, K., et al.: DNA polymerase programmed with a hairpin DNA incorporates a multiple-instruction architecture into molecular computing. Biosystems **83**(1), 18–25 (2006)

32. Masuda, Y., Seki, S., Ubukata, Y.: Towards the algorithmic molecular self-assembly of fractals by cotranscriptional folding. In: Câmpeanu, C. (ed.) CIAA 2018. LNCS, vol. 10977, pp. 261–273. Springer, Cham (2018). https://doi.org/10.1007/978-3-319-94812-6_22

33. Merkhofer, E.C., Hu, P., Johnson, T.L.: Introduction to cotranscriptional RNA splicing. Methods Mol. Biol. **1126**, 83–96 (2014). https://doi.org/10.1007/978-1-62703-980-2_6

34. Ota, M., Seki, S.: Ruleset design problems for oritatami systems. Theor. Comput. Sci. **671**, 26–35 (2017)

35. Parales, R., Bentley, D.: "Co-transcriptionality" - the transcription elongation complex as a nexus for nuclear transactions. Mol. Cell **36**(2), 178–191 (2009)

36. Rose, J.A., Komiya, K., Yaegashi, S., Hagiya, M.: Displacement whiplash PCR: optimized architecture and experimental validation. In: Mao, C., Yokomori, T. (eds.) DNA 2006. LNCS, vol. 4287, pp. 393–403. Springer, Heidelberg (2006). https://doi.org/10.1007/11925903_31

37. Rothemund, P.W.K.: Folding DNA to create nanoscale shapes and patterns. Nature **440**(7082), 297–302 (2006)

38. Sakamoto, K., et al.: Molecular comuptation by DNA hairpin formation. Science **288**, 1223–1226 (2000)

39. Sakamoto, K., et al.: State transitions by molecules. Biosystems **52**(1–3), 81–91 (1999)

40. Schwarz-Schilling, M., Dupin, A., Chizzolini, F., Krishnan, S., Mansy, S.S., Simmel, F.C.: Optimized assembly of a multifunctional RNA-protein nanostructure in a cell-free gene expression system. Nano Lett. **18**, 2650–2657 (2018)

41. Wang, H.: Proving theorems by pattern recognition. Bell Syst. Tech. J. **40**(1), 1–41 (1961)

42. Watters, K.E., Strobel, E.J., Yu, A.M., Lis, J.T., Lucks, J.B.: Cotranscriptional folding of a riboswitch at nucleotide resolution. Nat. Struct. Mol. Biol. **23**(12), 1124–1131 (2016)

43. Winfree, E.: Algorithmic self-assembly of DNA. Ph.D. thesis, Caltech, June 1998

44. Yurke, B., Turberfield Jr., A.J., Simmel, A.P.M.: A DNA-fuelled molecular machine made of DNA. Nature **406**, 605–608 (2000)

Regular Papers

A Linear Bound on the K-Rendezvous Time for Primitive Sets of NZ Matrices

Umer Azfar[1], Costanza Catalano[2(✉)], Ludovic Charlier[1],
and Raphaël M. Jungers[1]

[1] ICTEAM, UCLouvain, Av. Georges Lemaîtres 4-6, Louvain-la-Neuve, Belgium
{umer.azfar,ludovic.charlier}@student.uclouvain.be,
raphael.jungers@uclouvain.be
[2] Gran Sasso Science Institute, Viale Francesco Crispi 7, L'Aquila, Italy
costanza.catalano@gssi.it

Abstract. A set of nonnegative matrices is called primitive if there exists a product of these matrices that is entrywise positive. Motivated by recent results relating synchronizing automata and primitive sets, we study the length of the shortest product of a primitive set having a column or a row with k positive entries (the k-RT). We prove that this value is at most linear w.r.t. the matrix size n for small k, while the problem is still open for synchronizing automata. We then report numerical results comparing our upper bound on the k-RT with heuristic approximation methods.

Keywords: Primitive set of matrices · Synchronizing automaton · Černý conjecture

1 Introduction

Primitive Sets of Matrices. The notion of *primitive* matrix[1], introduced by Perron and Frobenius at the beginning of the 20th century in the theory that carries their names, can be extended to *sets* of matrices: a set of nonnegative matrices $\mathcal{M} = \{M_1, \ldots, M_m\}$ is called *primitive* if there exists some indices $i_1, \ldots, i_r \in \{1, \ldots, m\}$ such that the product $M_{i_1} \cdots M_{i_r}$ is entrywise positive. A product of this kind is called a *positive* product and the length of the shortest positive product of a primitive set $\mathcal{M}$ is called its *exponent* and it is denoted by $exp(\mathcal{M})$. The concept of primitive set was just recently formalized by Protasov and Voynov [31], but has been appearing before in different fields as in stochastic switching systems [20,30] and time-inhomogeneous Markov chains [19,34]. It has lately gained more importance due to its applications in consensus of discrete-time multi-agent systems [9], cryptography [12] and automata theory [4,6,15].

---

[1] A nonnegative matrix M is *primitive* if there exists $s \in \mathbb{N}$ such that $M^s > 0$ entrywise.

R.M. Jungers is a FNRS Research Associate. He is supported by the French Community of Belgium, the Walloon Region and the Innoviris Foundation.

P. Hofman and M. Skrzypczak (Eds.): DLT 2019, LNCS 11647, pp. 59–73, 2019.
https://doi.org/10.1007/978-3-030-24886-4_4

Deciding whether a set is primitive is a PSPACE-complete problem for sets of two matrices [15], while it is an NP-hard problem for sets of at least three matrices [4]. Computing the exponent of a primitive set is usually hard, namely it is an $FP^{NP[\log]}$-complete problem [15]; for the complexity of other problems related to primitivity and the computation of the exponent, we refer the reader to [15]. For sets of matrices having at least one positive entry in every row and every column (called *NZ* [15] or *allowable* matrices [18,20]), the primitivity problem becomes decidable in polynomial-time [31], although computing the exponent remains NP-hard [15]. Methods for approximating the exponent have been proposed [7] as well as upper bounds that depend just on the matrix size; in particular, if we denote with $exp_{NZ}(n)$ the maximal exponent among all the primitive sets of $n \times n$ NZ matrices, it is known that $exp_{NZ}(n) \leq (15617n^3 + 7500n^2 + 56250n - 78125)/46875$ [4,36]. Better upper bounds have been found for some classes of primitive sets (see e.g. [15] and [19], Theorem 4.1). The NZ condition is often met in applications and in particular in the connection with synchronizing automata.

Synchronizing Automata. A *(complete deterministic finite state) automaton* is a 3-tuple $\mathcal{A} = \langle Q, \Sigma, \delta \rangle$ where $Q = \{q_1, \ldots, q_n\}$ is a finite set of states, $\Sigma = \{a_1, \ldots, a_m\}$ is a finite set of input symbols (the *letters* of the automaton) and $\delta : Q \times \Sigma \to Q$ is the *transition function*. Let $i_1, i_2, \ldots, i_l \in \{1, \ldots, m\}$ be indices. Then $w = a_{i_1} a_{i_2} \ldots a_{i_l}$ is called a word and we define $\delta(q, w) = \delta(\delta(q, a_{i_1} a_{i_2} \ldots a_{i_{l-1}}), a_{i_l})$. An automaton is *synchronizing* if it admits a word w, called a *synchronizing* or a *reset* word, and a state q such that $\delta(q', w) = q$ for any state $q' \in Q$. In other words, the reset word w brings the automaton from every state to the same fixed state.

Remark 1. The automaton $\mathcal{A}$ can be equivalently represented by the set of matrices $\{A_1, \ldots, A_m\}$ where, for all $i = 1, \ldots, m$ and $l, k = 1, \ldots, n$, $(A_i)_{lk} = 1$ if $\delta(q_l, a_i) = q_k$, $(A_i)_{lk} = 0$ otherwise. The action of a letter a_i on a state q_j is represented by the product $e_j^T A_i$, where e_j is the j-th element of the canonical basis. Notice that the matrices $A_1, \ldots, A_m$ are binary[2] and row-stochastic, i.e. each of them has exactly one entry equal to 1 in every row and zero everywhere else. In this representation, the automaton $\mathcal{A}$ is synchronizing if and only if there exists a product of its matrices with a column whose entries are all equal to 1 (also called an *all-ones* column).

The idea of synchronization is quite simple: we want to restore control over a device whose current state is unknown. For this reason, synchronizing automata are often used as models of error-resistant systems [8,11], but they also find application in other fields such as in symbolic dynamics [25], in robotics [26] or in resilience of data compression [33,37]. For a recent survey on synchronizing automata we refer the reader to [42]. We are usually interested in the length of the shortest reset word of a synchronizing automaton $\mathcal{A}$, called its *reset threshold* and denoted by $rt(\mathcal{A})$. Despite the fact that determining whether an automaton is synchronizing can be done in polynomial time (see e.g. [42]), computing

---

[2] A *binary* matrix is a matrix having entries in $\{0, 1\}$.

its reset threshold is an NP-hard problem [11][3]. One of the most longstanding open questions in automata theory concerns the maximal reset threshold of a synchronizing automaton, presented by Černý in 1964 in his pioneering paper:

Conjecture 1. (The Černý conjecture [39]). Any synchronizing automaton on n states has a synchronizing word of length at most $(n-1)^2$.

Černý also presented in [39] a family of automata having reset threshold of exactly $(n-1)^2$, thus demonstrating that the bound in his conjecture (if true) cannot be improved. Exhaustive search confirmed the Černý conjecture for small values of n [2,5,24,38] and within certain classes of automata (see e.g. [22,35,41]), but despite a great effort has been made to prove (or disprove) it in the last decades, its validity still remains unclear. Indeed on the one hand, the best upper bound known on the reset threshold of any synchronizing n-state automaton is cubic in n [13,28,36], while on the other hand automata having quadratic reset threshold, called *extremal* automata, are very difficult to find and few of them are known (see e.g. [10,16,23,32]). Some of these families have been found by Ananichev et al. [3] by coloring the digraph of primitive matrices having large exponent; this has been probably the first time where primitivity has been successfully used to shed light on synchronization.

Connecting Primitivity and Synchronization. The following definition and theorem establish the connection between primitive sets of binary NZ matrices and synchronizing automata. From here on, we will use the matrix representation of deterministic finite automata as reported in Remark 1.

Definition 1. *Let $\mathcal{M}$ be a set of binary NZ matrices. The* automaton associated *to the set $\mathcal{M}$ is the automaton $Aut(\mathcal{M})$ such that $A \in Aut(\mathcal{M})$ if and only if A is a binary and row-stochastic matrix and there exists $M \in \mathcal{M}$ such that $A \le M$ (entrywise). We denote with $Aut(\mathcal{M}^T)$ the automaton associated to the set $\mathcal{M}^T = \{M_1^T, \dots, M_m^T\}$.*

Theorem 1. ([4] **Theorems 16–17**, [15] **Theorem 2**). *Let $\mathcal{M} = \{M_1, \dots, M_m\}$ be a primitive set of binary NZ matrices. Then $Aut(\mathcal{M})$ and $Aut(\mathcal{M}^T)$ are synchronizing and it holds that:*

$$rt\big(Aut(\mathcal{M})\big) \le exp(\mathcal{M}) \le rt\big(Aut(\mathcal{M})\big) + rt\big(Aut(\mathcal{M}^T)\big) + n - 1. \qquad (1)$$

Notice that the requirement in Theorem 1 that the set $\mathcal{M}$ has to be made of *binary* matrices is not restrictive, as the primitivity property does not depend on the magnitude of the positive entries of the matrices of the set. We can thus restrict ourselves to the set of binary matrices by using the Boolean product between them[4], that is setting for any A and B binary matrices, $(AB)_{ij} = 1$ any time that $\sum_s A_{is} B_{sj} > 0$. In this framework, primitivity can be also rephrased

---

[3] Moreover, even approximating the reset threshold of an n-state synchronizing automaton within a factor of $n^{1-\epsilon}$ is known to be NP-hard for any $\epsilon > 0$, see [14].

[4] In other words, we work with matrices over the Boolean semiring.

as a *membership problem* (see e.g. [27,29]), where we ask whether the all-ones matrix belongs to the semigroup generated by the matrix set. The following example reports a primitive set $\mathcal{M}$ of NZ matrices and the synchronizing automata $Aut(\mathcal{M})$ and $Aut(\mathcal{M}^T)$.

Example 1. Here we present a primitive set and its associated automata:

$$\mathcal{M} = \left\{ \left(\begin{smallmatrix} 0&1&0 \\ 0&0&1 \\ 1&0&0 \end{smallmatrix} \right), \left(\begin{smallmatrix} 0&1&0 \\ 1&0&1 \\ 0&0&1 \end{smallmatrix} \right) \right\}, Aut(\mathcal{M}) = \left\{ a = \left(\begin{smallmatrix} 0&1&0 \\ 0&0&1 \\ 1&0&0 \end{smallmatrix} \right), b_1 = \left(\begin{smallmatrix} 0&1&0 \\ 0&0&1 \\ 0&0&1 \end{smallmatrix} \right), b_2 = \left(\begin{smallmatrix} 0&1&0 \\ 0&0&1 \\ 0&0&1 \end{smallmatrix} \right) \right\},$$

$$Aut(\mathcal{M}^T) = \left\{ a' = \left(\begin{smallmatrix} 0&0&1 \\ 1&0&0 \\ 0&1&0 \end{smallmatrix} \right), b_1 = \left(\begin{smallmatrix} 0&1&0 \\ 1&0&0 \\ 0&0&1 \end{smallmatrix} \right), b_2' = \left(\begin{smallmatrix} 0&1&0 \\ 1&0&0 \\ 0&1&0 \end{smallmatrix} \right) \right\}$$

It holds that $exp(\mathcal{M}) = 7$, $rt\big(Aut(\mathcal{M})\big) = 2$ and $rt\big(Aut(\mathcal{M}^T)\big) = 3$. See also Fig. 1.

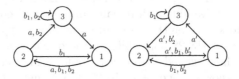

Fig. 1. The automata $Aut(\mathcal{M})$ (left) and $Aut(\mathcal{M}^T)$ (right) of Example 1.

Equation (1) shows that the behavior of the exponent of a primitive set of NZ matrices is tightly connected to the behavior of the reset threshold of its associated automaton. A primitive set $\mathcal{M}$ with quadratic exponent implies that one of the automata $Aut(\mathcal{M})$ or $Aut(\mathcal{M}^T)$ has quadratic reset threshold; in particular, a primitive set with exponent greater than $2(n - 1)^2 + n - 1$ would disprove the Černý conjecture. This property has been used by the authors in [6] to construct a randomized procedure for finding extremal synchronizing automata.

The synchronization problem for automata is about finding the length of the shortest word mapping the whole set of states onto one single state. We can weaken this request by asking what is the length of the shortest word w such that there exists a set of $k \geq 2$ states mapped by w onto one single state. In the matrix framework, we are asking what is the length of the shortest product having a column with k positive entries. The case $k = 2$ is trivial, as any synchronizing automaton has a letter mapping two states onto one; for $k = 3$ Gonze and Jungers [17] presented a quadratic upper bound in the number of the states of the automaton while, to the best of our knowledge, the cases $k \geq 4$ are still open. Clearly, the case $k = n$ is the problem of computing the reset threshold.

In view of the connection between synchronizing automata and primitive sets, we extend the above described problem to primitive sets by introducing the *k-rendezvous time* (k-RT): the k-RT of a primitive set $\mathcal{M}$ is the length of the shortest product having a row or a column with k positive entries. The following proposition shows how the k-RT of a primitive set $\mathcal{M}$ of NZ matrices (denoted by $rt_k(\mathcal{M})$) is linked to the length of the shortest word for which it exists a set of k states mapped by it onto a single state in the automata $Aut(\mathcal{M})$ and $Aut(\mathcal{M}^T)$ (lengths denoted respectively by $rt_k(Aut(\mathcal{M}))$ and $rt_k(Aut(\mathcal{M}^T))$).

Proposition 1. *Let $\mathcal{M}$ be a primitive set of $n \times n$ binary NZ matrices and let $Aut(\mathcal{M})$ and $Aut(\mathcal{M}^T)$ be the automata defined in Definition 1. Then for every $2 \leq k \leq n$, it holds that $rt_k(\mathcal{M}) = \min\{rt_k(Aut(\mathcal{M})), rt_k(Aut(\mathcal{M}^T))\}$.*

Proof. Omitted due to length restrictions.

Our Contribution. In this paper we prove that for any primitive set $\mathcal{M}$ of $n \times n$ NZ matrices, the k-rendezvous time $rt_k(\mathcal{M})$ is upper bounded by a linear function in n for any fixed $k \leq \sqrt{n}$, problem that is still open for synchronizing automata. Our result also implies that $\min\{rt_k(Aut(\mathcal{M})), rt_k(Aut(\mathcal{M}^T))\}$ is upper bounded by a linear function in n for any fixed $k \leq \sqrt{n}$, in view of Proposition 1. We then show that our technique for upper bounding $rt_k(\mathcal{M})$ cannot be much improved as it is, and so new strategies have to be implemented in order to possibly achieve better upper bounds. Finally, we report some numerical experiments comparing our theoretical upper bound on the k-RT with the real k-RT (or an approximation of it when it becomes too hard to compute it) for some examples of primitive sets.

2 Notation and Preliminaries

The set $\{1, \ldots, n\}$ is represented by $[n]$. The *support* of a nonnegative vector v is the set $supp(v) = \{i : v_i > 0\}$ and the *weight* of a nonnegative vector v is the cardinality of its support.

Given a matrix A, we denote by A_{*j} its j-th column and by A_{i*} its i-th row. A *permutation* matrix is a binary matrix having exactly one positive entry in every row and every column. We remind that an $n \times n$ matrix A is called *irreducible* if for any $i, j \in [n]$, there exists a natural number k such that $A_{ij}^k > 0$. A matrix A is called *reducible* if it is not irreducible.

Given $\mathcal{M}$ a set of matrices, we denote with $\mathcal{M}^d$ the set of all the products of at most d matrices from $\mathcal{M}$. A set of matrices $\mathcal{M} = \{M_1, \ldots, M_m\}$ is *reducible* if the matrix $\sum_i M_i$ is reducible, otherwise it is called *irreducible*. Irreducibility is a necessary but not sufficient condition for a matrix set to be primitive (see [31], Sect. 1). Given a directed graph $D = (V, E)$, we denote by $v \rightarrow w$ the directed edge leaving v and entering in w and with $v \rightarrow w \in E$ the fact that the edge $v \rightarrow w$ belongs to the digraph D.

Lemma 1. *Let $\mathcal{M}$ be an irreducible set of $n \times n$ NZ matrices, $A \in \mathcal{M}$ and $i, j \in [n]$. Then there exists a matrix $B \in \mathcal{M}^{n-1}$ such that $supp(A_{*i}) \subseteq supp((AB)_{*j})$.*

Proof. We consider the labeled directed graph $\mathscr{D}_{\mathcal{M}} = (V, E)$ where $V = [n]$ and $i \rightarrow j \in E$ iff there exists a matrix $A \in \mathcal{M}$ such that $A_{ij} > 0$. We label the edge $i \rightarrow j \in E$ by all the matrices $A \in \mathcal{M}$ such that $A_{ij} > 0$. We remind that a directed graph is *strongly connected* if there exists a directed path from any vertex to any other vertex. Notice that a path in $\mathscr{D}_{\mathcal{M}}$ from vertex k to vertex l having the edges sequentially labeled by the matrices $A_{s_1}, \ldots, A_{s_r}$ from $\mathcal{M}$ means that $(A_{s_1} \cdots A_{s_r})_{kl} > 0$. Since $\mathcal{M}$ is irreducible, it follows that $\mathscr{D}_{\mathcal{M}}$

is strongly connected and so, since V has cardinality n, any pair of vertices in $\mathcal{D}_{\mathcal{M}}$ are connected by a path of length at most $n-1$. Consider a path connecting vertex i to vertex j whose edges are sequentially labeled by the matrices $A_{s_1}, \ldots, A_{s_t}$ from $\mathcal{M}$ and let $B = A_{s_1} \cdots A_{s_t}$. Clearly $B \in \mathcal{M}^{n-1}$; furthermore it holds that $B_{ij} > 0$ and so $supp(A_{*i}) \subseteq supp((AB)_{*j})$.   □

Definition 2. *Let $\mathcal{M}$ be a finite set of $n \times n$ NZ matrices. We define the* pair digraph *of the set $\mathcal{M}$ as the labeled directed graph $\mathcal{PD}(\mathcal{M}) = (\mathcal{V}, \mathcal{E})$ where $\mathcal{V} = \{(i,j) : 1 \leq i \leq j \leq n\}$ is the vertex set and $(i,j) \to (i',j') \in \mathcal{E}$ if and only if there exists $A \in \mathcal{M}$ such that*

$$A_{ii'} > 0 \text{ and } A_{jj'} > 0, \text{ or } A_{ij'} > 0 \text{ and } A_{ji'} > 0. \tag{2}$$

An edge $(i,j) \to (i',j') \in \mathcal{E}$ is labeled by any matrix $A \in \mathcal{M}$ for which Eq. (2) holds. A vertex of the form (s,s) is called a singleton.

Lemma 2. *Let $\mathcal{M}$ be a finite set of $n \times n$ NZ matrices and let $\mathcal{PD}(\mathcal{M}) = (\mathcal{V}, \mathcal{E})$ be its pair digraph. Let $i, j, k \in [n]$ and suppose that there exists a path in $\mathcal{PD}(\mathcal{M})$ from the vertex (i,j) to the singleton (k,k) having the edges sequentially labeled by the matrices $A_{s_1}, \ldots, A_{s_l}$ from $\mathcal{M}$. Then it holds that for every $A \in \mathcal{M}$, $supp(A_{*i}) \cup supp(A_{*j}) \subseteq supp((AA_{s_1} \cdots A_{s_l})_{*k})$. Furthermore if $\mathcal{M}$ is irreducible, then $\mathcal{M}$ is primitive if and only if for any $(i,j) \in \mathcal{V}$ there exists a path in $\mathcal{PD}(\mathcal{M})$ from (i,j) to some singleton.*

Proof. By the definition of the pair digraph $\mathcal{PD}(\mathcal{M})$ (Definition 2), the existence of a path in $\mathcal{PD}(\mathcal{M})$ from vertex (i,j) to vertex (k,k) labeled by the matrices $A_{s_1}, \ldots, A_{s_l}$ implies that $(A_{s_1} \cdots A_{s_l})_{ik} > 0$ and $(A_{s_1} \cdots A_{s_l})_{jk} > 0$. By Lemma 1, it follows that $supp(A_{*i}) \cup supp(A_{*j}) \subseteq supp((AA_{s_1} \cdots A_{s_l})_{*k})$.

Suppose now that $\mathcal{M}$ is irreducible. If $\mathcal{M}$ is primitive, then there exists a product M of matrices from $\mathcal{M}$ such that for all i, j, $M_{ij} > 0$. By the definition of $\mathcal{PD}(\mathcal{M})$, this implies that any vertex in $\mathcal{PD}(\mathcal{M})$ is connected to any other vertex. On the other hand, if every vertex in $\mathcal{PD}(\mathcal{M})$ is connected to some singleton, then for every $i, j, k \in [n]$ there exists a product $A_{s_1} \cdots A_{s_l}$ of matrices from $\mathcal{M}$ such that $(A_{s_1} \cdots A_{s_l})_{ik} > 0$ and $(A_{s_1} \cdots A_{s_l})_{jk} > 0$. This suffices to establish the primitivity of $\mathcal{M}$ by Theorem 1 in [1][5].   □

3   The K-Rendezvous Time and a Recurrence Relation for Its Upper Bound

In this section, we define the k-rendezvous time of a primitive set of $n \times n$ NZ matrices and we prove a recurrence relation for a function $B_k(n)$ that upper bounds it.

---

[5] The theorem states that the following condition is sufficient for an irreducible matrix set $\mathcal{M}$ to be primitive: for all indices i, j, there exists an index k and a product M of matrices from $\mathcal{M}$ such that $M_{ik} > 0$ and $M_{jk} > 0$.

Definition 3. *Let $\mathcal{M}$ be a primitive set of $n \times n$ NZ matrices and $2 \leq k \leq n$. We define the k-rendezvous time (k-RT) to be the length of the shortest product of matrices from $\mathcal{M}$ having a column or a row with k positive entries and we denote it by $rt_k(\mathcal{M})$. We indicate with $rt_k(n)$ the maximal value of $rt_k(\mathcal{M})$ among all the primitive sets $\mathcal{M}$ of $n \times n$ NZ matrices.*

Our goal is to find, for any $n \geq 2$ and $2 \leq k \leq n$, a function $B_k(n)$ such that $rt_k(n) \leq B_k(n)$.

Definition 4. *Let n, k integers such that $n \geq 2$ and $2 \leq k \leq n-1$. We denote by $\mathcal{S}_n^k$ the set of all the $n \times n$ NZ matrices having every row and column of weight at most k and at least one column of weight exactly k. For any $A \in \mathcal{S}_n^k$, let $\mathcal{C}_A$ be the set of the indices of the columns of A having weight equal to k. We define $a_k^n(A) = \min_{c \in \mathcal{C}_A} |\{i : supp(A_{*i}) \not\subseteq supp(A_{*c})\}|$ and $a_k^n = \min_{A \in \mathcal{S}_n^k} a_k^n(A)$.*

In other words, $a_k^n(A)$ is the minimum over all the indices $c \in \mathcal{C}_A$ of the number of columns of A whose support is not contained in the support of the c-th column of A. Since the matrices are NZ, it clearly holds that for any $A \in \mathcal{S}_n^k$, $1 \leq a_k^n \leq a_k^n(A)$. The following theorem shows that for every $n \geq 2$, we can recursively define a function $B_k(n) \geq rt_k(n)$ on k by using the term a_k^n.

Theorem 2. *Let $n \geq 2$ integer. The following recursive function $B_k(n)$ is such that for all $2 \leq k \leq n$, $rt_k(n) \leq B_k(n)$.*

$$\begin{cases} B_2(n) = 1 \\ B_{k+1}(n) = B_k(n) + n(1 + n - a_k^n)/2 & for\ 2 \leq k \leq n-1. \end{cases} \tag{3}$$

Proof. We prove the theorem by induction.

Let $k = 2$. Any primitive set of NZ matrices must have a matrix with a row or a column with two positive entries, as otherwise it would be made of just permutation matrices and hence it would not be primitive. This trivially implies that $rt_2(n) = 1 \leq B_2(n)$.

Suppose now that $rt_k(n) \leq B_k(n)$, we show that $rt_{k+1}(n) \leq B_{k+1}(n)$. We remind that we denote with $\mathcal{M}^d$ the set of all the products of matrices from $\mathcal{M}$ having length smaller than or equal to d. If in $\mathcal{M}^{rt_k(\mathcal{M})+n-1}$ there exists a product having a column or a row with $k+1$ positive entries then $rt_{k+1}(\mathcal{M}) \leq rt_k(\mathcal{M}) + n - 1 \leq B_{k+1}(n)$. Suppose now that this is not the case. This means that in $\mathcal{M}^{rt_k(\mathcal{M})+n-1}$ every matrix has all the rows and columns of weight at most k. Let $A \in \mathcal{M}^{rt_k(\mathcal{M})}$ be a matrix having a row or a column of weight k, and suppose it is a column. The case when A has a row of weight k will be studied later. By Lemma 1 applied on the matrix A, for every $i \in [n]$ there exists a matrix $W_i \in \mathcal{M}^{rt_k(\mathcal{M})+n-1}$ having the i-th column of weight k (and all the other columns and rows of weight $\leq k$). Every W_i has at least a_k^n (see Definition 4) columns whose support is not contained in the support of the i-th column of W_i: let $c_i^1, c_i^2, \ldots, c_i^{a_k^n}$ be the indices of these columns. Notice that any product B of matrices from $\mathcal{M}$ of length l such that $B_{is} > 0$ and $B_{c_i^j s} > 0$ for some $s \in [n]$ and $j \in [a_k^n]$ would imply that $W_i B$ has the s-th column of weight at least $k+1$

and so $rt_{k+1}(\mathcal{M}) \leq rt_k(\mathcal{M}) + n - 1 + l$. We now want to minimize this length l over all $i, s \in [n]$ and $j \in [a_k^n]$: we will prove that there exists $i, s \in [n]$ and $j \in [a_k^n]$ such that $l \leq n(n - 1 - a_k^n)/2 + 1$. To do this, we consider the pair digraph $\mathcal{PD}(\mathcal{M}) = (\mathcal{V}, \mathcal{E})$ (see Definition 2) and the vertices

$$(1, c_1^1), (1, c_1^2), \ldots, (1, c_1^{a_k^n}), (2, c_2^1), \ldots, (2, c_2^{a_k^n}), \ldots, (n, c_n^1), \ldots, (n, c_n^{a_k^n}). \qquad (4)$$

By Lemma 2, for each vertex in Eq. (4) there exists a path in $\mathcal{PD}(\mathcal{M})$ connecting it to a singleton. By the same lemma, a path of length l from (i, c_i^j) to a singleton (s, s) would result in a product B_j of matrices from $\mathcal{M}$ of length l such that $W_i B_j$ has the s-th column of weight at least $k + 1$. We hence want to estimate the minimal length among the paths connecting the vertices in Eq. (4) to a singleton. Notice that Eq. (4) contains at least $\lceil na_k^n/2 \rceil$ different elements, since each element occurs at most twice. It is clear that the shortest path from a vertex in the list (4) to a singleton does not contain any other element from that list. The vertex set $\mathcal{V}$ of $\mathcal{PD}(\mathcal{M})$ has cardinality $n(n + 1)/2$ and it contains n vertices of type (s, s). It follows that the length of the shortest path connecting some vertex from the list (4) to some singleton is at most of $n(n + 1)/2 - n - \lceil na_k^n/2 \rceil + 1 \leq n(n - 1 - a_k^n)/2 + 1$. In view of what said before, we have that there exists a product B of matrices from $\mathcal{M}$ of length $\leq n(n - 1 - a_k^n)/2 + 1$ and $i \in [n]$ such that $W_i B_j$ has a column of weight at least $k + 1$. Since $W_i B_j$ belongs to $\mathcal{M}^{rt_k(\mathcal{M})+n-1+n(n-1-a_k^n)/2+1}$, it follows that $rt_{k+1}(\mathcal{M}) \leq rt_k(\mathcal{M}) + n(n + 1 - a_k^n)/2 \leq B_{k+1}(n)$.

Suppose now $A \in \mathcal{M}^{rt_k(\mathcal{M})}$ has a row of weight k. We can use the same argument as above on the matrix set $\mathcal{M}^T$ made of the transpose of all the matrices in $\mathcal{M}$. □

Notice that the above argument stays true if we replace a_k^n by a function $b(n, k)$ such that for all $n \geq 2$ and $2 \leq k \leq n - 1$, $1 \leq b(n, k) \leq a_k^n$. It follows that Eq. (3) still holds true if we replace a_k^n by $b(n, k)$.

4   Solving the Recurrence

We now find an analytic expression for a lower bound on a_k^n and we then solve the recurrence (3) in Theorem 2 by using this lower bound. We then show that this is the best estimate on a_k^n we can hope for.

Lemma 3. *Let n, k integers such that $n \geq 2$ and $2 \leq k \leq n - 1$, and let a_k^n as in Definition 4. It holds that $a_k^n \geq \max\{n - k(k - 1) - 1, \lceil (n - k)/k \rceil, 1\}$.*

Proof. We have that $a_k^n \geq 1$ since $k \leq n - 1$ and the matrices are NZ.
Let now $A \in S_n^k$ (see Definition 4) and let a be one of its columns of weight k. Let $S = supp(a)$; by assumption, the rows of A have at most k positive entries, so there can be at most $(k - 1)k$ columns of A different from a whose support is contained in S. Therefore, since A is NZ, there must exist at least $n - k(k - 1) - 1$ columns of A whose support is not contained in $supp(a)$ and so $a_k^n \geq n - k(k - 1) - 1$.

Let again $A \in S_n^k$ and let a be one of its columns of weight k. Let $S = [n]\setminus supp(a)$; S has cardinality $n - k$ and since A is NZ, for every $s \in S$ there exists $s' \in [n]$ such that $A_{ss'} > 0$. By assumption each column of A has weight of at most k, so there must exist at least $\lceil (n-k)/k \rceil$ columns of A different from a whose support is not contained in $supp(a)$. It follows that $a_k^n \geq \lceil (n-k)/k \rceil$. $\square$

Since $\lceil (n - k)/k \rceil \geq (n - k)/k$, $n - k(k - 1) - 1 \geq (n - k)/k$ for $k \leq \lfloor \sqrt{n} \rfloor$ and $(n - k)/k \geq 1$ for $k \leq \lfloor n/2 \rfloor$, the recursion (3) with a_k^n replaced by $\max\{n - k(k - 1) - 1, (n - k)/k, 1\}$ now reads as:

$$\tilde{B}_{k+1}(n) = \begin{cases} 1 & \text{if } k = 1 \\ \tilde{B}_k(n) + n(1 + k(k - 1)/2) & \text{if } 2 \leq k \leq \lfloor \sqrt{n} \rfloor \\ \tilde{B}_k(n) + n(1 + n(k - 1)/2k) & \text{if } \lfloor \sqrt{n} \rfloor + 1 \leq k \leq \lfloor n/2 \rfloor \\ \tilde{B}_k(n) + n^2/2 & \text{if } \lfloor n/2 \rfloor + 1 \leq k \leq n - 1 \end{cases} . \quad (5)$$

The following proposition shows the solution of the recursion (5):

Proposition 2. *Equation (5) is fulfilled by the following function:*

$$\tilde{B}_k(n) = \begin{cases} \dfrac{n(k^3 - 3k^2 + 8k - 12)}{6} + 1 & \text{if } 2 \leq k \leq \lfloor \sqrt{n} \rfloor \\ \tilde{B}_{\lfloor \sqrt{n} \rfloor}(n) + \dfrac{n(n + 2)(k - \lfloor \sqrt{n} \rfloor)}{2} - \dfrac{n^2}{2} \sum_{i=\lfloor \sqrt{n} \rfloor}^{k-1} \dfrac{1}{i} & \text{if } \lfloor \sqrt{n} \rfloor + 1 \leq k \leq \lfloor \tfrac{n}{2} \rfloor \\ \tilde{B}_{\lfloor \tfrac{n}{2} \rfloor}(n) + \dfrac{(k - \lfloor \tfrac{n}{2} \rfloor)n^2}{2} & \text{if } \lfloor \tfrac{n}{2} \rfloor + 1 \leq k \leq n \end{cases} \quad (6)$$

Therefore, for any constant k such that $k \leq \sqrt{n}$, the k-rendezvous time $rt_k(n)$ is at most linear in n.

Proof. If $2 \leq k \leq \lfloor \sqrt{n} \rfloor$, let $C_k(n) = \tilde{B}_k(n)/n$. By Eq. (5), it holds that $C_{k+1}(n) - C_k(n) = 1 + k(k - 1)/2$. By setting $C_k(n) = \alpha k^3 + \beta k^2 + \gamma k + \delta$, it follows that $3\alpha k^2 + (3\alpha + 2\beta)k + \alpha + \beta + \gamma = k^2/2 - k/2 + 1$. Since this must be true for all k, by equating the coefficients we have that $C_k(n) = k^3/6 - k^2/2 + 4k/3 + \delta$. Imposing the initial condition $\tilde{B}_2(n) = 1$ gives finally the desired result $\tilde{B}_k(n) = n(k^3 - 3k^2 + 8k - 12)/6 + 1$.

If $\lfloor \sqrt{n} \rfloor + 1 \leq k \leq \lfloor n/2 \rfloor$, let again $C_k(n) = \tilde{B}_k(n)/n$. By Eq. (5), it holds that $C_{k+1}(n) - C_k(n) = 1 + n(k - 1)/2k$ and so $C_k(n) = C_{\lfloor \sqrt{n} \rfloor}(n) + (k - 2)(1 + n/2) - (n/2) \sum_{i=\lfloor \sqrt{n} \rfloor}^{k-1} i^{-1}$. Since $C_{\lfloor \sqrt{n} \rfloor}(n) = \tilde{B}_{\lfloor \sqrt{n} \rfloor}(n)/n$, it follows that $\tilde{B}_k(n) = \tilde{B}_{\lfloor \sqrt{n} \rfloor}(n) + (k - \lfloor \sqrt{n} \rfloor)n(n + 2)/2 - (n^2/2) \sum_{i=\lfloor \sqrt{n} \rfloor}^{k-1} i^{-1}$.

If $\lfloor n/2 \rfloor + 1 \leq k \leq n - 1$, by Eq. (5) it is easy to see that $\tilde{B}_k(n) = \tilde{B}_{\lfloor n/2 \rfloor}(n) + (k - \lfloor n/2 \rfloor)n^2/2$, which concludes the proof. $\square$

We now show that $a_k^n = \max\{n - k(k - 1) - 1, \lceil (n - k)/k \rceil, 1\}$, and so we cannot improve the upper bound $\tilde{B}_k(n)$ on $rt_k(n)$ by improving our estimate of a_k^n.

Lemma 4. *Let n, k integers such that $n \geq 2$ and $2 \leq k \leq n - 1$. It holds that:*

$$1 \leq a_k^n \leq u(n,k) := \begin{cases} n - k(k-1) - 1 & \text{if } n - k(k-1) - 1 \geq \lceil (n-k)/k \rceil \\ \lceil (n-k)/k \rceil & \text{otherwise} \end{cases}.$$

Proof. We need to show that for every $n \geq 2$ and $2 \leq k \leq n - 1$, there exists a matrix $A \in \mathcal{S}_n^k$ such that $a_k^n(A) = u(n,k)$ (see Definition 4). We define the matrix $C_i^{m_1 \times m_2}$ as the $m_1 \times m_2$ matrix having all the entries of the i-th column equal to 1 and all the other entries equal to 0, and the matrix $R_i^{m_1 \times m_2}$ as the $m_1 \times m_2$ matrix having all the entries of the i-th row equal to 1 and all the other entries equal to 0. We indicate with $\mathbf{0}^{m_1 \times m_2}$ the $m_1 \times m_2$ matrix having all its entries equal to zero and with $\mathbf{I}^{m \times m}$ the $m \times m$ identity matrix. Let $v_k^n = \lceil (n-k)/k \rceil + 1$ and $q = n \mod k$.

Suppose that $n - k(k-1) - 1 \geq \lceil (n-k)/k \rceil$ and set $\alpha = n - k(k-1) - 1 - \lceil (n-k)/k \rceil$. Then the following matrix $\hat{A}$ is such that $a_k^n(\hat{A}) = n - k(k-1) - 1 = u(n,k)$:

$$\hat{A} = \left[\begin{array}{c|c} \begin{matrix} C_1^{k \times v_k^n} \\ C_2^{k \times v_k^n} \\ \vdots \\ C_{v_k^n - 1}^{k \times v_k^n} \\ C_{v_k^n}^{q \times v_k^n} \end{matrix} \begin{matrix} R_1^{k \times (k-1)} \;\; R_2^{k \times (k-1)} \;\; \cdots \;\; R_k^{k \times (k-1)} \\ \\ \mathbf{0}^{(n-k) \times [k(k-1)]} \end{matrix} & D \end{array} \right], \quad D = \begin{bmatrix} \mathbf{0}^{k \times \alpha} \\ \mathbf{I}^{\alpha \times \alpha} \\ \mathbf{0}^{(n-k-\alpha) \times \alpha} \end{bmatrix}.$$

Indeed by construction, the first column of $\hat{A}$ has exactly k positive entries. The columns of $\hat{A}$ whose support is not contained in $\hat{A}_{*1}$ are the columns $\hat{A}_{*i}$ for $i = 2, \ldots, v_k^n$ and all the columns of D. In total we have $\lceil (n-k)/k \rceil + \alpha = n - k(k-1) - 1$ columns, so it holds that $a_k^n(\hat{A}) = n - k(k-1) - 1$.

Suppose that $n - k(k-1) - 1 \leq \lceil (n-k)/k \rceil$. Then the following matrix $\tilde{A}$ is such that $a_k^n(\tilde{A}) = \lceil (n-k)/k \rceil = u(n,k)$:

$$\tilde{A} = \left[\begin{array}{c|c} \begin{matrix} C_1^{k \times v_k^n} \\ C_2^{k \times v_k^n} \\ \vdots \\ C_{v_k^n - 1}^{k \times v_k^n} \\ C_{v_k^n}^{q \times v_k^n} \end{matrix} & \begin{matrix} R_1^{k \times (k-1)} \;\; R_2^{k \times (k-1)} \;\; \cdots \;\; R_{k-1}^{k \times (k-1)} \;\; R_k^{k \times (n - v_k^n - (k-1)^2)} \\ \\ \mathbf{0}^{(n-k) \times (n - v_k^n)} \end{matrix} \end{array} \right]$$

Indeed by construction, the first column of $\tilde{A}$ has exactly k positive entries and the columns of $\tilde{A}$ whose support is not contained in $\tilde{A}_{*1}$ are the columns $\tilde{A}_{*i}$ for $i = 2, \ldots, v_k^n$. Therefore it holds that $a_k^n(\tilde{A}) = v_k^n - 1 = \lceil (n-k)/k \rceil$. $\square$

5 Numerical Results

We report here some numerical results that compare the theoretical bound $\tilde{B}_k(n)$ on $rt_k(n)$ of Eq. (6) with either the exact k-RT or with an heuristic approximation of the k-RT when the computation of the exact value is not computationally feasible. In Fig. 2 we compare our bound with the real k-RT of the primitive sets $\mathcal{M}_{CPR}$ and $\mathcal{M}_K$ reported here below:

$$\mathcal{M}_{CPR} = \left\{ \begin{pmatrix} 0 & 0 & 1 & 0 \\ 1 & 1 & 0 & 0 \\ 1 & 0 & 0 & 0 \\ 0 & 0 & 0 & 1 \end{pmatrix}, \begin{pmatrix} 1 & 0 & 0 & 0 \\ 0 & 0 & 1 & 0 \\ 0 & 0 & 0 & 1 \\ 0 & 1 & 0 & 0 \end{pmatrix} \right\}, \mathcal{M}_K = \left\{ \begin{pmatrix} 1 & 0 & 0 & 1 & 0 & 0 \\ 0 & 1 & 0 & 0 & 0 & 0 \\ 0 & 0 & 1 & 0 & 0 & 0 \\ 0 & 0 & 0 & 0 & 1 & 0 \\ 0 & 0 & 0 & 1 & 0 & 0 \\ 0 & 0 & 0 & 0 & 0 & 1 \end{pmatrix}, \begin{pmatrix} 0 & 0 & 0 & 0 & 1 & 0 \\ 0 & 0 & 1 & 0 & 0 & 0 \\ 0 & 0 & 0 & 1 & 0 & 0 \\ 0 & 1 & 0 & 0 & 0 & 0 \\ 0 & 0 & 0 & 0 & 0 & 1 \\ 1 & 0 & 0 & 0 & 0 & 0 \end{pmatrix} \right\}.$$

The sets $\mathcal{M}_K$ and $\mathcal{M}_{CPR}$ are primitive sets of matrices that are based on the Kari automaton [21] and the Černý-Piricka-Rozenaurova automaton [40] respectively. We can see that for small values of k, the upper bound is fairly close to the actual value of $rt_k(\mathcal{M})$.

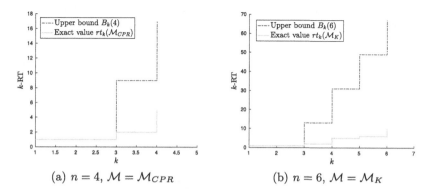

(a) $n = 4$, $\mathcal{M} = \mathcal{M}_{CPR}$ (b) $n = 6$, $\mathcal{M} = \mathcal{M}_K$

Fig. 2. Comparison between the bound $\tilde{B}_k(n)$, valid for all primitive NZ sets, and $rt_k(\mathcal{M})$ for $\mathcal{M} = \mathcal{M}_{CPR}$ (left) and $\mathcal{M} = \mathcal{M}_K$ (right).

When n is large, computing the k-RT for every $2 \leq k \leq n$ becomes hard, so we compare our upper bound on the k-RT with a method for approximating it. The *Eppstein heuristic* is a greedy algorithm developed by Eppstein in [11] for approximating the reset threshold of a synchronizing automaton. Given a primitive set $\mathcal{M}$ of binary NZ matrices, we can apply a slightly modified Eppstein heuristic to obtain, for any k, an upper bound on $rt_k(\mathcal{M})$. The description of this modified heuristic is not reported here due to length restrictions.

In Fig. 3 we compare our upper bound with the results of the Eppstein heuristic on the k-RT of the primitive sets with quadratic exponent presented by Catalano and Jungers in [6], Sect. 4; here we denote these sets by $\mathcal{M}_{C_n}$ where n is the matrix dimension. Finally, Fig. 4 compares the evolution of our bound with the results of the Eppstein heuristic on the k-RT of the family $\mathcal{M}_{C_n}$ for fixed $k = 4$ and as n varies. It can be noticed that the bound $\tilde{B}_k(n)$ does not increase very rapidly as compared to the Eppstein approximation.

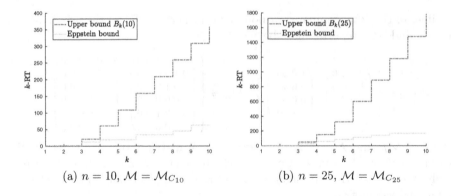

(a) $n = 10$, $\mathcal{M} = \mathcal{M}_{C_{10}}$ (b) $n = 25$, $\mathcal{M} = \mathcal{M}_{C_{25}}$

Fig. 3. Comparison between $\tilde{B}_k(n)$ and the Eppstein approx. of $rt_k(\mathcal{M})$, for $\mathcal{M} = \mathcal{M}_{C_{10}}$ (left) and $\mathcal{M} = \mathcal{M}_{C_{25}}$ (right). We recall that $\tilde{B}_k(n)$ is a generic bound valid for all primitive NZ sets, while the Eppstein bound is computed on each particular set.

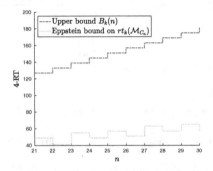

Fig. 4. Comparison between $\tilde{B}_k(n)$ and the Eppstein approx. of $rt_k(\mathcal{M}_{C_n})$ for $k = 4$. We recall that $\tilde{B}_k(n)$ is a generic bound valid for all primitive NZ sets, while the Eppstein bound is computed on each particular set.

6   Conclusions

In this paper we have shown that we can upper bound the length of the shortest product of a primitive NZ set $\mathcal{M}$ having a column or a row with k positive entries by a linear function of the matrix size n, for any constant $k \leq \sqrt{n}$. We have called this length the k-*rendezvous time* (k-RT) of the set $\mathcal{M}$, and we have shown that the same linear upper bound holds for $\min\{rt_k(Aut(\mathcal{M})), rt_k(Aut(\mathcal{M}^T))\}$, where $Aut(\mathcal{M})$ and $Aut(\mathcal{M}^T)$ are the synchronizing automata defined in Definition 1. We have also showed that our technique cannot be improved as it already takes into account the worst cases, so new strategies have to be implemented in order to possibly obtain a better upper bound on $rt_k(n)$. The notion of k-RT for primitive sets comes as an extension to primitive sets of the one introduced for synchronizing automata. For automata, the problem whether there exists a linear upper bound on the k-RT for small k is still open, as the only nontrivial result on the k-RT that appears in the literature, to the best of our knowledge, proves a quadratic upper bound on the 3-RT [17]. We believe that our result could help in shedding light to this problem and possibly to the Černý conjecture, in view of the connection between synchronizing automata and primitive NZ sets established by Theorem 1.

References

1. Al'pin, Y.A., Al'pina, V.S.: Combinatorial properties of irreducible semigroups of nonnegative matrices. J. Math. Sci. **191**(1), 4–9 (2013)
2. Ananichev, D.S., Gusev, V.V.: Approximation of reset thresholds with greedy algorithms. Fundam. Inform. **145**(3), 221–227 (2016)
3. Ananichev, D.S., Volkov, M.V., Gusev, V.V.: Primitive digraphs with large exponents and slowly synchronizing automata. J. Math. Sci. **192**(3), 263–278 (2013)
4. Blondel, V., Jungers, R.M., Olshevsky, A.: On primitivity of sets of matrices. Automatica **61**, 80–88 (2015)
5. de Bondt, M., Don, H., Zantema, H.: DFAs and PFAs with long shortest synchronizing word length. In: Charlier, É., Leroy, J., Rigo, M. (eds.) DLT 2017. LNCS, vol. 10396, pp. 122–133. Springer, Cham (2017). https://doi.org/10.1007/978-3-319-62809-7_8
6. Catalano, C., Jungers, R.M.: On randomized generation of slowly synchronizing automata. In: Mathematical Foundations of Computer Science, pp. 48:1–48:21 (2018)
7. Catalano, C., Jungers, R.M.: The synchronizing probability function for primitive sets of matrices. In: Hoshi, M., Seki, S. (eds.) DLT 2018. LNCS, vol. 11088, pp. 194–205. Springer, Cham (2018). https://doi.org/10.1007/978-3-319-98654-8_16
8. Chen, Y.B., Ierardi, D.J.: The complexity of oblivious plans for orienting and distinguishing polygonal parts. Algorithmica **14**(5), 367–397 (1995)
9. Chevalier, P.Y., Hendrickx, J.M., Jungers, R.M.: Reachability of consensus and synchronizing automata. In: IEEE Conference in Decision and Control, pp. 4139–4144 (2015)
10. Dzyga, M., Ferens, R., Gusev, V.V., Szykuła, M.: Attainable values of reset thresholds. In: Mathematical Foundations of Computer Science, vol. 83, pp. 40:1–40:14 (2017)
11. Eppstein, D.: Reset sequences for monotonic automata. SIAM J. Comput. **19**(3), 500–510 (1990)
12. Fomichev, V.M., Avezova, Y.E., Koreneva, A.M., Kyazhin, S.N.: Primitivity and local primitivity of digraphs and nonnegative matrices. J. Appl. Ind. Math. **12**(3), 453–469 (2018)
13. Frankl, P.: An extremal problem for two families of sets. Eur. J. Comb. **3**(3), 125–127 (1982)
14. Gawrychowski, P., Straszak, D.: Strong inapproximability of the shortest reset word. In: Italiano, G.F., Pighizzini, G., Sannella, D.T. (eds.) MFCS 2015. LNCS, vol. 9234, pp. 243–255. Springer, Heidelberg (2015). https://doi.org/10.1007/978-3-662-48057-1_19
15. Gerencsér, B., Gusev, V.V., Jungers, R.M.: Primitive sets of nonnegative matrices and synchronizing automata. SIAM J. Matrix Anal. Appl. **39**(1), 83–98 (2018)

16. Gonze, F., Gusev, V.V., Gerencsér, B., Jungers, R.M., Volkov, M.V.: On the interplay between babai and Černý's conjectures. In: Charlier, É., Leroy, J., Rigo, M. (eds.) DLT 2017. LNCS, vol. 10396, pp. 185–197. Springer, Cham (2017). https://doi.org/10.1007/978-3-319-62809-7_13

17. Gonze, F., Jungers, R.M.: On the synchronizing probability function and the triple Rendezvous time. In: Dediu, A.-H., Formenti, E., Martín-Vide, C., Truthe, B. (eds.) LATA 2015. LNCS, vol. 8977, pp. 212–223. Springer, Cham (2015). https://doi.org/10.1007/978-3-319-15579-1_16

18. Hajnal, J.: On products of non-negative matrices. Math. Proc. Cambr. Philos. Soc. **79**(3), 521–530 (1976)

19. Hartfiel, D.J.: Nonhomogeneous Matrix Products. World Scientific Publishing, London (2002)

20. Hennion, H.: Limit theorems for products of positive random matrices. Ann. Prob. **25**(4), 1545–1587 (1997)

21. Kari, J.: A counter example to a conjecture concerning synchronizing words in finite automata. Bull. EATCS **73**, 146 (2001)

22. Kari, J.: Synchronizing finite automata on eulerian digraphs. Theor. Comput. Sci. **295**(1), 223–232 (2003)

23. Kisielewicz, A., Szykuła, M.: Synchronizing automata with extremal properties. In: Italiano, G.F., Pighizzini, G., Sannella, D.T. (eds.) MFCS 2015. LNCS, vol. 9234, pp. 331–343. Springer, Heidelberg (2015). https://doi.org/10.1007/978-3-662-48057-1_26

24. Kisielewicz, A., Kowalski, J., Szykuła, M.: Experiments with synchronizing automata. In: Han, Y.-S., Salomaa, K. (eds.) CIAA 2016. LNCS, vol. 9705, pp. 176–188. Springer, Cham (2016). https://doi.org/10.1007/978-3-319-40946-7_15

25. Mateescu, A., Salomaa, A.: Many-valued truth functions, Černý's conjecture and road coloring. In: EATCS Bulletin, pp. 134–150 (1999)

26. Natarajan, B.K.: An algorithmic approach to the automated design of parts orienters. In: SFCS, pp. 132–142 (1986)

27. Paterson, M.: Unsolvability in 3×3 matrices. Stud. Appl. Math. **49**(1), 105–107 (1996)

28. Pin, J.E.: On two combinatorial problems arising from automata theory. In: International Colloquium on Graph Theory and Combinatorics, vol. 75, pp. 535–548 (1983)

29. Potapov, I., Semukhin, P.: Decidability of the membership problem for 2×2 integer matrices. In: ACM-SIAM Symposium on Discrete Algorithms, pp. 170–186 (2017)

30. Protasov, V.Y.: Invariant functions for the Lyapunov exponents of random matrices. Sbornik Math. **202**(1), 101 (2011)

31. Protasov, V.Y., Voynov, A.S.: Sets of nonnegative matrices without positive products. Linear Algebra Appl. **437**, 749–765 (2012)

32. Rystsov, I.K.: Reset words for commutative and solvable automata. Theor. Comput. Sci. **172**(1), 273–279 (1997)

33. Schützenberger, M.: On the synchronizing properties of certain prefix codes. Inf. Control **7**(1), 23–36 (1964)

34. Seneta, E.: Non-Negative Matrices and Markov Chains, 2nd edn. Springer, New York (1981). https://doi.org/10.1007/0-387-32792-4

35. Steinberg, B.: The averaging trick and the Černý conjecture. In: Gao, Y., Lu, H., Seki, S., Yu, S. (eds.) DLT 2010. LNCS, vol. 6224, pp. 423–431. Springer, Heidelberg (2010). https://doi.org/10.1007/978-3-642-14455-4_38

36. Szykuła, M.: Improving the upper bound the length of the shortest reset words. In: Symposium on Theoretical Aspects of Computer Science, vol. 96, pp. 56:1–56:16 (2018)
37. Biskup, M.T., Plandowski, W.: Shortest synchronizing strings for Huffman codes. Theor. Comput. Sci. **410**, 3925–3941 (2009)
38. Trahtman, A.: Notable trends concerning the synchronization of graphs and automata. Electron. Notes Discrete Math. **25**, 173–175 (2006)
39. Černý, J.: Poznámka k homogénnym eksperimentom s konečnými automatami. Matematicko-fysikalny Casopis SAV **14**(14), 208–216 (1964)
40. Černý, J., Piricka, A., Rosenaueriva, B.: On directable automata. Kybernetika **7**, 289–298 (1971)
41. Volkov, M.V.: Synchronizing automata preserving a chain of partial orders. In: Holub, J., Žd'árek, J. (eds.) CIAA 2007. LNCS, vol. 4783, pp. 27–37. Springer, Heidelberg (2007). https://doi.org/10.1007/978-3-540-76336-9_5
42. Volkov, M.V.: Synchronizing automata and the Černý conjecture. In: Martín-Vide, C., Otto, F., Fernau, H. (eds.) LATA 2008. LNCS, vol. 5196, pp. 11–27. Springer, Heidelberg (2008). https://doi.org/10.1007/978-3-540-88282-4_4

Words of Minimum Rank
in Deterministic Finite Automata

Jarkko Kari[1($\boxtimes$)], Andrew Ryzhikov[2], and Anton Varonka[3]

[1] University of Turku, Turku, Finland
jkari@utu.fi
[2] LIGM, Université Paris-Est, Marne-la-Vallée, France
[3] Belarusian State University, Minsk, Belarus

Abstract. The rank of a word in a deterministic finite automaton is the size of the image of the whole state set under the mapping defined by this word. We study the length of shortest words of minimum rank in several classes of complete deterministic finite automata, namely, strongly connected and Eulerian automata. A conjecture bounding this length is known as the Rank Conjecture, a generalization of the well known Černý Conjecture. We prove upper bounds on the length of shortest words of minimum rank in automata from the mentioned classes, and provide several families of automata with long words of minimum rank. Some results in this direction are also obtained for automata with rank equal to period (the greatest common divisor of lengths of all cycles) and for circular automata.

Keywords: Minimum rank word · Synchronizing automaton · Eulerian automaton

1 Introduction

A *complete deterministic finite automaton* (which we simply call an *automaton* in this paper) is a triple $\mathcal{A} = \langle Q, \Sigma, \delta \rangle$, where Q is a finite non-empty set of *states*, Σ is a finite non-empty *alphabet*, and $\delta : Q \times \Sigma \to Q$ is a complete *transition function*. We extend δ to $Q \times \Sigma^*$ and $2^Q \times \Sigma^*$ in the usual way: $\delta(q, w) = \delta(\delta(q, v), a)$ if $w = va$ for some word $v \in \Sigma^*$ and $a \in \Sigma$, and $\delta(S, w) = \{\delta(q, w) \mid q \in S\}$ for $S \subseteq Q$. We call the automaton *binary* or *ternary* if $|\Sigma| = 2$ or $|\Sigma| = 3$, respectively.

An automaton $\mathcal{A}$ is called *synchronizing* if there is a word w that resets it, that is, brings it to a particular state no matter at which state the word has been applied: $\delta(q, w) = \delta(q', w)$ for all $q, q' \in Q$. Any such word w is said to be a *synchronizing word* (or a *reset word*) for the automaton while the minimum

Jarkko Kari is supported by the Academy of Finland grant 296018. Anton Varonka is supported by Poland's National Science Centre (NCN) grant no. 2016/21/D/ST6/00491.

P. Hofman and M. Skrzypczak (Eds.): DLT 2019, LNCS 11647, pp. 74–87, 2019.
https://doi.org/10.1007/978-3-030-24886-4_5

length of a synchronizing word for $\mathcal{A}$ is called the *reset threshold* of $\mathcal{A}$ and is denoted rt($\mathcal{A}$).

A natural question arises: *how large can the reset threshold of n-state synchronizing automaton be?* In 1964 Černý [9] constructed an n-state synchronizing automaton $\mathcal{C}_n$ with two letters which reset threshold is $(n-1)^2$ for all $n > 1$. The state set of $\mathcal{C}_n$ is $Q = \{1, 2, \ldots, n\}$ and the letters a and b act on it as follows:

$$\delta(i, a) = \begin{cases} i, & \text{if } i > 1 \\ 2, & \text{if } i = 1; \end{cases} \quad \delta(i, b) = \begin{cases} i + 1, & \text{if } i < n \\ 1, & \text{if } i = n. \end{cases}$$

We refer to automata of this series as *the Černý automata.*

Some time later (e.g. [8]) it was conjectured that every synchronizing automaton with n states can be reset by a word of length $(n-1)^2$. This is known as *the Černý Conjecture* which remains open more than 50 years later (for a survey on this topic see [20]).

Given an automaton $\mathcal{A} = \langle Q, \Sigma, \delta \rangle$, the *rank* of a word $w \in \Sigma^*$ with respect to $\mathcal{A}$ is the number of states active after applying it, that is, the number $|\delta(Q, w)|$. When the automaton is clear from the context, we just call it the rank of w. The *rank* of an automaton is the minimum rank among all words with respect to the automaton. A *synchronizing* word (automaton) is thus a word (automaton) of rank 1. We call the length of a shortest word of minimum rank of an automaton $\mathcal{A}$ the *minimum rank threshold* of $\mathcal{A}$. We denote it mrt($\mathcal{A}$).

Pin [17] proposed the following generalization of the Černý Conjecture: for every n-state automaton having a word of rank at most r, there exists such a word of length at most $(n - r)^2$. A cubic upper bound is proved for this conjecture [16]. However, Kari [14] found a counterexample to the conjectured $(n - r)^2$ bound for $r = 2$, which is a binary automaton $\mathcal{K}$ with $n = 6$ states. As a consequence, a modification of this generalized conjecture was proposed by Pribavkina restricting it to r being the rank of the considered automaton ($\mathcal{K}$ is synchronizing but the Pin's bound is exceeded for a word of rank 2). This restricted case has not been disproved yet, and is sometimes referred to as the Rank Conjecture (or the Černý-Pin Conjecture in [1]). The case $r = 1$ is the Černý Conjecture.

It was pointed out in [2] that one of the reasons why the Černý Conjecture is so hard to tackle is the lack of examples of slowly synchronizing automata. The same is true concerning the Rank Conjecture. Pin [18] provided the following example. The automaton with two letters consists of r connected components, one of which is the Černý automaton $\mathcal{C}_{n-r+1}$ and $r - 1$ others are isolated states with loops labeled with both letters. The automaton thus constructed has n states, rank r and its minimum rank threshold is precisely $(n-r)^2$. However, this automaton is not strongly connected (an automaton is called *strongly connected* if any state can be mapped to any other state by some word), so this case in some sense reduces to the rank 1 case. No series of strongly connected automata with mrt($\mathcal{A}$) close to the $(n - r)^2$ bound were introduced so far.

In this paper, we propose a number of techniques to construct strongly connected automata of rank r with large minimum rank thresholds. The families of automata we obtain do not reach the conjectured bound $(n - r)^2$, but the minimum rank threshold is typically of the order $\frac{(n-r)^2}{r}$, or within a constant multiple of this. We provide families of automata having additional properties such as being Eulerian or circular, or having rank equal to the period (see Sect. 2 for definitions of these concepts). We also consider upper bounds: we prove the Rank Conjecture for Eulerian automata, and obtain an upper bound on the minimum rank threshold of circular automata.

The paper is organized as follows. In Sect. 2 we provide the main definitions and preliminary results. In Sect. 3 we provide constructions for turning a binary synchronizing automaton into a higher rank ternary (Sect. 3.1) or binary (Sect. 3.2) automaton having its minimum rank threshold close to the reset threshold of the original automaton. Applying these constructions on known series of synchronizing automata yield new series of automata of higher ranks $r > 1$. In Sect. 3.3 we show how upper bounds on the reset threshold can be turned into upper bounds on the minimum rank thresholds on automata with period equal to rank. In Sect. 4 we prove the Rank Conjecture for automata based on Eulerian digraphs, along with exhibiting lower bounds on minimum rank thresholds. In Sect. 4.2 we present a way to transform known bounds from Eulerian automata to circular automata. In particular, quadratic upper bounds on minimum rank thresholds for circular automata (including the reset threshold) are proved. In Sect. 4.3 we contribute to the Road Coloring Problem, presenting a nearly-linear algorithm of finding a coloring of minimum rank for an Eulerian digraph.

2   Main Definitions and Preliminary Results

All our digraphs are multigraphs and they are allowed to have loops. The *underlying digraph* $D(\mathcal{A})$ of an automaton $\mathcal{A} = \langle Q, \Sigma, \delta \rangle$ has vertex set Q, and for any $q, p \in Q$, there are as many edges from q to p as there are letters $a \in \Sigma$ such that $\delta(q, a) = p$. An automaton $\mathcal{A}$ is called a *coloring* of its multigraph $D(\mathcal{A})$. The underlying digraph of every automaton has the same outdegree at all its vertices. From now on, we consider only digraphs with this property.

A digraph D is called *strongly connected* if for every pair (v, v') of vertices there exists a directed path from v to v'. An automaton is *strongly connected* if its underlying digraph is strongly connected.

The *period* of a digraph D is the greatest common divisor of the lengths of its cycles, and the period of an automaton is defined as the period of its underlying digraph. Let us remark explicitly that digraphs with period $p > 1$ do not have synchronizing colorings. The following lemma is essential to understand the period of a digraph.

Lemma 1 ([5], **p. 29**). *Let D be a digraph with period p. Then the set V of vertices of D can be partitioned into p nonempty sets $V_1, V_2, \ldots, V_p$ where each edge of D goes from a vertex from V_i and enters some vertex in V_{i+1} for some i (the indices are taken modulo p).*

We will call this partition a *p-partition* of a digraph or of its coloring.

Much of the literature on synchronizing automata concentrates on the primitive case. A digraph is called *primitive* if it is strongly connected and the period is $p = 1$. In this paper we are interested in automata with underlying digraphs which are strongly connected but not necessarily primitive.

A digraph is *Eulerian* if for each vertex the outdegree is equal to the indegree. The automaton is *Eulerian* if it is strongly connected and its underlying digraph is Eulerian. Equivalently, at every state there must be exactly $|\Sigma|$ incoming transitions, where Σ is the alphabet of the automaton. An automaton is *circular* if there is a letter which acts on its set of states as a cyclic permutation.

3   Strongly Connected Automata

3.1   A Lower Bound for Ternary Automata

We start with a construction yielding a series of strongly connected ternary automata. We transform a synchronizing binary automaton $\mathcal{A}$ into a ternary automaton $\mathcal{A}'$ of a given rank $r > 1$ such that $\mathrm{mrt}(\mathcal{A}')$ is related to $\mathrm{rt}(\mathcal{A})$.

We start with a synchronizing binary automaton $\mathcal{A} = \langle Q, \{a, b\}, \delta \rangle$ with t states $q_1, \ldots, q_t$. We define a ternary automaton $\mathcal{A}' = \langle Q', \{a, b, c\}, \delta' \rangle$ of rank r with the size $n = r \cdot t$ state set $Q' = \bigcup_{i=0}^{r-1} Q_i$ where each Q_i contains t states $q_{i,1}, \ldots, q_{i,t}$. The action of the transition function δ' on the set Q_0 repeats the action of δ on set Q for the letters a, b: for $x = a$ and $x = b$ we have $\delta'(q_{0,j}, x) = q_{0,k}$ if and only if $\delta(q_j, x) = q_k$. On the other sets $Q_1, \ldots, Q_{r-1}$ the transitions by the letters a, b are self-loops: we set $\delta'(q_{i,k}, x) = q_{i,k}$ for $x = a$ and $x = b$, for all $i \neq 0$ and all k. Finally, the letter c shifts states of Q_i to the next set Q_{i+1}: we define $\delta'(q_{i,k}, c) = q_{i+1,k}$ where $i + 1$ is counted modulo r, that is, elements of Q_{r-1} are shifted to the set Q_0. Note that the construction preserves the property of the automaton to be strongly connected or Eulerian.

Since $\mathcal{A}$ is synchronizing, we certainly obtain an automaton of rank r as the result of this construction. No two states from different sets Q_i, Q_j with $i \neq j$ can be merged for the obvious reason. Each of them though can be mapped using the letter c to Q_0 which, in turn, can be mapped to a single state.

If w is a shortest reset word for $\mathcal{A}$, a trivial way to compose a word of rank r for $\mathcal{A}'$ is as follows. We use w to merge the states of Q_0 to one particular state, then use the letter c to shift the set at play and continue until every set Q_i is merged into one state. The resulting word $w' = wcw \ldots cw$ thus has length $\mathrm{rt}(\mathcal{A}) \cdot r + r - 1$. Moreover, w' is the shortest word of rank r. Indeed, since all the transitions in the sets $Q_1, Q_2, \ldots, Q_{r-1}$ are self-loops for a, b, the only place where merging of states takes place is inside Q_0. While states of some Q_i are treated there, the states of all $Q_j, j \neq i$, remain invariant. Obviously, c has to be applied at least $r - 1$ times. Hence, by the pigeonhole principle, the existence of a shorter word of minimum rank would imply that an automaton induced by the action of $\{a, b\}$ on Q_0 can be synchronized faster than in $\mathrm{rt}(\mathcal{A})$ steps.

If we apply the construction to the Černý automaton $\mathcal{C}_{\frac{n}{r}}$, we get the following.

Proposition 1. *For every n and every $r > 1$ such that r divides n, there exists a ternary strongly connected automaton with n states and rank r such that the length of its shortest word of minimum rank is $\frac{(n-r)^2}{r} + r - 1$.*

It is natural to ask for a lower bound on the minimum rank threshold for binary automata. There are some techniques known to decrease the alphabet size of an automaton while not changing the length of a shortest synchronizing word significantly. By carefully applying the construction encoding letters in states [4,21] one can get a lower bound of $\frac{n^2}{3r} - \frac{7}{3}n + 5r$ for the binary case. Another technique decreasing alphabet size, namely by encoding binary representation of letters in states [4, Lemma 3], does not yield any better bounds. Below we present some different ideas providing stronger lower bounds on $\mathrm{mrt}(\mathcal{A})$ in the class of binary strongly connected automata.

3.2   Lower Bounds for Binary Automata

In the ternary construction above we may represent the actions of words ac and bc by two new letters, and afterwards remove the original letters a, b, c. This yields a binary automaton of rank r. More generally, we can do this on the analogous construction from an automaton with alphabet size k to size $k + 1$, obtaining again an automaton with alphabet size k and having rank r.

The detailed construction goes as follows. Given a strongly connected synchronizing automaton $\mathcal{A} = \langle Q, \Sigma, \delta \rangle$ over any alphabet Σ and with state set $Q = \{q_1, \ldots, q_t\}$, we define the automaton $\mathcal{A}' = \langle Q', \Sigma, \delta' \rangle$ over the same alphabet as follows. As in the ternary construction, the state set is $Q' = \bigcup_{i=0}^{r-1} Q_i$ where each Q_i contains t states $q_{i,1}, \ldots, q_{i,t}$. The transitions from Q_0 to Q_1 imitate the transitions of $\mathcal{A}$: for every letter $a \in \Sigma$ we set $\delta'(q_{0,j}, a) = q_{1,k}$ if and only if $\delta(q_j, a) = q_k$. For the states in Q_i with $i \neq 0$ we define the transitions by just shifting a state to the state with the same index in the next set: for every $a \in \Sigma$ we set $\delta'(q_{i,j}, a) = q_{i+1,j}$, with the index $i + 1$ taken modulo p.

Observe that the action of the set of words Σ^r on the set Q_i in $\mathcal{A}'$ induces the automaton $\mathcal{A}$ (up to duplicating its letters). Moreover, the words of length $r - 1$ only shift the states of the set Q_1 to Q_0. Thus, any word synchronizing Q_1 is of length at least $\mathrm{rt}(\mathcal{A}) \cdot r$ over the initial alphabet. Clearly, this automaton has rank r, and its period is also r because $\mathcal{A}$ is synchronizing and thus primitive. We obtain the following result.

Proposition 2. *For every t-state strongly connected synchronizing automaton $\mathcal{A}$ and for every r there exists a tr-state strongly connected automaton $\mathcal{A}'$ over the same alphabet, with period and rank equal to r, such that $\mathrm{mrt}(\mathcal{A}') = \mathrm{rt}(\mathcal{A}) \cdot r$.*

Observe that the construction described preserves the property of the automaton to be strongly connected, circular or Eulerian. Applied to the Černý automaton this construction yields the following result.

Corollary 1. *For every n and every r such that r divides n, there exists an n-state circular binary automaton of period and rank r with minimum rank threshold $\frac{(n-r)^2}{r}$.*

The *Wielandt digraph* W_n has $n > 1$ vertices $0, \dots, n-1$. From each vertex $i > 0$ there are two edges to the next vertex $i+1$ modulo n, and from vertex 0 there are single edges to vertices 1 and 2. Introduced in [22], and studied in connection to synchronizing automata in [2], these digraphs have the interesting property that they admit only one coloring, when automata obtained by renaming letters are considered identical. The reset threshold of this n-state Wielandt automaton was proved in [2] to be $n^2 - 3n + 3$.

The Hybrid Černý-Road Coloring problem (see [2,7]) asks for the shortest length of a synchronizing word among all colorings of a fixed primitive digraph with n vertices. Since W_n has only one coloring, it provides the lower bound $n^2 - 3n + 3$ on this quantity. We can apply the binary construction of this section on the Wielandt automaton. The resulting automaton of rank r also admits only one coloring. Hence we get the following result in the spirit of the Hybrid Černý-Road Coloring problem, generalizing it to cases $r > 1$.

Corollary 2. *For every $n > 1$ and every r such that r divides n, there exists an n-vertex strongly connected digraph D of constant outdegree 2 such that all colorings of D are circular, have the same period and rank r, and for every coloring the length of a word of minimum rank is $\frac{(n-r)^2}{r} - n + 2r$.*

It is interesting to note that the digraphs D in Corollary 2 are the digraphs with the largest possible index, described in Theorem 4.3 of [13], after duplicating some edges to make all outdegrees equal to 2. Recall that the *index* of a strongly connected digraph with period r is the smallest k such that any pair of vertices are connected by a directed path of length k if and only if they are connected by a path of length $k+r$. In fact, one can easily show the following relationship (proof omitted), which also appears in [12] for the primitive case $r = 1$.

Proposition 3. *For a strongly connected n-state automaton $\mathcal{A}$ of rank r and period r the following holds:*

$$\mathrm{mrt}(\mathcal{A}) \geq k(\mathcal{A}) - n + r,$$

where $k(\mathcal{A})$ is the index of the underlying digraph of $\mathcal{A}$.

Since the index of D in Corollary 2 was proved in [13] to be $\frac{(n-r)^2}{r} + r$, we get from Proposition 3 the same lower bound as in Corollary 2.

We finish this section with a family of strongly connected binary automata that reach the same minimum rank threshold as the ternary automata in Proposition 1. Recall the n-state Černý automaton from Sect. 1. Let r be a number that divides n. Change in the Černý automaton the transition from state 1 by letter a to go into state $r+1$ instead of state 2. After this change, for any states i and j such that $i \equiv j$ modulo r, also $\delta(i,x) \equiv \delta(j,x)$ modulo r holds for both $x = a$ and $x = b$. This means that states in different residue classes modulo r cannot be merged, so that the rank of this automaton is at least r. Using the trick from [2], we introduce a new input letter c that acts as the word ab does. Now letters c and b define exactly the modified Wielandt automaton leading to

Corollary 2 above, so there is a word of rank r with letters c and b. Hence our automaton has rank r as well.

Since the action of word aa is the same as the action of a, a shortest minimum rank word w cannot contain factor aa. The word wb has also minimum rank, and it can be factored into ab's and b's. Viewing this as a word over letters c and b, we see that the number of c's and b's must be at least the minimum rank threshold $\frac{(n-r)^2}{r} - n + 2r$ from Corollary 2. Since b is a permutation and since c merges at most one pair of states, there must be at least $n - r$ letters c used. Each c counts as two letters over the alphabet $\{a, b\}$, so the length of word wb is at least

$$\frac{(n-r)^2}{r} - n + 2r + (n - r) = \frac{(n-r)^2}{r} + r.$$

Removing the last b from wb we obtain the following lower bound. Observe that the bound is exactly the same as in the ternary case in Proposition 1.

Proposition 4. *For every n and every $r > 1$ such that r divides n, there exists a binary n-state circular automaton $\mathcal{A}$ of rank r having* $\mathrm{mrt}(\mathcal{A}) = \frac{(n-r)^2}{r} + r - 1$.

3.3   Upper Bound in the Case When the Rank Equals the Period

Obviously, the period of an automaton is a lower bound on its rank. It is interesting to consider the special case of automata where these two values are equal. For lower bounds, observe that the rank r automata reported in Corollaries 1 and 2 have the same period as the rank. In this section we obtain upper bounds on the minimum rank threshold from any known upper bounds on the reset threshold, in the case that the rank equals the period.

For every n, let $f(n)$ denote the maximum of reset thresholds of n-state synchronizing automata.

Theorem 1. *Let $\mathcal{A}$ be an automaton of rank r and period r. Then* $\mathrm{mrt}(\mathcal{A}) \leq r^2 \cdot f(\frac{n}{r}) + (r - 1)$.

Proof. Let $\mathcal{A} = \langle Q, \Sigma, \delta \rangle$. By Lemma 1 there exists a partition of the set Q into the sets $Q_0, \ldots, Q_{r-1}$ such that every transition maps a state in Q_i to a state in Q_{i+1} (with the index $i + 1$ taken modulo r). Since the rank of $\mathcal{A}$ equals its period, each of the sets $Q_0, \ldots, Q_{r-1}$ is synchronizable (a set is called *synchronizable* if there is a word mapping this set to a single state). Assume without loss of generality that Q_0 is the smallest set in the partition. Consider then the automaton $\mathcal{A}^r = \langle Q_0, \Sigma^r, \delta' \rangle$ induced by the actions of all the words of length r on Q_0. This automaton is synchronizing, and by our assumption there is a word synchronizing it of length at most $f(|Q_0|) \leq f(\frac{n}{r})$ over the alphabet Σ^r. Over the alphabet Σ this word has length at most $r \cdot f(\frac{n}{r})$. Then to find a word of minimum rank it is enough to subsequently map each set $Q_1, \ldots, Q_{r-1}$ to Q_0 and apply the described word. In total we get a word of minimum rank of length at most $r^2 \cdot f(\frac{n}{r}) + (r - 1)$. □

For example, using the unconditional upper bound $f(n) \leq \frac{n^3-n}{6}$ on the reset threshold [17] we get that for every n-state automaton of rank r and period r we have $\mathrm{mrt}(\mathcal{A}) \leq \frac{n(n^2-r^2)}{6r} + (r-1)$, which is roughly r times stronger than the best known upper bound for the general case [16]. The Černý Conjecture implies the upper bound of $(n-r)^2 + (r-1)$. Thus, in the case of automata with rank equal to period the Rank Conjecture is implied by the Černý Conjecture up to an additive factor of $(r-1)$. However we conjecture that in this case the upper bound can be improved to $\frac{(n-r)^2}{r} + O(n)$.

4 Eulerian Automata

4.1 The Rank Conjecture

We continue our discussion on the Rank Conjecture proving it for a particular class of automata, namely the Eulerian automata. Eulerian automata have been widely studied, in particular, Kari [15] showed that $\mathrm{rt}(\mathcal{A}) \leq (n-1)(n-2)+1$ for any synchronizing Eulerian n-state automaton, thus proving the Černý Conjecture for this class of automata. We extend the mentioned result to the case of arbitrary minimum rank.

Theorem 2. *Let $\mathcal{A}$ be an n-state Eulerian automaton of rank r. Then $\mathcal{A}$ has a word of rank r of length at most $(n-r-1)(n-r)+1$.*

Proof. Let $\mathcal{A} = \langle Q, \Sigma, \delta \rangle$. Following [15], we consider the set Q, $|Q| = n$, of states as an orthonormal basis of $\mathbb{R}^n$ with subsets of states corresponding to the sums of the basis vectors. Thus, a set $S \subseteq Q$ is viewed as a vector $\sum_{q \in S} q$.

Every word $w \in \Sigma^*$ defines a state transition function $f_w : Q \to Q$ on the set of states, with $f_w(q) = \delta(q, w)$. Furthermore, $f_w^{-1}(q) = \{v \mid f_w(v) = q\}$. Since we know the values of f_w^{-1} on all the basis vectors, there is a unique way to extend it to a linear mapping $f_w^{-1} : \mathbb{R}^n \to \mathbb{R}^n$. Clearly, for a set $S \subseteq Q$ we have $f_w^{-1}(S) = \sum_{q \in S} f_w^{-1}(q)$. Moreover, for a vector $x = (x_1, \ldots, x_n)$ we define a linear *weight* function $|x|$ such that $|(x_1, \ldots, x_n)| = x_1 + \ldots + x_n$. The weight of a set $S \subseteq Q$ is just its cardinality.

Let $Z_1 \subseteq \mathbb{R}^n$ be the set of all *non-extendable* vectors, i.e. such vectors x that there exists no word w with $|f_w^{-1}(x)| \neq |x|$ (all the remaining vectors we call *extendable*). Observe that $\sum_{w \in \Sigma^k} |f_w^{-1}(S)| = |\Sigma|^k \cdot |S|$. Thus, if there exists a word w of length k such that $|f_w^{-1}(S)| \neq |S|$ then there is a word of the same length extending S (a word v is said to *extend* S if $|f_v^{-1}(S)| > |S|$). We will refer to that as the *averaging argument*.

Note that Z_1 is a linear subspace of $\mathbb{R}^n$ of dimension at least r. First we prove that it is a linear subspace. Indeed, consider a linear combination $\lambda_1 v_1 + \ldots + \lambda_k v_k$ of vectors from Z_1. Since the weight function is linear, any image of this combination under f_w^{-1} has the same weight, and thus the combination belongs to Z_1. To bound the dimension of Z_1 from below, consider a word w of minimum rank such that there exists a partition of Q into sets $S_1, \ldots, S_r$, such that each

S_i is a maximal synchronizable set. Such a word exists by Proposition 1 of [15]. The vectors corresponding to $S_1, \ldots, S_r$ are then non-extendable, and linearly independent since they have disjoint non-zero coefficients in the standard basis decomposition. We apply some linear algebra to obtain the following lemma.

Lemma 2. *For every extendable vector x there exists a word w of length at most $n - r$ such that $|f_w^{-1}(x)| \neq |x|$.*

Proof. Suppose the contrary: let x be extendable such that the shortest word w such that $|f_w^{-1}(x)| \neq |x|$ has length $m > n - r$. Note that for any words u, v we have $f_{uv}^{-1}(x) = f_u^{-1}(f_v^{-1}(x))$. Take Z_0 to be the orthogonal complement of Z_1. Since the dimension of Z_1 is at least r, the dimension of Z_0 is at most $n - r$. For every $i \leq m$ we denote $x_i = f_{w_i}^{-1}(x)$ where w_i is the suffix of w of length i, and we write $x_i = x_i^{(0)} + x_i^{(1)}$ for $x_i^{(0)} \in Z_0$ and $x_i^{(1)} \in Z_1$. Since m is greater than the dimension of Z_0, vectors $x_0^{(0)}, x_1^{(0)}, \ldots, x_{m-1}^{(0)}$ are linearly dependent. This means that for some $k < m$ the vector $x_k^{(0)}$ is a linear combination $\lambda_0 x_0^{(0)} + \cdots + \lambda_{k-1} x_{k-1}^{(0)}$ of vectors before it, with coefficients $\lambda_i \in \mathbb{R}$. The corresponding linear combination of vectors x_i is $\lambda_0 x_0 + \cdots + \lambda_{k-1} x_{k-1} = x_k + x'$ for some $x' \in Z_1$. Let $w = uv$ where v is the suffix of w of length k. Then, $f_u^{-1}(x_k) = f_u^{-1}(f_v^{-1}(x)) = f_w^{-1}(x)$. Moreover, for every $i < k$ we have $|f_u^{-1}(x_i)| = |x_i|$. Indeed, $f_u^{-1}(x_i) = f_u^{-1}(f_{w_i}^{-1}(x)) = f_{uw_i}^{-1}(x)$ has the same weight as x because uw_i is shorter than w, and of course $|x_i| = |x|$. Also, because x' is non-extendable, we have $|f_u^{-1}(x')| = |x'|$. Putting all together, using linearity of f_u^{-1} and the weight function, we obtain $|f_w^{-1}(x)| = |x|$, a contradiction. □

By the averaging argument we obtain from Lemma 2 that for any extendable set S of states there is a word w of length at most $n - r$ such that $|f_w^{-1}(S)| \geq |S| + 1$. Now we apply this extension procedure as follows. Start with a one-state set. Extend it step by step to a maximal synchronizable set (having size $\frac{n}{r}$). Then add another state to this maximal synchronizable set and extend this new set to a union of two disjoint maximal synchronizable sets. Repeat this procedure of adding a new state and extending the set to a union of several maximal synchronizable sets until the whole set of states of the automaton is reached. The extension is possible, since at every step the set S that we have to extend is a disjoint union of several maximal synchronizable subsets and a non-maximal synchronizable subset S'. Any word extending S' extends S, since f_w^{-1} preserves the weights of all the maximal synchronizable subsets for any word w (since otherwise by the averaging argument such sets are extendable).

For each step of this algorithm, we have a word of length at most $n - r$ to extend a set by one element. Each maximal synchronizable set has size $\frac{n}{r}$, and we have to reach r such sets, so the total length of the word is at most $(n - r)(\frac{n}{r} - 1)r = (n - r)^2$. We can initially choose a one-state set extendable by a word of length 1, which improves the bound to $(n - r)(n - r - 1) + 1$. □

To obtain a lower bound on the minimum rank threshold of Eulerian automata, recall the construction used to prove the bound of Proposition 1.

It was mentioned previously that applying it to an Eulerian automaton yields another Eulerian automaton. Thus, we repeat the same reasoning starting with a synchronizing n-state Eulerian automaton over alphabet of size 4 having reset threshold $\frac{n^2-3}{2}$, for any $n > 1$ such that $n \equiv 1 \pmod 4$, see [19].

Proposition 5. *For every n and every $r < n$ such that $n = (4p + 1)r$, there exists an n-state Eulerian automaton $\mathcal{A}$ of rank r with $\mathrm{mrt}(\mathcal{A}) = \frac{n^2-r^2}{2r} - 1$.*

The standard binarization methods cannot be applied to provide the lower bounds for binary Eulerian automata. However, we can apply the argument of Proposition 2 to the n-state binary Eulerian automaton whose reset threshold is at least $\frac{n^2-3n+4}{2}$ for odd $n \geq 3$ [12]. (This was proved for all odd $n \geq 5$ in [12] but the same construction also covers the case $n = 3$.) The automaton we obtain is also Eulerian.

Proposition 6. *For every n and every r such that r divides n and $n/r \geq 3$ is odd, there exists an n-state binary Eulerian automaton $\mathcal{A}$ of rank r having $\mathrm{mrt}(\mathcal{A}) \geq \frac{(n-2r)^2+nr}{2r}$.*

The multiplicative gap between the lower and the upper bounds consists intuitively of two parts. The factor of two comes from the gap between the known bounds on the reset threshold of Eulerian automata, while the factor r comes from the gap on the minimum rank threshold in general strongly connected automata that we see in the results in Sect. 3.

4.2   A Corollary for Circular Automata

In this section we provide a simple trick, similar to the idea of [6], which allows to transfer the results on Eulerian automata to the class of circular automata. Recall that an automaton is called circular if there is a letter which acts on its set of states as a cyclic permutation. The Černý Conjecture for this automata class was proved by Dubuc [11]. Note that the Černý automata are circular and possess the largest known reset thresholds.

Let us consider an n-state circular automaton $\mathcal{A} = \langle Q, \Sigma, \delta \rangle$ such that some letter $b \in \Sigma$ acts as a cyclic permutation on Q. Let us replace each $a \in \Sigma$ by n letters $a_0, \ldots, a_{n-1}$, where a_i acts on Q the same way as the word ab^i does in the original automaton. Let Σ' be the obtained new alphabet of size $n \cdot |\Sigma|$. It is not hard to prove that the obtained automaton is Eulerian (we omit the proof because of the space constraints).

Observe that this transformation preserves the synchronization properties of the initial automaton in the following sense. A word of rank r over Σ is clearly a word of rank r over Σ' because $\Sigma \subset \Sigma'$. The opposite holds as well since every word over Σ' can be rewritten as a word over Σ. It follows that the rank of the resulting automaton is equal to the rank of the initial one.

Theorem 3. *Every n-state circular automaton of rank $r < n$ has a minimum rank word of length at most $(2n - r - 1)(n - r - 1) + 1$.*

Proof. Let $\mathcal{A} = \langle Q, \Sigma, \delta \rangle$ be an n-state circular automaton with a cyclic permutation letter b. An Eulerian automaton $\mathcal{A}' = \langle Q, \Sigma', \delta' \rangle$ with n states is constructed as above. Now we show how to use the procedure described in Theorem 2 to get the upper bound.

Observe that any word over Σ' can be written as a concatenation of words over Σ. In other words, any extendable vector s can be extended by words made of letters in Σ only. Moreover, we can apply Lemma 2 for words over Σ, and get that the shortest word $w \in \Sigma^*$ such that $|f_w^{-1}(s)| \neq |s|$ has length at most $n - r$.

Let $w = cv$ where $c \in \Sigma$ and $v \in \Sigma^*$. Now consider all the words of the form σv with $\sigma \in \Sigma'$. Clearly, w is one of them. Because $\mathcal{A}'$ is Eulerian, we have

$$\sum_{\sigma \in \Sigma'} |f_{\sigma v}^{-1}(x)| = \sum_{\sigma \in \Sigma'} |f_\sigma^{-1}(f_v^{-1}(x))| = |\Sigma'| \cdot |f_v^{-1}(x)| = |\Sigma'| \cdot |x|.$$

Since there exists a word $w = cv$ such that $|f_w^{-1}(x)| \neq |x|$, the above equality implies that there is $u = \sigma v$ such that $|f_u^{-1}(x)| > |x|$. Notice that v is a word of length at most $n - r - 1$ over Σ, and hence u is of length $|\sigma| + |v| \leq n + (n - r - 1) = 2n - r - 1$ over Σ.

Thus we showed that every extendable set of states in $\mathcal{A}'$ can be extended by a word of length at most $2n - r - 1$ (over the alphabet Σ). We can now use the extension procedure described in Theorem 2 (starting from a one-state set extendable by a word of length 1) and get the upper bound of $(2n - r - 1)(n - r - 1) + 1$ on the length of a shortest word of minimum rank in $\mathcal{A}$. □

4.3   A Road Coloring Algorithm

As proved by Kari [15], every primitive strongly connected Eulerian digraph such that all its vertices have equal outdegrees has a synchronizing coloring. If the primitiveness condition is omitted, the period of a digraph is a lower bound on the rank of any coloring. A coloring of rank equal to period always exists and can be found in quadratic time [3]. We show that for Eulerian digraphs it can be found in almost linear time. We use the approach described in Sect. 3 of [15] and show how to generalize it and turn into an algorithm.

First observe that a permutation coloring (a coloring of rank n) of an Eulerian digraph with n vertices and constant outdegree k corresponds to a partition of a regular bipartite graph with n vertices and kn edges into k perfect matchings (Lemma 1 of [15]), and thus can be computed in $O(kn \log k)$ time [10].

The construction of a permutation coloring is used as a subroutine in order to construct a coloring with a stable pair of states. A pair of states p, q of an automaton is called *stable* if application of any word to this pair results in a synchronizable pair. For a permutation coloring $\mathcal{A} = \langle Q, \Sigma, \delta \rangle$ of a digraph take a state $x \in Q$ such that $y = \delta(x, a) \neq \delta(x, b) = z$ for some letters $a, b \in \Sigma$. Note that in a strongly connected digraph such state always exists, otherwise the digraph consists of one cycle and we have nothing to prove. We swap the letters coloring the edges $x \rightarrow y$ and $x \rightarrow z$. As proved in Theorem 1 of [15], the pair y, z is then stable in the resulting automaton $\mathcal{A}'$ and thus defines a congruence relation (that is, an equivalence relation invariant under application of any word) $\equiv$ on its state set. The quotient automaton $\mathcal{A}'/\equiv$ is then obtained by merging all the states of each congruence class. If $\mathcal{A}'$ is Eulerian, so is $\mathcal{A}'/\equiv$ [15].

Lemma 3. *Let $\mathcal{A}'$ be the Eulerian automaton, and y, z be the stable pair with corresponding congruence relation $\equiv$ obtained as described above. Then the quotient automaton $\mathcal{A}'/\equiv$ has at most half as many states as $\mathcal{A}'$.*

Proof. We compute $\mathcal{A}'/\equiv$ following the Merge procedure described in [3]. We start by merging the congruent pair y, z and then propagate this equivalence to the images of y, z under all the letters in Σ until we get a deterministic automaton. Observe that since we start with a permutation coloring, each state that has not yet been merged with some other state has all incoming edges of different colors. Thus, if there is such a state in the pair to be merged, the second state in this pair is different from it, and thus further calls of merging their successor will be performed. Moreover, assume that some state is not merged with any state during this procedure. Then there is such a state p having a transition going to it from some already merged state q, otherwise the digraph is not strongly connected. This means that during the first merging for q, merging for p has to be called, which is a contradiction. Hence, each state is in a congruence class of cardinality at least 2, and after taking the quotient, the number of states of $\mathcal{A}'/\equiv$ is at most half of the number of states $\mathcal{A}'$. □

Theorem 4. *Given a strongly connected Eulerian digraph of period r with n vertices and outdegree k, a coloring of rank r of this digraph can be found in $O((k \log k + \alpha(n)) \cdot n)$ time, where $\alpha(\cdot)$ is the inverse Ackermann function.*

Proof. The algorithm is recursive. At each iteration we start by finding a coloring with a stable pair as described above. Then we proceed by computing the quotient automaton as in Lemma 3. The automaton we obtain is Eulerian [15], moreover, it has the same period since no pair of states from different sets in a p-partition can be stable (since no such pair can be synchronized). If the automaton has rank r, we stop, otherwise we call the same algorithm for coloring it and then recover the final coloring by taking for every vertex the same permutation of the colors of outgoing edges as used for the equivalence class of this vertex (see Theorem 1 of [15]).

To analyze the time complexity, we estimate the complexity of one recursion step. Let ℓ be the size of the automaton at some iteration. As it was mentioned before, it takes $O(k\ell \log k)$ time to find a permutation coloring. The Merge procedure requires $O(k\ell)$ time for traversing and $O(\ell \alpha(\ell))$ time for merging the sets. Moreover, recovering the coloring from the smaller automaton can be done in $O(k\ell)$ time by storing the quotient automaton (together with the correspondence between the states and their equivalence classes) at each iteration. Hence, the time complexity of one iteration is $O(\ell(k \log k + \alpha(\ell)))$.

Now we can sum up the time complexity of all recursion steps. Lemma 3 implies that the number of states of each next automaton in the recursion call is decreased at least twice. Thus, the total time complexity is $O(n(k \log k + \alpha(n)))$, where n is the number of vertices of the initial digraph. □

References

1. Almeida, J., Steinberg, B.: Matrix Mortality and the Černý-Pin Conjecture. In: Diekert, V., Nowotka, D. (eds.) DLT 2009. LNCS, vol. 5583, pp. 67–80. Springer, Heidelberg (2009). https://doi.org/10.1007/978-3-642-02737-6_5
2. Ananichev, D., Gusev, V., Volkov, M.: Slowly synchronizing automata and digraphs. In: Hliněný, P., Kučera, A. (eds.) MFCS 2010. LNCS, vol. 6281, pp. 55–65. Springer, Heidelberg (2010). https://doi.org/10.1007/978-3-642-15155-2_7
3. Béal, M., Perrin, D.: A quadratic algorithm for road coloring. Discrete Appl. Math. **169**, 15–29 (2014). https://doi.org/10.1016/j.dam.2013.12.002
4. Berlinkov, M.V.: On two algorithmic problems about synchronizing automata. In: Shur, A.M., Volkov, M.V. (eds.) DLT 2014. LNCS, vol. 8633, pp. 61–67. Springer, Cham (2014). https://doi.org/10.1007/978-3-319-09698-8_6
5. Berman, A., Plemmons, R.: Nonnegative Matrices in the Mathematical Sciences. Classics in Applied Mathematics. Society for Industrial and Applied Mathematics, Philadelphia (1994)
6. Carpi, A., D'Alessandro, F.: Strongly transitive automata and the černý conjecture. Acta Informatica **46**(8), 591–607 (2009)
7. Carpi, A., D'Alessandro, F.: On the hybrid Černý-Road coloring problem and Hamiltonian paths. In: Gao, Y., Lu, H., Seki, S., Yu, S. (eds.) DLT 2010. LNCS, vol. 6224, pp. 124–135. Springer, Heidelberg (2010). https://doi.org/10.1007/978-3-642-14455-4_13
8. Černý, J., Pirická, A., Rosenauerova, B.: On directable automata. Kybernetika **7**(4), 289–298 (1971)
9. Černý, J.: Poznámka k homogénnym eksperimentom s konečnými automatami, Matematicko-fyzikalny Casopis Slovensk. Akad. Vied **14**(3), 208–216 (1964)
10. Cole, R., Ost, K., Schirra, S.: Edge-coloring bipartite multigraphs in $O(E \log D)$ time. Combinatorica **21**(1), 5–12 (2001)
11. Dubuc, L.: Sur les automates circulaires et la conjecture de černý. RAIRO - Theor. Inform. Appl. **32**(1–3), 21–34 (1998)
12. Gusev, V.V.: Lower bounds for the length of reset words in eulerian automata. Int. J. Found. Comput. Sci. **24**(2), 251–262 (2013). https://doi.org/10.1142/S0129054113400108
13. Heap, B.R., Lynn, M.S.: The structure of powers of nonnegative matrices: I. The index of convergence. SIAM J. Appl. Math. **14**(3), 610–639 (1966)
14. Kari, J.: A counter example to a conjecture concerning synchronizing words in finite automata. Bull. EATCS **73**, 146 (2001)
15. Kari, J.: Synchronizing finite automata on Eulerian digraphs. Theor. Comput. Sci. **295**(1), 223–232 (2003)
16. Klyachko, A.A., Rystsov, I.K., Spivak, M.A.: In extremal combinatorial problem associated with the bound on the length of a synchronizing word in an automaton. Cybernetics **23**(2), 165–171 (1987)
17. Pin, J.: On two combinatorial problems arising from automata theory. In: Berge, C., Bresson, D., Camion, P., Maurras, J., Sterboul, F. (eds.) Combinatorial Mathematics, North-Holland Mathematics Studies, vol. 75, pp. 535–548. North-Holland, Amsterdam (1983)
18. Pin, J.E.: Le problème de la synchronisation et la conjecture de Cerny. In: Luca, A.D. (ed.) Non-commutative structures in algebra and geometric combinatorics, vol. 109, pp. 37–48. Quaderni de la Ricerca Scientifica, CNR (Consiglio nazionale delle ricerche, Italy) (1981)

19. Szykuła, M., Vorel, V.: An extremal series of Eulerian synchronizing automata. In: Brlek, S., Reutenauer, C. (eds.) DLT 2016. LNCS, vol. 9840, pp. 380–392. Springer, Heidelberg (2016). https://doi.org/10.1007/978-3-662-53132-7_31

20. Volkov, M.V.: Synchronizing automata and the Černý conjecture. In: Martín-Vide, C., Otto, F., Fernau, H. (eds.) LATA 2008. LNCS, vol. 5196, pp. 11–27. Springer, Heidelberg (2008). https://doi.org/10.1007/978-3-540-88282-4_4

21. Vorel, V.: Subset synchronization and careful synchronization of binary finite automata. Int. J. Found. Comput. Sci. **27**(5), 557–577 (2016). https://doi.org/10.1142/S0129054116500167

22. Wielandt, H.: Unzerlegbare, nicht negative matrizen. Mathematische Zeitschrift **52**(1), 642–648 (1950)

On the Length of Shortest Strings Accepted by Two-Way Finite Automata

Egor Dobronravov, Nikita Dobronravov, and Alexander Okhotin$^{(\boxtimes)}$ (iD)

St. Petersburg State University, 7/9 Universitetskaya nab.,
Saint Petersburg 199034, Russia
yegordobronravov@mail.ru, dobronravov1999@mail.ru,
alexander.okhotin@spbu.ru

Abstract. Given a two-way finite automaton recognizing a non-empty language, consider the length of the shortest string it accepts, and, for each $n \geqslant 1$, let $f(n)$ be the maximum of these lengths over all n-state automata. It is proved that for n-state two-way finite automata, whether deterministic or nondeterministic, this number is at least $\Omega(8^{n/5})$ and less than $\binom{2n}{n+1}$, with the lower bound reached over an alphabet of size $\Theta(n)$. Furthermore, for deterministic automata and for a fixed alphabet of size $m \geqslant 1$, the length of the shortest string is at least $e^{(1+o(1))\sqrt{mn(\log n - \log m)}}$.

1 Introduction

For a one-way nondeterministic finite automaton (1NFA) with n states recognizing a non-empty language, the length of the shortest string it accepts is the length of the shortest path to an accepting state in the transition graph, and is accordingly at most $n - 1$. For other kinds of automata, the question of finding the exact length of the shortest string in the worst case is much more involved, and has been a subject of some research. Ellul et al. [4] proved that the greatest length of the shortest string *not* accepted by an n-state 1NFA is exponential in n. The length of the shortest string in the intersection of an m-state and an n-state deterministic automata (1DFA), as shown by Alpoge et al. [1], can be up to $mn-1$ for relatively prime m, n. Chistikov et al. [2] investigated the length of the shortest string for counter automata. For the intersection of a language defined by a formal grammar of a given size and a regular language, the length of a shortest string was estimated by Pierre [11].

This paper investigates the length of a shortest string accepted by a *two-way finite automaton*. A simple upper bound on this length follows from the work of Kapoutsis [7], who proved that every n-state 2NFA can be simulated by an 1NFA with $\binom{2n}{n+1}$ states; this binomial coefficient is of the order $\frac{1}{\sqrt{\pi n}}4^n$. Therefore, the shortest string accepted by an n-state 2NFA is of length at most $\binom{2n}{n+1} - 1$.

Supported by Russian Science Foundation, project 18-11-00100.

P. Hofman and M. Skrzypczak (Eds.): DLT 2019, LNCS 11647, pp. 88–99, 2019.
https://doi.org/10.1007/978-3-030-24886-4_6

Kapoutsis [7] also proved that this transformation of two-way automata to one-way automata is optimal in the worst case, that is, for every n, there is a language L_n recognized by an n-state 2DFA, but by no 1NFA with fewer than $\binom{2n}{n+1}$ states. However, since all strings in this language are of length 4, this example does not imply any lower bound on the length of the shortest string.

In this paper, the greatest length of the shortest string is determined up to a constant factor in the exponent, as $2^{\Theta(n)}$. First, there is a simple construction of an n-state 2DFA with a shortest string of length ca. $2^{n/2}$. This construction is then improved to obtain n-state 2DFA with shortest strings of length ca. $8^{n/5}$. In both cases, the size of the alphabet is exponential in n. For a fixed alphabet of size m, a series of n-state automata with shortest strings of length $e^{(1+o(1))\sqrt{mn\ln\frac{n}{m}}}$ is constructed.

2 Two-Way Finite Automata

Definition 1. *A nondeterministic two-way finite automaton (2NFA) is a quin-tuple $\mathcal{A} = (\Sigma, Q, q_0, \delta, F)$, in which:*

- Σ *is a finite alphabet, which is extended with a left end-marker $\vdash \notin \Sigma$, and a right end-marker $\dashv \notin \Sigma$;*
- Q *is a finite set of states;*
- $Q_0 \in Q$ *is the set of initial states;*
- $\delta\colon Q \times (\Sigma \cup \{\vdash, \dashv\}) \to 2^{Q \times \{-1,+1\}}$ *is the transition function, which lists possible transitions in a certain state while observing a certain tape symbol;*
- $F \subseteq Q$ *is the set of accepting states, effective at the right end-marker $\dashv$.*

Given an input string $w \in \Sigma^*$, a 2NFA operates on a read-only tape containing this string enclosed within end-markers ($\vdash w \dashv$). A 2NFA begins its computation in any initial state with the head observing the left end-marker ($\vdash$). At every step of the computation, when A is in a state $q \in Q$ and observes a square of the tape containing a symbol $a \in \Sigma \cup \{\vdash, \dashv\}$, the transition function specifies a set $\delta(q, a) \subseteq Q \times \{-1, +1\}$ of all the allowed actions, each being a pair of the next state and the direction of head's motion. If $\delta(q, a)$ contains multiple elements, then multiple continuations are possible, and, accordingly, a 2NFA may have multiple computations on the same input string. If the automaton eventually reaches an accepting state while at the right end-marker ($\dashv$), then this is an accepting computation.

The set of strings, on which there is at least one accepting computation, is the language recognized by the 2NFA, denoted by $L(\mathcal{A})$.

Other types of finite automata are obtained by restricting 2NFA. An automaton is *deterministic* (2DFA), if there is at most one possible action in each configuration, that is, if $|\delta(q, a)| \leqslant 1$ for all q and a.

A two-way automaton (2DFA for 2NFA) is called *sweeping* [12], if it can change its direction of motion only at the end-markers, and thus operates in alternating left-to-right sweeps and right-to-left sweeps. More precisely, the set of states Q is split into two disjoint subsets of *right-bound states* Q_{+1} and *left-bound states* Q_{-1}, so that all transitions in Q_d, except the transition on end-markers, move the head in the direction d.

For a less restrictive notion of a *direction-determinate automaton* [9], it is only required that every state $q \in Q$ can be entered by transitions from a single direction $d(q) \in \{-1, +1\}$. Every sweeping automaton is direction-determinate, but not vice versa.

An automaton is *one-way* (1NFA or 1NFA), if all its transitions move its head to the right, so that the automaton makes a single left-to-right pass, accepting or rejecting in the end. In one-way automata, the end-markers are of no use and are usually omitted from the definition.

3   Upper Bound

An upper bound on the length of a shortest string accepted by a two-way finite automaton follows from the known transformation of two-way automata to 1NFA, which is optimal for alphabets of unbounded size.

Theorem A (Kapoutsis [7]). *For every n-state 2NFA over an alphabet Σ, there exists a 1NFA with $\binom{2n}{n+1}$ states, which recognizes the same language. Conversely, for every n, there is such an alphabet Σ_n of size $\Theta(n^n)$, and such a language $L_n \subseteq \Sigma_n^*$ recognized by an n-state 2DFA, that every 1NFA recognizing L_n must have at least $\binom{2n}{n+1}$ states.*

Taking into account that the length of a shortest string accepted by a k-state 1NFA is at most $k - 1$, this has the following immediate consequence.

Corollary 1. *For every n-state 2NFA, the length of the shortest string it accepts is at most $\binom{2n}{n+1} - 1$.*

For direction-determinate automata, the method of Kapoutsis [7] can be adapted to produce fewer states. As proved by Geffert and Okhotin [6], the following transformation is optimal for alphabets with three or more symbols.

Theorem B (Geffert and Okhotin [6]). *For every n-state direction-determinate 2NFA over an alphabet Σ, there is a 1NFA with $\binom{n}{\lfloor n/2 \rfloor}$ states that recognizes the same language. Conversely, for every n, there exists a language L_n over a fixed 3-symbol alphabet, recognized by an n-state sweeping 2DFA, with the property that every 1NFA recognizing L_n has at least $\binom{n}{\lfloor n/2 \rfloor}$ states.*

Corollary 2. *The length of the shortest string accepted by an n-state direction-determinate 2NFA is at most $\binom{n}{\lfloor n/2 \rfloor}$.*

Using Stirling's approximation, these binomial coefficients are estimated as $\binom{2n}{n+1} = (1 + o(1))\frac{1}{\sqrt{\pi n}}4^n$ and as $\binom{n}{\lfloor n/2 \rfloor} = (1 + o(1))\sqrt{\frac{2}{\pi n}}2^n$, respectively.

This upper bound is the same for 2NFA and for 2DFA. In fact, as indicated by the following simple result, the length of shortest strings for 2NFA is the same as for 2DFA with the same number of states. However, there may still be some differences in the size of the alphabet necessary to achieve that bound.

Lemma 1. *For every n-state 2NFA (sweeping 2NFA) over an alphabet Σ, there exists an n-state 2DFA (sweeping 2DFA, respectively) over some alphabet Γ, which has the same length of the shortest accepted string. The number of symbols in Γ is at most $(2n)^n$ times the size of Σ.*

Proof. For every symbol $a \in \Sigma$, consider the 2NFA's transitions by that symbol. At each of the n states, there can be up to $2n$ possible transitions. For every choice of these transitions, let Γ contain a new symbol, which is a marked with that choice. The 2DFA's transitions by the marked symbols are defined to act deterministically according to that choice.

Then, for every string w accepted by the 2NFA, the new 2DFA accepts some string w' of the same length, with each symbol marked with the choices made by the 2NFA on the corresponding symbol of w. Conversely, for each string accepted by the 2DFA, the original 2NFA accepts the same string without markings. □

In view of this observation, the rest of this paper concentrates on the case of deterministic two-way automata.

4   Simple Lower Bound

The following two-way automata have long shortest accepted strings.

Lemma 2. *For every odd number $m \geqslant 1$, there exists a $2m$-state sweeping 2DFA, defined over an m-symbol alphabet, which recognizes a singleton language $\{w\}$, with $|w| = 2^m - 1$.*

Proof. Let the alphabet be $\Sigma = \{a_1, \ldots, a_m\}$. The automaton shall make m passes over the string. At each i-th pass, with $i \in \{1, \ldots, m\}$, the automaton marks whether it has encountered any symbol a_i since the last symbol with a number $i + 1$ or greater. When a symbol with a number $i + 1$ or greater is read, the automaton makes sure that it encountered exactly one a_i since the previous such symbol, and resets the mark. The same check is done in the end of each pass, upon seeing one of the end-markers.

The states are of the form $q_j^{(i)}$, with $i \in \{1, \ldots, m\}$ and $j \in \{0, 1\}$, which indicates making the i-th pass, having seen ($j = 1$) or not seen ($j = 0$) any symbol a_i.

$$Q = \{\, q_j^{(i)} \mid i \in \{1, \ldots, m\},\ j \in \{0, 1\} \,\}$$

The initial state is $q_0^{(1)}$, in which the automaton begins the first pass.

$$\delta(q_0^{(1)}, \vdash) = (q_0^{(1)}, +1)$$

For each i-th pass, let $d_i \in \{+1, -1\}$ be the direction of this pass, with $d_i = +1$ for odd i, and $d_i = -1$ for even i. The transitions at the i-th pass set the mark upon seeing the corresponding symbol a_i.

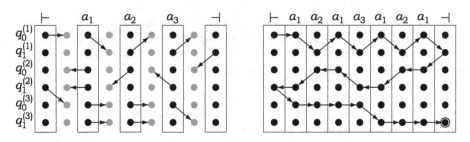

Fig. 1. A 6-state 2DFA with a shortest string of length $2^3 - 1 = 7$, constructed as in Lemma 2, with $m = 3$.

$$\delta(q_0^{(i)}, a_i) = (q_1^{(i)}, d_i), \qquad \text{for } i \in \{1, \ldots, m\},$$

For any of the symbols $a_{i+1}, \ldots, a_m$, the mark of having seen a_i is checked and then reset to false.

$$\delta(q_1^{(i)}, a_t) = (q_0^{(i)}, d_i), \qquad \text{for } i \in \{1, \ldots, m\}$$

All other input symbols are ignored, that is, the automaton passes them without changing its state.

$$\delta(q_j^{(i)}, a_t) = (q_j^{(i)}, d_i), \qquad \text{for } i \in \{1, \ldots, m\}, \, j \in \{0, 1\}, \, t \in \{1, \ldots, i-1\}$$

On each end-marker, the mark of having seen a_i is again checked, and then the automaton switches from the i-th pass to the $(i+1)$-th.

$$\delta(q_1^{(i)}, \dashv) = (q_0^{(i+1)}, -1), \qquad \text{for all odd } i < m$$
$$\delta(q_1^{(i)}, \vdash) = (q_0^{(i+1)}, -1), \qquad \text{for all even } i < m$$

The last pass leads the automaton to the right end-marker ($\dashv$), where it accepts in the state $q_1^{(m)}$. These transitions are illustrated in Fig. 1 for $m = 3$, along with the shortest accepted string of length 7.

Actually, the automaton always accepts a unique string. The following strings $w_0, w_1, \ldots, w_m$ are defined, with w_3 illustrated in Fig. 1(right).

$$w_0 = \varepsilon$$
$$w_i = w_{i-1} a_i w_{i-1} \qquad\qquad (1 \leqslant i \leqslant m)$$

The length of each w_i is $2^i - 1$, and one can verify that the last string w_m is accepted by tracing the automaton's computation. The goal is now to prove that w_m is the unique accepted string.

Claim. Let w be any string accepted by the automaton, let $i \in \{0, 1, \ldots, m\}$, and assume that the tape $\vdash w \dashv$ has a substring $\mathcal{c}u\$$, where $\mathcal{c} \in \{\vdash, a_{i+1}, \ldots, a_m\}$, $\$ \in \{\dashv, a_{i+1}, \ldots, a_m\}$ and $u \in \{a_1, \ldots, a_i\}^*$. Then, $u = w_i$.

The claim is proved by induction on i, from 0 to m.

The base case $i = 0$ is trivial: the string u is defined over an empty alphabet, and therefore must be ε.

For the induction step for i, consider the i-th pass in the automaton's computation, as it passes through the substring $\mathcal{c}u\$$, with the direction of traversal determined by the parity of i. As it enters the substring u from one side, the state is reset to $q_0^{(i)}$, and the automaton must emerge on the other side in the state $q_1^{(i)}$. For this to happen, u must contain exactly one instance of a_i, and therefore, $u = u_0 a_i u_1$, for some substrings $u_0, u_1 \in \{a_1, \ldots, a_{i-1}\}^*$. By the induction hypothesis for the substrings u_0 and for u_1, which are delimited by appropriate symbols, both are equal to w_{i-1}. Therefore, $u = w_{i-1} a_i w_{i-1} = w_i$.

For $i = m$, the above claim asserts that every accepted string must be w_m. $\square$

For each number n, Lemma 2 gives an n-state 2DFA with the shortest accepted string of length $2^{\lfloor \frac{n}{2} \rfloor} \approx 1.414^n$. Together with the upper bound $\binom{2n}{n+1} - 1$ given in Corollary 1, this shows that the maximal length of the shortest string for n-state 2DFA and 2NFA is between $(\sqrt{2})^n$ and 4^n. The question is, what is the precise base?

An easy improvement to this construction is given by *counting to 3* rather than to 2; then, the shortest string is of length $3^{\lfloor \frac{n-1}{3} \rfloor} \approx 1.442^n$. A construction that further improves this lower bound is presented in the next section.

5   Improved Lower Bound

A proposed improvement to the lower bound in Lemma 2 is based on the following example of an automaton with a shortest string of length 7, which has as few as 5 states, cf. 6 states in the automaton provided by Lemma 2.

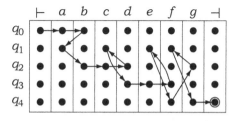

Fig. 2. A 5-state 2DFA with a shortest string of length 7, presented in Example 1.

Example 1. Let $\mathcal{A}$ be a 2DFA over the alphabet $\Sigma = \{a, b, c, d, e, f, g\}$, with the states $Q = \{q_0, q_1, q_2, q_3, q_4\}$, where q_0 is initial and q_4 is accepting, and with the following transitions: $\delta(q_0, \vdash) = (q_0, +1)$, $\delta(q_0, a) = (q_0, +1)$, $\delta(q_1, a) = (q_2, +1)$, $\delta(q_0, b) = (q_1, -1)$, $\delta(q_2, b) = (q_2, +1)$, $\delta(q_1, c) = (q_3, +1)$, $\delta(q_2, c) = (q_2, +1)$, $\delta(q_2, d) = (q_1, -1)$, $\delta(q_3, d) = (q_3, +1)$, $\delta(q_1, e) = (q_4, +1)$, $\delta(q_3, e) = (q_3, +1)$, $\delta(q_1, f) = (q_4, +1)$, $\delta(q_3, f) = (q_1, -1)$, $\delta(q_4, f) = (q_2, +1)$, $\delta(q_2, g) = (q_1, -1)$, $\delta(q_4, g) = (q_4, +1)$. Then, $\mathcal{A}$ is direction-determinate, with $d(q_1) = -1$ and $d(q) = +1$ in all other states.

The shortest string accepted by $\mathcal{A}$ is $w = abcdefg$, as illustrated in Fig. 2. To see that w is indeed the shortest string accepted by $\mathcal{A}$, it is sufficient to transform this automaton to the minimal equivalent partial 1DFA, which is presented in Fig. 3. The shortest string is clearly visible in the figure.

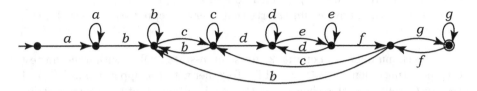

Fig. 3. The minimal 1DFA recognizing the same language as the 2DFA in Fig. 2.

The following lemma iteratively applies this example to construct arbitrarily large direction-determinate 2DFA with shortest accepted strings of length greater than in Lemma 2.

Lemma 3. *Let $\mathcal{A} = (\Sigma, Q, q_0, \delta, F)$ be a k-state direction-determinate 2DFA over some alphabet Σ, in which, for every state $q \in Q$, at most one of the following conditions may hold: (i) $\delta(q_0, \vdash) = q$; (ii) $q \in F$; (iii) $\delta(q, \vdash)$ is defined and $q \neq q_0$; (iv) $\delta(q, \dashv)$ is defined. Let $\ell - 1$ be the length of the shortest string accepted by $\mathcal{A}$. Then, for every odd number $m \geqslant 3$, there exists a km-state direction-determinate 2DFA $\mathcal{B}_m$, defined over an alphabet of size $m \cdot |\Sigma|$, which has the shortest accepted string of length $\ell^m - 1$.*

The construction in Lemma 3 actually generalizes that of Lemma 2, and before presenting it in the general case, it is useful to see how the earlier given construction fits the statement of Lemma 3. Let the base automaton $\mathcal{A}$ be a 2-state partial 1DFA recognizing the language $\{a\}$ over a one-symbol alphabet $\Sigma = \{a\}$. Then, during each i-th pass, the automaton in Lemma 2 simulates the base 1DFA on the symbols a_i, ignoring any symbols $\{a_1, \ldots, a_{i-1}\}$ encountered. A separate instance of the base 1DFA is executed for each block delimited by two symbols in $\{a_{i+1}, \ldots, a_m, \vdash, \dashv\}$.

It remains to extend the same construction to an arbitrary base automaton.

Proof. Let $\mathcal{A}$ be the given k-state direction-determinate 2DFA over an alphabet Σ. Let $Q = Q_{+1} \cup Q_{-1}$ be $\mathcal{A}$'s set of states, where the states in each Q_d are enterable only in the direction d. For $q \in Q_d$, denote by $d(q) = d$ the direction in which q is enterable. Let $F \subseteq Q$ be the set of accepting states of $\mathcal{A}$, effective at the right end-marker ($\dashv$).

The alphabet Ω of the new 2DFA $\mathcal{B}$ consists of symbols of the form $a^{(i)}$, where $a \in \Sigma$ is an input symbol of $\mathcal{A}$, and $i \in \{1, \ldots, m\}$.

$$\Sigma_i = \{\, a^{(i)} \mid a \in \Sigma \,\} \qquad\qquad (1 \leqslant i \leqslant m)$$

$$\Omega = \bigcup_{i=1}^{m} \Sigma_i$$

The new automaton's computation is organized into m passes. At each i-th pass, with $i \in \{1, \ldots, m\}$, the automaton $\mathcal{B}$ interprets its tape as $\vdash u_0 \#_1 u_1 \#_2 \ldots \#_z u_z \dashv$, where the separators $\#_1, \ldots, \#_z$ are any symbols of the form $a^{(j)}$, with $j > i$, and the substrings $u_0, \ldots, u_z$ are defined over the alphabet $\Sigma_1 \cup \ldots \cup \Sigma_i$. The substrings are processed one by one, from left to right for odd i, and from right to left for even i. For each string u_j, the automaton $\mathcal{B}$ simulates the computation of $\mathcal{A}$ on that string (if i is odd) or on its reverse (if i is even), taking into account only symbols $a^{(i)}$, with $a \in \Sigma$. All other symbols $a^{(j)}$, with $j < i$ and $a \in \Sigma$, are ignored by passing over them without changing the state or the direction; this is possible, because $\mathcal{A}$ is direction-determinate.

Each separator $\$_i$ acts both as a right delimiter for u_{i-1} and as a left delimiter for u_i. Conditions (i–iv) ensure that whenever $\mathcal{B}$ visits such a separator, it can always tell whether it is currently simulating a computation of $\mathcal{A}$ on u_{i-1} or on u_i.

The states of $\mathcal{B}$ are of the form $q^{(i)}$, which means simulating $\mathcal{A}$ in a state $q \in Q$ at the i-th pass.

$$Q = \{\, q^{(i)} \mid q \in Q, \, i \in \{1, \ldots, m\} \,\}$$

At odd-numbered passes, the substrings $u_0, \ldots, u_z$ are processed from left to right, and from right to left at even-numbered passes. Let $d(i)$ be the general direction of traversal at the i-th pass, defined by $d(i) = +1$ for odd i and $d(i) = -1$ for even i. The automaton $\mathcal{B}$ shall be direction-determinate with $d(q^{(i)}) = d(q) \cdot d(i)$.

Let q_0 be the initial state of $\mathcal{A}$, in which it makes the initial transition $\delta(q_0, \vdash) = r$. Then, the initial state of $\mathcal{B}$ is $q_0^{(1)}$, with the following initial transition.

$$\delta'(q_0^{(1)}, \vdash) = (r^{(1)}, +1)$$

At every i-th pass, with $i \in \{1, \ldots, m\}$, each $\mathcal{A}$'s transition $\delta(q, a) = (r, d(r))$, with $a \in \Sigma$ and $q, r \in Q$, is implemented by the following transition in $\mathcal{B}$.

$$\delta'(q^{(i)}, a^{(i)}) = (r^{(i)}, d(r) \cdot d(i))$$

Note that $\mathcal{A}$'s direction "$+1$" becomes "the direction of the i-th pass", whereas $\mathcal{A}$'s direction "-1" now goes in the opposite direction to the i-th pass' direction.

Each lesser symbol $a^{(j)}$, with $j < i$ and $a \in \Sigma$, is ignored by continuing in the same direction. This is where the direction-determinacy of $\mathcal{A}$ becomes essential.

$$\delta'(q^{(i)}, a^{(j)}) = (q^{(i)}, d(q) \cdot d(i)), \qquad \text{where } q \in Q, \; j < i, \; a \in \Sigma$$

Next, let $\mathfrak{c}_i$ and $\$_i$ be the end-markers at which the i-th pass begins and ends, respectively ($\mathfrak{c}_i = \vdash$ and $\$_i = \dashv$ for i odd, and vice versa for i even). For each $\mathcal{A}$'s transition $\delta(q, \dashv) = (r, -1)$ turning at the right end-marker, with $d(q) = +1$ and $d(r) = -1$, the new automaton executes the same turn on any separator symbols.

$$\delta'(q^{(i)}, s) = (r^{(i)}, -d(i)), \qquad \text{for } s \in \{\$_i\} \cup \Sigma_{i+1} \cup \ldots \cup \Sigma_m$$

Each turn at the left end-marker, $\delta(q, \vdash) = (r, +1)$, with $q \neq q_0$, $d(q) = -1$ and $d(r) = +1$, is implemented similarly.

$$\delta'(q^{(i)}, s) = (r^{(i)}, d(i)), \qquad \text{for } s \in \{\mathfrak{c}_i\} \cup \Sigma_{i+1} \cup \ldots \cup \Sigma_m$$

When $\mathcal{A}$ is about to accept at its right end-marker ($\dashv$) in a state $q \in F$, the simulating automaton $\mathcal{B}$ proceeds through a separator symbol to the next block, implementing the initial transition $\delta(q_0, \vdash) = r$ for the next block without actually entering q_0.

$$\delta'(q^{(i)}, s) = (r^{(i)}, d(i)), \qquad \text{for } s \in \Sigma_{i+1} \cup \ldots \cup \Sigma_m$$

At the end of the i-th pass, when $\mathcal{A}$'s accepting state $q \in F$ is reached while at the appropriate end-marker, $\mathcal{B}$ proceeds to the next pass by simulating the transition $\delta(q_0, \vdash) = r$ (as long as i is less than m).

$$\delta'(q^{(i)}, \$_i) = (r^{(i+1)}, d(i+1))$$

If that happens for $i = m$, the automaton $\mathcal{B}$ accepts instead.

Since the $\mathcal{B}$ proceeds to the next pass only at the end-markers, in order to accept a string, it needs to make $\frac{m-1}{2}$ left-to-right passes and $\frac{m+1}{2}$ right-to-left passes over the string, with each i-th pass made in the states from Q_i. The moment when the automaton enters any state from Q_{i+1}, it is said to have *completed the i-th pass*; the m-th pass is completed upon acceptance.

For every $i \in \{1, \ldots, m\}$, let $h_i : \Omega^* \to \Sigma^*$ be a homomorphism defined by $h_i(a_i) = a$ and $h_i(a_j) = \varepsilon$ for $j \neq i$: this is a projection to Σ_i.

Claim 1. *Let $w \in \Omega^*$ be any string, let $i_0 \in \{0, \ldots, m\}$. Then, $\mathcal{B}$ completes the i_0-th pass in its computation on w if and only if, for each $i \in \{1, 2, \ldots, i_0\}$, for the partition $w = u_0 \#_1 u_1 \#_2 \ldots \#_k u_k$, with $u_0, \ldots, u_k \in (\Sigma_1 \cup \ldots \cup \Sigma_i)^*$ and $\#_1, \ldots, \#_k \in \Sigma_{i+1} \cup \ldots \cup \Sigma_m$, each string $h_i(u_j)$ (the projection of u_j to Σ_i) is in $L(\mathcal{A})$ if i is odd, and in $L(\mathcal{A})^R$ if i is even.*

The proof is by induction on i. For every next i-th pass, with i odd, it is proved that $\mathcal{B}$ first simulates the computation of $\mathcal{A}$ on u_0; then, upon acceptance, on u_1; and so on until u_k. Each transition of $\mathcal{A}$ is simulated by a series of steps of $\mathcal{B}$: first implementing the original transition, and then skipping any intermediate symbols in $\Sigma_1 \cup \ldots \cup \Sigma_{i-1}$. A direct correspondence between these computations is established. The details of the proof are omitted due to space constraints.

It follows that $\mathcal{B}$ completes the last m-th pass if and only if the condition in Claim 1 is satisfied for all i.

With Claim 1 established, the language recognized by $\mathcal{B}$ can be described by the following formulae.

$$L_0 = \{\varepsilon\}$$

$$L_i = \bigcup_{a_1 \ldots a_z \in L(\mathcal{A})} L_{i-1} a_1^{(i)} L_{i-1} a_2^{(i)} L_{i-1} \ldots a_z^{(i)} L_{i-1}, \qquad \text{for odd } i > 1$$

$$L_i = \bigcup_{a_1 \ldots a_z \in L(\mathcal{A})} L_{i-1} a_z^{(i)} L_{i-1} a_{z-1}^{(i)} L_{i-1} \ldots a_1^{(i)} L_{i-1}, \qquad \text{for even } i > 1$$

$$L(\mathcal{B}) = L_m$$

Claim 2. *A string w is accepted by $\mathcal{B}$ if and only if, for all $i \in \{0, 1, \ldots, m\}$ and for every substring $\mathbf{c} v \$$ of the tape $\vdash w \dashv$, with $\mathbf{c} \in \{\vdash\} \cup \Sigma_{i+1} \cup \ldots \cup \Sigma_m$, $\$ \in \{\dashv\} \cup \Sigma_{i+1} \cup \ldots \cup \Sigma_m$ and $v \in (\Sigma_1 \cup \ldots \cup \Sigma_i)^*$, the string v is in L_i.*

First assume that $\mathcal{B}$ accepts w. The condition is proved by induction on i. The base case, $i = 0$, is trivial: the string v is defined over an empty alphabet and hence must be ε, and ε is in L_0.

For the induction step, let i be odd and let $\mathbf{c} v \$$ be a substring of the given form, with $v \in (\Sigma_1 \cup \ldots \cup \Sigma_i)^*$. Consider all occurrences of symbols from Σ_i in v, so that $v = v_0 a_1^{(i)} v_1 a_2^{(i)} v_2 \ldots a_z^{(i)} v_z$, with $v_0, \ldots, v_z \in (\Sigma_1 \cup \ldots \cup \Sigma_{i-1})^*$. By the induction hypothesis for each substring v_j, it belongs to L_{i-1}. On the other hand, since $\mathcal{B}$ completes its i-th pass, by Claim 1, the projection $h(v) = a_1 \ldots a_z$ is accepted by $\mathcal{A}$. This proves that v belongs to the language $L_{i-1} a_1^{(i)} L_{i-1} \ldots a_z^{(i)} L_{i-1}$ for some string $a_1 \ldots a_z \in L(\mathcal{A})$, confirming that v is in L_i. The proof for the case of even i is symmetric.

Conversely, let the condition in Claim 2 hold; the goal is to prove that the computation of $\mathcal{B}$ on w successfully completes all its m passes. For every subsequent i-th pass, let $w = u_0 \#_1 u_1 \#_2 \ldots \#_k u_k$, where $u_0, \ldots, u_k \in (\Sigma_1 \cup \ldots \cup \Sigma_i)^*$ and $\#_1, \ldots, \#_k \in \Sigma_{i+1} \cup \ldots \cup \Sigma_m$. The condition asserts that each string u_j is in L_i. Since the h_i-projection of every string in L_i is a string accepted by $\mathcal{A}$, it is known that $h_i(u_0), \ldots, h_i(u_k) \in L(\mathcal{A})$. Then, by Claim 1, $\mathcal{B}$ completes the i-th pass. The case of even i is again symmetric. This completes the proof of Claim 2.

Since the length of the shortest string in each L_i is $\ell^i - 1$, the shortest string accepted by $\mathcal{B}$ is of length $\ell^m - 1$, as claimed. $\qquad \square$

Substituting the 5-state automaton from Example 1 into Lemma 3 yields the following lower bound.

Theorem 1. *For every $n \geqslant 1$, there is an n-state direction-determinate 2DFA over an alphabet of size $7\lceil \frac{n}{5} \rceil$, with the shortest accepted string of length $8^{\lfloor \frac{n}{5} \rfloor} - 1$.*

6   Small Alphabets

The constructions in Lemmata 2 and 3 depend on using an alphabet of linear size. As it is often observed in the state complexity research, the assumption that the alphabet grows with the number of states is not always realistic, and the case of a fixed alphabet at least deserves a separate investigation.

For a unary alphabet, the expressive power of two-way automata is known quite well [3,5,8], and the maximal length of a shortest string can be determined precisely.

The ability of 2DFAs to count in unary notation is described by the following function, known as *Landau's function* [10].

$$g(n) = \max\{ \operatorname{lcm}(p_1, \ldots, p_k) \mid k \geqslant 1, \, p_1 + \ldots + p_k \leqslant n \} = e^{(1+o(1))\sqrt{n \ln n}}$$

The value $g(n)$ is known as the maximum order of an element in the group of permutations of n objects.

Theorem C. *For every $n \geqslant 2$, there is an n-state sweeping 2DFA recognizing the language $a^{g(n-1)-1}(a^{g(n-1)})^*$.*

Using this sweeping 2DFA as the base automaton in Lemma 3 leads to the following consequence.

Corollary 3. *Let Σ be a fixed m-symbol alphabet, with $m \geqslant 1$. Then, for every number $n \geqslant 1$, there exists an n-state 2DFA over the alphabet Σ, with the shortest accepted string of length $g\left(\lfloor \frac{n}{m} \rfloor - 1\right)^m - 1$, which is of the order $e^{(1+o(1))\sqrt{mn \ln \frac{n}{m}}}$.*

An interesting question is whether an exponential lower bound of the form $2^{\Omega(n)}$ can be obtained using a fixed alphabet.

7   On Improving the Estimation

The longest length of a shortest string in an n-state 2DFA is now known to be between 1.515^n and 4^n. The question is, what is the exact value?

An obvious way of improving the lower bound is to find a better base automaton for Lemma 3 than the one in Example 1. Any k-state direction-determinate automaton with the shortest accepting string of length $\ell - 1$ would improve over the existing construction if $\sqrt[k]{\ell} > \sqrt[5]{8}$. On the other hand, the method of Lemma 3 might have its limitations, and some entirely new methods might yield better lower bounds.

Turning to the upper bounds, perhaps the bounds in Corollaries 1 and 2 could be improved by analyzing the constructions in the corresponding Theorems A and B. One could also try improving the upper bound for small alphabets by investigating two-way transformation semigroups of Kunc and Okhotin [8].

References

1. Alpoge, L., Ang, T., Schaeffer, L., Shallit, J.: Decidability and shortest strings in formal languages. In: Holzer, M., Kutrib, M., Pighizzini, G. (eds.) DCFS 2011. LNCS, vol. 6808, pp. 55–67. Springer, Heidelberg (2011). https://doi.org/10.1007/978-3-642-22600-7_5

2. Chistikov, D., Czerwinski, W., Hofman, P., Pilipczuk, M., Wehar, M.: Shortest paths in one-counter systems. In: Jacobs, B., Löding, C. (eds.) FoSSaCS 2016. LNCS, vol. 9634. Springer, Heidelberg (2016). https://doi.org/10.1007/978-3-662-49630-5_27

3. Chrobak, M.: Finite automata and unary languages. Theor. Comput. Sci. **47**, pp. 149–158 (1986). https://doi.org/10.1016/0304-3975(86)90142-8. Errata: vol. 302, pp. 497–498 (2003).https://doi.org/10.1016/S0304-3975(03)00136-1

4. Ellul, K., Krawetz, B., Shallit, J., Wang, M.-W.: Regular expressions: new results and open problems. J. Autom. Lang. Comb. **10**(4), 407–437 (2005). https://doi.org/10.25596/jalc-2005-407

5. Geffert, V., Mereghetti, C., Pighizzini, G.: Converting two-way nondeterministic unary automata into simpler automata. Theor. Comput. Sci. **295**(1–3), 189–203 (2003). https://doi.org/10.1016/S0304-3975(02)00403-6

6. Geffert, V., Okhotin, A.: One-way simulation of two-way finite automata over small alphabets. In: NCMA 2013, Umeå, Sweden, 13–14 August 2013

7. Kapoutsis, C.A.: Removing bidirectionality from nondeterministic finite automata. In: Jędrzejowicz, J., Szepietowski, A. (eds.) MFCS 2005. LNCS, vol. 3618. Springer, Heidelberg (2005). https://doi.org/10.1007/11549345_47

8. Kunc, M., Okhotin, A.: Describing periodicity in two-way deterministic finite automata using transformation semigroups. In: Mauri, G., Leporati, A. (eds.) DLT 2011. LNCS, vol. 6795. Springer, Heidelberg (2011). https://doi.org/10.1007/978-3-642-22321-1_28

9. Kunc, M., Okhotin, A.: Reversibility of computations in graph-walking automata. In: Chatterjee, K., Sgall, J. (eds.) MFCS 2013. LNCS, vol. 8087, pp. 595–606. Springer, Heidelberg (2013). https://doi.org/10.1007/978-3-642-40313-2_53

10. Landau, E.: Über die Maximalordnung der Permutationen gegebenen Grades (On the maximal order of permutations of a given degree). Archiv der Mathematik und Physik, Ser. **3**(5), 92–103 (1903)

11. Pierre, L.: Rational indexes of generators of the cone of context-free languages. Theor. Comput. Sci. **95**(2), 279–305 (1992). https://doi.org/10.1016/0304-3975(92)90269-L

12. Sipser, M.: Lower bounds on the size of sweeping automata. In: STOC, pp. 360–364 (1979). https://doi.org/10.1145/800135.804429

Characterizing the Valuedness
of Two-Way Finite Transducers

Di-De Yen and Hsu-Chun Yen[✉]

Department of Electrical Engineering, National Taiwan University, Taipei 106,
Taiwan, ROC
bottle1116@hotmail.com, hcyen@ntu.edu.tw

Abstract. A transducer is infinite-valued if the maximal number of different outputs for an input string is not bounded by any constant. For one-way finite transducers, Weber gave sufficient and necessary conditions in terms of the structure of a transducer to characterize whether the transducer is infinite-valued or not. As crossing sequences in two-way automata often play similar roles as states in their one-way counterparts, we derive in this paper analogous criteria in the setting of crossing sequences to characterize the infinite-valuedness of two-way finite transducers.

Keywords: Crossing sequence · Finite transducer · Valuedness

1 Introduction

Finite transducers are finite automata with outputs. It is well known that one-way and two-way finite automate have the same expressive power as they both characterize the class of regular languages. Things change substantially when we switch from automata to transducers. In fact, two-way finite transducers (2FTs) are strictly more expressive than one-way finite transducers (1FTs).

Among various problems investigated in the literature for finite transducers, the *valuedness* problem has received considerable attention as it is related to several other problems in automata and formal languages. A finite transducer is k-*valued* if for every input, there are at most k different outputs. It is *single-valued* (or called *functional*) if $k = 1$. A transducer is *finite-valued* if it is k-valued for some k; otherwise it is *infinite-valued*. For 1FTs, the single-valuedness [2], the k-valuedness [8], as well as the finite-valuedness [12] problems are all decidable. For 2FTs, the single-valuedness problem and the k-valuedness problem were shown to be decidable in [4,5].

In [13], it was shown that a finite-valued 1FT can be effectively decomposed into finitely many single-valued ones. Likewise, a k-valued 1FT can be decomposed into exactly k single-valued ones as reported in [9,11,14]. For 1FTs,

Research supported in part by Ministry of Science and Technology, Taiwan, under grant MOST 106-2221-E-002-036-MY3.

P. Hofman and M. Skrzypczak (Eds.): DLT 2019, LNCS 11647, pp. 100–112, 2019.
https://doi.org/10.1007/978-3-030-24886-4_7

an important consequence of being finite-valued is the ability to apply known results/techniques available for single-valued ones to cope with problems for finite-valued counterparts taking advantage of the decomposition technique. As testing equivalence for single-valued transducers follows from the decidability of the functionality, the equivalence problem becomes decidable for k-valued finite transducers using the decomposition result. Note, in general, that the equivalence problem for finite transducers is undecidable [6]. The reader is referred to, e.g., [3,4,7] for more about decidability results for various types of one-way/two-way finite transducers.

To show the decidability of the finite-valuedness problem for 1FTs, Weber [12] gave two criteria in terms of the structure of a transducer to capture infinite-valuedness. As the structural criteria can easily be checked, the decidability of the finite-valuedness follows immediately. The aim of this paper is to investigate the finite-valuedness problem for 2FTs. Motivated by the fact that crossing sequences in two-way automata often play similar roles as states in their one-way counterparts, the main contribution of the paper is to derive a crossing-sequence version of Weber's criteria to characterize the infinite-valuedness of 2FTs. Our attempt starts with restricting our attention to bounded-crossing 2FTs, i.e., all the crossing sequences along an accepting computation are of finite length. It can easily be shown that if a 2FT is not bounded-crossing, then either an equivalent bounded-crossing one can be constructed or the transducer is infinite-valued. We then divide infinite-valued 2FTs into two kinds, i.e., with *length-conflicts* or with *position-conflicts*. We employ some of the ideas used in [9,10,12], to classify computations into finite classes, and utilize the notion of a so-called *pattern* introduced in this paper to provide a finer classification of computations. We feel that the techniques/results derived in the paper might have the potential to serve as a key for the decidability/complexity analysis of the valuedness problem and other problems for 2FTs.

2   Preliminaries

In this paper, we use $\mathbb{N}$ (resp., $\mathbb{Z}^+$) to denote the set of non-negative integers (resp., positive integers). For $n \in \mathbb{Z}^+$, We write $[n]$ to denote the set $\{1, \ldots, n\}$. We assume that the reader is familiar with the basic tenants of formal languages and automata theory. Given a set S, we let $|S|$ denote the cardinality of S. For a string w in Σ^*, $|w|$ is the length of w. Given a vector of strings $u = (u_1, \ldots, u_m)$, we write $|u|$ for $\sum_{i=1}^m |u_i|$, i.e., the sum of the lengths of strings in u. For a binary relation R, $Dom(R)$ and $Im(R)$ represent the domain and image of R, respectively.

A *two-way finite transducer* (*2FT*) is a 6-tuple $(Q, \Sigma, \Gamma, q_0, F, \Delta)$, where Q is a finite set of states, Σ is a finite input alphabet, Γ is a finite output alphabet, $q_0 \in Q$ is the initial state, $F \subseteq Q$ is the set of finial states, and $\Delta \subseteq Q \times (\Sigma \cup \{\triangleright, \triangleleft\}) \times Q \times \Gamma^* \times \{-1, 1\}$ is the finite set of transitions, where $\triangleright$ (the left endmarker) and $\triangleleft$ (the right endmarker) are two symbols not in Σ, -1 and 1 represent the left and right moves, respectively. T is called a *one-way finite transducer* (*1FT*) if the input head always moves to the right upon reading a symbol.

A *configuration* of a *2FT* T on string $\sigma(= \sigma_1 \cdots \sigma_m) \in (\Sigma \cup \{\triangleright, \triangleleft\})^*$ is a pair (q, i), meaning that T is in state $q(\in Q)$ reading $\sigma_i, i \in [m]$. We write $(q, i) \vdash (q', i + d)$ if $(q, \sigma_i, q', v, d) \in \Delta$, for some v. A *computation* is a sequence of configurations $\pi = (q_1, i_1) \ldots (q_n, i_n)$ such that $(q_k, i_k) \vdash (q_{k+1}, i_{k+1}), \forall k \in [n-1]$. The output string associated with the above π on string σ, written as $out_\pi(\sigma)$, is $v_1 v_2 \cdots v_{n-1}$, where $(q_k, \sigma_{i_k}, q_{k+1}, v_k, i_{k+1} - i_k)(\in \Delta)$, $v_k \in \Gamma^*$ and $k \in [n-1]$, is the transition executed in $(q_k, i_k) \vdash (q_{k+1}, i_{k+1})$. Computation $\pi = (q_1, i_1) \ldots (q_n, i_n)$ between input positions 1 and m is a *right traversal* if $i_1 = 1, i_n = m$; *left traversal* if $i_1 = m, i_n = 1$; *right U-turn* if $i_1 = 1, i_n = 1$; *left U-turn* if $i_1 = m, i_n = m$, and for each $2 \leq j \leq n-1, 1 < i_j < m$. If $q_1 = q_0$ (the initial state) and $q_n \in F$, then π is said to be an *accepting computation* on string σ. W.l.o.g., we assume that an accepting computation always ends in a configuration with the input head reading the right endmarker $\triangleleft$.

We write $T(u), u \in \Sigma^*$, to denote $\{out_\pi(\triangleright u \triangleleft) \mid \pi$ is an accepting computation on $\triangleright u \triangleleft\}$. The transduction of T, denoted by $R(T)$, is a binary relation $\{(u, v) \mid v \in T(u), u \in \Sigma^*\}$ over $\Sigma^* \times \Gamma^*$. $Dom(T)$ is the domain of $R(T)$. A transducer T is *k-valued* if $|\{v | (u, v) \in R(T)\}| \leq k$ for each $u \in \Sigma^*$. T is *single-valued* if $k = 1$. T is *finite-valued* if it is *k-valued*, for some k; otherwise it is *infinite-valued*.

A state $q \in Q$ is *useful* if there exist an input string u and an accepting computation $\pi = (q_1, i_1)(q_2, i_2) \ldots (q_n, i_n)$ on $\triangleright u \triangleleft$ such that $q_i = q$ for some $i \in [n]$, otherwise it is *useless*. In our subsequent discussion, we assume our *2FTs* to be always trim, i.e., all states are useful.

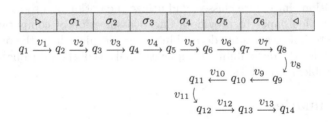

Fig. 1. The crossing sequence between cells σ_5 and σ_6 is $(q_7, 1)(q_{10}, -1)(q_{13}, 1)$, where 1 is for "right" and -1 is for "left". $C_\pi[7] = (q_7, 1)(q_{10}, -1)(q_{13}, 1)$, and $C_\pi[8] = (q_8, -1)(q_9, -1)(q_{14}, 0)$, where the "0" in q_{14} represents the end of the computation.

In what follows, we recall the notion of *crossing sequences* which play an important role in the analysis of various 2-way automata as reported in the literature. Intuitively, a crossing sequence captures the behavior of an automaton between two neighboring cells of the tape. See Fig. 1 for an example. The reader should notice that our definition of a crossing sequence here might be slightly different from some of those appearing in the literature. Given a crossing sequence $\mathbf{c} = (p_1, a_1) \ldots (p_m, a_m)$, we write $state(\mathbf{c}) = \{p_1, \ldots, p_m\}$, $state(\mathbf{c}, [p_i, p_j]) = \{p_i, \ldots, p_j\}$, $i \leq j$, and $state(\mathbf{c}, [p_i, p_j)) = \{p_i, \ldots, p_{j-1}\}$ (i.e., excluding q_j), $i < j$. Let $\pi = (q_1, i_1)(q_2, i_2) \ldots (q_n, i_l)$ be a computation on string $\triangleright \sigma_1 \cdots \sigma_m \triangleleft$. We use $C_\pi[k]$ to denote the crossing sequence w.r.t. the boundary between the $(k-1)$-th and the k-th positions along π, $1 \leq k \leq m+1$, where the $k = 0$ refers to the position left to the $\triangleright$.

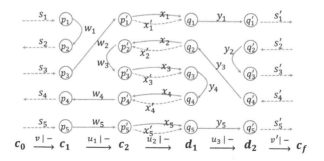

Fig. 2. The pattern from c_1 to c_2 is $(1,2)(3,1')(2',3')(4',4)(5,5')$, with $(1,2)$ a right U-turn, $(3,1')$ a right traversal, $(2',3')$ a left U-turn, $(4',4)$ a left traversal, and $(5,5')$ a right traversal.

In what follows, we define a binary relation $\xrightarrow{\sigma|\gamma}$ ($\sigma \in \Sigma \cup \{\triangleright, \triangleleft\}$ and $\gamma \in (\Gamma^*)^k$, for some k) between two crossing sequences c and c', written as $c \xrightarrow{\sigma|\gamma} c'$. Consider the first two crossing sequences c_1 and c_2 in Fig. 2. Suppose $u_1 = \sigma \in \Sigma$. The computation between c_1 and c_2 can be characterized by a sequence of *crossing pairs* (p_1, p_2) (p_3, p_1') (p_2', p_3') (p_4', p_4) (p_5, p_5'), each of which corresponds to a transition reading symbol σ. Furthermore, the output strings associated with the above sequence are $w_1, \ldots, w_5$. We therefore write $c_1 \xrightarrow{\sigma|(w_1,\ldots,w_5)} c_2$. The above is abbreviated as $c \xrightarrow{\sigma|-} c'$ if the vector of output strings is irrelevant.

In $c \xrightarrow{\sigma|-} c'$, we associate states along c (resp., c') from top to bottom with numbers $1, 2, \ldots, m$ (resp., $1', 2', \ldots, n'$), for some m, n. A valid sequence of crossing pairs $(s_1, t_1) \ldots (s_k, t_k)$ becomes a sequence of pairs of numbers in $\{1, \ldots, m\} \cup \{1', \ldots, n'\}$, which will be called a *pattern*. An $(i, i+1)$ (resp., $(i', (i+1)')$, (i, j'), and (i', j)) in a pattern is called a *right U-turn* (resp., *left U-turn*, *right traversal*, *left traversal*). It is not hard to see that with the sequences of states in c and c' given, a pattern corresponds to a valid sequence of crossing pairs. With a slight abuse of notations, we write $(p, q) \in z$, where p and q are states, to denote a crossing pair whose corresponding pair of numbers is in z.

A valid sequence δ of crossing pairs between two crossing sequences c and c' can be viewed as a layout of a (weighted) directed graph with states (in the given order) of c and c' placed as left and right columns and directed edges connecting nodes specified in δ. The weight of an edge corresponds to the output string associated with the pair of states. It should be noticed that as long as the nodes on the left and right columns respect the order given in the crossing sequences, edges do not cross as they are parts of a single computation from the initial state to a final state.

Given $c_1 \xrightarrow{\sigma_1|\gamma_1} c_2$ and $c_2 \xrightarrow{\sigma_2|\gamma_2} c_3$ (where $\sigma_1, \sigma_2 \in \Sigma$ and $\gamma_1 \in \Gamma^{k_1}, \gamma_2 \in \Gamma^{k_2}$, for some k_1, k_2) with valid sequences δ_1 and δ_2, respectively, we write $c_1 \xrightarrow{\sigma_1\sigma_2|\gamma_1\oplus\gamma_2} c_3$ to denote a valid sequence of crossing pairs $(s_1, t_1)\dots(s_m, t_m)$ (where $s_i, t_i \in state(c_1) \cup state(c_3)$), written as $\delta_1 \oplus \delta_2$, in the following way. $(s_i, t_i) \in \delta_1 \oplus \delta_2$ if there is a directed path from s_i to t_i possibly through states in c_2. Consider Fig. 2 in which the crossing pairs associated with $c_1 \xrightarrow{u_1|-} c_2$ and $c_2 \xrightarrow{u_2|-} d_1$ are δ_1 and δ_2, respectively. Then $\delta_1 \oplus \delta_2$ contains crossing pairs $(p_1, p_2)(p_3, q_1)(q_2, q_3)(q_4, p_4)(p_5, q_5)$, in which $q_2 \xrightarrow{\sigma_1\sigma_2|x_2w_3x_3} q_3$ is through intermediate states p_2' and p_3' of c_2. It is easy to see that the constructed $\delta_1 \oplus \delta_2$ satisfies the required conditions of a valid sequence. Let z_1 and z_2 be the patterns of δ_1 and δ_2, respectively. With a slight abuse of the use of notation $\oplus$, we write $z_1 \oplus z_2$ to denote the new pattern associated with $\delta_1 \oplus \delta_2$, and $\gamma_1 \oplus \gamma_2$ to denote the combined output vector of strings. In Fig. 2, $z_1 \oplus z_2$ is $(1, 2)(3, 1')(2', 3')(4', 4)(5, 5')$ and $\gamma_1 \oplus \gamma_2$ is $(w_1, w_2x_1, x_2w_3x_3, x_4w_4, w_5x_5)$. A pattern satisfying $z \oplus z = z$ is called *idempotent*. The interested reader is referred to [1] for a similar concept called *idempotent loops* in 2FTs.

We write $c \xrightarrow{\sigma_1\cdots\sigma_{m-1}|\gamma\oplus\cdots\oplus\gamma_{m-1}} c'$ if there exist crossing sequences $c_1, \dots, c_m$, such that $c = c_1$, $c' = c_m$ and $c_i \xrightarrow{\sigma_i|\gamma_i} c_{i+1}$, where $\sigma_i \in \Sigma \cup \{\triangleright, \triangleleft\}$, $\gamma_i \in (\Gamma^*)^{k_i}$, for some k_i, $1 \leq i \leq m - 1$. We write $c \xrightarrow[z]{\sigma|(\gamma)_z} c'$ if it is important to specify the pattern z associated with the computation from c to c'.

Let $z = (a_1, b_1)\dots(a_n, b_n)$ be the pattern associated with a computation $c \xrightarrow[z]{u|w} d$. If we partition z into two factors z_1 and z_2, then c (resp., d) can also be partitioned into two factors c_1' and c_2' with $c = c_1'c_2'$ (resp., d_1' and d_2' with $d = d_1'd_2'$) such that $c_1' \xrightarrow[z_1]{u|w_1} d_1'$ and $c_2' \xrightarrow[z_2]{u|w_2} d_2'$ and $w = w_1w_2$. For instance, if we partition the pattern between c_1 and c_2 in Fig. 2 into $z_1 = (1, 2)(3, 1')(2', 3')$ and $z_2 = (4', 4)(5, 5')$, then such a partition induces two subcomputations $c_1' \xrightarrow[z_1]{u|v_1} d_1'$ and $c_2' \xrightarrow[z_2]{u|v_2} d_2'$ with $v_1 = (w_1, w_2, w_3)$ and $v_2 = (w_4, w_5)$.

For *1FTs*, if $p \xrightarrow{u_1|v_1} q$ and $q \xrightarrow{u_2|v_2} r$, then $p \xrightarrow{u_1u_2|v_1v_2} r$, where p, q, r are states. Regarding crossing sequences, we have the following result, whose proof follows from the definition of patterns.

Lemma 1. *The following properties hold:*

(1) (Transitivity) If $c \xrightarrow[z_1]{u_1|(v_1,\dots,v_l)_{z_1}} d$ *and* $d \xrightarrow[z_2]{u_2|(w_1,\dots,w_m)_{z_2}} e$, *then* $c \xrightarrow[z]{u_1u_2|(x_1,\dots,x_n)_z} e$, *for some strings* $x_1, \dots, x_n$ *and pattern* z, *and* $\sum_{i=1}^{n}|x_i| = \sum_{i=1}^{l}|v_i| + \sum_{i=1}^{m}|w_i|$. *For ease of expression, the new computation is also written as* $c \xrightarrow[z_1\oplus z_2]{u_1u_2|(v_1,\dots,v_l)_{z_1}\oplus(w_1,\dots,w_m)_{z_2}} e$.

(2) (Interchangeability) If $\mathbf{c} \xrightarrow{\ u|(v_1,\cdots,v_n)_z\ }_z \mathbf{d}$ *and* $\mathbf{c} \xrightarrow{\ u|(w_1,\cdots,w_n)_z\ }_z \mathbf{d}$, *then*
$\mathbf{c} \xrightarrow{\ u|(x_1,\cdots,x_n)_z\ }_z \mathbf{d}$ *where* $x_i \in \{v_i, w_i\}$ *for each* $i \in [n]$.

The following result concerning patterns will be used later in the paper.

Lemma 2. *Let z be a pattern. If $z(\oplus z)^{n-1}$ exists for all $n \in \mathbb{Z}^+$, then there is a $p \in \mathbb{Z}^+$ such that $z' = z(\oplus z)^{p-1}$ and $z' \oplus z' = z'$, i.e., z' is idempotent.*

Given $v_1, v_2 \in \Gamma^*$ with $v_1 \neq v_2$, one of the following statements is true:

(1) $|v_1| \neq |v_2|$.
(2) $v_1(i) \neq v_2(i)$ for some $i \in [|v_1|] \cap [|v_2|]$.

We call the first case a *length-conflict* and the second case a *position-conflict*.

If for every $n \in \mathbb{Z}^+$, there exist a $u \in \Sigma^*$ and $v_1, v_2, \ldots, v_n \in \Gamma^*$ such that $(u, v_i) \in R(T)$, $1 \leq i \leq n$, v_i and v_j have a length-conflict (resp., position-conflict), $\forall 1 \leq i, j \leq n, i \neq j$, then T (or $R(T)$) is said to have length-conflicts (resp., position-conflicts). It is not hard to see that a *2FT* T is infinite-valued iff T has length-conflicts or position-conflicts.

Regarding the cardinality of $T(u)$, $u \in \Sigma^*$, there are two possibilities: (1) $T(u)$ is finite for all $u \in Dom(T)$, and (2) $T(u)$ is infinite for some $u \in Dom(T)$. If the second condition holds, T clearly has length-conflicts, and hence, it is infinite-valued. However, T could still be infinite-valued if the first but not the second condition holds, as the size of $T(u)$ may grow unboundedly.

In what follows, we give a sufficient and necessary condition to characterize the existence of a $u \in Dom(T)$ such that $T(u)$ is infinite, i.e., Condition (2) above.

Lemma 3. *Given a 2FT T, $T(u)$ is infinite for some $u \in Dom(T)$ iff there exists an accepting computation π on u and a crossing sequence $\mathbf{c} = (q_1, a_1) \ldots (q_n, a_n)$, $q_i \in Q, a_i \in \{1, -1\}, 1 \leq i \leq n$, such that $(q_j, a_j) = (q_k, a_k)$, for some $1 \leq j \neq k \leq n$, where the output string associated with the computation from state q_j to state q_k of $\mathbf{c}$ along π is not ϵ.*

A 2FT T is *bounded-crossing* if there is a constant k such that for every input string u, no tape cell is read more than k times for T on u. Throughout the rest of the paper, we assume our 2FTs to be bounded-crossing; otherwise, either it can be made bounded-crossing by removing loops of ϵ outputs, or it is infinite-valued as we have shown above.

3   Some Properties of Bounded-Crossing 2FTs

For convenience, the following notations regarding a 2FT $T = (Q, \Sigma, \Gamma, q_0, F, \Delta)$ will be used throughout this paper.

- N_C: the number of crossing sequences.
- N_S: the number of different subsets of crossing sequences, i.e., $N_S = 2^{N_C}$.
- $\psi = 2 \times d \times |Q| \times (N_C)^3$, where $d = Max\{|v| | (p, u, q, v, d) \in \Delta\}$.

Notice that each of the above is in fact a constant.

Let C and D be two sets of crossing sequences. D is said to be *accessible* from C (written as $C \succeq D$) if there is a $u \in \Sigma^*$ such that for every $\mathbf{c} \in C$, there exists a $\mathbf{d} \in D$ such that $\mathbf{c} \xrightarrow{u|-} \mathbf{d}$, and for any $\mathbf{d} \in D$, there is a $\mathbf{c} \in C$ such that $\mathbf{c} \xrightarrow{u|-} \mathbf{d}$. The u is called a *witnessing string* for $C \succeq D$. It is easy to see that $C \succeq D$ and $D \succeq E$ imply $C \succeq E$, hence, $\succeq$ is transitive. C and D are said to be *equivalent*, denoted by $C \cong D$, if $C \succeq D$ and $D \succeq C$. Notice that witnessing strings for $C \succeq D$ and $D \succeq C$ need not be the same. Let u be an input string and C_i denote the set $\{C_\pi[i] \mid \pi \text{ is an accepting computation on } u\}$ for each $i \in [|u| + 2]$, i.e., C_i is the set of crossing sequences each of which appears at position i in some accepting computation. Obviously, $C_i \succeq C_j$ for every $i \leq j$.

The following lemma plays a key role in our subsequent discussion:

Lemma 4. *Given an input $u \in Dom(T)$, there exists a sequence $1 = i_1 < i_2 < \ldots < i_k = |u| + 2$, for some $k \leq N_S$, such that*

(1) $C_{i_{j+1}} \ncong C_{i_j} \; \forall j \in [k-1]$, and
(2) $C_l \cong C_m \; \forall j \in [k-1], \forall l, m \in [i_j, i_{j+1} - 1]$.

We now give some properties concerning computations of 2FTs without length-conflicts. Similar results for 1FTs can be found in [9].

Lemma 5. *Given a bounded-crossing 2FT $T = (Q, \Sigma, \Gamma, q_0, F, \Delta)$ having no length-conflicts, let $\mathbf{c}, \mathbf{d}, \mathbf{e}, \mathbf{f}$ be crossing sequences, $u, u_1, u_2 \in \Sigma^*$, $v_1, \ldots, v_n$, $v_1', \ldots, v_n' \in \Gamma^*$, $x_1, x_2, x_1', x_2', w, x, y$ be vectors of strings over Γ^*, and a pattern z, the following hold:*

(1) If $\mathbf{c} \xrightarrow{u|-} \mathbf{c}$, $\mathbf{c} \xrightarrow[z]{u|(v_1, \ldots, v_n)z} \mathbf{d}$, $\mathbf{c} \xrightarrow[z]{u|(v_1', \ldots, v_n')z} \mathbf{d}$, and $\mathbf{d} \xrightarrow{u|-} \mathbf{d}$, then $||v_i| - |v_i'|| \leq \psi, \forall 1 \leq i \leq n$.

(2) If $\mathbf{c} \xrightarrow{u_1 u_2|-} \mathbf{c}$, $\mathbf{c} \xrightarrow{u_1|x_1} \mathbf{e}$, $\mathbf{c} \xrightarrow{u_1|x_1'} \mathbf{f}$, $\mathbf{e} \xrightarrow{u_2|x_2} \mathbf{d}$, $\mathbf{f} \xrightarrow{u_2|x_2'} \mathbf{d}$, and $\mathbf{d} \xrightarrow{u_1 u_2|-} \mathbf{d}$, then $||x_i| - |x_i'|| \leq \psi$, for $i = 1, 2$.

(3) If $\mathbf{c} \xrightarrow{u|w} \mathbf{c}$, $\mathbf{c} \xrightarrow{u|x} \mathbf{d}$, and $\mathbf{d} \xrightarrow{u|y} \mathbf{d}$, then $|w| = |y|$.

Lemma 6. *If a 2FT T has length-conflicts, for each $N \in \mathbb{N}$, there are two crossing sequences $\mathbf{c}, \mathbf{d}$, a string u, and two vectors of strings v, w such that $\mathbf{c} \xrightarrow{u|v} \mathbf{c}$, $\mathbf{c} \xrightarrow{u|w} \mathbf{d}$, $\mathbf{d} \xrightarrow{u|-} \mathbf{d}$, and $||v| - |w|| \geq N$.*

4   Sufficient and Necessary Conditions for the Infinite-Valuedness of 2FTs

In [12], Weber gave two criteria, IV1 and IV2 (depicted in Figs. 3(a) and (b)), to characterize the infinite-valuedness of *1FTs*. For IV1 in Fig. 3(a), $|y_1| \neq |y_2|$, and for IV2 in Fig. 3(b), $v_1 \neq \epsilon$ and $v_2(i) \neq v_3(i)$ for some $i \in [|v_2|] \cap [|v_3|]$. IV1 captures length-conflicts, whereas IV2 is a sufficient condition but not a necessary condition for position-conflicts.

Consider the analogous versions of IV1 (called *CIV1*) and IV2 (called *CIV2*) in the setting of crossing sequences. To understand the structure of CIV1 better, the reader is referred to Fig. 3(a) by replacing p, q, q_1, q_2, q_3 with crossing sequences $\mathbf{c}, \mathbf{d}, \mathbf{d}_1, \mathbf{d}_2, \mathbf{d}_3$, respectively, and strings x_i, y_i, z_i with $(x_1^i, ..., x_{s_i}^i)$, $(y_1^i, ..., y_{k_i}^i)$, $(z_1^i, ..., z_{t_i}^i)$, respectively, and for CIV2, replacing p and q in Fig. 3(b) with $\mathbf{c}$ and $\mathbf{d}$, respectively, and v_1, v_2, v_3, v_4 with $(w_1, \ldots, w_l)$, $(x_1, \ldots, x_m)$, $(x_1', \ldots, x_m')$, and $(y_1, \ldots, y_n)$, respectively.

(CIV1) There exists an accepting computation π along which there are crossing sequences $\mathbf{c}, \mathbf{d}_1, \mathbf{d}_2, \mathbf{d}_3, \mathbf{d}$, indices $s_i, k_i, t_i \in N$, strings $u, v, w \in \Sigma^*$, and vectors of strings $(x_1^i, ..., x_{s_i}^i)$, $(y_1^i, ..., y_{k_i}^i)$, $(z_1^i, ..., z_{t_i}^i)$ over Γ^*, $1 \le i \le 3$, such that

(1) $\mathbf{c} \xrightarrow{u|(x_1^i,...,x_{s_i}^i)} \mathbf{d}_i$ for $i = 1, 2$,

(2) $\mathbf{d} \xrightarrow{u|(x_1^3,...,x_{s_3}^3)} \mathbf{d}_3$,

(3) $\mathbf{d}_i \xrightarrow{v|(y_1^i,...,y_{k_i}^i)} \mathbf{d}_i$ for $i = 1, 2, 3$,

(4) $\mathbf{d}_1 \xrightarrow{w|(z_1^1,...,z_{t_1}^1)} \mathbf{c}$, and

(5) $\mathbf{d}_i \xrightarrow{w|(z_1^i,...,z_{t_i}^i)} \mathbf{d}$ for $i = 2, 3$, and

(6) $\sum_{j=1}^{k_1} |y_j^1| \ne \sum_{j=1}^{k_2} |y_j^2|$.

We now have our first main result.

Theorem 1. *A 2FT T has length-conflicts iff it satisfies criterion CIV1.*

(CIV2) There exists an accepting computation π along which there are crossing sequences $\mathbf{c}, \mathbf{d}$, patterns z_1, z_2, z_3, strings $u \in \Sigma^+$, $w_1, \ldots, w_l$, $x_1, \ldots, x_m$, $x_1', \ldots, x_m'$, $y_1, \ldots, y_n \in \Gamma^*$,

(1)

- $\mathbf{c} \xrightarrow[z_1]{u|(w_1,...,w_l)z_1} \mathbf{c}$,

- $\mathbf{c} \xrightarrow[z_2]{u|(x_1,...,x_m)z_2} \mathbf{d}$,

- $\mathbf{c} \xrightarrow[z_2]{u|(x_1',...,x_m')z_2} \mathbf{d}$,

- $\mathbf{d} \xrightarrow[z_3]{u|(y_1,...,y_n)z_3} \mathbf{d}$,

and for some index $\iota \in [m]$, there is a position-conflict between x_ι and x_ι'

(2) x_ι (x_ι') corresponds to either a left or a right traversal between some state p in $\mathbf{c}$ and some state q in $\mathbf{d}$, and

- (right traversal): if $\pi : \cdots p_1 \xrightarrow{u|w_j} p \xrightarrow{u|x_\iota} q \xrightarrow{u|y_k} q_1 \cdots$, then $\sum_{t=1}^{j} |w_t| \ne \sum_{t=1}^{k-1} |y_t|$

- (left traversal): if $\pi : \cdots q_1 \xrightarrow{u|y_k} q \xrightarrow{u|x_\iota} p \xrightarrow{u|w_j} p_1 \cdots$, then $\sum_{t=1}^{j-1} |w_t| \ne \sum_{t=1}^{k} |y_t|$

To understand the intuition behind CIV2, consider Fig. 2. Assume $\mathbf{c}_1 = \mathbf{c}_2$ $(= \mathbf{c})$, $\mathbf{d}_1 = \mathbf{d}_2 (= \mathbf{d})$ and $u_1 = u_2 = u_3 (= u \in \Sigma^*)$. Suppose x_4 and x_4' have a position-conflict. It is not hard to see that there is an accepting computation associated with input $vu^n v'$, for all $n \ge 1$. Consider the

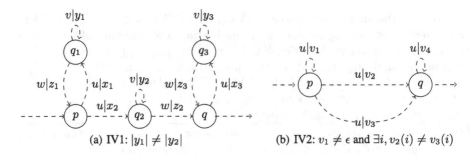

(a) IV1: $|y_1| \neq |y_2|$ (b) IV2: $v_1 \neq \epsilon$ and $\exists i, v_2(i) \neq v_3(i)$

Fig. 3. Weber's Criteria for Infinite-valuedness of $1FT$s.

$$\text{computation } \mathbf{c}_0 \xrightarrow[z]{\;v|(s_1,\ldots,s_5)_z\;} \mathbf{c} \overbrace{\xrightarrow[z_1]{\;u|(w_1,\ldots,w_5)_{z_1}\;} \cdots \xrightarrow[z_1]{\;u|(w_1,\ldots,w_5)_{z_1}\;}}^{i} \mathbf{c} \xrightarrow[z_2]{\;u|(x_1,\ldots,x_5)_{z_2}\;}$$

$$\overbrace{\mathbf{d} \xrightarrow[z_3]{\;u|(y_1,\ldots,y_5)_{z_3}\;} \cdots \xrightarrow[z_3]{\;u|(y_1,\ldots,y_5)_{z_3}\;} \mathbf{d}}^{j} \xrightarrow[z']{\;v'|(s'_1,\ldots,s'_5)_{z'}\;} \mathbf{c}_f,$$ where $i + j = n$ and $\mathbf{c}_0$ and

$\mathbf{c}_f$ are the initial and accepting crossing sequences, respectively. The output is
$\bar{w}x_4\bar{w}'$, for some $\bar{w}$ and $\bar{w}'$, where $|\bar{w}| = \sum_{t=1}^{3}|s_t| + (\sum_{t=1}^{3}|w_t|)^i + \sum_{t=1}^{3}|x_t| +$
$(\sum_{t=1}^{4}|y_t|)^j + \sum_{t=1}^{4}|s'_t|$. Suppose $\sum_{t=1}^{3}|w_t| \neq \sum_{t=1}^{4}|y_t|$, different combinations
of i and j (with $i+j = n$) result in $\bar{w}$ of different lengths. Hence, for each $1 \leq i \leq n$,
the ability to choose between $(x_1,...,x_5)$ and $(x'_1,...,x'_5)$ (both are of pattern z_2)
will result in the transducer being infinite-valued.

Consider Fig. 5(left), in which a position-conflict occurs between x_i and x'_i (a
right traversal). The w_j (resp., y_k) in the above description of CIV2 corresponds
to w_{l_2} (resp., y_{n_1+1}) in Fig. 5(left). As a result, $\sum_{t=1}^{j}|w_t| \neq \sum_{t=1}^{k-1}|y_t|$ in CIV2
simply means $\sum_{t=1}^{l_2}|w_t| \neq \sum_{t=1}^{n_1}|y_t|$ in Fig. 5(left).

Lemma 7. *If T be a 2FT satisfying CIV2, then T has position-conflicts and
hence is infinite-valued.*

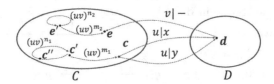

Fig. 4. Crossing sequences $\mathbf{c} \in C$ and $\mathbf{d} \in D$.

To show CIV2 to be necessary for *2FT*s without length-conflicts to exhibit
position-conflicts, we employ some of the ideas used in [9]. Consider Fig. 4 in
which $\mathbf{c} \in C, \mathbf{d} \in D$ and $C \cong D$, and a position-conflict occurs between output

strings x and y upon reading u from $\mathbf{c}$ to $\mathbf{d}$. The first step to prove the necessity of CIV2 is to show the presence of some sort of "pumpable loops" before $\mathbf{c}$ and after $\mathbf{d}$. With such pumpable loops, an unbounded number of position-conflicts in output strings can be obtained by pumping the two loops provided they have a "disparity in length" which will be clarified later.

Lemma 8. *Given an infinite-valued 2FT T without length-conflicts, there exists a $\bar{u} \in \Sigma^*$ which can be divided into $u_1 u_2 \cdots u_k$ (based on the $\cong$ relation, see Lemma 4), there exist $\mathbf{c} \in C_h$ and $\mathbf{d} \in C_{h'}$, $C_h \cong C_{h'}$, h and h' are positions falling inside u_r, for some $1 \leq r \leq k$, such that*

(1) $\mathbf{c} \xrightarrow{\;u|(w_1,\ldots,w_l)z_1\;}_{z_1} \mathbf{c},$

(2) $\mathbf{c} \xrightarrow{\;u|(x_1,\ldots,x_m)z_2\;}_{z_2} \mathbf{d},$

(3) $\mathbf{c} \xrightarrow{\;u|(x'_1,\ldots,x'_m)z_2\;}_{z_2} \mathbf{d},$

(4) $\mathbf{d} \xrightarrow{\;u|(y_1,\ldots,y_n)z_3\;}_{z_3} \mathbf{d},$

(5) $|x_i| = |x'_i|, 1 \leq i \leq m$, x_ι and x'_ι have a position conflict, for some ι,

(6) $|x_\iota| = |x'_\iota| > 2\psi$, and

(7) z_1 and z_3 are idempotent.

for some $u \in \Sigma^+$.

Lemma 8 guarantees that Condition (1) in the statement of CIV2 holds. It remains to show Condition (2) also holds. To see this, we first discuss two base cases and then show how the general cases can be reduced to the base cases.

- **(Base case: traversal)**

  Consider Fig. 5 (left). Let π: $\mathbf{c_2} \xrightarrow{\;u|(w_1,\ldots,w_l)z_1\;}_{z_1} \mathbf{c_1} \xrightarrow{\;u|(x_1,\ldots,x_m)z_2\;}_{z_2} \mathbf{d_1}$ $\xrightarrow{\;u|(y_1,\ldots,y_n)z_3\;}_{z_3} \mathbf{d_2}$ be a computation on u^3 (where $\mathbf{c_1} = \mathbf{c_2} = \mathbf{c}$ and $\mathbf{d_1} = \mathbf{d_2} = \mathbf{d}$), along which x_ι and x'_ι (both are **right-traversals** from $p \in \mathbf{c}$ to $q \in \mathbf{d}$) have a position-conflict. The left-traversal case is similar and is therefore omitted here. The conditions for this base case require

  (i) $(p, p') \in z_1$, $(q', q) \in z_3$ are right traversals, for some p' and q', and
  (ii) for every $s \in state(\mathbf{c_1}, [p', p\rangle)$, (resp., $state(\mathbf{d_1}, [q, q'\rangle))$, if $(s, t) \in z_1$ or z_2 (resp., z_3 or z_2), then the pair must be a U-turn.

The (ii) above simply says that all the crossing pairs from p' to p in $\mathbf{c_1}$ (and q to q' in $\mathbf{d_1}$) are U-turns. As z_1 and z_3 are idempotent, it is not hard to see that p' to p in $\mathbf{c_2}$ (as well as q to q' in $\mathbf{d_2}$) is also composed of a sequence of U-turns. To show Condition (2) of CIV2 holds, if suffices to show (A) $\sum_{i=1}^{l_1} |w_i| = \sum_{i=1}^{n_1} |y_i|$, and (B) $\sum_{i=l_1+1}^{l_2} |w_i| \neq 0$, which together imply $\sum_{i=1}^{l_2} |w_i| > \sum_{i=1}^{n_1} |y_i|$. The intuitive idea behind proving (A) above relies on the ability to shift the block containing $(x_1 \cdots x_{m_1})$ (i.e., the red block) to the right with the original location replaced by the block $(w_1 \cdots w_{l_1})$. Notice that the original crossing sequence $\mathbf{d_1}$ might change. As such a shifting can be done to the left or to the right for an arbitrary number of times, we are able to yield length-conflicts (due to Statement (3) in Lemma 5) if

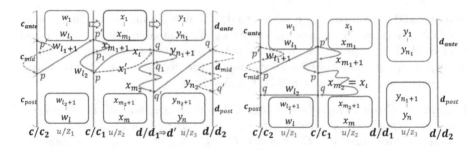

Fig. 5. Base case: traversal (left); U-turn (right).

$\sum_{i=1}^{l_1} |w_i| \neq \sum_{i=1}^{n_1} |y_i|$. (B) can be shown using a similar idea except that we shift the block $(x_\iota \ldots x_{m_2})$ to the left.

- **(Base case: U-turn)**

  Consider Fig. 5 (right). Suppose x_ι and x'_ι are right U-turns from p to q in $\mathbf{c}_1$. The left U-turn case is similar. The conditions for this base case require

  (i) $(p, p') \in z_1$ and $(q, q) \in z_1$ are right and left traversals, respectively, and
  (ii) for every $s \in state(\mathbf{c}_1, [p', p))$, if $(s, t) \in z_1$ or z_2, then the pair must be a U-turn,

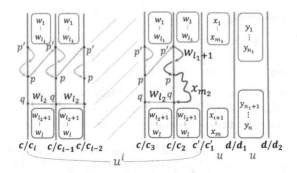

Fig. 6. On u^{i+2}, contracting the subcomputation from p to q in $\mathbf{c}_2$ of Fig. 5(right) with the right U-turn labeled x_{m_2} in $\mathbf{c}_1 \xrightarrow{u|-} \mathbf{d}_1$.

It is not hard to see $\mathbf{c}_2 \xrightarrow[\substack{z'_1}]{u|(w_1, \ldots, w_{l_1+f-1}, x_\iota, w_{l_2+1}, \ldots, w_l)_{z'_1}} \mathbf{c}'_1 \xrightarrow{uu|-} \mathbf{d}_2$, for some $\mathbf{c}'_1$, z'_1 and w_{l_1+f} is the output from p to p', i.e., the computation from p to q in $\mathbf{c}_2$ is replaced by $x_{m_2} = x_\iota$. See Fig. 6. According to Statement (2) in Lemma 5, $|\sum_{i=l_1+f}^{l_2} |w_i| - |x_\iota||$ is bounded by ψ. As $|x_\iota| > 2\psi$, $\sum_{i=l_1+1}^{l_2} |w_i| \neq 0$.

By contracting k copies of $\mathbf{c} \xrightarrow{u|-} \mathbf{c}$ in a way shown in Fig. 6, we have

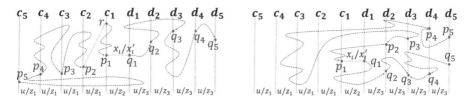

for any $0 \le k < i$. Because T has no length-conflicts, $\sum_{i=l_1+1}^{l_2} |w_i| = 0$; otherwise, there will be k outputs of different lengths.

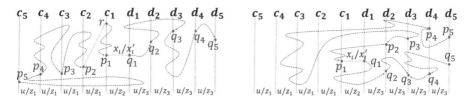

Fig. 7. General case: traversal (left); U-turn (right).

Due to the above contradicting results, the right U-turn case does not exist.

- **(General case)**

  Consider Fig. 7(left) in which $\mathbf{c_2} \xrightarrow[z_1]{u|-} \mathbf{c_1} \xrightarrow[z_2]{u|-} \mathbf{d_1} \xrightarrow[z_3]{u|-} \mathbf{d_2}$ on u^3 witnesses a position-conflict between x_ι and x'_ι, and the two base cases do not apply. That is, either $p_1 \ne p_2$ or $q_1 \ne q_2$. We show in the following how to locate another witnessing computation such that one of the two base cases holds. As z_1 and z_3 are idempotent (i.e., $z_1 \oplus z_1 = z_1$ and $z_3 \oplus z_3 = z_3$), $\mathbf{c_2} \xrightarrow[z_1]{u|-} \mathbf{c_1}$
  (resp., $\mathbf{d_1} \xrightarrow[z_3]{u|-} \mathbf{d_2}$) can be "pumped" an arbitrary number of times to yield
  $\mathbf{c_{i+1}} \xrightarrow[z_1]{u|-} \mathbf{c_i}$ with $\mathbf{c_i} = \mathbf{c_1}$ (resp., $\mathbf{d_i} \xrightarrow[z_3]{u|-} \mathbf{d_{i+1}}$ with $\mathbf{d_i} = \mathbf{d_1}$), $i = 2, ...,$ as
  shown in Fig. 7, while retaining the same pattern z_1 (resp., z_3). From p_2, we trace the computation backward until reaching either $\mathbf{c_3}$ or $\mathbf{d_3}$, and let the state be p_3. Likewise, q_3 is obtained by tracing the computation forward from q_2 until reaching either $\mathbf{c_3}$ or $\mathbf{d_3}$. The p_i and q_i, $i \ge 4$, are obtained iteratively in the same way.

  Suppose (p_2, q_2) is a right traversal on u^3 and p_3 is located in $\mathbf{c_3}$ (see Fig. 7(left)). Let $(p_2, r) \in z_1$, for some r. In $\mathbf{c_3} \xrightarrow{u^2|-} \mathbf{c_1}$, we have $(p_3, r) \in z_1 \oplus z_1 \ (= z_1)$, as z_1 is an idempotent. Hence, $p_3 = p_2$. Likewise, if q_3 is located in $\mathbf{d_3}$ (i.e., q_2 to q_3 is a right traversal), then $q_2 = q_3$.

  Figure 7(right) displays the case when (p_2, q_2) is a left U-turn, p_3 to p_2 is a left traversal, and q_2 to q_3 is a right traversal. As $(z_1\oplus)^i z_2(\oplus z_3)^i = z_1 \oplus z_2 \oplus z_3$

for each $i \in \mathbb{Z}^+$, we have $p_2 = p_3$ and $q_2 = q_3$. In fact, in either case in Fig. 7, $p_i = p_2$, $q_i = q_2$, for each $i \geq 3$.

In the case of Fig. 7(left), by letting $u' = u^3$, the computation $\mathbf{c}_5 \xrightarrow{u'|-}$ $\mathbf{c}_2 \xrightarrow{u'|-} \mathbf{d}_2 \xrightarrow{u'|-} \mathbf{d}_5$ is a right traversal meeting the conditions of a base case. The remaining cases are similar.

The above, together with Lemma 7, yields our second main result:

Theorem 2. *Let T be a bounded-crossing 2FT having no length-conflicts. T is infinite-valued iff it satisfies CIV2.*

References

1. Baschenis, F., Gauwin, O., Muscholl, A., Puppis, G.: One-way definability of two-way word transducers. Logical Methods Comput. Sci. **14**, 1–54 (2018)
2. Blattner, M., Head, T.: Single-valued a-transducers. J. Comput. Syst. Sci. **15**(3), 310–327 (1977)
3. Blattner, M., Head, T.: The decidability of equivalence for deterministic finite transducers. J. Comput. Syst. Sci. **19**, 45–49 (1979)
4. Culik II, K., Karhumäki, J.: The equivalence of finite valued transducers (on hdt0l languages) is decidable. Theor. Comput. Sci. **47**(1), 71–84 (1986)
5. Culik II, K., Karhumäki, J.: The equivalence problem for single-valued two-way transducers (on NPDTOL languages) is decidable. SIAM J. Comput. **16**(2), 221–230 (1987)
6. Griffiths, T.V.: The unsolvability of the equivalence problem for λ-free nondeterministic generalized machines. J. ACM **15**(3), 409–413 (1968)
7. Gurari, E.: The equivalence problem for deterministic two-way sequential transducers is decidable. SIAM J. Comput. **11**, 448–452 (1982)
8. Gurari, E., Ibarra, O.H.: A note on finite-valued and finitely ambiguous transducers. Math. Syst. Theor. **16**(1), 61–66 (1983)
9. Muchnik, A.A., Gorbunova, K.Y.: Algorithmic aspects of decomposition and equivalence of finite-valued transducers. Probl. Inf. Transm. **51**(3), 267–288 (2015)
10. Sakarovitch, J., de Souza, R.: On the decidability of bounded valuedness for transducers. Math. Found. Comput. Sci., 588–600 (2008)
11. Sakarovitch, J., de Souza, R.: Lexicographic decomposition of k-valued transducers. Theor. Comput. Syst. **47**(3), 758–785 (2010)
12. Weber, A.: On the valuedness of finite transducers. Acta Informatica **27**(8), 749–780 (1990)
13. Weber, A.: Decomposing finite-valued transducers and deciding their equivalence. SIAM J. Comput. **22**(1), 175–202 (1993)
14. Weber, A.: Decomposing a k-valued transducer into k unambiguous ones. RAIRO - Theoretical Informatics and Applications - Informatique Théorique et Applications **30**(5), 379–413 (1996)

Input-Driven Pushdown Automata for Edit Distance Neighborhood

Viliam Geffert[(✉)], Zuzana Bednárová, and Alexander Szabari

Department of Computer Science, P. J. Šafárik University,
Jesenná 5, 04154 Košice, Slovakia
{viliam.geffert,zuzana.bednarova,alexander.szabari}@upjs.sk

Abstract. Edit distance ℓ-neighborhood of a language $\mathcal{L}$ is the set of strings that can be obtained by at most ℓ elementary edit operations—deleting or inserting one symbol in the string—from some string in $\mathcal{L}$. We show that if $\mathcal{L}$ is recognized by a nondeterministic input-driven pushdown automaton (PDA) with $\|\Gamma\|$ pushdown symbols and $\|Q\|$ states, then its edit distance ℓ-neighborhood can be recognized by a nondeterministic input-driven PDA with $2 \cdot \|\Gamma\| + 1$ pushdown symbols and $\mathcal{O}(\|Q\| \cdot \ell \cdot \|\Gamma\|^{\ell})$ states, which improves the known upper bound. We have obtained also a lower bound, namely, at least $(\|Q\| - 1) \cdot \|\Gamma\|^{\ell}$ states are required. If the measure of edit distance includes also the operation of rewriting one symbol with another, the edit distance ℓ-neighborhood can be recognized with $2 \cdot \|\Gamma\| + 1$ pushdown symbols and $\mathcal{O}(\|Q\| \cdot \ell \cdot \|\Gamma\|^{2 \cdot \ell})$ states.

Keywords: Context-free languages · Edit distance ·
Input-driven pushdown automata

1 Introduction

Edit distance is the standard measure of similarity between two strings, defined as the smallest number of elementary edit operations—such as inserting or removing one symbol in the string—that is required to transform one string into another. Based on this, we can consider $\mathcal{E}_\ell(\mathcal{L})$, an *edit distance ℓ-neighborhood* of a given language $\mathcal{L} \subseteq \Sigma^*$: this is the set of all strings at edit distance at most ℓ from some string in $\mathcal{L}$.

The notion of edit distance was first used by Levenshtein [12]; the algorithm for computing edit distance between two strings was presented in [23]. However, several independent early papers utilized this idea, e.g., [1,7,15], in applications devoted, among others, to self-correcting codes, to correction of spelling errors, and to parsing for context-free languages with error-recovery. See also [6,11,20] for overview and history, and [5,6,9,14] for other applications, like, e.g., the edit distance between two languages.

Supported by the Slovak grant contracts VEGA 1/0056/18 and APVV-15-0091.

P. Hofman and M. Skrzypczak (Eds.): DLT 2019, LNCS 11647, pp. 113–126, 2019.
https://doi.org/10.1007/978-3-030-24886-4_8

It turned out that most programming languages used in real life can be parsed by pushdown automata (PDAs) that are *input-driven*, for which the current input symbol determines whether the automaton should push one symbol on top of the pushdown store, pop one symbol from top, or leave the pushdown store untouched. These machines were introduced by Mehlhorn in [13], under the name *visibly pushdown automata*, and later studied in [2,3]. This language class has nice closure properties, among others, it is closed under all Boolean operations, concatenation, and Kleene star. The edit-distance between two languages accepted by input-driven automata is computable [8], which does not hold for general context-free languages [14]. Moreover, nondeterministic and deterministic variants of input-driven PDAs are equivalent in power and can be simulated deterministically in $\log n$ space [4,21]. For a survey, see also [17].

It is known that the regular languages are closed under ℓ-neighborhood [16,22]; the same holds for context-free languages, which can be derived by the use of a grammar [1] for parsing a context-free language with error-recovery.

It was shown that even the input-driven PDAs are closed under edit distance ℓ-neighborhood [18]: if $\mathcal{L}$ is recognized by a nondeterministic input-driven PDA with $\|\Gamma\|$ pushdown symbols and $\|Q\|$ states, then $\mathcal{E}_1(\mathcal{L})$ can be recognized with $\mathcal{O}(\|\Gamma\|^2)$ pushdown symbols and $\mathcal{O}(\|Q\|\cdot\|\Gamma\|)$ states. Since $\mathcal{E}_\ell(\mathcal{L}) = \mathcal{E}_1(\mathcal{E}_{\ell-1}(\mathcal{L}))$, the ℓ-neighborhood can be obtained by applying this construction ℓ times. However, this way we use more than $\|\Gamma\|^{2^\ell}$ pushdown symbols and $\|Q\|\cdot\|\Gamma\|^{2^\ell-1}$ states. In [19], the journal version of [18] (published online only three days before closing submissions for DLT'19, pointed to us by one of the reviewers), the authors improved this to $\|\Gamma\|+1$ pushdown symbols and $\|Q\|\cdot(2\cdot\|\Gamma\|+3)$ states for $\mathcal{E}_1(\mathcal{L})$ which, iterated, gives $\|\Gamma\|+\ell$ pushdown symbols and $\|Q\|\cdot\prod_{i=0}^{\ell-1}(2\cdot\|\Gamma\|+3+2\cdot i)$ states for $\mathcal{E}_\ell(\mathcal{L})$. Still, this requires at least $\|Q\|\cdot 2^\ell\cdot(\|\Gamma\| + \frac{3}{2})^\ell$ states, so the gap between this bound and our upper bound presented below broadens with growing ℓ quite rapidly.

In this paper, we show that $2\cdot\|\Gamma\|+1$ pushdown symbols and $\mathcal{O}(\|Q\|\cdot\ell\cdot\|\Gamma\|^\ell)$ states are sufficient[1] to recognize $\mathcal{E}_\ell(\mathcal{L})$ by a nondeterministic input-driven PDA. We have also obtained a delicate lower bound, depending on $\|Q\|$, ℓ, and $\|\Gamma\|$: for each $\|\Gamma\| \geq 2$ and $\|Q\| > \|\Gamma\|$, there exists a language $\mathcal{L}$ that can be recognized by a deterministic input-driven PDA using $\|\Gamma\|$ pushdown symbols and $\|Q\|$ states but, for each $\ell \geq 1$, any nondeterministic input-driven PDA recognizing $\mathcal{E}_\ell(\mathcal{L})$ needs at least $(\|Q\|-1)\cdot\|\Gamma\|^\ell$ states. Last but not least, we obtain the machine for the ℓ-neighborhood by a single straightforward construction. (To obtain a machine for $\mathcal{E}_\ell(\mathcal{L})$ by the use of [18,19], one has to combine six separate constructions—for insertions/deletions of neutral/pushing/popping symbols— and iterate them ℓ times.)

By increasing the number of finite control states to $\mathcal{O}(\|Q\|\cdot\ell\cdot\|\Gamma\|^{\ell+1})$, we can reduce the size of the pushdown alphabet in the machine for $\mathcal{E}_\ell(\mathcal{L})$ to $\|\Gamma\|+1$. If, beside deleting or inserting one symbol in the string, the measure of edit

---

[1] Throughout the paper, the notation $\mathcal{O}(f(\ell, \|Q\|, \|\Gamma\|))$ represents a function the exact value of which is at most $c\cdot f(\ell, \|Q\|, \|\Gamma\|)$, for some constant $c > 0$. This bound involves all positive values $\ell, \|Q\|, \|\Gamma\|$.

distance includes the operation of *rewriting one symbol with another*, then $2 \cdot \|\Gamma\| + 1$ pushdown symbols with $\mathcal{O}(\|Q\| \cdot \ell \cdot \|\Gamma\|^{2 \cdot \ell})$ states are sufficient.

2 Input-Driven Pushdown Automata

We assume the reader is familiar with the standard models of finite state automata and pushdown automata (see, e.g., [10]).

Definition 1. *A nondeterministic input-driven pushdown automaton (PDA, for short) is a septuplet $\mathcal{A} = \langle Q, \Sigma, \Gamma, q_{\mathrm{I}}, \bot, H, F \rangle$, in which Q is a finite set of states, $\Sigma = \Sigma_0 \cup \Sigma_+ \cup \Sigma_-$ is an input alphabet, partitioned into three disjoint sets, namely, Σ_0 — the set of neutral input symbols, Σ_+ — the set of pushing input symbols, and Σ_- — the set of popping input symbols. Γ denotes a pushdown alphabet, $q_{\mathrm{I}} \in Q$ is an initial state, $\bot \notin \Gamma$ a special push-down bottom endmarker, $F \subseteq Q$ a set of accepting (final) states, and $H \subseteq (Q \times \Sigma_0 \times Q) \cup (Q \times \Sigma_+ \times Q \times \Gamma) \cup (Q \times \Sigma_- \times (\Gamma \cup \{\bot\}) \times Q) \cup (Q \times Q)$ is a transition relation. A transition from the set H establishes a machine's instruction with the following meaning:*

(I) *$(q, a_0) \rightarrow (q')$: if the next input symbol is $a_0 \in \Sigma_0$, the machine $\mathcal{A}$ gets from the state $q \in Q$ to $q' \in Q$ by reading a_0, not using the pushdown store.*

(II) *$(q, a_+) \rightarrow (q', A)$: if the next input symbol is $a_+ \in \Sigma_+$, the machine gets from q to q' by reading a_+ and pushing the symbol $A \in \Gamma$ onto the pushdown.*

(III) *$(q, a_-, A) \rightarrow (q')$: if the next input symbol is $a_- \in \Sigma_-$ and the symbol on top of the pushdown is $A \in \Gamma$, the machine gets from q to q' by reading a_- and popping A from the pushdown store.*

(III') *$(q, a_-, \bot) \rightarrow (q')$: if the next input symbol is $a_- \in \Sigma_-$ and the symbol on top of the pushdown is $\bot$, the machine gets from q to q' by reading a_-. However, the bottom endmarker $\bot$ is not popped.*

(IV) *$(q) \rightarrow (q')$: the machine $\mathcal{A}$ gets from the state q to the state q' without using the input tape or the pushdown store.*

An accepting computation begins in the state q_{I} with the pushdown store containing only the bottom endmarker $\bot$ and ends in an accepting state $q' \in F$ after reading the entire input. $\mathcal{A}$ is ε-free, if there are no transitions of type (IV).

A *local configuration* of $\mathcal{A}$ is an ordered pair $\langle q, \varphi \rangle \in Q \times \Gamma^*$, in which q is the current finite control state and φ the current pushdown contents, with the topmost symbol displayed on the left. The bottom endmarker $\bot$ is not displayed.

Traditionally, transitions are given by a set of partial transition functions $\{\delta_a : a \in \Sigma\}$ of different types, depending on whether the input symbol a is neutral, pushing, or popping. (See, e.g., [2,4,17,18].) For example, a transition of type (II) corresponds to $(q', A) \in \delta_{a_+}(q)$ in [17,18], while a transition of type (III) to $q' \in \delta_{a_-}(q, A)$. However, apart from notation, the machine model introduced by Definition 1 agrees with the standard model in the literature. The only difference is that the traditional literature does not allow ε-moves of type (IV); the machine must move forward along the input in each step.

Theorem 1. *For each input-driven* PDA $\mathcal{A}$ *with ε-transitions, there exists an equivalent input-driven* PDA $\mathcal{A}'$ *without ε-transitions. Moreover, $\mathcal{A}'$ uses the same finite control states, the same pushdown alphabet, and the same partitioning of the input alphabet to neutral, pushing, and popping symbols.*

Proof. The machine $\mathcal{A} = \langle Q, \Sigma, \Gamma, q_1, \perp, H, F \rangle$ is replaced by $\mathcal{A}' = \langle Q, \Sigma, \Gamma, q_1, \perp, H', F' \rangle$, in which, for each sequence of ε-moves $(q_0) \to (q_1)$, $\ldots$, $(q_{r-1}) \to (q_r)$ in H, with $r \in \{0, \ldots, \|Q\|-1\}$ (not excluding sequences of length zero, with $q_r = q_0$), we include the following transitions in H':

- If $(q_r, a_0) \to (q') \in H$, then $(q_0, a_0) \to (q') \in H'$.
- If $(q_r, a_+) \to (q', A) \in H$, then $(q_0, a_+) \to (q', A) \in H'$.
- If $(q_r, a_-, A) \to (q') \in H$, then $(q_0, a_-, A) \to (q') \in H'$,
  not excluding the special case of $A = \perp$.

Analogically, we establish the set of accepting states: if $q_r \in F$, then $q_0 \in F'$. □

3   Edit Distance Neighborhood

For the purposes of our main construction, we found it useful to introduce also $\widetilde{\mathcal{E}}_\ell(\mathcal{L})$, an edit distance ℓ-neighborhood *with marked corrections*. To give an idea, consider the following example. Let the string $w' = $ "missspeldd" be in $\mathcal{E}_4(\mathcal{L})$, and let $w = $ "misspelled" be in $\mathcal{L}$. The corresponding string with marked corrections will be $\widetilde{w} = $ "missspeld$\overline{\underline{l}}$ ed", in which all deletions are overlined and all insertions are underlined. (This string is not unique.) In general, having given $w' \in \mathcal{E}_\ell(\mathcal{L})$, we replace each letter $a \in \Sigma$ to be deleted by its overlined version $\overline{a} \in \overline{\Sigma}$ and insert each $a \in \Sigma$ in its underlined version $\underline{a} \in \underline{\Sigma}$. Here $\overline{\Sigma}$ and $\underline{\Sigma}$ denote two new copies of the original input alphabet Σ, and hence $\widetilde{w} \in \widetilde{\Sigma}^*$, where $\widetilde{\Sigma} = \Sigma \cup \overline{\Sigma} \cup \underline{\Sigma}$. The original input $w' \in \mathcal{E}_\ell(\mathcal{L})$ can be reconstructed from $\widetilde{w}$ by using $w' = h'(\widetilde{w})$, the corrected version $w \in \mathcal{L}$ by $w = h(\widetilde{w})$, and the number of used edit changes transforming w' into w is equal to $|h_{\mathrm{err}}(\widetilde{w})|$, where h', h, h_{err} are homomorphisms from $\widetilde{\Sigma}^*$ to Σ^* defined as follows:

$$\begin{aligned}
h'(a) &= a, & h'(\overline{a}) &= a, & h'(\underline{a}) &= \varepsilon, \\
h(a) &= a, & h(\overline{a}) &= \varepsilon, & h(\underline{a}) &= a, \\
h_{\mathrm{err}}(a) &= \varepsilon, & h_{\mathrm{err}}(\overline{a}) &= a, & h_{\mathrm{err}}(\underline{a}) &= a.
\end{aligned} \tag{1}$$

By definition, $\widetilde{w} \in \widetilde{\mathcal{E}}_\ell(\mathcal{L})$, if the corrected version w is in $\mathcal{L}$ and the number of marked edit operations is bounded by ℓ. This leads to the following definition of $\widetilde{\mathcal{E}}_\ell(\mathcal{L})$, which gives also an alternative characterization of $\mathcal{E}_\ell(\mathcal{L})$:

$$\begin{aligned}
\widetilde{\mathcal{E}}_\ell(\mathcal{L}) &= \{\widetilde{w} \in \widetilde{\Sigma}^* : h(\widetilde{w}) \in \mathcal{L} \text{ and } |h_{\mathrm{err}}(\widetilde{w})| \leq \ell\}, \\
\mathcal{E}_\ell(\mathcal{L}) &= \{w' \in \Sigma^* : w' = h'(\widetilde{w}) \text{ for some } \widetilde{w} \in \widetilde{\mathcal{E}}_\ell(\mathcal{L})\}.
\end{aligned} \tag{2}$$

Now we can turn our attention to the main problem. Let $\mathcal{A}$ be an input-driven PDA accepting a language $\mathcal{L} \subseteq \Sigma^*$. For the given $\ell \geq 0$, this machine

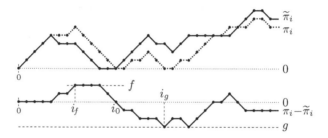

Fig. 1. Pushdown heights $\pi_i, \widetilde{\pi}_i$ along the inputs $h(\widetilde{w})$ and $\widetilde{w}$ (top), and their difference $\pi_i - \widetilde{\pi}_i$ (bottom).

should be transformed to an input-driven PDA for $\mathcal{E}_\ell(\mathcal{L})$. Recall that, since $\mathcal{A}$ is *input-driven*, we have a partitioning of input symbols to $\Sigma = \Sigma_0 \cup \Sigma_+ \cup \Sigma_-$, depending on whether they are processed as neutral, pushing, or popping.

As the first step, we shall convert $\mathcal{A}$ to an input-driven PDA with ε-transitions accepting $\widetilde{\mathcal{E}}_\ell(\mathcal{L}) \subseteq \widetilde{\Sigma}^*$. By definition of $\widetilde{\mathcal{E}}_\ell(\mathcal{L})$, the input symbols in $\widetilde{\Sigma}$ are partitioned to $\widetilde{\Sigma} = \Sigma \cup \overline{\Sigma} \cup \underline{\Sigma}$, depending on whether they are kept untouched, marked as deleted, or marked as inserted. Taking also into account partitioning given by $\mathcal{A}$, we shall therefore work with the following input alphabet:

$$\widetilde{\Sigma} = \Sigma_0 \cup \Sigma_+ \cup \Sigma_- \cup \overline{\Sigma}_0 \cup \overline{\Sigma}_+ \cup \overline{\Sigma}_- \cup \underline{\Sigma}_0 \cup \underline{\Sigma}_+ \cup \underline{\Sigma}_- \,.$$

All these sets are pairwise disjoint. For future use, we fix partitioning of $\widetilde{\Sigma}$ to neutral, pushing, and popping symbols as follows:

$$\begin{aligned}
\widetilde{\Sigma}_0 &= \Sigma_0 \cup \overline{\Sigma}_0 \cup (\underline{\Sigma}_0 \cup \underline{\Sigma}_+ \cup \underline{\Sigma}_-)\,, \\
\widetilde{\Sigma}_+ &= \Sigma_+ \cup \overline{\Sigma}_+\,, \\
\widetilde{\Sigma}_- &= \Sigma_- \cup \overline{\Sigma}_-\,.
\end{aligned} \tag{3}$$

Before passing further, we need also more details about the pushdown heights.

Definition 2. *Let $\mathcal{A}$ be an input-driven PDA accepting a language $\mathcal{L} \subseteq \Sigma^*$, let $\widetilde{\mathcal{A}}$ be any input-driven PDA with ε-transitions that works with the partitioning of $\widetilde{\Sigma}$ given by (3)—not necessarily accepting $\widetilde{\mathcal{E}}_\ell(\mathcal{L})$, and let $\widetilde{w} = b_1 b_2 \cdots b_{|\widetilde{w}|} \in \widetilde{\Sigma}^*$ be an input for $\widetilde{\mathcal{A}}$. Now, for these given $\mathcal{A}$, $\widetilde{\mathcal{A}}$, and $\widetilde{w}$, let*

$\widetilde{\pi}_i$ denote the pushdown height of $\widetilde{\mathcal{A}}$ (i.e., the number of symbols stored in the pushdown, not counting $\bot$) at the moment when $\widetilde{\mathcal{A}}$ has read the prefix $b_1 \cdots b_i$, and let

π_i be the corresponding pushdown height of $\mathcal{A}$ at the moment when $\mathcal{A}$ has read the string $h(b_1 \cdots b_i)$, where h is the homomorphism introduced by (1).

The values $\widetilde{\pi}_i, \pi_i$ are illustrated by Fig. 1. These values $\widetilde{\pi}_i, \pi_i$ are given unambiguously. As an example, $\widetilde{\pi}_i = \max\{\widetilde{\pi}_{i-1}-1, 0\}$, if $b_i \in \Sigma_- \cup \overline{\Sigma}_-$. On the other hand, $\pi_i = \max\{\pi_{i-1}-1, 0\}$ for $b_i \in \Sigma_-$, but $\pi_i = \pi_{i-1}$ for $b_i \in \overline{\Sigma}_-$, because $h(b_1 \cdots b_i) = h(b_1 \cdots b_{i-1})$. By analysis of all cases in $\widetilde{\Sigma}$, we get:[2]

$$\pi_0 = \widetilde{\pi}_0 = 0,$$
$$\pi_i - \widetilde{\pi}_i = (\pi_{i-1} - \widetilde{\pi}_{i-1}) + \delta_i, \text{ for some } \delta_i \in \{-1, 0, +1\},$$
$$|\pi_i - \widetilde{\pi}_i| \le |\pi_{i-1} - \widetilde{\pi}_{i-1}|, \qquad \text{if } b_i \notin \overline{\Sigma} \cup \underline{\Sigma}. \tag{4}$$

By the use of (4) for $\widetilde{w} \in \widetilde{\mathcal{E}}_\ell(\mathcal{L})$, we can easily see that $-\ell \le \pi_i - \widetilde{\pi}_i \le +\ell$ for each i, since there are at most ℓ marked edit changes along this input. We are now going to narrow the range for $\pi_i - \widetilde{\pi}_i$:

Lemma 1. *For any given $\ell \ge 1$, PDAs $\mathcal{A}, \widetilde{\mathcal{A}}$, and input $\widetilde{w} = b_1 \cdots b_{|\widetilde{w}|} \in \widetilde{\mathcal{E}}_\ell(\mathcal{L})$ (see Definition 2), there exists $g \in \{-\ell, \ldots, 0\}$ such that the machine $\mathcal{A}$ has an accepting computation path on $h(\widetilde{w})$ satisfying $\pi_i - \widetilde{\pi}_i \in \{g, \ldots, g+\ell\}$ for each $i \in \{0, \ldots, |\widetilde{w}|\}$.*

We are now ready to present a PDA $\widetilde{\mathcal{A}}_\ell$ for $\widetilde{\mathcal{E}}_\ell(\mathcal{L})$. By (1) and (2), to decide whether the given input $\widetilde{w} \in \widetilde{\Sigma}^*$ is in $\widetilde{\mathcal{E}}_\ell(\mathcal{L})$, it is sufficient to simulate the machine $\mathcal{A}$ on $w = h(\widetilde{w}) \in \Sigma^*$ and, in parallel, to count the number of marked edit changes along the input in the finite state control, up to ℓ. During this simulation, we skip each input symbol $\overline{a} \in \overline{\Sigma}$ (marked deletion) as if it were not present and interpret each $\underline{a} \in \underline{\Sigma}$ (marked insertion) in the same way as the corresponding $a \in \Sigma$. If, at the end of the input, we reach an accepting state of $\mathcal{A}$ and the number of marked edit changes does not exceed ℓ, we accept.

However, for future use, the new PDA $\widetilde{\mathcal{A}}_\ell$ should be input-driven in accordance with the partitioning given by (3). That is, marked deletions should push and pop the pushdown store as if they were their unmarked counterparts and marked insertions should not manipulate the pushdown at all.

The underlying idea for solving this is based on Lemma 1: for a "properly" chosen $g \in \{-\ell, \ldots, 0\}$, the original machine accepts $h(\widetilde{w})$ along a path satisfying $\pi_i - \widetilde{\pi}_i \in \{g, \ldots, g+\ell\}$ at each input position $i \in \{0, \ldots, |\widetilde{w}|\}$. Thus, if we take $g' = (-g) \in \{0, \ldots, \ell\}$ and put g' copies of some new symbol "□" into the pushdown store at the beginning, the updated heights will satisfy $(\pi_i+g') - \widetilde{\pi}_i \in \{0, \ldots, \ell\}$ during the course of the computation. This allows us to represent the pushdown store of $\mathcal{A}$, now of updated height π_i+g', by two quantities, keeping the topmost $(\pi_i+g') - \widetilde{\pi}_i$ symbols in a "buffer"—in the finite state control—and the remaining $\widetilde{\pi}_i$ symbols in the "real" pushdown store of $\widetilde{\mathcal{A}}_\ell$. The symbols are pushed and popped on top of the buffer, as the simulation of $\mathcal{A}$ demands, but, *independently*, the symbols are moved from the bottom of the buffer to the top of the real pushdown store—or the other way round—depending on whether the input symbol is neutral, pushing, or popping, in accordance with (3).

---

[2] The last inequality in (4) cannot be changed to "=" because the bottom endmarker $\perp$ is never popped out. Namely, if $b_i \in \Sigma_-$, and either $\widetilde{\pi}_{i-1} > \pi_{i-1} = 0$ or $\pi_{i-1} > \widetilde{\pi}_{i-1} = 0$, we have $|\pi_i - \widetilde{\pi}_i| = |\pi_{i-1} - \widetilde{\pi}_{i-1}| - 1$.

The only trouble-making case is a transition of type (III') in Definition 1, at the moment when the buffer is empty and the next input symbol is some $\underline{a}_- \in \widetilde{\Sigma}_-$: at this moment, the simulation requires to verify that the original pushdown store of $\mathcal{A}$ is empty, i.e., apart from $\square^{g'}$, we have no more symbols stored below the bottom of the buffer. This could be checked by testing the top of the real pushdown store of $\widetilde{\mathcal{A}}_\ell$. However, since $\underline{a}_- \in \widetilde{\Sigma}_- \subseteq \widetilde{\Sigma}_0$, this is forbidden by (3). To fix this, we need a more detailed implementation.

Theorem 2. *For each $\ell \geq 1$ and each input-driven* PDA *$\mathcal{A} = \langle Q, \Sigma, \Gamma, q_1, \bot, H, F \rangle$ accepting a language $\mathcal{L}$, there exists an input-driven* PDA *$\widetilde{\mathcal{A}}_\ell$ with ε-transitions accepting the language $\widetilde{\mathcal{E}}_\ell(\mathcal{L})$, using at most $2\cdot\|\Gamma\|+1$ pushdown symbols and $\mathcal{O}(\|Q\|\cdot\ell\cdot\|\Gamma\|^\ell)$ states, if $\|\Gamma\| \geq 2$. Moreover, $\widetilde{\mathcal{A}}_\ell$ works with the partitioning of the input alphabet given by (3).*

Proof. The machine $\widetilde{\mathcal{A}}_\ell$ simulates $\mathcal{A}$ on $h(\widetilde{w})$ along the input $\widetilde{w}$ as follows. If the pushdown store of $\mathcal{A}$ contains some $\varphi = A_{\pi_i}\cdots A_2 A_1 \in \Gamma^*$ after reading the first i input symbols, with A_{π_i} on top, the machine $\widetilde{\mathcal{A}}_\ell$ keeps the string $\varphi' = \varphi^\bot \square^{g'} = A_{\pi_i}\cdots A_2 A_1^\bot \square^{g'}$, where $A_1^\bot \in \Gamma^\bot$ is a new copy of the original pushdown symbol $A_1 \in \Gamma$ and $\square \notin \Gamma$ is a new symbol. The value $g' \in \{0,\ldots,\ell\}$ has been fixed nondeterministically at the very beginning. The string φ' is partitioned to $\varphi' = \gamma\,\gamma'$, with γ of length $(\pi_i+g') - \widetilde{\pi}_i \in \{0,\ldots,\ell\}$ kept in a "buffer" and γ' of length $\widetilde{\pi}_i$ kept in the "real" pushdown store of $\widetilde{\mathcal{A}}_\ell$.

However, in the case of $\varphi = \varepsilon$, the machine $\widetilde{\mathcal{A}}_\ell$ keeps $\varphi' = \gamma\gamma' = \varepsilon^\bot \square^{g'}$, where "$\varepsilon^\bot$" is a new special symbol, a placeholder for carrying the "$\bot$" mark. γ' is of length $\widetilde{\pi}_i$ also in this special case but, because of the placeholder, γ is one symbol longer than in the standard case. The special symbol $\varepsilon^\bot$ can *never* be pushed to the real pushdown store of $\widetilde{\mathcal{A}}_\ell$ (but $A^\bot \in \Gamma^\bot$ can).

Thus, whenever the special "$\bot$" mark is absent in the buffer, it is present on the deepest symbol of φ, placed in the real pushdown store of $\widetilde{\mathcal{A}}_\ell$ below the bottom of the buffer, and hence $\varphi \neq \varepsilon$. This way we can test whether $\varphi = \varepsilon$ without testing the real pushdown store of $\widetilde{\mathcal{A}}_\ell$ at all.

The current state $q \in Q$ of $\mathcal{A}$ is manipulated in a straightforward way. In parallel, $\widetilde{\mathcal{A}}_\ell$ counts also the number of marked edit changes along the input, for $e = 0,\ldots,\ell$. The values e, q, γ are kept in the finite state control. For the "proper" nondeterministic choice of $g' \in \{0,\ldots,\ell\}$, Lemma 1 ensures that $|\gamma| \in \{0,\ldots,\ell\}$, and hence the buffer does not overflow/underflow. This leads to the following construction of $\widetilde{\mathcal{A}}_\ell = \langle \widetilde{Q}_\ell, \widetilde{\Sigma}, \widetilde{\Gamma}, \widetilde{q}_1, \bot, \widetilde{H}_\ell, \widetilde{F}_\ell \rangle$:

- $\widetilde{\Gamma} = \Gamma \cup \Gamma^\bot \cup \{\square\}$, where $\Gamma^\bot = \{A^\bot : A \in \Gamma\}$ is a new copy of the original pushdown alphabet and $\square \notin \Gamma$ is a new pushdown symbol,
- $\varepsilon^\bot$ is yet another new auxiliary symbol — the "placeholder" $\varepsilon^\bot \notin \widetilde{\Gamma}$,
- $\widetilde{\mathcal{G}}_\ell = \{\gamma \in \Gamma^* \cup \Gamma^*\cdot\Gamma^\bot\cdot\{\square\}^* : 0 \leq |\gamma| \leq \ell\} \cup \{\varepsilon^\bot \square^i : 0 \leq i \leq \ell\}$ is an auxiliary set — the "buffer",
- $\widetilde{Q}_\ell = \{0,\ldots,\ell\}\times Q\times\widetilde{\mathcal{G}}_\ell \cup \{\widetilde{q}_1\}$, where $\widetilde{q}_1$ is a new state,
- $\widetilde{F}_\ell = \{\langle e, q, \gamma\rangle \in \widetilde{Q}_\ell : q \in F\}$,
- $\widetilde{\Sigma}$ is the input alphabet, partitioned to $\widetilde{\Sigma}_0, \widetilde{\Sigma}_+, \widetilde{\Sigma}_-$ as shown by (3) above.

We are now ready to present the machine's transitions in $\widetilde{H}_\ell$.

Initially, we set $e = 0$, $q = q_{\mathrm{I}}$, and $\gamma = \varepsilon^\perp \square^{g'}$, for a nondeterministically chosen g'. Since the initial contents of the real pushdown store is $\gamma' = \varepsilon$, this gives the initial value $\gamma\gamma' = \varepsilon^\perp \square^{g'}$. For this reason,

(I) $(\widetilde{q}_{\mathrm{I}}) \rightarrow (\langle 0, q_{\mathrm{I}}, \varepsilon^\perp \square^{g'} \rangle) \in \widetilde{H}_\ell$, for each $g' \in \{0, \ldots, \ell\}$.

Transitions for "untouched" (i.e., not marked) input symbols work as follows. As the simulation of $\mathcal{A}$ demands, the symbols are pushed/popped on *top* of the buffer (the left end of γ). The real pushdown store of $\widetilde{\mathcal{A}}_\ell$ must be pushed/popped as well, so we pop or push, respectively, some other symbol from/to the *bottom* of the buffer (the right end of γ) and use this symbol to push or pop on top of the real pushdown store, carrying also the "$\perp$" mark, if present. However, if the buffer is empty, the symbols are pushed/popped directly on top the real pushdown store of $\widetilde{\mathcal{A}}_\ell$. There are several special cases for processing a popping symbol $a_- \in \Sigma_-$, depending on whether the pushdown store of $\mathcal{A}$ is empty and/or the pushdown store of $\widetilde{\mathcal{A}}_\ell$ is empty. All these cases are detected easily; by checking whether $\gamma = \varepsilon$; whether $\varepsilon^\perp$ is on top of the buffer; and/or whether $\perp$ is on top of the real pushdown. Finally, the counter for detected marked deletions/insertions does not change. The following transitions are therefore defined for each $e \in \{0, \ldots, \ell\}$:

(II) If $(q, a_0) \rightarrow (q') \in H$, then
   $(\langle e, q, \psi \rangle, a_0) \rightarrow (\langle e, q', \psi \rangle) \in \widetilde{H}_\ell$, provided that $\psi \in \widetilde{\mathcal{G}}_\ell$.
(III) If $(q, a_+) \rightarrow (q', A) \in H$, then
   $(\langle e, q, \psi B \rangle, a_+) \rightarrow (\langle e, q', A\psi \rangle, B) \in \widetilde{H}_\ell$, provided that $\psi B, A\psi \in \widetilde{\mathcal{G}}_\ell$,
   $(\langle e, q, \varepsilon \rangle, a_+) \rightarrow (\langle e, q', \varepsilon \rangle, A) \in \widetilde{H}_\ell$,
   $(\langle e, q, \varepsilon^\perp \square^{i+1} \rangle, a_+) \rightarrow (\langle e, q', A^\perp \square^i \rangle, \square) \in \widetilde{H}_\ell$, provided that $\varepsilon^\perp \square^{i+1} \in \widetilde{\mathcal{G}}_\ell$,
   $(\langle e, q, \varepsilon^\perp \rangle, a_+) \rightarrow (\langle e, q', \varepsilon \rangle, A^\perp) \in \widetilde{H}_\ell$.
(IV) If $(q, a_-, A) \rightarrow (q') \in H$, then
   $(\langle e, q, A\psi \rangle, a_-, B) \rightarrow (\langle e, q', \psi B \rangle) \in \widetilde{H}_\ell$, provided that $A\psi, \psi B \in \widetilde{\mathcal{G}}_\ell$,
   $(\langle e, q, A^\perp \square^i \rangle, a_-, \square) \rightarrow (\langle e, q', \varepsilon^\perp \square^{i+1} \rangle) \in \widetilde{H}_\ell$, provided that $A^\perp \square^i \in \widetilde{\mathcal{G}}_\ell$,
   $(\langle e, q, \varepsilon \rangle, a_-, A) \rightarrow (\langle e, q', \varepsilon \rangle) \in \widetilde{H}_\ell$,
   $(\langle e, q, \varepsilon \rangle, a_-, A^\perp) \rightarrow (\langle e, q', \varepsilon^\perp \rangle) \in \widetilde{H}_\ell$,
   $(\langle e, q, A\psi \rangle, a_-, \perp) \rightarrow (\langle e, q', \psi \rangle) \in \widetilde{H}_\ell$, provided that $A\psi \in \widetilde{\mathcal{G}}_\ell$,
   $(\langle e, q, A^\perp \square^i \rangle, a_-, \perp) \rightarrow (\langle e, q', \varepsilon^\perp \square^i \rangle) \in \widetilde{H}_\ell$, provided that $A^\perp \square^i \in \widetilde{\mathcal{G}}_\ell$.
(IV') If $(q, a_-, \perp) \rightarrow (q') \in H$, then
   $(\langle e, q, \varepsilon^\perp \square^i \rangle, a_-, \square) \rightarrow (\langle e, q', \varepsilon^\perp \square^{i+1} \rangle) \in \widetilde{H}_\ell$, provided that $\varepsilon^\perp \square^{i+1} \in \widetilde{\mathcal{G}}_\ell$,
   $(\langle e, q, \varepsilon^\perp \square^i \rangle, a_-, \perp) \rightarrow (\langle e, q', \varepsilon^\perp \square^i \rangle) \in \widetilde{H}_\ell$, provided that $\varepsilon^\perp \square^i \in \widetilde{\mathcal{G}}_\ell$.

Transitions for marked deletions push and pop the real pushdown store in accordance with (3), but the simulation of $\mathcal{A}$ is temporarily interrupted. Thus, we push or pop one symbol to/from the top of real pushdown and, respectively, pop or push this symbol from/to the bottom of the buffer, so that the value $\gamma\gamma'$ does not change. If the real pushdown store of $\widetilde{\mathcal{A}}_\ell$ is empty, no symbol moves from the real pushdown to the buffer. Processing a marked deletion requires to increase e, the counter for marked edit changes. If the limit on the number of edit changes has been exhausted, i.e., if $e = \ell$, the computation is aborted by undefined transition. The same holds for buffer overflow/underflow, which may happen due to a wrong nondeterministic choice of g' in the past. By this reasoning, the following transitions are defined for each $e \in \{0, \ldots, \ell-1\}$:

(V) For each $\overline{a}_0 \in \overline{\Sigma}_0$ and $q \in Q$,

$(\langle e, q, \psi \rangle, \overline{a}_0) \rightarrow (\langle e+1, q, \psi \rangle) \in \widetilde{H}_\ell$, provided that $\psi \in \widetilde{\mathcal{G}}_\ell$.

(VI) For each $\overline{a}_+ \in \overline{\Sigma}_+$, $q \in Q$, and $B \in \widetilde{\Gamma}$,

$(\langle e, q, \psi B \rangle, \overline{a}_+) \rightarrow (\langle e+1, q, \psi \rangle, B) \in \widetilde{H}_\ell$, provided that $\psi B \in \widetilde{\mathcal{G}}_\ell$.

(VII) For each $\overline{a}_- \in \overline{\Sigma}_-$, $q \in Q$, and $B \in \widetilde{\Gamma}$,

$(\langle e, q, \psi \rangle, \overline{a}_-, B) \rightarrow (\langle e+1, q, \psi B \rangle) \in \widetilde{H}_\ell$, provided that $\psi B \in \widetilde{\mathcal{G}}_\ell$,

$(\langle e, q, \psi \rangle, \overline{a}_-, \bot) \rightarrow (\langle e+1, q, \psi \rangle) \in \widetilde{H}_\ell$, provided that $\psi \in \widetilde{\mathcal{G}}_\ell$.

Transitions for marked insertions simulate $\mathcal{A}$ by manipulating the topmost symbols of the original pushdown in the buffer, without touching the real pushdown store of $\widetilde{\mathcal{A}}_\ell$ at all. By checking whether $\varepsilon^\bot$ is on top of the buffer, we test whether the original pushdown is empty. Processing a marked insertion increases the counter e. If $e = \ell$ or the buffer overflows/underflows, the computation is aborted. This gives the following transitions, for each $e \in \{0, \ldots, \ell-1\}$:

(VIII) If $(q, a_0) \rightarrow (q') \in H$, then

$(\langle e, q, \psi \rangle, \underline{a}_0) \rightarrow (\langle e+1, q', \psi \rangle) \in \widetilde{H}_\ell$, provided that $\psi \in \widetilde{\mathcal{G}}_\ell$.

(IX) If $(q, a_+) \rightarrow (q', A) \in H$, then

$(\langle e, q, \psi \rangle, \underline{a}_+) \rightarrow (\langle e+1, q', A\psi \rangle) \in \widetilde{H}_\ell$, provided that $A\psi \in \widetilde{\mathcal{G}}_\ell$

$(\langle e, q, \varepsilon^\bot \Box^i \rangle, \underline{a}_+) \rightarrow (\langle e+1, q', A^\bot \Box^i \rangle) \in \widetilde{H}_\ell$, provided that $A^\bot \Box^i \in \widetilde{\mathcal{G}}_\ell$.

(X) If $(q, a_-, A) \rightarrow (q') \in H$, then

$(\langle e, q, A\psi \rangle, \underline{a}_-) \rightarrow (\langle e+1, q', \psi \rangle) \in \widetilde{H}_\ell$, provided that $A\psi \in \widetilde{\mathcal{G}}_\ell$,

$(\langle e, q, A^\bot \Box^i \rangle, \underline{a}_-) \rightarrow (\langle e+1, q', \varepsilon^\bot \Box^i \rangle) \in \widetilde{H}_\ell$, provided that $A^\bot \Box^i \in \widetilde{\mathcal{G}}_\ell$.

(X') If $(q, a_-, \bot) \rightarrow (q') \in H$, then

$(\langle e, q, \varepsilon^\bot \Box^i \rangle, \underline{a}_-) \rightarrow (\langle e+1, q', \varepsilon^\bot \Box^i \rangle) \in \widetilde{H}_\ell$, provided that $\varepsilon^\bot \Box^i \in \widetilde{\mathcal{G}}_\ell$.

By induction on $i \in \{0, \ldots, |\widetilde{w}|\}$, analyzing all cases presented by items (II)–(X'), it is easy to show that, if the number of marked edit changes in $b_1 \cdots b_i$ is equal to some $e \leq \ell$ and $\mathcal{A}$ can get from the local configuration $\langle q_1, \varepsilon \rangle \in Q \times \Gamma^*$ to $\langle q, \varphi \rangle$ by a computation path reading the string $h(b_1 \cdots b_i) \in \Sigma^*$, then the machine $\widetilde{\mathcal{A}}_\ell$ can get from the local configuration $\langle \langle 0, q_1, \varepsilon^\bot \Box^{g'} \rangle, \varepsilon \rangle \in \widetilde{Q}_\ell \times \widetilde{\Gamma}^*$ to the local configuration $\langle \langle e, q, \gamma \rangle, \gamma' \rangle$ by a computation path reading the string $b_1 \cdots b_i \in \widetilde{\Sigma}^*$, where $\gamma \gamma' = \varphi^\bot \Box^{g'}$ and $|\gamma'| = \widetilde{\pi}_i$, *provided that*, for the given g', the buffer does not overflow/underflow, i.e., provided that, at each input tape position $j \leq i$, we have $(\pi_j + g') - \widetilde{\pi}_j \in \{0, \ldots, \ell\}$. However, if $\widetilde{w} = b_1 \cdots b_{|\widetilde{w}|}$ is in $\widetilde{\mathcal{E}}_\ell(\mathcal{L})$, this condition is ensured by Lemma 1 for at least one value $g' \in \{0, \ldots, \ell\}$, and hence $\widetilde{w}$ is accepted by $\widetilde{\mathcal{A}}_\ell$, guessing the value g' at the very beginning.

Conversely, by induction on $i \in \{0, \ldots, |\widetilde{w}|\}$ again, we get that if, for some $g' \in \{0, \ldots, \ell\}$, the machine $\widetilde{\mathcal{A}}_\ell$ can get from $\langle \langle 0, q_1, \varepsilon^\bot \Box^{g'} \rangle, \varepsilon \rangle$ to $\langle \langle e, q, \gamma \rangle, \gamma' \rangle$ by a computation path reading $b_1 \cdots b_i \in \widetilde{\Sigma}^*$, the number of marked symbols in $b_1 \cdots b_i$

is equal to $e \leq \ell$. In addition, $\gamma \gamma' = \varphi^\perp \square^{g'}$, for some $\varphi^\perp \in \Gamma^* \Gamma^\perp \cup \{\varepsilon^\perp\}$, such that the machine $\mathcal{A}$ can get from $\langle q_1, \varepsilon \rangle$ to $\langle q, \varphi \rangle$ by a path reading $h(b_1 \cdots b_i) \in \Sigma^*$. Thus, if $\widetilde{w} = b_1 \cdots b_{|\widetilde{w}|}$ is accepted by $\widetilde{\mathcal{A}}_\ell$, it is in $\widetilde{\mathcal{E}}_\ell(\mathcal{L})$.

It only remains to bound the number of states. First, for each $i \in \{1, \ldots, \ell\}$, the number of strings of length i in $\widetilde{\mathcal{G}}_\ell$ can be bounded by

$$G_i = \|\Gamma\|^i + \sum_{j=1}^{i} \|\Gamma\|^j + 1 \leq \frac{2 \cdot \|\Gamma\| - 1}{\|\Gamma\| - 1} \cdot \|\Gamma\|^i,$$

using $\|\Gamma\| \geq 2$. There is also one string of length 0, namely, ε, and one string of length $\ell+1$, namely, $\varepsilon^\perp \square^\ell$. This gives $G_0 + G_{\ell+1} = 2 \leq (2 \cdot \|\Gamma\| - 1)/(\|\Gamma\| - 1) \cdot \|\Gamma\|^0$. But then the total number of different strings in $\widetilde{\mathcal{G}}_\ell$ is

$$\|\widetilde{\mathcal{G}}_\ell\| = G_0 + G_{\ell+1} + \sum_{i=1}^{\ell} G_i \leq \sum_{i=0}^{\ell} \frac{2 \cdot \|\Gamma\| - 1}{\|\Gamma\| - 1} \cdot \|\Gamma\|^i = \frac{2 \cdot \|\Gamma\| - 1}{\|\Gamma\| - 1} \cdot \frac{\|\Gamma\|^{\ell+1} - 1}{\|\Gamma\| - 1}$$

$$\leq \frac{2 \cdot \|\Gamma\| - 1}{\|\Gamma\| - 1} \cdot \frac{\|\Gamma\|}{\|\Gamma\| - 1} \cdot \|\Gamma\|^\ell = (2 + \frac{1}{\|\Gamma\| - 1}) \cdot (1 + \frac{1}{\|\Gamma\| - 1}) \cdot \|\Gamma\|^\ell \leq 3 \cdot 2 \cdot \|\Gamma\|^\ell.$$

Finally, $\|\widetilde{Q}_\ell\| = 1 + (\ell+1) \cdot \|Q\| \cdot \|\widetilde{\mathcal{G}}_\ell\| \leq \mathcal{O}(\|Q\| \cdot \ell \cdot \|\Gamma\|^\ell)$. □

Now we are ready to convert the input-driven PDA $\widetilde{\mathcal{A}}_\ell$ accepting $\widetilde{\mathcal{E}}_\ell(\mathcal{L}) \subseteq \widetilde{\Sigma}^*$ to an input-driven PDA $\mathcal{A}_\ell$ accepting the language $\mathcal{E}_\ell(\mathcal{L}) \subseteq \Sigma^*$, in which corrections are not marked. This is based on the homomorphic characterization of $\mathcal{E}_\ell(\mathcal{L})$ by $\widetilde{\mathcal{E}}_\ell(\mathcal{L})$, presented by (2), and heavy use of ε-transitions:

Theorem 3. *For each $\ell \geq 1$ and each input-driven PDA $\mathcal{A} = \langle Q, \Sigma, \Gamma, q_1, \perp, H, F \rangle$ accepting a language $\mathcal{L}$, there exists an input-driven PDA $\mathcal{A}_\ell$ with ε-transitions accepting the language $\mathcal{E}_\ell(\mathcal{L})$, using at most $2 \cdot \|\Gamma\| + 1$ pushdown symbols and $\mathcal{O}(\|Q\| \cdot \ell \cdot \|\Gamma\|^\ell)$ states, if $\|\Gamma\| \geq 2$. Moreover, $\mathcal{A}_\ell$ uses the same partitioning of the input alphabet to neutral, pushing, and popping symbols as does $\mathcal{A}$.*

Proof. The machine $\widetilde{\mathcal{A}}_\ell = \langle \widetilde{Q}_\ell, \widetilde{\Sigma}, \widetilde{\Gamma}, \widetilde{q}_1, \perp, \widetilde{H}_\ell, \widetilde{F}_\ell \rangle$ for $\widetilde{\mathcal{E}}_\ell(\mathcal{L})$, presented in Theorem 2, is replaced by $\mathcal{A}_\ell = \langle \widetilde{Q}_\ell, \Sigma, \widetilde{\Gamma}, \widetilde{q}_1, \perp, H_\ell, \widetilde{F}_\ell \rangle$. The new machine uses the same states and pushdown symbols; only the input alphabet and the set of transitions are modified, so that $\mathcal{A}_\ell$ gets, in one step, from a local configuration $\langle p, \phi \rangle$ to some local configuration $\langle p', \phi' \rangle$ by reading $h'(b) \in \Sigma \cup \{\varepsilon\}$ from the input if and only if $\widetilde{\mathcal{A}}_\ell$ gets, in one step, from $\langle p, \phi \rangle$ to $\langle p', \phi' \rangle$ by reading $b \in \widetilde{\Sigma}$. This will hold for each $p, p' \in \widetilde{Q}_\ell$, each $b \in \widetilde{\Sigma}$, and each $\phi, \phi' \in \widetilde{\Gamma}^*$. Here h' denotes the homomorphism introduced by (1), that is, $h'(a) = h'(\overline{a}) = a$ and $h'(\underline{a}) = \varepsilon$. Thus, if $\widetilde{\mathcal{A}}_\ell$ accepts $\widetilde{w} = b_1 b_2 \cdots b_{|\widetilde{w}|} \in \widetilde{\Sigma}^*$ along some computation path, $\mathcal{A}_\ell$ accepts the input $w' = h'(\widetilde{w}) \in \Sigma^*$ along the corresponding path. Vice versa, if $w' \in \Sigma^*$ is accepted by $\mathcal{A}_\ell$, the machine $\widetilde{\mathcal{A}}_\ell$ has an accepting computation path for some $\widetilde{w} \in \widetilde{\Sigma}^*$ satisfying $h'(\widetilde{w}) = w'$. By (2), we thus have that $\mathcal{A}_\ell$ accepts the language $\mathcal{E}_\ell(\mathcal{L})$. To see that the new machine $\mathcal{A}_\ell$ stays input-driven, we need a more detailed description of the updated transition set H_ℓ.

First, the initial ε-transitions are not changed. That is:

(I) If $(\widetilde{q_1}) \rightarrow (\boldsymbol{p'}) \in \widetilde{H}_\ell$, then $(\widetilde{q_1}) \rightarrow (\boldsymbol{p'}) \in H_\ell$.

Also the transitions for "untouched" (i.e., not marked) input symbols are preserved, since $h'(a) = a$ for each $a \in \Sigma$:

(II) If $(\boldsymbol{p}, a_0) \rightarrow (\boldsymbol{p'}) \in \widetilde{H}_\ell$, then $(\boldsymbol{p}, a_0) \rightarrow (\boldsymbol{p'}) \in H_\ell$.
(III) If $(\boldsymbol{p}, a_+) \rightarrow (\boldsymbol{p'}, \boldsymbol{B}) \in \widetilde{H}_\ell$, then $(\boldsymbol{p}, a_+) \rightarrow (\boldsymbol{p'}, \boldsymbol{B}) \in H_\ell$.
(IV) If $(\boldsymbol{p}, a_-, \boldsymbol{B}) \rightarrow (\boldsymbol{p'}) \in \widetilde{H}_\ell$, then $(\boldsymbol{p}, a_-, \boldsymbol{B}) \rightarrow (\boldsymbol{p'}) \in H_\ell$,
not excluding $\boldsymbol{B} = \bot$, which covers also (IV') in the proof of Theorem 2.

Next, since $h'(\overline{a}) = a$ for each $\overline{a} \in \overline{\Sigma}$, the machine $\mathcal{A}_\ell$ processes each marked deletion as not deleted:

(V) If $(\boldsymbol{p}, \overline{a}_0) \rightarrow (\boldsymbol{p'}) \in \widetilde{H}_\ell$, then $(\boldsymbol{p}, a_0) \rightarrow (\boldsymbol{p'}) \in H_\ell$.
(VI) If $(\boldsymbol{p}, \overline{a}_+) \rightarrow (\boldsymbol{p'}, \boldsymbol{B}) \in \widetilde{H}_\ell$, then $(\boldsymbol{p}, a_+) \rightarrow (\boldsymbol{p'}, \boldsymbol{B}) \in H_\ell$.
(VII) If $(\boldsymbol{p}, \overline{a}_-, \boldsymbol{B}) \rightarrow (\boldsymbol{p'}) \in \widetilde{H}_\ell$, then $(\boldsymbol{p}, a_-, \boldsymbol{B}) \rightarrow (\boldsymbol{p'}) \in H_\ell$,
not excluding the case of $\boldsymbol{B} = \bot$.

Finally, since $h'(\underline{a}) = \varepsilon$ for each $\underline{a} \in \underline{\Sigma}$, the machine $\mathcal{A}_\ell$ processes each marked insertion as not inserted, which changes transitions reading these symbols to ε-transitions:

(VIII) If $(\boldsymbol{p}, \underline{a}_0) \rightarrow (\boldsymbol{p'}) \in \widetilde{H}_\ell$, then $(\boldsymbol{p}) \rightarrow (\boldsymbol{p'}) \in H_\ell$.
(IX) If $(\boldsymbol{p}, \underline{a}_+) \rightarrow (\boldsymbol{p'}) \in \widetilde{H}_\ell$, then $(\boldsymbol{p}) \rightarrow (\boldsymbol{p'}) \in H_\ell$.
(X) If $(\boldsymbol{p}, \underline{a}_-) \rightarrow (\boldsymbol{p'}) \in \widetilde{H}_\ell$, then $(\boldsymbol{p}) \rightarrow (\boldsymbol{p'}) \in H_\ell$,
which covers also (X') in the proof of Theorem 2.

Summing up, we have obtained the following four types of transitions in H_ℓ: $(\boldsymbol{p}, a_0) \rightarrow (\boldsymbol{p'})$, with $a_0 \in \Sigma_0$, $(\boldsymbol{p}, a_+) \rightarrow (\boldsymbol{p'}, \boldsymbol{B})$, with $a_+ \in \Sigma_+$, $(\boldsymbol{p}, a_-, \boldsymbol{B}) \rightarrow (\boldsymbol{p'})$, with $a_- \in \Sigma_-$, and $(\boldsymbol{p}) \rightarrow (\boldsymbol{p'})$, covering also the case of $\boldsymbol{p} = \widetilde{q_1}$. $\qquad\square$

Now, by applying Theorem 1 on $\mathcal{A}_\ell$ constructed in Theorem 3, we can get the standard input-driven PDA without ε-transitions:

Theorem 4 (Upper Bound). *For each $\ell \geq 1$ and each input-driven PDA $\mathcal{A} = \langle Q, \Sigma, \Gamma, q_1, \bot, H, F \rangle$ accepting a language $\mathcal{L}$, there exists an ε-free input-driven PDA $\mathcal{A}'_\ell$ accepting $\mathcal{E}_\ell(\mathcal{L})$, the edit distance ℓ-neighborhood of $\mathcal{L}$, using at most $2 \cdot \|\Gamma\| + 1$ pushdown symbols and $\mathcal{O}(\|Q\| \cdot \ell \cdot \|\Gamma\|^\ell)$ states, if $\|\Gamma\| \geq 2$. Moreover, $\mathcal{A}'_\ell$ uses the same partitioning of the input alphabet to neutral, pushing, and popping symbols as does $\mathcal{A}$.*

The corresponding lower bound is also single exponential in ℓ:

Theorem 5 (Lower Bound). *For each $\|\Gamma\| \geq 2$ and each $\|Q\| > \|\Gamma\|$, there exists a language $\mathcal{L}$ that can be recognized by a deterministic input-driven PDA $\mathcal{A}$ using $\|\Gamma\|$ pushdown symbols and $\|Q\|$ states but, for each $\ell \geq 1$, any nondeterministic input-driven PDA $\mathcal{A}'$ recognizing the language $\mathcal{E}_\ell(\mathcal{L})$ with the same partitioning of the input alphabet to neutral, pushing, and popping symbols needs at least $(\|Q\| - 1) \cdot \|\Gamma\|^\ell$ states.*

We conclude this section with some variants. First, by increasing the number of states, we can reduce the size of the pushdown alphabet to $\|\Gamma\|+1$:

Corollary 1. *For each $\ell \geq 1$ and each input-driven PDA $\mathcal{A} = \langle Q, \Sigma, \Gamma, q_1, \perp, H, F \rangle$ accepting a language $\mathcal{L}$, there exists an ε-free input-driven PDA accepting $\mathcal{E}_\ell(\mathcal{L})$, using at most $\|\Gamma\|+1$ pushdown symbols and $\mathcal{O}(\|Q\| \cdot \ell \cdot \|\Gamma\|^{\ell+1})$ states, if $\|\Gamma\| \geq 2$. This machine uses the same partitioning of the input alphabet to neutral, pushing, and popping symbols as does $\mathcal{A}$.*

The definition of edit distance sometimes includes the operation of rewriting one symbol with another. This establishes $\mathcal{R}_\ell(\mathcal{L})$, an edit distance ℓ-neighborhood *with rewritings*: this is the set of all strings that can be obtained by at most ℓ deletions, insertions, or rewritings from some string in the given language $\mathcal{L}$. A rewriting can be implemented as a combination of one deletion followed, at the same input position, by one insertion. (Thus, "$\texttt{miss}\overline{\texttt{s}}\texttt{peld}\overline{\texttt{l}}\texttt{\_ed}$" can be viewed as containing one deletion, one rewriting, and one insertion.) Therefore, each $w' \in \mathcal{R}_\ell(\mathcal{L})$ is in $\mathcal{E}_{2\cdot\ell}(\mathcal{L})$. Using the homomorphisms introduced by (1), the string w' is in $\mathcal{R}_\ell(\mathcal{L})$ if and only if $w' = h'(\widetilde{w})$ for some $\widetilde{w} \in \widetilde{\Sigma}^*$, such that $h(\widetilde{w}) \in \mathcal{L}$ and the number of marked deletions, insertions, and rewritings in $\widetilde{w}$ is bounded by ℓ. A marked rewriting is displayed in $\widetilde{w}$ by a combination of two letters, as $\overline{a}\underline{a}' \in \overline{\Sigma} \cdot \underline{\Sigma}$. The set of such strings $\widetilde{w}$ will be denoted by $\widetilde{\mathcal{R}}_\ell(\mathcal{L})$. Note that, passing through a marked rewriting $\overline{a}\underline{a}'$ along the input, we count the number of marked edit changes as follows: $e_i = e_{i-1} = e_{i-2}+1$. This gives:

Theorem 6. *For each $\ell \geq 1$ and each input-driven PDA $\mathcal{A} = \langle Q, \Sigma, \Gamma, q_1, \perp, H, F \rangle$ accepting a language $\mathcal{L}$, there exists an ε-free input-driven PDA accepting $\mathcal{R}_\ell(\mathcal{L})$, the edit distance ℓ-neighborhood of $\mathcal{L}$ with rewritings, using at most $2 \cdot \|\Gamma\|+1$ pushdown symbols and $\mathcal{O}(\|Q\| \cdot \ell \cdot \|\Gamma\|^{2\cdot\ell})$ states, if $\|\Gamma\| \geq 2$. This machine uses the same partitioning of the input alphabet to neutral, pushing, and popping symbols as does $\mathcal{A}$.*

Independently, using $\|\Gamma\|+\ell$ pushdown symbols and $\mathcal{O}(\|Q\| \cdot \ell^{2\cdot\ell} \cdot \|\Gamma\|^{2\cdot\ell})$ states, an upper bound for $\mathcal{R}_\ell(\mathcal{L})$ appears as Lemma 11 in [6].

4   Concluding Remarks

We tackled the problem of converting a nondeterministic input-driven PDA recognizing a language $\mathcal{L}$ with $\|\Gamma\|$ pushdown symbols and $\|Q\|$ states into a machine recognizing $\mathcal{E}_\ell(\mathcal{L})$, the edit distance ℓ-neighborhood. We have improved the upper bound, from above $\|Q\| \cdot 2^\ell \cdot (\|\Gamma\|+\frac{3}{2})^\ell$ states, presented in [19], to $\mathcal{O}(\|Q\| \cdot \ell \cdot \|\Gamma\|^\ell)$. The following techniques were essential: First, as an intermediate step, we have constructed a machine for $\widetilde{\mathcal{E}}_\ell(\mathcal{L})$, the set of strings at edit distance at most ℓ in which all deletions and insertions are marked. Second, to construct this machine, we have used ε-transitions. Such machine is then converted into a standard ε-free input-driven PDA for the standard $\mathcal{E}_\ell(\mathcal{L})$, using the homomorphic characterization of $\mathcal{E}_\ell(\mathcal{L})$ by $\widetilde{\mathcal{E}}_\ell(\mathcal{L})$. Both edit distance neighborhood with marked corrections and input-driven PDAs with ε-transitions are of independent interest. (As the next step, we are going to reduce the number of states down to $\mathcal{O}(\|Q\|\cdot\|\Gamma\|^{\ell})$, that is, to eliminate the cost of the counter for edit changes and match asymptotically the lower bound $(\|Q\|-1)\cdot\|\Gamma\|^{\ell}$. Because of the page limit, this recent improvement will appear in a full version of the paper only.)

Some questions were left open. First, Theorem 5 provides the lower bound $(\|Q\|-1)\cdot\|\Gamma\|^{\ell}$ on the number of states only if $\|Q\| > \|\Gamma\|$, the case of $\|Q\| \leq \|\Gamma\|$ is open. Second, in Corollary 1, we have shown that already $\|\Gamma\|+1$ pushdown symbols are sufficient for an input-driven PDA to recognize $\mathcal{E}_{\ell}(\mathcal{L})$. We conjecture that $\|\Gamma\|$ symbols are not sufficient, however, the argument is an open problem. Finally, we do not have a corresponding lower bound for Theorem 6.

References

1. Aho, A., Peterson, T.: A minimum distance error-correcting parser for context-free languages. SIAM J. Comput. **1**, 305–312 (1972)
2. Alur, R., Madhusudan, P.: Visibly pushdown languages. In: Proceedings ACM Symposium Theory of Computing, pp. 202–211 (2004)
3. Alur, R., Madhusudan, P.: Adding nesting structure to words. J. Assoc. Comput. Mach. **56**(3) (2009). Art. No.16
4. von Braunmühl, B., Verbeek, R.: Input driven languages are recognized in $\log n$ space. Ann. Discrete Math. **24**, 1–20 (1985)
5. Chatterjee, K., Henzinger, T.A., Ibsen-Jensen, R., Otop, J.: Edit distance for pushdown automata. Logical Methods Comput. Sci. **13**(3:23), 1–23 (2017)
6. Cheon, H., Han, Y.-S., Ko, S.-K., Salomaa, K.: The relative edit-distance between two input-driven languages. DLT 2019. LNCS, vol. 11647, pp. 127–139. Springer, Heidelberg (2019)
7. Damerau, F.: A technique for computer detection and correction of spelling errors. Comm. Assoc. Comput. Mach. **7**, 171–176 (1964)
8. Han, Y.-S., Ko, S.-K.: Edit-distance between visibly pushdown languages. In: Steffen, B., Baier, C., van den Brand, M., Eder, J., Hinchey, M., Margaria, T. (eds.) SOFSEM 2017. LNCS, vol. 10139, pp. 387–401. Springer, Cham (2017). https://doi.org/10.1007/978-3-319-51963-0_30
9. Han, Y.-S., Ko, S.-K., Salomaa, K.: The edit-distance between a regular language and a context-free language. Int. J. Found. Comput. Sci. **24**, 1067–1082 (2013)
10. Hopcroft, J., Motwani, R., Ullman, J.: Introduction to Automata Theory, Languages, and Computation. Addison-Wesley, Harlow (2001)
11. Kruskal, J.: An overview of sequence comparison. In: Sankoff, D., Kruskal, J. (eds.) Time Warps, String Edits, and Macromolecules: The Theory and Practice of Sequence Comparison, pp. 1–44. Addison-Wesley, Stanford (1983)
12. Levenshtein, V.: Binary codes capable of correcting deletions, insertions and reversals. Soviet Phys. Dokl. **10**, 707–710 (1966)
13. Mehlhorn, K.: Pebbling mountain ranges and its application to DCFL-recognition. In: de Bakker, J., van Leeuwen, J. (eds.) ICALP 1980. LNCS, vol. 85, pp. 422–435. Springer, Heidelberg (1980). https://doi.org/10.1007/3-540-10003-2_89
14. Mohri, M.: Edit-distance of weighted automata: general definitions and algorithms. Int. J. Found. Comput. Sci. **14**, 957–982 (2003)
15. Morgan, H.: Spelling correction in systems programs. Commun. Assoc. Comput. Mach. **13**, 90–94 (1970)

16. Ng, T., Rappaport, D., Salomaa, K.: State complexity of neighbourhoods and approximate pattern matching. Int. J. Found. Comput. Sci. **29**, 315–329 (2018)
17. Okhotin, A., Salomaa, K.: Complexity of input-driven pushdown automata. SIGACT News **45**, 47–67 (2014)
18. Okhotin, A., Salomaa, K.: Edit distance neighbourhoods of input-driven pushdown automata. In: Weil, P. (ed.) CSR 2017. LNCS, vol. 10304, pp. 260–272. Springer, Cham (2017). https://doi.org/10.1007/978-3-319-58747-9_23
19. Okhotin, A., Salomaa, K.: Edit distance neighbourhoods of input-driven pushdown automata. Theoret. Comput. Sci. (2019). https://www.sciencedirect.com/science/article/pii/S0304397519301525
20. Pighizzini, G.: How hard is computing the edit distance? Inform. Comput. **165**, 1–13 (2001)
21. Rytter, W.: An application of Mehlhorn's algorithm for bracket languages to $\log n$ space recognition of input-driven languages. Inform. Process. Lett. **23**, 81–84 (1986)
22. Salomaa, K., Schofield, P.N.: State complexity of additive weighted finite automata. Int. J. Found. Comput. Sci. **18**, 1407–1416 (2007)
23. Wagner, R.A., Fischer, M.J.: The string-to-string correction problem. J. Assoc. Comput. Mach. **21**, 168–173 (1974)

The Relative Edit-Distance Between Two Input-Driven Languages

Hyunjoon Cheon[1], Yo-Sub Han[1], Sang-Ki Ko[2(✉)], and Kai Salomaa[3]

[1] Department of Computer Science, Yonsei University, 50, Yonsei-Ro,
Seodaemun-Gu, Seoul 120-749, Republic of Korea
{hyunjooncheon,emmous}@yonsei.ac.kr
[2] AI Research Center, Korea Electronics Technology Institute, Seongnam-si,
Gyeonggi-do, Republic of Korea
sangkiko@keti.re.kr
[3] School of Computing, Queen's University, Kingston, ON K7L 3N6, Canada
ksalomaa@queensu.ac.kr

Abstract. We study the relative edit-distance problem between two input-driven languages. The relative edit-distance is closely related to the language inclusion problem, which is a crucial problem in formal verification. Input-driven languages are a robust subclass of context-free languages that enable to model program analysis questions within tractable time complexity. For instance, the language inclusion (or equivalence) problem is undecidable for context-free languages whereas the problem is solvable in polynomial time for input-driven languages specified by deterministic input-driven pushdown automata (IDPDAs) and is EXPTIME-complete for nondeterministic IDPDAs. Our main contribution is to prove that the relative edit-distance problem for two input-driven languages is decidable by designing a polynomial time IDPDA construction, based on the edit-distance, that recognizes a neighbourhood of a given input-driven language. In fact, the relative edit-distance problem between two input-driven languages turns out to be EXPTIME-complete when the neighbourhood distance threshold is fixed as a constant.

Keywords: Input-driven languages · Visibly pushdown languages · Edit-distance · Algorithm · Decidability · Complexity

1 Introduction

Edit-distance between two strings is the smallest number of insertion, deletion and substitution operations required to transform one string into the other [12]. We can use the edit-distance as a similarity measure between two strings; the shorter distance implies that the two strings are more similar. We can compute the distance between two strings using a bottom-up dynamic programming algorithm [21]. The edit-distance problem arises in many areas such as computational

© Springer Nature Switzerland AG 2019
P. Hofman and M. Skrzypczak (Eds.): DLT 2019, LNCS 11647, pp. 127–139, 2019.
https://doi.org/10.1007/978-3-030-24886-4_9

biology, text processing and speech recognition [14,18,20] and can be used to compute the similarity or dissimilarity between languages [5,9,11,14].

There are two types of metrics for measuring the distance between two languages L_1 and L_2. The minimum edit-distance between two languages is defined as the minimum edit-distance of two strings, where one string is from L_1 and the other string is from L_2. Mohri [14] considered the problem of computing the edit-distance between two regular languages given by finite-state automata (FAs) of sizes m and n, and presented an $O(mn \log mn)$ time algorithm. He also proved that it is undecidable to compute the edit-distance between two context-free languages using the undecidability of the intersection emptiness of two context-free languages. As an intermediate result, Han et al. [9] considered the edit-distance between an FA and a pushdown automaton (PDA) and proposed a poly-time algorithm. Ko et al. [11] studied the approximate matching problem between a regular language given by an FA and a context-free language given by a context-free grammar. Recently, two of the authors studied the minimum edit-distance between two IDPDAs and established its decidability and computational complexity [8].

The second approach, which is of our interest, is called the *relative edit-distance*. The relative edit-distance is the supremum over all strings in L_1 of the distance of the string to L_2. Note that the relative edit-distance is non-symmetric. Given two languages L_1 and L_2, the relative edit-distance problem is to compute the relative edit-distance $d_{\mathsf{rel}}(L_1, L_2)$ from L_1 to L_2. It is easy to see that the relative edit-distance problem is a generalization of the language inclusion problem since the relative edit-distance is 0 if and only if $L_1 \subseteq L_2$. The *Hausdorff distance* is $\max\{d_{\mathsf{rel}}(L_1, L_2), d_{\mathsf{rel}}(L_2, L_1)\}$, thus symmetric. Choffrut and Pighizzini [5] studied the Hausdorff distance between languages by investigating the properties of relations and proved that the Hausdorff distance can be computed between regular languages. Benedikt et al. [2] considered this problem as a software verification task and defined two types of problem called the *bounded repairability problem* and the *threshold problem*. The former is to decide whether the relative edit-distance is bounded by a constant and the latter is to compute the actual relative edit-distance between two languages. They showed that computing the relative edit-distance is PSPACE-complete when the two languages are given by DFAs or NFAs. Bourhis et al. [3] studied the bounded repairability problem for regular tree languages and proved that the problem is coNEXP-complete between two bottom-up tree automata. Chatterjee et al. [17] proved that the relative edit-distance problem is EXPTIME-complete if L_1 is given by a (deterministic) PDA and L_2 is given by a (deterministic) FA. They also showed that the undecidability holds when L_2 is deterministic context-free and L_1 is regular.

Input-driven languages are recognizable by input-driven pushdown automata (IDPDAs), which are a special type of pushdown automata for which stack behavior is driven by the input symbols according to a partition of the alphabet. Note that these automata were originally introduced by Mehlhorn [13] with the name of *input-driven pushdown automata* in 1980. Later in 2004, Alur and

Table 1. Complexity of the language inclusion problem from $\mathcal{L}_1$ to $\mathcal{L}_2$.

$\mathcal{L}_1$	$\mathcal{L}_2$					
	DFA	NFA	DIDPDA	NIDPDA	DPDA	NPDA
(D,N)FA	P	PSPACE-c	P (Proposition 2)	EXPTIME-c (Proposition 1)	P	Undec.
(D,N)IDPDA		EXPTIME-c (Theorem 3)		EXPTIME-c [1]	Undec. (Corollary 5)	
(D,N)PDA		EXPTIME-c [17]	Undec. (Theorem 4)		Undec	

Table 2. Complexity of the relative edit-distance problem from $\mathcal{L}_1$ to $\mathcal{L}_2$. (*) The PSPACE-hardness for DFAs and NFAs holds if the threshold k is given by a unary notation. (**) The EXPTIME upper bound holds even when the threshold k is given by a unary notation. Note that the other entries hold for fixed k.

$\mathcal{L}_1$	$\mathcal{L}_2$		
	DFA, NFA	DIDPDA, NIDPDA	(D,N)PDA
(D,N)FA	PSPACE-complete [2]*	EXPTIME-complete (Theorem 13)	Undec. [17]
(D,N)IDPDA	EXPTIME-complete (Theorem 9)**		
(D,N)PDA	EXPTIME-complete [17]	Undec. (Corollary 14)	

Madhusudan [1] reintroduced the model under the name of *visibly pushdown automata*. The class of input-driven languages lies in between the class of regular languages and the class of context-free languages. They are useful to describe program analysis queries because these queries can be answered within a tractable time complexity. Recently, there have been many results about input-driven languages because of nice closure properties. Note that context-free languages are not closed under intersection and complement and deterministic context-free languages are not closed under union, intersection, concatenation, and Kleene-star. On the other hand, input-driven languages are closed under all these operations. Moreover, language inclusion, equivalence and universality are all decidable for input-driven languages whereas they are undecidable for context-free languages.

We first study the language inclusion problem for IDPDAs and further investigate the relative edit-distance problem for IDPDAs since the language inclusion problem is the simplest case of the relative edit-distance problem. Since the relative edit-distance is not symmetric, we distinguish the two languages L_1 and L_2 by calling L_1 a *source language* and L_2 a *target language*. It is EXPTIME-complete for the inclusion problem from DIDPDAs to NFAs. The inclusion problem is in P when the source language is described by an NIDPDA and the target language is described by a DIDPDA. The problem turns out to be undecidable when the source language is deterministic context-free and the target language is an input-driven language. The main complexity results on the language inclusion problem are summarized in Table 1.

The most interesting contribution of our paper is the EXPTIME-completeness of the relative edit-distance problem when both the source and target languages are input-driven languages. We also establish that the undecidability holds when the source language is deterministic context-free using the undecidability of the inclusion problem. Our main contributions on the relative edit-distance problem for IDPDAs are presented in Table 2.

2   Preliminaries

We recall some basic definitions and fix notation. For more detailed knowledge in automata theory, the reader may refer to textbooks [10,22].

The size of a finite set S is $|S|$. Let Σ denote a finite alphabet and Σ^* denote the set of all finite strings over Σ. For $m \in \mathbb{N}$, $\Sigma^{\leq m}$ is the set of strings of length at most m over Σ. A language over Σ is a subset of Σ^*. Given a set X, 2^X denotes the power set of X. The symbol λ denotes the empty string.

A *nondeterministic finite automaton* (NFA) is specified by a tuple $A = (Q, \Sigma, \delta, I, F)$, where Q is a finite set of states, Σ is an input alphabet, $\delta : Q \times \Sigma \to 2^Q$ is a multi-valued transition function, $I \subseteq Q$ is a set of initial states and $F \subseteq Q$ is a set of final states. The automaton A is a *deterministic finite automaton* (DFA) if $|I| = 1$ and $|\delta(q,a)| \leq 1$ for all $q \in Q$ and $a \in \Sigma$. A string $x \in \Sigma^*$ is accepted by A if there is a labeled path from $s \in I$ to a final state in F such that this path spells out x, namely, $\delta(s, x) \cap F \neq \emptyset$. The language $L(A)$ is the set of all strings accepted by A. It is well-known that NFAs and DFAs both recognize the class of regular languages [10,22].

A *nondeterministic pushdown automaton* (NPDA) is an extended computation model from NFA by adding a stack of unbounded size. An NPDA is specified by a tuple $P = (Q, \Sigma, \Gamma, \delta, I, F)$, where Q is a finite set of states, Σ is a finite input alphabet, Γ is a finite stack alphabet, $\delta : Q \times (\Sigma \cup \{\lambda\}) \times \Gamma \to 2^{Q \times \Gamma^*}$ is a transition function, $I \subseteq Q$ is a set of initial states, and $F \subseteq Q$ is a set of final states. An NPDA is a *deterministic pushdown automaton* (DPDA) if I is a singleton set and there is at most one applicable transition with any label $a \in \Sigma \cup \{\lambda\}$. It is also well-known that NPDAs recognize the class of context-free languages whereas DPDAs only recognize a proper subclass of context-free languages— deterministic context-free languages.

A *nondeterministic input-driven pushdown automaton* (NIDPDA) [1,13] is a restricted version of a PDA, where the input alphabet consists of three disjoint sets—$\Sigma_c \cup \Sigma_r \cup \Sigma_l$. The class of the input alphabet determines the type of stack operation. The automaton always pushes a symbol onto the stack when it reads a *call symbol* in Σ_c. If the input symbol is a *return symbol* in Σ_r, then the automaton pops a symbol from the stack. Finally, the automaton neither uses the stack nor even examines the content of the stack for the *local symbols* in Σ_l. Formally, the input alphabet is defined as a triple $\widetilde{\Sigma} = (\Sigma_c, \Sigma_r, \Sigma_l)$, where three components are finite disjoint sets.

An NIDPDA is specified by a tuple $A = (Q, \widetilde{\Sigma}, \Gamma, \delta, I, F)$, where Q is a finite set of states, $\Sigma = \Sigma_c \cup \Sigma_r \cup \Sigma_l$ is an input alphabet, Γ is a finite set of stack symbols, $I \subseteq Q$ is a set of initial states, $F \subseteq Q$ is a set of final states, and $\delta = \delta_c \cup \delta_r \cup \delta_l$ is a set of transitions, where $\delta_c \subseteq Q \times \Sigma_c \times Q \times \Gamma$ is the set of transitions for push operations, $\delta_r \subseteq Q \times \Sigma_r \times (\Gamma \cup \{\bot\}) \times Q$ is the set of transitions for pop operations, and $\delta_l \subseteq Q \times \Sigma_l \times Q$ is the set of transitions for local symbols. We use $\bot \notin \Gamma$ to denote the top of an empty stack.

A *configuration* of A is a triple (q, w, v), where $q \in Q$ is a current state, $w \in \Sigma^*$ is a remaining input, and $v \in \Gamma^*$ is a stack content. Let $C(A)$ denote the set of configurations of A. Then, we define the single step computation with the relation $\vdash_A \subseteq C(A) \times C(A)$ as follows:

- **Push:** $(q, aw, v) \vdash_A (q', w, \gamma v)$ for all $a \in \Sigma_c, (q, a, q', \gamma) \in \delta_c, \gamma \in \Gamma, w \in \Sigma^*$ and $v \in \Gamma^*$.
- **Pop:** $(q, aw, \gamma v) \vdash_A (q', w, v)$ for all $\in \Sigma_r, (q, a, \gamma, q') \in \delta_r, \gamma \in \Gamma, w \in \Sigma^*$ and $v \in \Gamma^*$; furthermore, $(q, aw, \lambda) \vdash_A (q', w, \lambda)$, for all $a \in \Sigma_r, (q, a, \bot, q') \in \delta_r$ and $w \in \Sigma^*$.
- **Local:** $(q, aw, v) \vdash_A (q', w, v)$, for all $a \in \Sigma_l, (q, a, q') \in \delta_l, w \in \Sigma^*$ and $v \in \Gamma^*$.

An *initial configuration* of an NIDPDA $A = (\widetilde{\Sigma}, \Gamma, Q, I, F, \delta_c, \delta_r, \delta_l)$ is (s, w, λ), where $s \in I$ is an initial state, w is an input string and λ implies an empty stack. An NIDPDA accepts w if A arrives at a final state after processing w from the initial configuration. Then, the language $L(A)$ recognized by A is

$$L(A) = \{w \in \Sigma^* \mid (s, w, \lambda) \vdash_A^* (q, \lambda, v) \text{ for some } s \in I, q \in F, \text{ and } v \in \Gamma^*\}.$$

An NIDPDA is *deterministic* (DIDPDA) if there is only one initial state, and for each configuration with at least one remaining input symbol, the next configuration is uniquely determined. It should be noted that NIDPDAs and DIDPDAs recognize the same class of languages—*input-driven languages*. The class of input-driven languages is a proper subclass of deterministic context-free languages and a proper superclass of regular languages. Input-driven languages are closed under complementation and intersection, as well as other basic operations such as concatenation, union, and Kleene-star.

3   Edit-Distance

We define a function $d : \Sigma^* \times \Sigma^* \to \mathbb{N}_0$ to be a *distance* if it satisfies the followings for all $x, y, z \in \Sigma^*$:

(i) $d(x, y) = 0$ if and only if $x = y$,   (identity)
(ii) $d(x, y) = d(y, x)$, and   (symmetry)
(iii) $d(x, z) \leq d(x, y) + d(y, z)$.   (triangle inequality)

In other words, a distance between two strings is a function from $\Sigma^* \times \Sigma^*$ to the non-negative integers that (i) has value zero only for two identical strings, (ii) is symmetric, and (iii) satisfies the triangle inequality [6].

The Levenshtein distance (edit-distance) between two strings is the smallest number of operations that transform one string to the other [12]. In the edit-distance, atomic edit operations on a string x consist of substituting an element of Σ by another element of Σ, deleting an element of Σ from x, or inserting an element of Σ into x. Then, given a non-negative integer r and a language L, we define a language L_r to be the edit-distance neighbourhood of L of radius r if every string in L_r has an edit-distance of at most r from a string in L—$L_r = \{w \in \Sigma^* \mid \exists u \in L \; d(u, w) \leq r\}$.

We can define the edit-distance between languages by extending the distance function to two languages. Let L_1 and L_2 be two languages. One way of defining an edit-distance between L_1 and L_2 is to find a most similar pair of strings $w_1 \in L_1$ and $w_2 \in L_2$, and compute their edit-distance. Formally, the edit-distance between L_1 and L_2 is $d_{\min}(L_1, L_2) = \inf\{d(w_1, w_2) \mid w_1 \in L_1, w_2 \in L_2\}$. We call this distance the *minimum edit-distance* between L_1 and L_2. Note that the minimum edit-distance implies the degree of difference between two most similar strings from L_1 and L_2. Thus, even if two languages are quite different, the minimum edit-distance becomes zero if both have one same string.

Another way of defining the distance between L_1 and L_2 is to consider all strings from L_1 and look for the most similar counterpart string from L_2 for each string, and compute the edit-distance between a string from L_1 and its most similar string from L_2. Then, we compute the maximum distance d among all pairs—if the relative edit-distance from L_1 to L_2 is at most k, then for any string $w_1 \in L_1$ there exists $w_2 \in L_2$ such that $d(w_1, w_2) \leq k$. We call this distance the *relative edit-distance* from L_1 to L_2 and formally define it as follows:

$$d_{\mathsf{rel}}(L_1, L_2) = \sup_{w_1 \in L_1} \inf_{w_2 \in L_2} d(w_1, w_2).$$

It is easy to see that the relative edit-distance from L_1 to L_2 is 0 if and only if L_1 is included in L_2. When we compute the relative distance from L_1 to L_2, we call L_1 the *source language* and L_2 the target language. We also note that the functions $d_{\min}$ and d_{rel} are not distance functions since they are not satisfying (i) the identity property and (ii) symmetry property, respectively. For example, $d_{\min}(\{a, aa\}, \{a\}) = 0$, $d_{\mathsf{rel}}(\{a, aa\}, \{a\}) = 1$, and $d_{\mathsf{rel}}(\{a\}, \{a, aa\}) = 0$.

We are now ready to formally present our main problem. Let $k \in \mathbb{N}$ be a constant and consider two classes X and Y of automata, where $X, Y \in \{\mathrm{DFA}, \mathrm{NFA}, \mathrm{DPDA}, \mathrm{NPDA}, \mathrm{DIDPDA}, \mathrm{NIDPDA}\}$.

The *relative k-edit-distance problem* from class X to class Y is to decide, for an automaton A in class X and an automaton B in class Y, whether or not $d_{\mathsf{rel}}(L(A), L(B)) \leq k$. For simplicity, we just use *relative edit-distance problem* in the rest of the paper.

4   Inclusion Problem for IDPDAs

Before we tackle the relative edit-distance problem between two NIDPDAs, we first study the language inclusion problem for NIDPDAs since the inclusion problem is a special case of the relative edit-distance problem. The following two results are easy consequences from well-known facts for NIDPDAs [1].

Proposition 1. Given an NFA (or a DFA) A and an NIDPDA B, the problem of deciding whether or not $L(A) \subseteq L(B)$ is **EXPTIME**-complete.

Proposition 2. Given an NIDPDA A and a DIDPDA B, the problem of deciding whether or not $L(A) \subseteq L(B)$ can be solved in polynomial time.

Now we consider the language inclusion problem from a DIDPDA (or an NIDPDA) to an NFA and establish the EXPTIME-completeness result. Note that we also use the reduction from the membership problem of linear-space alternating Turing machines (ATM), which is known to be EXPTIME-complete [4]. Our proof is inspired by the EXPTIME-completeness proof of the inclusion problem for DPDAs by Chatterjee et al. [17] but the computation trees of linear-space alternating Turing machine in our proof are encoded in a different manner due to additional restrictions imposed on the IDPDAs. For instance, the original encoding of computation trees in Chatterjee et al. [17] does not work for IDPDAs since the proof utilizes the same characters for pushing and popping stack symbols at the same time, which is not allowed in the IDPDAs. In order to operate with the restrictions of IDPDAs, we encode the computation trees in a different way—the IDPDAs can process the encoded strings without any conflict.

Theorem 3. *Given a DIDPDA (or an NIDPDA) A and an NFA B, the problem of deciding whether or not $L(A) \subseteq L(B)$ is* EXPTIME-*complete.*

Proof. It is known that the complement of an NFA B is constructed in exponential time. Moreover, $L(A) \subseteq L(B)$ if and only if $L(A) \cap L(B)^c = \emptyset$, and we can compute the intersection $L(A) \cap L(B)^c$ in polynomial-time in the sizes of A and the NFA for $L(B)^c$. Hence, the inclusion problem from NIDPDAs to NFAs is decidable in EXPTIME.

For the EXPTIME-hardness, we reduce the membership problem of linear-space alternating Turing machine (ATM) M, which is to decide whether M accepts a given string w over an alphabet Σ with the tape of size linear in $|w|$. The membership problem on an ATM is known to be EXPTIME-complete [4].

We make a language L of strings that encode every valid accepting computation of M on the given input w of length n. Let $M = (Q, \Sigma, \delta, q_0, g)$ be a linear-space ATM, where Q is a finite set of states, Σ is an input alphabet, $\delta : Q \times \Sigma \rightarrow 2^{Q \times \Sigma \times \{L, R\}}$ is the transition function, $q_0 \in Q$ is the initial state, $g : Q \rightarrow \{\wedge, \vee, \text{accept}, \text{reject}\}$ specifies the type of each state. Without loss of generality, we assume that existential and universal transitions of M alternate. We encode a configuration of M on $w \in \Sigma^n$ as a string of length $n + 1$ of the form $\Sigma^i q \Sigma^{n-i}$, where $q \in Q$ is a state of M. Let C_1 be the initial configuration $q_0 w$ of M on w. If the state q_0 is an existential state, an existential transition takes M to the successor configuration C_2 that contains an occurrence of a universal state q' of M.

From the configuration C_2, an universal transition of M branches into two successor configurations C_3 and C_4. We can encode such a computation tree as $C_1(C_2^R \$_l C_3(\cdots) \$_r C_4(\cdots))$, where C_i^R is the reversal of a configuration C_i. Note that '$\cdots$' after the configuration C_3 (resp., C_4) implies the substring encoding the successor configurations of C_3 (resp., C_4).

A computation of M on the input string w is *accepting* if every leaf node of the computation tree is accepting. Therefore, any string over the alphabet

$\Sigma' = \Sigma \cup Q \cup \{\$_l, \$_r, (,)\}$ encodes an accepting computation of M on w when the following four conditions are satisfied:

(i) the string encodes a tree,
(ii) the initial configuration is $q_0 w$,
(iii) the successive configurations are valid, and
(iv) every final configuration is accepting.

Then, we construct a DIDPDA A and an NFA B over Σ' that satisfy the following conditions. The DIDPDA A accepts strings that satisfy the condition (i) and a part of the condition (iii) which is about the validity of the right successor of a universal configuration (namely, from C_2 to C_4). The NFA B accepts strings that *violate* any of the conditions (ii), (iv), and a part of (iii) which is about the validity of the successor of an existential configuration (namely, from C_1 to C_2) and the left successor of a universal configuration (from C_2 to C_3).

First, we present the construction of the NFA B. It is easy to verify that we can check whether or not strings violate the condition (ii) or (iv) with a DFA of polynomial size. The DFA accepts strings that violate the condition (ii) by checking whether the sequence of first $|w| + 1$ symbols is not $q_0 w$ and strings that violate the condition (iv) by checking whether there exists a substring that corresponds to a *non-accepting* final configuration. We can also check the validity of the successive configurations (from C_1 to C_2 and from C_2 to C_3) by an NFA as follows. First, the NFA B nondeterministically guesses the position while reading the configuration C_1 (or C_2^R) in the first phase (*reading phase*) and check whether or not the corresponding part in the successive configuration C_2^R (or C_3) is valid in the second phase (*checking phase*).

In the reading phase, the NFA B reads the first configuration, say C_1, and nondeterministically guess a position where there exists an inconsistency between two configurations (C_1 and the following configuration C_2^R) considering the transition function δ of M. Since we only need to compare at most three symbols to check the inconsistency, we only need a polynomial number of states to remember the sub-configuration consisting of three symbols. In the checking phase, B goes to the position where we nondeterministically guessed in the reading phase and compare (at most) three symbols to check whether the successive configurations are valid. By taking the union of these NFAs, we construct the desired NFA B which still has polynomially many states.

The DIDPDA A construction is rather simple. Note that '(' and the symbols that encode a universal configuration (C_2) are push symbols, and ')' and the symbols for a right successor (C_4) are pop symbols. We can deterministically validate the input string by pushing '(' and following symbols that encode C_2, letting the subtree rooted at C_3 be processed recursively, reading $\$_r$ that indicates the starting of right successor, compare C_4 using the stack symbols that pushed while reading C_2, and pop '(' while reading ')'.

From the constructions, we can see that the intersection of $L(B)^c$ and $L(A)$ contains only the strings that encode valid accepting computations of M on a given string w, thus checking the intersection emptiness is EXPTIME-hard.

Since $L(B)^c \cap L(A) = \emptyset$ and $L(A) \subseteq L(B)$ are logically equivalent, the inclusion problem from DIDPDAs to NFAs is EXPTIME-hard.   □

Next, we consider the case when the source language is deterministic context-free and the target language is non-regular. If the target language is also deterministic context-free, then the inclusion problem is already proved to be undecidable [10].

We improve the current undecidability result by showing that the undecidability holds even when the target is an input-driven language.

Theorem 4. *Given a DPDA A and a DIDPDA B, the problem of deciding whether or not $L(A) \subseteq L(B)$ is undecidable.*

Proof. Let $M = (Q, \Sigma, \delta, q_0, F)$ be a linear bounded automaton (LBA). A *valid computation* of M is a string $w_1 \# w_2^R \# w_3 \# w_4^R \cdots \in (\Sigma \cup Q \cup \{\#\})^*$ such that

(i) each w_i is a configuration of M of the form $\Sigma^* q \Sigma^*$ for a state $q \in Q$,
(ii) w_1 is the initial configuration of the form $q_0 w$ for the input string $w \in \Sigma^*$,
(iii) w_n is a final configuration of the form $\Sigma^* q_f \Sigma^*$ for a final state $q_f \in F$, and
(iv) w_{i+1} is a successor configuration of w_i by the transition function δ for $1 \leq i < n$.

Without loss of generality, '#' is a border symbol in neither Q nor Σ. We construct a DPDA A and a DIDPDA B that accept strings $x_1 \# x_2 \# \cdots \# x_m \# \in (\Sigma \cup Q \cup \{\#\})^*$.

We use A to check the validity of two consecutive configurations x_i and x_{i+1} for odd i's and B for even i's. The important thing is that the symbols encoding the ith configuration for even i's should be call symbols and the symbols for odd i's should be return symbols of B. Therefore, we need to use two disjoint sets of symbols to encode configurations. We make a copy (denoted by $\overline{\Sigma}$ and $\overline{Q}$) of Σ and Q of M. We make a disjoint copy of $\Sigma \cup Q$ and denote it by $\overline{\Sigma} \cup \overline{Q}$. Then, we use $\Sigma \cup Q$ to encode the configurations in even positions and use $\overline{\Sigma} \cup \overline{Q}$ to encode configurations in odd positions.

The DPDA A also checks if x_1 is the initial configuration. We can also check if x_m is a final configuration by A or B depending on m being odd or even, respectively. It is immediate from the construction that $L(A) \cap L(B)$ is the set of all valid computations of M. Since the class of input-driven languages is closed under complement, we can compute a DIDPDA B' for $L(B)^c$ and $L(A) \subseteq L(B')$ implies that there is no valid computation of M and, thus, $L(M)$ is empty. Since the emptiness problem of LBAs is undecidable, the inclusion problem from DPDAs to DIDPDAs is also undecidable.   □

Using a simple modification of the proof of Theorem 4, we also establish:

Corollary 5. *Given a DPDA A and a DIDPDA B, the problem of deciding whether or not $L(B) \subseteq L(A)$ is undecidable.*

5   Relative Edit-Distance Problem

Recall that the relative edit-distance problem is a generalization of the inclusion problem in the sense that the relative edit-distance problem with zero threshold is the inclusion problem. Hence, every lower bound for the complexity or the decidability of the inclusion problem naturally carries over to the relative edit-distance problem.

First, we show that the relative edit-distance problem from NIDPDAs to NFAs is in EXPTIME. Our EXPTIME algorithm is based on the following proposition.

Proposition 6 ([15,19]). *Let A be an NFA with n states and $r \in \mathbb{N}$. The neighbourhood of $L(A)$ of radius r can be recognized by an NFA B with $n \cdot (r+1)$ states. The NFA B can be constructed in time that depends polynomially on n and r.*

Lemma 7. *Given an NIDPDA A and an NFA B, the relative edit-distance problem from $L(A)$ to $L(B)$ is decidable in EXPTIME.*

Proof. Let n be the number of states in B. Based on Proposition 6, we construct an NFA B' with $n \cdot (r+1)$ states that recognizes the neighbourhood of $L(B)$ of radius r. Then, the size of the DFA B'' for $L(B')^c$ is $2^{n \cdot (r+1)}$ in the worst-case. We can decide $L(A) \subseteq L(B')$ by checking whether or not $L(A) \cap L(B')^c$ is empty, which is decidable in polynomial-time in the sizes of A and B''. Hence, it follows that the relative edit-distance problem is decidable in exponential time in the sizes of A and B. □

Language inclusion is a special case of the relative edit distance problem. This means that Theorem 3 implies that the relative edit-distance problem from DIDPDAs to NFAs is EXPTIME-hard. We further have the following lemma for the lower bound for the problem from DIDPDAs even to DFAs. The proof is a modification of the proof of Lemma 10 in Otop et al. [17] showing that the relative edit-distance problem from DPDAs to DFAs is EXPTIME-hard.

Lemma 8. *Given a DIDPDA A and a DFA B, the relative edit-distance problem from $L(A)$ to $L(B)$ is EXPTIME-hard.*

Proof. We reduce the inclusion problem from a DIDPDA A to an NFA B, which is EXPTIME-complete by Theorem 3. Let us change the name of the NFA B used in Theorem 3, to A_N for notational convenience.

By construction, the transition set δ_N of the NFA A_N can be partitioned into two sets $\delta_{N,1}$ and $\delta_{N,2}$ where $\delta_{N,1}$ is a function and every accepting path in A_N uses exactly one transition from the set $\delta_{N,2}$. Recall that the transitions of $\delta_{N,2}$ are used to make a nondeterministic guess of the position where two successive configurations are not valid.

For all transitions in $\delta_{N,2}$, we extend the alphabet Σ of A_N to Σ' by adding new symbols where each symbol corresponds to a transition in $\delta_{N,2}$.

Namely, $\Sigma' = \Sigma \cup \{\diamond_{(q,a,p)} \mid (q,a,p) \in \delta_{N,2}\}$. After then, we replace the character used in the transition of $\delta_{N,2}$ by the corresponding symbol to make A_N deterministic. For instance, if there is a transition (q,a,p) in $\delta_{N,2}$, then we replace the transition by $(q, \diamond_{(q,a,p)}, p)$. It is easy to verify that the resulting NFA A_D does not have nondeterministic transition anymore.

Note that every string accepted by the DFA A_D is different from the corresponding original string in $L(A_N)$ at exactly one position. This in turn implies that, for every string w in $L(A)$, there exists a string in $L(A_D)$ which is different from w at exactly one position. Hence, $L(A) \subseteq L(A_N)$ (over Σ) is reduced to $d_{\mathsf{rel}}(L(A), L(A_D)) \leq 1$ (over Σ'). Since the inclusion problem is EXPTIME-complete, the relative edit-distance problem is EXPTIME-hard. $\qquad\square$

From Lemmas 7 and 8, we prove that the following theorem holds.

Theorem 9. *Given an NIDPDA (or a DIDPDA) A and an NFA (or a DFA) B, the relative edit-distance problem from $L(A)$ to $L(B)$ is EXPTIME-complete.*

Recently, Okhotin and Salomaa [16] showed that the class of input-driven languages is closed under the edit distance neighbourhood operation. In other words, the neighbourhood of an input-driven language is still an input-driven language. They presented a neighbourhood automaton construction of size $O(nm^r)$, where n is the number of states of an input IDPDA, m is the number of stack symbols, and $r \in \mathbb{N}$ is the radius of the neighbourhood. In their construction, they only considered two basic operations—insertion and deletion—for constructing its neighbourhood. We revise the construction to cope with substitution and establish the following result.

Lemma 10. *Let A be an NIDPDA with m states and n stack symbols. The neighbourhood of $L(A)$ of radius one can be recognized by an NIDPDA with $O(mn^2)$ states and $n + 1$ stack symbols.*

By iteratively applying the construction in the proof of Lemma 10, we establish the following descriptional complexity for the complete edit-distance neighbourhood of the input-driven languages.

Lemma 11. *Given an NIDPDA A of m states and n stack symbols and a nonnegative integer $r \in \mathbb{N}$, it is possible to construct an NIDPDA B recognizing the neighbourhood of $L(A)$ of radius r in size $O(m \cdot (n + r)^{2r})$.*

We have to mention that there is a very recent result by Geffert et al. [7] on the descriptional complexity of IDPDAs for the complete edit-distance neighbourhood. For the radius r neighbourhood of an NIDPDA with m states and n stack symbols Geffert et al. [7] construct an NIDPDA with $O(mr \cdot n^{2r})$ states and $2n + 1$ stack symbols. The upper bound is slightly better than the bound given by Lemma 11. Both constructions yield the same EXPTIME upper bound for the complexity of deciding the relative edit-distance problem of NIDPDAs.

Based on the NIDPDA construction of the edit-distance neighbourhood of $L(A)$, we obtain the EXPTIME upper bound on the complexity of the relative edit-distance problem for two NIDPDAs.

Lemma 12. *Given two NIDPDAs A and B, the relative edit-distance problem from $L(B)$ to $L(A)$ is decidable in* EXPTIME.

Proof. We can construct an NIDPDA A' recognizing the radius r neighbourhood of $L(A)$ in polynomial time in the size of A as r is fixed by the problem definition. Then, the relative edit-distance problem from $L(B)$ to $L(A)$ is equivalent to the problem of deciding whether or not $L(B) \subseteq L(A')$.

Since $L(B) \subseteq L(A')$ if and only if $L(B) \cap L(A')^c \neq \emptyset$, we obtain the complement of $L(A')$ and decide whether or not the intersection between $L(B)$ and $L(A')^c$ is empty. Note that the problem belongs to EXPTIME since the size of the neighbourhood automaton is polynomial in the size of A and only the complementation of $L(A')$ involves exponential blow-up in size. □

Following Lemmas 8 and 12, we have the tight complexity bound for the relative edit-distance problem as follows:

Theorem 13. *Given two NIDPDAs A and B, the relative edit-distance problem from $L(B)$ to $L(A)$ is* EXPTIME-*complete.*

Finally, we mention that the relative edit-distance problem from DPDAs to DIDPDAs is undecidable following the undecidability of the inclusion problem in Theorem 4.

Corollary 14. *Given a DIDPDA A and a DPDA B, the relative edit-distance problem from $L(B)$ to $L(A)$ is undecidable.*

6 Conclusions

The class of input-driven languages is interesting both from theoretical and practical viewpoints since many computational problems are decidable whereas the same problems are undecidable even for deterministic context-free languages. We have investigated the unknown computational complexity results regarding the inclusion problem, which is one of the most fundamental problems in formal verification. Moreover, we have considered a more general version of the inclusion problem called the relative edit-distance problem that is relaxed by allowing a fixed number of errors.

For the inclusion problem, we have proved that the problem between IDPDAs and PDAs (or DPDAs) is undecidable and the problem from NFAs to NIDPDAs is EXPTIME-complete. We also have established that the relative edit-distance problem is EXPTIME-complete if both languages are input-driven, and undecidable if one of the languages is deterministic context-free.

References

1. Alur, R., Madhusudan, P.: Visibly pushdown languages. In: Proceedings of the 36th Annual ACM Symposium on Theory of Computing, pp. 202–211 (2004)

2. Benedikt, M., Puppis, G., Riveros, C.: Bounded repairability of word languages. J. Comput. Syst. Sci. **79**(8), 1302–1321 (2013)
3. Bourhis, P., Puppis, G., Riveros, C., Staworko, S.: Bounded repairability for regular tree languages. ACM Trans. Database Syst. **41**(3), 18:1–18:45 (2016)
4. Chandra, A.K., Kozen, D.C., Stockmeyer, L.J.: Alternation. J. ACM **28**(1), 114–133 (1981)
5. Choffrut, C., Pighizzini, G.: Distances between languages and reflexivity of relations. Theor. Comput. Sci. **286**(1), 117–138 (2002)
6. Deza, M.M., Deza, E.: Encyclopedia of Distances, pp. 1–583. Springer, Heidelberg (2009). https://doi.org/10.1007/978-3-642-00234-2_1
7. Geffert, V., Bednárová, Z., Szabari, A.: Input-driven pushdown automata for edit distance neighborhood. In: Hofman, P., Skrzypczak, M. (eds.) DLT 2019. LNCS, vol. 11647, pp. 113–126. Springer, Cham (2019)
8. Han, Y.-S., Ko, S.-K.: Edit-distance between visibly pushdown languages. In: Steffen, B., Baier, C., van den Brand, M., Eder, J., Hinchey, M., Margaria, T. (eds.) SOFSEM 2017. LNCS, vol. 10139, pp. 387–401. Springer, Cham (2017). https://doi.org/10.1007/978-3-319-51963-0_30
9. Han, Y.S., Ko, S.K., Salomaa, K.: The edit-distance between a regular language and a context-free language. Int. J. Found. Comput. Sci. **24**(7), 1067–1082 (2013)
10. Hopcroft, J.E., Ullman, J.D.: Introduction to Automata Theory, Languages, and Computation, 2nd edn. Addison-Wesley, Reading (1979)
11. Ko, S.K., Han, Y.S., Salomaa, K.: Approximate matching between a context-free grammar and a finite-state automaton. Inf. Comput. **247**, 278–289 (2016)
12. Levenshtein, V.I.: Binary codes capable of correcting deletions, insertions, and reversals. Sov. Phys. Dokl. **10**(8), 707–710 (1966)
13. Mehlhorn, K.: Pebbling mountain ranges and its application to DCFL-recognition. In: de Bakker, J., van Leeuwen, J. (eds.) ICALP 1980. LNCS, vol. 85, pp. 422–435. Springer, Heidelberg (1980). https://doi.org/10.1007/3-540-10003-2_89
14. Mohri, M.: Edit-distance of weighted automata: general definitions and algorithms. Int. J. Found. Comput. Sci. **14**(6), 957–982 (2003)
15. Ng, T., Rappaport, D., Salomaa, K.: State complexity of neighbourhoods and approximate pattern matching. In: Proceedings of the 19th International Conference on Developments in Language Theory, pp. 389–400 (2015)
16. Okhotin, A., Salomaa, K.: Edit distance neighbourhoods of input- driven pushdown automata. Theor. Comput. Sci. (2019). https://doi.org/10.1016/j.tcs.2019.03.005
17. Otop, J., Ibsen-Jensen, R., Henzinger, T.A., Chatterjee, K.: Edit distance for pushdown automata. Log. Methods Comput. Sci. **13** (2017)
18. Pevzner, P.A.: Computational Molecular Biology - An Algorithmic Approach. MIT Press, Cambridge (2000)
19. Povarov, G.: Descriptive complexity of the Hamming neighborhood of a regular language. In: Proceedings of the 1st International Conference on Language and Automata Theory and Applications, pp. 509–520 (2007)
20. Thompson, K.: Regular expression search algorithm. Commun. ACM **11**(6), 419–422 (1968)
21. Wagner, R.A., Fischer, M.J.: The string-to-string correction problem. J. ACM **21**, 168–173 (1974)
22. Wood, D.: Theory of Computation. Harper & Row, New York (1987)

On Shrinking Restarting Automata of Window Size One and Two

František Mráz[1] and Friedrich Otto[2]([✉])

[1] Faculty of Mathematics and Physics, Department of Computer Science,
Charles University, Malostranské nám. 25, 118 00 Prague 1, Czech Republic
`frantisek.mraz@mff.cuni.cz`
[2] Fachbereich Elektrotechnik/Informatik, Universität Kassel, 34109 Kassel, Germany
`f.otto@uni-kassel.de`

Abstract. Here we study the expressive power of shrinking RWW- and RRWW-automata the window size of which is just one or two. We show that for shrinking RRWW-automata that are nondeterministic, window size one suffices, while for nondeterministic shrinking RWW-automata, we already need window size two to accept all growing context-sensitive languages. In the deterministic case, shrinking RWW- and RRWW-automata of window size one accept only regular languages, while those of window size two characterize the Church-Rosser languages. In addition, we study shrinking RWW- and RRWW-automata of window size one that are monotone.

Keywords: Restarting automaton · Weight function · Language class · Window size

1 Introduction

The restarting automaton was introduced in [3] as a formal model for the linguistic technique of 'analysis by reduction'. A restarting automaton, RRWW-automaton for short, is a device M that consists of a finite-state control, a flexible tape containing a word delimited by sentinels, and a read/write window of fixed finite size. This window is moved along the tape by move-right steps until the control decides (nondeterministically) that the contents of the window should be rewritten by some *shorter* string. In fact, the new string may contain auxiliary symbols that do not belong to the input alphabet. After a rewrite, M can continue to move its window until it either halts and accepts, or halts and rejects, or restarts, which means that it places its window over the left end of the tape and reenters its initial state. It follows that each computation of M can be described through a sequence of cycles and a tail computation, where a cycle is a part of a computation that begins after a restart step (or by the first step from an initial configuration) and that ends with the next restart step, and the tail is the part of a computation that begins after the last restart step, that is,

© Springer Nature Switzerland AG 2019
P. Hofman and M. Skrzypczak (Eds.): DLT 2019, LNCS 11647, pp. 140–153, 2019.
https://doi.org/10.1007/978-3-030-24886-4_10

it ends with either an accept step or with M getting stuck in a configuration to which no transition applies.

By requiring that an RRWW-automaton always performs a restart step immediately after executing a rewrite operation, we obtain the so-called RWW-automaton. Within any cycle such an automaton cannot scan the suffix of the tape contents that is to the right of the position at which the rewrite operation is performed. Although the definition of the RWW-automaton is clearly much more restricted than that of the RRWW-automaton, it is a long-standing open problem whether the class of languages $\mathcal{L}(\mathsf{RWW})$ accepted by RWW-automata coincides with the class of languages $\mathcal{L}(\mathsf{RRWW})$ accepted by RRWW-automata.

In order to investigate the relationship between RWW- and RRWW-automata, a generalization of the restarting automaton, called *shrinking restarting automaton*, was introduced in [5]. A shrinking restarting automaton M is defined just like an RRWW-automaton with the one exception that it is no longer required that each rewrite step $u \to v$ of M must be length-reducing. Instead there must exist a weight function ω that assigns a positive integer $\omega(a)$ to each letter a of M's tape alphabet Γ such that, for each rewrite step $u \to v$ of M, $\omega(u) > \omega(v)$ holds. Here the function ω is extended to a morphism $\omega : \Gamma^* \to \mathbb{N}$ as usual.

In [4] it was shown that the monotone variants (see Sect. 3) of the nondeterministic RWW- and RRWW-automaton accept exactly the context-free languages, while the corresponding deterministic automata characterize the class of deterministic context-free languages. In [17] Schluter proves that the context-free languages are already accepted by monotone RWW-automata of window size two, and in [12] a corresponding result has been established for deterministic monotone RWW-automata. In fact, these results carry over to shrinking RWW-automata (see, e.g., [16]). Further, it is shown in [17] that for nondeterministic RRWW-automata, window size two suffices, while for deterministic RWW-and RRWW-automata, which characterize the Church-Rosser languages [13,14], it is still open whether there exists an infinite ascending hierarchy of language classes based on window size. Finally, it has been noted that deterministic RWW- and RRWW-automata of window size one just accept the regular languages [6,10].

Here we study the expressive power of shrinking RWW- and RRWW-automata of window size one and two. We will see that for nondeterministic shrinking RRWW-automata, already window size one suffices. On the other hand, for nondeterministic shrinking RWW-automata, window size nine suffices, but window size one does not, as for these automata we already need window size two to accept all growing context-sensitive languages. In fact, it remains open whether window size nine is the smallest possible, that is, whether shrinking RWW-automata of window size eight are really less powerful than those of window size nine.

We also consider shrinking RWW-automata and monotone shrinking RRWW-automata of window size one and their deterministic variants. We will see that deterministic shrinking RWW- and RRWW-automata of window size one just accept the regular languages, as do the monotone shrinking

RWW-automata of window size one. However, shrinking RWW-automata and monotone shrinking RRWW-automata of window size one are strictly more expressive.

This paper is structured as follows. After presenting the necessary definitions and some notation in Sect. 2, we concentrate on monotone nondeterministic and deterministic shrinking RWW- and RRWW-automata of window size one and two in Sect. 3, and in the next section we study non-monotone automata. The paper closes with Sect. 5 in which we summarize our results using a diagram displaying all the language classes considered and state some open problems.

2   Definitions and Notation

Throughout the paper λ will denote the empty word, and $\mathbb{N}_+$ will denote the set of all positive integers, while $\mathbb{N}$ is used to denote the set of all non-negative integers. Further, for any type of automaton X, we will use the notation $\mathcal{L}(\mathsf{X})$ to denote the class of languages that are accepted by automata of type X.

A (one-way) *restarting automaton*, RRWW-automaton for short, is a one-tape machine that is described by an 8-tuple $M = (Q, \Sigma, \Gamma, \cent, \$, q_0, k, \delta)$, where Q is a finite set of states, Σ is a finite input alphabet, Γ is a finite tape alphabet containing Σ, the symbols $\cent, \$ \notin \Gamma$, called *sentinels*, serve as markers for the left and right borders of the work space, respectively, $q_0 \in Q$ is the initial state, $k \geq 1$ is the size of the *read/write window*, and

$$\delta : Q \times \mathcal{PC}^{(k)} \to \mathcal{P}((Q \times (\{\mathsf{MVR}\} \cup \mathcal{PC}^{\leq(k-1)})) \cup \{\mathsf{Restart}, \mathsf{Accept}\})$$

is the *transition relation*. Here $\mathcal{P}(S)$ denotes the powerset of the set S, $\mathcal{PC}^{(k)}$ is the set of *possible contents* of the read/write window of M, where

$$\mathcal{PC}^{(i)} := (\{\cent\} \cdot \Gamma^{i-1}) \cup \Gamma^i \cup (\Gamma^{\leq i-1} \cdot \{\$\}) \cup (\{\cent\} \cdot \Gamma^{\leq i-2} \cdot \{\$\}) \quad (i \geq 0),$$

and

$$\Gamma^{\leq n} := \bigcup_{i=0}^{n} \Gamma^i \quad \text{and} \quad \mathcal{PC}^{\leq(k-1)} := \bigcup_{i=0}^{k-1} \mathcal{PC}^{(i)}.$$

For any contents $u \in \mathcal{PC}^{(k)}$ of the read/write window and a state $q \in Q$, the transition relation $\delta(q, u)$ can contain four different types of transition steps:

1. A *move-right step* is of the form $(q', \mathsf{MVR}) \in \delta(q, u)$, where $q' \in Q$ and $u \neq \$$. If M is in state q and sees the string u in its read/write window, then this move-right step causes M to shift the read/write window one position to the right and to enter state q'. However, if the contents u of the read/write window is only the symbol $\$$, then no shift to the right is possible.
2. A *rewrite step* is of the form $(q', v) \in \delta(q, u)$, where $q' \in Q$, $u \neq \$$, and $v \in \mathcal{PC}^{\leq(k-1)}$ such that $|v| < |u|$. It causes M to replace the contents u of the read/write window by the string v, thereby shortening the tape, and to enter state q'. Further, the read/write window is placed immediately to the

right of the string v. However, some additional restrictions apply in that the sentinels ¢ and \$ must not disappear from the tape nor that new occurrences of these symbols are created.

3. A *restart step* is of the form Restart $\in \delta(q, u)$. It causes M to place the read/write window over the left end of the tape, so that the first symbol it sees is the left sentinel ¢, and to reenter the initial state q_0.

4. An *accept step* of the form Accept $\in \delta(q, u)$ causes M to halt and accept.

If $\delta(q, u) = \emptyset$ for some $q \in Q$ and $u \in \mathcal{PC}^{(k)}$, then M necessarily halts when it is in state q with the string u in its window, and we say that M *rejects* in this situation. There is one additional restriction that the transition relation must satisfy. This restriction says that, when ignoring move operations, *rewrite steps and restart steps alternate* within any computation of M, with a rewrite step coming first.

A *configuration* of M can be described by a string $\alpha q \beta$, where $q \in Q$, and either $\alpha = \lambda$ and $\beta \in \{¢\} \cdot \Gamma^* \cdot \{\$\}$ or $\alpha \in \{¢\} \cdot \Gamma^*$ and $\beta \in \Gamma^* \cdot \{\$\}$; here q represents the current state, $\alpha\beta$ is the current contents of the tape, and it is understood that the window contains the first k symbols of β or all of β when $|\beta| \leq k$. A *restarting configuration* is of the form $q_0 ¢ w \$$, where $w \in \Gamma^*$; if $w \in \Sigma^*$, then $q_0 ¢ w \$$ is an *initial configuration*. Thus, initial configurations are a particular type of restarting configurations.

A phase of a computation of M, called a *cycle*, begins with a restarting configuration, the window moves along the tape performing MVR operations and a single rewrite operation until a restart operation is performed and, thus, a new restarting configuration is reached. Hence, a computation consists of a sequence of cycles that is followed by a *tail*, which is the part of a computation that comes after the last restart operation. By $\vdash_M^c$ we denote the relation on restarting configurations that is induced through the execution of a cycle, and we use $\vdash_M^{c*}$ to denote its reflexive and transitive closure. The above restriction on the transition relation implies that M performs *exactly one* rewrite operation during each cycle – thus each new phase starts on a shorter word than the previous one, and that it executes at most one rewrite operation during a tail computation.

An input word $w \in \Sigma^*$ is *accepted* by M, if there is a computation which, starting with the initial configuration $q_0 ¢ w \$$, finishes by executing an accept step. By $L(M)$ we denote the language consisting of all (input) words accepted by M; we say that M *accepts the language* $L(M)$.

In general, an RRWW-automaton is nondeterministic, that is, for some pairs (q, u), there may be more than one applicable transition step. If this is not the case, then the automaton is deterministic. We use the prefix det- to denote classes of deterministic restarting automata.

An *RWW-automaton* is an RRWW-automaton that is required to execute a restart step immediately after performing a rewrite step. Accordingly, for RWW-automata we combine a rewrite step with the subsequent restart step into a single *combined rewrite/restart step* to simplify the notation:

– A *combined rewrite/restart step* is of the form $v \in \delta(q, u)$, where $q, q' \in Q$, $u \in \mathcal{PC}^{(k)}$, $u \neq \$$, and $v \in \mathcal{PC}^{\leq(k-1)}$ such that $|v| < |u|$. It causes M to replace the contents u of the read/write window by the string v, thereby shortening the tape, to place the read/write window over the left end of the tape, so that the first symbol it sees is the left sentinel ¢, and to reenter the initial state q_0.

The size of the read/write window is an essential parameter of a restarting automaton. For each $k \geq 1$, we use the notation $X(k)$ to denote those restarting automata of type X that have a read/write window of size k.

Recall that the computation of a restarting automaton proceeds in cycles, where each cycle contains exactly one rewrite step. Thus, each cycle C contains a unique configuration of the form $\alpha q \beta$ in which a rewrite step is applied. Now $|\beta|$ is called the *right distance* of C, which is denoted by $D_r(C)$.

A sequence of cycles $S = (C_1, C_2, \ldots, C_n)$ is called *monotone* if $D_r(C_1) \geq D_r(C_2) \geq \cdots \geq D_r(C_n)$. A computation is *monotone*, if the corresponding sequence of cycles is monotone. Observe that here the tail of the computation is not taken into account. Finally, a restarting automaton is called *monotone*, if all its computations that start with an initial configuration are monotone. The prefix mon- is used to denote the various classes of monotone restarting automata.

The following result is an extension of the characterization of the (deterministic) context-free languages by (deterministic) monotone restarting automata that is presented in [4].

Theorem 1 [12, 17]
(a) CFL $= \mathcal{L}(\text{mon-RWW}(2))$ $= \mathcal{L}(\text{mon-RRWW}(2))$.
(b) DCFL $= \mathcal{L}(\text{det-mon-RWW}(2)) = \mathcal{L}(\text{det-mon-RRWW}(2))$.

Concerning window size one, the following results are known.

Theorem 2 [6, 10]
(a) REG $= \mathcal{L}((\text{mon-})\text{RWW}(1)) = \mathcal{L}(\text{det-(mon-)}\text{RRWW}(1))$.
(b) REG $\subsetneq \mathcal{L}(\text{mon-RRWW}(1)) \subsetneq$ CFL.

Thus, window size one restricts the expressive power of monotone deterministic and non-deterministic RWW- and RRWW-automata considerably.

3   On Monotone Shrinking Restarting Automata

The shrinking restarting automaton, which was introduced in [5], is a generalized type of restarting automaton. A *shrinking restarting automaton* M is defined just like an RRWW-automaton with the one exception that it is no longer required that each rewrite step $u \to v$ of M must be length-reducing. Instead there must exist a weight function ω that assigns a positive integer $\omega(a)$ to each letter a of M's tape alphabet Γ such that, for each rewrite step $u \to v$ of M, $\omega(u) > \omega(v)$ holds. Here the function ω is extended to a morphism $\omega : \Gamma^* \to \mathbb{N}$ by taking $\omega(\lambda) = 0$ and $\omega(wa) = \omega(w) + \omega(a)$ for all words $w \in \Gamma^*$ and all letters $a \in \Gamma$.

We will use the notation sRRWW and sRWW to denote shrinking RRWW- and RWW-automata.

It has been observed that the simulations of monotone RRWW-automata by pushdown automata presented in [4] extend to shrinking RRWW-automata, both in the nondeterministic as well as in the deterministic case [16]. Thus, we immediately obtain the following result from Theorem 1.

Corollary 3 [12,17]
(a) CFL $= \mathcal{L}(\text{mon-sRWW}(2))$ $= \mathcal{L}(\text{mon-sRRWW}(2))$.
(b) DCFL $= \mathcal{L}(\text{det-mon-sRWW}(2)) = \mathcal{L}(\text{det-mon-sRRWW}(2))$.

Next we study monotone sRWW- and sRRWW-automata of window size one. Concerning the former we have the following result which extends the corresponding result for monotone RWW(1)-automata.

Theorem 4. $\mathcal{L}(\text{mon-sRWW}(1)) = \text{REG}$.

Proof. This result can be proved by using a construction that turns a monotone sRWW(1)-automaton M into a stateless ORWW-automaton M_s such that $L(M_s) = L(M)$. Here an ORWW-automaton is an sRWW(3)-automaton the rewrite steps of which just replace the symbol in the middle of the window by a smaller letter, that is, by a letter with less weight. These ORWW-automata have been studied in [8,9]. An ORWW-automaton is called stateless, if it has no other states but the initial one. It is known that stateless ORWW-automata just accept the regular languages [8]. □

For monotone sRRWW(1)-automata, we have the following result.

Theorem 5. REG $\subsetneq \mathcal{L}(\text{mon-RRWW}(1)) \subsetneq \mathcal{L}(\text{mon-sRRWW}(1))$.

Proof. Let $M = (Q, \{a, b\}, \{a, b\}, \mathcal{c}, \$, q_0, 1, \delta)$ be the RRWW(1)-automaton that is defined by taking $Q = \{q_0, q_1, q_2, p_0, p_1, p_2\}$ and by defining the transition relation δ as follows:

(1) $\delta(q_0, \mathcal{c}) = \{(q_0, \text{MVR})\}$,
(2) $\delta(q_0, \$) = \{\text{Accept}\}$,
(3) $\delta(q_0, a) = \{(p_0, \lambda), (q_2, \text{MVR})\}$,
(4) $\delta(q_1, a) = \{(p_2, \lambda), (q_2, \text{MVR})\}$,
(5) $\delta(q_2, a) = \{(p_1, \lambda), (q_1, \text{MVR})\}$,
(6) $\delta(p_0, \$) = \{\text{Accept}\}$,

(7) $\delta(q_1, b) = \{(p_1, \lambda)\}$,
(8) $\delta(q_2, b) = \{(p_2, \lambda)\}$,
(9) $\delta(p_1, b) = \{(p_2, \text{MVR})\}$,
(10) $\delta(p_2, b) = \{(p_1, \text{MVR})\}$,
(11) $\delta(p_2, \$) = \{\text{Restart}\}$.

We claim that $L(M) = \{\, a^m b^n \mid m \in \{n, n+1\}, n \geq 0 \,\}$, which is not a regular language. Obviously, M accepts the empty word λ and the word a. Further, it is easily seen that M only accepts words from the regular language $a^* \cdot b^*$. Now let $w = a^m b^n$ be given as input, that is, we have the initial configuration $q_0 \mathcal{c} a^m b^n \$$. If M deletes one of the first $m - 1$ occurrences of the letter a, then it gets stuck immediately thereafter. Hence, we see that M either deletes the last occurrence of the letter a or the first occurrence of the letter b, which implies that M is monotone. From the indices of the states used, we see that to complete a cycle through the restart operation (11), M must delete the last occurrence of the letter a, if m and n do not have the same parity mod 2, and M must delete the first occurrence of the letter b, if m and n have the same parity mod 2. Indeed, if m is even, then depending on the parity of n, we have the following cycles:

$$q_0 \mathcal{c} a^{2r} b^{2s+1} \$ \vdash_M^{2r} \mathcal{c} a^{2r-1} q_2 a b^{2s+1} \$ \vdash_M \mathcal{c} a^{2r-1} p_1 b^{2s+1} \$$$
$$\vdash_M^{2s+1} \mathcal{c} a^{2r-1} b^{2s+1} p_2 \$ \vdash_M q_0 \mathcal{c} a^{2r-1} b^{2s+1} \$,$$

or

$$q_0 \mathcal{c} a^{2r} b^{2s} \$ \vdash_M^{2r+1} \mathcal{c} a^{2r} q_1 b^{2s} \$ \vdash_M \mathcal{c} a^{2r} p_1 b^{2s-1} \$$$
$$\vdash_M^{2s-1} \mathcal{c} a^{2r} b^{2s-1} p_2 \$ \vdash_M q_0 \mathcal{c} a^{2r} b^{2s-1} \$,$$

and analogously for the case that m is uneven. Further, in each of these cases, if another occurrence of the letter b is added, in this way changing the relative parities of a's and b's, then M reaches the right sentinel while being in state p_1, and hence, it gets stuck. It follows that $L(M) = L_2'$.

By replacing the first letter a by an auxiliary letter a' and verifying that the number of a's has the same parity mod 2 as the number of b's on the tape during the first cycle, the monotone RRWW(1)-automaton above is turned into a monotone sRRWW(1)-automaton for the language $L_2 = \{\, a^m b^m \mid m \geq 0 \,\}$. However, it is easily seen that this language is not accepted by any RRWW(1)-automaton. □

In fact, even the language $L_{\mathrm{pal},c} = \{\, wcw^R \mid w \in \{a,b\}^* \,\}$ of marked palindromes is accepted by a monotone sRRWW(1)-automaton. Currently it remains open whether all context-free languages can be accepted by monotone sRRWW-automata of window size one.

4   On Non-monotone Shrinking Restarting Automata

In [5] the following result has been established, where FA denotes the class of finite-change automata from [18]. A *finite-change automaton* is a nondeterministic linear-bounded automaton that does not change the contents of any tape cell more than r times during any accepting computation, where $r \geq 1$ is a constant.

Theorem 6 [5]. $\mathcal{L}(\mathsf{FA}) = \mathcal{L}(\mathsf{sRWW}) = \mathcal{L}(\mathsf{sRRWW})$.

In the proof of Lemma 17 in [5] it is shown that a finite-change automaton A can be simulated by an sRRWW-automaton M of window size one. In fact, the sRRWW(1)-automaton M just performs rewrites that replace a single letter by another single letter. Hence, M can be interpreted as an ordered RRWW-automaton (ORRWW-automaton) as defined in [7]. These are sRRWW-automata that have a window of size three, but the rewrite steps of which just replace the symbol in the middle of the window by a smaller letter, that is, by a letter of less weight. This yields the following consequence.

Corollary 7. $\mathcal{L}(\mathsf{FA}) = \mathcal{L}(\mathsf{sRRWW}(1)) = \mathcal{L}(\mathsf{ORRWW})$.

The simulation of an sRRWW-automaton of window size k by an sRWW-automaton given in [5] yields that the latter has window size $\max\{2k, 9\}$, which gives the following result.

Corollary 8. $\mathcal{L}(\mathsf{FA}) = \mathcal{L}(\mathsf{sRWW}(9))$.

It remains open whether sRWW-automata of window size $k \in \{2, 3, \ldots, 8\}$ are really less expressive than finite-change automata. However, concerning sRWW(1)-automata we have the following result. Recall that an ORWW-automaton is an sRWW(3)-automaton the rewrite steps of which just replace the symbol in the middle of the window by a smaller letter, that is, by a letter with less weight [8, 9].

Theorem 9. REG $\subsetneq \mathcal{L}(\mathsf{sRWW}(1)) \subseteq \mathcal{L}(\mathsf{ORWW})$.

Proof. As a finite-state acceptor can be simulated by an sRWW(1)-automaton that does not use any rewrite/restart operations, REG $\subseteq \mathcal{L}(\mathsf{sRWW}(1))$. To prove that this is a proper inclusion, we consider the example language $L_{\geq} = \{a^{m+n}b^n \mid m, n \geq 0\}$, which is easily seen to be a deterministic context-free language that is not regular. An sRWW(1)-automaton $M_{\geq} = (Q, \{a, b\}, \Gamma, \mathord{\mathrm{c}}, \$, q_0, 1, \delta)$ for this language can be defined by taking $Q = \{q_0, q_1, q_2, p_0, p_1, p_2\}$, $\Gamma = \{a, b, a_1, a_2, a_3, b_1, b_2\}$, and by defining the transition relation δ as follows:

(1) $\delta(q_0, \mathord{\mathrm{c}}) = \{(q_0, \mathsf{MVR})\}$,
(2) $\delta(q_0, \$) = \{\mathsf{Accept}\}$,
(3) $\delta(q_0, a) = \{a_1\}$,
(4) $\delta(q_0, a_1) = \{(q_1, \mathsf{MVR}), a_2\}$,
(5) $\delta(q_0, a_2) = \{(q_2, \mathsf{MVR}), a_3\}$,
(6) $\delta(q_0, a_3) = \{(q_0, \mathsf{MVR})\}$,
(7) $\delta(q_0, b_2) = \{(p_0, \mathsf{MVR})\}$,
(8) $\delta(p_0, b_2) = \{(p_0, \mathsf{MVR})\}$,
(9) $\delta(p_0, \$) = \{\mathsf{Accept}\}$,
(10) $\delta(q_1, a) = \{(q_1, \mathsf{MVR})\}$,
(11) $\delta(q_1, b) = \{b_1\}$,
(12) $\delta(q_1, b_2) = \{(p_1, \mathsf{MVR})\}$,
(13) $\delta(q_1, \$) = \{\mathsf{Accept}\}$,
(14) $\delta(q_2, a) = \{(q_2, \mathsf{MVR})\}$,
(15) $\delta(q_2, b_1) = \{b_2\}$,
(16) $\delta(q_2, b_2) = \{(p_2, \mathsf{MVR})\}$,
(17) $\delta(p_1, b_2) = \{(p_1, \mathsf{MVR})\}$,
(18) $\delta(p_1, b) = \{b_1\}$,
(19) $\delta(p_1, \$) = \{\mathsf{Accept}\}$,
(20) $\delta(p_2, b_2) = \{(p_2, \mathsf{MVR})\}$,
(21) $\delta(p_2, b_1) = \{b_2\}$.

From the form of the transitions it is easily seen that $M_{\geq}$ performs an accepting tail computation iff the tape contents is of the form $z = a_3^m b_2^n$ for some $m, n \geq 0$ or of the form $a_3^m a_1 a^r b_2^n$ for some $m, n, r \geq 0$. Thus, the corresponding input is of the form $a^s b^t$ for some $s, t \geq 0$. During an accepting computation on an input of this form, the occurrences of the letter a are rewritten, from left to right, first into a_1, then into a_2, and finally into a_3. Analogously, the occurrences of the letter b are rewritten, from left to right, first into b_1 and then into b_2. However, an occurrence of b can only be rewritten into b_1 if in that cycle, the rightmost occurrence of the letter a that has already been rewritten happens to be an a_1, and an occurrence of b_1 can only be rewritten into b_2 if in that cycle, the rightmost occurrence of the letter a that has already been rewritten happens to be an a_2. It follow that $s \geq t$, that is, $L(M_{\geq}) = L_{\geq}$. Thus, REG is indeed a proper subclass of $\mathcal{L}(\mathsf{sRWW}(1))$.

Next we prove that each $\mathsf{sRWW}(1)$-automaton can be simulated by an ORWW-automaton. Let $M = (Q, \Sigma, \Gamma, \mathcal{c}, \$, q_0, 1, \delta)$ be an $\mathsf{sRWW}(1)$-automaton that is compatible with the weight function $\varphi : \Gamma \to \mathbb{N}_+$, and let $c = \max\{ \varphi(X) \mid X \in \Sigma \}$. Without loss of generality we can assume that M only accepts with its read/write window on the right sentinel $\$$.

We define an ORWW-automaton $M_o = (Q, \Sigma, \Delta, \mathcal{c}, \$, q_0, 3, \delta_o, >)$ as follows. First let $\Delta = \Sigma \cup \{ [\alpha] \mid \alpha \in \Gamma^*, \varphi(\alpha) \leq c \}$. Here the symbol $[\alpha]$ encodes the word $\alpha \in \Gamma^*$, where the weight $\varphi(\alpha)$ is bounded by the constant c. As the weight of each letter $a \in \Gamma$ is positive, we see that there are only finitely many words from Γ^* with weight bounded from above by c. Hence, Δ is indeed a finite alphabet. We define a morphism $\psi : \Delta^* \to \Gamma^*$ through $\psi(a) = a$ for all $a \in \Sigma$ and $\psi([\alpha]) = \alpha$ for all $[\alpha] \in \Delta \smallsetminus \Sigma$, and we define the partial ordering $>$ on Δ by taking, for all $a, b \in \Sigma$, $a > [a]$, and for all $x, y \in \Delta \smallsetminus \Sigma$, $x > y$ if $\varphi(\psi(x)) > \varphi(\psi(y))$. Finally we specify the transition relation δ_o as follows, where $\vdash_{\mathrm{MVR}}$ denotes the single-step computation relation that is induced by the MVR steps of M, $a, b \in \Sigma$, $u, v, z, \alpha, \gamma \in \Gamma^*$, $\omega \in \Delta$, $X, Y \in \Gamma$, and $q, q_1, q_2 \in Q$:

(1) $\delta_o(q_0, \mathcal{c}\$) \quad = \{\mathsf{Accept}\}$, if $q_0 \mathcal{c}\$ \vdash_{\mathrm{MVR}} \mathcal{c} q_1 \$$ and $\delta(q_1, \$) = \{\mathsf{Accept}\}$,

(2) $\delta_o(q_0, \mathcal{c}a\$) \quad = \{\mathcal{c}[a]\$\}$,

(3) $\delta_o(q_0, \mathcal{c}[u]\$) \quad = \{\mathsf{Accept}\}$, if $q_0 \mathcal{c} u \$ \vdash_{\mathrm{MVR}}^{|u|+1} \mathcal{c} u q_1 \$$ and $\delta(q_1, \$) = \{\mathsf{Accept}\}$,

(4) $\delta_o(q_0, \mathcal{c}[uXv]\$) \ni \mathcal{c}[uzv]\$$, if $q_0 \mathcal{c} u X v \$ \vdash_{\mathrm{MVR}}^{|u|+1} \mathcal{c} u q_1 X v \$$ and $\delta(q_1, X) \ni z$,

(5) $\delta_o(q_0, \mathcal{c}ab) \quad = \{\mathcal{c}[a]b\}$,

(6) $\delta_o(q_0, \mathcal{c}[u]\omega) \ni (q_1, \mathsf{MVR})$, if $q_0 \mathcal{c} u \psi(\omega) \vdash_{\mathrm{MVR}}^{|u|+1} \mathcal{c} u q_1 \psi(\omega)$,

(7) $\delta_o(q_0, \mathcal{c}[uXv]\omega) \ni \mathcal{c}[uzv]\omega$, if $q_0 \mathcal{c} u X v \vdash_{\mathrm{MVR}}^{|u|+1} \mathcal{c} u q_1 X v$ and $\delta(q_1, X) \ni z$,

(8) $\delta_o(q_1, [\alpha]ab) \quad = \{[\alpha][a]b\}$,

(9) $\delta_o(q_1, [\alpha][u]\omega) \ni (q_2, \mathsf{MVR})$, if $q_1 u \psi(\omega) \vdash_{\mathrm{MVR}}^{|u|} u q_2 \psi(\omega)$,

(10) $\delta_o(q_1, [\alpha][uXv]\omega) \ni [\alpha][uzv]\omega$, if $q_1 u X v \vdash_{\mathrm{MVR}}^{|u|} u q_2 X v$ and $\delta(q_2, X) \ni z$,

(11) $\delta_o(q_1, [\alpha]a\$) \quad = \{[\alpha][a]\$\}$,

(12) $\delta_o(q_1, [\alpha][u]\$) \quad = \{\mathsf{Accept}\}$, if $q_1 u \$ \vdash_{\mathrm{MVR}}^{|u|} u q_2 \$$ and $\delta(q_2, \$) = \{\mathsf{Accept}\}$,

(13) $\delta_o(q_1, [\alpha][uXv]\$) \ni [\alpha][uzv]\$$, if $q_1 u X v \vdash_{\mathrm{MVR}}^{|u|} u q_2 X v$ and $\delta(q_2, X) \ni z$.

All rewrite steps of M_o do either replace an input letter a by the auxiliary letter $[a]$ or they simulate a rewrite step of M on some auxiliary symbol. Hence, each rewrite step replaces a letter by a smaller one with respect to the partial ordering $>$. Thus, we see that M_o is indeed an ORWW-automaton.

It remains to prove that M_o accepts the same language as M. It is easily seen from the definition of δ_o that M_o accepts on input λ iff M accepts on input λ. So let $w = a_1 a_2 \cdots a_n$ be given as input, where $n \geq 1$ and $a_1, a_2, \ldots, a_n \in \Sigma$. Assume that $w \in L(M)$, that is, M has an accepting computation on input w.

As M only accepts with its read/write window on the right sentinel $\$$, this computation looks as follows:

$$q_0 \mathbb{c} w \$ = q_0 \mathbb{c} a_1 a_2 \cdots a_n \$ \vdash^c_M q_0 \mathbb{c} w_1 \$ \vdash^c_M q_0 \mathbb{c} w_2 \$$$
$$\vdash^c_M \quad \cdots \quad \vdash^c_M q_0 \mathbb{c} w_m \$ \vdash^+_{MVR} \mathbb{c} w_m q_+ \$ \vdash_M \text{Accept},$$

where $q_+ \in Q$, $\delta(q_+, \$) = \{\text{Accept}\}$, and $w_1, w_2, \ldots, w_m \in \Gamma^*$. As M is shrinking and has window size one, each word w_i can be factored as $w_i = u_{i,1} u_{i,2} \cdots u_{i,n}$, where $u_{i,j}$ is the factor of w_i that is obtained from the input letter a_j by those rewrite steps in the above computation that have been applied to a_j and to the j-th factors of $w_2, w_3, \ldots, w_{i-1}$.

Now the ORWW-automaton M_o proceeds as follows. On input $w = a_1 a_2 \cdots a_n$, it replaces each letter a_j by the auxiliary symbol $[a_j]$ using instructions (2), (5), (8), and (11). Then it simulates the cycles of M by performing the rewrite steps from M's computation within the corresponding auxiliary symbols, that is, if in a cycle

$$q_0 \mathbb{c} w_i \$ = q_0 \mathbb{c} u_{i,1} u_{i,2} \cdots u_{i,j-1} u_{i,j} u_{i,j+1} \cdots u_{i,n} \$$$
$$\vdash^c_M q_0 \mathbb{c} u_{i,1} u_{i,2} \cdots u_{i,j-1} u_{i+1,j} u_{i,j+1} \cdots u_{i,n} \$$$
$$= q_0 \mathbb{c} w_{i+1} \$$$

the factor $u_{i,j}$ is rewritten into the factor $u_{i+1,j}$, then M_o executes the cycle

$$q_0 \mathbb{c} w'_i \$ = q_0 \mathbb{c} [u_{i,1}][u_{i,2}] \cdots [u_{i,j-1}][u_{i,j}][u_{i,j+1}] \cdots [u_{i,n}] \$$$
$$\vdash^c_M q_0 \mathbb{c} [u_{i,1}][u_{i,2}] \cdots [u_{i,j-1}][u_{i+1,j}][u_{i,j+1}] \cdots [u_{i,n}] \$$$
$$= q_0 \mathbb{c} w'_{i+1} \$$$

by rewriting the letter $[u_{i,j}]$ into the letter $[u_{i+1,j}]$, using one of the instructions (4), (7), (10), and (13). Here it is possible that some of the factors $u_{i,j+1}$ to $u_{i,n}$ are just input letters that have not yet been rewritten by M_o into auxiliary symbols. Finally, as

$$q_0 \mathbb{c} w_m \$ = q_0 \mathbb{c} u_{m,1} u_{m,2} \cdots u_{m,n} \$ \vdash^*_{MVR} \mathbb{c} u_{m,1} u_{m,2} \cdots u_{m,n} q_+ \$$$

and $\delta(q_+, \$) = \{\text{Accept}\}$, M_o can execute an accepting tail computation starting from the configuration

$$q_0 \mathbb{c} w'_m \$ = q_0 \mathbb{c} [u_{m,1}][u_{m,2}] \cdots [u_{m,n}] \$$$

using instructions (3), (6), (9), and (12).

Conversely, it is easily seen that each accepting computation of M_o is just the simulation of an accepting computation of M. Thus, $L(M_o) = L(M)$ follows, which completes the proof of Theorem 9. $\square$

The technique used in the construction of the sRWW(1)-automaton for the language $L_\geq$ can easily be extended to show that also the following language

$$L'_{\text{copy}} = \{ w \# u \mid w, u \in \{a, b\}^*, |w|, |u| \geq 2, u \text{ is a scattered subword of } w \}$$

is accepted by an sRWW(1)-automaton. In [8] it is shown that this language is not even growing context-sensitive.

Based on a pumping lemma for ORWW-automata, it is shown in [9] that the deterministic linear language $L = \{ a^n b^n \mid n \geq 0 \}$ is not accepted by any ORWW-automaton. Thus, $\mathcal{L}(\text{ORWW})$ is clearly a proper subclass of $\mathcal{L}(\text{sRWW}) = \mathcal{L}(\text{FA})$. It remains open whether the inclusion $\mathcal{L}(\text{sRWW}(1)) \subseteq \mathcal{L}(\text{ORWW})$ is proper.

Now we turn to sRWW-automata of window size two. We will see that these automata accept all growing context-sensitive languages. The growing context-sensitive languages (GCSL) are generated by growing grammars, that is, a language $L \subseteq \Sigma^*$ is *growing context-sensitive* if it is generated by a grammar $G = (N, \Sigma, S, P)$ such that, for each production $(\ell \to r) \in P$, $\ell = S$ or $|\ell| < |r|$ (see, e.g., [2]), but they have also been characterized by shrinking two-pushdown automata (sTPDA) in [1]. Based on this characterization and the fact that GCSL $\subsetneq \mathcal{L}(\text{sRWW}) = \mathcal{L}(\text{FA})$, the following inclusion result can be derived.

Theorem 10. GCSL $\subsetneq \mathcal{L}(\text{sRWW}(2))$.

Proof. As the language L'_{copy} mentioned above is accepted by an sRWW(1)-automaton, we see that $\mathcal{L}(\text{sRWW}(2))$ contains a language that is not growing context-sensitive. On the other hand, it can be shown that each sTPDA can be simulated by an sRWW(2)-automaton.   □

Further, it is easily seen that each ORWW-automaton can be simulated by an sRWW(2)-automaton, that is, we also have the following proper inclusion.

Corollary 11. $\mathcal{L}(\text{ORWW}) \subsetneq \mathcal{L}(\text{sRWW}(2))$.

Finally, we consider deterministic sRWW- and sRRWW-automata. The construction in the second part of the proof of Theorem 9 carries over to the deterministic case, and it can easily be extended to simulate a det-sRRWW(1)-automaton by a det-ORRWW-automaton. As det-ORRWW-automata and det-ORRWW-automata only accept regular languages (see [7,11]), we obtain the following results.

Theorem 12. (a) $\mathcal{L}(\text{det-sRWW}(1)) = \mathcal{L}(\text{det-ORWW}) = \text{REG}$.
(b) $\mathcal{L}(\text{det-sRRWW}(1)) = \mathcal{L}(\text{det-ORRWW}) = \text{REG}$.

Also the simulation of an sTPDA by an sRWW(2)-automaton in the proof of Theorem 10 carries over to the deterministic case. As deterministic sTPDAs characterize the class CRL of Church-Rosser languages [15], this yields the following result.

Corollary 13. $\mathcal{L}(\text{det-sRWW}(2)) = \mathcal{L}(\text{det-sRRWW}(2)) = \text{CRL}$.

5   Conclusion

We have studied the expressive power of shrinking restarting automata of small window size. We have seen that for sRRWW-automata, already window size one suffices, while for monotone and/or deterministic sRWW- and sRRWW-automata, window size two is required to obtain the full expressive power of these types of automata. In particular, we have seen that for deterministic shrinking RWW- and RRWW-automata, the hierarchy based on window size consists of only two levels: window size one yields the regular languages, and window size $k \geq 2$ yields the Church-Rosser languages. The corresponding question is still open for deterministic RWW- and RRWW-automata (see [12]). Also it remains open whether sRWW(1)-automata are as powerful as ORWW-automata, whether window size nine is really needed to obtain the full power of

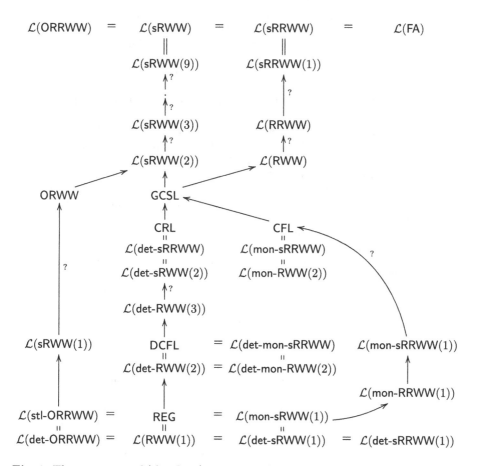

Fig. 1. The taxonomy of (shrinking) restarting automata with small window size. An arrow $\rightarrow$ denotes a proper inclusion, while $\rightarrow^?$ denotes an inclusion which is not known to be proper.

sRWW-automata, and whether monotone sRRWW(1)-automata accept all context-free languages. The diagram in Fig. 1 summarizes the characterizations and inclusion relations that we have obtained for (shrinking) restarting automata of small window size.

References

1. Buntrock, G., Otto, F.: Growing context-sensitive languages and Church-Rosser languages. Inf. Comput. **141**, 1–36 (1998)
2. Dahlhaus, E., Warmuth, M.: Membership for growing context-sensitive grammars is polynomial. J. Comput. Syst. Sci. **33**, 456–472 (1986)
3. Jančar, P., Mráz, F., Plátek, M., Vogel, J.: Restarting automata. In: Reichel, H. (ed.) FCT 1995. LNCS, vol. 965, pp. 283–292. Springer, Heidelberg (1995). https://doi.org/10.1007/3-540-60249-6_60
4. Jančar, P., Mráz, F., Plátek, M., Vogel, J.: On monotonic automata with a restart operation. J. Aut. Lang. Comb. **4**, 287–311 (1999)
5. Jurdziński, T., Otto, F.: Shrinking restarting automata. Int. J. Found. Comput. Sci. **18**, 361–385 (2007)
6. Kutrib, M., Reimann, J.: Succinct description of regular languages by weak restarting automata. In: Loos, R., Fazekas, S., Martin-Vide, C. (eds.) Preproc., LATA 2007, pp. 343–354. Report 35/07, Research Group on Mathematical Linguistics, Universitat Rovira i Virgili, Tarragona (2007)
7. Kwee, K., Otto, F.: On ordered RRWW-automata. In: Brlek, S., Reutenauer, C. (eds.) DLT 2016. LNCS, vol. 9840, pp. 268–279. Springer, Heidelberg (2016). https://doi.org/10.1007/978-3-662-53132-7_22
8. Kwee, K., Otto, F.: On the effects of nondeterminism on ordered restarting automata. In: Freivalds, R.M., Engels, G., Catania, B. (eds.) SOFSEM 2016. LNCS, vol. 9587, pp. 369–380. Springer, Heidelberg (2016). https://doi.org/10.1007/978-3-662-49192-8_30
9. Kwee, K., Otto, F.: Nondeterministic ordered restarting automata. Int. J. Found. Comput. Sci. **29**, 663–685 (2018)
10. Mráz, F.: Lookahead hierarchies of restarting automata. J. Aut. Lang. Comb. **6**, 493–506 (2001)
11. Mráz, F., Otto, F.: Ordered restarting automata for picture languages. In: Geffert, V., Preneel, B., Rovan, B., Štuller, J., Tjoa, A.M. (eds.) SOFSEM 2014. LNCS, vol. 8327, pp. 431–442. Springer, Cham (2014). https://doi.org/10.1007/978-3-319-04298-5_38
12. Mraz, F., Otto, F.: Window size two suffices for deterministic monotone RWW-automata. In: Freund, R., Holzer, M., Sempere, J. (eds.) Proceedings of NCMA 2019, books@ocg.at, vol. 336, pp. 139–154. Österreichische Computer Gesellschaft, Wien (2019)
13. Niemann, G., Otto, F.: Restarting automata, Church-Rosser languages, and representations of r.e. languages. In: Rozenberg, G., Thomas, W. (eds.) Proceedings of DLT 1999, pp. 103–114. World Scientific, Singapore (2000)
14. Niemann, G., Otto, F.: Further results on restarting automata. In: Ito, M., Imaoka, T. (eds.) Words, Languages and Combinatorics III, Proceedings, pp. 352–369. World Scientific, Singapore (2003)
15. Niemann, G., Otto, F.: The Church-Rosser languages are the deterministic variants of the growing context-sensitive languages. Inf. Comput. **197**, 1–21 (2005)

16. Otto, F.: On shrinking restarting automata. In: Freund, R., Mráz, F., Průša, D. (eds.) Proceedings of NCMA 2017, books@ocg.at, vol. 329, pp. 181–195. Österreichische Computer Gesellschaft, Wien (2017)
17. Schluter, N.: Restarting automata with auxiliary symbols restricted by lookahead size. Int. J. Comput. Math. **92**, 908–938 (2015)
18. von Braunmühl, B., Verbeek, R.: Finite-change automata. In: Weihrauch, K. (ed.) GI-TCS 1979. LNCS, vol. 67, pp. 91–100. Springer, Heidelberg (1979). https://doi.org/10.1007/3-540-09118-1_11

The Teaching Complexity of Erasing Pattern Languages with Bounded Variable Frequency

Ziyuan Gao[✉]

Department of Mathematics, National University of Singapore,
10 Lower Kent Ridge Road, Singapore 119076, Republic of Singapore
matgaoz@nus.edu.sg

Abstract. Patterns provide a concise, syntactic way of describing a set of strings, but their expressive power comes at a price: a number of fundamental decision problems concerning (erasing) pattern languages, such as the membership problem and inclusion problem, are known to be NP-complete or even undecidable, while the decidability of the equivalence problem is still open; in learning theory, the class of pattern languages is unlearnable in models such as the distribution-free (PAC) framework (if $\mathcal{P}/poly \neq \mathcal{NP}/poly$). Much work on the algorithmic learning of pattern languages has thus focussed on interesting subclasses of patterns for which positive learnability results may be achieved. A natural restriction on a pattern is a bound on its variable frequency – the maximum number m such that some variable occurs exactly m times in the pattern. This paper examines the effect of limiting the variable frequency of all patterns belonging to a class Π on the worst-case minimum number of labelled examples needed to uniquely identify any pattern of Π in cooperative teaching-learning models. Two such models, the teaching dimension model as well as the preference-based teaching model, will be considered.

1 Introduction

In the context of this paper, a *pattern* is a string made up of symbols from two disjoint sets, a countable set X of *variables* and an alphabet Σ of *constants*. The *non-erasing pattern language* generated by a pattern π is the set of all words obtained by substituting nonempty words over Σ for all the variables in π, under the condition that for any variable, all of its occurrences in π must be replaced with the same word; the *erasing pattern language* generated by π is defined analogously, the only difference being that the variables in π may be replaced with the empty string. Unless stated otherwise, all pattern languages in the present paper refer to erasing pattern languages. In computational learning theory, the non-erasing pattern languages were introduced by Angluin [3] as a motivating example for her work on the identification of uniformly decidable families of languages in the limit. Shinohara [28] later introduced the class of

© Springer Nature Switzerland AG 2019
P. Hofman and M. Skrzypczak (Eds.): DLT 2019, LNCS 11647, pp. 154–167, 2019.
https://doi.org/10.1007/978-3-030-24886-4_11

erasing pattern languages, proving that the class of all such languages generated by *regular* patterns (patterns in which every variable occurs at most once) is polynomial-time learnable in the limit. Patterns and allied notions – such as that of an extended regular expression [1,8,13,26], which has more expressive power than a pattern – have also been studied in other fields, including word combinatorics and pattern matching. For example, the membership problem for pattern languages is closely related to the problem of matching 'patterns' with variables (based on various definitions of 'pattern') in the pattern matching community [2,6,9–11].

The present paper considers the problem of uniquely identifying pattern languages from labelled examples – where a labelled example for a pattern language L is a pair $(w, *)$ such that $*$ is "+" if w belongs to L and "−" otherwise – based on formal teaching-learning models. We shall study two such models in the computational learning theory literature: the well-known teaching dimension (TD) model [16,27] and the preference-based teaching (PBT) model [15] (c.f. Sect. 3). Given a model $\mathcal{T}$ and any class Π of patterns to be learnt, the maximum size of a sample (possibly ∞) needed for a learner to successfully identify any pattern in Π based on the teaching-learning algorithm of $\mathcal{T}$ is known as the teaching complexity of Π (according to $\mathcal{T}$). The broad question we try to partly address is: what properties of the patterns in a given class Π of patterns influence the teaching complexity of Π according to the TD and PBT models? More specifically, let Π_m be a class of patterns π such that the maximum number of times any single variable occurs in π (known here as the *variable frequency* of π) is at most m; how does the teaching complexity of Π_m vary with m? The variable frequency of a pattern is quite a natural parameter that has been investigated in other problems concerning pattern languages. For example, Matsumoto and Shinohara [21] established an upper bound on the query complexity of learning (non-erasing) pattern languages in terms of the variable frequency of the pattern and other parameters; Fernau and Schmid [12] proved that the membership problem for patterns remains NP-complete even when the variable frequency is restricted to 2 (along with other parameter restrictions).

In this paper, one motivation for concentrating on the variable frequency of a pattern rather than, say, the number of distinct variables occurring in the pattern, comes from examining the teaching complexity of some basic patterns. Take the constant pattern 0, where 0 is a letter in the alphabet Σ of constants. The language generated by this pattern cannot be finitely distinguished (i.e., distinguished using a finite set of labelled examples) from every other pattern language, even only those generated by a pattern with at most one variable. Indeed, any finite set $\{(0, +), (w_1, -), \ldots, (w_k, -)\}$ of labelled examples for the pattern 0 is also consistent with the pattern $0x^m$ where $m = \max_{1 \leq i \leq k} |w_i|$. The latter observation depends crucially on the fact that a variable may occur any number of times in a pattern, and less so on the number of distinct variables occurring in a pattern. A similar remark applies to the pattern languages generated by patterns with a constant part of length at least 2 [7, Theorem 3]. On the other hand, if one were to teach the singleton language $\{0\}$ w.r.t. all languages generated by patterns with variable frequency at most k for some fixed

k, then a finite distinguishing set for $\{0\}$ could consist of $(0, +)$ plus all negative examples $(0^n, -)$ with $2 \le n \le k + 1$. This seems to suggest that the maximum variable frequency of the patterns in a class of patterns may play a crucial role in determining whether or not the languages generated by members of this class are finitely distinguishable.

The first section of this work studies the teaching complexity of *simple block-regular* patterns, which are equivalent to patterns of the shape $x_1 a_1 x_2 a_2 \ldots a_{n-1} x_n$, where $x_1, \ldots, x_n$ are distinct variables and $a_1, \ldots, a_{n-1}$ are constants. They make up one of the simplest, non-trivial classes of patterns that have a restriction on the variable frequency. Bayeh et al. [7] showed that over alphabets of size at least 4, the languages generated by such patterns are precisely those that are finitely distinguishable; we refine this result by determining, over any alphabet, the TD and PBT dimensions of the class of simple block-regular patterns. Further, we calculate the TD of these patterns w.r.t. the class of regular patterns and provide an asymptotic lower bound for the TD of any given simple block-regular pattern w.r.t. the whole class of patterns. In the subsequent section, we proceed to the more general problem of determining, for various natural classes Π of patterns that have a uniformly bounded variable frequency, those members of Π that are finitely distinguishable. It will be proven that all m-quasi-regular patterns (i.e. every variable of the pattern occurs exactly m times) and m-regular (i.e. every variable occurs at most m times) non-cross patterns are finitely distinguishable w.r.t. the class of m-quasi-regular and m-regular non-cross patterns respectively; moreover, the TD of the class of m-regular non-cross patterns is even finite and in fact sublinear in m. Next, we present partial results on the problem of determining the subclass of m-regular patterns that have a finite TD. Over any infinite alphabet, *every* m-regular pattern is finitely distinguishable – contrasting quite sharply with the previously mentioned theorem that over alphabets with at least 4 letters, the only patterns with a finite TD are the simple block-regular ones. Over binary alphabets, on the other hand, there are patterns that are not finitely distinguishable even when the variable frequency is restricted to 4.

Due to space constraints, most proofs have been omitted. The full version of the paper is available at https://arxiv.org/pdf/1905.07737.pdf.

2   Preliminaries

$\mathbb{N}_0$ denotes the set of natural numbers $\{0, 1, 2, \ldots\}$ and $\mathbb{N} = \mathbb{N}_0 \setminus \{0\}$. Let $X = \{x_1, x_2, x_3, \ldots\}$ be an infinite set of variable symbols. An alphabet is a finite or countably infinite set of symbols, disjoint from X. Fix an alphabet Σ. A *pattern* is a nonempty finite string over $X \cup \Sigma$. The class of patterns over any alphabet Σ with $z = |\Sigma|$ is denoted by Π^z; this notation reflects the fact that all the properties of patterns and classes of patterns considered in the present work depend only on the size of the alphabet and not on the actual letters of the alphabet. The *erasing pattern language* $L(\pi)$ generated by a pattern π over Σ consists of all strings generated from π when replacing variables in π with any string over Σ, where all occurrences of a single variable must be replaced by the same string [28]. Patterns π and τ over Σ are said to be *equivalent* iff $L(\pi) = L(\tau)$; they are *similar* iff $\pi = \alpha_1 u_1 \alpha_2 u_2 \ldots u_n \alpha_n$ and $\tau = \beta_1 u_1 \beta_2 u_2 \ldots u_n \beta_n$ for some $u_1, u_2, \ldots, u_n \in \Sigma^+$ and $\alpha_1, \ldots, \alpha_n, \beta_1, \ldots, \beta_n \in X^*$. Unless specified otherwise, we identify any pattern π belonging to a class Π of patterns with every other $\pi' \in \Pi$ such that $L(\pi) = L(\pi')$. $\text{Var}(\pi)$ (resp. $\text{Const}(\pi)$) denotes the set of all distinct variables (resp. constant symbols) occurring in π.

For any symbol a and $n \in \mathbb{N}_0$, a^n denotes the string equal to n concatenated copies of a. For any alphabets A and B, a *morphism* is a function $h : A^* \to B^*$ with $h(uv) = h(u)h(v)$ for all $u, v \in A^*$. A *substitution* is a morphism $h : (\Sigma \cup X)^* \to \Sigma^*$ with $h(a) = a$ for all $a \in \Sigma$. By abuse of notation, we will often use the same symbol h to represent the morphism $(X \cup \Sigma)^* \mapsto \Sigma^*$ that coincides with the substitution h on individual variables and with the identity function on letters from Σ. $\mathcal{I}_{h,\pi}$ denotes the mapping of closed intervals of positions of π to closed intervals of positions of $h(\pi)$ induced by h; $\pi(\varepsilon)$ denotes the word obtained from π by substituting ε for every variable in π. Let $\sqsubseteq$ denote the *subsequence* relation on Σ^*: $u \sqsubseteq v$ holds iff there are numbers $i_1 < i_2 < \ldots < i_{|u|}$ such that $v_{i_j} = u_j$ for all $j \in \{1, \ldots, |u|\}$. Given any $u, v \in \Sigma^*$, the *shuffle product* of u and v, denoted by $u \sqcup\!\sqcup v$, is the set $\{u_1 v_1 u_2 v_2 \ldots u_k v_k : u_i, v_i \in \Sigma^* \land u_1 u_2 \ldots u_k = u \land v_1 v_2 \ldots v_k = v\}$. Given any $A, B \subseteq \Sigma^*$, the *shuffle product* of A and B, denoted by $A \sqcup\!\sqcup B$, is the set $\bigcup_{u \in A \land v \in B} u \sqcup\!\sqcup v$. If $A = \{u\}$, we will often write $A \sqcup\!\sqcup B$ as $u \sqcup\!\sqcup B$.

3   Teaching Dimension and Preference-Based Teaching Dimension

Machine teaching focusses on the problem of designing, for any given learning algorithm, an optimal training set for every concept belonging to a class of concepts to be learnt [29]. Such a training set is sometimes known as a *teaching set*. In this work, an "optimal" teaching set for a pattern π is one that has the minimum number of examples labelled consistently with π needed for the algorithm to successfully identify π (up to equivalence). We study the design of optimal teaching sets for various classes of pattern languages w.r.t. (i) the classical *teaching dimension* model [16,27], where it is only assumed that the learner's hypotheses are always consistent with the given teaching set; (ii) the *preference-based teaching* model [15], where the learner has, for any given concept class, a particular "preference relation" on the class, and the learner's hypotheses are always not only consistent with the given teaching set, but also not less preferred to any other concept in the class w.r.t. the preference relation.

Fix an alphabet Σ. Let Π be any class of patterns, and suppose $\pi \in \Pi$. A *teaching set for* π *w.r.t.* Π is a set $T \subseteq \Sigma \times \{+, -\}$ that is consistent with π but with no other pattern in Π (up to equivalence), that is, $w \in L(\pi)$ for all $(w, +) \in T$ and $w \notin L(\pi)$ for all $(w, -) \in T$. The *teaching dimension of* π *w.r.t.* Π, denoted by $\text{TD}(\pi, \Pi)$ is defined as $\text{TD}(\pi, \Pi) = \inf\{|T| : T \text{ is a teaching set for } \pi \text{ w.r.t. } \Pi\}$. Furthermore, if $\Pi' \subseteq \Pi$, then the *teaching dimension of* Π' *w.r.t.* Π, denoted by $\mathrm{TD}(\Pi',\Pi)$, is defined as $\mathrm{TD}(\Pi',\Pi) = \sup\{\mathrm{TD}(\pi,\Pi) : \pi \in \Pi'\}$. The *teaching dimension of* Π, denoted by $\mathrm{TD}(\Pi)$, is defined as $\mathrm{TD}(\Pi,\Pi)$.

In real-world learning scenarios, even the smallest possible teaching set for a given concept relative to some concept class may be impractically large. Learning algorithms often make predictions based on a set of assumptions known as the *inductive bias*, which may allow the algorithm to infer a target concept from a small set of data even when there is more than one concept in the class that is consistent with the data. Certain types of bias impose an a priori preference ordering on the learner's hypothesis space; for example, an algorithm that adheres to the Minimum Description Length (MDL) principle favours hypotheses that have shorter descriptions based on some given description language. The preference-based teaching model, to be defined shortly, considers learning algorithms with an inductive bias that specifies a preference ordering of the learner's hypotheses.

Let $\prec$ be a *strict partial order* on Π, i.e., $\prec$ is asymmetric and transitive. The partial order that makes every pair $\pi, \pi' \in \Pi$ (where $L(\pi) \neq L(\pi')$) incomparable is denoted by $\prec_\emptyset$. For every $\pi \in \Pi$, let $\Pi_{\prec\pi} = \{\pi' \in \Pi : \pi' \prec \pi\}$ be the set of patterns over which π is strictly preferred (as mentioned earlier, equivalent patterns are identified with each other). A *teaching set for* π *w.r.t.* $(\Pi, \prec)$ is defined as a teaching set for π w.r.t. $\Pi \setminus \Pi_{\prec\pi}$. Furthermore define $\mathrm{PBTD}(\pi, \Pi, \prec) = \inf\{|T| : T$ is a teaching set for π w.r.t. $(\Pi, \prec)\} \in \mathbb{N}_0 \cup \{\infty\}$. The number $\mathrm{PBTD}(\Pi, \prec) = \sup_{\pi \in \Pi} \mathrm{PBTD}(\pi, \Pi, \prec) \in \mathbb{N}_0 \cup \{\infty\}$ is called the *teaching dimension of* $(\Pi, \prec)$. The *preference-based teaching dimension of* Π is given by $\mathrm{PBTD}(\Pi) = \inf\{\mathrm{PBTD}(\Pi, \prec) : \prec$ is a strict partial order on $\Pi\}$. For all pattern classes Π and Π' with $\Pi' \subseteq \Pi$, $K(\Pi') \leq K(\Pi)$ for $K \in \{\mathrm{TD}, \mathrm{PBTD}\}$ (i.e. the TD and PBTD are monotonic) and $\mathrm{PBTD}(\Pi) \leq \mathrm{TD}(\Pi)$ [15].

4   Simple Block-Regular Patterns

Fix an alphabet Σ of size $z \leq \infty$. A pattern $\pi \in \Pi^z$ is said to be *simple block-regular* if it is of the shape $X_1 a_1 X_2 a_2 \ldots a_{n-1} X_n$, where $X_1, \ldots, X_n \in X^+$, $a_1, \ldots, a_{n-1} \in \Sigma$, and for all $i \in \{1, \ldots, n\}$, X_i contains a variable that does not occur in any other variable block X_j with $j \neq i$. Every simple block-regular pattern is equivalent to a pattern π' of the shape $y_1 a_1 y_2 a_2 \ldots a_k y_{k+1}$, where $k \geq 0$, $a_1, a_2, \ldots, a_k \in \Sigma$ and $y_1, y_2, \ldots, y_{k+1}$ are $k+1$ distinct variables [17, Theorem 6(b)]. $\mathrm{SR}\Pi^z$ denotes the class of all simple block-regular patterns in Π^z. $\mathrm{SR}\Pi^z$ is a subclass of the family of *regular* patterns (denoted by $\mathrm{R}\Pi^z$), which are patterns in which every variable occurs at most once.

As mentioned in the introduction, the simple block-regular patterns constitute precisely the subclass of finitely distinguishable patterns over any alphabet of size at least 4 [7, Theorem 3]. The language generated by a simple block-regular pattern is known as a *principal shuffle ideal* in word combinatorics [19, §6.1], and the family of all such languages is an important object of study in the PAC learning model [5].

The goal of this section is to determine the teaching complexity of the class of simple block-regular patterns over any alphabet Σ w.r.t. three classes: $SR\Pi^{|\Sigma|}$ itself, $R\Pi^{|\Sigma|}$ and $\Pi^{|\Sigma|}$. It will be shown that $TD(SR\Pi^{|\Sigma|}) <$ $TD(SR\Pi^{|\Sigma|}, R\Pi^{|\Sigma|}) < TD(SR\Pi^{|\Sigma|}, \Pi^{|\Sigma|})$. To this end, we introduce a uniform construction of a certain negative example for any given pattern π; this example is powerful enough to distinguish π from every simple block-regular pattern whose constant part is a proper subsequence (not necessarily contiguous) of the constant part of π.

Notation 1. *For any word $w = \delta_1^{m_1} \delta_2^{m_2} \ldots \delta_k^{m_k}$, where $\delta_1, \ldots, \delta_k \in \Sigma$ and $\delta_i \neq \delta_{i+1}$ whenever $1 \leq i < k$, $m_1, \ldots, m_k \geq 1$ and $k \geq 1$, define*

$$\widehat{w} := \underbrace{\delta_1^{m_1-1} \delta_2^{m_2} \delta_1}_{} \underbrace{\delta_2^{m_2-1} \delta_3^{m_3} \delta_2}_{} \ldots \underbrace{\delta_i^{m_i-1} \delta_{i+1}^{m_{i+1}} \delta_i}_{} \ldots \underbrace{\delta_{k-1}^{m_{k-1}-1} \delta_k^{m_k} \delta_{k-1}}_{} \delta_k^{m_k-1}. \quad (1)$$

(In particular, if $m \geq 1$, then $\widehat{\delta_1^m} = \delta_1^{m-1}$.)

Lemma 2. *Fix any $z \in \mathbb{N} \cup \{\infty\}$ and any $\pi, \tau \in SR\Pi^z$ with $\pi(\varepsilon) \neq \varepsilon$. Then $\widehat{\pi(\varepsilon)} \notin L(\pi)$. Furthermore, if $\tau(\varepsilon) \sqsubseteq \pi(\varepsilon)$, then $\widehat{\pi(\varepsilon)} \in L(\tau)$.*

Proof. Suppose $\pi(\varepsilon) = \delta_1^{m_1} \delta_2^{m_2} \ldots \delta_k^{m_k}$, where $\delta_1, \ldots, \delta_k \in \Sigma$ and $\delta_i \neq \delta_{i+1}$ whenever $1 \leq i < k$, $m_1, \ldots, m_k \geq 1$ and $k \geq 1$. That $\widehat{\pi(\varepsilon)} \notin L(\pi)$ may be argued as follows: if $k = 1$, then $\widehat{\pi(\varepsilon)} = \delta_1^{m_1-1} \sqsubset \pi(\varepsilon)$ is immediate; if $k \geq 2$, then one shows by induction that for $i = 1, \ldots, k - 1$, $\delta_1^{m_1} \delta_2^{m_2} \ldots \delta_i^{m_i} \delta_{i+1} \not\sqsubseteq$ $\underbrace{\delta_1^{m_1-1} \delta_2^{m_2} \delta_1}_{} \underbrace{\delta_2^{m_2-1} \delta_3^{m_3} \delta_2}_{} \ldots \underbrace{\delta_i^{m_i-1} \delta_{i+1}^{m_{i+1}} \delta_i}_{}$. For the second part of the lemma,

suppose $\tau(\varepsilon) = \delta_1^{n_1} \delta_2^{n_2} \ldots \delta_k^{n_k}$, where $0 \leq n_i \leq m_i$ for all $i \in \{1, \ldots, k\}$ and $n_{i_0} \leq m_{i_0} - 1$ for some least number i_0. Taking $w = \pi(\varepsilon)$ in Eq. (1), observe that $\delta_i^{n_i} \sqsubseteq \delta_i^{m_i-1} \delta_{i+1}^{m_{i+1}} \delta_i$ for all $i < i_0$, $\delta_{i_0}^{n_{i_0}} \sqsubseteq \delta_{i_0}^{m_{i_0}-1}$, and $\delta_j^{n_j} \sqsubseteq \delta_j^{m_j} \delta_{j-1} \delta_j^{m_j-1}$ for all $j > i_0$. Thus, since τ is simple block-regular, one has that $\widehat{\pi(\varepsilon)} \in L(\tau)$.   ∎

Lemma 2 now provides a tool for establishing the TD of $SR\Pi^z$.

Theorem 3. *For any $z \in \mathbb{N} \cup \{\infty\}$, $TD(SR\Pi^z) = 2$ and $PBTD(SR\Pi^z) = 1$.*

Proof. Fix any $0 \in \Sigma$. The pattern $\pi := x_1 0 x_2$ needs to be taught with at least one negative example in order to distinguish it from x_1. Suppose a teaching set for π contains $(w_1 w_2 \ldots w_k, -)$, where $w_1, \ldots, w_k \in \Sigma$. For any $m \geq 3$, $w_1 w_2 \ldots w_k \notin L(\pi')$, where $\pi' := x_1 w_1 x_2 w_2 x_3 \ldots x_k w_k x_{k+1} 0 x_{k+2} 0 \ldots 0 x_{k+m}$. Since π' is simple block-regular and $L(\pi') \neq L(\pi)$, at least one additional example is required to distinguish π from π'. Hence $TD(SR\Pi^z) \geq 2$.

Let π be any simple block-regular pattern. Since x_1 can be taught with the single example $(\varepsilon, +)$, we will suppose that $\pi(\varepsilon) \neq \varepsilon$. A teaching set for π consists of the two examples $(\pi(\varepsilon), +)$ and $(\widehat{\pi(\varepsilon)}, -)$. By Lemma 2, $(\widehat{\pi(\varepsilon)}, -)$ is consistent with π and $(\widehat{\pi(\varepsilon)}, -)$ distinguishes π from all patterns π' such that $\pi'(\varepsilon) \sqsubseteq \pi(\varepsilon)$, while $(\pi(\varepsilon), +)$ distinguishes π from all patterns π'' such that $\pi''(\varepsilon) \not\sqsubseteq \pi(\varepsilon)$.

Let $\prec$ be a preference relation on $SR\Pi^z$ such that for any $\pi, \tau \in SR\Pi^z$ with $L(\pi) \neq L(\tau)$, $\pi \prec \tau$ iff $|\pi(\varepsilon)| < |\tau(\varepsilon)|$. Every $\pi \in SR\Pi^z$ can be taught w.r.t. $(SR\Pi^z, \prec)$ using the example $(\pi(\varepsilon), +)$: for every $\tau \in SR\Pi^z$ such that $L(\tau) \neq L(\pi)$ and $\pi(\varepsilon) \in L(\tau)$, $\tau(\varepsilon) \sqsubset \pi(\varepsilon)$; thus $|\tau(\varepsilon)| < |\pi(\varepsilon)|$ and so $\pi \succ \tau$. ∎

Not surprisingly, the TD of a simple block-regular pattern is in general larger w.r.t. the whole class of regular patterns than w.r.t. the restricted class of simple block-regular patterns. It might be worth noting that a smallest teaching set for a simple block-regular pattern π need not necessarily contain $\pi(\varepsilon)$ as a positive example, as the proof of the following result shows.

Theorem 4. $TD(SR\Pi^z, R\Pi^z) = 3$.

To prove the lower bound in Theorem 4, it suffices to observe that any teaching set (w.r.t. the whole class of regular patterns) for a non-constant regular pattern not equivalent to x_1 must contain at least two positive examples and one negative example; for a very similar proof, see [7, Theorem 12.1]. We prove the upper bound. If $z = 1$, then $R\Pi^z$ is the union of $SR\Pi^z$ and all constant patterns (up to equivalence). By the proof of Theorem 3, any $\pi \in SR\Pi^z$ can be distinguished from every non-equivalent $\tau \in SR\Pi^z$ with one positive example or one positive and one negative example; to distinguish π from any constant pattern, at most one additional positive example is needed. Suppose $z \geq 2$. The proof will be split into the cases (i) $|\Sigma| = 2$ and (ii) $|\Sigma| \geq 3$.

Lemma 5. If $\pi \in SR\Pi^2$, then $TD(\pi, R\Pi^2) \leq 3$.

The basic proof idea of Lemma 5 – using positive examples to exclude certain types of constant segments of the target pattern – can also be generalised to the case $|\Sigma| \geq 3$, although the details of the construction are more tedious.

Lemma 6. Suppose $z = |\Sigma| \geq 3$. If $\pi \in SR\Pi^z$, then $TD(\pi, R\Pi^z) \leq 3$.

The next result determines upper (for $|\Sigma| \in \{1, \infty\}$) and lower (for $|\Sigma| \in \mathbb{N} \cup \{\infty\}$) bounds for the TD of any given simple block-regular pattern w.r.t. the whole class of patterns. It turns out that these bounds vary with the alphabet size.

Theorem 7. Suppose $z \in \mathbb{N} \cup \{\infty\}$ and $\pi = x_1 c_1 x_2 \ldots c_{n-1} x_n$ for some $c_1, \ldots, c_{n-1} \in \Sigma$ and $n \geq 2$. (i) If $z \in \{1, \infty\}$, then $TD(\pi, \Pi^z) \in \{1, 3\}$. (ii) If $2 \leq z < \infty$, then $TD(\pi, \Pi^z) = \Omega(|\pi|)$.

We do not know whether the lower bound given in Assertion (ii) of Theorem 7 is also an upper bound (up to numerical constant factors). In the proof of [7, Proposition 4], it was shown that the TD of every simple block-regular pattern π is $O(2^{|\pi|})$.

5   Finite Distinguishability of m-Quasi-Regular, Non-cross m-Regular and m-Regular Patterns

This section studies the problem of determining the subclass of finitely distinguishable patterns w.r.t. three classes: the m-quasi-regular patterns, the non-cross m-regular patterns, and the m-regular patterns. The first two classes are interesting from an algorithmic learning perspective as they provide natural examples of pattern language families that are learnable in the limit[1] [22,24]. The m-regular patterns are a fairly natural generalisation of the m-quasi-regular patterns; as will be seen later, the class of constant-free 4-regular patterns is not identifiable in the limit over binary alphabets, and in particular, not all m-regular patterns are finitely distinguishable over binary alphabets.

Notation 8. *Fix any $\ell \geq 0$ and $z, m \geq 1$. An ℓ-variable pattern is one that has at most ℓ distinct variables. Let $\Pi_{\ell,m}^z$ denote the class of ℓ-variable patterns π such that every variable occurs at most m times in π; if $\ell = \infty$, then there is no uniform upper bound on the number of distinct variables occurring in any $\pi \in \Pi_{\ell,m}^z$; if $m = \infty$, then there is no uniform upper bound on the number of times any variable can occur. We call every $\pi \in \Pi_{\infty,m}^z$ an m-regular pattern. $\Pi_{\infty,m,cf}^z$ denotes the class of all constant-free m-regular patterns.*

Let $QR\Pi_{\ell,m}^z$ denote the class of all ℓ-variable patterns π such that every variable of π occurs exactly m times; again, if $\ell = \infty$, then there is no uniform upper bound on the number of distinct variables occurring in any $\pi \in QR\Pi_{\ell,m}^z$. Every $\pi \in QR\Pi_{\infty,m}^z$ is known as an m-quasi-regular pattern [22]. We denote the class of constant-free m-quasi-regular patterns by $QR\Pi_{\infty,m,cf}^z$.

Mitchell [22] showed that for any $m \geq 1$, the class of m-quasi-regular pattern languages is learnable in the limit. The next theorem shows that for all $z \geq 1$, every m-quasi-regular pattern even has a finite teaching set w.r.t. $QR\Pi_{\infty,m}^z$. Thus, at least as far as m-quasi-regular patterns are concerned, version space learning with a helpful teacher is just as powerful as learning in the limit. We begin with a lemma, which states that for any given m-quasi-regular pattern π and every m-quasi-regular pattern τ with $L(\tau) \not\subseteq L(\pi)$, there is some $S \subseteq \text{Var}(\tau)$ of size at most linear in $|\text{Var}(\pi)|$ for which $L\left(\tau|_{\Sigma \cup S}\right) \not\subseteq L(\pi)$; for any $S' \subseteq X \cup \Sigma$, $\tau|_{S'}$ is the subsequence of τ obtained by deleting symbols not in S'.

Lemma 9. *Fix Σ with $z = |\Sigma| \geq 2$ and $\{0,1\} \subseteq \Sigma$. Suppose $m \geq 1$ and $\pi, \tau \in QR\Pi_{\infty,m}^z$. If $\tau(\varepsilon) = \pi(\varepsilon)$ and $L(\tau) \not\subseteq L(\pi)$, then there is some $S \subseteq \text{Var}(\tau)$ with $|S| \leq 1 + (|\pi(\varepsilon)| + m + 4) \cdot |\text{Var}(\pi)|$ such that $L\left(\tau|_{\Sigma \cup S}\right) \not\subseteq L(\pi)$.*

---

[1] Roughly speaking, a class of languages is learnable in the limit if there is a learning algorithm such that, given any infinite sequence of all positive examples for any language L in the class, the algorithm outputs a corresponding sequence of guesses for the target language (based on a representation system for the languages in the class) that converges to a fixed representation for L; this model is due to Gold [14].

Theorem 10. *If $z = 1$, then $TD(QR\Pi^z_{\infty,m}) = 3$. If $z \geq 2$, then for every $\pi \in QR\Pi^z_{\infty,m}$, $TD(\pi, QR\Pi^z_{\infty,m}) = O(2^{|\pi(\varepsilon)|} + D \cdot (|\pi(\varepsilon)| + D \cdot m)^{D \cdot m})$, where $D := \max(\{(1/m) \cdot (2 \cdot |\pi| - |\pi(\varepsilon)|), 1 + (|\pi(\varepsilon)| + m + 4) \cdot |Var(\pi)|\})$.*

Next, we show that the PBTD of the class of constant-free m-quasi-regular pattern languages is exactly 1 for large enough alphabet sizes. We establish this value by observing that if the adjacency graph of a constant-free m-quasi-regular pattern π [20, Chapter 3] has a colouring satisfying certain conditions, where each colour corresponds to a letter in the alphabet, then such a colouring can be used to construct a positive example for π that distinguishes it from all shorter constant-free m-quasi-regular patterns.

Theorem 11. *For any $z \geq 1$, $TD(QR\Pi^z_{\infty,1,cf}) = PBTD(QR\Pi^z_{\infty,1,cf}) = 0$. Suppose $m \geq 2$. If $z = |\Sigma| \geq 4m^2 + 1$, then $PBTD(QR\Pi^z_{\infty,m,cf}) = 1$.*

While the PBTD of the class of m-quasi-regular patterns remains open in full generality, we observe that over unary alphabets, the PBTD of this class is exactly 2 for any $m \geq 1$.

Proposition 12. *For any $m \geq 1$, $PBTD(QR\Pi^1_{\infty,m}) = 2$. If $z \geq 2$, then $PBTD(QR\Pi^z_{\infty,m}) \geq 2$.*

A *non-cross pattern* π is a constant-free pattern of the shape $x_0^{n_0} x_1^{n_1} \ldots x_k^{n_k}$, where $n_0, n_1, \ldots, n_k \in \mathbb{N}$. Let $NC\Pi^z_{\infty,m}$ denote the class of all non-cross patterns π over any Σ with $|\Sigma| = z$ such that every variable of π occurs at most m times. $NC\Pi^z_{\infty,\infty}$ coincides with $NC\Pi^z$, the class of all non-cross patterns. The next main result shows that for any fixed m, the TD of every pattern in $NC\Pi^z_{\infty,m}$ is not only finite, but also has a uniform upper bound depending only on m. Slightly more interestingly, the teaching complexity of $NC\Pi^z_{\infty,m}$ in the preference-based teaching model varies with the alphabet size when $m \geq 2$: over unary alphabets, the PBTD of this class is exactly linear in m, while over alphabets of size at least 2, the PBTD is exactly 1. In the following lemma, we observe certain properties of an "unambiguous" word that was constructed in [24, Lemma 13].

Lemma 13 *(Based on [24, Lemma 13]).* *Suppose $\{0,1\} \subseteq \Sigma$. Fix any $m \geq 2$, and let $\pi = x_0^{n_0} \ldots x_k^{n_k}$, where $n_0, \ldots, n_k \in \{2, \ldots, m\}$. Suppose there are positive numbers ℓ and $i_1, \ldots, i_\ell$ such that*

$$w := \underbrace{(01)^{i_1}}_{I_1} \underbrace{(001)^{i_2}}_{I_2} \ldots \underbrace{(0^j 1)^{i_j}}_{I_j} \ldots \underbrace{(0^{\ell-1} 1)^{i_{\ell-1}}}_{I_{\ell-1}} \underbrace{(0^\ell 1)^{i_\ell}}_{I_\ell} \in L(\pi), \qquad (2)$$

where, for each $j \in \{1, \ldots, \ell\}$, I_j is the closed interval of positions of w occupied by the subword $(0^j 1)^{i_j}$ as indicated with braces in Eq. (2). For each $j \in \{0, \ldots, k\}$, let J_j denote the closed interval of positions of π occupied by $x_j^{n_j}$. Let h be any substitution such that $h(\pi) = w$ and $h(x_i) \neq \varepsilon$ for all $i \in \{0, \ldots, k\}$. Then the following hold.

(i) For all $j \in \{0, \ldots, k\}$, $h(x_j)$ is of the shape $(0^{j'} 1)^{i'}$ for some $j' \in \{1, \ldots, \ell\}$ and $i' \in \{1, \ldots, i_{j'}\}$.

(ii) For each $j \in \{1, \ldots, \ell\}$, there are $g_j \in \{0, \ldots, k\}$ and $h_j \in \{0, \ldots, k - g_j\}$ such that $I_j = \coprod_{l=0}^{h_j} \mathcal{I}_{h,\pi}(J_{g_j+l})$.

Theorem 14. For all $z \in \mathbb{N} \cup \{\infty\}$, $TD(NC\Pi_{\infty,1}^z) = PBTD(NC\Pi_{\infty,1}^z) = 0$. Suppose $m \geq 2$.

(i) If $z = 1$, then $TD(NC\Pi_{\infty,m}^z) = \Theta(m)$ and $PBTD(NC\Pi_{\infty,m}^z) = \Theta(m)$.

(ii) For any $n \in \mathbb{N}_0$, let $\omega(n)$ denote the number of distinct prime factors of n and let $\Pi(n)$ denote the number of prime powers not exceeding n. If $z \geq 2$, then $\max(\{\omega(n) : n \leq m\}) \leq TD(NC\Pi_{\infty,m}^z) \leq 2 + \Pi(m - 1)$ and $PBTD(NC\Pi_{\infty,m}^z) = PBTD(NC\Pi^z) = 1$. In particular, $\max(\{\omega(n) : n \leq m\}) \leq TD(NC\Pi_{\infty,m}^z) < O\left((m - 1)^{\frac{1}{2}} \log(m - 1)\right) + \dfrac{1.25506(m - 1)}{\log(m - 1)}$.

It is possible that neither the lower bound nor the upper bound on $TD(NC\Pi_{\infty,m}^z)$ given in Theorem 14 is tight for almost all m. The proof of Theorem 14 shows that the TD of any general non-cross pattern π w.r.t. $NC\Pi_{\infty,m}^z$ (for any fixed $z \geq 2$ and $m \geq 2$) is at most 2 plus the number of maximal proper prime factors of the variable frequencies of π, but as the following example shows, this upper bound is not always sharp even for non-cross succinct patterns with three variables; a pattern π is *succinct* [22,25] iff there is no pattern τ such that $L(\tau) = L(\pi)$ and $|\tau| < |\pi|$.

Example 15. Suppose $\{0, 1\} \subseteq \Sigma$. Let $\pi = x_1^4 x_2^8 x_3^9$. There are 3 *maximal proper prime power factors* of $4, 8$ and 9, namely, $2, 4$ and 3, and so by the proof of Theorem 14, the TD of π w.r.t. $NC\Pi_{\infty,9}^{|\Sigma|}$ is at most $2 + 3 = 5$. However, π has a teaching set of size 4.

The next result exemplifies the general observation that a larger alphabet allows pattern languages to be distinguished using a relatively smaller number of labelled examples.

Theorem 16. $PBTD(\Pi^\infty) = 2$ and for any $m \geq 1$, $PBTD(\Pi_{\infty,m}^1) = \Theta(m)$.

The next series of results deal with the finite distinguishability problem for the general class of m-regular patterns. We begin with a few preparatory results. The first part of Theorem 17 gives a sufficient criterion for the inclusion of pattern languages, and it was observed by Jiang, Kinber, Salomaa and Yu [18]; the second part, due to Ohlebusch and Ukkonen [23], states that the existence of a constant-preserving morphism from π to τ (where π and τ are similar) also implies $L(\tau) \subseteq L(\pi)$ if Σ contains at least two letters that do not occur in π or τ. The second result is based on a few lemmas due to Reidenbach [25, Lemmas 4–6], adapted to the case of general patterns over an infinite alphabet.

Theorem 17 [18,23]. *Let Σ be an alphabet, and let $\pi, \tau \in \Pi^{|\Sigma|}$. Then $L(\pi) \subseteq L(\tau)$ if there exists a constant-preserving morphism $g : (X \cup \Sigma)^* \mapsto (X \cup \Sigma)^*$ with $g(\tau) = \pi$. If $|\Sigma| \geq |Const(\pi)| + 2, |\Sigma| \geq |Const(\tau)| + 2$ and π is similar to τ, then $L(\pi) \subseteq L(\tau)$ only if there exists a constant-preserving morphism $g : (X \cup \Sigma)^* \mapsto (X \cup \Sigma)^*$ with $g(\tau) = \pi$.*

Lemma 18 *(Based on [25]). Suppose $|\Sigma| = \infty$. Fix any $\pi \in \Pi^\infty$ such that π is succinct. Let $Y = \{y_1, y_2, \ldots\}$ be an infinite set of variables such that $Y \cap Var(\pi) = \emptyset$. Suppose $\tau \in \pi \sqcup Y^*$. Then $L(\tau) = L(\pi)$ iff*

(i) *For all $Y' \in Y^+$ and $\delta, \delta' \in Const(\pi)$, the following hold: (a) $Y'\delta$ is not a prefix of τ, (b) $\delta Y'$ is not a suffix of τ, (c) $\delta Y'\delta'$ is not a substring of τ;*

(ii) *There is a constant-preserving morphism $g : (X \cup \Sigma)^* \mapsto (X \cup \Sigma)^*$ such that $g(\pi) = \tau$;*

(iii) *For all constant-preserving morphisms $h : (X \cup \Sigma)^* \mapsto (X \cup \Sigma)^*$ with $h(\pi) = \tau$ and for all $x \in Var(\pi)$, if there exist $Y_1, Y_2 \in Y^*$ such that $Y_1 x Y_2$ is a substring of τ and Y_1 (resp. Y_2) is not immediately preceded (resp. succeeded) by any $y \in Y$ w.r.t. τ, then there are splittings $Y_1^1 Y_1^2$ and $Y_2^1 Y_2^2$ of Y_1 and Y_2 respectively for which $h(x) = Y_1^2 x Y_2^1$.*

The next crucial lemma shows that for any fixed $m \geq 1$, only finitely many negative examples are needed to distinguish a succinct pattern π from all patterns $\pi' \in \Pi^\infty_{\infty,m}$ obtained by shuffling π with an infinite set Y of variables such that Y and $Var(\pi)$ are disjoint.

Lemma 19. *Fix Σ with $|\Sigma| = \infty$. Suppose $k \geq 0$, $m \geq 1$ and $\pi \in \Pi^\infty_{k,m}$. Let $Y = \{y_1, y_2, \ldots\}$ be an infinite set of variables such that $Y \cap Var(\pi) = \emptyset$. Suppose $\tau \in (\pi \sqcup Y^*) \cap \Pi^\infty_{\infty,m}$. There is some $\tau' \in \Pi^\infty_{4mk+|\pi|+2,m}$ such that $\tau' = \tau|_{\Sigma \cup Var(\pi) \cup S}$ for some finite $S \subset Y$, and if $L(\pi) \subset L(\tau)$, then $L(\pi) \subset L(\tau')$.*

Theorem 20. *Suppose $m \geq 1$.*

(i) *$TD(\Pi^1_{\infty,m}) \leq 2^m + m + 1$ and for all $\pi \in \Pi^\infty_{k,m}$ with $k \geq 1$, $TD(\pi, \Pi^\infty_{\infty,m}) = O((D+1)^D)$, where $D := (4mk + |\pi| + 2) \cdot m$.*

(ii) *Let $1\Pi^z_m$ denote the class of patterns π over any alphabet of size z such that π contains at most one variable that occurs more than m times. Suppose $\pi \in 1\Pi^z_m$. If $z \geq 4$, then $TD(\pi, 1\Pi^z_m) < \infty$ only if π contains a variable that occurs more than m times or $\pi \in SR\Pi^z$. If $z = \infty$, then $TD(\pi, 1\Pi^z_m) < \infty$ if π contains a variable that occurs more than m times or $\pi \in SR\Pi^z$.*

The next result shows that over binary alphabets, even the class of constant-free 4-regular pattern languages contains patterns with infinite TD. We prove this by modifying Reidenbach's [24] proof of the non-learnability of $x_1^2 x_2^2 x_3^2$ so that every pattern constructed in the proof has variable frequency at most 4.

Theorem 21 *(Based on [24, Theorem 5]). Suppose $\pi = x_1^2 x_2^2 x_3^2$. For any $m \geq 4$, $TD(\pi, \Pi^2_{\infty,m,cf}) = \infty$.*

Remark 22. The lower bound 4 on m in Theorem 21 is tight in the sense that the TD of $\pi := x_1^2 x_2^2 x_3^2$ w.r.t. $\Pi_{\infty,3}^2$ is finite. In fact, $T := \{(\varepsilon, +), (0^2 1^2 0^2, +), (0, -), (01^2 0, -), (0^3, -), ((01)^2 (0^2 1)^2 (0^3 1)^2 (0^4 1)^2, -)\}$ is a teaching set for π w.r.t. $\Pi_{\infty,3}^2$.

6   Conclusion

Table 1 summarises some of the main results of this paper. For three types of pattern classes studied – the simple block-regular, m-quasi-regular and m-regular non-cross patterns – it was found that over any alphabet size, every pattern in the class is finitely distinguishable; in the case of simple block-regular and m-regular non-cross patterns, one also has an upper bound on the TD of the class of such patterns that is, depending on the alphabet size, constant, linear or sublinear in m. The most delicate questions appear to be those concerning the m-regular patterns for finite alphabets of size at least 2; we only know that for all $m \geq 4$, there are patterns in $\Pi_{\infty,m,cf}^2$ that are not finitely distinguishable (and even not learnable in the limit). We note that the class of non-cross patterns over any alphabet and the class of all patterns over infinite alphabets are learnable

Table 1. TD and PBTD of various pattern classes. In each entry, $m \geq 1$, the universal (resp. existential) quantifier is taken over all patterns belonging to the class in the corresponding row and Π refers to the class in the corresponding row.

	$z = 1$	$2 \leq z < \infty$	$z = \infty$
SRΠ^z	TD = 2,	TD = 2,	TD = 2,
	PBTD = 1 (Theorem 3)	PBTD = 1 (Theorem 3)	PBTD = 1 (Theorem 3)
QR$\Pi_{\infty,m}^z$	TD = 3 (Theorem 10)	$(\forall \pi)[\text{TD}(\pi, \Pi) < \infty]$ (Theorem 10)	$(\forall \pi)[\text{TD}(\pi, \Pi) < \infty]$ (Theorem 10)
	PBTD = 2 (Proposition 12)	PBTD ≥ 2 (Proposition 12)	PBTD = 2 (Proposition 12, Theorem 16)
NC$\Pi_{\infty,m}^z$	TD/PBTD = $\Theta(m), m \geq 2$, TD/PBTD = 0, $m = 1$ (Theorem 14)	TD = $o(m)$, PBTD = 1, $m \geq 2$, PBTD = 0, $m = 1$ (Theorem 14)	TD = $o(m)$, PBTD = 0, $m = 1$ (Theorem 14)
$\Pi_{\infty,m}^z$	TD = $O(2^m)$ (Theorem 20(i))	$(\exists \pi)[\text{TD}(\pi, \Pi_{\infty,4,cf}^2) = \infty]$ (Theorem 21)	$(\forall \pi)[\text{TD}(\pi, \Pi) < \infty]$ (Theorem 20(i))
	PBTD = $\Theta(m)$ (Theorem 16)	PBTD ≥ 2 (Proposition 12)	PBTD = 2 (Proposition 12, Theorem 16)

in the limit[2] [22,24], but they have relatively restricted subclasses of finitely distinguishable patterns [7, Theorems 3,10]. Thus the fact that every pattern in the m-regular versions of these classes has a finite TD suggests that the variable frequency of a pattern class may play a role in determining whether any given pattern π can be finitely distinguished from all π' such that $L(\pi') \nsubseteq L(\pi)$. On the other hand, we have seen in Theorem 20(ii) that even constant patterns cannot be finitely distinguished w.r.t. the class of patterns with at most one variable (but no uniform upper bound on the number of variable occurrences). It might be interesting to know whether there is a 'natural' class Π of m-regular patterns such that Π is learnable in the limit but $TD(\pi, \Pi) = \infty$ for some $\pi \in \Pi$. We also suspect that $TD(\Pi^\infty_{\infty,m}) = \infty$ for some $m \geq 2$ and $TD(QR\Pi^z_{\infty,m}) = \infty$ for some finite $z \geq 2$ and $m \geq 1$, but as yet do not know how to prove this.

Acknowledgements. The author was supported (as RF) by the Singapore Ministry of Education Academic Research Fund grant MOE2016-T2-1-019/R146-000-234-112. I sincerely thank Fahimeh Bayeh, Sanjay Jain and Sandra Zilles for proofreading the manuscript; their numerous suggestions for corrections and improvements (such as studying the PBTD of m-quasi-regular patterns over unary alphabets) are gratefully acknowledged. Many thanks are also due to the anonymous referees of this paper for their very helpful comments and suggestions.

References

1. Aho, A.V.: Algorithms for finding patterns in strings. In: van Leeuwen, J. (ed.) Handbook of Theoretical Computer Science. Algorithms and Complexity, vol. A, chap. 5, pp. 257–300. MIT Press, Oxford (1990)
2. Amir, A., Nor, I.: Generalized function matching. J. Disc. Algorithms 5(3), 514–523 (2007)
3. Angluin, D.: Finding patterns common to a set of strings. J. Comput. Syst. Sci. **21**, 46–62 (1980)
4. Angluin, D.: Inductive inference of formal languages from positive data. Inf. Control **45**(2), 117–135 (1980)
5. Angluin, D., Aspnes, J., Eisenstat, S., Kontorovich, A.: On the learnability of shuffle ideals. J. Mach. Learn. Res. **14**, 1513–1531 (2013)
6. Baker, B.S.: Parameterized pattern matching: algorithms and applications. J. Comput. Syst. Sci. **52**(1), 28–42 (1996)
7. Bayeh, F., Gao, Z., Zilles, S.: Erasing pattern languages distinguishable by a finite number of strings. In: ALT, pp. 72–108 (2017)
8. Campeanu, C., Salomaa, K., Yu, S.: A formal study of practical regular expressions. Int. J. Found. Comput. Sci. **14**(6), 1007–1018 (2003)
9. Day, J.D., Fleischmann, P., Manea, F., Nowotka, D.: Local patterns. In: FSTTCS, pp. 24:1–24:14 (2017)

---

[2] This implies that for every pattern π belonging to any one of these classes, $L(\pi)$ contains a finite set that distinguishes π from all π' in the class such that $L(\pi') \subset L(\pi)$ [4, Theorem 1].

10. Day, J.D., Fleischmann, P., Manea, F., Nowotka, D., Schmid, M.L.: On matching generalised repetitive patterns. In: Hoshi, M., Seki, S. (eds.) DLT 2018. LNCS, vol. 11088, pp. 269–281. Springer, Cham (2018). https://doi.org/10.1007/978-3-319-98654-8_22

11. Fernau, H., Manea, F., Mercas, R., Schmid, M.L.: Pattern matching with variables: fast algorithms and new hardness results. In: STACS, pp. 302–315 (2015)

12. Fernau, H., Schmid, M.L.: Pattern matching with variables: a multivariate complexity analysis. Inf. Comput. **242**, 287–305 (2015)

13. Freydenberger, D.D., Schmid, M.L.: Deterministic regular expressions with back-references. In: STACS, pp. 33:1–33:14 (2017)

14. Gold, E.M.: Language identification in the limit. Inf. Control **10**, 447–474 (1967)

15. Gao, Z., Ries, C., Simon, H.U., Zilles, S.: Preference-based teaching. J. Mach. Learn. Res. **18**, 1–32 (2017)

16. Goldman, S.A., Kearns, M.J.: On the complexity of teaching. J. Comput. Syst. Sci **50**, 20–31 (1995)

17. Jain, S., Ong, Y.S., Stephan, F.: Regular patterns, regular languages and context-free languages. Inf. Proc. Lett. **110**(24), 1114–1119 (2010)

18. Jiang, T., Kinber, E., Salomaa, A., Salomaa, K., Yu, S.: Pattern languages with and without erasing. Int. J. Comput. Math. **50**, 147–163 (1994)

19. Lothaire, M.: Combinatorics on Words, Cambridge Mathematical Library. Cambridge University Press, Cambridge (1997). Corrected reprint of the 1983 original

20. Lothaire, M.: Algebraic Combinatorics on Words. Encyclopedia of Mathematics and its Applications. Cambridge University Press, Cambridge (2002)

21. Matsumoto, S., Shinohara, A.: Learning pattern languages using queries. In: Ben-David, S. (ed.) EuroCOLT 1997. LNCS, vol. 1208, pp. 185–197. Springer, Heidelberg (1997). https://doi.org/10.1007/3-540-62685-9_16

22. Mitchell, A.R.: Learnability of a subclass of extended pattern languages. In: COLT, pp. 64–71 (1998)

23. Ohlebusch, E., Ukkonen, E.: On the equivalence problem for e-pattern languages. Theor. Comput. Sci **186**(1–2), 231–248 (1997)

24. Reidenbach, D.: A non-learnable class of e-pattern languages. Theor. Comput. Sci **350**(1), 91–102 (2006)

25. Reidenbach, D.: Discontinuities in pattern inference. Theor. Comput. Sci **397**, 166–193 (2008)

26. Schmid, M.L.: Characterising REGEX languages by regular languages equipped with factor-referencing. Inf. Comput. **249**, 1–17 (2016)

27. Shinohara, A., Miyano, S.: Teachability in computational learning. New Gener. Comput. **8**(4), 337–347 (1991)

28. Shinohara, T.: Polynomial time inference of extended regular pattern languages. In: Goto, E., Furukawa, K., Nakajima, R., Nakata, I., Yonezawa, A. (eds.) RIMS Symposia on Software Science and Engineering. LNCS, vol. 147, pp. 115–127. Springer, Heidelberg (1983). https://doi.org/10.1007/3-540-11980-9_19

29. Zhu, X., Singla, A., Zilles, S., Rafferty, A.N.: An overview of machine teaching (2018, manuscript). http://arxiv.org/abs/1801.05927

On Timed Scope-Bounded
Context-Sensitive Languages

D. Bhave[1], S. N. Krishna[1], R. Phawade[2]([⊠]), and A. Trivedi[3]

[1] IIT Bombay, Mumbai, India
{devendra,krishnas}@cse.iitb.ac.in
[2] IIT Dharwad, Dharwad, India
prb@iitdh.ac.in
[3] CU Boulder, Boulder, USA
ashutosh.trivedi@colorado.edu

Abstract. Perfect languages, characterized by closure under Boolean operations and decidable emptiness problem, form the basis for decidable automata-theoretic model-checking for the corresponding class of models. Regular languages and visibly pushdown languages are paradigmatic examples of perfect languages. In a previous work authors have established a timed context-sensitive perfect language characterized by multistack pushdown automata (MPA) with an explicit bound on number of rounds where in each round at most one stack is used. This paper complements the results of on bounded-round timed MPA by characterizing an alternative restriction on timed context-sensitive perfect languages called the scope-bounded multi-stack timed push-down automata where every stack symbol must be popped within a bounded number of stack contexts. The proposed model uses visibly-pushdown alphabet and event clocks to recover a bounded-scope MPA with decidable emptiness, closure under Boolean operations, and an equivalent logical characterization.

1 Introduction

The Vardi-Wolper [18] recipe for an automata-theoretic model-checking for a class of languages requires that class to be closed under Boolean operations and have decidable emptiness problem. Esparza, Ganty, and Majumdar [11] coined the term "perfect languages" for the classes of languages satisfying these properties. However, several important extensions of regular languages, such as pushdown automata and timed automata, do not satisfy these requirements. In order to lift the automata-theoretic model-checking framework for these classes of languages, appropriate restrictions have been studied including visibly pushdown automata [5] (VPA) and event-clock automata [4] (ECA). Tang and Ogawa [17] introduced a perfect class of timed context-free languages generalized both visibly pushdown automata and event-clock automata to introduce event-clock visibly pushdown automata (ECVPA). This paper proposes a perfect class of

Partially supported by grant MTR/2018/001098.

P. Hofman and M. Skrzypczak (Eds.): DLT 2019, LNCS 11647, pp. 168–181, 2019.
https://doi.org/10.1007/978-3-030-24886-4_12

timed context-sensitive languages inspired by the scope-bounded restriction on multi-stack visibly pushdown languages introduced by La Torre, Napoli, and Parlato [13] and presents a logical characterization for the proposed subclass.

Automata Characterizing Perfect Context-Free Languages. Alur and Madhusudan [5] introduced visibly pushdown automata as a specification formalism where the call and return edges are made visible in a structure of the word. This notion is formalized by giving an explicit partition of the alphabet into three disjoint sets of call, return, and internal or local symbols and the visibly pushdown automata must push one symbol to the stack while reading a call symbol, and must pop one symbol (given the stack is non-empty) while reading a return symbol, and must not touch the stack while reading an internal symbol.

Automata Characterizing Perfect Timed Regular Languages. Alur-Dill timed automata [3] is a generalization of finite automata with continuous variables called clocks that grow with uniform rate in each control location and their valuation can be used to guard the transitions. Each transition can also reset clocks, and that allows one to constrain transitions based on the duration since a previous transition has been taken. However, the power of reseting clocks contributed towards timed automata not being closed under complementation. In order to overcome this limitation, Alur, Fix, and Henzinger [4] introduced event-clock automata where input symbol dictate the resets of the clocks. In an event-clock automata every symbol a is implicitly associated with two clocks x_a and y_a, where the recorder clock x_a records the time since the last occurrence of the symbol a, and the predictor clock y_a predicts the time of the next occurrence of symbol a. Hence, event-clock automata do not permit explicit reset of clocks and it is implicitly governed by the input timed word.

Proposed Model For Perfect Context-Sensitive Timed Languages. We study dense-time event-clock multistack visibly pushdown automata (dt-ECMVPA) that combines event-clock dynamics of event-clock automata with multiple visibly pushdown stacks. We assume a partition of the alphabet among various stacks, and partition of the alphabet of each stack into call, return, and internal symbols. Moreover, we associate recorder and predictor clocks with each symbol. Inspired by Atig et al. [1] we consider our stacks to be dense-timed, i.e. we allow stack symbols to remember the time elapsed since they were pushed to the stack.

A finite timed word over an alphabet Σ is a sequence $(a_1, t_1), \ldots, (a_n, t_n) \in (\Sigma \times \mathbb{R}_{\geq 0})^*$ such that $t_i \leq t_{i+1}$ for all $1 \leq i \leq n - 1$. Alternatively, we can represent timed words as tuple $(\langle a_1, \ldots, a_n \rangle, \langle t_1, \ldots, t_n \rangle)$. We may use both of these formats depending on the context and for technical convenience. Let $T\Sigma^*$ denote the set of finite timed words over Σ.

We briefly discuss the concepts of rounds and scope as introduced by [13]. Consider an pushdown automata with n stacks. We say that for a stack h, a (timed) word is a stack-h context if all of its symbols belong to the alphabet of stack h. A *round* is fixed sequence of exactly n contexts one for each stack. Given a timed word, it can be partitioned into sequences of contexts of various stacks. The word is called k-round if it can be partitioned into k rounds. We say that a timed word is k-scoped if for each return symbol of a stack its matching call symbol occurs within the last k contexts of that stack. A visibly-pushdown multistack event-clock automata is *scope-bounded* if all of the accepting words are k-scoped for a fixed $k \in \mathbb{N}$.

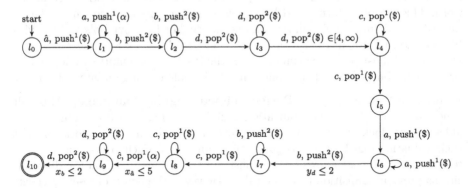

Fig. 1. A dense-time multistack visibly pushdown automata (from Example 1).

Example 1. Consider the timed language whose untimed component is of the form $L = \{\hat{a}a^x b^y d^y c^l a^l b^z c^x \hat{c} d^z \mid x, l, z \geq 1, \ y \geq 2\}$ with the critical timing restrictions among various symbols in the following manner. The time delay between the first occurrence of b and the last occurrence of d in the substring $b^y d^y$ is at least 4 time-units. The time-delay between this last occurrence of d and the next occurrence of b is at most 2 time-units. Finally the last d of the input string must appear within 2 time units of the last b, and $\hat{c}$ must occur within 5 time units of corresponding $\hat{a}$. This language is accepted by a dt-ECMVPA with two stacks shown in Fig. 1. We annotate a transition with the symbol and corresponding stack operations if any. We write pop^i or $push^i$ to emphasize pushes and pops to the i-th stack. We also use $pop^i(X) \in I$ to check if the age of the popped symbol X belongs to the interval I. In addition, we use simple constraints on predictor/recorder clock variables corresponding to the symbols. Let $a, \hat{a}$ and $c, \hat{c}$ (b and d, resp.) be call and return symbols for the first (second, resp.) stack. The Stack alphabet for the first stack is $\Gamma^1 = \{\alpha, \$\}$ and for the second stack is $\Gamma^2 = \{\$\}$. In Fig. 1 clock x_a measures the time since the occurrence of the last a, while constraints $pop(\gamma) \in I$ checks if the age of the popped symbol γ is in a given interval I. This language is 3-scoped and is accepted by a 6-round dt-ECMVPA. But if we consider the Kleene star of this language, it will be still 3-scoped and its machine can be built by fusing states l_0 and l_{10} in Fig. 1.

The formalisms of timed automata and pushdown stack have been combined before. First such attempt was timed pushdown automata [9] by Bouajjani, et al. and was proposed as a timed extension of pushdown automata which uses global clocks and timeless stack. We follow the dense-timed pushdown automata by Abdulla et al. [1]. The reachability checking of a given location from an initial one was shown to be decidable for this model. Trivedi and Wojtczak [16] studied the recursive timed automata in which clock values can be pushed onto a stack using mechanisms like pass-by-value and pass-by-reference. They studied reachability and termination problems for this model. Nested timed automata (NeTA) proposed by Li et al. [15] is a relatively recent model which, an instance of timed automata itself can be pushed on the stack along with the clocks. The clocks of pushed timed automata progress uniformly while on the stack. From the perspective of logical characterization, timed matching logic, an existential fragment of second-order logic, identified by Droste and Perevoshchikov [10] characterizes dense-timed pushdown automata.

We earlier [6] studied MSO logic for dense-timed visibly pushdown automata which form a subclass of timed context-free languages. This subclass is closed under union, intersection, complementation and determinization. The work presented in this paper extends the results from [7] for bounded-round dt-ECMVPA to the case of bounded-scope dt-ECMVPA. *We study bounded-scope dt-ECMVPA and show that they are closed under Boolean operations with decidable emptiness problem. We also present a logical characterization for these models.*

In the next section we recall the definitions of event clock and visibly pushdown automata. In Sect. 3 we define k-scope dense time multiple stack visibly push down automata with event clocks and its properties. In the following section these properties are used to decide emptiness checking and determinizability of k-scope ECMVPA with event clocks. Building upon these results, we show decidability of these properties for k-scope dt-ECMVPA with event clocks. In Sect. 5 we give a logical characterization for models introduced.

2 Preliminaries

Due to space limitation, we only give a very brief introduction of required concepts in this section, and for a detailed background on these concepts we refer the reader to [2,4,5]. We assume that the reader is comfortable with standard concepts such as context-free languages, pushdown automata, MSO logic from automata theory; and clocks, event clocks, clock constraints, and valuations from timed automata. Before we introduce our model, we revisit the definitions of event-clock automata.

The general class of TA [2] are not closed under Boolean operations. An important class of TA which is determinizable is Event-clock automata (ECA) [4], and hence closed under Boolean operations. Here the determinizability is achieved by making clock resets "visible".

To make clock resets visible we have two clocks which are associated with every action $a \in \Sigma$: x_a the "recorder" clock which records the time of the last occurrence of action a, and y_a the "predictor" clock which predicts the time of the next occurrence of action a. For example, for a timed word $w = (a_1, t_1), (a_2, t_2), \ldots, (a_n, t_n)$, the value of the event clock x_a at position j is $t_j - t_i$

where i is the largest position preceding j where an action a occurred. If no a has occurred before the jth position, then the value of x_a is undefined denoted by a special symbol $\vdash$. Similarly, the value of y_a at position j of w is undefined if symbol a does not occur in w after the jth position. Otherwise, it is $t_k - t_j$ where k is the first occurrence of a after j.

We write C for the set of all event clocks and we use $\mathbb{R}_{>0}^{\vdash}$ for the set $\mathbb{R}_{>0} \cup \{\vdash\}$. Formally, the clock valuation after reading j-th prefix of the input timed word w, $\nu_j^w : C \mapsto \mathbb{R}_{>0}^{\vdash}$, is defined as follows: $\nu_j^w(x_q) = t_j - t_i$ if there exists an $0 \leq i < j$ such that $a_i = q$ and $a_k \neq q$ for all $i < k < j$, otherwise $\nu_j^w(x_q) = \vdash$ (undefined). Similarly, $\nu_j^w(y_q) = t_m - t_j$ if there is $j < m$ such that $a_m = q$ and $a_l \neq q$ for all $j < l < m$, otherwise $\nu_j^w(y_q) = \vdash$. A clock constraint over C is a boolean combination of constraints of the form $z \sim c$ where $z \in C$, $c \in \mathbb{N}$ and $\sim \in \{\leq, \geq\}$. Given a clock constraint $z \sim c$ over C, we write $\nu_i^w \models (z \sim c)$ to denote if $\nu_j^w(z) \sim c$. For any boolean combination φ, $\nu_i^w \models \varphi$ is defined in an obvious way: if $\varphi = \varphi_1 \wedge \varphi_2$, then $\nu_i^w \models \varphi$ iff $\nu_i^w \models \varphi_1$ and $\nu_i^w \models \varphi_2$. Likewise, the other Boolean combinations are defined. Let $\Phi(C)$ define all the clock constraints defined over C.

3   Dense-Time Visibly Pushdown Multistack Automata

A visibly pushdown alphabet is a tuple $\langle \Sigma_c, \Sigma_r, \Sigma_l \rangle$ where Σ_c is *call* alphabet, Σ_r is a *return* alphabet, and Σ_l is *internal* alphabet. This section introduces scope-bounded dense-timed multistack visibly pushdown automata and give some properties about words and languages accepted by these machines.

Let $\Sigma = \langle \Sigma_c^h, \Sigma_r^h, \Sigma_l^h \rangle_{h=1}^n$ where $\Sigma_x^i \cap \Sigma_r^j = \emptyset$ whenever either $i \neq j$ or $x \neq y$, and $x, y \in \{c, r, l\}$. Let $\Sigma^h = \langle \Sigma_c^h, \Sigma_r^h, \Sigma_l^h \rangle$. Let Γ^h be the stack alphabet of the h-th stack and $\Gamma = \bigcup_{h=1}^n \Gamma^h$. For notational convenience, we assume that each symbol $a \in \Sigma^h$ has a unique recorder x_a and predictor y_a clock assigned to it. Let C_h denote the set of event clocks corresponding to stack h and $\Phi(C_h)$ denote the set of clock constraints defined over C_h. Let $cmax$ be the maximum constant used in the clock constraints $\Phi(C^h)$ of all stacks. Let $\mathcal{I}$ denote the finite set of intervals $\{[0,0], (0,1), [1,1], (1,2), \ldots, [cmax, cmax], (cmax, \infty)\}$.

Definition 2. *A dense-timed visibly pushdown multistack automata (dt-ECMVPA) over* $\langle \Sigma_c^h, \Sigma_r^h, \Sigma_l^h \rangle_{h=1}^n$ *is a tuple* $(L, \Sigma, \Gamma, L^0, F, \Delta = (\Delta_c^h \cup \Delta_r^h \cup \Delta_l^h)_{h=1}^n)$ *where*

- L *is a finite set of locations including a set* $L^0 \subseteq L$ *of initial locations,*
- Γ^h *is the finite alphabet of stack* h *and has special end-of-stack symbol* $\perp_h$,
- $\Delta_c^h \subseteq (L \times \Sigma_c^h \times \Phi(C_h) \times L \times (\Gamma^h \setminus \{\perp_h\}))$ *is the set of call transitions,*
- $\Delta_r^h \subseteq (L \times \Sigma_r^h \times \mathcal{I} \times \Gamma^h \times \Phi(C_h) \times L)$ *is set of return transitions,*
- $\Delta_l^h \subseteq (L \times \Sigma_l^h \times \Phi(C_h) \times L)$ *is set of internal transitions, and*
- $F \subseteq L$ *is the set of final locations.*

Let $w = (a_0, t_0), \ldots, (a_e, t_e)$ be a timed word. A configuration of the dt-ECMVPA is a tuple $(\ell, \nu_i^w, (\gamma^1 \sigma^1, age(\gamma^1 \sigma^1)), \ldots, (\gamma^n \sigma^n, age(\gamma^n \sigma^n)))$ where ℓ is the current location of the dt-ECMVPA, function ν_i^w gives the valuation of all the event clocks at position $i \leq |w|$, $\gamma^h \sigma^h \in \Gamma^h(\Gamma^h)^*$ is the content of stack h with γ^h being the topmost symbol, and σ^h the string representing stack contents below γ^h, while $age(\gamma^h \sigma^h)$ is a sequence of real numbers denoting the ages (the time elapsed since a stack symbol was pushed on to the stack) of all the stack symbols in $\gamma^h \sigma^h$. We follow the assumption that $age(\perp^h) = \langle \vdash \rangle$ (undefined). If for some string $\sigma^h \in (\Gamma^h)^*$ we have $age(\sigma^h) = \langle t_1, t_2, \ldots, t_g \rangle$ and for $\tau \in \mathbb{R}_{\geq 0}$ then we write $age(\sigma^h) + \tau$ for the sequence $\langle t_1 + \tau, t_2 + \tau, \ldots, t_g + \tau \rangle$. For a sequence $\sigma^h = \langle \gamma_1^h, \ldots, \gamma_g^h \rangle$ and a stack symbol γ^h we write $\gamma^h :: \sigma^h$ for $\langle \gamma^h, \gamma_1^h, \ldots, \gamma_g^h \rangle$.

A run of a dt-ECMVPA on a timed word $w = (a_0, t_0), \ldots, (a_e, t_e)$ is a sequence of configurations:

$$(\ell_0, \nu_0^w, ((\langle \perp^1 \rangle, \langle \vdash \rangle), \ldots, ((\langle \perp^n \rangle, \langle \vdash \rangle)), (\ell_1, \nu_1^w, ((\sigma_1^1, age(\sigma_1^1)), \ldots, (\sigma_1^n, age(\sigma_1^n)))),$$
$$\ldots, (\ell_{e+1}, \nu_{e+1}^w, (\sigma_{e+1}^1, age(\sigma_{e+1}^1)), \ldots, (\sigma_{e+1}^n, age(\sigma_{e+1}^n)))) \text{ where } \ell_i \in L, \ell_0 \in L^0,$$
$\sigma_i^h \in (\Gamma^h)^* \perp^h$, and for each i, $0 \leq i \leq e$, we have:

- If $a_i \in \Sigma_c^h$, then there is $(\ell_i, a_i, \varphi, \ell_{i+1}, \gamma^h) \in \Delta_c^h$ such that $\nu_i^w \models \varphi$. The symbol $\gamma^h \in \Gamma^h \backslash \{\perp^h\}$ is then pushed onto the stack h, and its age is initialized to zero, i.e. $(\sigma_{i+1}^h, age(\sigma_{i+1}^h)) = (\gamma^h :: \sigma_i^h, 0 :: (age(\sigma_i^h) + (t_i - t_{i-1})))$. All symbols in all other stacks are unchanged, and they age by $t_i - t_{i-1}$.
- If $a_i \in \Sigma_r^h$, then there is $(\ell_i, a_i, I, \gamma^h, \varphi, \ell_{i+1}) \in \Delta_r^h$ such that $\nu_i^w \models \varphi$. Also, $\sigma_i^h = \gamma^h :: \kappa \in \Gamma^h(\Gamma^h)^*$ and $age(\gamma^h) + (t_i - t_{i-1}) \in I$. The symbol γ^h is popped from stack h obtaining $\sigma_{i+1}^h = \kappa$ and ages of remaining stack symbols are updated i.e., $age(\sigma_{i+1}^h) = age(\kappa) + (t_i - t_{i-1})$. However, if $\gamma^h = \langle \perp^h \rangle$, then γ^h is not popped. The contents of all other stacks remains unchanged, and simply age by $(t_i - t_{i-1})$.
- If $a_i \in \Sigma_l^h$, then there is $(\ell_i, a_i, \varphi, \ell_{i+1}) \in \Delta_l^h$ such that $\nu_i^w \models \varphi$. In this case all stacks remain unchanged i.e. $\sigma_{i+1}^h = \sigma_i^h$, but their contents age by $t_i - t_{i-1}$ i.e. $age(\sigma_{i+1}^h) = age(\sigma_i^h) + (t_i - t_{i-1})$ for all $1 \leq h \leq n$.

A run ρ of a dt-ECMVPA M is accepting if it terminates in a final location. A timed word w is an accepting word if there is an accepting run of M on w. The language $L(M)$ of a dt-ECMVPA M, is the set of all timed words w accepted by M and is called dt-ECMVPL.

A dt-ECMVPA $M = (L, \Sigma, \Gamma, L^0, F, \Delta)$ is said to be *deterministic* if it has exactly one start location, and for every configuration and input action exactly one transition is enabled. Formally, we have the following conditions: for any two moves $(\ell, a, \phi_1, \ell', \gamma_1)$ and $(\ell, a, \phi_2, \ell'', \gamma_2)$ of Δ_c^h, condition $\phi_1 \wedge \phi_2$ is unsatisfiable; for any two moves $(\ell, a, I_1, \gamma, \phi_1, \ell')$ and $(\ell, a, I_2, \gamma, \phi_2, \ell'')$ in Δ_r^h, either $\phi_1 \wedge \phi_2$ is unsatisfiable or $I_1 \cap I_2 = \emptyset$; and for any two moves (ℓ, a, ϕ_1, ℓ') and (ℓ, a, ϕ_2, ℓ') in Δ_l^h, condition $\phi_1 \wedge \phi_2$ is unsatisfiable.

An Event clock multi stack visibly push down automata (ECMVPA) is a dt-ECMVPA where the stacks are untimed i.e., a dt-ECMVPA $(L, \Sigma, \Gamma, L^0, F, \Delta)$, with $I = [0, +\infty]$ for every $(\ell, a, I, \gamma, \phi, \ell') \in \Delta_r^h$, is an ECMVPA.

A dtECVPA is a dt-ECMVPA restricted to single stack.

We now define a *matching relation* $\sim_h$ on the positions of input timed word w which identifies matching call and return positions for each stack h. Note that this is possible because of the visibility of the input symbols.

Definition 3 (Matching relation). *Consider a timed word w over Σ. Let $\mathcal{P}_c^h$ (resp. $\mathcal{P}_r^h$) denote the set of positions in w where a symbol from Σ_c^h i.e. a call symbol (resp. Σ_r^h i.e. a return symbol) occurs. Position i (resp. j) is called* call position *(resp.* return position*). For each stack h the timed word w, defines a* matching relation $\sim_h \subseteq \mathcal{P}_c^h \times \mathcal{P}_r^h$ *satisfying the following conditions:*

1. *for all positions i, j with $i \sim_h j$ we have $i < j$,*
2. *for any call position i of $\mathcal{P}_c^h$ and any return position j of $\mathcal{P}_r^h$ with $i < j$, there exists l with $i \leq l \leq j$ for which either $i \sim_h l$ or $l \sim_h j$,*
3. *for each call position $i \in \mathcal{P}_c^h$ (resp. $i \in \mathcal{P}_r^h$) there is at most one return position $j \in \mathcal{P}_r^h$ (resp. $j \in \mathcal{P}_c^h$) with $i \sim_h j$ (resp. $j \sim_h i$).*

For $i \sim_h j$, position i (resp. j) is called *matching call (resp. matching return).*

This definition of matching relation extends that defined by La Torre, et al. [14] to timed words. As matching relation is completely determined by stacks and timestamps of the input word does not play any role, we claim that above definition uniquely identifies matching relation for a given input word w using uniqueness proof from [14].

Fix a k from $\mathbb{N}$. A *stack-h context* is a word in $\Sigma^h(\Sigma^h)^*$. Given a word w and a stack h, the word w has k maximal h-contexts if $w \in (\Sigma^h)^*((\bigcup_{h \neq h'} \Sigma^{h'})^*(\Sigma^h)^*)^{k-1}$. A timed word over Σ is k-**scoped** if for each matching call of stack h, its corresponding return occurs within at most k maximal stack-h contexts.

Let $Scope(\Sigma, k)$ denote the set of all k-scope timed words over Σ. For any fixed k, a k-scope dt-ECMVPA over Σ is a tuple $A = (k, M)$ where $M = (L, \Sigma, \Gamma, L^0, F, \Delta)$ is a dt-ECMVPA over Σ. The language accepted by A is $L(A) = L(M) \cap Scope(\Sigma, k)$ and is called k-scope dense-timed multistack visibly pushdown language (k-scoped-dt-ECMVPL). We define k-scoped-ECMVPL in a similar fashion. We now recall some key definitions from La Torre [13,14] which help us extend the notion of scoped words from untimed to timed words.

Definition 4 (k-scoped splitting [13,14]). *A* cut *of w is $w_1{:}w_2$ where $w = w_1 w_2$. The cutting of w is marked by ":". A cut is* h-consistent *with matching relation $\sim_h$ if no call occuring in w_1 matches with a return in w_2 in $\sim_h$. A* splitting *of w is a set of cuts $w_1 \ldots w_i : w_{i+1} \ldots w_m$ such that $w = w_1 \ldots w_i w_{i+1} \ldots w_m$ for each i in $\{1, \ldots, m-1\}$. An* h-consistent splitting *of w is the one in which each specified cut is h-consistent. A* context-splitting *of word w is a splitting $w_1 : w_2 : \ldots : w_m$ such that each w_i is an h-context for some stack h and $i \in \{1, \ldots, m\}$. A* canonical context-splitting *of word is a context-splitting of w in which no two consecutive contexts belong to the same stack.*

Given a context-splitting of timed word w, we obtain its h-projection by removing all non stack-h contexts. Observe that an h-projection is a context-splitting. An ordered tuple of m h-contexts is k-bounded if there there exists a h-consistent splitting of this tuple, where each component of the cut in the splitting is a concatenation of at most k consecutive h-contexts of given tuple. A k-scoped splitting of word w is the canonical splitting of w equipped with additional cuts for each stack h such that, if we take h-projection of w with these cuts it is k-bounded. The main purpose for introducing all the above definitions is to come up with a scheme which will permit us to split any arbitrary length input timed word into k-scoped words. Using [13,14] for untimed words we get the following Lemma.

Lemma 5. *A timed word w is k-scoped iff there is a k-scoped splitting of w.*

Next we describe the notion of switching vectors for timed words [6], which are used in determinization of k-scope dt-ECMVPA.

3.1   Switching Vectors

Let A be k-scoped dt-ECMVPA over Σ and let w be a timed word accepted by A. Our aim is to simulate A on w by n different dtECVPAs, A^h for each stack-h inputs. We insert a special symbol $\#$ at the end of each maximal context, to obtain word w' over $\Sigma \cup \{\#, \#'\}$. We also have recorder clocks $x_\#$ and predictor clocks $y_\#$ for symbol $\#$. For h-th stack, let dtECVPA A^h be the restricted version of A over alphabet $\Sigma \cup \{\#, \#'\}$ which simulates A on input symbols from Σ^h. Then, it is clear that at the symbol before $\#$, stack h may be touched by dt-ECMVPA A and at the first symbol after $\#$, stack h may be touched again. But it may be the case that at positions where $\#$ occurs stack h may not be empty i.e., cut defined position of $\#$ may be not be h-consistent.

To capture the behaviour of A^h over timed word w we have a notion of switching vector. Let m be the number of maximal h-contexts in word w and w^h be the h-projection of w i.e., $w^h = u_1^h \ldots u_m^h$. In particular, m could be more than k. A switching vector $\mathbb{V}^h$ of A for word w is an element of $(L, \mathcal{I}, L)^m$, where $\mathbb{V}^h[l] = (q, I_l, q')$ if in the run of A over w^h we have $q \xrightarrow{u_l^h} q'$. Let $w'^h = u_1^h \# u_2^h \# \ldots u_m^h \#$, where $u_i^h = (a_{i1}^h, t_{i1}^h), (a_{i2}^h, t_{i2}^h) \ldots (a_{i,s_i}^h, t_{i,s_i}^h)$ is a stack-h context, where $s_i = |u_i^h|$. Now we assign time stamps of the last letter read in the previous contexts to the current symbol $\#$ to get the word $\kappa^h = u_1^h(\#, t_{1,s_1}^h) u_2^h(\#, t_{2,s_2}^h) \ldots u_m^h(\#, t_{m,s_m}^h)$.

We take the word w'^h and looking at this word we construct another word $\bar{w}^h$ by inserting symbols $\#'$ at places where the stack is empty after popping some symbol, and if $\#'$ is immediately followed by $\#$ then we drop $\#$ symbol. We do this in a very canonical way as follows: In this word w'^h look at the first call position c_1 and its corresponding return position r_1. Then we insert $\#'$ after position r_1 in w^h. Now we look for next call position c_2 and its corresponding return position r_2 and insert symbol $\#'$ after r_2. We repeat this construction for all call and its corresponding return positions in w'^h to get a timed word $\bar{w}^h$ over $\Sigma \cup \{\#, \#'\}$. Let $\bar{w}^h = \bar{u}_1^h \widehat{\#} \bar{u}_2^h \widehat{\#} \ldots \widehat{\#} \bar{u}_z^h$, where $\widehat{\#}$ is either $\#$ or $\#'$, and $\bar{u}_i^h = (\bar{a}_{i1}^h, \bar{t}_{i1}^h), (\bar{a}_{i2}^h, \bar{t}_{i2}^h) \ldots (\bar{a}_{i,s_i}^h, \bar{t}_{i,s_i}^h)$, is a timed word.

The restriction of A which reads $\bar{w}^h$ is denoted by A_k^h. Assign timestamps of the last letter read in the previous contexts to the current symbol $\widehat{\#}$ to get the word $\bar{\kappa}^h = \bar{u}_1^h(\widehat{\#}, \bar{t}_{1,s_1}^h) \bar{u}_2^h(\widehat{\#}, \bar{t}_{2,s_2}^h) \ldots \bar{u}_z^h(\widehat{\#}, \bar{t}_{z,s_z}^h)$, where $s_i = |\bar{u}_i^h|$ for i in

$\{1, \ldots, z\}$. A stack-h *switching vector* $\bar{\mathbb{V}}^h$ is a z-tuple of the form $(L, \mathcal{I}, L)^z$, where $z > 0$ and for every $j \leq z$ if $\bar{\mathbb{V}}^h[j] = (q_j, I_j, q'_j)$ then there is a run of A^h from location q_j to q'_j.

By definition of k-scoped word we are guaranteed to find maximum k number of # symbols from c_j to r_j. And we also know that stack-h is empty whenever we encounter #' in the word. In other words, if we look at the switching vector $\bar{\mathbb{V}}^h$ of A reading $\bar{w}^h$, it can be seen as a product of switching vectors of A each having a length less than k. Therefore, $\bar{\mathbb{V}}^h = \Pi_{i=1}^r V_i^h$ where $r \leq z$ and $V_i^h = (L \times \mathcal{I} \times L)^{\leq k}$. When we look at a timed word and refer to the switching vector corresponding to it, we view it as tuples of switching pairs, but when we look at the switching vectors as a part of state of A_k^h then we see at a product of switching vectors of length less than k.

A *correct sequence of context switches* for A_k^h wrt $\bar{\kappa}^h$ is a sequence of pairs $\bar{\mathbb{V}}^h = P_1^h P_2^h \ldots P_z^h$, where $P_i^h = (\ell_i^h, I_i^h, \ell_i'^h)$, $2 \leq h \leq n$, $P_1^h = (\ell_1^h, \nu_1^h, \ell_1'^h)$ and $I_i^h \in \mathcal{I}$ such that

1. Starting in ℓ_1^h, with the h-th stack containing $\perp^h$, and an initial valuation ν_1^h of all recorders and predictors of Σ^h, the dt-ECMVPA A processes u_1^h and reaches some $\ell_1'^h$ with stack content σ_2^h and clock valuation $\nu_1'^h$. The processing of u_2^h by A then starts at location ℓ_2^h, and a time $t \in I_2^h$ has elapsed between the processing of u_1^h and u_2^h. Thus, A starts processing u_2^h in (ℓ_2^h, ν_2^h) where ν_2^h is the valuation of all recorders and predictors updated from $\nu_1'^h$ with respect to t. The stack content remains same as σ_2^h when the processing of u_2^h begins.
2. In general, starting in (ℓ_i^h, ν_i^h), $i > 1$ with the h-th stack containing σ_i^h, and ν_i^h obtained from ν_{i-1}^h by updating all recorders and predictors based on the time interval I_i^h that records the time elapse between processing u_{i-1}^h and u_i^h, A processes u_i^h and reaches $(\ell_i'^h, \nu_i'^h)$ with stack content σ_{i+1}^h. The processing of u_{i+1}^h starts after time $t \in I_{i+1}^h$ has elapsed since processing u_i^h in a location ℓ_{i+1}^h, and stack content being σ_i^h.

These switching vectors were used in to get the determinizability of k-round dt-ECMVPA [6] In a k-round dt-ECMVPA, we know that there at most k-contexts of stack-h and hence the length of switching vector (whichever it is) is at most k for any given word w. See for example the MVPA corresponding to Kleene star of language given in the Example 1. In k-scope MVPA for a given w, we do not know beforehand what is the length of switching vector. So we employ not just one switching vector but many one after another for given word w, and we maintain that length of each switching vector is at most k. This is possible because of the definition of k-scope dt-ECMVPA and Lemma 5.

Lemma 6 (*Switching Lemma for A_k^h*). *Let $A = (k, L, \Sigma, \Gamma, L^0, F, \Delta)$ be a k-scope-dt-ECMVPA. Let w be a timed word with m maximal h-contexts and accepted by A . Then we can construct a dtECVPA A_k^h over $\Sigma^h \cup \{\#, \#'\}$ such that A_k^h has a run over $\bar{w}^h$ witnessed by a switching sequence $\bar{\mathbb{V}}^h = \Pi_{i=1}^r \bar{\mathbb{V}}_i^h$ where $r \leq z$ and $\bar{\mathbb{V}}_i^h = (L \times \mathcal{I} \times L)^{\leq k}$ which ends in the last component $\bar{\mathbb{V}}_r^h$ of $\bar{\mathbb{V}}^h$ iff there exists a k-scoped switching sequence $\bar{\mathbb{V}}'^h$ of switching vectors of A such that for any v' of $\bar{\mathbb{V}}'^h$ there exist v_i and v_j in $\bar{\mathbb{V}}'$ with $i \leq j$ and $v'[1] = v_i[1]$ and $v'[|v'|] = v_j[|v_j|]$.*

Proof. We construct a dtECVPA $A_h^k = (L^h, \Sigma \cup \{\#, \#'\}, \Gamma^h, L^0, F^h = F, \Delta^h)$ where, $L^h \subseteq (L \times \mathcal{I} \times L)^{\leq k} \times \Sigma \cup \{\#, \#'\}$ and Δ^h are given below.

1. For a in Σ:
   $(P_1^h, \ldots, P_i^h = (q, I_i^h, q'), b) \xrightarrow{a, \phi} (P_1'^h, \ldots, P_i'^h = (q, I_i'^h, q''), a)$, when $q' \xrightarrow{a, \phi} q''$ is in Δ, and $b \in \Sigma$.

2. For a in Σ:
   $(P_1^h, \ldots, P_i^h = (q, I_i^h, q'), \#) \xrightarrow{a, \phi \wedge x_\# = 0} (P_1'^h, \ldots, P_i'^h = (q, I_i'^h, q''), a)$, when $q' \xrightarrow{a, \phi} q''$ is in Δ, and $b \in \Sigma$.

3. For a in Σ:
   $(P_1^h, \ldots, P_i^h = (q, I_i^h, q'), \#') \xrightarrow{a, \phi \wedge x_{\#'} = 0} (P_1'^h, \ldots, P_i'^h = (q, I_i'^h, q''), a)$, when $q' \xrightarrow{a, \phi} q''$ is in Δ, and $b \in \Sigma$.

4. For $a = \#$,
   $(P_1^h, \ldots, P_i^h = (q, I_i^h, q'), b) \xrightarrow{a, \phi \wedge x_b \in I_{i+1}'^h} (P_1^h, \ldots, P_{i+1}'^h = (q'', I_{i+1}'^h, q'), \#)$, when $q' \xrightarrow{a, \phi} q''$ is in Δ.

5. For $a = \#'$,
   $(P_1^h, \ldots, P_i^h = (q, I_i^h, q'), a) \xrightarrow{a, \phi, x_{\#'} \in \hat{I}_1^h} (\hat{P}_1^h = (q', \hat{I}_1^h, q'), \#')$, when $q' \xrightarrow{a, \phi} q''$ is in Δ.

Given a timed word w accepted by A, when A is restricted to A^h then it is running on w'^h, the projection of w on Σ^h, interspersed with $\#$ separating the maximal h-contexts in original word w. Let $v_1, v_2, \ldots, v_m$ be the sequence of switching vectors witnessed by A^h while reading w'^h.

Now when w'^h is fed to the constructed machine A_h^k, it is interspersed with new symbols $\#'$ whenever the stack is empty just after a return symbol is read. Now $\bar{w}^h$ thus constructed is again a collection of z stack-h contexts which possibly are more in number than in w'^h. And each newly created context is either equal to some context of w'^h or is embedded in exactly one context of w'^h. These give rise to sequence of switching vectors $v_1', v_2', \ldots, v_z'$, where $m \leq z$. That explains the embedding of switching vectors witnessed by A_h^k, while reading $\bar{w}^h$, into switching vectors of A, while reading w^h. □

Let w be in $L(A)$. Then as described above we can have a sequence of switching vectors $\bar{\mathbb{V}}_h$ for stack-h machine A_k^h. Let d^h be the number of h-contexts in the k-scoped splitting of w i.e., the number of h-contexts in $\bar{w}^h$. Then we have those many tuples in the sequence of switching vectors $\bar{\mathbb{V}}^h$. Therefore, $\bar{\mathbb{V}}^h = \Pi_{y \in \{1, \ldots, d_h\}} \langle l_y^h, I_y^h, l_y'^h \rangle$.

We define the relation between elements of $\bar{\mathbb{V}}^h$ across all such sequences. While reading the word w, for all h and h' in $\{1, \ldots, n\}$ and for some y in $\{1, \ldots, d_h\}$ and some y' in $\{1, \ldots, d_{h'}\}$ we define a relation $follows(h, y) = (h'y')$ if y-th h-context is followed by y'-th h'-context.

A collection of correct sequences of context switches given via switching vectors $(\bar{\mathbb{V}}^1, \ldots, \bar{\mathbb{V}}^n)$ is called **globally correct** if we can stitch together runs of all A_k^hs on $\bar{w}^h$ using these switching vectors to get a run of A on word w.

In the reverse direction, if for a given k-scoped word w over Σ which is in $L(A)$ then we have, collection of globally correct switching vectors $(\bar{\mathbb{V}}^1, \ldots, \bar{\mathbb{V}}^n)$. The detailed proof of the following lemma is given in [8].

Lemma 7 (Stitching Lemma). *Let $A = (k, L, \Sigma, \Gamma, L^0, F, \Delta)$ be a k-scope dt-ECMVPA. Let w be a k-scoped word over Σ. Then $w \in L(A)$ iff there exist a collection of globally correct sequences of switching vectors for word w.*

4   Scope-Bounded ECMVPA and dt-ECMVPA

Fix a $k \in \mathbb{N}$. Decidability of emptiness checking of k-round ECMVPA has been shown in [7]. This proof works for any general ECMVPA as the notion k-round has not been used and we use the same for emptiness checking of k-scope ECMVPA. Detailed proofs for the theorems in this section are given in [8].

Theorem 8. *Emptiness checking for k-scope ECMVPA is decidable.*

Using Lemmas 6 and 7 we get the following theorem.

Theorem 9. *The class of k-scope ECMVPA are determinizable.*

To prove the decidability of emptiness checking for k-scope dt-ECMVPA, we first do untime its stack to get k-scope ECMVPA for which emptiness is shown to be decidable in Theorem 8.

Theorem 10. *The emptiness checking for k-scope dt-ECMVPA is decidable.*

Theorem 11. *The k-scope dt-ECMVPA are determinizable.*

Proof (sketch). From a k-scope dt-ECMVPA using the stack untiming construction we get a k-scope ECMVPA, which is determinized using Theorem 9. We convert this back to get deterministic k-scope dt-ECMVPA.

It is easy to show that k-scoped ECMVPAs and k-scoped dt-ECMVPAs are closed under union and intersection; using Theorems 9 and 11 we get closure under complementation.

Theorem 12. *The classes of k-scoped ECMVPLs and k-scoped dt-ECMVPLs are closed under Boolean operations.*

5   Logical Characterization of k-dt-ECMVPA

Let $w = (a_1, t_1), \ldots, (a_m, t_m)$ be a timed word over alphabet $\Sigma = \langle \Sigma_c^i, \Sigma_l^i, \Sigma_r^i \rangle_{i=1}^n$ as a *word structure* over the universe $U = \{1, 2, \ldots, |w|\}$ of positions in w. We borrow definitions of predicates $Q_a(i)$, $\lhd_a(i)$, $\rhd_a(i)$ from [6]. Following [12], we use the matching binary relation $\mu_j(i, k)$ which evaluates to true iff the ith position is a call and the kth position is its matching return corresponding to the jth stack. We introduce the predicate $\theta_j(i) \in I$ which evaluates to true on the word structure iff

$w[i] = (a, t_i)$ with $a \in \Sigma_r^j$ and $w[i] \in \Sigma_r^j$, and there is some $k < i$ such that $\mu_j(k, i)$ evaluates to true and $t_i - t_k \in I$. The predicate $\theta_j(i)$ measures time elapsed between position k where a call was made on the stack j, and position i, its matching return. This time elapse is the age of the symbol pushed onto the stack during the call at position k. Since position i is the matching return, this symbol is popped at i, if the age lies in the interval I, the predicate evaluates to true. We define MSO(Σ), the MSO logic over Σ, as:

$$\varphi := Q_a(x) \mid x \in X \mid \mu_j(x, y) \mid \lhd_a(x) \in I \mid \rhd_a(x) \in I \mid \theta_j(x) \in I \mid \neg\varphi \mid \varphi \vee \varphi \mid \exists x.\varphi \mid \exists X.\varphi$$

where $a \in \Sigma$, $x_a \in C_\Sigma$, x is a first order variable and X is a second order variable.

The models of a formula $\phi \in$ MSO(Σ) are timed words w over Σ. The semantics is standard where first order variables are interpreted over positions of w and second order variables over subsets of positions. We define the language $L(\varphi)$ of an MSO sentence φ as the set of all words satisfying φ.

Words in $Scope(\Sigma, k)$, for some k, can be captured by an MSO formula $Scope_k(\psi) = \bigwedge_{1 \leq j \leq n} Scope_k(\psi)^j$, where n is number of stacks, where

$$Scope_k(\psi)^j \stackrel{def}{=} \forall y Q_a(y) \wedge a \in \Sigma_j^r \Rightarrow (\exists x \mu_j(x, y) \wedge (\psi_{kcnxt}^j \wedge \psi_{matcnxt}^j \wedge \psi_{noxcnxt}))$$

where ψ_{kcnxt}^j, $\psi_{matcnxt}^j$, and $\psi_{noxcnxt}$ are defined as

$$\psi_{kcnxt}^j = \exists x_1 \dots k (x_1 \leq \dots \leq x_k \leq y \bigwedge_{1 \leq q \leq k} (Q_a(x_q) \wedge a \in \Sigma_j \wedge (Q_b(x_q - 1) \Rightarrow b \notin \Sigma_j)),$$

$$\psi_{matcnxt}^j = \bigvee_{1 \leq q \leq k} \forall x_i (x_q \leq x_i \leq x(Q_c(x_i) \Rightarrow c \in \Sigma_j)), \text{ and}$$

$$\psi_{noxcnxt} = \exists x_l (x_1 \leq x_l \leq y)(Q_a(l) \wedge a \in \Sigma_j \wedge Q_b(x_l - 1) \wedge b \in \Sigma_j) \Rightarrow 1 \leq l \leq k.$$

Formulas $\psi_{noextracnxt}$ and ψ_{kcnxt} say that there are at most k contexts of j-th stack, while formula $\psi_{matcnxt}$ says where matching call position x of return position y is found. Conjuncting the formula obtained from a dt-ECMVPA M with $Scope(\psi)$ accepts only those words which lie in $L(M) \cap Scope(\Sigma, k)$. Likewise, if one considers any MSO formula $\zeta = \varphi \wedge Scope(\psi)$, it can be shown that the dt-ECMVPA M constructed for ζ will be a k-dt-ECMVPA. Hence we have the following MSO characterization.

Theorem 13. *A language L over Σ is accepted by an k-scope dt-ECMVPA iff there is a MSO sentence φ over Σ such that $L(\varphi) \cap Scope(\Sigma, k) = L$.*

The two directions, dt-ECMVPA to MSO, as well as MSO to dt-ECMVPA can be handled using standard techniques, and can be found in [8].

References

1. Abdulla, P.A., Atig, M.F., Stenman, J.: Dense-timed pushdown automata. In: Proceedings of the 27th Annual IEEE Symposium on Logic in Computer Science, LICS 2012, Dubrovnik, Croatia, pp. 35–44, 25–28 June 2012. IEEE Computer Society. https://doi.org/10.1109/LICS.2012.15

2. Alur, R., Dill, D.: A theory of timed automata. Theoret. Comput. Sci. **126**, 183–235 (1994)
3. Alur, R., Dill, D.: Automata for modeling real-time systems. In: Paterson, M.S. (ed.) ICALP 1990. LNCS, vol. 443, pp. 322–335. Springer, Heidelberg (1990). https://doi.org/10.1007/BFb0032042
4. Alur, R., Fix, L., Henzinger, T.A.: Event-clock automata: a determinizable class of timed automata. Theoret. Comput. Sci. **211**(1–2), 253–273 (1999)
5. Alur, R., Madhusudan, P.: Visibly pushdown languages. In: Babai, L. (ed.) Proceedings of the 36th Annual ACM Symposium on Theory of Computing, Chicago, IL, USA, pp. 202–211, 13–16 June 2004. ACM. https://doi.org/10.1145/1007352.1007390
6. Bhave, D., Dave, V., Krishna, S.N., Phawade, R., Trivedi, A.: A logical characterization for dense-time visibly pushdown automata. In: Dediu, A.-H., Janoušek, J., Martín-Vide, C., Truthe, B. (eds.) LATA 2016. LNCS, vol. 9618, pp. 89–101. Springer, Cham (2016). https://doi.org/10.1007/978-3-319-30000-9_7
7. Bhave, D., Dave, V., Krishna, S.N., Phawade, R., Trivedi, A.: A perfect class of context-sensitive timed languages. In: Brlek, S., Reutenauer, C. (eds.) DLT 2016. LNCS, vol. 9840, pp. 38–50. Springer, Heidelberg (2016). https://doi.org/10.1007/978-3-662-53132-7_4
8. Bhave, D., Krishna, S.N., Phawade, R., Trivedi, A.: On timed scope-bounded context-sensitive languages. Technical report, IIT Bombay (2019). www.cse.iitb.ac.in/internal/techreports/reports/TR-CSE-2019-77.pdf
9. Bouajjani, A., Echahed, R., Habermehl, P.: On the verification problem of non-regular properties for nonregular processes. In: Proceedings, 10th Annual IEEE Symposium on Logic in Computer Science, San Diego, California, USA, pp. 123–133, 26–29 June 1995. IEEE Computer Society. https://doi.org/10.1109/LICS.1995.523250
10. Droste, M., Perevoshchikov, V.: A logical characterization of timed pushdown languages. In: Beklemishev, L.D., Musatov, D.V. (eds.) CSR 2015. LNCS, vol. 9139, pp. 189–203. Springer, Cham (2015). https://doi.org/10.1007/978-3-319-20297-6_13
11. Esparza, J., Ganty, P., Majumdar, R.: A perfect model for bounded verification. In: Proceedings of the 27th Annual IEEE Symposium on Logic in Computer Science, LICS 2012, Dubrovnik, Croatia, pp. 285–294, 25–28 June 2012. https://doi.org/10.1109/LICS.2012.39
12. La Torre, S., Madhusudan, P., Parlato, G.: A robust class of context-sensitive languages. In: LICS, pp. 161–170 (2007)
13. La Torre, S., Napoli, M., Parlato, G.: Scope-bounded pushdown languages. In: Shur, A.M., Volkov, M.V. (eds.) DLT 2014. LNCS, vol. 8633, pp. 116–128. Springer, Cham (2014). https://doi.org/10.1007/978-3-319-09698-8_11
14. La Torre, S., Napoli, M., Parlato, G.: Scope-bounded pushdown languages. Int. J. Found. Comput. Sci. **27**(2), 215–234 (2016)
15. Li, G., Cai, X., Ogawa, M., Yuen, S.: Nested timed automata. In: Braberman, V., Fribourg, L. (eds.) FORMATS 2013. LNCS, vol. 8053, pp. 168–182. Springer, Heidelberg (2013). https://doi.org/10.1007/978-3-642-40229-6_12
16. Trivedi, A., Wojtczak, D.: Recursive timed automata. In: Bouajjani, A., Chin, W.-N. (eds.) ATVA 2010. LNCS, vol. 6252, pp. 306–324. Springer, Heidelberg (2010). https://doi.org/10.1007/978-3-642-15643-4_23

17. Van Tang, N., Ogawa, M.: Event-clock visibly pushdown automata. In: Nielsen, M., Kučera, A., Miltersen, P.B., Palamidessi, C., Tůma, P., Valencia, F. (eds.) SOFSEM 2009. LNCS, vol. 5404, pp. 558–569. Springer, Heidelberg (2009). https://doi.org/10.1007/978-3-540-95891-8_50
18. Vardi, M., Wolper, P.: Reasoning about infinite computations. Inform. Comput. **115**(1), 1–37 (1994)

Logics for Reversible Regular Languages and Semigroups with Involution

Paul Gastin[1], Amaldev Manuel[2(✉)], and R. Govind[3,4]

[1] LSV, ENS Paris-Saclay & CNRS, University Paris-Saclay, Cachan, France
[2] Indian Institute of Technology Goa, Ponda, India
devmanuel@gmail.com
[3] Chennai Mathematical Institute, Chennai, India
[4] LaBRI, University of Bordeaux, Bordeaux, France

Abstract. We present MSO and FO logics with predicates 'between' and 'neighbour' that characterise various fragments of the class of regular languages that are closed under the reverse operation. The standard connections that exist between MSO and FO logics and varieties of finite semigroups extend to this setting with semigroups extended with an involution. The case is different for FO with neighbour relation where we show that one needs additional equations to characterise the class.

1 Introduction

In this paper we look closely at the class of regular languages that are closed under the reverse operation. We fix a finite alphabet A for the rest of our discussion. The set A^* (respectively A^+) denotes the set of all (resp. non-empty) finite words over the alphabet A. If $w = a_1 \cdots a_k$ with $a_i \in A$ is a word then $w^r = a_k \cdots a_1$ denotes the reverse of w. This notion is extended to sets of words pointwise, i.e. $L^r = \{w^r \mid w \in L\}$ and we can talk about reverse of languages. A regular language $L \subseteq A^*$ is *closed under reverse* or simply *reversible* if $L^r = L$. We let Rev denote the class of all reversible regular languages. Clearly Rev is a strict subset of the class of all regular languages.

The class Rev is easily verified to be closed under union, intersection and complementation. It is also closed under homomorphic images, and inverse homomorphic images under alphabetic (i.e. length preserving) morphisms. However they are not closed under quotients. For instance, the language $L = (abc)^* + (cba)^*$ is closed under reverse but the quotient $a^{-1}L = bc(abc)^*$ is not closed under reverse. Thus the class Rev fails to be a *variety* of languages—i.e. a class closed under Boolean operations, inverse morphic images and quotients. However reversible languages are closed under bidirectional quotients, i.e. quotients of the form $u^{-1}Lv^{-1} \cup (v^r)^{-1} L (u^r)^{-1}$, given words u, v. Thus, to a good extent, Rev shares properties similar to that of regular languages. Hence it makes sense to ask the question

Partly supported by UMI ReLaX. The work was carried out at Chennai Mathematical Institute.

P. Hofman and M. Skrzypczak (Eds.): DLT 2019, LNCS 11647, pp. 182–191, 2019.
https://doi.org/10.1007/978-3-030-24886-4_13

"are there good logical characterisations for the class Rev *and its well behaved subclasses?"*.

Our Results. We suggest a positive answer to the above question. We introduce two predicates *between* (bet(x, y, z) is true if position y is between positions x and z) and *neighbour* (N(x, y) is true if positions x and y are adjacent). The predicates *between* and *neighbour* are the natural analogues of the order relation $<$ and successor relation $+1$ in the undirected case. In fact this analogy extends to the case of logical definability. We show that Rev is the class of monadic second order (MSO) definable languages using either of the predicates, i.e. MSO(bet) or MSO(N). This is analogous to the classical Büchi-Elgot-Trakhtenbrot theorem relating regular languages and MSO logic. This connection extends to the case of first order logic as well. We show that FO(bet) definable languages are precisely the reversible languages definable in FO($<$). However the case of successor relation is different, i.e. the class of FO(N) definable languages is a strict subset of reversible languages definable in FO($+1$). The precise characterisation of this class is one of our main contributions.

The immediate question that arises from the above characterisations is one of definability: *Given a reversible language is it definable in the logic?"*. The case of FO(bet) is decidable due to Schützenberger-McNaughton-Papert theorem that states that syntactic monoids of FO($<$) definable languages are aperiodic (equivalent to the condition that the monoid contains no groups as subsemigroups) [8,9]. However the question for FO(N) is open. We prove a partial characterisation in terms of semigroups with involution. It is to be noted that the characterisation of FO($+1$) is a tedious one that goes via categories [11].

Related Work. A different but related *between* predicate (namely $a(x, y)$, for $a \in A$, is true if there is an a-labelled position between positions x and y) was introduced and studied in [5–7]. Such a predicate is not definable in FO^2($<$), the two variable fragment of first-order logic (which corresponds to the well known semigroup variety DA [12]). The authors of [5–7] study the expressive power of FO^2($<$) enriched with the between predicates $a(x, y)$ for $a \in A$, and show an algebraic characterisation of the resulting family of languages. The between predicate (predicates rather) in [5] is strictly less expressive than the between predicate introduced in this paper. However the logics considered in [5] have the between predicates in conjunction with order predicates $<$ and $+1$. Hence their results are orthogonal to ours.

Another line of work that has close parallels with the one in this paper is the variety theory of involution semigroups (also called $\star$-semigroups) (see [3] for a survey). Most investigations along these lines have been on subvarieties of *regular* $\star$-semigroups (i.e. $\star$-semigroups satisfying the equation $xx^\star x = x$). As far as we are aware the equation introduced in this paper has not been studied before.

Structure of the Paper. In Sect. 2 we introduce the predicates and present our logical characterisations. This is followed by a characterisation of FO(N). In Sect. 3

we discuss semigroups with involution, a natural notion of syntactic semigroups for reversible languages. In Sect. 4 we conclude.

2   Logics with *Between* and *Neighbour*

As usual we represent a word $w = a_1 \cdots a_n$ as a structure containing positions $\{1, \ldots, n\}$, and unary predicates P_a for each letter a in the alphabet. The predicate P_a is precisely true at those positions labelled by letter a. The atomic predicate $x < y$ (resp. $x + 1 = y$) is true if position y is after (resp. immediately after) position x. The logic FO is the logic containing atomic predicates, boolean combinations ($\phi \vee \psi$, $\phi \wedge \psi$, $\neg \psi$ whenever ϕ, ψ are formulas of the logic), and first order quantifications ($\exists x \, \psi$, $\forall x \, \psi$ if ψ is a formula of the logic). The logic MSO in addition contains second order quantification as well ($\exists X \, \psi$, $\forall X \, \psi$ if ψ is a formula of the logic)—i.e. quantification over sets of positions. By FO(τ) or MSO(τ) we mean the corresponding logic with atomic predicates τ in addition to the unary predicates P_a. The classical result relating MSO and regular languages states that MSO($<$) = MSO($+1$) defines all regular languages. We introduce two analogous predicates for the class Rev of reversible regular languages.

2.1   MSO(bet), MSO(N) and FO(bet)

The ternary *between* predicate $bet(x, y, z)$ is true for positions x, y, z when y is in between x and z, i.e.

$$bet(x, y, z) \quad := \quad x < y < z \text{ or } z < y < x.$$

Example 1. The set of all words containing the subword $a_1 a_2 \cdots a_k$ or $a_k a_{k-1} \cdots a_1$ is defined by the formula

$$\exists x_1 \exists x_2 \cdots \exists x_k \bigwedge_{i=1}^{k} P_{a_i}(x_i) \ \wedge \ \bigwedge_{i=2}^{k-1} bet(x_{i-1}, x_i, x_{i+1}).$$

The 'successor' relation of bet is the binary predicate *neighbour* $N(x, y)$ that holds true when x and y are neighbours, i.e.

$$N(x, y) \quad := \quad x + 1 = y \text{ or } y + 1 = x.$$

Example 2. The set of words of even length is defined by the formula

$$\exists X (X(e_1) \wedge \neg X(e_2) \wedge \forall x \forall y (N(x, y) \rightarrow (X(x) \leftrightarrow \neg X(y))))$$

where e_1, e_2 are the endpoints, i.e. the two positions with exactly one neighbour (defined easily in FO(N)).

The relation $N(x, y)$ can be defined in terms of bet using first-order quantifiers as $x \neq y \wedge \forall z \, \neg bet(x, z, y)$. One can also define $bet(x, y, z)$ in terms of N, but using second-order set quantification. To do this we assert that any subset X of positions

- that contains x, z and at least some other position
- and such that any position in X, except for x and z, has exactly two neighbours in X, contains the position y.

Proposition 1. *For definable languages,* MSO(bet) = MSO(N) = Rev.

Proof. Clearly from the discussion above, MSO(bet) = MSO(N) $\subseteq$ Rev. To show the other inclusion, let L be a reversible regular language and let φ be a formula in MSO($<$) defining it. Pick an endpoint e of the given word, an endpoint is a position with exactly one neighbour, a property expressible in FO(N) $\subseteq$ FO(bet). We relativize the formula φ with respect to e by replacing all occurrences of $x < y$ in the formula by $(e = x \neq y) \vee \text{bet}(e, x, y)$. Let $\varphi'(e)$ be the formula obtained in this way and let $\psi(e) = \neg \exists x, y \, (x \neq y \wedge N(e, x) \wedge N(e, y))$ be the FO(N) formula asserting that e is an endpoint, then we claim that

$$\chi = \exists e \, (\psi(e) \wedge \varphi'(e))$$

defines the language L. Let w be a word of length $k \geq 1$ then,

$$w \models \chi \Leftrightarrow w, 1 \models \varphi'(e) \text{ or } w, k \models \varphi'(e)$$
$$\Leftrightarrow w \models \varphi \text{ or } w^r \models \varphi$$
$$\Leftrightarrow w \models \varphi \text{ (since } L \text{ is reversible)}$$

Hence $L(\chi) = L(\varphi) = L$. $\qquad\square$

The above proposition says that MSO(bet) = MSO($<$) $\cap$ Rev. This carries down to the first-order case using the same relativization idea. In fact the result holds for the prefix class Σ_i (first-order formulas in prenex normal form with i blocks of alternating quantifiers starting with $\exists$-block).

Proposition 2. *The following is true for definable languages.*

1. FO(bet) = FO($<$) $\cap$ Rev.
2. Σ_i(bet) = Σ_i($<$) $\cap$ Rev.

Proof. Given an FO($<$) formula in prenex form defining a language in Rev, we replace every occurrence of $x < y$ by $(e = x \neq y) \vee \text{bet}(e, x, y)$ as before, where e is asserted to be an endpoint with $\psi(e) = \forall x, y \, \neg\text{bet}(x, e, y)$. For every formula in Σ_i($<$), $i \geq 2$ this results in an equivalent formula in Σ_i(bet). For the case of Σ_1, let us note that every formula in Σ_1($<$) defines a union of languages of the form $A^* a_1 A^* a_2 A^* \cdots A^* a_k A^*$. Such a language can be written as a disjunction of formulas like the one in Example 1. $\qquad\square$

2.2 FO(N)

Next we address the expressive power of FO with the neighbour predicate.

We start by detailing the class of *locally threshold testable languages.* Recall that word y is a factor of word u if $u = xyz$ for some x, z in A^*. We use $\sharp(u, y)$ to denote the number of times the factor y appears in u.

Let $\approx_k^t$, for $k, t > 0$, be the equivalence on A^*, whereby two words u and v are equivalent if either they both have length at most $k - 1$ and $u = v$, or otherwise they have

1. the same prefix of length $k - 1$,
2. the same suffix of length $k - 1$,
3. and the same number of occurrences, upto threshold t, for all factors of length $\leq k$, i.e. for each word $y \in A^*$ of length at most k, either $\sharp(u, y) = \sharp(v, y) < t$, or $\sharp(u, y) \geq t$ and $\sharp(v, y) \geq t$.

Example 3. We have $ababab \approx_2^1 abab \not\approx_2^1 abbab$. Indeed, all the words start and end with the same letter. In the first two words the factors ab as well as ba appear at least once. While in the last word the factor bb appears once while it is not present in the word $abab$. Notice also that $ababab \not\approx_2^2 abab$ due to the factor ba.

A language is *locally threshold testable* (or LTT for short) if it is a union of $\approx_k^t$ classes, for some $k, t > 0$.

Example 4. The language $(ab)^*$ is LTT. In fact it is *locally testable* (the special case of locally threshold testable with $t = 1$). Indeed, $(ab)^*$ is the union of three classes: $\{\varepsilon\}$, $\{ab\}$ and $abab(ab)^*$ which is precisely the set of words that begin with a, end with b, and the only factors are ab and ba.

A language that is definable in FO($<$) and not LTT is $c^*ac^*bc^*$. In this language if a and b are sufficiently separated by c-blocks then the order between a and b cannot be differentiated. It can be proved that for any t, k there is a sufficiently large n such that $c^n ac^n bc^n \approx_k^t c^n bc^n ac^n$.

Locally threshold testable languages are precisely the class of languages definable in FO($+1$) [1,13]. Since we can define the neighbour predicate N using $+1$, clearly FO(N) $\subseteq$ FO($+1$) $\cap$ Rev = LTT $\cap$ Rev. But this inclusion is strict as shown in Example 6.

Example 5. Consider the language $L = ua^* + a^*u^r$ of words which have either u as prefix and followed by an arbitrary number of a's, or u^r as suffix and preceded by an arbitrary number of a's. The language L is in FO(N). When $u = a_1 \cdots a_n$, it can be defined by a formula of the form $\exists x_1, \ldots, x_n \, \psi$ where ψ states that x_1 is an endpoint, $\bigwedge_{1 \leq i < n} N(x_i, x_{i+1})$, $\bigwedge_{1 < i < n} x_{i-1} \neq x_{i+1}$, $\bigwedge_{1 \leq i \leq n} P_{a_i}(x_i)$, and all other positions are labelled a.

Example 6. Consider the language L over the alphabet $\{a, b, c\}$,

$$L = \{w \mid \sharp(w, ab) = 2, \sharp(w, ba) = 1 \text{ or } \sharp(w, ab) = 1, \sharp(w, ba) = 2\}.$$

Since L is locally threshold testable and reverse closed, $L \in$ FO($+1$) $\cap$ Rev.
We can show that $L \notin$ FO(N) by showing that the words,

$$c^k \, ab \, c^k \, ba \, c^k ab \, c^k \in L \qquad c^k \, ab \, c^k \, ab \, c^k \, ab \, c^k \notin L$$

for $k > 0$ are indistinguishable by an FO(N) formula of quantifier depth k. For showing the latter claim, one uses Ehrenfeucht-Fraïssé games and argues that in the k-round EF-game the duplicator has a winning strategy. The strategy is roughly described below:

$$\underline{c^k abc^k b}\, ac^k abc^k \qquad c^k abc^k a\, \underline{bc^k abc^k}$$

Any move of the spoiler is mimicked by the duplicator in the corresponding underlined or non-underlined part of the other word, while maintaining the neighbourhood relation between positions. For instance, if the spoiler plays the first b on the underlined part of the first word, then the duplicator chooses the last b on the underlined portion of the word on the right. Similarly, if the spoiler plays the first a on the non-underlined part of the first word, the duplicator chooses the last a on the non-underlined portion of the word on the right. Note that, since no order on positions in the words can be checked with the neighbour predicate, there is no way to distinguish between these words, if the duplicator plays in the above way ensuring that the position played has the same neighbourhood relation as the position played by the spoiler. Therefore, the Neighbour predicate will not be able to distinguish between ab and ba when they are sufficiently separated by c's.

From the above example, we get,

Proposition 3. *For definable languages,* $\mathsf{FO}(\mathsf{N}) \subsetneq \mathsf{FO}(+1) \cap \mathsf{Rev} = \mathsf{LTT} \cap \mathsf{Rev}.$

Next we will characterise the class of languages accepted by FO(N). For $t > 0$ we define the equality with threshold t on the set $\mathbb{N}$ of natural numbers by $i =^t j$ if $i = j$ or $i, j \geq t$. Recall that $\sharp(w, v)$ denotes the number of occurrences of v in w, i.e. the number of pairs (x, y) such that $w = xvy$. We extend this to $\sharp^r(w, v)$ which counts the number of occurrences of v or v^r in w, i.e. the number of pairs (x, y) such that $w = xvy$ or $w = xv^r y$. Notice that $\sharp^r(w, v) = \sharp^r(w, v^r) = \sharp^r(w^r, v) = \sharp^r(w^r, v^r)$.

We define now the *locally-reversible threshold testable* (LRTT) equivalence relation. Let $k, t > 0$. Two words $w, w' \in A^*$ are (k, t)-LRTT equivalent, denoted $w \approx_k^{rt} w'$ if $|w| < k$ and $w' \in \{w, w^r\}$, or

- w, w' are both of length at least k, and
- $\sharp^r(w, v) =^t \sharp^r(w', v)$ for all $v \in A^{\leq k}$, and
- if x, x' are the prefixes of w, w' of length $k - 1$ and y, y' are the suffixes of w, w' of length $k - 1$ then $\{x, y^r\} = \{x', y'^r\}$.

Notice that $w \approx_k^{rt} w^r$ for all $w \in A^*$ and $w \approx_k^t w'$ implies $w \approx_k^{rt} w'$ for all $w, w' \in A^*$. Notice also that $\approx_k^{rt}$ is not a congruence. Indeed, we have $ab \approx_k^{rt} ba$ but $aba \not\approx_k^{rt} baa$. On the other hand, if $v \approx_k^{rt} w$ then for all $u \in A^*$ we have $uv \approx_k^{rt} uw$ or $uv \approx_k^{rt} uw^r$, and similarly $vu \approx_k^{rt} wu$ or $vu \approx_k^{rt} w^r u$.

Definition 1 (Locally-Reversible Threshold Testable Languages). *A language L is* locally-reversible threshold testable, *LRTT for short, if it is a union of equivalence classes of $\approx_k^{rt}$ for some $k, t > 0$.*

Theorem 1. *Languages defined by* FO(N) *are precisely the class of locally-reversible threshold testable languages.*

Proof. ($\Leftarrow$) Assume we are given an LRTT language, i.e. a union of $\approx_k^{rt}$-classes for some $k, t > 0$. We explain how to write an FO(N) formula for each $\approx_k^{rt}$-class. Consider a word $v = a_1 a_2 \cdots a_n \in A^+$. For $m \in \mathbb{N}$, we can say that v or its reverse occurs at least m times in a word $w \in A^*$, i.e. $\sharp^r(w, v) \geq m$, by the formula

$$\varphi_v^{\geq m} = \exists x_{1,1} \cdots \exists x_{1,n} \cdots \exists x_{m,1} \cdots \exists x_{m,n}$$

$$\bigwedge_{i=1}^{m} \Big(\bigwedge_{j=1}^{n-1} \mathsf{N}(x_{i,j}, x_{i,j+1}) \wedge \bigwedge_{j=2}^{n-1} (x_{i,j-1} \neq x_{i,j+1}) \wedge \bigwedge_{j=1}^{n} P_{a_j}(x_{i,j}) \Big)$$

$$\wedge \bigwedge_{1 \leq i < j \leq m} \neg((x_{i,1} = x_{j,1} \wedge x_{i,n} = x_{j,n}) \vee (x_{i,1} = x_{j,n} \wedge x_{i,n} = x_{j,1})).$$

Similarly, we can write a formula $\psi_v \in$ FO(N) that says that a word belongs to $\{v, v^r\}$. Finally, given two words of same length $u, v \in A^n$, we can write a formula $\chi_{u,v} \in$ FO(N) that says that u, v occur at two different end points of a word w, i.e. that $\{x, y^r\} = \{u, v\}$ where x, y are the prefix and suffix of w of length n.

($\Rightarrow$) Hanf's theorem [4] states that two structures A and B are m-equivalent (i.e. indistinguishable by any FO formula of quantifier rank at most m), for some $m \in \mathbb{N}$ if for each 3^m ball type S, both A and B have the same number of 3^m balls of type S upto a threshold $m \times e$, where $e \in \mathbb{N}$. Applying Hanf's theorem to undirected path graphs, we obtain that given an FO(N) formula Φ, there exist $k, t > 0$ such that the fact that a word w satisfies Φ only depends on its $\approx_k^{rt}$-class. The set of all such words is therefore an LRTT language.   □

3   Semigroups with Involution

In this section we address the question of definability of a language—"is the given reversible regular language definable by a formula in the logic?"—in the previously defined logics. We show that in the case of FO(bet) the existing theorems provide an algorithm for the problem, while for FO(N) the answer is not yet known.

First we recall the notion of recognisability by a finite semigroup. A finite semigroup $(S, \cdot)$ is a finite set S with an associative binary operation $\cdot : S \times S \to S$. If the semigroup operation has an identity, then it is necessarily unique and is denoted by 1. In this case S is called a monoid. A semigroup morphism from $(S, \cdot)$ to $(T, +)$ is a map $h : S \to T$ that preserves the semigroup operation, i.e. $h(a \cdot b) = h(a) + h(b)$ for a, b in S. Further if S and T are monoids the map is a monoid morphism if h maps the identity of S to the identity of T.

The set A^* (resp. A^+) under concatenation forms a free monoid (resp. free semigroup). A language $L \subseteq A^*$ is *recognised* by a semigroup (or monoid) $(S, \cdot)$, if there is a morphism $h : A^* \to (S, \cdot)$ and a set $P \subseteq S$, such that $L = h^{-1}(P)$.

Given a language L, the *syntactic congruence* of L, denoted as $\sim_L$ is the congruence on A^*,

$$x \sim_L y \quad \text{if} \quad uxv \in L \Leftrightarrow uyv \in L \text{ for all } u, v \in A^*.$$

The quotient $A^*/\sim_L$, (resp. $A^+/\sim_L$) denoted as $M(L)$, is called the *syntactic monoid* (resp. *syntactic semigroup*). It recognises L and is the unique minimal object with this property: any monoid S recognising L has a surjective morphism from a submonoid of S to $M(L)$ [11].

In the particular case of reversible languages the syntactic monoid described above admits further properties. The observation is that the reverse operation can be extended to congruence classes of the syntactic congruence by letting $[x]^r = [x^r]$ for each word x and it is well defined since if $x \sim_L y$ then $x^r \sim_L y^r$ as can be easily verified. Moreover this operation is an involution, i.e. $([x]^r)^r = ([x^r])^r = [(x^r)^r] = [x]$, and an anti-isomorphism on the congruence classes, i.e. $([x] \cdot [y])^r = ([x \cdot y])^r = [(x \cdot y)^r] = [y^r \cdot x^r] = [y^r] \cdot [x^r] = [y]^r \cdot [x]^r$. Therefore one can enrich the notion of semigroups for recognisability in the case of reversible languages as below.

A *semigroup with involution* (also called a $\star$-semigroup) $(S, \cdot, \star)$ is a semigroup $(S, \cdot)$ extended with an operation $\star \colon S \to S$ (called the involution) such that

1. the operation $\star$ is an involution on S, i.e. $(a^\star)^\star = a$ for all elements a of S,
2. the operation $\star$ is an anti-automorphism on S (isomorphism between S and opposite of S), i.e. $(a \cdot b)^\star = b^\star \cdot a^\star$ for any a, b in S.

It is a $\star$-monoid if S is a monoid. It is easy to see that in the case of $\star$-monoids, necessarily $1^\star = 1$. Clearly the free monoid A^* with the reverse operation r as the involution is a $\star$-monoid, since $(w^r)^r = w$ and $(v \cdot w)^r = w^r \cdot v^r$. When there is no ambiguity, we just write A^* to refer to the $\star$-monoid $(A^*, \cdot, r)$.

A map $h \colon S \to T$ between two $\star$-semigroups $(S, \cdot, \star)$ and $(T, +, \dagger)$ is a morphism if it is a morphism between the semigroups $(S, \cdot)$ and $(T, +)$ that preserves the involution, i.e. $h(a^\star) = h(a)^\dagger$.

A language $L \subseteq A^*$ is said to be recognised by a $\star$-semigroup $(S, \cdot, \star)$, if there is a morphism $h \colon (A^*, \cdot, r) \to (S, \cdot, \star)$ and a set $P \subseteq S$, such that $P^\star = P$ and $L = h^{-1}(P)$. The following proposition summarises the discussion so far.

Proposition 4. *The following are equivalent for a language L.*

1. *L is a reversible regular language,*
2. *L is recognised by a finite $\star$-monoid,*
3. *$M(L)$ with the reverse operation is a finite $\star$-monoid with $P = P^\star$ where $P = \{[u] \mid u \in L\}$, i.e. $(M(L), \cdot, r)$ recognises L as a $\star$-monoid.*

A semigroup (or monoid) is aperiodic if there is some $n \in \mathbb{N}$ such that $a^n = a^{n+1}$ for each element a of the semigroup. Schützenberger-McNaughton-Papert theorem states that a language L is definable in $FO(<)$ if and only if the syntactic monoid is aperiodic. This theorem in conjunction with Proposition 2 gives that,

Proposition 5. *A reversible language L is definable in* FO(bet) *if and only if* $M(L)$ *is aperiodic.*

The above theorem hence yields an algorithm for definability of a language in FO(bet), i.e. check if the language is reversible, if so compute the syntactic monoid (which is also a monoid with an involution) and test for aperiodicity.

Next we look at the logic FO(N). The characterisation theorem for FO(+1) due to Brzozowski and Simon [2], and Beauquier and Pin [1], is stated below. Recall that an element of a semigroup e is an *idempotent* if $e \cdot e = e$.

Theorem 2 (Brzozowski-Simon, Beauquier-Pin). *The following are equivalent.*

1. *L is locally threshold testable.*
2. *L is definable in* FO(+1).
3. *The syntactic semigroup of L is finite, aperiodic and satisfies the identity*
   $e\,x\,f\,y\,e\,z\,f = e\,z\,f\,y\,e\,x\,f$ *for all $e, f, x, y, z \in M(L)$ with e, f idempotents.*

Because of Proposition 3 we need to add more identities to characterise the logic FO(N) in terms of $\star$-semigroups.

Theorem 3. *The syntactic $\star$-semigroup of an* FO(N)*-definable language satisfies the identity*
$$exe^\star = ex^\star e^\star,$$
where e is an idempotent, and x is any element of the semigroup.

Proof. Assume we are given an FO(N)-language L, with its syntactic $\star$-semigroup $M = (A^+/\sim_L, \cdot, \star)$, and $h \colon A^+ \to M$ the canonical morphism recognising L. Let e be an idempotent of M, and let x be an element of M. Pick nonempty words u and s such that $h(u) = e$ and $h(s) = x$.

By definition of the involution, $h(u^r) = e^\star$ and $h(s^r) = x^\star$. We are going to show that $usu^r \sim_L us^r u^r$ and hence they will correspond to the same element in the syntactic $\star$-semigroup, proving that $exe^\star = ex^\star e^\star$.

Since L is FO(N) definable, we know by Theorem 1 that L is a union of $\approx_k^{rt}$ equivalence classes for some $k, t > 0$. Consider the words $w = (u^k)s(u^k)^r$ and $w^r = (u^k)s^r(u^k)^r$, obtained by pumping the words corresponding to e and $e^\star$. Since $e, e^\star$ are idempotents, it is clear that $h(w) = h(usu^r) = exe^\star$ and $h(w^r) = h(us^r u^r) = ex^\star e^\star$.

For all contexts $\alpha, \beta \in A^*$, we show below that $\alpha w \beta \approx_k^{rt} \alpha w^r \beta$, which implies $\alpha w \beta \in L$ iff $\alpha w^r \beta \in L$ since L is a union of $\approx_k^{rt}$ classes. It follows that $w \sim_L w^r$ and therefore $h(w) = h(w^r)$, which will conclude the proof.

Fix some contexts $\alpha, \beta \in A^*$. Since $u \neq \varepsilon$, the words $\alpha w \beta$ and $\alpha w^r \beta$ have the same prefix of length $k-1$ and the same suffix of length $k-1$. Now, consider $v \in A^k$. If an occurrence of v (resp. v^r) in $\alpha w \beta$ overlaps with α or β then we have the very same occurrence in $\alpha w^r \beta$. Using $w \approx_k^{rt} w^r$, we deduce that $\sharp^r(\alpha w \beta, v) =^t \sharp^r(\alpha w^r \beta, v)$. Therefore, $\alpha w \beta \approx_k^{rt} \alpha w^r \beta$. $\square$

The converse direction is open. The similar direction in the case of FO(+1) goes via categories [14] and uses the Delay theorem of Straubing [10,11].

4 Conclusion

The logics MSO(bet), MSO(N) and FO(bet) behave analogously to the classical counterparts MSO(<), MSO(+1) and FO(<). But the logic FO(N) gives rise to a new class of languages, locally-reversible threshold testable languages. The quest for characterising the new class takes us to the formalism of involution semigroups. The full characterisation of the new class is the main question we leave open. Another line of investigation is to study the equationally-defined classes that arise naturally from automata theory.

References

1. Beauquier, D., Pin, J.: Languages and scanners. Theor. Comput. Sci. **84**(1), 3–21 (1991)
2. Brzozowski, J.A., Simon, I.: Characterizations of locally testable events. In: Proceedings of the 12th Annual Symposium on Switching and Automata Theory (Swat 1971), pp. 166–176. SWAT 1971 (1971)
3. Crvenković, S., Dolinka, I.: Varieties of involution semigroups and involution semirings: a survey. In: Proceedings of the International Conference "Contemporary Developments in Mathematics" (Banja Luka, 2000), pp. 7–47. Bulletin of Society of Mathematicians of Banja Luka (2000)
4. Ebbinghaus, H., Flum, J.: Finite Model Theory. Perspectives in Mathematical Logic. Springer, Heidelberg (1995). https://doi.org/10.1007/978-3-662-03182-7
5. Krebs, A., Lodaya, K., Pandya, P., Straubing, H.: Two-variable logic with a between relation. In: Proceedings of the 31st Annual ACM/IEEE Symposium on Logic in Computer Science, LICS 2016, pp. 106–115 (2016)
6. Krebs, A., Lodaya, K., Pandya, P.K., Straubing, H.: An Algebraic Decision Procedure for Two-Variable Logic with a Between Relation. In: 27th EACSL Annual Conference on Computer Science Logic (CSL 2018), Leibniz International Proceedings in Informatics (LIPIcs), vol. 119, pp. 28:1–28:17 (2018)
7. Krebs, A., Lodaya, K., Pandya, P.K., Straubing, H.: Two-variable logics with some betweenness relations: expressiveness, satisfiability and membership. arXiv preprint arXiv:1902.05905 (2019)
8. McNaughton, R., Papert, S.A.: Counter-Free Automata (M.I.T. Research Monograph No. 65). The MIT Press (1971)
9. Schützenberger, M.P.: On finite monoids having only trivial subgroups. Inf. Control **8**(2), 190–194 (1965)
10. Straubing, H.: Finite semigroup varieties of the form V ∗ D. J. Pure Appl. Algebra **36**, 53–94 (1985)
11. Straubing, H.: Finite Automata, Formal Logic, and Circuit Complexity. Birkhäuser Verlag, Basel (1994)
12. Tesson, P., Therien, D.: Diamonds are forever: the variety DA. In: Semigroups, Algorithms, Automata and Languages, Coimbra (Portugal) 2001, pp. 475–500. World Scientific (2002)
13. Thomas, W.: Classifying regular events in symbolic logic. J. Comput. Syst. Sci. **25**(3), 360–376 (1982)
14. Tilson, B.: Categories as algebra: an essential ingredient in the theory of monoids. J. Pure Appl. Algebra **48**(1–2), 83–198 (1987)

Eventually Safe Languages

Simon Iosti[1] and Denis Kuperberg[2(✉)]

[1] Verimag, Université Grenoble-Alpes, Saint-Martin-d'Hères, France
[2] CNRS, LIP, ENS, Lyon, France
denis.kuperberg@ens-lyon.fr

Abstract. Good-for-Games (GFG) automata constitute a sound alternative to determinism as a way to model specifications in the Church synthesis problem. Typically, inputs for the synthesis problem are in the form of LTL formulas. However, the only known examples where GFG automata present an exponential gap in succinctness compared to deterministic ones are not LTL-definable. We show that GFG automata still enjoy exponential succinctness for LTL-definable languages. We introduce a class of properties called "eventually safe" together with a specification language $E\nu$TL for this class. We finally give an algorithm to produce a Good-for-Games automaton from any $E\nu$TL formula, thereby allowing synthesis for eventually safe properties.

1 Introduction

Synthesis is one of the most classical applications of automata theory. It asks, given a specification, whether there exists a reactive system complying with it. We also want to automatically build such a system when it exists. The specification is typically given in a logic such as Linear Temporal Logic (LTL). The problem was solved positively by Büchi and Landweber [5] for the case of ω-regular specifications. The usual approach to this problem consists in building a deterministic automaton from the specification, and then solving a game based on this automaton. Henzinger and Piterman [11] have proposed a model oproblem was solved positively byf Good-For-Games (GFG) automata as a weakening of determinism that is still sound for solving the synthesis problem. An automaton is GFG if there exists a strategy that resolves the non-deterministic choices, by taking into account only the prefix of the input ω-word read so far. The strategy must guarantee to build an accepting run whenever the input word is in the language of the automaton. In [15], the question of succinctness of GFG automata compared to deterministic ones is answered. A family (L_n) of languages is exhibited, such that for each n there is a GFG coBüchi automaton of size n for L_n, but any deterministic Streett automaton for L_n must have size exponential in n. Therefore, GFG automata offer a promising alternative to deterministic ones for synthesis, and this work is part of an effort to systematically study their applicability in this context.

However, one of the potential issues with the use of GFG automata for synthesis lies in the fact that the most usual specification formalism for synthesis

P. Hofman and M. Skrzypczak (Eds.): DLT 2019, LNCS 11647, pp. 192–205, 2019.
https://doi.org/10.1007/978-3-030-24886-4_14

is LTL. It is therefore natural to ask whether GFG automata can be useful in this context. We show that the languages L_n witnessing succinctness of GFG automata are not LTL-definable. Moreover, a close look at the structure of GFG coBüchi automata, as studied in [15], suggests that the ability to permute states is an essential feature of non-trivial GFG automata. It is therefore plausible that GFG automata are no longer succinct (compared to deterministic ones) for LTL-definable languages, where such permutations are forbidden [7].

We answer this question here, by building a family (K_n) of LTL-definable languages presenting the same succinctness gap as the family (L_n) between GFG and deterministic automata. Although this shows that GFG automata are still succinct for LTL-definable languages, the issue of practicability is still unclear, due to the fact that the LTL formulas representing K_n have exponential size. Moreover, we show that there are simple μ-calculus formulas of linear size for the same languages. Interestingly, a by-product of this work is the exhibition of the family K_n as a candidate witness for an exponential gap succinctness of linear μ-calculus compared to LTL, a problem that is open to our knowledge. This suggests that μ-calculus is more suited than LTL for describing specifications that are recognized by small GFG automata. We therefore aim at proposing a framework based on μ-calculus for building succinct GFG automata.

This leads us to a second issue standing in the way of bringing GFG automata to practical applications. Due to their semantic definition, building GFG automata is a hard problem and requires an understanding of their syntactical shape. A first way to achieve this has been given in [14], building GFG automata in an incremental way from non-deterministic ones. The algorithm tries bigger and bigger automata until a GFG one is reached, the worst case being when a full determinization construction is needed. The only knowledge about GFG automata that is used in this construction is in the subroutine used to test whether an automaton is GFG. We propose here an alternative approach, building automata that are GFG by construction, using the understanding acquired in [15] about the structure of GFG coBüchi automata.

Considering restricted classes of specifications is a classical way to try to tackle the difficulty of the synthesis problem. The classes of safety and liveness properties [1] have gathered particular interest [18,20], as they simplify algorithms while expressing typical requirements on reactive systems. We introduce a class of properties called "eventually safe" and noted $ESafe$, for which we give a specification language $E\nu$TL and an algorithm systematically producing GFG automata from this language. The class $ESafe$ can be seen as a natural compromise between safety and liveness, and is defined as the class of languages of the form $\Sigma^* L_{safe}$ where L_{safe} is a suffix-closed safety language. Equivalently, the class $ESafe$ is the class of prefix-independent coBüchi languages. As an example, the following specification can be formalized in $ESafe$: "after being started, the system must eventually start interacting with external agents, and must answer their requests within a fixed finite time".

Both families (L_n) and (K_n) are expressible in the logic $E\nu$TL in a very natural way and with formulas of size linear in n. This approach is orthogonal to the one from [14] that we outlined above. Here, we restrict the class of inputs to the class *ESafe* that is natural for verification purposes, and for which GFG automata are well-suited. We show that unfortunately, translating a formula of $E\nu$TL to a GFG automaton is still doubly exponential in the worst case. This is not surprising, as it was shown in [4] that this is already the case for translating LTL (or linear μ-calculus) formulas for "bounded" languages, i.e. languages that are both safe and co-safe, to GFG automata. However we believe that this model is worth exploring, in order to understand the power and possible limitations of GFG automata for synthesis. Moreover, recent works such as [8,13] rely on a modular treatment of specifications, and can call subroutines to build automata for restricted fragments of LTL. This is particularly suitable to embed GFG automata for well-behaved fragments, and the present work brings a clearer understanding of the possibilities and theoretical limitations of this approach.

Let us give another example of application of the $E\nu$TL formalism, in the spirit of this modular approach. Properties required of systems are often subject to fairness assumptions. This is expressed by specifications of the form $\psi \Rightarrow \varphi$ for some fairness assumption ψ, that typically consists in liveness properties. This can be treated by building a GFG automaton for $\neg\psi$, in addition to the automaton for φ. In this context, $E\nu$TL would for example allow to model the fairness assumption that a finite set of agents (that can be dynamically renamed) will all be activated infinitely many times, as the complement of such a language is similar to the language L_n discussed in this work.

Outline of the Paper

We start by recalling definitions on logical formalisms and automata in Sect. 2. In Sect. 3, we recall the definition of the (L_n) language family from [15], and show that it is not LTL-definable. In Sect. 4, we define the (K_n) family, show that it also witnesses succinctness of GFG automata compared to deterministic ones, and give a family of LTL formulas of exponential size for the languages (K_n). In Sect. 5, we define the safety fragment $S\nu$TL of linear μ-calculus, show that it is equivalent to safety languages, and build the logic $E\nu$TL based on its syntax by using an alternative semantic. We show that both families of languages (K_n) and (L_n) have linear-size representations in $E\nu$TL, and give a generic algorithm to translate an $E\nu$TL formula to a GFG coBüchi automaton. We also exhibit an $E\nu$TL formula witnessing that the translation to GFG coBüchi automata is doubly exponential in the worst case. Detailed proofs can be found in the appendix of the online version.

2   Definitions

We will use Σ to denote an arbitrary finite alphabet. The empty word is denoted ε. If $i \leq j$, the set $\{i, i+1, i+2, \ldots, j\}$ is denoted $[i, j]$. The set of finite words on Σ is denoted Σ^*, and the set of infinite words Σ^ω. We note $\Sigma^\infty = \Sigma^* \cup \Sigma^\omega$. If $X \subseteq \Sigma^\omega$, we note $pref(X)$ the set of finite prefixes of words in X, and $suff(X)$ the set of infinite suffixes of words in X. A set $X \subseteq \Sigma^\omega$ is *prefix-independent* if for all $u, v \in \Sigma^*$ and $w \in \Sigma^\omega$, we have $uw \in X \Leftrightarrow vw \in X$. A set $X \subseteq \Sigma^\omega$ is *suffix-closed* if $suff(X) = X$.

2.1 Logic

We define here the linear temporal logic (LTL) and the linear μ-calculus.

The syntax of LTL is defined with the following grammar, where a ranges over Σ:

$$\varphi := a \mid \varphi \vee \varphi \mid \neg\varphi \mid \bigcirc\varphi \mid \varphi \mathbf{U}\varphi$$

The semantic $\llbracket\varphi\rrbracket \subseteq \Sigma^\omega$ of a formula φ of LTL is defined recursively on the formula:

- $\llbracket a \rrbracket = \{aw \mid w \in \Sigma^\omega\}$,
- $\llbracket\varphi \vee \psi\rrbracket = \llbracket\varphi\rrbracket \cup \llbracket\psi\rrbracket$,
- $\llbracket\neg\varphi\rrbracket = \Sigma^\omega \setminus \llbracket\varphi\rrbracket$,
- $\llbracket\bigcirc\varphi\rrbracket = \{aw \in \Sigma^\omega \mid a \in \Sigma, w \in \llbracket\varphi\rrbracket\}$,
- $\llbracket\varphi\mathbf{U}\psi\rrbracket = \{a_0a_1 \cdots \in \Sigma^\omega \mid \exists i \in \mathbb{N}, \forall j < i, a_ja_{j+1} \cdots \in \llbracket\varphi\rrbracket$, and $a_ia_{i+1} \cdots \in \llbracket\psi\rrbracket\}$.

Let a be an arbitrary letter in Σ and φ, ψ be LTL formulas. We will use the syntactic sugar $\varphi \wedge \psi$, $\top$, $\bot$, $\mathbf{F}\varphi$, $\mathbf{G}\varphi$ and $\varphi\mathbf{W}\mathbf{U}\psi$ as shorthands for $\neg((\neg\varphi) \vee (\neg\psi))$, $a \vee \neg a$, $\neg\top$, $\top\mathbf{U}\varphi$, $\neg\mathbf{F}\neg\varphi$ and $\mathbf{G}\varphi \vee \varphi\mathbf{U}\psi$ respectively.

The linear μ-calculus has the following syntax, where a ranges over Σ, and X over a countable set V of variables:

$$\varphi := a \mid X \mid \varphi \vee \varphi \mid \neg\varphi \mid \bigcirc\varphi \mid \mu X.\varphi \mid \nu X.\varphi$$

Its semantic $\llbracket\varphi\rrbracket_{\mu,val}$ relative to a valuation $val : V \to 2^{\Sigma^\omega}$ of the variables is defined similarly to the semantic of LTL for their common symbols (using the μ-calculus semantic instead of the LTL semantic), with the following additional rules for the new symbols, where gfp and lfp denote the greatest fixed point and the least fixed point operators respectively, and $val[X \to S]$ is the valuation val except for $val(X) = S$:

- $\llbracket X \rrbracket_{\mu,val} = val(X)$;
- $\llbracket\mu X.\varphi\rrbracket_{\mu,val} = lfp(S \to \llbracket\varphi\rrbracket_{\mu,val[X \to S]})$;
- $\llbracket\nu X.\varphi\rrbracket_{\mu,val} = gfp(S \to \llbracket\varphi\rrbracket_{\mu,val[X \to S]})$.

The semantic $\llbracket\varphi\rrbracket_\mu$ of a closed formula φ is $\llbracket\varphi\rrbracket_{\mu,\emptyset}$ where $\emptyset$ is the empty valuation.

The *DAG-size* of a formula is a measure of the size of the formula using the directed acyclic graph (DAG) representing the formula instead of the syntactic tree. We define formally the DAG-size $|\varphi|_{dag}$ of a formula φ as the size of the set $sub(\varphi)$ of subformulas of φ. This representation of a formula as a DAG is usually the one used in algorithms taking as input LTL or μ-calculus formulas (e.g. the translation from a LTL formula to a Büchi automaton), and is therefore a more sensible measure of the size of a formula than the size of its syntactic tree.

2.2   Automata

A non-deterministic automaton $\mathcal{A}$ is a tuple $(Q, \Sigma, q_0, \Delta, F)$ where Q is the set of states, Σ is a finite alphabet, $q_0 \in Q$ is the initial state, $\Delta : Q \times \Sigma \to 2^Q$ is the transition function, and $F \subseteq Q$ is the set of accepting states. If for all $(p, a) \in Q \times \Sigma$ there is at most one $q \in Q$ such that $q \in \Delta(p, a)$, we say that $\mathcal{A}$ is *deterministic*.

If $u = a_1 \ldots a_n$ is a finite word of Σ^*, a run of $\mathcal{A}$ on u is a sequence $q_0 q_1 \ldots q_n$ such that for all $i \in [1, n]$, we have $q_i \in \Delta(q_{i-1}, a_i)$. The run is said to be *accepting* if $q_n \in F$. If $u = a_1 a_2 \ldots$ is an infinite word of Σ^ω, a run of $\mathcal{A}$ on u is a sequence $q_0 q_1 q_2 \ldots$ such that for all $i > 0$, we have $q_i \in \Delta(q_{i-1}, a_i)$. A run is said to be *Büchi accepting* if it contains infinitely many accepting states, and *coBüchi accepting* if it contains finitely many non-accepting states. Automata on infinite words will be called Büchi and coBüchi automata, to specify their acceptance condition.

We will note NFA (resp. DFA) for a non-deterministic (resp. deterministic) automaton on finite words, and NCW (resp. DCW) for a non-deterministic (resp. deterministic) coBüchi automaton. An automaton $\mathcal{A}$ is a *safety* automaton if $F = Q$, and every run is accepting.

Non-deterministic automata can be generalized to *alternating* automata, where the transition function associates to each pair $(p, a) \in Q \times \Sigma$ a positive boolean combination of states instead of a disjunction. We refer the reader to [9] for formal definitions and basic constructions on alternating automata.

We also mention the *Rabin condition* on infinite words: it consists of a list of pairs $(E_i, F_i) \in 2^Q \times 2^Q$ and an infinite run is accepting if there is i such that some states from E_i are seen infinitely often and all states from F_i are seen finitely often. Its dual, the negation of a Rabin condition, is called a *Streett condition*. They both generalize the parity condition.

The language of an automaton $\mathcal{A}$, noted $L(\mathcal{A})$, is the set of words on which the automaton $\mathcal{A}$ has an accepting run. Two automata are *equivalent* if they recognise the same language. For a property P of automata (e.g. safety, or coBüchi), a language is said to be P if it is the language of a P automaton.

An automaton $\mathcal{A}$ is *determinisable by pruning* (DBP) if an equivalent deterministic automaton can be obtained from $\mathcal{A}$ by removing some transitions.

An automaton $\mathcal{A}$ is *Good-For-Games* (GFG) if there exists a function $\sigma \colon \Sigma^* \to Q$ (called *GFG strategy*) that resolves the non-determinism of $\mathcal{A}$ depending only on the prefix of the input word read so far: over every word $u = a_1 a_2 a_3 \ldots$ (finite or infinite depending on the type of automaton considered), the sequence of states $\sigma(\varepsilon)\sigma(a_1)\sigma(a_1 a_2)\sigma(a_1 a_2 a_3) \ldots$ is a run of $\mathcal{A}$ on u, and it is accepting whenever $u \in L(\mathcal{A})$. For instance every DBP automaton is GFG. See [2] for more introductory material and examples on GFG automata.

Lemma 1. *GFG automata are closed under the standard union and intersection constructions using cartesian products.*

3   The Original Family L_n

We start by recalling the family of languages L_n from [15], witnessing an exponential blow-up in the state space for determinisation of GFG automata.

The language L_n is defined on alphabet $\Sigma = \{\iota, \sigma, \pi, \sharp\}$. Each letter represents a permutation of the set $[0, 2n-1]$: ι is the identity, σ is the cycle $(0\ 1\ 2\ \ldots 2n-1)$, π is the transposition $(0\ 1)$, and $\sharp$ is the identity on $[1, 2n-1]$ and is undefined on 0.

An infinite word $w \in \Sigma^\omega$ describes an infinite graph noted $\mathrm{Graph}(w)$ with vertices $[0, 2n-1] \times \mathbb{N}$, where letter $w(i)$ representing a permutation α induces edges from vertice (k, i) to $(\alpha(k), i+1)$ for each $k \in [0, 2n-1]$ where α is defined. An example is given below for $n = 2$.

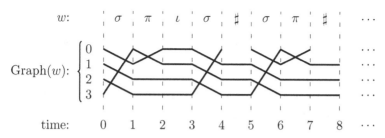

The language L_n is then defined as

$$L_n = \{w \in \Sigma^\omega \mid \mathrm{Graph}(w) \text{ contains an infinite path}\}$$

The infinite path required in the definition of L_n needs not start at time 0. Notice that L_n is suffix-closed and prefix-independent.

Theorem 2 [15]. *There is a GFG-NCW with $2n + 1$ states for L_n, but any deterministic Streett[1] automaton for L_n has at least $\dfrac{2^n}{2n+1}$ states.*

However, this example does not settle the blowup problem for languages represented by LTL formulas. Indeed, for any $n \geq 1$, the language L_n is not LTL-definable:

Lemma 3. *For all $n \geq 1$, there is no LTL formula for the language L_n.*

Proof. We use the characterization of LTL-definable languages as aperiodic languages [7]. Let M be the syntactic monoid of L_n, and $h : \Sigma^* \to M$ be the corresponding syntactic morphism. Assume there is $u, v \in \Sigma^*$ such that for infinitely many $k \in \mathbb{N}$, $(u^k v)^\omega \in L_n$ and $(u^{k+1} v)^\omega \notin L_n$. Then we have $h(u)^k \neq h(u)^{k+1}$ for infinitely many k, so the syntactic monoid of L_n cannot be aperiodic, and therefore L_n is not LTL-definable. Hence it suffices to find such u, v to prove that L_n is not LTL-definable. We can take here $u = \sigma$ and $v = \sharp$. Indeed, if k is a multiple of $2n$, we have $(\sigma^k \sharp)^\omega \in L_n$ and $(\sigma^{k+1} \sharp)^\omega \notin L_n$.

---

[1] Note that the Streett acceptance condition is not specified in [15], but it is in the relevant result of [2]. The Streett condition for $\mathcal{D}$ is needed so that the condition of the form "$\mathcal{A}$ accepts or $\mathcal{D}$ rejects" is Rabin, and the game admits positional strategies.

Moreover, it is shown in [15] that in some sense, the languages L_n essentially constitute the canonical example for coBüchi GFG automata. Indeed, in order to show that deciding whether a NCW is GFG can be done in polynomial time, it is shown that GFG-NCW are very close to the following structure: the automaton deterministically follows a safe path, and when a coBüchi state is encountered, the automaton jumps to another such safe path ; in particular, the safe paths can in some sense be "permuted", and a bad choice of path for the automaton can eventually be corrected by jumping to the right path later, provided the GFG strategy has enough memory to remember how paths were permuted. It is thus plausible that the reason exponential memory is needed in GFG-NCW is the presence of arbitrary permutations, and that this could not happen for LTL-definable languages, where permutations of states are forbidden in the run-DAG of the corresponding automaton [7].

We show in the next section that this is not the case: this exponential blowup result still holds for LTL-definable languages. This gives hope for the use of GFG automata in the context of LTL synthesis.

4   A Family of LTL-definable Languages K_n with Succinct GFG Representations

We will define for every $n \geq 1$ a LTL-language K_n. We show that for all $n \geq 1$ there is a GFG-NCW of size $2n+1$ recognizing K_n, but there is no deterministic Streett automaton recognizing K_n of size less than $\frac{2^n}{2n+1}$.

4.1   Definition of the Language K_n

The language K_n is defined on alphabet $\Sigma = \{\iota, a_0, a_1, \ldots a_{2n-2}, b_0, b_1 \ldots b_{2n-2}\}$.

As in L_n, each letter $x \in L$ is mapped to a bipartite graph $G(x)$ describing a partial function $[0, 2n - 1] \rightarrow [0, 2n - 1]$. A word $w = x_1 x_2 \ldots$ is in K_n if and only if the DAG Graph(w) with vertices $[0, 2n - 1] \times \mathbb{N}$ obtained by concatenating all the slices $G(x_1)G(x_2)\ldots$ contains an infinite path, not necessarily starting in $[0, 2n - 1] \times \{0\}$, so we define $K_n = \{w \in \Sigma^\omega \mid$ Graph(w) contains an infinite path$\}$.

The graph $G(\iota)$ will represent the identity function. For all $i \in [0, 2n-2]$, the graph $G(a_i)$ maps i to $i+1$, is undefined on $i+1$, and leaves $[0, 2n-1] \setminus \{i, i+1\}$ unchanged. For all $i \in [0, 2n - 2]$, the graph $G(b_i)$ maps $i + 1$ to i, is undefined on i, and leaves $[0, 2n - 1] \setminus \{i, i+1\}$ unchanged. An example of Graph(w) for $n = 2$ is given below.

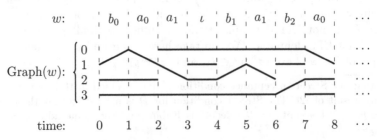

4.2   Aperiodicity of K_n and Succinctness of GFG Automaton

Theorem 4. *There is a GFG coBüchi automaton of size $2n+1$ for K_n, but any deterministic Streett automaton for K_n has at least $\dfrac{2^n}{2n+1}$ states.*

Proof (Scheme). The same proof scheme as the one from [15] showing the exponential blowup for the family L_n can be used here. We need to adapt it to account for the specificities of K_n, namely modify the construction to avoid crossings of paths.

Lemma 5. *K_n is LTL-definable, via a formula of DAG-size at least exponential in n.*

Proof (Scheme). LTL definability is shown via the aperiodicity of K_n [7]. We also provide an explicit formula, defined by induction on n, where each induction steps doubles the depth of the formula.

Conjecture 6. There is no LTL formula for K_n with DAG-size polynomial in n.

In the next section, we define a specification logic more suited to this setting.

5   A Modal Logic for Eventually Safe Properties

5.1   The Safety Logic $S\nu$TL

We recall here the formalism $S\nu$TL, a fragment of linear μ-calculus designed to express safety properties. This fragment has been studied in several works, usually in the branching time setting ; see for example [19], from which we extract (in Theorem 7 below) part of the characterization of $S\nu$TL as the safety fragment of the μ-calculus. A similar characterization for LTL is sketched in the conclusions of [18].

Formulas of $S\nu$TL are given by the following syntax, where a stands for letters of Σ.

$$\varphi := a \mid \neg a \mid \varphi \vee \varphi \mid \varphi \wedge \varphi \mid \odot\varphi \mid X \mid \nu X.\varphi$$

If φ is a formula of $S\nu$TL, we will note $[\![\varphi]\!]$ its semantic as a linear μ-calculus formula.

Theorem 7. *A language is definable in $S\nu$TL if and only if it is a safety language.*

Proof (Scheme). For the left to right implication, we follow a more general construction that has been proposed in [19], for branching μ-calculus. In our case, the states of the constructed alternating safety automaton are subformulas of the input $S\nu$TL formula ψ, and the transition function describes the subformulas that should be true after reading a letter, using alternation to encode the disjunctions and conjunctions. Since alternating safety automata are equivalent to safety languages through standard powerset constructions we are done. For the right to left implication, we build a $S\nu$TL formula from a non-deterministic safety automaton by encoding into the formula the transition function; loops in the automaton are encoded using the operator νX.

5.2   The Logic $E\nu$TL for Eventually Safe Properties

We introduce here a second semantic $[\![\cdot]\!]_E$ for $S\nu$TL formulas, called the *eventual semantic*, in the following way:

$$[\![\varphi]\!]_E := \{uw \in \Sigma^\omega \mid w \in \mathit{suff}([\![\varphi]\!])\}.$$

That is to say, $[\![\varphi]\!]_E$ denotes infinite words that have a suffix that is also a suffix of $[\![\varphi]\!]$. This logic can be seen as a way to specify what we mean by a safe behaviour, letting the semantic automatically generate the language of eventually safe behaviours. Notice that since GFG automata are closed under union and intersection by Lemma 1, the technique introduced in this paper can be combined with others in order to treat more advanced specifications.

We call $E\nu$TL the logic $S\nu$TL equipped with the eventual semantic.

Lemma 8. *A language is definable in $E\nu$TL if and only if it is of the form $\Sigma^* L_{safe}$, where L_{safe} is a suffix-closed safety language.*

Proof. If L is defined in $E\nu$TL via the formula φ, then $L = \Sigma^* \mathit{suff}([\![\varphi]\!])$, which is of the wanted form. Conversely, if $L = \Sigma^* L_{safe}$ with L_{safe} a suffix-closed safety language, then by Theorem 7 there is a formula φ of $S\nu$TL such that $[\![\varphi]\!] = L_{safe}$, and we obtain $L = [\![\varphi]\!]_E$.

Let us call *ESafe* the class of such languages. Notice that $E\nu$TL uses a syntax for safety properties, but with our semantics, the languages defined by $E\nu$TL are actually liveness properties [1]: if $L \in ESafe$, any finite word can be extended to a word in L.

5.3   Properties of the Class *ESafe*

The following theorem states that the class *ESafe* captures exactly prefix-independent coBüchi languages, and that it is equivalent to represent a language from *ESafe* directly with a NCW, or via its suffix-closed safety language L_{safe}.

Theorem 9. *CobCaract ESafe is equal to the class of prefix-independent coBüchi languages. Moreover, if $L = \Sigma^* L_{safe}$ is accepted by a NCW C, we can build a non-deterministic safety automaton $\mathcal{A}_{safe}$ from C recognizing L_{safe} with the same number of states. Conversely, if we have a non-deterministic safety automaton for L_{safe}, we can build a NCW C for L with one more state.*

Lemma 10. *Given a regular language L, it is decidable whether it is in ESafe. If L is given by a DCW, the problem is in NL, whereas it is PSPACE-complete if L is given by a NCW.*

The complexity of deciding whether an arbitrary regular language (given by various models of automata and LTL formulas) is coBüchi-recognizable, and obtaining an equivalent DCW or NCW automaton, is studied in [3]. This completes the picture for the problem of deciding whether an arbitrary language can be represented using $E\nu$TL.

5.4 A Succinct $E\nu\mathrm{TL}$ Formula for the Language K_n

The formula we aim to build will describe the safety languages of words for which the path starting in $(0,0)$ is infinite. It recognizes K_n via the eventually safe semantic. We use the weak until operator **WU** as syntactic sugar, defined as $\varphi\mathbf{WU}\psi := \nu X.\psi \vee (\varphi \wedge \odot X)$.

The pure LTL formula for K_n from Lemma 5 has DAG-size at least exponential in n. The formulas we will define here will instead be linear in n. Let $N = 2n - 1$. Let $\alpha_i = \Sigma \setminus \{a_{i-1}, a_i, b_i, b_{i+1}\}$ be the subalphabet leaving i unchanged. We define inductively the formulas ψ_i for i from N to 0, each one containing X_{i-1} as a free variable, except for ψ_0 which is closed:

$$\psi_N = \nu X_N.((\alpha_N \wedge \odot X_N) \vee (b_{N-1} \wedge \odot X_{N-1}))$$
$$\text{For } 0 < i < N : \psi_i = \nu X_i.((\alpha_i \wedge \odot X_i) \vee (a_i \wedge \odot \psi_{i+1}) \vee (b_{i-1} \wedge \odot X_{i-1}))$$
$$\psi_0 = \nu X_0.((\alpha_0 \wedge \odot X_0) \vee (a_0 \wedge \odot \psi_1))$$

We finally define $\Phi := \psi_0$.

Lemma 11. *The formula Φ has size linear in n, and $[\![\Phi]\!]_E = K_n$.*

We note that a similar formula can be explicited for the original family of languages (L_n) witnessing exponential succinctness of GFG automata. This formula allows to encode the examples of specifications on interacting agents given in the introduction.

5.5 From $E\nu\mathrm{TL}$ to GFG CoBüchi Automata

In this section, we describe a general algorithm for translating any $E\nu\mathrm{TL}$ formula to an equivalent GFG-NCW. Recall that since GFG automata are sound for synthesis [11], this translation can be used as a blackbox for solving synthesis of *ESafe* properties, specified via the logic $E\nu\mathrm{TL}$. As explained before, this translation can also be used in a modular way, and combined with other deterministic or GFG automata as shown in Lemma 1. We now describe the algorithm, taking as input an $E\nu\mathrm{TL}$ formula ψ. We can view ψ as a $S\nu\mathrm{TL}$ formula and build an alternating safety automaton $\mathcal{A}_{\mathrm{alt}}$ recognizing $[\![\psi]\!]$ as described in the proof of Theorem 7.

We use a powerset construction to obtain an equivalent non-deterministic safety automaton $\mathcal{A}_{\mathrm{nd}}$. Determinizing $\mathcal{A}_{\mathrm{nd}}$ to a deterministic safety automaton $\mathcal{A}_{\mathrm{det}}$ through another powerset construction is standard. Since $\mathcal{A}_{\mathrm{det}}$ can be equivalently seen as a safety DFA, it can be minimized into a safety deterministic automaton $\mathcal{A}_{\mathrm{min}} = (Q, \Sigma, q_0, \Delta)$ using standard techniques. Minimization techniques can also be applied on the intermediate automaton $\mathcal{A}_{\mathrm{nd}}$, for instance using bisimulation equivalence [17]. Here we omitted the accepting states of $\mathcal{A}_{\mathrm{min}}$, since all runs are accepting. We assume that all states of $\mathcal{A}_{\mathrm{min}}$ are reachable from q_0.

We will now build a GFG coBüchi automaton $\mathcal{C} = (Q', \Sigma, q_0, \Delta, F)$ for $[\![\psi]\!]_E$, based on $\mathcal{A}_{\mathrm{min}}$. We take $Q' = Q \cup \{\bot\}$, $F = Q$, and

$$\Delta' = \Delta \cup \{(p, a, \bot) \mid \forall q \in Q, (p, a, q) \notin \Delta\} \cup (\{\bot\} \times \Sigma \times Q)$$

The following theorem states that the algorithm is correct.

Theorem 12. $\mathcal{C}$ *is a GFG-NCW for* $[\![\psi]\!]_E$.

Proof (Scheme). $\mathcal{C}$ will deterministically follow paths made of safe transitions, and will go to $\bot$ when the path it is currently following is cut. The only non-determinism to resolve is: where to jump from $\bot$? It suffices to jump to the path that has been uncut for the longest time.

Remark 13. An alternative construction where strongly connected components of $\mathcal{A}_{nd}$ are determinized separately is also possible and allows more optimizations, we discuss this in the appendix of the online version. This can yield smaller GFG automata in cases where the size of the biggest strongly connected component of $\mathcal{A}_{nd}$ is small in front of its total size, or if some components cover the safe languages of others.

The complexity of this algorithm is doubly exponential in terms of number of states. The following theorem shows that this cannot be avoided.

Theorem 14. *The translation of EνTL formulas to GFG-NCW is doubly exponential.*

Proof. This result for general LTL formulas has been proven in [4] using a language family $(\mathcal{L}_n)$ defined in [16], itself adapted from a language of finite words given in [6]. However, the particular structure of the class *ESafe* prevents us from using the results of [4,6,16] as blackboxes. The language $\mathcal{L}_n$ as defined by the LTL formula from [16] is $F_n \sharp^\omega$ where F_n is the language defined by $F_n = \{\{0,1,\#\}^* \cdot \# \cdot w \cdot \# \cdot \{0,1,\#\}^* \cdot \$ \cdot w \mid w \in \{0,1\}^n\}$. We will use similar ideas here, while taking care of the special semantic of EνTL.

Let $\Sigma = \{0,1,\#,\$,\flat\}$. We change the formula from [16] so that we iterate the closure of F_n, with $\flat$ as separator. Intuitively, the $S\nu$TL formula φ_n states that any word on $\{0,1\}^*$ immediately following a $\$$ has length n, is followed by a $\flat$, and is identical to a word that occurred between the last $\flat$ and the $\$$ following it. Let $\Theta = 0 \vee 1$ and $\Theta_\sharp = \Theta \vee \sharp$, we define the following formulas:

$$\varphi_{\text{word}}(X) = \Theta \wedge \odot(\Theta \wedge \overset{n}{\cdots} \odot(\Theta \wedge \odot(\flat \wedge \odot X))\cdots)$$
$$\varphi_{i,x} = (\odot^i x \wedge (\Theta_\sharp \mathbf{WU}(\$ \wedge \odot^i x))) \qquad \text{for } 1 \le i \le n \text{ and } x \in \{0,1\}$$
$$\varphi_{\text{match}} = \bigwedge\nolimits_{1 \le i \le n}(\varphi_{i,0} \vee \varphi_{i,1})$$
$$\varphi_n = \nu X.\Theta_\sharp \overline{\mathbf{WU}}[\# \wedge \varphi_{\text{match}} \wedge (\Theta_\sharp \mathbf{WU}(\$ \wedge \odot\varphi_{\text{word}}(X)))]$$

The formula $\varphi_{\text{word}}(X)$ checks for $\{0,1\}^n \flat X$, where X is a free variable. The formula $\varphi_{i,x}$ checks that i^{th} letter is x and that it is again the case after the next $\$$. The formula φ_{match} enforces that the current word $u \in \{0,1\}^n$ must be matched by a $\$u$ at the next $\$$. Finally, φ_n ensures that before the next $\$$, we encounter some $\sharp u$ where u is further matched by $\$u\flat$, after which we reiterate the constraint. Notice that $|\varphi_n|$ is quadratic in n, and $[\![\varphi_n]\!]_E \cap (\Sigma^* \flat)^\omega = \Sigma^*(F_n \flat)^\omega$. Let us assume that we have a GFG-NCW automaton $\mathcal{C}$ for $[\![\varphi_n]\!]_E$. We show that $\mathcal{C}$ must have at least 2^{2^n-1} states. Let Q be the set of states of $\mathcal{C}$ and $\sigma : \Sigma^* \to Q$ be the GFG strategy of $\mathcal{C}$. Let us assume that $|Q| < 2^{2^n-1}$. We call the *type* of a finite run of $\mathcal{C}$ the pair (c, q), where c is a bit specifying whether a rejecting state has been seen, and q is the last state of the run. The number of possible types is $2|Q| < 2^{2^n}$. To any set of words $X = \{u_1, u_2, \ldots, u_k\} \subseteq \{0,1\}^n$, we associate a word $w_X = \#u_1\#u_2\#\ldots\#u_k$, where the u_i's are lexicographically sorted. Since there are 2^{2^n} such sets, there must be $X_1 \neq Y_1 \subseteq \{0,1\}^n$ such that $\sigma(w_{X_1})$ and $\sigma(w_{Y_1})$ have same type. Without loss of generality let $w_1 \in X_1 \setminus Y_1$, we have $w_{X_1}\$w_1 \in F_n$ but $w_{Y_1}\$w_1 \notin F_n$. Again, there are X_2, Y_2, q_2, w_2 such that $\sigma(w_{X_1}\$w_1 \flat w_{X_2})$ and $\sigma(w_{Y_1}\$w_1 \flat w_{Y_2})$ have same type on the suffix starting with $\$w_1\flat$, and $w_2 \in X_2 \setminus Y_2$. By iterating this construction, we build two infinite words $v = w_{X_1}\$w_1 \flat w_{X_2}\$w_2\flat\ldots$ and $v' = w_{Y_1}\$w_1\flat w_{Y_2}\$w_2\flat\ldots$ such that σ accepts v if and only if σ accepts v', but we have $v \in [\![\varphi_n]\!]_E$ while $v' \notin [\![\varphi_n]\!]_E$. We obtain a contradiction with the fact that $\mathcal{C}$ recognizes $[\![\varphi_n]\!]_E$ with GFG strategy σ.

However, our algorithm can perform well in practice, as witnessed by the languages K_n and L_n. Indeed, if the input is the formula Φ from Sect. 5.4 (resp. φ_0, see online version) describing the language K_n (resp. L_n), the algorithm computes an automaton of size linear in n, while any deterministic automaton would be exponential, by Theorem 4 (resp. Theorem 2).

6 Conclusion

We showed that GFG automata still enjoy an exponential succinctness gap compared to deterministic automata for the class of LTL-definable languages, by giving a family of languages (K_n) witnessing this gap. However, the LTL formula we give for K_n is exponential in n, while there is an equivalent μ-calculus formula that is linear in n. We conjecture that the family (K_n) can be used as a witness to prove an exponential gap in succinctness between the linear μ-calculus and LTL. We defined and studied a class *ESafe* of eventually safe languages, a natural compromise between safety and liveness specifications. We defined a fragment of linear μ-calculus, the logic $E\nu$TL, that describes the class *ESafe*, and can be translated to GFG coBüchi automata.

The idea of using automata that are allowed to non-deterministically jump to a new path to improve performances in LTL synthesis was implemented in [10], but the so-called "shift automaton" was based on a powerset construction, and the notion of Good-for-Games was not identified, replaced by the weaker condition of being Determinisable by Pruning. Prior to the discovery of succinctness of GFG automata, a GFG-based algorithm for model-checking of Markov decision process has been implemented in [12], where it turned out that this particular approach was not more efficient than standard ones.

As future work, we plan to implement our approach that makes use of newly discovered features of GFG automata, in order to compare benchmarks with those present in [10, 12]. A related open challenge is to find fragments of LTL or other logics that can be translated to GFG automata with only a single exponential blowup.

References

1. Alpern, B., Schneider, F.B.: Defining liveness. Inf. Process. Lett. **21**(4), 181–185 (1985)
2. Boker, U., Kuperberg, D., Kupferman, O., Skrzypczak, M.: Nondeterminism in the presence of a diverse or unknown future. In: Fomin, F.V., Freivalds, R., Kwiatkowska, M., Peleg, D. (eds.) ICALP 2013. LNCS, vol. 7966, pp. 89–100. Springer, Heidelberg (2013). https://doi.org/10.1007/978-3-642-39212-2_11
3. Boker, U., Kupferman, O.: Co-büching them all. In: Hofmann, M. (ed.) FoSSaCS 2011. LNCS, vol. 6604, pp. 184–198. Springer, Heidelberg (2011). https://doi.org/10.1007/978-3-642-19805-2_13
4. Boker, U., Kupferman, O., Skrzypczak, M.: How deterministic are Good-For-Games automata? In: FSTTCS 2017–37th IARCS Annual Conference on Foundations of Software Technology and Theoretical Computer Science. Leibniz International Proceedings in Informatics (LIPIcs) (2017)
5. Büchi, J.R., Landweber, L.H.: Solving sequential conditions by finite-state strategies. Trans. Am. Math. Soc. **138**, 295–311 (1969)
6. Chandra, A.K., Kozen, D., Stockmeyer, L.J.: Alternation. J. ACM **28**(1), 114–133 (1981)
7. Diekert, V., Gastin, P.: First-order definable languages. Logic and Automata: History and Perspectives. Texts in Logic and Games, pp. 261–306. Amsterdam University Press, Amsterdam (2008)
8. Esparza, J., Kretínský, J., Sickert, S.: One theorem to rule them all: a unified translation of LTL into ω-automata. In: Proceedings of the 33rd Annual ACM/IEEE Symposium on Logic in Computer Science, LICS 2018, pp. 384–393, Oxford, UK, 09–12 July 2018
9. Fellah, A., Jürgensen, H., Sheng, Y.: Constructions for alternating finite automata. Int. J. Comput. Math. **35**(1–4), 117–132 (1990)
10. Harding, A., Ryan, M., Schobbens, P.-Y.: A new algorithm for strategy synthesis in LTL games. In: Halbwachs, N., Zuck, L.D. (eds.) TACAS 2005. LNCS, vol. 3440, pp. 477–492. Springer, Heidelberg (2005). https://doi.org/10.1007/978-3-540-31980-1_31
11. Henzinger, T.A., Piterman, N.: Solving games without determinization. In: Proceedings of Computer Science Logic, 20th International Workshop, CSL2006, 15th Annual Conference of the EACSL, pp. 395–410, Szeged, Hungary, 25–29 September 2006
12. Klein, J., Müller, D., Baier, C., Klüppelholz, S.: Are good-for-games automata good for probabilistic model checking? In: Proceedings of Language and Automata Theory and Applications - 8th International Conference, LATA 2014, pp. 453–465, Madrid, Spain, 10–14 March 2014
13. Kretínský, J., Meggendorfer, T., Sickert, S., Ziegler, C.: Rabinizer 4: from LTL to your favourite deterministic automaton. In: Chockler, H., Weissenbacher, G. (eds.) CAV 2018. LNCS, vol. 10981, pp. 567–577. Springer, Cham (2018). https://doi.org/10.1007/978-3-319-96145-3_30
14. Kuperberg, D., Majumdar, A.: Width of non-deterministic automata. In 35th International Symposium on Theoretical Aspects of Computer Science, STACS, 29th February–3rd March 2018, p. 2018, Caen, France (2018)
15. Kuperberg, D., Skrzypczak, M.: On determinisation of good-for-games automata. In: Halldórsson, M.M., Iwama, K., Kobayashi, N., Speckmann, B. (eds.) ICALP 2015. LNCS, vol. 9135, pp. 299–310. Springer, Heidelberg (2015). https://doi.org/10.1007/978-3-662-47666-6_24

16. Kupferman, O., Vardi, M.Y.: From linear time to branching time. ACM Trans. Comput. Log. **6**(2), 273–294 (2005)

17. Paige, R., Tarjan, R.E.: Three partition refinement algorithms. SIAM J. Comput. **16**(6), 973–989 (1987)

18. Sistla, A.P.: Safety, liveness and fairness in temporal logic. Formal Aspects Comput. **6**(5), 495–511 (1994)

19. Wilke, T.: Alternating tree automata, parity games, and modal μ-calculus. Bull. Belg. Math. Soc. Simon Stevin **8**(2), 359 (2001)

20. Zhu, S., Tabajara, L.M., Li, J., Pu, G., Vardi, M.Y.: A symbolic approach to safety LTL synthesis. Hardware and Software: Verification and Testing. LNCS, vol. 10629, pp. 147–162. Springer, Cham (2017). https://doi.org/10.1007/978-3-319-70389-3_10

Coinductive Algorithms for Büchi Automata

Denis Kuperberg[(⊠)], Laureline Pinault, and Damien Pous

Univ Lyon, CNRS, ENS de Lyon, UCB Lyon 1, LIP, Lyon, France
denis.kuperberg@ens-lyon.fr

Abstract. We propose a new algorithm for checking language equivalence of non-deterministic Büchi automata. We start from a construction proposed by Calbrix, Nivat and Podelski, which makes it possible to reduce the problem to that of checking equivalence of automata on finite words. Although this construction generates large and highly non-deterministic automata, we show how to exploit their specific structure and apply state-of-the art techniques based on coinduction to reduce the state-space that has to be explored. Doing so, we obtain algorithms which do not require full determinization or complementation.

Keywords: Büchi automata · Language equivalence · Coinduction

1 Introduction

Büchi automata are machines which make it possible to recognise sets of infinite words. They form a natural counterpart to finite automata, which operate on finite words. They play a crucial role in logic for their links with monadic second order logic (MSO) [5], and in program verification. For instance, they are widely used in model-checking tools, in order to check whether a given program satisfies a linear temporal logic formula (LTL) [13, 29].

A key algorithmic property of Büchi automata is that checking whether two automata recognise the same language is decidable, and in fact PSPACE-complete, like in the finite case with non-deterministic finite automata. This is how one obtains model-checking algorithms. Several algorithms have been proposed in the literature [1, 5, 14, 18] and implemented in various tools [15, 24, 28].

Two families of algorithms were discovered for non-deterministic automata on finite words, which drastically improved over the pre-existing ones in practice: antichain-based algorithms [3, 10, 30] and algorithms based on bisimulations up to congruence [4]. In both cases, those algorithms explore the starting automata

This work has been funded by the European Research Council (ERC) under the European Union's Horizon 2020 programme (CoVeCe, grant agreement No 678157), and was supported by the LABEX MILYON (ANR-10-LABX-0070) of Université de Lyon, within the program "Investissements d'Avenir" (ANR-11-IDEX-0007) operated by the French National Research Agency (ANR).

P. Hofman and M. Skrzypczak (Eds.): DLT 2019, LNCS 11647, pp. 206–220, 2019.
https://doi.org/10.1007/978-3-030-24886-4_15

by resolving non-determinism on the fly through the powerset construction, and they exploit subsumption techniques to avoid the need to explore all reachable states (which can be exponentially many). The algorithms based on bisimulations up to congruence improve over those based on antichains by using simultaneously the antichain techniques and an older technique for deterministic automata, due to Hopcroft and Karp [17]. Note that both families of algorithms require exponential space (and time) in worst-case complexity, for a problem which is only PSPACE. In practice however, they perform better than existing PSPACE algorithms, because the latter require exponential time even for best cases.

The antichain-based algorithms could be adapted to Büchi automata by exploiting constructions to compute the complement of a Büchi automaton, either Ramsey-based [11,12] or rank-based [9,10]. Unfortunately, those complementation operations do not make it possible to adapt the algorithms based on bisimulations up to congruence: those require a proper powerset construction for determinization, which is not available for Büchi automata. Here we propose to circumvent this difficulty using a construction by Calbrix, Nivat, and Podelski [6], which makes it possible to reduce the problem of checking Büchi automata equivalence to that of checking equivalence of automata on finite words.

The first observation, which is used implicitly in the so-called Ramsey-based algorithms from the literature [1,11,12], is that it suffices to consider ultimately periodic words: if the languages of two Büchi automata differ, then they must differ on an ultimately periodic word. The second observation is that the set of ultimately periodic words accepted by a Büchi automaton can be faithfully represented as a rational language of finite words, for which Calbrix et al. give an explicit non-deterministic finite automaton. This automaton contains two layers: one for the prefixes of the ultimately periodic words, and one for their periods. We show that algorithms like HKC [4] can readily be used to reason about the prefix layer, without systematically determinising it. The period layer requires more work in order to avoid paying a doubly exponential price. We show how to analyse it to compute *discriminating sets* that summarize the periodic behaviour of the automaton, and suffice to check language equivalence.

We first recall the algorithms from [4] for checking equivalence of automata on finite words (Sect. 2). Then we revisit the construction of Calbrix et al., making their use of the Büchi transition monoid [25] explicit (Sect. 3). We define the new algorithm HKC$^\omega$ in Sect. 4. We conclude with directions for future work in Sect. 5.

Notation. We denote sets by capital letters $X, Y, S, T \ldots$ and functions by lower case letters $f, g, \ldots$ Given sets X and Y, $X \times Y$ is their Cartesian product, $X \uplus Y$ is the disjoint union, X^Y is the set of functions $f \colon Y \to X$. The collection of subsets of S is denoted by $\mathcal{P}(S)$. The collection of relations on S is denoted by $Rel(S) = \mathcal{P}(S^2)$. Given a relation $R \in Rel(X)$, we write $x \, R \, y$ for $\langle x, y \rangle \in R$. We fix an arbitrary alphabet A ranged over using lowercase letters a, b. We write A^* for the set of all finite words over A; ϵ the empty word; $w_1 w_2$ the concatenation of words $w_1, w_2 \in A^*$; and $|w|$ for the length of a word w and w_i for its ith letter (when $i < |w|$). We write A^+ for the set of non-empty words and A^ω for the set of infinite words over A . We use 2 for the set $\{0,1\}$ (Booleans).

A semilattice is a tuple $\langle O, +, 0 \rangle$ where O is a set of elements, $+: O^2 \to O$ is an associative, commutative and idempotent binary operation, and $0 \in O$ is a neutral element for $+$. For instance, $\langle 2, max, 0 \rangle$ is a semilattice. More generally $\langle \mathcal{P}(X), \cup, \emptyset \rangle$ is a semi-lattice for every set X.

2   Coinductive Algorithms for Finite Automata

We will need to work with *Moore machines*, which generalise finite automata by allowing output values in an arbitrary set rather than Booleans. We keep the standard automata terminology for the sake of readability.

A deterministic finite automaton (DFA) over the alphabet A and with outputs in O is a triple $\langle S, o, t \rangle$, where S is a finite set of states, $o: S \to O$ is the output function, and $t: A \times S \to S$ is the transition function which returns, for each letter $a \in A$ and for each state x, the next state $t_a(x)$. Note that we do not specify an initial state in the definition of DFA: rather than comparing two DFAs, we shall compare two states in a single DFA (obtained as disjoint union if necessary).

Every DFA $\mathcal{A} = \langle S, o, t \rangle$ induces a function $[\cdot]_\mathcal{A} : S \to O^{A^*}$, mapping each state to a weighted language with weights in O. This function is defined by $[x]_\mathcal{A}(\epsilon) = o(x)$ for the empty word, and $[x]_\mathcal{A}(aw) = [t_a(x)]_\mathcal{A}(w)$ otherwise. We shall omit the subscript $\mathcal{A}$ when it is clear from the context. For a state x of a DFA, $[x]$ is called the language accepted by x. The languages accepted by some state in a DFA with Boolean outputs are the *rational languages*.

2.1   Deterministic Automata: Hopcroft and Karp's Algorithm

We fix a DFA $\langle S, o, t \rangle$. Coinductive algorithms for checking language equivalence proceed by trying to find a *bisimulation* relating the given starting states.

Definition 1 (Bisimulation). *Let $g: Rel(S) \to Rel(S)$ be the function on relations defined as*

$$g(R) = \{\langle x, y \rangle \mid o(x) = o(y) \text{ and } \forall a \in A, \ t_a(x) \ R \ t_a(y)\}$$

A bisimulation is a relation R such that $R \subseteq g(R)$.

The above function g being monotone, it admits the union of all bisimulations as a greatest fixpoint, by Knaster-Tarski's theorem [19,27]. This greatest-fixpoint is actually language equivalence:

Theorem 1. *For all $x, y \in S$, $[x] = [y]$ iff there is a bisimulation R with $x \ R \ y$.*

This theorem yields two families of algorithms: on the one hand, backward algorithms like partition-refinement [16] make it possible to compute the largest bisimulation, and thus to minimize DFA; on the other hand, forward algorithms make it possible to compute the smallest bisimulation containing a given pair of states (if any), and thus to check language equivalence locally, between two states [17]. The latter problem is the one we are interested in in this paper. (Unlike with languages of finite words, there is no canonical notion of minimal automaton for Büchi automata.) For deterministic automata on finite words this problem is slightly easier complexity-wise: when the starting automaton has size n, minimisation can be solved in time $o(n\ln(n))$ while language equivalence of two given states can be tested in almost linear time [26].

> **input** : A DFA $\mathcal{A} = \langle S, o, t \rangle$ and two states $x, y \in S$
> **output** : true if $[x]_\mathcal{A} = [y]_\mathcal{A}$; false otherwise
>
> 1 $R := \emptyset$; $todo := \{\langle x, y \rangle\}$;
> 2 **while** $todo \neq \emptyset$ **do**
>   // **invariant**: $\langle x, y \rangle \in R \subseteq g(f(R \cup todo))$
> 3   extract $\langle x', y' \rangle$ from $todo$;
> 4   **if** $o(x') \neq o(y')$ **then return** *false*;
> 5   **if** $\langle x', y' \rangle \in f(R \cup todo)$ **then** skip;
> 6   **forall** $a \in A$ **do**
> 7 | insert $\langle t_a(x'), t_a(y') \rangle$ in $todo$;
> 8   insert $\langle x', y' \rangle$ in R;
> 9 **return** *true*; // **because**: $\langle x, y \rangle \in R \subseteq g(f(R))$

Fig. 1. Coinductive algorithm for language equivalence in a DFA; the function f on line 5 ranges over the identity for the naive algorithm ($\texttt{Naive}(\mathcal{A}, x, y)$) or e for Hopcroft & Karp's algorithm ($\texttt{HK}(\mathcal{A}, x, y)$).

A preliminary algorithm for checking language equivalence of two states $x, y \in S$ is obtained as follows: try to complete the relation $\{\langle x, y \rangle\}$ into a bisimulation, by adding the successors along all letters and checking that o agrees on all inserted pairs. This algorithm is described in Fig. 1; it is quadratic in worst case since a pair of states is added to the relation R at each iteration. The standard and almost linear algorithm by Hopcroft and Karp [17,26], can be seen as an improvement of this naive algorithm where one searches for bisimulations up to equivalence rather than plain bisimulations:

Definition 2. *Let* $e \colon Rel(S) \to Rel(S)$ *be the function mapping a relation R to the least equivalence relation containing R. A bisimulation up to equivalence is a relation R such that* $R \subseteq g(e(R))$.

This coarser notion makes it possible to take advantage of the fact that language equivalence is indeed an equivalence relation, so that one can skip pairs of states whose equivalence follows by transitivity from the previously visited pairs. The soundness of this technique is established by the following Proposition:

Proposition 1 ([4, Thm. 1]). *If R is a bisimulation up to equivalence, then $e(R)$ is a bisimulation.*

Complexity-wise, when looking for bisimulations up to equivalence in a DFA with n states, at most n pairs can be inserted in R in the algorithm in Fig. 1: at the beginning, $e(R)$ corresponds to a discrete partition with n equivalence classes; at each iteration, two classes of $e(R)$ are merged.

Note that Hopcroft and Karp's algorithm proceeds forward and computes the smallest bisimulation up to equivalence containing the starting pair of states, if any. As mentioned above, this contrasts with partition-refinement algorithms [16], which proceed backward: they start with a coarse partition (accepting v.s. non-accepting states), which they refine by reading transitions backward.

2.2   Non-deterministic Automata: HKC

A *non-deterministic finite automaton* (NFA) over the alphabet A and with outputs in O is a triple $\langle S, o, t \rangle$, where S is a finite set of states, $o: S \to O$ is the output function, and $t: A \times S \to \mathcal{P}(S)$ is the transition function which returns, for each letter $a \in A$ and for each state x, a set $t_a(x)$ of potential successors. Like for DFA, we do not specify a set of initial states in the definition of NFA.

We fix an NFA $\langle S, o, t \rangle$ in this section and we assume that the set O of outputs is a semilattice. Under this assumption, an NFA $\mathcal{A} = \langle S, o, t \rangle$ can be transformed into a DFA $\mathcal{A}^{\#} = \langle \mathcal{P}(S), o^{\#}, t^{\#} \rangle$ using the well-known powerset construction:

$$o^{\#}(X) = \sum_{x \in X} o(x) \qquad\qquad t_a^{\#}(X) = \bigcup_{x \in X} t_a(x)$$

This construction makes it possible to extend the function $[\cdot]$ into a function from sets of states of a given NFA to weighted languages. It also gives immediately algorithms to decide language equivalence in NFA: just use algorithms for DFA on the resulting automaton. Note that when doing so, it is not always necessary to compute the determinised automaton beforehand. For instance, with coinductive algorithms like in Fig. 1, the determinised automaton can be explored on the fly. This is useful since this DFA can have exponentially many states, even when restricting to reachable subsets.

The key idea behind the HKC algorithm [4] is that one can actually do better than Hopcroft and Karp's algorithm by exploiting the semilattice structure of the state-space of NFA determinised through the powerset construction. This is done using *bisimulations up to congruence*.

Definition 3. *Let $c: Rel(\mathcal{P}(S)) \to Rel(\mathcal{P}(S))$ be the function mapping a relation R to the least equivalence relation $\mathcal{H}$ containing R and such that $X \mathrel{\mathcal{H}} Y$ and $X' \mathrel{\mathcal{H}} Y'$ entail $(X \cup X') \mathrel{\mathcal{H}} (Y \cup Y')$ for all $X, X', Y, Y' \in \mathcal{P}(S)$. A bisimulation up to congruence is a relation R such that $R \subseteq g(c(R))$.*

The function g here is defined as in Sect. 2.1, but with respect to the determinized DFA with state space $\mathcal{P}(S)$, so its type is $Rel(\mathcal{P}(S)) \to Rel(\mathcal{P}(S))$.

Proposition 2 ([4, Thm. 2]). *If R is a bisimulation up to congruence, then $c(R)$ is a bisimulation.*

Checking whether a pair of sets belongs to the congruence closure of a finite relation can be done algorithmically (see [4, Sect. 3.4]). The algorithm HKC [4] is obtained by running the algorithm from Fig. 1 on $\mathcal{A}^\#$, replacing the function f on 1.5 with the congruence closure function c. We provide a variant of this algorithm in Fig. 2, where we prepare the ground for the algorithms we will propose for Büchi automata. There, we only explore the transitions of the determinised automaton, leaving aside the verification that the output function agrees on all pairs. This corresponds to using a function g' instead of g, defined as

$$g'(R) = \{\langle x, y \rangle \mid \forall a \in A, \; t_a^\#(x) \, R \, t_a^\#(y)\}$$

---

input : A NFA $\mathcal{A} = \langle S, o, t \rangle$ and two sets of states $X, Y \subseteq S$
output : a relation R such that $[X] = [Y]$ iff $\forall \langle X', Y' \rangle \in R, \; o^\#(X') = o^\#(Y')$

1 $R := \emptyset$; $todo := \{\langle X, Y \rangle\}$;
2 **while** $todo \neq \emptyset$ **do**
    // invariant: $\langle X, Y \rangle \in R \subseteq g'(c(R \cup todo))$
3   extract $\langle X', Y' \rangle$ from $todo$;
4   **if** $\langle X', Y' \rangle \in c(R \cup todo)$ **then** skip;
5   **forall** $a \in A$ **do**
6 | insert $\langle t_a^\#(X'), t_a^\#(Y') \rangle$ in $todo$;
7   insert $\langle X', Y' \rangle$ in R;
8 **return** R;

Fig. 2. HKC'$(\mathcal{A}, X, Y)$: computing a pre-bisimulation up to congruence in a NFA.

Indeed, while this verification step is usually done on the fly in order to fail faster when a counter-example is found (as in Fig. 1, line 4), it will be useful later to perform this step separately.

As mentioned in the Introduction, the advantage of HKC over HK is that in practice it often makes it possible to skip reachable subsets from the determinised automaton, even when the algorithm answers positively, thus achieving substantial gains in terms of performance: there are families of examples where it answers positively in polynomial time even though the underlying minimal DFA has exponential size. Actually it can also improve exponentially over the more recent antichain-based algorithms [4, Sect. 4]. These latter gains can be explained by the fact that we focus on language equivalence rather than language inclusion: while the two problems are interreducible (e.g., $[X] \subseteq [Y]$ iff $[X \cup Y] = [Y]$), working with equivalence relations makes it possible to strengthen the coinductive argument used implicitly by both algorithms.

3   From Büchi Automata to Finite Words Automata

Let 3 be the set $\{0, 1, \star\}$. A *(non-deterministic) Büchi automaton* (NBW) over the alphabet A is a tuple $\langle S, T \rangle$ where S is a finite set of states, and $T \colon A \to 3^{S^2}$

is the transition function. Like for DFA and NFA, we do not include a set of initial states in the definition. We work with Büchi automata with Büchi transitions rather than Büchi states, hence the type of T (the two models are equivalent and the one we chose is slightly more succinct). We write T_a for $T(a)$, $x \xrightarrow{a} x'$ when $T_a(x, x') \neq 0$, and $x \overset{a}{\Rightarrow} x'$ when $T_a(x, x') = \star$; the latter denote Büchi transitions, that should be fired infinitely often in order to accept an infinite word.

Given a NBW $\mathcal{A} = \langle S, T \rangle$ and $w \in A^\omega$ an infinite word, we say that a sequence of states $\chi \in S^\omega$ accepts w if the sequence $(T_{w_i}(\chi_i, \chi_{i+1}))_{i \in \mathbb{N}}$ contains infinitely many $\star$ and no 0. The ω-language $[X]_\mathcal{A}$ of a set of states $X \subseteq S$ is the set of infinite words accepted by a sequence χ such that $\chi_0 \in X$. The ω-languages accepted by some set of states in a NBW are the *rational ω-languages* [5].

Given a finite word $u \in A^*$ and a finite non-empty word $v \in A^+$, write uv^ω for the infinite word $w \in A^\omega$ defined by $w_i = u_i$ if $i < |u|$ and $w_i = v_{(i-|u|) mod |v|}$ otherwise. *Ultimately periodic words* are (infinite) words of the form uv^ω for some $u, v \in A^* \times A^+$. Given an ω-language $L \subseteq A^\omega$, we set

$$UP(L) = \{uv^\omega \mid uv^\omega \in L\} \qquad\qquad L^\$ = \{u\$v \mid uv^\omega \in L\}$$

$UP(L)$ is a ω-language over A while $L^\$$ is a language of finite words over the alphabet $A^\$ = A \uplus \{\$\}$. The first key observation is that the ultimately periodic words of a rational ω-language fully characterize it:

Proposition 3 ([6, **Fact 1**]). *For all rational ω-languages L, L', we have that $UP(L) = UP(L')$ entails $L = L'$.*

Proof. Consequence of the closure of rational ω-languages under Boolean operations [5], and the fact that every non-empty rational ω-language contains at least one ultimately periodic word. □

As a consequence, to compare the ω-languages of two sets of states in a NBW, it suffices to compare the ω-languages of ultimately periodic words they accept. Calbrix et al. show that these ω-languages can be faithfully represented as rational languages (of finite words):

Proposition 4 ([6, **Prop. 4**]). *If $L \subseteq A^\omega$ is ω-regular, then $L^\$$ is regular.*

To prove it, Calbrix et al. construct a NFA for $L^\$$ from a NBW $\mathcal{A}$ for L, with two layers. The first layer recognizes the prefixes (the u in uv^ω). This is a copy of the NBW for L (without accepting states, and where the Büchi status of the transitions is ignored). This layer guesses non-deterministically when to read the $\$$ symbol and then jumps into the second layer, whose role is to recognise the period (the v in uv^ω). We depart from [6] here, by using notions from [25] which make the presentation easier and eventually make it possible to propose our algorithm. We use the *(Büchi) transition monoid* of the NBW $\mathcal{A} = \langle S, T \rangle$ [25] to define the second layer.

Consider the set 3 as an idempotent semiring, using the following operations:

+	0	1	$\star$
0	0	1	$\star$
1	1	1	$\star$
$\star$	$\star$	$\star$	$\star$

$\cdot$	0	1	$\star$
0	0	0	0
1	0	1	$\star$
$\star$	0	$\star$	$\star$

Write $\mathcal{M} = 3^{S^2}$ for the set of square matrices over 3 indexed by S; it forms a Kleene algebra [7,20] and in particular a semiring. Let I denote the identity matrix of $\mathcal{M}$. The transition function of $\mathcal{A}$ has type $A \to \mathcal{M}$; we extend it to finite words by setting $T_\epsilon = I$ and $T_{u_1 \ldots u_n} = T_{u_1} \cdot \ldots \cdot T_{u_n}$. We have that $T_u(x, x')$ is $\star$ if there is a path along u from x to x' visiting an accepting transition, 0 if there is no path from x to x' along u, and 1 otherwise. We extend the notations $x \xrightarrow{u} x'$ and $x \overset{u}{\Rightarrow} x'$ to words accordingly.

A periodic word v^ω is accepted from a state x in $\mathcal{A}$ if and only if there is a *lasso* for v starting from x: a state y and two natural numbers n, m such that $x \xrightarrow{v^n} y \overset{v^m}{\Rightarrow} y$. This information can be computed from the matrix T_v: given a matrix M, compute[1] its Kleene star M^* and set

$$\omega(M) = \{x \in S \mid \exists y \in S,\ M^*(x, y) \neq 0 \wedge M^*(y, y) = \star\}. \tag{†}$$

At this point, one can notice that with the previously defined operations, matrices and subsets form the *Wilke algebra* associated to the NBW as in [25].

Lemma 1. *For all words v, v^ω is accepted from a state x iff $x \in \omega(T_v)$.*

We can now formally define the desired NFA: set $\mathcal{A}^\$ = \langle S^\$, o^\$, T^\$ \rangle$, where $S^\$ = S \uplus S \times \mathcal{M}$ is the disjoint union of S and $|S|$ copies of $\mathcal{M}$, and

$$\begin{cases} T_a^\$(x) = \{x' \mid T_a(x, x') \neq 0\} \\ T_a^\$(\langle x, M \rangle) = \{\langle x, M \cdot T_a \rangle\} \end{cases} \quad \begin{cases} T_\$^\$(x) = \{\langle x, I \rangle\} \\ T_\$^\$(\langle x, M \rangle) = \emptyset \end{cases} \quad \begin{cases} o^\$(x) = 0 \\ o^\$(\langle x, M \rangle) = x \in \omega(M) \end{cases}$$

The set $\mathcal{M}$ can be replaced here by its accessible part $\mathcal{M}' = \{T_u \mid u \in A^*\}$. The main difference with the construction from [6] is that we use deterministic automata in the second layer, which enable a streamlined presentation in terms of matrices—which are not mentioned explicitly in [6]. The construction of $\mathcal{A}^\$$ preserves the semantics of all sets of states, up to $L \mapsto L^\$$:

Theorem 2. *For all sets X of states from $\mathcal{A}$, we have $[X]_{\mathcal{A}^\$} = ([X]_{\mathcal{A}})^\$$.*

---

[1] To compute M^*, one can use the fact that $M^* = (I + M)^n$ with $n = |S|$, and use iterated squaring.

Example 1. To illustrate this construction, consider the NBW depicted on the left in Fig. 3. The state 0 accepts the words with a finite but non-zero number of b's; the state 1 only accepts the word a^ω. Accordingly, we have $[0]^{\$}_{\mathcal{A}} = (a+b)^*ba^*\$a^+$ and $[1]^{\$}_{\mathcal{A}} = a^*\$a^+$. These are indeed the languages respectively recognized by the states 0 and 1 from the NFA $\mathcal{A}^{\$}$ on the right.

We only depicted the relevant part of the second layer: the only reachable matrices are those of the form T_u for some word u. There are only three of them in this example since $T_a \cdot T_b = T_b \cdot T_a = T_b \cdot T_b = T_b$ and $T_a \cdot T_a = T_a$. We might want to prune $\mathcal{A}^{\$}$ so that all states may reach an accepting state, but we want in the sequel to exploit the structure shared by the copies of the transition monoid: they only differ by the accepting status of their states, by definition.

Note that since the second layer of $\mathcal{A}^{\$}$ is already deterministic, one can determinise $\mathcal{A}^{\$}$ into a DFA with at most $2^n + 2^n 3^{n^2}$ states, where n is the number of states of $\mathcal{A}$. This is slightly better than the $2^n + 2^{2n^2+n}$ bound obtained in [6].

We summarize the operations defined so far on languages and automata in Fig. 4; we define the operations in the right-most column in the following section.

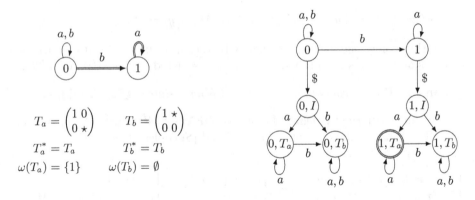

Fig. 3. A NBW $\mathcal{A}$ (left) and the reachable part of its associated NFA $\mathcal{A}^{\$}$ (right).

ω-regular	ultimately periodic	rational	A^+-weigthed
$\mathcal{L} : A^\omega \to 2$	$\mathcal{L} : A^\omega \to 2$	$\mathcal{L}^{\$} : (A^{\$})^* \to 2$	$\mathcal{L}^{\pounds} : A^* \to \mathcal{P}(A^+)$
$\mathcal{L}_1 = \mathcal{L}_2 \quad \Leftrightarrow$	$UP(\mathcal{L}_1) = UP(\mathcal{L}_2) \quad \Leftrightarrow$	$\mathcal{L}_1^{\$} = \mathcal{L}_2^{\$} \quad \Leftrightarrow$	$\mathcal{L}_1^{\pounds} = \mathcal{L}_2^{\pounds}$

NBW		NFA	weighted NFA
$\mathcal{A}$	$\longrightarrow$	$\mathcal{A}^{\$}$ $\longrightarrow$	$\mathcal{A}^{\pounds}$
$[X]_{\mathcal{A}} = [Y]_{\mathcal{A}}$	$\Leftrightarrow$	$[X]_{\mathcal{A}^{\$}} = [Y]_{\mathcal{A}^{\$}} \quad \Leftrightarrow$	$[X]_{\mathcal{A}^{\pounds}} = [Y]_{\mathcal{A}^{\pounds}}$
Ramsey/ranked based		HKC	HKC$^\omega$

Fig. 4. Summary of the operations and algorithms on languages and automata.

4   HKC for Büchi Automata

By Proposition 3 and Theorem 2, given two sets of states X, Y of a NBW $\mathcal{A}$, we have $[X]_{\mathcal{A}} = [Y]_{\mathcal{A}}$ iff $[X]_{\mathcal{A}^\$} = [Y]_{\mathcal{A}^\$}$. One can thus use any algorithm for language equivalence on NFA to solve language equivalence on NBW. Given the structure (and size) of $\mathcal{A}^\$$, this would however be inefficient: each time the letter $\$$ is read, the algorithm would explore one of the automata for the second layer, without ever realising that the transition structure of those automata is always the same, only the accepting status of their states differ. We show in this section that we can do better, by using a weighted automata.

Given a an ω-language L, the language $L^\$$ can be seen as a weighted language $L^{\pounds} : A^* \to \mathcal{P}(A^+)$ with weights in the semilattice $\langle \mathcal{P}(A^+), \cup, \emptyset \rangle$:

$$L^{\pounds} : u \mapsto \{ v \in A^+ \mid uv^\omega \in L \}$$

Given a NBW $\mathcal{A} = \langle S, T \rangle$, one can immediately construct a NFA $\mathcal{A}^{\pounds} = \langle S^{\pounds}, T^{\pounds}, o^{\pounds} \rangle$ such that for every set of states X, $[X]_{\mathcal{A}}^{\pounds} = [X]_{\mathcal{A}^{\pounds}}$. This is just the first layer from the previous construction: set $S^{\pounds} = S$ and

$$T_a^{\pounds}(x) = \{ x' \mid T_a(x, x') \neq 0 \} \qquad o^{\pounds}(x) = \{ v \in A^+ \mid v^\omega \in [x]_{\mathcal{A}} \}$$

> **input**   : A NBW $\mathcal{A} = \langle S, T \rangle$
> **output** : The set of discriminating sets $\mathcal{D} = \{ \omega(T_v) \mid v \in A^* \}$
>
> 1 $\mathcal{D} := \emptyset$; $\mathcal{M} := \emptyset$; $todo := \{I\}$;
> 2   **while** $todo \neq \emptyset$ **do**
> 3 $\quad$ extract M from $todo$;
> 4 $\quad$ **if** $M \in \mathcal{M}$ **then** skip;
> 5 $\quad$ **forall** $a \in A$ **do**
> 6 $\quad\quad |$ insert $M \cdot T_a$ in $todo$;
> 7 $\quad$ insert M in $\mathcal{M}$; insert $\omega(M)$ in $\mathcal{D}$;
> 8   **return** $\mathcal{D}$;

Fig. 5. Discr($\mathcal{A}$): exploring the Büchi transition monoid of a NBW $\mathcal{A}$ to compute discriminating sets.

Let $\mathcal{A}^{\pounds\#}$ be the powerset automaton of $\mathcal{A}^{\pounds}$. To use algorithms such as HKC on $\mathcal{A}^{\pounds}$, it suffices to be able to compare the outputs of any two states of $\mathcal{A}^{\pounds\#}$, i.e., compare the languages $o^{\pounds\#}(X)$ and $o^{\pounds\#}(Y)$ for any two sets $X, Y \subseteq S$. Since those languages are rational (using the second layer of the previous construction), it might be tempting to use algorithms such as HK or HKC to perform this task. We proceed differently in order to exploit the shared structure of those languages.

Lemma 2. *For all states $x \in S$ and sets $X \subseteq S$, we have*

$$o^{\pounds}(x) = \{ v \in A^+ \mid x \in \omega(T_v) \}$$
$$o^{\pounds\#}(X) = \{ v \in A^+ \mid X \cap \omega(T_v) \neq \emptyset \}$$

Proof. Immediate consequence of Lemma 1 and the definitions of $o^{\mathcal{L}}$ and $o^{\mathcal{L}\#}$. Note that allowing empty v would not change the statement since $\omega(T_\epsilon) = \omega(I) = \emptyset$.

Proposition 5. *For all sets* $X, Y \subseteq S$,

$$o^{\mathcal{L}\#}(X) = o^{\mathcal{L}\#}(Y) \quad iff \quad forall \ v \in A^+, X \cap \omega(T_v) = \emptyset \Leftrightarrow Y \cap \omega(T_v) = \emptyset.$$

This result shows that an explicit computation of $o^{\mathcal{L}\#}$ is not necessary, as the knowledge of $\{\omega(T_v), v \in A^+\}$ is enough to assess whether X and Y have same output. Let $\mathcal{D} = \{\omega(T_v) \mid v \in A^+\}$. We call the sets in $\mathcal{D}$ *discriminating sets*. Again, allowing empty v here would make no difference: the discriminating set $\emptyset$ is useless to distinguish two sets $X, Y \subseteq S$. As subsets of S, there are at most $2^{|S|}$ discriminating sets. Those can be enumerated since the T_v range over finitely many matrices (at most $3^{|S|^2}$). This is what is done in the algorithm from Fig. 5.

We finally obtain the algorithm in Fig. 6 for language equivalence in a NBW: we compute the discriminating sets ($\mathcal{D}$) and a relation (R) which is almost a bisimulation up to congruence: the outputs of its pairs must be checked against the discriminating sets, which we achieve with a simple loop (lines 2-4).

---

input : A NBW $\mathcal{A} = \langle S, T \rangle$ and two sets $X, Y \subseteq S$
output : true if $[X]_{\mathcal{A}} = [Y]_{\mathcal{A}}$; false otherwise

1   $R := \text{HKC}'(\mathcal{A}^{\mathcal{L}}, X, Y)$ $||$ $\mathcal{D} := \text{Discr}(\mathcal{A})$;
2   **forall** $\langle X', Y' \rangle \in R, \ D \in \mathcal{D}$ **do**
3 | **if** $X' \cap D = \emptyset \nLeftrightarrow Y' \cap D = \emptyset$ **then return** *false*;
4   **return** *true*;

Fig. 6. $\text{HKC}^\omega(\mathcal{A}, X, Y)$: checking language equivalence in a NBW using bisimulations up to congruence.

Example 2. We execute HKC^ω on the NBW on the left below, starting with states $\{0\}$ and $\{1\}$. The transition monoid has 13 elements (see [21, App A]). They give rise to three discriminating sets: $\emptyset$, $\{0, 1\}$, and $\{0, 1, 2\}$, which arise for instance from the three matrices on the right, using formula (†) on page 8:

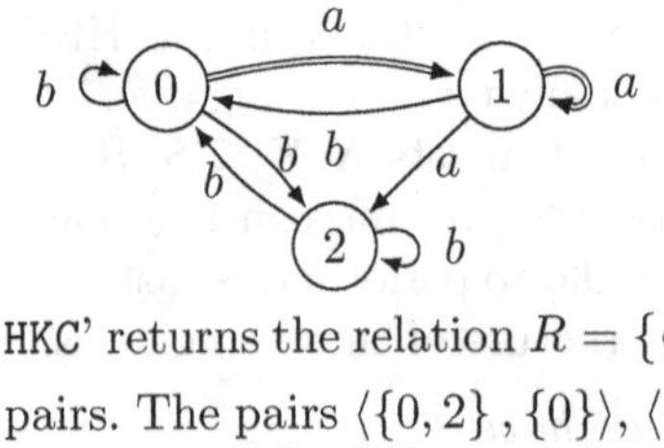

$$T_b = \begin{pmatrix} 1 & 0 & 1 \\ 1 & 0 & 0 \\ 1 & 0 & 1 \end{pmatrix} \quad T_a = \begin{pmatrix} 0 \star 0 \\ 0 \star 1 \\ 0 \ 0 \ 0 \end{pmatrix} \quad T_{ba} = \begin{pmatrix} 0 \star 0 \\ 0 \star 0 \\ 0 \star 0 \end{pmatrix}$$

HKC' returns the relation $R = \{\langle \{0\}, \{1\} \rangle, \langle \{1\}, \{1, 2\} \rangle\}$, which contains only two pairs. The pairs $\langle \{0, 2\}, \{0\} \rangle$, $\langle \{1, 2\}, \{1, 2\} \rangle$, and $\langle \{0\}, \{0, 2\} \rangle$, which are reachable from $\langle \{0\}, \{1\} \rangle$ by reading the words b, aa, and ab, are skipped thanks to the up to congruence technique. For instance to obtain the pair $\langle \{0, 2\}, \{0\} \rangle$, starting from $\langle \{0\}, \{1\} \rangle$ and $\langle \{1\}, \{1, 2\} \rangle$ we can obtain $\langle \{0\}, \{1, 2\} \rangle$ by transitivity, from which we deduce $\langle\{0,2\},\{1,2\}\rangle$ by union with $\langle\{2\},\{2\}\rangle$. By transitivity and symmetry we can finally obtain $\langle\{0,2\},\{0\}\rangle$.

The two pairs of R cannot be told apart using the three discriminating sets and HKC^ω returns *true*. States 0 and 1 are indeed equivalent: they accept the words with infinitely many a's. If instead we start HKC^ω from sets $\{0\}$ and $\{2\}$, it returns *false*: the discriminating set $\{0,1\}$ distinguishes $\{0\}$ and $\{2\}$. Indeed, the state 2 recognises the words starting with b and with infinitely many a's.

Note that HKC^ω can be instrumented to return a counterexample in case of failure: it suffices to record the finite word u that lead to each pair in R as well the finite word v that lead to each discriminating set in $\mathcal{D}$: if the check on line 3 fails, the corresponding word uv^ω is a counter-example to language equivalence.

Also note that HKC^ω is intrinsically parallel: the computations of $\mathcal{D}$ and R can be done in parallel, and the checks in lines 2–4 can be performed using a producer-consumer pattern where they are triggered whenever new values are inserted in $\mathcal{D}$ or R. Alternatively, those checks can be delegated to a SAT solver. Indeed, given a discriminating set D, define the following formula with $2|D|$ variables $\{x_d \mid d \in D\} \cup \{y_d \mid d \in D\}$:

$$\varphi_D = \bigvee_{d\in D} x_d \Leftrightarrow \bigvee_{d\in D} y_d$$

For all sets $X, Y \subseteq S$, we have $X \cap D = \emptyset \Leftrightarrow Y \cap D = \emptyset$ iff φ_D evaluates to *true* under the assignment $x_d \mapsto d \in X$ and $y_d \mapsto d \in Y$. Given the set of discriminating sets $\mathcal{D}$, it thus suffices to build the formula $\varphi_{\mathcal{D}} = \bigwedge_{D\in\mathcal{D}} \varphi_D$ with $2|S|$ variables, and to evaluate it on all pairs from the relation R returned by HKC'. The main advantage of proceeding this way is that the SAT solver might be able to represent $\varphi_{\mathcal{D}}$ in a compact and efficient way. If we moreover use an incremental SAT solver, this formula can be built incrementally, thus avoiding the need to store explicitly the set $\mathcal{D}$.

One can also use a (incremental) SAT solver in a symmetrical way: Given a pair of sets $\langle X, Y \rangle \in S^2$, define the following formula with $|S|$ variables $\{x_s \mid s \in S\}$:

$$\psi_{\langle X,Y\rangle} = \bigvee_{s\in X} x_s \Leftrightarrow \bigvee_{s\in Y} x_s$$

For all sets D, we have $X \cap D = \emptyset \Leftrightarrow Y \cap D = \emptyset$ iff $\psi_{\langle X,Y\rangle}$ evaluates to *true* under the assignment $x_s \mapsto s \in D$. Like previously, one can thus construct incrementally the formula $\psi_R = \bigwedge_{p\in R} \psi_p$ before evaluating it on all discriminating sets.

5   Conclusion and Future Work

We presented an algorithm for checking language equivalence of non-deterministic Büchi automata. This algorithm exploits advanced coinductive techniques to analyse the finite prefixes of the considered languages, through bisimulations up to congruence, as in the algorithm HKC for NFA. The periodic part of the considered languages is also analysed coinductively, in order to compute the discriminating sets. Those sets make it possible to classify the periodic words accepted by the various states of the starting automaton, thus providing all the necessary information together with the analysis of the finite prefixes.

A prototype implementation is available; it makes it possible to test several combinations of up-to techniques [22].

Our algorithm stems from the construction of Calbrix et al. [6], which we revisited using notions from [25] in Sect. 3. HKC$^\omega$ is rather close to *Ramsey-based* algorithms [1,11] (as opposed to *rank-based* ones [8–10,23]). In particular, our matrices are often called *super-graphs* in Ramsey-based algorithms. A key difference is that we focus on language equivalence, thus enabling stronger coinductive proof principles.

The next step is to design up-to techniques in order to reduce the exploration of the periodic layer, to compute the discriminating sets more efficiently. We provide two such techniques in the extended version of this abstract [21], namely coinduction up to unions and coinduction up to equivalence. Using the two techniques at the same time is likely to be possible, i.e., using coinduction up to congruence; this however requires further investigations, especially in order to find reasonably efficient ways to perform the corresponding tests.

Along the same vein, we also want to investigate how to exploit techniques using simulation relations, which were successfully used in [1,2,10,24] and which tend to nicely fit in the coinductive framework we propose here [4, Sect. 5].

Acknowledgements. We would like to thank Dmitriy Traytel for pointing us to the work of Calbrix et al. [6].

References

1. Abdulla, P.A., et al.: Simulation subsumption in Ramsey-based Büchi automata universality and inclusion testing. In: Touili, T., Cook, B., Jackson, P. (eds.) CAV 2010. LNCS, vol. 6174, pp. 132–147. Springer, Heidelberg (2010)

2. Abdulla, P.A., et al.: Advanced Ramsey-Based Büchi automata inclusion testing. In: Katoen, J.-P., König, B. (eds.) CONCUR 2011. LNCS, vol. 6901, pp. 187–202. Springer, Heidelberg (2011). https://doi.org/10.1007/978-3-642-14295-6_14

3. Abdulla, P.A., Chen, Y.-F., Holík, L., Mayr, R., Vojnar, T.: When simulation meets antichains. In: Esparza, J., Majumdar, R. (eds.) TACAS 2010. LNCS, vol. 6015, pp. 158–174. Springer, Heidelberg (2010). https://doi.org/10.1007/978-3-642-12002-2_14

4. Bonchi, F., Pous, D.: Checking NFA equivalence with bisimulations up to congruence. In: Proceedings POPL, pp. 457–468. ACM (2013). https://doi.org/10.1145/2429069.2429124

5. Büchi, J.R.: On a decision method in restricted second order arithmetic. In: Mac Lane, S., Siefkes, D. (eds.) The Collected Works of J. Richard Büchi, pp. 425–435. Springer, New York (1990). https://doi.org/10.1007/978-1-4613-8928-6_23

6. Calbrix, H., Nivat, M., Podelski, A.: Ultimately periodic words of rational w-languages. In: Brookes, S., Main, M., Melton, A., Mislove, M., Schmidt, D. (eds.) MFPS 1993. LNCS, vol. 802, pp. 554–566. Springer, Heidelberg (1994). https://doi.org/10.1007/3-540-58027-1_27

7. Conway, J.H.: Regular Algebra and Finite Machines. Chapman and Hall, London (1971)

8. Doyen, L., Raskin, J.-F.: Improved Algorithms for the Automata-Based Approach to Model-Checking. In: Grumberg, O., Huth, M. (eds.) TACAS 2007. LNCS, vol. 4424, pp. 451–465. Springer, Heidelberg (2007). https://doi.org/10.1007/978-3-540-71209-1_34

9. Doyen, L., Raskin, J.: Antichains for theautomata-based approach to model-checking. Logical Meth. Comput. Sci. **5**, 1 (2009). http://dx.doi.org/10.2168/LMCS-5(1:5)2009

10. Doyen, L., Raskin, J.-F.: Antichain algorithms for finite automata. In: Esparza, J., Majumdar, R. (eds.) TACAS 2010. LNCS, vol. 6015, pp. 2–22. Springer, Heidelberg (2010). https://doi.org/10.1007/978-3-642-12002-2_2

11. Fogarty, S., Vardi, M.Y.: Büchi complementation and size-change termination. In: Kowalewski, S., Philippou, A. (eds.) TACAS 2009. LNCS, vol. 5505, pp. 16–30. Springer, Heidelberg (2009). https://doi.org/10.1007/978-3-642-00768-2_2

12. Fogarty, S., Vardi, M.Y.: Efficient Büchi universality checking. In: Esparza, J., Majumdar, R. (eds.) TACAS 2010. LNCS, vol. 6015, pp. 205–220. Springer, Heidelberg (2010). https://doi.org/10.1007/978-3-642-12002-2_17

13. Gastin, P., Oddoux, D.: Fast LTL to Büchi automata translation. In: Berry, G., Comon, H., Finkel, A. (eds.) CAV 2001. LNCS, vol. 2102, pp. 53–65. Springer, Heidelberg (2001). https://doi.org/10.1007/3-540-44585-4_6

14. Gurumurthy, S., Kupferman, O., Somenzi, F., Vardi, M.Y.: On Complementing Nondeterministic Büchi Automata. In: Geist, D., Tronci, E. (eds.) CHARME 2003. LNCS, vol. 2860, pp. 96–110. Springer, Heidelberg (2003). https://doi.org/10.1007/978-3-540-39724-3_10

15. Holzmann, G.J.: The model checker spin. IEEE Trans., Softw. Eng. **23**(5), 279–295 (1997)

16. Hopcroft, J.E.: An n log n algorithm for minimizing in a finite automaton. In: Proceedings International Symposium of Theory of Machines and Computations, 189–196. Academic Press, Cambridge (1971)

17. Hopcroft, J.E., Karp, R.M.: A linear algorithm for testing equivalence of finite automata. Technical report, 114, Cornell University, December 1971. http://techreports.library.cornell.edu:8081/Dienst/UI/1.0/Display/cul.cs/TR71-114

18. Hutagalung, M., Lange, M., Lozes, E.: Revealing vs. concealing: more simulation games for Büchi inclusion. In: Dediu, A.-H., Martín-Vide, C., Truthe, B. (eds.) LATA 2013. LNCS, vol. 7810, pp. 347–358. Springer, Heidelberg (2013). https://doi.org/10.1007/978-3-642-37064-9_31

19. Knaster, B.: Un théorème sur les fonctions d'ensembles. Annales de la Société Polonaise de Mathématiques **6**, 133–134 (1928)

20. Kozen, D.: A completeness theorem for Kleene algebras and the algebra of regular events. Inf. Comput. **110**(2), 366–390 (1994). https://doi.org/10.1006/inco.1994.1037

21. Kuperberg, D., Pinault, L., Pous, D.: Extended version of this abstract (2018). https://hal.archives-ouvertes.fr/hal-01928701/

22. Kuperberg, D., Pinault, L., Pous, D.: Web appendix for this paper (2019). http://perso.ens-lyon.fr/damien.pous/covece/hkcw

23. Kupferman, O., Vardi, M.Y.: Weak alternating automata are not that weak. ACM Trans. Comput. Log. **2**(3), 408–429 (2001). https://doi.org/10.1145/377978.377993
24. Mayr, R., Clemente, L.: Advanced automata minimization. In: 2013 Proceedings POPL, pp. 63–74. ACM (2013). https://doi.org/10.1145/2429069.2429079
25. Perrin, D., Pin, J.É.: Semigroups and automata on infinite words. NATO ASI Series C Mathematical and Physical Sciences-Advanced Study Institute **466**, 49–72 (1995)
26. Tarjan, R.E.: Efficiency of a good but not linear set union algorithm. J. ACM **22**(2), 215–225 (1975). https://doi.org/10.1145/321879.321884
27. Tarski, A.: A lattice-theoretical fixpoint theorem and its applications. Pac. J. Math. **5**(2), 285–309 (1955)
28. Tsai, M.-H., Tsay, Y.-K., Hwang, Y.-S.: GOAL for games, omega-automata, and logics. In: Sharygina, N., Veith, H. (eds.) CAV 2013. LNCS, vol. 8044, pp. 883–889. Springer, Heidelberg (2013). https://doi.org/10.1007/978-3-642-39799-8_62
29. Vardi, M.Y.: An automata-theoretic approach to linear temporal logic. In: Moller, F., Birtwistle, G. (eds.) Logics for Concurrency. LNCS, vol. 1043, pp. 238–266. Springer, Heidelberg (1996). https://doi.org/10.1007/3-540-60915-6_6
30. De Wulf, M., Doyen, L., Henzinger, T.A., Raskin, J.-F.: Antichains: a new algorithm for checking universality of finite automata. In: Ball, T., Jones, R.B. (eds.) CAV 2006. LNCS, vol. 4144, pp. 17–30. Springer, Heidelberg (2006). https://doi.org/10.1007/11817963_5

Hole-Free Partially Directed Animals

Paolo Massazza[(✉)]

Dipartimento di Scienze teoriche e applicate, Università degli studi dell'Insubria,
Varese, Italy
paolo.massazza@uninsubria.it

Abstract. We consider the class HFPDA of hole-free partially directed animals. This is the class of all polyominoes P such that every cell of P can be reached from any cell in the first column of P with a path (inside P) which makes only North, South and East steps, and such that there is not a finite region of empty unitary squares which is surrounded by cells belonging to P. We provide a generation algorithm that allows us to enumerate HFPDA(n) in constant amortized time using $O(n)$ space.

1 Introduction

A *polyomino* is a finite and connected union of unitary squares (called cells) in the plane $\mathbb{Z} \times \mathbb{Z}$, considered up to translations [11]. The number of cells of a polyomino is its *area*. To classify polyominoes and to tackle some difficult questions about them (for instance, counting and exhaustive generation), several subclasses have been introduced in literature. For instance, the class of convex polyominoes (*i.e.* polyominoes whose intersection with any vertical or horizontal line is connected) and its subclasses have been studied under several points of view [2, 5–8].

In this paper we consider a class of polyominoes contained in the class PDA of partially directed animals [17]. A polyomino P is in PDA if and only if every cell of P can be reached from any cell in the first column of P with a path (inside P) which makes only North, South and East steps, see Fig. 1. Furthermore, if P belongs to PDA and has no holes (a hole is a closed region of cells not in P, that is, a finite set of cells not in P surrounded by cells of P), then it belongs to HFPDA (Hole-Free Partially Directed Animals), see Fig. 1(b).

We see that the set of polyominoes of area n in HFPDA can be generated by an algorithm that runs in Constant Amortized Time (CAT) and uses space $O(n)$. We recall that suitable families of directed animals (obtained by considering paths made of North and East steps) have been enumerated in [1].

CAT algorithms for the exhaustive generation by area of the class of convex polyominoes and of many of its subclasses have been recently presented [3, 4, 14–16]. The problem of efficiently generating non-convex polyominoes is of particular interest. The most used algorithm to generate the whole class of polyominoes runs in exponential time and exponential space [12]. This algorithm has been used to compute the exact number of polyominoes of area n for $n \leq 56$.

P. Hofman and M. Skrzypczak (Eds.): DLT 2019, LNCS 11647, pp. 221–233, 2019.
https://doi.org/10.1007/978-3-030-24886-4_16

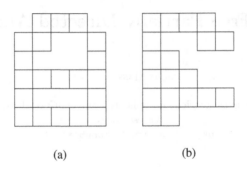

(a)   (b)

Fig. 1. A partially directed animal with two holes (a) and a hole-free partially directed animal (b).

The number of polyominoes of area n seems to grow as $\frac{c\lambda^n}{n}$ for two values c, λ estimated as $c = 0.3169$ and $\lambda = 4.0626$, see [13]. Very recently, CAT generation algorithms for PDA and for the class of 2-Polyominoes have been presented in [9, 10].

In Sect. 2 we give some preliminaries and notation, whereas in Sect. 3 we define a discrete dynamical system that is used to generate polyominoes in HFPDA column-by-column. In Sect. 4 we describe the algorithm and the data structure used to represent a polyomino. Time and space complexity are then discussed. Finally, in Sect. 5 we give some brief conclusions.

2   Notation and Preliminaries

The *area* $A(P)$ of a polyomino P is the number of its cells. A polyomino can be seen as a finite sequence of columns. A *column* of a polyomino consists of a sequence of *vertical segments* separated by empty unitary squares. A *vertical segment* is a sequence of cells $q_1, q_2, \ldots, q_k$ which are in the same column and such that q_i is edge-adjacent to q_{i+1} for $1 \leq i < k$ (two cells are edge-adjacent if they have a common edge). The *position* of a cell is its y-coordinate. The position of the top (resp., bottom) cell of a segment s is denoted by $\text{Top}(s)$ (resp., $\text{Bot}(s)$). We represent a segment s of a column by means of the pair $(A(s), \text{Top}(s))$. Segments belonging to the same column are numbered from the top to the bottom, thus a column with p segments is simply a sequence of disjoint segments $\mathbf{c} = (s_1, \ldots, s_p)$, with $\text{Top}(s_i) < \text{Top}(s_{i-1}) - A(s_{i-1})$ for $1 < i \leq p$. Furthermore, the position of $\mathbf{c}$ is the position of its first segment, $\text{Top}(\mathbf{c}) = \text{Top}(s_1)$. Similarly, we set $\text{Bot}(\mathbf{c}) = \text{Bot}(s_p)$. Given a segment s and an integer j such that $\text{Top}(s) > j \geq \text{Bot}(s)$, we denote by $s_{>j}$ (resp., $s_{\leq j}$) the part of s consisting of the cells with position greater than j (resp., smaller than or equal to j). The part of a column $\mathbf{c}$ that is above a position j is $\mathbf{c}_{>j}$ ($\mathbf{c}_{\geq j}$, $\mathbf{c}_{\leq j}$ and $\mathbf{c}_{<j}$ are defined similarly). Given two segments s and t with $\text{Bot}(s) > \text{Top}(t)$, their *distance* is $\text{Dist}(s, t) = \text{Bot}(s) - \text{Top}(t) - 1$.

Segments can be ordered with respect to their position and their area.

Definition 1 (< **on segments**). *Let u and v be two segments. Then, one has $u < v$ if and only if $Top(u) > Top(v)$ or $Top(u) = Top(v)$ and $A(u) > A(v)$.*

A total order on columns (denoted by $\prec$) can be obtained by extending $<$.

Definition 2 ($\prec$ **on columns**). *Let $\mathbf{b} = (s_1, \ldots, s_p)$ and $\mathbf{c} = (t_1, \ldots, t_q)$ be two columns. Then, one has $\mathbf{b} \prec \mathbf{c}$ if and only if either $A(\mathbf{b}) > A(\mathbf{c})$, or $A(\mathbf{b}) = A(\mathbf{c})$ and there exists m with $1 \leq m \leq \min(p, q)$ such that $s_j = t_j$ for all $j < m$ and $s_m < t_m$.*

We assume that the position of the bottom cell of the last segment of the first column of a polyomino is 0. We denote by $\mathsf{Pol}(n)$ the set of polyominoes of area n. If $P \in \mathsf{Pol}(n)$ then $P_{\leq i}$ and P_i indicate the i-prefix of P (the sequence of the first i columns of P) and the i-th column of P, respectively. Notice that $P_{\leq i}$ is not necessarily a polyomino, as well as an arbitrary sequence of columns does not generally represent a polyomino but a set of polyominoes. The *width* $w(P)$ of a polyomino P is the number of its columns. A segment s of P_i is *left-adjacent* (l-adjacent for short) to a segment t of P_{i-1} if there exists a cell of s that is edge-adjacent to a cell of t. We consider an alternative (but equivalent) definition for the class of polyominoes known as partially directed animals [17,18].

Definition 3 (**The class PDA**). *The class $\mathsf{PDA}(n)$ of Partially Directed Animals of area n is the class containing all $P \in \mathsf{Pol}(n)$ such that $P_{\leq i}$ is a polyomino for all $i \in \mathbb{N}$ with $1 \leq i \leq w(P)$.*

Given $P \in \mathsf{PDA}$, we say that P has a *hole* if there exists a maximal set S of empty unit squares such that:

1. for any two squares a and b in S, there exists a path connecting a to b, which makes only North, West, South and East steps, and that crosses only squares in S;
2. for any two empty unit squares $c \notin S$ and $a \in S$, there is not a path connecting c to a that uses only North, West, South and East steps, and that crosses only empty unit squares.

We are interested in a particular subclass of PDA, called HFPDA (Hole-Free Partially Directed Animals), which contains all polyominoes in PDA without holes. It is immediate to prove that any polyomino in HFPDA has the following property.

Lemma 1. *Let $P \in \mathsf{HFPDA}$. Then, for all $i \in \mathbb{N}$, $1 < i \leq w(P)$, any segment of P_i is l-adjacent to exactly one segment of P_{i-1}.*

As a matter of fact, any two consecutive columns of a polyomino in $\mathsf{HFPDA}(n)$ satisfy a particular relation called *compatibility*.

Definition 4 (**Compatibility of columns**). *Given $P \in \mathsf{Pol}(n)$, P_i is compatible with P_{i-1}, denoted by $P_i \ \square \ P_{i-1}$, if every segment of P_i is l-adjacent to exactly one segment of P_{i-1}.*

Remark 1. For any $n > 0$, a one-column polyomino $(((n), n - 1))$ consisting of one segment of area n is in HFPDA(n). Then, a polyomino P is in HFPDA if and only if for all i, with $1 < i \leq w(P)$, one has $P_{\leq i-1} \in$ HFPDA and $P_i \,\square\, P_{i-1}$.

The set of all columns that are compatible with a column $\mathbf{a}$ and have area r is indicated by $\text{Comp}(\mathbf{a}, r) = \{\mathbf{b} \mid \mathbf{b} \,\square\, \mathbf{a} \text{ and } A(\mathbf{b}) = r\}$.

The (right) *column concatenation* $\mid$ is the operation which takes a polyomino $P \in$ HFPDA and a column $\mathbf{c}$ such that $\mathbf{c} \,\square\, P_{w(P)}$, and produces a polyomino $P' = P|\mathbf{c}$, with $w(P) + 1$ columns, which is still in HFPDA. The main idea of the paper is to generate all polyominoes in HFPDA(n) according to the following total order.

Definition 5 (Order on HFPDA). *Given* $P, Q \in$ HFPDA(n), $P < Q$ *if there exists i such that* $P_{\leq i} = Q_{\leq i}$ *and* $P_i \prec Q_i$.

From here on, given a segment s of P_i, the two segments immediately above and below s are denoted by $s^\uparrow$ and $s_\downarrow$, respectively. The second segment below s is $s_{\downarrow\downarrow}$, and the segment of P_{i-1} to which s is l-adjacent is indicated by $\overleftarrow{s}$.

3   A Dynamical System for Columns

In this section we are going to define a family $f_{\mathbf{a},r}$ of discrete dynamical systems depending on two parameters: a column $\mathbf{a}$ and an integer r. For fixed values of the parameters, $f_{\mathbf{a},r}$ takes in input a column $\mathbf{b}$ such that $\mathbf{b} \,\square\, \mathbf{a}$ and $A(\mathbf{b}) = r$, and outputs $\mathbf{c}$ such that $\mathbf{c} \,\square\, \mathbf{a}$ $A(\mathbf{c}) = r$ and $\mathbf{b} \prec \mathbf{c}$.

Given $\mathbf{a}$, the initial state of the system is the column $\mathbf{b} = \min_{\prec}\{\mathbf{c} \mid \mathbf{c} \,\square\, \mathbf{a}, A(\mathbf{c}) = r\}$. This is a column consisting of one segment of area r whose bottom cell has position $\text{Top}(\mathbf{a})$, $\mathbf{b} = ((r, \text{Top}(\mathbf{a}) + r - 1))$. The evolution rule of $f_{\mathbf{a},r}$ rearranges the cells of the column given in input according to three operations called *moves*. Informally, a move in a column $\mathbf{b}$ can only occur in a position j occupied by a cell of a segment s of $\mathbf{b}$. It can be of three different types, namely a *split* move or a *shift* move or a *shift-and-split* move. A split move occurs when $\text{Bot}(s) \leq j < \text{Top}(s)$ and $\text{Top}(\overleftarrow{s}) > j$. In this case, s is split into two parts, $s_{>j}$ and $s_{\leq j}$. The segment $s_{>j}$ remains in its position (so it is l-adjacent to $\overleftarrow{s}$) whereas $s_{\leq j}$ is shifted k positions downwards, where k is the smallest integer greater than 0 such that the shifted segment is l-adjacent either to $\overleftarrow{s}$ or to $(\overleftarrow{s})_\downarrow$ (possibly it joins $s_\downarrow$, unless $\text{Dist}(s, s_\downarrow) = 1$, $j > \text{Bot}(\overleftarrow{s})$ and $\overleftarrow{s} \neq \overleftarrow{s_\downarrow}$), see Fig. 2(a). If such a k does not exist then the move is not defined.

A shift move at j has the effect of shifting the segment s of $\mathbf{b}$ with $\text{Top}(s) = j$. In this case, s is shifted k positions downwards, where k is the smallest integer greater than 0 such that the shifted segment is l-adjacent either to $\overleftarrow{s}$ or to $(\overleftarrow{s})_\downarrow$, see Fig. 2(a) (with $k = 1$). Possibly, the shifted segment joins $s_\downarrow$ (unless $\text{Dist}(s, s_\downarrow) = 1$, $\text{Top}(s) > \text{Bot}(\overleftarrow{s})$ and $\overleftarrow{s} \neq \overleftarrow{s_\downarrow}$). The move is undefined if such a k does not exist.

Lastly, a shift-and-split move at j occurs when $j = \text{Top}(s)$, $A(s) > 1$, $\text{Bot}(s) = \text{Top}(\overleftarrow{s})$, $\text{Dist}(s, s_\downarrow) = 1$ and $\overleftarrow{s} \neq \overleftarrow{s_\downarrow}$. In this case s is shifted one

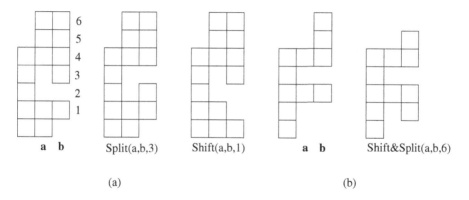

Fig. 2. A column admitting a split move at 3 and a shift move at 1 (a). A column admitting a Split-and-Shift move at 6 (b).

position downwards and joins $s_\downarrow$, producing a new segment that is l-adjacent both to $\overleftarrow{s}$ and to $\overleftarrow{s}_\downarrow$, which is then split at $\mathrm{Top}(\overleftarrow{s}) - 1$ to satisfy the property in Lemma 1, see Fig. 2(b). We denote by $\mathrm{Split}(\mathbf{a}, \mathbf{b}, j)$, $\mathrm{Shift}(\mathbf{a}, \mathbf{b}, j)$ and $\mathrm{Shift\&Split}(\mathbf{a}, \mathbf{b}, j)$ the three operations applied to the position j of a column $\mathbf{b}$ such that $\mathbf{b} \,\square\, \mathbf{a}$.

When the column $\mathbf{a}$ is clear from the context, we simply write $\mathbf{b} \xrightarrow{j} \mathbf{b}'$ if either $\mathbf{b}' = \mathrm{Shift}(\mathbf{a}, \mathbf{b}, j)$ or $\mathbf{b}' = \mathrm{Split}(\mathbf{a}, \mathbf{b}, j)$ or $\mathbf{b}' = \mathrm{Shift\&Split}(\mathbf{a}, \mathbf{b}, j)$. Furthermore, we indicate by $\mathrm{Mc}(\mathbf{b})$ the set of positions where a move can occur in $\mathbf{b}$, that is, $\mathrm{Mc}(\mathbf{b}) = \{j \in \mathbb{N} \mid \mathbf{b} \xrightarrow{j} \mathbf{b}'\}$. In particular, we are interested in the move occurring at position $\min(\mathrm{Mc}(\mathbf{b}))$. This move occurs in the last segment s of $\mathbf{b}$ if and only if $\mathrm{Top}(s) > \mathrm{Bot}(t)$, where t is the last segment of $\mathbf{a}$. Otherwise, one has $\mathrm{Top}(s) = \mathrm{Bot}(t)$ and the move occurs in $s^\uparrow$. More precisely, one has:

Lemma 2. *Let $\mathbf{a}$, $\mathbf{b}$ be two columns such that $\mathbf{b} \,\square\, \mathbf{a}$, and let s (resp., t) be the lowest segment in $\mathbf{b}$ (resp., $\mathbf{a}$). Then, one has $\min(\mathrm{Mc}(\mathbf{b})) = j$, where*

$$
j = \begin{cases}
Bot(s^\uparrow) & \text{if } Top(s) = Bot(t) \wedge \left(A(s^\uparrow) = 1 \vee Bot(s^\uparrow) < Top\left(\overleftarrow{(s^\uparrow)}\right)\right) \\
Top(s^\uparrow) & \text{if } Top(s) = Bot(t) \wedge A(s^\uparrow) > 1 \wedge Bot(s^\uparrow) = Top\left(\overleftarrow{(s^\uparrow)}\right) \\
Top(s) & \text{if } Top(s) > Bot(t) \wedge Bot(s) = Top(\overleftarrow{s}) \\
Bot(s) & \text{if } Bot(s) > Bot(t) \wedge Bot(s) < Top(\overleftarrow{s}) \\
Bot(t) + 1 & \text{if } Top(s) > Bot(t) \wedge Bot(s) \leq Bot(t)
\end{cases}
$$

Proof. Figure 3 illustrates the five cases (in order from left to right). First, consider the case $\mathrm{Top}(s) = \mathrm{Bot}(t)$. Obviously, no move can occur in s otherwise there would be a segment that is not l-adjacent to a segment of $\mathbf{a}$. If $A(s^\uparrow) = 1$ then $\mathrm{Shift}(\mathbf{a}, \mathbf{b}, \mathrm{Top}(s^\uparrow))$ is always defined (possibly $s^\uparrow$ joins s, and the new segment is l-adjacent to exactly one segment of $\mathbf{a}$). Similarly, $A(s^\uparrow) > 1 \wedge \mathrm{Bot}(s^\uparrow) < \mathrm{Top}\left(\overleftarrow{(s^\uparrow)}\right)$ implies that $\mathrm{Split}(\mathbf{a}, \mathbf{b}, \mathrm{Bot}(s^\uparrow))$ is defined.

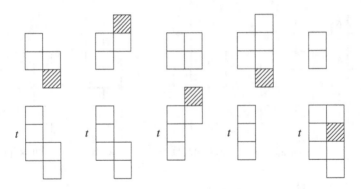

Fig. 3. The lowest move in a column: the cell where the move occurs is shaded.

So, consider the case $A(s^\uparrow) > 1$ and $\text{Bot}(s^\uparrow) = \text{Top}(\overleftarrow{(s^\uparrow)})$. For all j with $\text{Bot}(s^\uparrow) \le j < \text{Top}(s^\uparrow)$, the move $\text{Split}(\mathbf{a}, \mathbf{b}, j)$ is not defined since it would produce a segment that is not l-adjacent to a segment of $\mathbf{a}$. So, if $\text{Dist}(s^\uparrow, s) > 1$ or $\overleftarrow{(s^\uparrow)} = \overleftarrow{s}$ then $\text{Shift}(\mathbf{a}, \mathbf{b}, \text{Top}(s^\uparrow))$ is defined (more precisely, $s^\uparrow$ is shifted one position downwards). Otherwise one has $\text{Dist}(s^\uparrow, s) = 1$ and $\overleftarrow{(s^\uparrow)} \ne \overleftarrow{s}$, and the move $\text{Shift\&Split}(\mathbf{a}, \mathbf{b}, \text{Top}(s^\uparrow))$ is defined.

Now, consider the case $\text{Top}(s) > \text{Bot}(t)$. If $\text{Bot}(s) = \text{Top}(\overleftarrow{s})$ then, for all j such that $\text{Bot}(s) \le j < \text{Top}(s)$, the move $\text{Split}(\mathbf{a}, \mathbf{b}, j)$ is not defined, whereas $\text{Shift}(\mathbf{a}, \mathbf{b}, \text{Top}(s))$ is defined. Otherwise, one has $\text{Bot}(s) < \text{Top}(\overleftarrow{s})$ and either $\text{Split}(\mathbf{a}, \mathbf{b}, \text{Bot}(s))$ (if $\text{Bot}(s) > \text{Bot}(t)$) or $\text{Split}(\mathbf{a}, \mathbf{b}, \text{Bot}(t) + 1)$ (if $\text{Bot}(s) < \text{Bot}(t)$ and $\text{Top}(s) > \text{Bot}(t) + 1$) or $\text{Shift}(\mathbf{a}, \mathbf{b}, \text{Bot}(t) + 1)$ (if $\text{Bot}(s) < \text{Bot}(t)$ and $\text{Top}(s) = \text{Bot}(t) + 1$)) is defined.   □

The lowest move in $\mathbf{b}$ determines a particular column, called the *grand ancestor* of $\mathbf{b}$ with respect to $\mathbf{a}$ and denoted by $\text{GA}(\mathbf{b}, \mathbf{a})$. The grand ancestor $\text{GA}(\mathbf{b}, \mathbf{a})$ is defined so that it allows to get the column that follows $\mathbf{b}$ in the ordered (with respect to $\prec$) sequence of columns belonging to $\text{Comp}(\mathbf{a}, A(\mathbf{b}))$.

Definition 6 (Grand ancestor). *Let $\mathbf{a}$ and $\mathbf{b}$ be two columns such that $\mathbf{b} \,\square\, \mathbf{a}$. Consider the last segment s of $\mathbf{b}$ and the position j of the lowest move, $j = \min(Mc(\mathbf{b}))$. If $j \le \text{Top}(s)$ or $j = \text{Top}(s^\uparrow)$ and $\text{Shift\&Split}(\mathbf{a}, \mathbf{b}, j)$ is defined, then $\text{GA}(\mathbf{b}, \mathbf{a}) = \mathbf{b}$. Otherwise, one has $\text{Top}(s) = \text{Bot}(\mathbf{a}) \wedge j \in \{\text{Top}(s^\uparrow), \text{Bot}(s^\uparrow)\}$ (see Lemma 2) and*

$$\text{GA}(\mathbf{b}, \mathbf{a}) = \min_{\prec}\{\mathbf{c} \,|\, A(\mathbf{c}) = A(\mathbf{b}), \mathbf{c}_{<\text{Bot}(\mathbf{b}')-2} \,\square\, \mathbf{a}, \mathbf{c}_{\ge \text{Bot}(\mathbf{b}')-2} = \mathbf{b}'\},$$

where $\mathbf{b}'$ is obtained from $\mathbf{b}$ by deleting s and replacing $s^\uparrow$ by a segment t with $\text{Top}(t) = \text{Top}(s^\uparrow)$ and $A(t) = A(s^\uparrow) + p$, for a suitable integer p which is determined as follows. Let $\delta_1 = \min(A(s), \text{Dist}(s^\uparrow, v_\downarrow) - 1)$, $\delta_2 = \min(A(s), \text{Dist}(s^\uparrow, v_\downarrow) - 2, 0)$, $\Delta_1 = \min(A(s), \text{Dist}(s^\uparrow, v_{\downarrow\downarrow}) - 1)$ and $\Delta_2 = \min(A(s), \text{Dist}(s^\uparrow, v_{\downarrow\downarrow}) - 2)$. One has:

$(v = \overleftarrow{s})$ $p = A(s)$;

$(v_\downarrow = \overleftarrow{s})$ *if $j \le Bot(v)$ then $p = A(s)$. Otherwise, one has $j > Bot(v)$ and either*
$p = \delta_1$ *(if $Top(s) < Top(v_\downarrow)$) or $p = \delta_2$ (if $Top(s) = Top(v_\downarrow)$);*

$(\mathbf{Top}(v_{\downarrow\downarrow}) \ge \mathbf{Top}(s))$ *if $j \le Bot(v)$ then either $p = \Delta_1$ (if $Top(s) < Top(v_{\downarrow\downarrow})$) or*
$p = \Delta_2$ *(if $Top(s) = Top(v_{\downarrow\downarrow})$). Otherwise, one has $j > Bot(v)$ and $p = \delta_1$.*

In general, $GA(\mathbf{b}, \mathbf{a})$ is not compatible with $\mathbf{a}$, since the segment t of $\mathbf{b'}$ such that $Bot(t) \le j \le Top(t)$ may be l-adjacent to two segments of $\mathbf{a}$ (a property that does not hold after the move at j). Nevertheless, it follows by Definition 6 that it is possible to make a move at $j = \min(Mc(\mathbf{b}))$ in $GA(\mathbf{b}, \mathbf{a})$, $GA(\mathbf{b}, \mathbf{a}) \xrightarrow{j} \mathbf{c}$, obtaining a compatible column $\mathbf{c}$, $\mathbf{c} \,\square\, \mathbf{a}$. The construction of the column $GA(\mathbf{b}, \mathbf{a})$ is straightforward. Indeed, once the column $\mathbf{b'}$ of Definition 6 has been determined it is sufficient to add all the segments obtained by applying the following procedure (based on Definition 2). Let $k_1 = A(\mathbf{b}) - A(\mathbf{b'})$ be the number of cells to add. Determine the highest position p_1 (with $p_1 \le Bot(\mathbf{b'}) - 2$) for a segment t_1 of maximal area $a_1 \le k_1$ and such that $t_1 = (a_1, p_1)$ is l-adjacent to exactly one segment of $\mathbf{a}$. Add t_1 to $\mathbf{b'}$ and get a column $\mathbf{b''}$. If $a_1 = k_1$ then $GA(\mathbf{b}, \mathbf{a}) = \mathbf{b''}$, otherwise iterate the procedure on $\mathbf{b''}$ (with $k_2 = k_1 - a_1$ cells to add), that is, find the highest position p_2 smaller than $Bot(\mathbf{b''}) - 1$ for an l-adjacent segment t_2 of maximal area $a_2 \le k_2$, and so on. Obviously, after at most $A(s)$ steps the column $GA(\mathbf{b}, \mathbf{a})$ is obtained, see Fig. 4.

Remark: a particular case occurs when the procedure adds a segment s' that is l-adjacent to the second to last segment t of $\mathbf{a}$, with $A(t_\downarrow) = 1$ and $Bot(s') = Top(t_\downarrow) + 1$. In this case, if the area of the column is smaller than $A(\mathbf{b})$ then s' has to be shortened (*i.e.* $Bot(s') = Top(t_\downarrow) + 2$) so that a segment $s'_\downarrow$ (with $Top\left(s'_\downarrow\right) = Top(t_\downarrow)$) can be added to obtain the smallest compatible column.

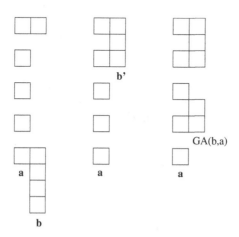

Fig. 4. The grand ancestor.

We define a discrete dynamical system $f_{\mathbf{a},r}: \text{Comp}(\mathbf{a},r) \to \text{Comp}(\mathbf{a},r)$ over columns as follows.

Definition 7. *Let* $\mathbf{a}$, $\mathbf{b}$ *be two columns such that* $\mathbf{b} \in \text{Comp}(\mathbf{a},r)$ *for a suitable integer* $r > 0$. *Then,*

$$f_{\mathbf{a},r}(\mathbf{b}) = \begin{cases} \mathbf{c} & GA(\mathbf{b},\mathbf{a}) \xrightarrow{j} \mathbf{c}, \ j = \min(Mc(\mathbf{b})) \\ ((r, Bot(\mathbf{a})) & \textit{if } Mc(\mathbf{b}) = \emptyset \end{cases}$$

Remark that $((r, Bot(\mathbf{a}))$ is a fixed point for $f_{\mathbf{a},r}$. We denote by $f_{\mathbf{a},r}^n$ the n-fold composition of $f_{\mathbf{a},r}$ with itself.

For simplicity's sake, $f_{\mathbf{a},r}$ is defined for a given column $\mathbf{a}$, extending the definition to polyominoes in HFPDA is straightforward. The main properties of the dynamical system are stated in the following lemma.

Lemma 3. *Fix an integer* r *and a column* $\mathbf{a}$. *Then, for all* $\mathbf{b} \in \text{Comp}(\mathbf{a},r)$ *it holds:*

1. $f_{\mathbf{a},r}^n(\mathbf{b}) \prec f_{\mathbf{a},r}^{n+1}(\mathbf{b})$ *for* $\mathbf{b} \neq ((r, Bot(\mathbf{a})))$;
2. $\bigcup_{n \in \mathbb{N}} f_{\mathbf{a},r}^n(((r, Top(\mathbf{a}) + r - 1)) = \text{Comp}(\mathbf{a},r)$.

Proof. (outline)

1. The column $\mathbf{c} = f_{\mathbf{a},r}(\mathbf{b})$ is such that for $j = \min(Mc(\mathbf{b}))$ one has $\mathbf{c}_{>j} = \mathbf{b}_{>j}$. Furthermore, the position j is empty in $\mathbf{c}$ whereas in $\mathbf{b}$ it is occupied by a cell of a segment, hence $\mathbf{b} \prec \mathbf{c}$ by Definition 2.

2. We argue by contradiction and let $\mathbf{c}'$ be the smallest column that is missing. We distinguish two cases. First, suppose that $\mathbf{b} = f_{\mathbf{a},r}(\mathbf{b})$ and $\mathbf{b} \prec \mathbf{c}'$. Since $\mathbf{b} = ((r, Bot(\mathbf{a})))$, the relation $\mathbf{b} \prec \mathbf{c}'$ implies that any segment in $\mathbf{c}'$ is not l-adjacent to a segment of $\mathbf{a}$, hence $\mathbf{c}' \notin \text{Comp}(\mathbf{a},r)$.

   Now, suppose that there exists $\mathbf{b} = (\ldots, s^{\uparrow}, s)$ such that $\mathbf{b} \prec \mathbf{c}' \prec \mathbf{c}$, where $\mathbf{c} = f_{\mathbf{a},r}(\mathbf{b})$. We distinguish five cases depending on j (see Lemma 2).

   If $j = Bot(s)$ then $\mathbf{b} = GA(\mathbf{b},\mathbf{a})$, and $\mathbf{c}$ is obtained by shifting downwards the cell with position j in $\mathbf{b}$. Since $\mathbf{c}_{>j} = \mathbf{b}_{>j} = \mathbf{c}'_{>j}$, the two columns $\mathbf{c}'$ and $\mathbf{c}$ differ only in their last segments, say v' and v respectively, with $A(v') = A(v) = 1$. By recalling how the moves Shift, Split and Shift&Split are defined, it follows that the position of v can not be smaller than the position of v', hence $\mathbf{c}' \not\prec \mathbf{c}$ or $\mathbf{c}' \notin \text{Comp}(\mathbf{a},r)$. The same reasoning holds if $j = Top(s)$ and the whole segment s is shifted. Thus, consider the case $j = Bot(\overleftarrow{s}) + 1$ and $j > Bot(s)$ (occurring when $Bot(\overleftarrow{s}) = Bot(\mathbf{a})$ and $Bot(\mathbf{a}) > Bot(s)$). In this case $\mathbf{c}$ is obtained from $\mathbf{b}$ by shifting $s_{\leq j}$ one position downwards, that is by placing a segment v with $Top(v) = Bot(\mathbf{a})$. Hence, $\mathbf{c}' \prec \mathbf{c}$ implies that in $\mathbf{c}'$ there exists a segment v' that is not l-adjacent to a segment of $\mathbf{a}$ since $Top(v') < Bot(\mathbf{a})$.

   Now, consider the case $j = Bot(s^{\uparrow})$. Since $Top(s) = Bot(\mathbf{a})$ (otherwise a move would occur in s), the relation $\mathbf{b} \prec \mathbf{c}'$ implies that in $\mathbf{c}'$ the position j is empty. Let v' be the first segment of $\mathbf{c}'$ such that $Top(v') < j$. By Definition 6, the first segment v of $\mathbf{c}$ with $Top(v) < j$ has the highest position so that the column is compatible with $\mathbf{a}$. Furthermore, once the position is determined, v has also the largest possible area, hence $v < v'$ or $v' = v$. All the segments below v have the highest possible position and the largest area. So, if $v' = v$ then either $v_\downarrow < v'_\downarrow$ or $v'_\downarrow = v_\downarrow$, and so on. Finally, we get the contradiction $\mathbf{c} \prec \mathbf{c}'$ or $\mathbf{c} = \mathbf{c}'$.

Lastly, let $j = \mathrm{Top}(s^\uparrow)$. This means that $\mathrm{A}(s^\uparrow) = 1$ or $\mathrm{Bot}(s^\uparrow) = \mathrm{Top}(\overleftarrow{s^\uparrow})$. In both cases the relation $\mathbf{b} \prec \mathbf{c}'$ implies that the position j is empty in $\mathbf{c}'$. Indeed, either $\mathbf{c}'$ has an empty unitary square at j or it has a segment v' such that $v' = (\mathrm{A}(s^\uparrow), \mathrm{Top}(s^\uparrow))$ and $s < v'_\downarrow$. This implies that $v'_\downarrow$ is not l-adjacent to a segment of $\mathbf{a}$, hence $\mathbf{c}' \notin \mathrm{Comp}(\mathbf{a}, r)$. So, let v' (resp., v) be the first segment in $\mathbf{c}'$ (resp., in $\mathbf{c}$) having a position smaller than j. Note that v is obtained by shifting the segment t with $\mathrm{Top}(t) = j$ in $\mathrm{GA}(\mathbf{b}, \mathbf{a})$. By Definition 6, t is shifted downwards as few positions as possible in order to obtain a compatible column. Furthermore, the area of t is as large as possible. Hence $v < v'$ or $v = v'$. The same remarks about the position and the area hold for all segments below v, so we obtain the contradiction $\mathbf{c} \prec \mathbf{c}'$ or $\mathbf{c} = \mathbf{c}'$.   □

4   Exhaustive Generation

An algorithm for generating HFPDA(n) can be obtained from Lemma 3 by adopting an inductive approach. We suppose that at step i we have already generated a polyomino $P_{\leq i} \in$ HFPDA$(n - r)$. Thus, the aim is to add all compatible $(i+1)$-th columns of area at most r (one at a time, by exploiting Lemma 3). Then, for each of these columns we recursively add all compatible $(i + 2)$-th columns, and so on until we obtain a polyomino $P \in$ HFPDA(n).

The computation starts by calling HFPDAGEN(n) (see Algorithm 1), which sets the first column of the polyomino (a segment of area r, with $1 \leq r \leq n$) and then calls COLGEN to (recursively) add all subsequent columns, until the area reaches the value n. The procedure COLGEN(i, r) (see Algorithm 2) adds all i-th columns that are compatible with the column P_{i-1} of the polyomino $P_{\leq i-1} \in$ HFPDA$(n - r)$, which has been already generated. Notice that the order of generation derives from Definition 5, and that the area of the columns is at most r, the number of remaining cells. As a matter of fact, the Procedure COLGEN is an application of Lemma 3 and consists of a while-loop (lines 5–9) where at each iteration a move is executed (line 7). The polyomino is given in output if the area is n; otherwise a recursive call is made (line 8). The Procedure GRAN(P_i, P_{i-1}) restores the grand ancestor of the current column P_i (w.r.t. P_{i-1}) and returns $\min(\mathrm{Mc}(P_i))$. The procedure call MOVE(i, j) at line 7 executes a move at j in the grand ancestor (either a Shift or a Split or a Shift&Split).

4.1   Data Structure

A polyomino P is simply a sequence of columns, where a column $\mathbf{b}$ is represented by a doubly-linked list $L_\mathbf{b}$ associated with the sequence of segments in $\mathbf{b}$ (as many nodes as segments). So, a node of the list corresponds to a segment s and contains five entries $(\mathrm{A}(s), \mathrm{Top}(s), l_1, l_2, l_3)$ where:

- l_1 is the link to the preceding node in the list L_b (for $s^\uparrow$);
- l_2 is the link to the next node in the list L_b (for $s_\downarrow$);
- l_3 is a link to the node associated with $\overleftarrow{s}$ (in the previous list).

Algorithm 1. Generation of HFPDA(n).

1: PROCEDURE HFPDAGEN(n)
2: $P := ((n, n-1))$; OUTPUT(P);
3: **for** $r := n-1$ to 1 **do**
4:    $P_1 := ((r, r-1)))$; COLGEN($2, n-r$);
5: **end for**

Algorithm 2. Generation of columns.

1: PROCEDURE COLGEN(i, r)
2: **for** $d := r$ downto 1 **do**
3:    $P_i := ((d, \text{Top}(P_{i-1}) + d - 1))$; {the smallest column w.r.t. $\prec$}
4:    **if** $d < r$ **then** COLGEN($i+1, r-d$); **else** OUTPUT(P); **endif**
5:    **while not** ISFIXEDPOINT(P_i) **do**
6:       $j := $GRAN($P_i, P_{i-1}$); {restore the grand ancestor}
7:       MOVE(i, j); {P_i is changed according to a move in the position j}
8:       **if** $d < r$ **then** COLGEN($i+1, r-d$); **else** OUTPUT(P); **endif**
9:    **end while**
10: **end for**

Figure 5 shows the data structure representing the polyomino in Fig. 1(b). Lemma 2 states that the move in the position min(Mc(**b**)) regards either the last or the second to last segment of **b**. Thus, P is represented by an array of records, where the i-th record has two fields, the area of P_i and a link to the node associated with the last segment of P_i.

4.2   Complexity

Obviously, the data structure used to represent a polyomino of area n requires space $O(n)$. In order to determine the time complexity, notice that the execution of HFPDAGEN(n) is described by a tree with the following properties:

- the root corresponds to the procedure call HFPDAGEN(n);
- an internal node v at the level i, with $i > 0$, corresponds to the procedure call COLGEN($i+1, r$) for a suitable $r > 0$. Such a call adds all compatible $(i+1)$-th columns of area at most r (associated with the children of v) to a particular polyomino with i columns and area $n - r$, uniquely identified by the path from the root of the tree to v;
- there is a one-to-one mapping between the leaves and the polyominoes in HFPDA(n);
- each internal node has at least two children or the only child is a leaf.

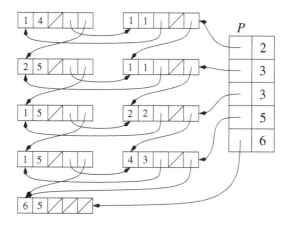

Fig. 5. The data structure for the polyomino of Fig. 1(b).

The complexity of COLGEN depends on the complexity of the procedures ISFIXEDPOINT, GRAN and MOVE. First, by using the data structure described in Sect. 4.1, one can easily develop a function ISFIXEDPOINT that runs in constant time. Indeed, a column P_i of area d is a fixed point if and only if $P_i = ((d, \text{Bot}(P_{i-1})))$.

The procedure $\text{GRAN}(P_i, P_{i-1})$ is used to restore the grand ancestor of the current column P_i with respect to P_{i-1}. By Lemma 2, the value $j = \min(\text{Mc}(P_i))$ indicates a cell in the last two segments of P_i, and it can be determined in time $O(1)$. Unfortunately, the construction of the grand ancestor does not always run in time $O(1)$ (as in the case $P_i = \text{GA}(P_i, P_{i-1})$). Indeed, it runs in time $O(\min(p, \text{A}(s)))$, where p is the number of segments of the column P_{i-1} and s is the last segment of P_i, see also Fig. 4. Nevertheless, an amortized analysis leads to the following result.

Lemma 4. *Let* **b**, **c** *be two columns in* $\text{Comp}(P_{i-1}, r)$ *such that* $\text{GRAN}(\mathbf{b}, P_{i-1})$ *and* $\text{GRAN}(\mathbf{c}, P_{i-1})$ *have cost* $\Theta(p_1)$ *and* $\Theta(p_2)$, *respectively. Then there exist two sets* $T_1, T_2 \subseteq \text{Comp}(P_{i-1}, r)$, *with* $|T_1| = \Omega(p_1)$, $|T_2| = \Omega(p_2)$ *and* $T_1 \cap T_2 = \emptyset$, *such that* $\text{GRAN}(\mathbf{d}, P_{i-1})$ *has cost* $O(1)$ *for any* $\mathbf{d} \in T_1 \cup T_2$.

Proof. (outline) Let t be the last segment of $\mathbf{a} = P_{i-1}$. Consider $\text{GA}(\mathbf{b}, \mathbf{a}) = (\ldots, s_e, v, \ldots)$ and the column $\mathbf{b}' = (\ldots, s_e, v', \ldots)$, where $\text{GA}(\mathbf{b}, \mathbf{a}) \xrightarrow{j} \mathbf{b}'$, $j = \min(\text{Mc}(\mathbf{b}))$ and $\text{Bot}(v) \leq j \leq \text{Top}(v)$. If the construction of $\text{GA}(\mathbf{b}, \mathbf{a})$ has cost $\Theta(p_1)$ then in $\mathbf{a}$ there exist $\Theta(p_1)$ segments with position smaller than $\text{Bot}(v)$, with $\text{A}(\mathbf{b}'_{<\text{Bot}(v)}) \geq p_1$. Define the set

$$T_1 = \{\mathbf{c} \in \text{Comp}(\mathbf{a}, r) | \mathbf{c} = (\ldots, s_e, v', \ldots, (1, \text{Bot}(t^\uparrow)), (k, \text{Bot}(t))), 1 \leq k < p_1\}.$$

It is immediate that $|T_1| = \Omega(p_1)$ and that for $\mathbf{d} \in T_1$ the call $\text{GRAN}(\mathbf{d}, \mathbf{a})$ has cost $O(1)$.

Now, consider $\mathbf{c}$ and let h be the integer such that $\mathbf{b}_{>h} = \mathbf{c}_{>h}$ and $\mathbf{b}_{\geq h} \neq \mathbf{c}_{\geq h}$. Furthermore, let $GA(\mathbf{c}, \mathbf{a}) = (\ldots, t_f, w, \ldots)$ and $\mathbf{c}' = (\ldots, t_f, w', \ldots)$, where $GA(\mathbf{c}, \mathbf{a}) \overset{k}{\to} \mathbf{c}'$, $k = \min(Mc(\mathbf{c}))$ and $Bot(w) \leq k \leq Top(w)$. Define the set

$$T_2 = \{\mathbf{c} \in Comp(\mathbf{a}, r) | \mathbf{c} = (\ldots, t_f, w', \ldots, (1, Bot(t^\uparrow)), (k, Bot(t))), 1 \leq k < p_2\}.$$

If $h > j$ then for $\mathbf{p} \in T_1$ and $\mathbf{q} \in T_2$ it holds $\mathbf{p}_{\geq h} \neq \mathbf{q}_{\geq h}$, hence $T_i \cap T_2 = \emptyset$.

Otherwise, one has $h \leq j$. Notice that $j \neq k$ implies $\mathbf{p}_{\geq h} \neq \mathbf{q}_{\geq h}$ and then $T_i \cap T_2 = \emptyset$. Lastly, the case $j = k$ can not occur. Indeed, suppose that $j = k$. Without loss of generality, let $\mathbf{b} \prec \mathbf{c}$ (this means that the position h identifies a segment in $\mathbf{b}$ and an empty cell in $\mathbf{c}$). By hypothesis, the construction of $GA(\mathbf{b}, \mathbf{a})$ (resp., $GA(\mathbf{c}, \mathbf{a})$) has cost $\Theta(p_1)$ (resp., $\Theta(p_2)$). This means that the position j (resp., k) is occupied by the second to last segment u (resp. z) of $\mathbf{b}$ (resp., $\mathbf{c}$). Furthermore, one necessarily has $h \geq Bot(u)$, otherwise $\mathbf{b}$ and $\mathbf{c}$ have not the same area. As $Bot(z) > h$, by Lemma 2 it follows that $j = Top(u)$, which means that $u_{>Bot(u)}$ is not l-adjacent. Finally, if $u_{>Bot(u)}$ is not l-adjacent then also z is not l-adjacent and $\mathbf{c}$ is not compatible with $\mathbf{a}$.   □

From Lemma 4 one easily obtains the following lemma and the main result.

Lemma 5. *Let $P_{\leq i} \in HFPDA$. Then $COLGEN(i+1, r)$ runs in time $O(t)$ where t is the number of all $(i+1)$-th columns $\mathbf{c}$ (of area at most r) that can be added to $P_{\leq i}$ so that $P_{\leq i}|\mathbf{c} \in HFPDA$.*

As a matter of fact, the running time of $HFPDAGEN(n)$ is just the sum of the running times of all the procedure calls $COLGEN(i, r)$ associated with the internal nodes of the execution tree of $HFPDAGEN(n)$. The properties of such a tree imply that the number of internal nodes is $O(C(n))$, where $C(n) = |HFPDA(n)|$. Thus, by Lemma 5 we obtain:

Theorem 1. *$HFPDAGEN(n)$ runs in constant amortized time.*

5   Conclusions and Further Work

This paper further deepens the approach to polyominoes generation based on discrete dynamical systems, which has been used in [9, 10] for the class of partially directed animals and of 2-polyominoes, respectively. Furthermore, by combining the dynamical system of Sect. 3 and the one used in [9], we can obtain a CAT algorithm for the class of partially directed animals with at most k holes, for any $k \geq 0$. An implementation of such an algorithm is ongoing and will appear in the full version of this paper, together with the counting sequences associated with these classes of polyominoes.

References

1. Barcucci, E., Del Lungo, A., Pergola, E., Pinzani, R.: Directed animals, forests and permutations. Discrete Math. **204**(1–3), 41–71 (1999)

2. Bousquet-Mélou, M.: A method for the enumeration of various classes of column-convex polygons. Discrete Math. **154**(1–3), 1–25 (1996)
3. Brocchi, S., Castiglione, G., Massazza, P.: On the exhaustive generation of k-convex polyominoes. Theor. Comput. Sci. **664**, 54–66 (2017)
4. Castiglione, G., Massazza, P.: An efficient algorithm for the generation of Z-convex polyominoes. In: Barneva, R.P., Brimkov, V.E., Šlapal, J. (eds.) IWCIA 2014. LNCS, vol. 8466, pp. 51–61. Springer, Cham (2014). https://doi.org/10.1007/978-3-319-07148-0_6
5. Castiglione, G., Restivo, A.: Reconstruction of L-convex polyominoes. Electron. Notes Discrete Math. **12**, 290–301 (2003)
6. Del Lungo, A., Duchi, E., Frosini, A., Rinaldi, S.: On the generation and enumeration of some classes of convex polyominoes. Electron. J. Comb. **11**(1), 60 (2004)
7. Delest, M.-P., Viennot, G.: Algebraic languages and polyominoes enumeration. Theor. Comput. Sci. **34**(1–2), 169–206 (1984)
8. Duchi, E., Rinaldi, S., Schaeffer, G.: The number of Z-convex polyominoes. Adv. Appl. Math. **40**(1), 54–72 (2008)
9. Formenti, E., Massazza, P.: From tetris to polyominoes generation. Electron. Notes Discrete Math. **59**, 79–98 (2017)
10. Formenti, E., Massazza, P.: On the generation of 2-polyominoes. In: Konstantinidis, S., Pighizzini, G. (eds.) DCFS 2018. LNCS, vol. 10952, pp. 101–113. Springer, Cham (2018). https://doi.org/10.1007/978-3-319-94631-3_9
11. Golomb, S.W.: Checker boards and polyominoes. Am. Math. Mon. **61**, 675–682 (1954)
12. Jensen, I.: Enumerations of lattice animals and trees. J. Stat. Phys. **102**(3), 865–881 (2001). https://doi.org/10.1023/A:1004855020556
13. Jensen, I., Guttmann, A.J.: Statistics of lattice animals (polyominoes) and polygons. J. Phys. A: Math. Gen. **33**(29), L257–L263 (2000)
14. Mantaci, R., Massazza, P.: From linear partitions to parallelogram polyominoes. In: Mauri, G., Leporati, A. (eds.) DLT 2011. LNCS, vol. 6795, pp. 350–361. Springer, Heidelberg (2011). https://doi.org/10.1007/978-3-642-22321-1_30
15. Massazza, P.: On the generation of L-convex polyominoes. In: Proceedings of GAS-Com12, Bordeaux, 25–27 June 2012
16. Massazza, P.: On the generation of convex polyominoes. Discrete Appl. Math. **183**, 78–89 (2015)
17. Privman, V., Barma, M.: Radii of gyration of fully and partially directed lattice animals. Z. Phys. B: Condens. Matter **57**(1), 59–63 (1984). https://doi.org/10.1007/BF01679926
18. Redner, S., Yang, Z.R.: Size and shape of directed lattice animals. J. Phys. A: Math. Gen. **15**(4), L177–L187 (1982)

First Lower Bounds for Palindromic Length

Anna E. Frid[(✉)]

Aix Marseille University, CNRS, Centrale Marseille, I2M, Marseille, France
anna.e.frid@gmail.com

Abstract. We study possible behaviour of the function of prefix palindromic length $PPL_u(n)$ of an infinite word u, that is, the minimal number of palindromes to which the prefix of length n of u can be decomposed. In a 2013 paper with Puzynina and Zamboni we stated the conjecture that $PPL_u(n)$ is unbounded for every infinite word u which is not ultimately periodic. Up to now, the conjecture has been proved only for some particular cases including all fixed points of morphisms and, later, Sturmian words.

To give an upper bound for the palindromic length, it is in general sufficient to point out a decomposition of a given word to a given number of palindromes. Proving that such a decomposition does not exist is a trickier question. In this paper, we summarize the existing techniques which can be used for lower bounds on the palindromic length. In particular, we completely describe the prefix palindromic length of the Thue-Morse word and use appropriate numeration systems to give a lower bound for the palindromic length of some Toeplitz words.

1 Introduction

As usual, a palindrome is a finite word $p = p[1] \cdots p[n]$ on a finite alphabet such that $p[i] = p[n - i + 1]$ for every i. We consider decompositions of a finite word s to a minimal number of palindromes which we call a *palindromic length* of s: for example, the palindromic length of $abbaba$ is equal to 3 since this word is not a concatenation of two palindromes, but $abbaba = (abba)(b)(a) = (a)(bb)(aba)$. A decomposition to a minimal possible number of palindromes is called *optimal*.

In this paper, we are interested in the palindromic length of prefixes of an infinite word $u = u[1] \cdots u[n] \cdots$. The palindromic length of the prefix of u of length n is denoted by $PPL_u(n)$ and is the main object studied in this paper.

The length of the shortest prefix of u of palindromic length k is denoted by $SP_u(k)$ and can be considered as a kind of an inverse function to $PPL_u(n)$. Clearly, $SP_u(k)$ can be infinite: for example, if $u = abababab \cdots$, $SP_u(k) = \infty$ for every $k \geq 3$.

The following conjecture was first formulated, in slightly different terms, in our 2013 paper [7] with Puzynina and Zamboni.

Conjecture 1.1. For every non ultimately periodic word u, the function $PPL_u(n)$ is unbounded, or, which is the same, $SP_u(k) < \infty$ for every $k \in \mathbb{N}$.

© Springer Nature Switzerland AG 2019
P. Hofman and M. Skrzypczak (Eds.): DLT 2019, LNCS 11647, pp. 234–243, 2019.
https://doi.org/10.1007/978-3-030-24886-4_17

Note that in fact, two versions of the conjecture were considered in [7], one with the prefix palindromic length and the other with the palindromic length of any factor of u. However, Saarela [10] later proved the equivalence of these two statements.

In [7], the conjecture was proved for the case when u is k-power-free for some k, as well as for the more general case when a so-called (k, l)-condition, discussed below in Sect. 5, holds for some k and l. For the other cases the conjecture remains unsolved, except for Sturmian words [5]. Most of published papers on palindromic length concern algorithmic aspects; in particular, there exist several fast effective algorithms for computing $PPL_u(n)$ [4,8,9].

Among rare combinatorial results on the palindromic length, I mention the paper [2] by Ambrož et al. where some upper bounds were obtained on the palindromic length of fixed points of morphisms from a so-called class $\mathcal{P}$ discussed below in Sect. 4. However, these are not upper but lower bounds which are more difficult to obtain and which may lead to proving Conjecture 1.1. So, in this paper we focus on them.

The original proof of Conjecture 1.1 for the k-power-free words is not constructive. The upper bound for a length N such that $PPL(N) \geq k$ for a given k is given as a solution of a transcendental equation and grows with k faster than any exponential function. However, this bound does not look the best possible. So, it is reasonable to state the following conjecture.

Conjecture 1.2. If a word u is P-power free for some P, then $\limsup \frac{PPL_u(n)}{\ln n} > 0$, or, which is the same, $SP_u(k) \leq C^k$ for some C. The constant C can be chosen independently of u as a function of P.

The first cases for which we prove this conjecture here are the Thue-Morse word and a special family of Toeplitz words. Even for k-power-free Sturmian words including the Fibonacci word, the conjecture remains open, as well as for the general fixed points of morphisms from the class $\mathcal{P}$. Proofs for these families of words, which we leave to further research, can contribute to the proof of Conjecture 1.2.

The notion of palindromic length (or palindromic width) is independently studied in groups not semigroups (see [3,10]).

Throughout the paper, we use the notation $w(i..j] = w[i+1]..w[j]$ for a factor of a finite or infinite word w starting at position $i + 1$ and ending at j.

2 General Properties

The following lemma is a particular case of Lemma 6 from [10].

Lemma 2.1. *For every word u and for every $n \geq 0$, we have*

$$PPL_u(n) - 1 \leq PPL_u(n + 1) \leq PPL_u(n) + 1.$$

In other terms, first differences of the prefix palindromic length can be equal only to -1, 0, or 1. It is not clear, however, if this condition is sufficient or not. We can only prove the following

Lemma 2.2. *For every non-decreasing function $f : \mathbb{N} \to \mathbb{N}$ such that $f(1) = 1$ and $f(n + 1) \leq f(n) + 1$, there exists a ternary word u with $PPL_u(n) = f(n)$ for all n.*

PROOF. It is sufficient to define $u[1] = a$ and $u[n + 1] = u[n] + f(n + 1) - f(n)$, where the addition is defined as $a + 1 = b$, $b + 1 = c$, $c + 1 = a$. So, for example, if $f(n) = 1, 1, 1, 2, 2, 3, 4, 5, 5, 5, \cdots$, we obtain $u = aaabbcabbb \cdots$. Clearly, all palindromes in u are powers of letters, which proves the lemma. □

3   Prefix Palindromic Length of the Thue-Morse Word

In this section, it is convenient to consider the famous Thue-Morse word

$$t = abbabaabbaababba \cdots$$

as the fixed point starting with a of the morphism

$$\tau : \begin{cases} a \to abba, \\ b \to baab. \end{cases}$$

It is convenient since both images of letters under this morphism, the square of the usual Thue-Morse morphism $a \to ab, b \to ba$, are palindromes.

Theorem 3.1. *The following identities hold for all $n \geq 0$:*

$$PPL_t(4n) = PPL_t(n), \tag{1}$$
$$PPL_t(4n + 1) = PPL_t(n) + 1, \tag{2}$$
$$PPL_t(4n + 2) = \min(PPL_t(n), PPL_t(n + 1)) + 2, \tag{3}$$
$$PPL_t(4n + 3) = PPL_t(n + 1) + 1. \tag{4}$$

Before proving the theorem, let us discuss what it means in terms of the first differences of the prefix palindromic length defined as the sequence $(d_t(n))_{n=0}^{\infty}$, where $d_t(n) = PPL_t(n + 1) - PPL_t(n)$; here we set $PPL_t(0) = 0$. Due to Lemma 2.1, $d_t(n) \in \{-1, 0, +1\}$ for every n; so, it is a sequence on a finite alphabet which we prefer to denote $\{-, 0, +\}$.

The following corollaries of Theorem 3.1 are more or less straightforward.

Corollary 3.2. *The sequence $(d_t(n))$ is the fixed point of the morphism*

$$\delta : \begin{cases} + & \mapsto & + + 0 -, \\ 0 & \mapsto & + + - -, \\ - & \mapsto & + 0 - -. \end{cases}$$

To prove this corollary, it is sufficient to see that there three possible differences $d_t(n) = PPL_t(n + 1) - PPL_t(n)$, described by the signs $+$, 0 or $-$. The equality (2) means that the first symbol of any morphic image of δ is $+$;

the equality (4) means that the last symbol of any morphic image of δ is $-$; the two symbols in the middle are clear from (3) and depend on $d_t(n)$.

In particular, this means that in all cases,

$$PPL_t(4n + 2) > PPL_t(4n + 4). \tag{5}$$

The next corollary is a direct consequence of basic properties of k-regular sequences in the sense of [1].

Corollary 3.3. *The sequence $PPL_t(n)$ is 4-regular.*

At last, the next corollary can be obtained from Theorem 3.1 by elementary computations.

Corollary 3.4. *We have $SP_t(1) = 1$, $SP_t(2) = 2$, $SP_t(3) = 6$ and for all $k > 0$,*

$$SP_t(k + 3) = 16SP_t(k) - 6.$$

To prove Theorem 3.1, we need several observations. First of all, the shortest non-empty palindrome factors in the Thue-Morse word are $a, b, aa, bb, aba, bab,$ $abba, baab$. All the longer palindromes are of even length and have aa or bb in the center: if $t(i..i + 2k]$ is a palindrome, then $t(i + k - 1, i + k + 1] = aa$ or bb.

Let us say that an occurrence of a palindrome $t(i..j]$ is of type (i', j') if i' is the residue of i and j' is the residue of j modulo 4. For example, the palindrome $t(5..7] = aa$ is of type $(1, 3)$, the palindrome $t(4, 8] = baab$ is of type $(0, 0)$, and the palindrome $t(7..9] = bb$ is of type $(3, 1)$.

Proposition 3.5. *Every occurrence of a palindromic factor of length not equal to one or three to the Thue-Morse word is of a type $(m, 4 - m)$ for some $m \in \{0, 1, 2, 3\}$.*

PROOF. Every such a palindrome in the Thue-Morse word is of even length which we denote by $2k$, and every its occurrence is of the form $t(i..i + 2k]$. Its center $t(i + k - 1, i + k + 1]$ is equal to aa or bb, and these two words always appear in t at positions of the same parity: $t(i + k - 1, i + k + 1] = xx = t(2l - 1, 2l + 1]$, where $x = a$ or $x = b$, for some $l \geq 1$. So, $i + k - 1 = 2l - 1$, meaning that $i = 2l - k$ and $i + 2k = 2l + k$. So, modulo 4, we have $i + (i + 2k) = 4l \equiv 0$, that is, $i \equiv -(i + 2k)$. □

Note that the palindromes of odd length in the Thue-Morse word are, first, a and b, which can be of type $(0, 1)$, $(1, 2)$, $(2, 3)$ or $(3, 0)$, and second, aba and bab, which can only be of type $(2, 1)$ or $(3, 2)$.

Proposition 3.6. *Let $t(i..i + k]$ for $i > 0$ be a palindrome of length $k > 0$ and of type $(m, 4 - m)$ for some $m \neq 0$. Then $t(i - 1..i + k + 1]$ is also a palindrome, as well as $t(i + 1..i + k - 1]$.*

PROOF. The type of the palindrome is not $(0, 0)$, meaning that its first and last letters $t[i + 1]$ and $t[i + k]$ are not the first the last letters of τ-images of letters. Since these first and last letters are equal and their positions in τ-images of letters are symmetric and determine their four-blocks $abba$ or $baab$, the letters

$t[i]$ and $t[i+k+1]$ are also equal, and thus $t(i-1..i+k+1]$ is a palindrome. As for $t(i+1..i+k-1]$, it is a palindrome since is obtained from the palindrome $t(i..i+k]$ by erasing the first and the last letters.   □

Let us say that a decomposition of $t(0..4n]$ to palindromes is a 0-*decomposition* if all palindromes in it are of type $(0,0)$. The minimal number of palindromes in a 0-decomposition is denoted by $PPL_t^0(4n)$.

Proposition 3.7. *For every* $n \geq 1$, *we have* $PPL_t(n) = PPL_t^0(4n) \geq PPL_t(4n)$.

PROOF. It is sufficient to note that τ is a bijection between all palindromic decompositions of $t(0..n]$ and 0-decompositions of $t(0..4n]$.   □

PROOF OF THEOREM 3.1. The proof is done by induction on n. Clearly, $PPL_t(0) = 0$, $PPL_t(1) = PPL_t(4) = 1$, and $PPL_t(2) = PPL_t(3) = 2$, the equalities (1)–(4) hold for $n = 0$, and moreover, (1) is true for $n = 1$. Now suppose that they all, and, as a corollary, (5), hold for all $n < N$, and (1) holds also for $n = N$. We fix an $N > 0$ and prove for it the following sequence of propositions.

Proposition 3.8. *An optimal decomposition to palindromes of the prefix* $t(0..4N+1]$ *cannot end by a palindrome of length 3.*

PROOF. Suppose the opposite: some optimal decomposition of $t(0..4N+1]$ ends by the palindrome $t(4N-2..4N+1]$. This palindrome is preceded by an optimal decomposition of $t(0..4N-2]$. So, $PPL_t(4N+1) = PPL_t(4N-2)+1$; but by (5) applied to $N-1$, which we can use by the induction hypothesis, $PPL_t(4N-2) > PPL_t(4N)$. So, $PPL_t(4N+1) > PPL_t(4N)+1$, contradicting to Lemma 2.1.   □

Proposition 3.9. *There exists an optimal decomposition to palindromes of the prefix* $t(0..4N+2]$ *which does not end by a palindrome of length 3.*

PROOF. The opposite would mean that all optimal decompositions of $t(0..4N+2]$ end by the palindrome $t(4N-1..4N+2]$ preceded by an optimal decomposition of $t(0..4N-1]$. So, $PPL_t(4N+2) = PPL_t(4N-1)+1$; by the induction hypothesis, $PPL_t(4N-1) = PPL_t(4N)+1$. So, $PPL_t(4N+2) = PPL_t(4N)+2$, and thus another optimal decomposition of $t(0..4N+2]$ can be obtained as an optimal decomposition of $t(0..4N]$ followed by two palindromes of length 1. A contradiction.   □

Proposition 3.10. *For every* $m \in \{1,2,3\}$ *and every* $n \geq 0$, *the equality holds*

$$PPL_t(4N+m) = \min(PPL_t(4N+m-1), PPL_t(4N+m+1)) + 1.$$

PROOF. Consider an optimal decomposition $t(0..4N+m] = p_1 \cdots p_k$, where $k = PPL_t(4N+m)$. Denote the ends of palindromes as $0 = e_0 < e_1 < \cdots < e_k = 4N+m$, so that $p_i = t(e_{i-1}, e_i]$ for each i. Since $m \neq 0$ and due to Proposition 3.5, there exist some palindromes of length 1 or 3 in this decomposition. Let p_j be the last of them.

Suppose first that $j = k$. Then due to the two previous propositions, p_k is of length 1 not 3, so that $t(0..4N + m - 1] = p_1 \cdots p_{k-1}$ is decomposable to $k - 1$ palindromes. Due to Lemma 2.1, we have $PPL_t(4N + m - 1) = k - 1$, and thus $PPL_t(4N + m) = PPL_t(4N + m - 1) + 1$. Again due to Lemma 2.1, we have $PPL_t(4N + m + 1) \geq PPL_t(4N + m) - 1 = PPL_t(4N + m - 1)$, and so the statement holds.

Now suppose that $j < k$, so that $e_{j-1} = e_j - 1$ and $e_j \equiv -e_{j+1} \equiv e_{j+2} \equiv \cdots \equiv (-1)^{k-j} e_k \mod 4$. Since p_j is the last palindrome in the optimal decomposition of $p_1 \cdots p_j$, it is of length 1 not 3 due to the two previous propositions applied to some smaller length. Here $e_k \equiv m \neq 0 \mod 4$, so, applying Proposition 3.6, we see that $p'_j = t(e_j - 1..e_{j+1} + 1]$ is a palindrome, as well as $p'_{j+1} = t(e_{j+1} + 1..e_{j+2} - 1]$ and so on up to $p'_{k-1} = t(e_{k-1} + (-1)^{k-j}..e_k - (-1)^{k-j}]$. Since $e_k = 4N + m$, we see that $p_1 \cdots p_{j-1} p'_j \cdots p'_{k-1}$ is a decomposition of $t(0..4N + m - (-1)^{k-j}]$ to $k - 1$ palindromes. So, as above, $PPL_t(4N + m) = PPL_t(4N + m - (-1)^{k-j}) + 1$, and since $PPL_t(4N + m + (-1)^{k-j}) \geq PPL_t(4N + m) - 1 = PPL_t(4N + m - (-1)^{k-j})$, the proposition holds. $\qquad\square$

Proposition 3.11. *Every optimal palindromic decomposition of $t(0..4N + 4]$ is a 0-decomposition, and thus $PPL_t(4N + 4) = PPL_t(N + 1)$.*

PROOF. Suppose the opposite; then the last palindrome in the optimal decomposition which is not of type $(0,0)$ is of type $(m, 0)$ and thus is of length 1 not 3. Since (1) holds for all $n < N + 1$, this is the very last palindrome of the optimal decomposition, and so $PPL_t(4N + 4) = PPL_t(4N + 3) + 1$. Now let us use Proposition 3.10 applied to $m = 3, 2, 1$; every time we get $PPL_t(4N + m) = PPL_t(4N + m - 1) + 1$. Summing up these inequalities, we get $PPL_t(4N + 4) = PPL_t(4N) + 4$, which is impossible since $PPL_t(4N) = PPL_t(N)$ and $PPL_t(4N + 4) \leq PPL_t(N + 1) \leq PPL_t(N) + 1$. A contradiction. $\qquad\square$

We have proved (1) for $n = N + 1$. It remains to prove (2)–(4) for $n = N$. Indeed, we know that

$$-1 \leq PPL_t(4N + 4) - PPL_t(4N) = PPL_t(N + 1) - PPL_t(N) \leq 1. \quad (6)$$

Now to prove (2) suppose by contrary that $PPL_t(4N + 1) \leq PPL_t(4N) = PPL_t(N)$. Due to Proposition 3.10, this means that $PPL_t(4N + 1) = PPL_t(4N + 2) + 1$, that is, $PPL_t(4N + 2) < PPL_t(4N)$, and, again by Proposition 3.10, $PPL_t(N + 1) = PPL_t(4N + 2) - 2$. Thus, $PPL_t(N) - PPL_t(N + 1) \geq 3$, a contradiction to (6). So, (2) is proved.

The equality (4) is proved symmetrically. Now (3) follows from them both and Proposition 3.10. $\qquad\square$

4   A Lower Bound for Toeplitz Morphisms

Usually, any result proved for the Thue-Morse word can immediately be generalized to fixed points of at least some other morphisms. For this problem, it would be natural to work with the morphism from the class $\mathcal{P}$. Following [2], we say that a morphism ψ belongs to the class $\mathcal{P}$ if it is primitive (meaning that every letter a appears in some power $\psi^k(b)$ for any letter b) and there exist palindromes p and q_a for each letter $a \in \Sigma$, such that for every $a \in \Sigma$

$$\psi(a) = pq_a.$$

So, the Thue-Morse morphism τ of length 4 belongs to the class $\mathcal{P}$ with the empty p and $q_a = abba$, $q_b = baab$.

In [2], it was proved that $\limsup \frac{PPL_u(n)}{\ln n}$, and, moreover, the palindromic length of *every* factor of u, is bounded (from above) for every fixed point of a morphism of the class $\mathcal{P}$. In this paper it would be nice to add to that result a lower bound or even a precise description of the function $PPL_u(n)$ if u is such a fixed point. However, even for the period doubling word, which is the fixed point of the morphism $a \to ab, b \to aa$, the problem looks not so easy. At the moment, except for the Thue-Morse word, we are able to prove a lower bound for $\sup \frac{PPL_t(n)}{\ln n}$ only for the following family.

Denote by φ_d, $d \geq 2$, the morphism

$$\varphi_d : \begin{cases} a \to a^{d-1}b, \\ b \to a^d. \end{cases}$$

Clearly, the period-doubling morphism $a \to ab, b \to aa$ is φ_2; the main result of this section, Theorem 4.5, holds however only for $d \geq 3$.

In several following propositions, we write numbers in d-ary notation, separating digits by the sign $|$ to avoid ambiguity with multiplication or with decimal notation: $n = x_l| \cdots |x_0$ means $n = \sum_{i=0}^{l} x_i d^i$, where $0 \leq x_i \leq d-1$. We also denote $\overline{x} = d - 1 - x$; here normally x and $\overline{x}$ are digits between 0 and $d-1$.

Proposition 4.1. *For every $d \geq 2$, a factor $v_d(i..j]$ is a palindrome if and only if at least one of the following properties holds:*

1. $i = x_l| \cdots |x_m| \cdots |x_0$ *and* $j = x_l| \cdots |x_{m+1}|y_m|\overline{x_{m-1}}| \cdots |\overline{x_0}$ *for some digits* $x_0, \cdots, x_l, y_m \in \{0, \ldots, d-1\}$, $y_m > x_m$;
2. $i = s.d^{m+2} + (d-1)|x_m| \cdots |x_0$ *and* $j = (s+1)d^{m+2} + 0|y_m|\overline{x_{m-1}}| \cdots |\overline{x_0}$. *Here again* $x_0, \cdots, x_m, y_m$ *are digits from* $\{0, \ldots, d-1\}$ *and s is a positive integer; note that the d-ary representation of i (j) is just a concatenation of the d-ary representation of s ($s+1$) and the described last $m+2$ digits.*

The respective palindromes will be called below palindromes of the first or the second type.

Example 4.2. Consider $d = 4$ and the word $v_4 = aaabaaabaaabaaaaaaab$ $aaab\cdots$. For the palindrome $v_4(18..21] = aba$ we have $18 = 1|0|2$ and $21 = 1|1|1$, so, this is a palindrome of the first type with $l = 2$ and $m = 1$; here $1 = \overline{2}$. For the palindrome $v_4(12, 17] = aaaaa$, we have $12 = (0)|3|0$ and $17 = 1|0|1$, so, it is a palindrome of the second type with $s = 0$ and $m = 0$. For the palindrome $v_4(12, 19] = aaaaaaa$, we have $12 = (0)|3|0$ and $19 = 1|0|3$, so, it is a palindrome of both types.

Proposition 4.3. *Denote by $L_d(i)$ the number of digits not equal to 0 or $d-1$ in the d-representation of an integer i. Then for every $d \geq 3$ and for every palindrome $v_d(i..j]$, we have $L_d(j) \leq L_d(i) + 2$.*

PROOF. The operation $x \to \bar{x}$ preserves the function L_d, so, if the palindrome is of the first type, the only digit which may add 1 to L_d is that at position m. If the palindrome is of the second type, however, in addition to the position m, a new symbol not equal to 0 or $d-1$ may appear in the d-decomposition of the number s which turns into $s+1$ (as in the palindrome $v_4(12, 17]$ in the previous example). □

Proposition 4.4. *For every $d \geq 3$, consider the length $n_k = 1^{2k-1}$ in the d-ary numeration system. Then $PPL_{v_d}(n_k) \geq k$.*

PROOF. The statement follows directly from the previous proposition and the fact that the prefix palindrome $v_d(0..i]$ of any decomposition cannot be of the second type. □

The following theorem is a direct corollary of Proposition 4.4.

Theorem 4.5. *For every $d \geq 3$,*

$$\limsup \frac{PPL_{v_d}(n)}{\ln n} \geq \frac{1}{2\ln d}.$$

The lower bound from Theorem 4.5 looks not at all optimal. In particular, the calculations show that we have $PPL_{v_3}(1^k) = k$. So, we may state a conjecture that $\limsup \frac{PPL_{v_d}(n)}{\ln n} = \frac{1}{\ln d}$, but its proof will not be so easy.

5   Words with Longer Powers

The proof of Theorem 4.5 can be immediately extended to a wider class of words. Namely, consider a sequence $\mathbf{d} = (d_n)$ of integers, $d_n \geq 2$, and the word

$$v_{\mathbf{d}} = \varphi_{d_1} \circ \varphi_{d_2} \circ \cdots \circ \varphi_{d_n} \circ \cdots (a).$$

Clearly, it is well-defined, and if $d_i = d$ for all i, we have $v_{\mathbf{d}} = v_d$. If by contrary the sequence $\mathbf{d}$ is unbounded, we obtain one of the easiest possible examples of an infinite word which does not satisfy any (k, l)-condition formulated in [7]. This means exactly the following: for every l and every k there exists a position in the word covered by at least l different k-powers (here different powers mean powers of primitive words of different lengths).

Clearly, if $\mathbf{d}$ is unbounded, then the very first position in $v_{\mathbf{d}}$ is covered by an infinite number of k-powers for every k. Another example of words not satisfying any (k, l)-condition are Sturmian words with the unbounded directive sequence considered in [5], but the words $f_{\mathbf{d}}$ form an even simpler family.

For each such word, we can construct a respective numeration system, in which a number N is represented as

$$N = \sum_{i=0}^{n}(d_1 \cdots d_i)x_i = x_0 + x_1d_1 + x_2d_1d_2 + \cdots + x_n\prod_{i=1}^{n}d_i,$$

where $0 \le x_i < d_{i+1}$. In this case, the choice of x_i is unique up to leading zeros, and the word N can be written as $N = x_n|\ldots|x_0$. If $d_i = d$ for all i, it is just a usual d-ary numeration system.

Propositions 4.1 and 4.3 can be directly extended to such numeration systems, with only one change of notation: the digit x_i changes between 0 and $d_{i+1} - 1$, and $\overline{x_i}$ is defined as $d_{i+1} - 1 - x_i$. So, instead of Proposition 4.4, we can state the following.

Theorem 5.1. *Consider a word $v_\mathbf{d}$ corresponding to a sequence $\mathbf{d}$ with $d_{n_i} > 2$ for an infinite sequence of digits (n_i). Consider a number $N_k = x_{n_{2k-1}}|\cdots|x_0$ such that $x_{n_i} = 1$ for $i = 1, \ldots, 2k - 1$ and $x_j = 0$ for $j \ne n_i$. Then $PPL_{v_\mathbf{d}}(N_k) \ge k$.*

6   Conclusion

At the moment, up to my knowledge, the only existing lower bounds for the lim sup of the prefix palindromic length are the following:

- A general bound for k-power-free words from [7], obtained as a solution of a transcendental equation and growing slower than any logarithmic function.
- A bound for Sturmian words which are not k-power-free, described in [5] in terms of the Ostrowski numeration systems.
- The bounds obtained here for the Thue-Morse word (together with the explicit function $PPL_t(n)$) and Toeplitz words $v_\mathbf{d}$, under the conditions described in Theorems 4.5 and 5.1.

At the same time, even for famous and simple examples like the period doubling word or the Fibonacci word, the only existing lower bounds are those from [7], even though in [6], some calculations allowed to state a reasonable exponential conjecture on the $SP(k)$ of the Fibonacci word. So, the following range of the open questions can be added to Conjectures 1.1 and 1.2.

Problem 6.1. Find a precise formula for the prefix palindromic length of the period-doubling word, or a lower bound for its lim sup.

Problem 6.2. Find a precise formula for the prefix palindromic length of the Fibonacci word, or a lower bound for its lim sup.

Problem 6.3. Is it true that the function $PPL_u(n)$ is d-regular for any d-automatic word u? Fibonacci-regular for the Fibonacci word?

Problem 6.4. Describe all functions $\mathbb{N} \to \mathbb{N}$ which can be prefix palindromic length functions of an infinite word.

As for Conjecture 1.1, it seems that the remaining case when no (k, l)-condition holds can be treated with the help of specially constructed numeration systems, like in [5] or here in Theorem 5.1. The proof of this kind will inevitably be very technical.

References

1. Allouche, J.-P., Shallit, J.: Automatic Sequences: Theory, Applications, Generalizations. Cambridge University Press, Cambridge (2003)
2. Ambrož, P., Kadlec, O., Masáková, Z., Pelantová, E.: Palindromic length of words and morphisms in class $\mathcal{P}$. Preprint. https://arxiv.org/abs/1812.00711
3. Bardakov, V., Shpilrain, V., Tolstykh, V.: On the palindromic and primitive widths of a free group. J. Algebra **285**, 574–585 (2005)
4. Fici, G., Gagie, T., Kärkkäinen, J., Kempa, D.: A subquadratic algorithm for minimum palindromic factorization. J. Discr. Alg. **28**, 41–48 (2014)
5. Frid, A.E.: Sturmian numeration systems and decompositions to palindromes. Eur. J. Combin. **71**, 202–212 (2018)
6. Frid, A.: Representations of palindromes in the Fibonacci word. In: Proceedings of Numeration, pp. 9–12 (2018)
7. Frid, A., Puzynina, S., Zamboni, L.: On palindromic factorization of words. Adv. Appl. Math. **50**, 737–748 (2013)
8. Borozdin, K., Kosolobov, D., Rubinchik, M., Shur, A.M.: Palindromic length in linear time. In: CPM 2017, pp. 23:1–23:12 (2017)
9. Rubinchik, M., Shur, A.M.: EERTREE: an efficient data structure for processing palindromes in strings. Eur. J. Combin. **68**, 249–265 (2018)
10. Saarela, A.: Palindromic length in free monoids and free groups. In: Brlek, S., Dolce, F., Reutenauer, C., Vandomme, É. (eds.) WORDS 2017. LNCS, vol. 10432, pp. 203–213. Springer, Cham (2017). https://doi.org/10.1007/978-3-319-66396-8_19

On Palindromic Length of Sturmian Sequences

Petr Ambrož$^{(\boxtimes)}$ and Edita Pelantová

FNSPE, Czech Technical University in Prague, Trojanova 13,
120 00 Praha 2, Czech Republic
{petr.ambroz,edita.pelantova}@fjfi.cvut.cz

Abstract. Frid, Puzynina and Zamboni (2013) defined the palindromic length of a finite word w as the minimal number of palindromes whose concatenation is equal to w. For an infinite word u we study pal_u, that is, the function that assigns to each positive integer n, the maximal palindromic length of factors of length n in u. Recently, Frid (2018) proved that $\limsup_{n \to \infty} \mathrm{pal}_u(n) = +\infty$ for any Sturmian word u. We show that there is a constant $K > 0$ such that $\mathrm{pal}_u(n) \leq K \ln n$ for every Sturmian word u, and that for each non-decreasing function f with property $\lim_{n \to \infty} f(n) = +\infty$ there is a Sturmian word u such that $\mathrm{pal}_u(n) = \mathcal{O}(f(n))$.

Keywords: Palindromes · Palindromic length · Sturmian words

1 Introduction

Palindromic length of a word v, denoted by $|v|_{\mathrm{pal}}$, is the minimal number K of palindromes $p_1, p_2, \dots, p_K$ such that $v = p_1 p_2 \cdots p_K$. This notion has been introduced by Frid, Puzynina and Zamboni [3] along with the following conjecture.

Conjecture 1. If there is a positive integer P such that $|v|_{\mathrm{pal}} \leq P$ for every factor v of an infinite word w then w is eventually periodic.

Frid et al. proved validity of the conjecture for r-power-free infinite words, i.e., for words which do not contain factors of the form $v^r = vv \cdots v$ (r times for some integer $r \geq 2$). By result of Mignosi [6] the conjecture thus holds for any Sturmian word whose slope has bounded coefficients in its continued fraction. Recently, Frid [2] proved the conjecture for all Sturmian words.

In this paper we study asymptotic growth of function $\mathrm{pal}_u : \mathbb{N} \to \mathbb{N}$ defined for an infinite word u by

$$\mathrm{pal}_u(n) = \max\{|v|_{\mathrm{pal}} : v \text{ is factor of length } n \text{ in } u\}.$$

The aforementioned result by Frid can be stated, using function pal_u, in the form of the following theorem.

© Springer Nature Switzerland AG 2019
P. Hofman and M. Skrzypczak (Eds.): DLT 2019, LNCS 11647, pp. 244–250, 2019.
https://doi.org/10.1007/978-3-030-24886-4_18

Theorem 1 ([2]). *Let u be a Sturmian word. Then $\limsup_{n\to\infty} \mathrm{pal}_u(n) = +\infty$.*

We prove the following two theorems about the rate of growth of function pal_u for Sturmian words.

Theorem 2. *Let $f : \mathbb{N} \to \mathbb{R}$ be a non-decreasing function with $\lim_{n\to\infty} f(n) = +\infty$. Then there is a Sturmian word u such that $\mathrm{pal}_u(n) = o(f(n))$.*

Theorem 3. *There is a constant K such that for every Sturmian word u we have $\mathrm{pal}_u(n) \leq K \ln n$.*

In other words, pal_u may grow into infinity arbitrarily slow (Theorem 2) and not faster than $\mathcal{O}(\ln n)$ (Theorem 3). Let us stress that the constant K in Theorem 3 is universal for every Sturmian word.

Both theorems refer to upper estimates on the growth of pal_u. Indeed, it is much more difficult to obtain a lower bound on the growth, such bound is not known even for the Fibonacci word. Recently, Frid [1] considered a certain sequence of prefixes of the Fibonacci word, denoted $(w^{(n)})$, and she formulated a conjecture about the precise value of $|w^{(n)}|_{\mathrm{pal}}$. This conjecture can be rephrased in the following way (cf. Remark 1).

Conjecture 2. Let f be the Fibonacci word, that is, the fixed point of the morphism $0 \mapsto 01$, $1 \mapsto 0$. Then

$$\limsup_{n\to\infty} \frac{\mathrm{pal}_f(n)}{\ln n} \geq \frac{1}{3 \ln \tau},$$

where τ is the golden ratio.

We propose (see Remark 1 for more details) the following extension of this so far unproved statement.

Conjecture 3. Let u be a Sturmian word whose slope has bounded coefficients in its continued fraction. Then

$$\limsup_{n\to\infty} \frac{\mathrm{pal}_u(n)}{\ln n} > 0.$$

2   Preliminaries

An *alphabet* A is a finite set of *letters*. A finite sequence of letters of A is called a (finite) *word*. The *length* of a word $w = w_1 w_2 \cdots w_n$, that is, the number of its letters, is denoted $|w| = n$. The notation $|w|_a$ is used for the number of occurrences of the letter a in w. The *empty word* is the unique word of length 0, denoted by ε. The set of all finite words over A (including the empty word) is denoted by A^*, equipped with the operation of concatenation of words A^* is a free monoid with ε as its neutral element. We consider also *infinite words* $u = u_0 u_1 u_2 \cdots$, the set of infinite words over A is denoted by $A^{\mathbb{N}}$.

A word w is called a *factor* of $v \in A^*$ if there exist words $w^{(1)}, w^{(2)} \in A^*$ such that $v = w^{(1)} w w^{(2)}$. The word w is called a *prefix* of v if $w^{(1)} = \varepsilon$, it is called a *suffix* of v if $w^{(2)} = \varepsilon$. The notions of factor and prefix can be easily extended to infinite words. The set of all factors of an infinite word $\boldsymbol{u}$, called the *language* of $\boldsymbol{u}$, is denoted by $\mathcal{L}(\boldsymbol{u})$. Let w be a prefix of v, that is, $v = wu$ for some word u. Then we write $w^{-1}v = u$.

The *slope* of a nonempty word $w \in \{0,1\}^*$ is the number $\pi(w) = \frac{|w|_1}{|w|}$. Let $\boldsymbol{u} = (u_n)_{n \geq 0}$ be an infinite word. Then the limit

$$\rho = \lim_{n \to \infty} \pi(u_0 \cdots u_{n-1}) = \frac{|u_0 \cdots u_{n-1}|_1}{n} \tag{1}$$

is the *slope* of the infinite word. Obviously, the slope of $\boldsymbol{u}$ is equal to the frequency of the letter 1 in $\boldsymbol{u}$.

In this paper we are concerned with the so-called *Sturmian words* [8]. These are infinite words over a binary alphabet that have exactly $n+1$ factors of length n for each $n \geq 0$. Sturmian words admit several equivalent definitions and have many interesting properties. We will need the following two fact above all. The limit in (1) exists, and thus the slope of a Sturmian word is well defined, and, moreover, it is an irrational number [4]. Two Sturmian words have the same language if and only if they have the same slope [5].

A *morphism* of the free monoid A^* is a map $\varphi : A^* \to A^*$ such that $\varphi(vw) = \varphi(v)\varphi(w)$ for all $v, w \in A^*$. A morphism φ is called *Sturmian* if $\varphi(\boldsymbol{u})$ is a Sturmian word for every Sturmian word $\boldsymbol{u}$. The set of all Sturmian morphisms coincides with the so-called *Monoid of Sturm* [7], it is the monoid generated by the following three morphisms

$$E : \begin{matrix} 0 \mapsto 1 \\ 1 \mapsto 0 \end{matrix}, \qquad G : \begin{matrix} 0 \mapsto 0 \\ 1 \mapsto 01 \end{matrix}, \qquad \tilde{G} : \begin{matrix} 0 \mapsto 0 \\ 1 \mapsto 10 \end{matrix}.$$

3   Images of Sturmian Words

In this section we study length and palindromic length of images of words under morphisms $\psi_b : \{0,1\}^* \to \{0,1\}^*$, where $b \in \mathbb{N}$, $b \geq 1$ and

$$\begin{aligned} \psi_b(0) &= 10^{b-1}, \\ \psi_b(1) &= 10^b. \end{aligned} \tag{2}$$

Note that ψ_b is a Sturmian morphism since $\psi_b = \tilde{G}^{b-1} \circ E \circ G$.

Lemma 1. *Let $b, c \in \mathbb{N}$, $b, c \geq 1$ and let $v \in \{0,1\}^*$. Then*

(i) $|\psi_b(v)| \geq b|v|$,
(ii) $|(\psi_c \circ \psi_b)(v)| \geq 2|v|$.

Proof. (i) Let $x = |v|_0$ and $y = |v|_1$. Then $\psi_b(v)$ contains $x' := (b-1)x + by$ zeros and $y' := x + y$ ones. Thus $|\psi_b(v)| = x' + y' = bx + (b+1)y \geq b(x+y) = b|v|$.

(ii) The word $(\psi_c \circ \psi_b)(v)$ contains $x'' := (c-1)x' + cy'$ zeros and $y'' := x' + y'$ ones. Thus $|(\psi_c \circ \psi_b)(v)| = x'' + y'' = cx' + (c+1)y' \geq x' + 2y' \geq 2y' = 2(x+y) = 2|v|$. $\qquad\square$

Lemma 2. *Let $b \in \mathbb{N}$, $b \geq 1$ and let $v \in \{0,1\}^*$. Then $|\psi_b(v)|_{pal} \leq |v|_{pal} + 1$.*

Proof. One can easily check that if p is a palindrome then both $\psi_b(p)1$ and $1^{-1}\psi_b(p)$ are palindromes.

If $v = p_1 p_2 \cdots p_{2q}$, where all p_i are palindromes, then

$$\psi_b(v) = \underbrace{\psi_b(p_1)1}_{p_1'} \cdot \underbrace{1^{-1}\psi_b(p_2)}_{p_2'} \cdot \underbrace{\psi_b(p_3)1}_{p_3'} \cdot \underbrace{1^{-1}\psi_b(p_4)}_{p_4'} \cdots \underbrace{\psi_b(p_{2q-1})1}_{p_{2q-1}'} \cdot \underbrace{1^{-1}\psi_b(p_{2q})}_{p_{2q}'}$$

is a factorization of $\psi_b(v)$ into $2q$ palindromes and therefore we have $|\psi_b(v)|_{pal} \leq |v|_{pal}$.

On the other hand, if $|v|_{pal}$ is odd the factorization of $\psi_b(v)$ is almost the same with the only exception that at the end there is (possibly non-palindromic) image of the last palindrome, i.e., $\psi_b(p_{2q+1})$. The statement follows from the fact that $\psi_b(p_{2q+1}) = 1 \cdot 1^{-1}\psi_b(v_{2q+1})$. $\qquad\square$

Lemma 3. *Let u be a Sturmian word with slope $\alpha \in (0,1)$ and let the continued fraction of α be $\alpha = [0, a_1, a_2, a_3, \ldots]$. Then $\psi_b(u)$ is a Sturmian word with slope β, where $\beta = [0, b, a_1, a_2, a_3, \ldots]$.*

Proof. Recall that α is the frequency of the letter 1 in u, that is,

$$\alpha = \lim_{|v| \to \infty} \frac{|v|_1}{|v|_0 + |v|_1}, \quad \text{where } v \in \mathcal{L}(u).$$

Let us consider the image of $v \in \mathcal{L}(u)$ under ψ_b. We have $|\psi_b(v)|_0 = (b-1)|v|_0 + b|v|_1$ and $|\psi_b(v)|_1 = |v|_0 + |v|_1$. Therefore

$$\beta = \lim_{|v| \to \infty} \frac{|\psi_b(v)|_1}{|\psi_b(v)|_0 + |\psi_b(v)|_1} = \lim_{|v| \to \infty} \frac{|v|_0 + |v|_1}{b|v|_0 + (b+1)|v|_1}$$

$$= \lim_{|v| \to \infty} \frac{1}{b + \frac{|v|_1}{|v|_0 + |v|_1}} = \frac{1}{b + \alpha}.$$

$\qquad\square$

Lemma 4. *Let $v \in \{0,1\}^*$ be a factor of a Sturmian word u with slope $\beta = [0, b, a_1, a_2, a_3, \ldots]$ and let $|v|_1 \geq 2$. Then there are words v', v_L, v_R such that $v' \neq \varepsilon$ is a factor of a Sturmian word with slope $\alpha = [0, a_1, a_2, a_3, \ldots]$, v_L is a proper suffix of $\psi_k(x)$ and v_R is a proper prefix of $\psi_k(y)$ for some $x, y \in \{0,1\}$, and*

(i) $v = v_L \psi_b(v') v_R$,
(ii) $|v|_{pal} \leq 4 + |v'|_{pal}$.

Proof. (i) Let $\boldsymbol{u}$ be a Sturmian word with slope $\alpha = [0, a_1, a_2, a_3, \ldots]$. By Lemma 3, $\psi_k(\boldsymbol{u})$ has slope $\beta = [0, b, a_1, a_2, a_3, \ldots]$. Recall that the language of a Sturmian word is entirely determined by its slope, thus we have $v \in \mathcal{L}(\psi_b(\boldsymbol{u}))$. Since by assumption v contains at least two ones, we can unambiguously write it in the required form.

(ii) This statement then follows from inequalities $|v|_{\mathrm{pal}} \leq |v_L|_{\mathrm{pal}} + |\psi_b(v')|_{\mathrm{pal}} + |v_R|_{\mathrm{pal}}$, $|v_L|_{\mathrm{pal}} \leq 1$, $|v_R|_{\mathrm{pal}} \leq 2$ and from Lemma 2.   □

4   Proofs of Main Theorems

Both proofs make use of the following idea. Let $\boldsymbol{u}$ be a Sturmian word with slope $\alpha = [0, a_1, a_2, a_3, \ldots]$. Let $v = v^{(1)} \in \mathcal{L}(\boldsymbol{u})$. By successive application of Lemma 4 we find words $v^{(2)}, v^{(3)}, \ldots, v^{(j+1)}$ such that for every $i = 1, 2, \ldots, j$ we have

(i) $v^{(i)}$ is a factor of a Sturmian word with slope $[0, a_i, a_{i+1}, a_{i+2}, \ldots]$,
(ii) $|v^{(i)}| \geq |\psi_{a_i}(v^{(i+1)})| \geq a_i |v^{(i+1)}|$ (this follows from Lemmas 1 and 4),
(iii) $|v^{(i)}|_{\mathrm{pal}} \leq 4 + |v^{(i+1)}|_{\mathrm{pal}}$,
(iv) $v^{(j+1)}$ does not contain two ones, in particular $|v^{(j+1)}|_{\mathrm{pal}} \leq 2$ and $|v^{(j+1)}| \geq 1$.

Altogether we have

$$|v| = |v^{(1)}| \geq a_1 a_2 \cdots a_j,$$
$$|v|_{\mathrm{pal}} \leq 4j + 2. \tag{3}$$

Proof (of Theorem 2). Let $f : \mathbb{N} \to \mathbb{R}$ be a non-decreasing function with $\lim_{n \to \infty} f(n) = +\infty$. We find $a_1 \in \mathbb{N}$, $a_1 \geq 2$ such that $f(a_1) \geq 1$, then $a_2 \in \mathbb{N}$, $a_2 \geq 2$ such that $f(a_1 a_2) \geq 2^2$, and so on, i.e., we proceed recurrently to find $a_k \in \mathbb{N}$, $a_k \geq 2$ such that

$$f(a_1 a_2 \cdots a_k) \geq k^2 \quad \text{for all } k \in \mathbb{N}, k \geq 1. \tag{4}$$

Using (3), (4) and monotony of f we can estimate

$$\frac{|v|_{\mathrm{pal}}}{f(|v|)} \leq \frac{4j + 2}{f(a_1 a_2 \cdots a_j)} \leq \frac{4j + 2}{j^2}.$$

Obviously $j \to \infty$ as $|v| = n \to \infty$ and therefore

$$\limsup_{n \to \infty} \frac{\mathrm{pal}_{\boldsymbol{u}}(n)}{f(n)} \leq \lim_{j \to \infty} \frac{4j + 2}{j^2} = 0.$$

□

Proof (of Theorem 3). The estimate $|v| \geq a_1 a_2 \cdots a_j$ is weak in the case where most of the coefficients of the continued fraction are equal to 1. Therefore, we use the fact that $v^{(i)}$ contains factor $(\psi_{a_i} \circ \psi_{a_{i+1}})(v^{(i+2)})$. By Lemma 1 we have $|v^{(i)}| \geq 2|v^{(i+2)}|$ and thus $|v| \geq 2^{\lfloor \frac{j}{2} \rfloor}$. Using this estimate we get

$$\frac{|v|_{\text{pal}}}{\ln |v|} \leq \frac{4j + 2}{\frac{j-1}{2} \ln 2} \xrightarrow{j \to \infty} \frac{8}{\ln 2}.$$

Statement of the theorem follows, using $K = \frac{8}{\ln 2}$.   □

Remark 1. In [1], Frid defined the sequence $(w^{(n)})$ of prefixes of the Fibonacci word $\boldsymbol{f}$, where $|w^{(n)}|$ has representation $(100)^{2n-1}101$ in the Ostrowski numeration system.

Using the Fibonacci sequence $(F_n)_{n \geq 0}$ (given by $F_0 = 1$, $F_2 = 2$ and $F_{n+2} = F_{n+1} + F_n$ for $n \in \mathbb{N}$) one gets $|w^{(n)}| = F_0 + F_2 + \sum_{k=1}^{2n-1} F_{3k+2} < F_{6n}$. Frid proved that $|w^{(n)}|_{\text{pal}} \leq 2n+1$, while she conjectured that the equality $|w^{(n)}|_{\text{pal}} = 2n+1$ holds. Since $F_n = \frac{1}{\sqrt{5}} \tau^{n+2}(1 + o(1))$, the validity of Frid's conjecture would imply

$$\frac{|w^{(n)}|_{\text{pal}}}{\ln |w^{(n)}|} \geq \frac{2n+1}{\ln F_{6n}} = \frac{2n+1}{(6n+2) \ln \tau (1 + o(1))} \xrightarrow{n \to \infty} \frac{1}{3 \ln \tau} \tag{5}$$

as stated in Conjecture 2.

In her proof of the fact that for a Sturmian word $\boldsymbol{u}$ the function $\text{pal}_u(n)$ is not bounded, Frid considered only prefixes of $\boldsymbol{u}$. This was made possible by the following result by Saarela [9]: for a factor x of a word y we have $|x|_{\text{pal}} \leq 2|y|_{\text{pal}}$. Computer experiments do indicate that the prefixes $w^{(n)}$ have the highest possible ratio $\frac{|w|_{\text{pal}}}{\ln |w|}$ (among all prefixes of $\boldsymbol{f}$). However, it is still possible that there is a sequence of factors (not prefixes) of $\boldsymbol{f}$ which can be used to enlarge the constant $\frac{1}{3 \ln \tau}$ in (5).

Acknowledgements. This work was supported by the project CZ.02.1.01/0.0/ 0.0/16_019/0000778 from European Regional Development Fund. We also acknowledge financial support of the Grant Agency of the Czech Technical University in Prague, grant No. SGS14/205/OHK4/3T/14.

References

1. Frid, A.: Representations of palindromes in the Fibonacci word. In: Numeration 2018, pp. 9–12 (2018). https://numeration2018.sciencesconf.org/data/pages/num18_abstracts.pdf
2. Frid, A.E.: Sturmian numeration systems and decompositions to palindromes. Eur. J. Combin. **71**, 202–212 (2018). https://doi.org/10.1016/j.ejc.2018.04.003
3. Frid, A.E., Puzynina, S., Zamboni, L.Q.: On palindromic factorization of words. Adv. Appl. Math. **50**(5), 737–748 (2013). https://doi.org/10.1016/j.aam.2013.01.002
4. Lothaire, M.: Algebraic combinatorics on words. In: Encyclopedia of Mathematics and its Applications, vol. 90. Cambridge University Press, Cambridge (2002). https://doi.org/10.1017/CBO9781107326019

5. Mignosi, F.: Infinite words with linear subword complexity. Theoret. Comput. Sci. **65**(2), 221–242 (1989). https://doi.org/10.1016/0304-3975(89)90046-7

6. Mignosi, F.: On the number of factors of Sturmian words. Theoret. Comput. Sci. **82**(1), 71–84 (1991). https://doi.org/10.1016/0304-3975(91)90172-X

7. Mignosi, F., Séébold, P.: Morphismes sturmiens et règles de Rauzy. J. Théor. Nombres Bordeaux **5**(2), 221–233 (1993). http://jtnb.cedram.org/item?id=JTNB_1993_5_2_221_0

8. Morse, M., Hedlund, G.A.: Symbolic dynamics II Sturmian trajectories. Amer. J. Math. **62**, 1–42 (1940). https://doi.org/10.2307/2371431

9. Saarela, A.: Palindromic length in free monoids and free groups. In: Brlek, S., Dolce, F., Reutenauer, C., Vandomme, É. (eds.) WORDS 2017. LNCS, vol. 10432, pp. 203–213. Springer, Cham (2017). https://doi.org/10.1007/978-3-319-66396-8_19

Separating Many Words by Counting Occurrences of Factors

Aleksi Saarela[(✉)][iD]

Department of Mathematics and Statistics, University of Turku,
20014 Turku, Finland
amsaar@utu.fi

Abstract. For a given language L, we study the languages X such that for all distinct words $u, v \in L$, there exists a word $x \in X$ appearing a different number of times as a factor in u and in v. In particular, we are interested in the following question: For which languages L does there exist a finite language X satisfying the above condition? We answer this question for all regular languages and for all sets of factors of infinite words.

Keywords: Combinatorics on words · Regular language ·
Infinite word · k-abelian equivalence · Separating words problem

1 Introduction

The motivation for this article comes from three sources.

First, a famous question about finite automata is the *separating words problem*. If $\mathrm{sep}(u, v)$ is the size of the smallest DFA that accepts one of the words u, v and rejects the other, then what is the maximum of the numbers $\mathrm{sep}(u, v)$ when u and v run over all words of length at most n? This question was first studied by Goralčík and Koubek [8], and they proved an upper bound $o(n)$ and a lower bound $\Omega(\log n)$. The upper bound was improved to $O(n^{2/5}(\log n)^{3/5})$ by Robson [18], and this remains the best known result. A survey and some additional results can be found in the article by Demaine, Eisentat, Shallit and Wilson [6]. Several variations of the problem exist. For example, NFAs [6] or context-free grammars [5] could be used instead of DFAs. More generally, we could try to separate two disjoint languages A and B by providing a language X from some specified family of languages such that $A \subseteq X$ and $B \cap X = \varnothing$. As an example related to logic, see [16]. Alternatively, we could try to separate many words $w_1, \ldots, w_k$ by providing languages $X_1, \ldots, X_k$ with some specific properties such that $w_i \in X_j$ if and only if $i = j$. As an example, see [9].

Let $|w|_x$ denote the number of occurrences of a factor x in a word w. A simple observation that can be made about the separating words problem is that if $|u|_x \neq |v|_x$, then $|u|_x \not\equiv |v|_x \pmod{p}$ for some relatively small prime p (more specifically, $p = O(\log(|uv|))$), and the number of occurrences modulo a prime can be easily counted by a DFA. So if u and v have a different number of

© Springer Nature Switzerland AG 2019
P. Hofman and M. Skrzypczak (Eds.): DLT 2019, LNCS 11647, pp. 251–264, 2019.
https://doi.org/10.1007/978-3-030-24886-4_19

occurrences of some short factor x, then $\text{sep}(u, v)$ is small, see [6] for more details. Unfortunately, this approach does not provide any general bounds, and more complicated ideas are required to prove the results mentioned in the previous paragraph.

In this article, we are interested in the question of how well words can be separated if we forget about automata and only consider the simple idea of counting occurrences of factors. For any two distinct words u and v of length n, we can find a factor x of length $\lfloor n/2 \rfloor + 1$ or less such that $|u|_x \neq |v|_x$. A proof of this simple fact can be found in an article by Manuch [13]. See [19] for a variation where also the positions of the occurrences modulo a certain number are taken into account. The question becomes more interesting if we want to separate more than two words (possibly infinitely many) at once, and we can do this by counting the numbers of occurrences of more than one factor. We are particularly interested in the following question.

Question 1.1. Given a language L, does there exist a finite language X such that for all distinct words $u, v \in L$, there exists $x \in X$ such that $|u|_x \neq |v|_x$?

The second source of motivation is an old guessing game for two players, let us call them Alice and Bob: From a given set of options, Alice secretly picks one. Bob is allowed to ask any yes-no questions, and he is trying to figure out what Alice picked. Two famous versions are the game "Twenty Questions" and the children's board game "Guess Who". In their simplest forms, these kinds of games are easy to analyze: The required number of questions is logarithmic with respect to the number of options. However, many more complicated variations have been studied. As examples, see [15] and [1].

In this article, we are interested in a variation where the options are words and, instead of arbitrary yes-no questions, Bob is allowed to ask for the number of occurrences of any factor in the word Alice has chosen. Usually in games like this, Bob can decide every question based on the previous answers, but we can also require that Bob needs to decide all the questions in advance.

Question 1.2. Given a language from which Alice has secretly picked one word w, can Bob find a finite language X such that the answers to the questions "What is $|w|_x$?" for all $x \in X$ are guaranteed to reveal the correct word w?

It is easy to see that Questions 1.1 and 1.2 are equivalent. In this article, we will use the formulation of Question 1.1 instead of talking about games.

The third source of motivation is k-abelian complexity. For a positive integer k, words u and v are said to be k-abelian equivalent if $|u|_x = |v|_x$ for all factors x of length at most k. The factor complexity of an infinite word w is a function that maps a number n to the number of factors of w of length n. The k-abelian complexity of w similarly maps a number n to the number of k-abelian equivalence classes of factors of w of length n. k-abelian equivalence was first studied by Karhumäki [10]. Many basic properties were proved by Karhumäki, Saarela and Zamboni in the article [11], where also k-abelian complexity was introduced. Several articles have been published about k-abelian complexity [3, 4, 12], and about abelian complexity (that is, the case $k = 1$) already earlier [17]. Perhaps the most interesting one from the point of view of this paper is [3], where the relationships between the k-abelian complexities of an infinite word for different values of k were studied. However, the following simple question was not considered in that article.

Question 1.3. Given an infinite word, does there exist a number $k \geq 1$ such that the k-abelian complexity of the word is the same as the usual factor complexity of the word?

For a given language, we can define its growth function and k-abelian growth function as concepts analogous to the factor complexity and k-abelian complexity of an infinite word. Then the above question can be generalized. We are specifically interested in the case of regular languages. Some connections between k-abelian equivalence and regular languages have been studied by Cassaigne, Karhumäki, Puzynina and Whiteland [2].

Question 1.4. Given a language, does there exist a number $k \geq 1$ such that the growth function of the language is the same as the k-abelian growth function of the language?

In this article, we first define some concepts related to Question 1.1 and prove basic properties about them. As stated above, Questions 1.1 and 1.2 are equivalent, and so is Question 1.4, but this requires a short proof. We answer these questions for two families of languages: Sets of factors of infinite words (this corresponds to Question 1.3) and regular languages. In the first case, the result is not surprising: The answer is positive if and only if the word is ultimately periodic. Our main result is a characterization in the case of regular languages: The answer is positive if and only if the language does not have a subset of the form xw^*yw^*z for any words w, x, y, z such that $wy \neq yw$.

2   Preliminaries

Throughout the article, we use the symbol Σ to denote an alphabet. All words are over Σ unless otherwise specified.

Primitive Words and Lyndon Words. A nonempty word is *primitive* if it is not a power of any shorter word. The *primitive root* of a nonempty word w is the unique primitive word p such that $w \in p^+$. It is well known that nonempty words u, v have the same primitive root if and only if they commute, that is, $uv = vu$.

Words u and v are *conjugates* if there exist words p, q such that $u = pq$ and $v = qp$. All conjugates of a primitive word are primitive. If two nonempty words are conjugates, then their primitive roots are conjugates.

We can assume that the alphabet Σ is ordered. This order can be extended to a lexicographic order of Σ^*. A *Lyndon word* is a primitive word that is lexicographically smaller than all of its other conjugates. We use Lyndon words when we need to pick a canonical representative from the conjugacy class of a primitive word. The fact that this representative happens to be lexicographically minimal is not actually important in this article.

The *Lyndon root* of a nonempty word w is the unique Lyndon word that is conjugate to the primitive root of w.

Occurrences. Let u and w be words. An *occurrence of u in w* is a triple (x, u, y) such that $w = xuy$. The number of occurrences of u in w is denoted by $|w|_u$.

Let (x, u, y) and (x', u', y') be occurrences in w. If

$$\max(|x|, |x'|) < \min(|xu|, |x'u'|),$$

then we say that these occurrences have an *overlap* of length

$$\min(|xu|, |x'u'|) - \max(|x|, |x'|).$$

If $|x| \geq |x'|$ and $|y| \geq |y'|$, then we say that (x, u, y) is *contained* in (x', u', y').

If (x, u, y) is an occurrence in w and $u \in L$, then (x, u, y) is an *L-occurrence in w*. It is a *maximal L-occurrence in w* if it is not contained in any other L-occurrence in w.

k-abelian Equivalence. Let k be a positive integer. Words $u, v \in \Sigma^*$ are *k-abelian equivalent* if $|u|_x = |v|_x$ for all $x \in \Sigma^{\leq k}$. k-abelian equivalence is an equivalence relation and it is denoted by $\equiv_k$.

Here are some basic facts about k-abelian equivalence (see [11]): $u, v \in \Sigma^{\geq k-1}$ are k-abelian equivalent if and only if they have a common prefix of length $k - 1$ and $|u|_x = |v|_x$ for all $x \in \Sigma^k$. The condition about prefixes can be replaced by a symmetric condition about suffixes. Words of length $2k - 1$ or less are k-abelian equivalent if and only if they are equal. k-abelian equivalence is a congruence, that is, if $u \equiv_k u'$ and $v \equiv_k v'$, then $uv \equiv_k u'v'$.

We are going to use the following simple fact a couple of times when showing that two words are k-abelian equivalent: If $u, v, w, x \in \Sigma^*$, $|v| = k - 1$, and $|x| = k$, then

$$|uvw|_x = |uv|_x + |vw|_x.$$

Example 2.1. The words $aabab$ and $abaab$ are 2-abelian equivalent: They have the same prefix of length one, one occurrence of aa, two occurrences of ab, one occurrence of ba, and no occurrences of bb.

The words aba and bab have the same number of occurrences of every factor of length two, but they are not 2-abelian equivalent, because they have a different number of occurrences of a.

Let $k \geq 1$. The words $u = a^k ba^{k-1}$ and $v = a^{k-1}ba^k$ are k-abelian equivalent: They have the same prefix of length $k - 1$, and $|u|_x = 1 = |v|_x$ if $x = a^k$ or $x = a^i ba^{k-i-1}$ for some $i \in \{0, \ldots, k-1\}$, and $|u|_x = 0 = |v|_x$ for all other factors x of length k. On the other hand, u and v are not $(k + 1)$-abelian equivalent, because they have a different prefix of length k.

Growth Functions and Factor Complexity. The *growth function* of a language L is the function

$$\mathcal{P}_L : \mathbb{Z}_{\geq 0} \to \mathbb{Z}_{\geq 0}, \; \mathcal{P}_L(n) = |L \cap \Sigma^n|$$

mapping a number n to the number of words of length n in L. The *factor complexity* of an infinite word w, denoted by $\mathcal{P}_w$, is the growth function of the set of factors of w (technically, the domain of $\mathcal{P}_w$ is often defined to be $\mathbb{Z}_+$ instead of $\mathbb{Z}_{\geq 0}$).

We can also define k-abelian versions of these functions. The k-abelian growth function of a language L is the function

$$\mathcal{P}_L^k : \mathbb{Z}_{\geq 0} \to \mathbb{Z}_{\geq 0}, \; \mathcal{P}_L(n) = |(L \cap \Sigma^n)/ \equiv_k |,$$

where $(L \cap \Sigma^n)/ \equiv_k$ denotes the set of equivalence classes of elements of $L \cap \Sigma^n$. The *k-abelian complexity* of an infinite word w, denoted by $\mathcal{P}_w^k$, is the k-abelian growth function of the set of factors of w.

An infinite word w is *ultimately periodic* if there exist finite words u, v such that $w = uv^\omega$. An infinite word is *aperiodic* if it is not ultimately periodic. It was proved by Morse and Hedlund [14] that if w is ultimately periodic, then $\mathcal{P}_w(n) = O(1)$, and if w is aperiodic, then $\mathcal{P}_w(n) \geq n + 1$ for all n.

3   Separating Sets of Factors

A language X is a *separating set of factors* (SSF) of a language L if for all distinct words $u, v \in L$, there exists $x \in X$ such that $|u|_x \neq |v|_x$. The set X is *size-minimal* if no set of smaller cardinality is an SSF of L, and it is *inclusion-minimal* if X does not have a proper subset that is an SSF of L.

Example 3.1. Let $\Sigma = \{a, b\}$. The language a^* has two inclusion-minimal SSFs: $\{\varepsilon\}$ and $\{a\}$. The language $\Sigma^2 = \{aa, ab, ba, bb\}$ has eight inclusion-minimal SSFs:

$$\{a, ab\}, \{a, ba\}, \{b, ab\}, \{b, ba\}, \{aa, ab, ba\}, \{aa, ab, bb\}, \{aa, ba, bb\}, \{ab, ba, bb\}.$$

The first four are size-minimal.

Example 3.2. Let $\Sigma = \{a, b, c, d, e, f\}$. The language $L = \{ac, ad, be, bf\}$ has a size-minimal SSF $\{a, c, e\}$. In terms of the guessing game mentioned in the introduction, this means that if Alice has chosen $w \in L$, then Bob can ask for the numbers $|w|_a, |w|_c, |w|_e$, and this will always reveal w. Actually, two questions are enough if Bob can choose the second question after hearing the answer to the first one: He can first ask for $|w|_a$, and then for either $|w|_c$ or $|w|_e$ depending on whether $|w|_a = 1$ or $|w|_a = 0$.

The following lemma contains some very basic results related to the above definitions. In particular, it proves that every language has an inclusion-minimal SSF, and all SSFs are completely characterized by the inclusion-minimal ones.

Lemma 3.3. *Let L and X be languages.*

1. *If $L \neq \varnothing$, then L has a proper subset that is an SSF of L.*
2. *If X is an SSF of L and $K \subseteq L$, then X is an SSF of K.*
3. *If X is an SSF of L and $X \subseteq Y$, then Y is an SSF of L.*
4. *If X is an SSF of L, then X has a subset that is an inclusion-minimal SSF of L.*

Proof. To prove the first claim, let $w \in L$ be of minimal length and let $X = L \smallsetminus \{w\}$. Let $u, v \in L$ and $u \neq v$. By symmetry, we can assume that $|u| \leq |v|$ and $v \neq w$. Then $v \in X$ and $|u|_v = 0 \neq 1 = |v|_v$. This shows that X is an SSF of L.

The second and third claims follow directly from the definition of an SSF.

The fourth claim is easy to prove if X is finite. In the general case, it can be proved by Zorn's lemma as follows. Consider the partially ordered (by inclusion) family of all subsets of X that are SSFs of L. The family contains at least X, so it is nonempty. By Zorn's lemma, if every nonempty chain (that is, a totally ordered subset of the family) C has a lower bound in this family, then the family has a minimal element, which is then an inclusion-minimal SSF of L. We show that the intersection I of the sets in C is an SSF of L, and therefore it is the required lower bound. For any $u, v \in L$ such that $u \neq v$ and for any $Y \in C$, there exists $y \in Y$ such that $|u|_y \neq |v|_y$. Then y must be a factor of u or v, so if u and v are fixed, then there are only finitely many possibilities for y. Thus at least one of the words y is in all sets Y and therefore also in I. This shows that I is an SSF of L. This completes the proof.   □

The next lemma shows a connection between SSFs and k-abelian equivalence.

Lemma 3.4. *Let L be a language.*

1. *Let $k \in \mathbb{Z}_+$. The language $\Sigma^{\leq k}$ is an SSF of L if and only if the words in L are pairwise k-abelian nonequivalent.*
2. *The language L has a finite SSF if and only if there exists a number k such that the words in L are pairwise k-abelian nonequivalent.*

Proof. The first claim follows directly from the definitions of an SSF and k-abelian equivalence. The "only if" and "if" directions of the second claim can be proved as follows: If a finite set X is an SSF of L, then $X \subseteq \Sigma^{\leq k}$ for some k, and then the words in L are pairwise k-abelian nonequivalent. Conversely, if the words in L are pairwise k-abelian nonequivalent, then $\Sigma^{\leq k}$ is an SSF of L.   □

Note that the condition "the words in L are pairwise k-abelian nonequivalent" can be equivalently expressed as "$\mathcal{P}_L = \mathcal{P}_L^k$". This means that Lemma 3.4 proves the equivalence of Questions 1.1 and 1.4.

Example 3.5. Let $w, x, y, z \in \{a, b\}^*$ and $L = \{awa, axb, bya, bzb\}$. No two words in L have both a common prefix and a common suffix of length one, so the words are pairwise 2-abelian nonequivalent. By the first claim of Lemma 3.4, $\{a, b\}^{\leq 2}$

is an SSF of L. This SSF is not size-minimal (by the first claim of Lemma 3.3, L has an SSF of size three), but it has the advantage of consisting of very short words and not depending on w, x, y, z. Actually, also $\{\varepsilon, a, aa, ab, ba\}$ is an SSF of L. This follows from the fact that $|u|_b = |u|_\varepsilon - |u|_a - 1$ and $|u|_{bb} = |u|_\varepsilon - |u|_{aa} - |u|_{ab} - |u|_{ba} - 2$ for all $u \in \{a, b\}^*$.

Example 3.6. In a list of about 140000 English words (found in the SCOWL database[1]), there are no 4-abelian equivalent words. Therefore, by Lemma 3.4, $\Sigma^{\leq 4}$ is an SSF of the language formed by these words (the alphabet Σ here contains the 26 letters from a to z and also many accented letters and other symbols). The only pairs of 3-abelian equivalent words are $reregister, registerer$ and $reregisters, registerers$. The number of other pairs of 2-abelian equivalent words is also small enough that they can be listed here:

$indenter, intender$	$indenters, intenders$
$pathophysiologic, physiopathologic$	$pathophysiological, physiopathological$
$pathophysiology, physiopathology$	$pathophysiologies, physiopathologies$
$tamara, tarama$	$tamaras, taramas$
$tantarara, tarantara$	$tantararas, tarantaras$
$tantaras, tarantas$	

This means that most words of length 4 and 3 are not needed in the SSF. For example, the set $\Sigma^{\leq 2} \cup \{rere, hop, ind, tan, tar\}$ is an SSF of the language. We did not try to find a minimal SSF.

In the next lemma, we consider whether the properties of having or not having a finite SSF are preserved under the rational operations union, concatenation and Kleene star.

Lemma 3.7. *Let K and L be languages.*

1. *If L has a finite SSF and F is a finite language, then $L \cup F$ has a finite SSF.*
2. *If L does not have a finite SSF, then $L \cup K$ does not have a finite SSF.*
3. *If L has a finite SSF and w is a word, then wL and Lw have finite SSFs.*
4. *If L does not have a finite SSF and $K \neq \varnothing$, then neither KL nor LK have finite SSFs.*
5. *L^* has a finite SSF if and only if there exists a word w such that $L \subseteq w^*$.*
6. *If the symmetric difference of K and L is finite, then either both or neither have a finite SSF.*

Proof. 1. Let X be a finite SSF of L. Let $u, v \in L \cup F$ and $u \neq v$. First, if $u, v \in L$, then $|u|_x \neq |v|_x$ for some $x \in X$. Second, if $u \in F$ and $|u| = |v|$, then $|u|_u \neq |v|_u$. Finally, if $|u| \neq |v|$, then $|u|_\varepsilon \neq |v|_\varepsilon$. Thus $X \cup F \cup \{\varepsilon\}$ is an SSF of $L \cup F$.

2. If a finite set is an SSF of $L \cup K$, then it is also an SSF of L.

---

[1] http://wordlist.aspell.net/.

3. Let wL have no finite SSF. Let $k \in \mathbb{Z}_+$ and $k' = k + |w|$. By Lemma 3.4, there exist two k'-abelian equivalent words $wu, wv \in wL$. Then u and v have a common prefix p of length $k - 1$. For all $x \in \Sigma^k$,

$$|u|_x = |wu|_x - |wp|_x = |wv|_x - |wp|_x = |v|_x,$$

so $u \equiv_k v$. We have shown that for all $k \geq 1$, there exist two k-abelian equivalent words in L. By Lemma 3.4, L does not have a finite SSF. The case of Lw is symmetric.

4. Let L have no finite SSF and let $w \in K$. Let $k \in \mathbb{Z}_+$. By Lemma 3.4, there exist two k-abelian equivalent words $u, v \in L$, and then $wu, wv \in KL$ are k-abelian equivalent. We have shown that for all $k \geq 1$, there exist two k-abelian equivalent words in KL. By Lemma 3.4, KL does not have a finite SSF. The case of LK is symmetric.

5. If $L \subseteq w^*$, then $\{w\}$ is an SSF of L. If there does not exist w such that $L \subseteq w^*$, then there exist $u, v \in L$ such that $uv \neq vu$. For all $k \in \mathbb{Z}_+$, the words $u^k v u^{k-1}, u^{k-1} v u^k \in L^*$ are distinct. They have the same prefix of length $k - 1$. If u_1 is the prefix and u_2 is the suffix of u^{k-1} of length $k - 1$, then

$$|u^k v u^{k-1}|_x = |u^k|_x + |u_2 v u_1|_x + |u^{k-1}|_x = |u^{k-1} v u^k|_x$$

for all $x \in \Sigma^k$, so $u^k v u^{k-1} \equiv_k u^{k-1} v u^k$. We have shown that for all $k \geq 1$, there exist two k-abelian equivalent words in L^*. By Lemma 3.4, L^* does not have a finite SSF.

6. If K has a finite SSF, then so does $K \cap L$. If $L \setminus K$ is finite, then also L has a finite SSF by the first claim of this lemma. Similarly, if L has a finite SSF and $K \setminus L$ is finite, then also K has a finite SSF.   □

Example 3.8. We give an example showing that the property of having a finite SSF is not always preserved by union and concatenation. Let $L = \{a^k b a^{k-1} \mid k \in \mathbb{Z}_+\}$. Then both L and Laa have the finite SSF $\{\varepsilon\}$. On the other hand, $L\{\varepsilon, aa\} = L \cup Laa$ contains the k-abelian equivalent words $a^k b a^{k-1}$ and $a^{k-1} b a^k$ for all $k \geq 2$, so by Lemma 3.4, $L \cup Laa$ does not have a finite SSF even though both L and Laa do have a finite SSF, and $L\{\varepsilon, aa\}$ does not have a finite SSF even though both L and $\{\varepsilon, aa\}$ do have a finite SSF.

4   Infinite Words

In this section, we give an answer to Question 1.3.

Theorem 4.1. *Let w be an infinite word. There exists $k \in \mathbb{Z}_+$ such that $\mathcal{P}_w = \mathcal{P}_w^k$ if and only if w is ultimately periodic.*

Proof. First, let w be ultimately periodic. Then we can write $w = uv^\omega$, where v is primitive and v is not a suffix of u. Let $k = |uv| + 1$ and let x, y be k-abelian equivalent factors of w. If x and y are shorter than uv, then $x = y$. Otherwise x and y have a common prefix of length $k - 1 = |uv|$ and we can write $x = u'v'x'$

and $y = u'v'y'$, where $|u'| = |u|$ and $|v'| = |v|$. Here v' is a factor of v^ω, so it must be a conjugate of v, and it is followed by a $(v')^\omega$. Thus x' and y' are prefixes of $(v')^\omega$ and they are of the same length, so $x' = y'$ and thus $x = y$. We have proved that no two factors of w are k-abelian equivalent. It follows that $\mathcal{P}_w = \mathcal{P}_w^k$.

Second, let w be aperiodic and let $k \geq 2$ be arbitrary. Let $n = \mathcal{P}_w(k-1)+1$. There must exist a word u of length $(k-1)n$ that occurs infinitely many times in w as a factor. We can write $u = x_1 \cdots x_n$, where $x_1, \ldots, x_n \in \Sigma^{k-1}$. By the definition of n, there exist two indices $i, j \in \{1, \ldots, n\}$ such that $x_i = x_j$. Let $i < j$, $x = x_i = x_j$ and $y = x_{i+1} \cdots x_{j-1}$. Then xyx is a factor of u and thus occurs infinitely many times in w as a factor. Therefore we can write $w = z_0xyxz_1xyxz_2xyx \cdots$ for some infinite sequence of words $z_0, z_1, z_2, \ldots$. If the words xy and xz_i have the same primitive root p for all $i \in \mathbb{Z}_+$, then $w = z_0 p^\omega$, which contradicts the aperiodicity of w. Thus there exists i such that xy and xz_i have a different primitive root. Then $xyxz_ix \neq xz_ixy$ and thus $xyxz_ix \neq xz_ixyx$. On the other hand, $xyxz_ix$ and xz_ixyx are k-abelian equivalent because they have the same prefix x of length $k-1$ and

$$|xyxz_ix|_t = |xyx|_t + |xz_ix|_t = |xz_ix|_t + |xyx|_t = |xz_ixyx|_t$$

for all $t \in \Sigma^k$. Moreover, $xyxz_ix$ and xz_ixyx are factors of w. It follows that $\mathcal{P}_w \neq \mathcal{P}_w^k$. □

Corollary 4.2. *The set of factors of an infinite word w has a finite SSF if and only if w is ultimately periodic.*

Proof. Follows from Theorem 4.1 and Lemma 3.4. □

5   Regular Languages

In this section, we give an answer to Question 1.1 for regular languages.

Lemma 5.1. *If a language L has a subset of the form xw^*yw^*z for some words w, x, y, z such that $wy \neq yw$, then L does not have a finite SSF.*

Proof. For all $k \in \mathbb{Z}_+$, the words $xw^kyw^{k-1}z$ and $xw^{k-1}yw^kz$ are distinct. They have the same prefix of length $k-1$. If w_1 is the prefix and w_2 is the suffix of w^{k-1} of length $k-1$, then

$$|xw^kyw^{k-1}z|_t = |xw_1|_t + |w^k|_t + |w_2yw_1|_t + |w^{k-1}|_t + |w_2z|_t = |xw^{k-1}yw^kz|_t$$

for all $t \in \Sigma^k$, so $xw^kyw^{k-1}z \equiv_k xw^{k-1}yw^kz$. We have shown that for all $k \geq 1$, there exist two k-abelian equivalent words in L. By Lemma 3.4, L does not have a finite SSF. □

A language L is *bounded* if it is a subset of a language of the form

$$v_1^* \cdots v_n^*,$$

where $v_1, \ldots, v_n$ are words. It was proved by Ginsburg and Spanier [7] that a regular language is bounded if and only if it is a finite union of languages of the form

$$u_0 v_1^* u_1 \cdots v_n^* u_n,$$

where $u_0, \ldots, u_n$ are words and $v_1, \ldots, v_n$ are nonempty words.

Lemma 5.2. *Every regular language is bounded or has a subset of the form* $xw^* yw^* z$ *for some words* w, x, y, z *such that* $wy \neq yw$.

Proof. The proof is by induction. Every finite language is bounded. We assume that A and B are regular languages that have the claimed property and prove that also $A \cup B$, AB and A^* have the claimed property.

First, we consider $A \cup B$. If both A and B are bounded, then so is $A \cup B$ by the characterization of Ginsburg and Spanier. If at least one of A and B has a subset of the form $xw^* yw^* z$ for some words w, x, y, z such that $wy \neq yw$, then $A \cup B$ has this same subset.

Next, we consider AB. If both A and B are bounded or if one of them is empty, then AB is bounded by the definition of bounded languages. If A and B are nonempty and at least one of them has a subset of the form $xw^* yw^* z$ for some words w, x, y, z such that $wy \neq yw$, then AB has a subset of the same form with a different x or z.

Finally, we consider A^*. If $A \subseteq u^*$ for some word u, then $A^* \subseteq u^*$ is bounded. If A is not a subset of u^* for any word u, then there exist $w, y \in A$ such that $wy \neq yw$, and A^* has $w^* yw^*$ as a subset. □

By Lemmas 5.1 and 5.2, if a regular language is not bounded, then it does not have a finite SSF. Thus we can concentrate on bounded regular languages. We continue with a technical lemma.

Lemma 5.3. *Let L be a bounded regular language. There exist numbers $n, k \geq 0$ and a finite set of Lyndon words P such that the following are satisfied:*

1. *If $p, q \in P$, $p \neq q$, and $l, m \geq 0$, then p^l and q^m do not have a common factor of length n.*
2. *If $u \in L$ and $p \in P$, then either there is at most one maximal $p^{\geq n}$-occurrence in u or L has a subset of the form $x(p^m)^* y(p^m)^* z$, where $py \neq yp$ and $m \geq 1$.*
3. *If $u \in L$ and x is a factor of u of length at least k, then x has a factor p^{n+1} for some $p \in P$.*

Proof. If L is finite, then the claim is basically trivial. If L is infinite, then

$$L = \bigcup_{i=1}^{s} u_{i0} \prod_{j=1}^{r_i} v_{ij}^* u_{ij},$$

where $s \geq 1$ and $r_1, \ldots, r_s \geq 0$, $r_i \geq 1$ for at least one i, and the words v_{ij} are nonempty. We can let P be the set of Lyndon roots of the words v_{ij} and

$$n = 2 \cdot \max \left\{ \left| u_{i0} \prod_{j=1}^{r_i} v_{ij} u_{ij} \right| \; \middle| \; i \in \{1, \ldots, s\} \right\},$$

$$k = \max \left\{ \left| u_{i0} \prod_{j=1}^{r_i} v_{ij}^{n+2} u_{ij} \right| \; \middle| \; i \in \{1, \ldots, s\} \right\}.$$

The proof can be found in the arXiv version of this paper.[2] □

Now we are ready to prove our main theorem.

Theorem 5.4. *A regular language L has a finite SSF if and only if L does not have a subset of the form xw^*yw^*z for any words w, x, y, z such that $wy \neq yw$.*

Proof. The "only if" direction follows from Lemma 5.1. To prove the "if" direction, let n, k, P be as in Lemma 5.3 (L is bounded by Lemma 5.2). Let $u, v \in L$ be k-abelian equivalent. We are going to show that $u = v$. This proves the theorem by Lemma 3.4. If $|u| = |v| < k$, then trivially $u = v$, so we assume that $|u| = |v| \geq k$.

Let $P_j = \{p^i \mid p \in P, i \geq j\}$ for all j. Let the maximal P_n-occurrences in u be

$$(x_1, p_1^{m_1}, x_1'), \ldots, (x_r, p_r^{m_r}, x_r'), \tag{1}$$

where $p_1, \ldots, p_r \in P$. It follows from $|u| \geq k$ and Condition 3 of Lemma 5.3 that $r \geq 1$. We can assume that the occurrences have been ordered so that $|x_1| \leq \cdots \leq |x_r|$. By Condition 2 of Lemma 5.3, the words $p_1, \ldots, p_r$ are pairwise distinct. All P_n-occurrences in u are contained in one of the maximal occurrences (1). By Condition 1 of Lemma 5.3, p^n cannot be a factor of $p_j^{m_j}$ if $p \in P \setminus \{p_j\}$, so if $p \in P \setminus \{p_1, \ldots, p_r\}$, then there are no $p^{\geq n}$-occurrences in u, and all $p_i^{\geq n}$-occurrences are $(x_i p_i^l, p_i^j, p_i^{m_i - j - l} x_i')$ for $j \in \{n, \ldots, m_i\}$ and $l \in \{0, \ldots, m_i - j\}$. In particular, $|u|_{p_i^n} = m_i - n + 1$.

Similarly, let the maximal P_n-occurrences in v be

$$(y_1, q_1^{n_1}, y_1'), \ldots, (y_s, q_s^{n_s}, y_s'),$$

where $s \geq 1$ and $q_1, \ldots, q_s \in P$. As above, we can assume that the occurrences have been ordered so that $|y_1| \leq \cdots \leq |y_s|$, and we can prove that the words $q_1, \ldots, q_s$ are pairwise distinct, p^n cannot be a factor of $q_j^{n_j}$ if $p \in P \setminus \{q_j\}$, and if $p \in P \setminus \{q_1, \ldots, q_s\}$, then there are no $p^{\geq n}$-occurrences in v, all $q_i^{\geq n}$-occurrences are $(y_i q_i^l, q_i^j, q_i^{n_i - j - l} y_i')$ for $j \in \{n, \ldots, n_i\}$ and $l \in \{0, \ldots, n_i - j\}$, and $|v|_{q_i^n} = n_i - n + 1$.

If $p \in P$, then $|p^n| < k$ by Condition 3 of Lemma 5.3, and then $|u|_{p^n} = |v|_{p^n}$ because $u \equiv_k v$. It follows that $r = s$ and $\{p_1, \ldots, p_r\} = \{q_1, \ldots, q_s\}$. We have seen that $|u|_{p_i^n} = m_i - n + 1$ and $|v|_{q_j^n} = n_j - n + 1$, so if $p_i = q_j$, then $m_i = n_j$.

---

[2] http://arxiv.org/abs/1905.07223.

We prove by induction that $(x_i, p_i, m_i) = (y_i, q_i, n_i)$ for all $i \in \{1, \ldots, r\}$. First, we prove the case $i = 1$. The words u and v have prefixes $x_1 p_1^n$ and $y_1 q_1^n$, respectively. There is only one P_n-occurrence and no P_{n+1}-occurrences in $x_1 p_1^n$. Similarly, there is only one P_n-occurrence and no P_{n+1}-occurrences in $y_1 q_1^n$. By Condition 3 of Lemma 5.3, $|x_1 p_1^n| < k$ and $|y_1 q_1^n| < k$. Because u and v are k-abelian equivalent, they have the same prefix of length $k - 1$, and thus one of $x_1 p_1^n$ and $y_1 q_1^n$ is a prefix of the other. If, say, $x_1 p_1^n$ is a prefix of $y_1 q_1^n$, then $y_1 q_1^n$ has an occurrence (x_1, p_1^n, z) for some word z, and this must be the unique P_n-occurrence $(y_1, q_1^n, \varepsilon)$. It follows that $x_1 = y_1$ and $p_1 = q_1$, and then also $m_1 = n_1$.

Next, we assume that $(x_i, p_i, m_i) = (y_i, q_i, n_i)$ for some $i \in \{1, \ldots, r - 1\}$ and prove that $(x_{i+1}, p_{i+1}, m_{i+1}) = (y_{i+1}, q_{i+1}, n_{i+1})$. Let $x_{i+1} = x_i p_i^{m_i - n} x_i''$ and $y_{i+1} = y_i q_i^{n_i - n} y_i'' = x_i p_i^{m_i - n} y_i''$. The unique shortest factor in u beginning with p_i^n and ending with p^n for some $p \in P \setminus \{p_i\}$ is the factor $x_i'' p_{i+1}^n$ starting at position $|x_i p_i^{m_i - n}|$ and ending at position $|x_{i+1} p_{i+1}^n|$. Similarly, the unique shortest factor in v beginning with p_i^n and ending with p^n for some $p \in P \setminus \{p_i\}$ is the factor $y_i'' q_{i+1}^n$ starting at position $|y_i q_i^{n_i - n}| = |x_i p_i^{m_i - n}|$ and ending at position $|y_{i+1} q_{i+1}^n|$. There are no P_{n+1}-occurrences in these factors, so they are of length less than k by Condition 3 of Lemma 5.3, and they must be equal because $u \equiv_k v$. It follows that $p_{i+1} = q_{i+1}$, $x_i'' = y_i''$, and $x_{i+1} = y_{i+1}$, and then also $m_{i+1} = n_{i+1}$.

It follows by induction that $x_r p_r^{m_r} = y_r q_r^{n_r}$. Because $|u| = |v|$, it must be $|x_r'| = |y_r'|$. Because x_r' does not have any P_{n+1}-occurrences, $|x_r'| < k$ by Condition 3 of Lemma 5.3. Because u and v are k-abelian equivalent, they have the same suffix of length $k - 1$, so $x_r' = y_r'$. Thus $u = v$. This completes the proof. $\square$

Example 5.5. First, consider the language $K = a^*(abab)^*ba(ba)^*$. It has a subset $(abab)^*ba(ba)^* = (abab)^*b(ab)^*a$, which has a subset $(abab)^*b(abab)^*a$. It follows from Theorem 5.4 that K does not have a finite SSF.

Then, consider the language $L = a^*(abab)^*aba(ba)^* = a^*(abab)^*(ab)^*aba = a^*(ab)^*aba$. It can be proved that if L has a subset xw^*yw^*z with $w \neq \varepsilon$, then the Lyndon root of w is a or ab, and $wy = yw$. It follows from Theorem 5.4 that L has a finite SSF.

6   Conclusion

In this article, we have defined and studied separating sets of factors. In particular, we have considered the question of whether a given language has a finite SSF. We have answered this question for sets of factors of infinite words and for regular languages. In the future, this question could be studied for other families of languages. We can also ask the following questions:

- Given a language with a finite SSF, what is the minimal size of an SSF of this language? For example, this could be considered for Σ^n.
- Given a language with no finite SSF, how "small" can the growth function of an SSF of this language be? For example, this could be considered for Σ^*.

References

1. Ambainis, A., Bloch, S.A., Schweizer, D.L.: Delayed binary search, or playing twenty questions with a procrastinator. Algorithmica **32**(4), 641–650 (2002). https://doi.org/10.1007/s00453-001-0097-4
2. Cassaigne, J., Karhumäki, J., Puzynina, S., Whiteland, M.A.: k-abelian equivalence and rationality. Fund. Inform. **154**(1–4), 65–94 (2017). https://doi.org/10.3233/FI-2017-1553
3. Cassaigne, J., Karhumäki, J., Saarela, A.: On growth and fluctuation of k-abelian complexity. Eur. J. Combin. **65**, 92–105 (2017). https://doi.org/10.1016/j.ejc.2017.05.006
4. Chen, J., Lü, X., Wu, W.: On the k-abelian complexity of the cantor sequence. J. Combin. Theory Ser. A **155**, 287–303 (2018). https://doi.org/10.1016/j.jcta.2017.11.010
5. Currie, J., Petersen, H., Robson, J.M., Shallit, J.: Separating words with small grammars. J. Autom. Lang. Comb. **4**(2), 101–110 (1999)
6. Demaine, E.D., Eisenstat, S., Shallit, J., Wilson, D.A.: Remarks on separating words. In: Holzer, M., Kutrib, M., Pighizzini, G. (eds.) DCFS 2011. LNCS, vol. 6808, pp. 147–157. Springer, Heidelberg (2011). https://doi.org/10.1007/978-3-642-22600-7_12
7. Ginsburg, S., Spanier, E.H.: Bounded regular sets. Proc. Amer. Math. Soc. **17**, 1043–1049 (1966). https://doi.org/10.2307/2036087
8. Goralčík, P., Koubek, V.: On discerning words by automata. In: Kott, L. (ed.) ICALP 1986. LNCS, vol. 226, pp. 116–122. Springer, Heidelberg (1986). https://doi.org/10.1007/3-540-16761-7_61
9. Holub, V., Kortelainen, J.: On partitions separating words. Int. J. Algebra Comput. **21**(8), 1305–1316 (2011). https://doi.org/10.1142/S0218196711006650
10. Karhumäki, J.: Generalized Parikh mappings and homomorphisms. Inf. Control **47**(3), 155–165 (1980). https://doi.org/10.1016/S0019-9958(80)90493-3
11. Karhumäki, J., Saarela, A., Zamboni, L.Q.: On a generalization of Abelian equivalence and complexity of infinite words. J. Combin. Theory Ser. A **120**(8), 2189–2206 (2013). https://doi.org/10.1016/j.jcta.2013.08.008
12. Karhumäki, J., Saarela, A., Zamboni, L.Q.: Variations of the Morse-Hedlund theorem for k-abelian equivalence. Acta Cybernet. **23**(1), 175–189 (2017). https://doi.org/10.14232/actacyb.23.1.2017.11
13. Maňuch, J.: Characterization of a word by its subwords. In: Proceedings of the 4th DLT, pp. 210–219. World Scientific Publication (2000). https://doi.org/10.1142/9789812792464_0018
14. Morse, M., Hedlund, G.A.: Symbolic dynamics. Amer. J. Math. **60**(4), 815–866 (1938). https://doi.org/10.2307/2371264
15. Pelc, A.: Solution of Ulam's problem on searching with a lie. J. Combin. Theory Ser. A **44**(1), 129–140 (1987). https://doi.org/10.1016/0097-3165(87)90065-3
16. Place, T., Zeitoun, M.: Separating regular languages with first-order logic. Log. Methods Comput. Sci. **12**(1), 31 (2016). https://doi.org/10.2168/LMCS-12(1:5)2016. Paper No. 5
17. Richomme, G., Saari, K., Zamboni, L.Q.: Abelian complexity of minimal subshifts. J. Lond. Math. Soc. **83**(1), 79–95 (2011). https://doi.org/10.1112/jlms/jdq063

18. Robson, J.M.: Separating strings with small automata. Inform. Process. Lett. **30**(4), 209–214 (1989). https://doi.org/10.1016/0020-0190(89)90215-9
19. Vyalyĭ, M.N., Gimadeev, R.A.: On separating words by the occurrences of subwords. Diskretn. Anal. Issled. Oper. **21**(1), 3–14 (2014). https://doi.org/10.1134/S1990478914020161

k-Spectra of Weakly-c-Balanced Words

Joel D. Day[1], Pamela Fleischmann[2(✉)], Florin Manea[2], and Dirk Nowotka[2]

[1] Loughborough University, Loughborough, UK
J.Day@lboro.ac.uk
[2] Kiel University, Kiel, Germany
{fpa,flm,dn}@informatik.uni-kiel.de

Abstract. A word u is a scattered factor of w if u can be obtained from w by deleting some of its letters. That is, there exist the (potentially empty) words $u_1, u_2, ..., u_n$, and $v_0, v_1, .., v_n$ such that $u = u_1 u_2 ... u_n$ and $w = v_0 u_1 v_1 u_2 v_2 ... u_n v_n$. We consider the set of length-k scattered factors of a given word w, called here k-spectrum and denoted $\mathrm{ScatFact}_k(w)$. We prove a series of properties of the sets $\mathrm{ScatFact}_k(w)$ for binary weakly-0-balanced and, respectively, weakly-c-balanced words w, i.e., words over a two-letter alphabet where the number of occurrences of each letter is the same, or, respectively, one letter has c-more occurrences than the other. In particular, we consider the question which cardinalities $n = |\mathrm{ScatFact}_k(w)|$ are obtainable, for a positive integer k, when w is either a weakly-0-balanced binary word of length $2k$, or a weakly-c-balanced binary word of length $2k - c$. We also consider the problem of reconstructing words from their k-spectra.

1 Introduction

Given a word w, a scattered factor (also called scattered subword, or simply subword in the literature) is a word obtained by removing one or more factors from w. More formally, u is a scattered factor of w if there exist $u_1, \ldots, u_n \in \Sigma^*$, $v_0, \ldots, v_n \in \Sigma^*$ such that $u = u_1 u_2 \ldots u_n$ and $w = v_0 u_1 v_1 u_1 \ldots u_n v_n$. Consequently a scattered factor of w can be thought of as a representation of w in which some parts are missing. As such, there is considerable interest in the relationship of a word and its scattered factors from both a theoretical and practical point of view. For an introduction to the study of scattered factors, see Chapter 6 of [9]. On the one hand, it is easy to imagine how, in any situation where discrete, linear data is read from an imperfect input – such as when sequencing DNA or during the transmission of a digital signal – scattered factors form a natural model, as multiple parts of the input may be missed, but the rest will remain unaffected and in-sequence. For instance, various applications and connections of this model in verification are discussed in [6,14] within a language theoretic framework, while applications of the model in DNA sequencing are discussed in [4] in an algorithmic framework. On the other hand, from a more algebraic perspective, there have been efforts to bridge the gap between the non-commutative field of combinatorics on words with traditional commutative

© Springer Nature Switzerland AG 2019
P. Hofman and M. Skrzypczak (Eds.): DLT 2019, LNCS 11647, pp. 265–277, 2019.
https://doi.org/10.1007/978-3-030-24886-4_20

mathematics via Parikh matrices (cf. e.g., [11,13]) which are closely related to, and influenced by the topic of scattered factors.

The set (or also in some cases, multi-set) of scattered factors of a word w, denoted ScatFact(w) is typically exponentially large in the length of w, and contains a lot of redundant information in the sense that, for $k' < k \leq |w|$, a word of length k' is a scattered factor of w if and only if it is a scattered factor of a scattered factor of w of length k. This has led to the idea of k-spectra: the set of all length-k scattered factors of a word. For example, the 3-spectrum of the word ababbb is the set $\{$aab, aba, abb, bab, bbb$\}$. Note that unlike some literature, we do not consider the k-spectra to be the multi-set of scattered factors in the present work, but rather ignore the multiplicities. This distinction is non-trivial as there are significant variations on the properties based on these different definitions (cf. e.g., [10]). Also, the notion of k-spectra is closely related to the classical notion of factor complexity of words, which counts, for each positive integer k, the number of distinct factors of length k of a word. Here, the cardinality of the k-spectrum of a word gives the number of the word's distinct *scattered* factors of length k.

One of the most fundamental questions about k-spectra of words, and indeed sets of scattered factors in general, is that of recognition: given a set S of words (of length k), is S the subset of a k-spectrum of some word? In general, it remains a long standing goal of the theory to give a "nice" descriptive characterisation of scattered factor sets (and k-spectra), and to better understand their structure [9]. Another fundamental question concerning k-spectra, and one well motivated in several applications, is the question of reconstruction: given a word w of length n, what is the smallest value k such that the k-spectrum of w is uniquely determined? This question was addressed and solved successively in a variety of cases. In particular, in [3], the exact bound of $\frac{n}{2}+1$ is given in the general case. Other variations, including for the definition of k-spectra where multiplicities are also taken into account, are considered in [10], while [7] considers the question of reconstructing words from their palindromic scattered factors.

In the current work, we consider k-spectra in the restricted setting of a binary alphabet $\Sigma = \{$a, b$\}$. For such an alphabet, we can always identify the natural number $c \in \mathbb{N}_0$ which describes how weakly balanced a word is: c is the difference between the amount of as and bs. Thus, it seems natural to categorise all words over Σ according to this difference: a binary word where one letter has exactly c more occurrences than the other one is called weakly-c-balanced. In Section 3 the cardinalities of k-spectra of weakly-c-balanced words of length $2k - c$ are investigated. Our first results concern the minimal and maximal cardinality ScatFact$_k$ might have. We show that the cardinality ranges for weakly-0-balanced between $k + 1$ and 2^k, and determine exactly for which words of length $2k$ these values are reached. In the case of weakly-c-balanced words, we are able to replicate the result regarding the minimal cardinality of ScatFact$_k$, but the case of maximal cardinality seems to be more complicated. To this end, it seems that the words containing many alternations between the two letters of the alphabet have larger sets ScatFact$_k$. Therefore, we first investigate the scattered factors of the words which are prefixes of $(\mathtt{ab})^{\omega}$ and give a precise description of all scattered factors of any length of such words. That is, not only we compute the cardinality of $\mathrm{ScatFact}_k(w)$, for all such words w, but also describe a way to obtain directly the respective scattered factors, without repetitions. We use this to describe exactly the sets $\mathrm{ScatFact}_i$ for the word $(\mathtt{ab})^{k-c}\mathtt{a}^c$, which seems a good candidate for a weakly-*c*-balanced word with many distinct scattered factors.

Further, in Sect. 4, we explore more the cardinalities of $\mathrm{ScatFact}_k(w)$ for weakly-0-balanced words w of length $2k$. We obtain for these words that the smallest three numbers which are possible cardinalities for their *k*-spectra are $k+1$, $2k$, and $3k-3$, thus identifying two gaps in the set of such cardinalities. Among other results on this topic, we show that for every constant i there exist a word w of length $2k$ such that $|\mathrm{ScatFact}_k(w)| \in \Theta(n^i)$; we also show how such a word can be constructed.

Finally, in Sect. 5, we also approach the question of reconstructing weakly-0-balanced words from *k*-spectra in the specific case that the spectra are also limited to weakly-0-balanced words only. While we are not able to resolve the question completely, we conjecture that the situation is similar to the general case: the smallest value k such that the *k*-spectrum of w is uniquely determined is $k = \frac{|w|}{2} + 1$ if $\frac{|w|}{2}$ is odd and $k = \frac{|w|}{2} + 2$, otherwise, in the case when w contains at most two blocks of bs.

After introducing a series of basic definitions, preliminaries, and notations, the organisation of the paper follows the description above. The proofs can be found in [2].

2 Preliminaries

Let $\mathbb{N}$ be the set of natural numbers, $\mathbb{N}_0 = \mathbb{N} \cup \{0\}$, and let $\mathbb{N}_{\geq k}$ be all natural numbers greater than or equal to k. Let $[n]$ denote the set $\{1, \ldots, n\}$ and $[n]_0 = [n] \cup \{0\}$ for an $n \in \mathbb{N}$.

We consider words w over the alphabet $\Sigma = \{\mathtt{a}, \mathtt{b}\}$. Σ^* denotes the set of all finite words over Σ, also called binary words. Σ^{ω} the set of all infinite words over Σ, also called binary infinite words. The *empty word* is denoted by ε and Σ^+ is the free semigroup $\Sigma^* \backslash \{\varepsilon\}$. The length of a word w is denoted by $|w|$. Let $\Sigma^{\leq k} := \{w \in \Sigma^* \mid |w| \leq k\}$ and Σ^k be the set of all words of length exactly $k \in \mathbb{N}$. The number of occurrences of a letter $\mathtt{a} \in \Sigma$ in a word $w \in \Sigma^*$ is denoted by $|w|_{\mathtt{a}}$. The $\mathrm{i^{th}}$ letter of a word w is given by $w[i]$ for $i \in [|w|]$. For a given word $w \in \Sigma^n$ the *reversal* of w is defined by $w^R = w[n]w[n-1]\ldots w[2]w[1]$. The powers of $w \in \Sigma^*$ are defined recursively by $w^0 = \varepsilon$, $w^n = ww^{n-1}$ for $n \in \mathbb{N}$.

A word $w \in \Sigma^*$ is called *weakly-c-balanced* if $||w|_a - |w|_b| = c$ for $c \in \mathbb{N}_0$. Thus weakly-0-balanced words have the same number of as and bs. Let Σ^*_{wzb} be the set of all weakly-0-balanced words over Σ. For example, $\mathtt{abaa}$ is weakly-2-balanced, $\mathtt{aba}$ is weakly-1-balanced, while $\mathtt{abbaba}$ is weakly-0-balanced.

A word $u \in \Sigma^*$ is a *factor* of $w \in \Sigma^*$, if $w = xuy$ holds for some words $x, y \in \Sigma^*$. Moreover, u is a *prefix* of w if $x = \varepsilon$ holds and a *suffix* if $y = \varepsilon$ holds. The factor of w from the $\mathrm{i^{th}}$ to the $\mathrm{j^{th}}$ letter will be denoted by $w[i..j]$ for

$0 \leq i \leq j \leq |w|$. Given a letter $\mathsf{a} \in \Sigma$ and a word $w \in \Sigma^*$, a *block* of a is a factor $u = w[i..j]$ with $u = \mathsf{a}^{j-i}$, such that either $i = 1$ or $w[i-1] = \mathsf{b} \neq \mathsf{a}$ and either $j = |w|$ or $w[j+1] = \mathsf{b} \neq \mathsf{a}$. For example the word $\mathsf{abaaabaabb}$ has 3 a-blocks and 3 b-blocks. Scattered factors and k-spectra are defined as follows.

Definition 1. A word $u = a_1 \ldots a_n \in \Sigma^n$, for $n \in \mathbb{N}$, is a *scattered factor* of a word $w \in \Sigma^+$ if there exists $v_0, \ldots, v_n \in \Sigma^*$ with $w = v_0 a_1 v_1 \ldots v_{n-1} a_n v_n$. Let $\mathrm{ScatFact}(w)$ denote the set of w's scattered factors and consider additionally $\mathrm{ScatFact}_k(w)$ and $\mathrm{ScatFact}_{\leq k}(w)$ as the two subsets of $\mathrm{ScatFact}(w)$ which contain only the scattered factors of length $k \in \mathbb{N}$ or the ones up to length $k \in \mathbb{N}$.

The sets $\mathrm{ScatFact}_{\leq k}(w)$ and $\mathrm{ScatFact}_k(w)$ are also known as *full k-spectrum* and, respectively, *k-spectrum* of a word $w \in \Sigma^*$ (see [1,10,12]) and moreover, scattered factors are often called *subwords* or *scattered subwords*. Obviously the k-spectrum is empty for $k > |w|$ and contains exactly w's letters for $k = 1$ and only w for $k = |w|$. Considering the word $w = \mathsf{abba}$, the other spectra are given by $\mathrm{ScatFact}_2(w) = \{\mathsf{a}^2, \mathsf{b}^2, \mathsf{ab}, \mathsf{ba}\}$ and $\mathrm{ScatFact}_3(w) = \{\mathsf{ab}^2, \mathsf{aba}, \mathsf{b}^2\mathsf{a}\}$.

It is worth noting that if u is a scattered factor of w, and v is a scattered factor of u, then v is a scattered factor of w. Additionally, notice two important symmetries regarding k-spectra. For $w \in \Sigma^*$ and the *renaming morphism* $\bar{\cdot}$: $\Sigma \to \Sigma$ with $\bar{\mathsf{a}} = \mathsf{b}$ and $\bar{\mathsf{b}} = \mathsf{a}$ we have $\mathrm{ScatFact}(w^R) = \{u^R \mid u \in \mathrm{ScatFact}(w)\}$ and $\mathrm{ScatFact}(\overline{w}) = \{\overline{u} \mid u \in \mathrm{ScatFact}(w)\}$. Thus, from a structural point of view, it is sufficient to consider only one representative from the equivalence classes induced by the equivalence relation where w_1 is equivalent to w_2 whenever w_2 is obtained by a composition of reversals and renamings from w_1. Considering w.l.o.g. the order $\mathsf{a} < \mathsf{b}$ on Σ, we choose the lexicographically smallest word as representative from each class. As such, we will mostly analyse the k-spectra of words starting with a. We shall make use of this fact extensively in Sect. 4.

3   Cardinalities of k-Spectra of Weakly-c-Balanced Words

In the current section, we consider the combinatorial properties of k-spectra of weakly-c-balanced finite words. In particular, we are interested in the cardinalities of the k-spectra and in the question: which cardinalities are (not) possible? Since the k-spectra of a^n and b^n are just a^k and b^k respectively for all $n \in \mathbb{N}_0$ and $k \in [n]_0$, we assume $|w|_\mathsf{a}, |w|_\mathsf{b} > 0$ for $w \in \Sigma^*$. It is a straightforward observation that not every subset of Σ^k is a k-spectrum of some word w. For example, for $k = 2$, aa and bb can only be scattered factors of a word containing both as and bs, and therefore having either ab or ba as a scattered factor as well. Thus, there is no word w such that $\mathrm{ScatFact}_2(w) = \{\mathsf{aa}, \mathsf{bb}\}$.

In general, for any word containing only as or only bs, there will be exactly one scattered factor of each length, while for words containing both a's and b's, the smallest k-spectra are realised for words of the form $w = \mathsf{a}^n\mathsf{b}$ (up to renaming and reversal), for which $\mathrm{ScatFact}_k(w) = \{\mathsf{a}^k, \mathsf{a}^{k-1}\mathsf{b}\}$ for each $k \in [|w|]$. On the other hand, as Proposition 5 shows, the maximal k-spectra are those containing all words of length k – and hence have size 2^k, achieved by e.g. $w = (\mathsf{ab})^n$

for $n \geq k$. Note that when weakly-0-balanced words are considered, the same maximum applies, since $(\mathsf{ab})^n$ is weakly-0-balanced, while the minimum does not, since $\mathsf{a}^n\mathsf{b}$ is not weakly-0-balanced.

It is straightforward to enumerate all possible k-spectra, and describe the words realising them for $k \leq 2$, hence we shall generally consider only k-spectra in the sequel for which $k \geq 3$. Our first result generalises the previous observation about minimal-size k-spectra.

Theorem 2. *For* $k \in \mathbb{N}_{\geq 3}$, $c \in [k-1]_0$, $i \in [c]_0$, *and a weakly-c-balanced word* $w \in \Sigma^{2k-c}$, *we have* $|\operatorname{ScatFact}_{k-i}(w)| \geq k - c + 1$, *where equality holds if and only if* $w \in \{\mathsf{a}^k\mathsf{b}^{k-c}, \mathsf{a}^{k-c}\mathsf{b}^k, \mathsf{b}^k\mathsf{a}^{k-c}, \mathsf{b}^{k-c}\mathsf{a}^k\}$. *Moreover, if* $w \in \Sigma^{2k}_{wzb}\backslash\{\mathsf{a}^k\mathsf{b}^k\}$, *then* $|\operatorname{ScatFact}_k(w)| \geq k + 3$.

Remark 3. Theorem 2 answers immediately the question, whether a given set $S \subseteq \Sigma^k$, with $|S| < k+1$ or $|S| = k+2$, is a k-spectrum of a word $w \in \Sigma^{2k}_{wzb}$ in the negative.

Theorem 2 shows that the smallest cardinality of the k-spectrum of a word w is reached when the letters in w are *nicely ordered*, both for weakly-0-balanced words as well as for weakly-*c*-balanced words with $c > 0$. The largest cardinality is, not surprisingly, reached for words where the alternation of a and b letters is, in a sense, maximal, e.g., for $w = (\mathsf{ab})^k$. To this end, one can show a general result.

Theorem 4. *For* $w \in \Sigma^*$, *the k-spectrum of w is* Σ^k *if and only if*

$$\{\mathsf{ab}, \mathsf{ba}\}^k \cap \operatorname{ScatFact}_{2k}(w) \neq \emptyset.$$

The previous theorem has an immediate consequence, which exactly characterises the weakly-0-balanced words of length $2k$ for which the maximal cardinality of $\operatorname{ScatFact}_k(w)$ is reached.

Proposition 5. *For* $k \in \mathbb{N}_{\geq 3}$ *and* $w \in \Sigma^{2k}_{wzb}$ *we have* $w \in \{\mathsf{ab}, \mathsf{ba}\}^k$ *if and only if* $\operatorname{ScatFact}_k(w) = \Sigma^k$.

To see why from $w \in \{\mathsf{ab}, \mathsf{ba}\}^k$ it follows that $\operatorname{ScatFact}_k(w) = \Sigma^k$, note that, by definition, a word $w \in \{\mathsf{ab}, \mathsf{ba}\}^k$ is just a concatenation of k blocks from $\{\mathsf{ab}, \mathsf{ba}\}$. To construct the scattered factors of w, we can simply select from each block either the a or the b. The resulting output is a word of length k, where in each position we could choose freely the letter. Consequently, we can produce all words in Σ^k in this way. The other implication follows by induction.

Generalising Proposition 5 for weakly-*c*-balanced words requires a more sophisticated approach. A generalisation would be to consider $w \in \{\mathsf{ab}, \mathsf{ba}\}^{k-c}\mathsf{a}^c$. By Theorem 4 we have $\operatorname{ScatFact}_{k-c}(w) = \Sigma^{k-c}$. But the size of $\operatorname{ScatFact}_{k-i}(w)$ for $i \in [c]_0$ depends on the specific choice of w. To see why, consider the words $w_1 = \mathsf{baabba}$ and $w_2 = (\mathsf{ba})^3$. Then by Proposition 5, $|\operatorname{ScatFact}_3(w_1)| = 8 = |\operatorname{ScatFact}_3(w_2)|$. However, when we append an a to the end of both w_1 and w_2, we see that in fact $|\text{ScatFact}_4(w_1\text{a})| = 11 \neq 12 = |\text{ScatFact}_4(w_2\text{a})|$. The main difference between weakly-0-balanced and weakly-c-balanced words for $c > 0$, regarding the maximum cardinality of the scattered factors-sets, comes from the role played by the factors a^2 and b^2 occurring in w.

In the remaining part of this section we present a series of results for weakly-c-balanced words. Intuitively, the words with many alternations between a and b have more distinct scattered factors. So, we will focus on such words mainly. Our first result is a direct consequence from Theorem 4. The second result concerns words avoiding a^2 and b^2 gives a method to identify efficiently the ℓ-spectra of words which are prefixes of $(\text{ab})^\omega$, for all ℓ. Finally, we are able to derive a way to efficiently enumerate (and count) the scattered factors of length k of $(\text{ab})^{k-c}\text{a}^c$.

Corollary 6. *For $k \in \mathbb{N}_{\geq 3}$, $c \in [k]_0$, and $w \in \Sigma^{2k-c}$ weakly-c-balanced, the cardinality of $\text{ScatFact}_{k-c}(w)$ is exactly 2^{k-c} if and only if $\text{ScatFact}_{2(k-c)}(w) \cap \{\text{ab}, \text{ba}\}^{k-c} \neq \emptyset$.*

As announced, we further focus our investigation on the words $w = (\text{ab})^{k-c}\text{a}^c$. By Theorem 4 we have $|\text{ScatFact}_i(w)| = \Sigma^i$ for all $i \in [k - c]_0$. For all i with $k - c < i \leq k$, a more sophisticated counting argument is needed. Intuitively, a scattered factor of length i of $(\text{ab})^{k-c}\text{a}^c$ consists of a part that is a scattered factor (of arbitrary length) of $(\text{ab})^{k-c}$ followed by a (possibly empty) suffix of as. Thus, a full description of the ℓ-spectra of words that occur as prefixes of $(\text{ab})^\omega$, for all appropriate ℓ, is useful. To this end, we introduce the notion of a deleting sequence: for a word w and a scattered factor u of w the deleting sequence contains (in a strictly increasing order) w's positions that have to be deleted to obtain u.

Definition 7. *For $w \in \Sigma^*$, $\sigma = (s_1, \ldots, s_\ell) \in [|w|]^\ell$, with $\ell \leq |w|$ and $s_i < s_{i+1}$ for all $i \in [\ell - 1]$, is a deleting sequence. The scattered factor u_σ associated to a deleting sequence σ is $u_\sigma = u_1 \ldots u_{\ell+1}$, where $u_1 = w[1..s_1 - 1]$, $u_{\ell+1} = w[s_\ell + 1..|w|]$, and $u_i = w[s_{i-1} + 1..s_i - 1]$ for $2 \leq i \leq \ell$. Two sequences σ, σ' with $u_\sigma = u_{\sigma'}$ are called equivalent.*

For the word $w = \text{abbaa}$ and $\sigma = (1, 3, 4)$ the associated scattered factor is $u_\sigma = \text{ba}$. Since ba can also be generated by $(1, 3, 5)$, $(1, 2, 4)$ and $(1, 2, 5)$, these sequences are equivalent.

In order to determine the ℓ-spectrum of a word $w \in \Sigma^n$ for $\ell, n \in \mathbb{N}$, we can determine how many equivalence classes does the equivalence defined above have, for sequences of length $k = n - \ell$. The following three lemmas characterise the equivalence of deleting sequences.

Lemma 8. *Let $w \in \Sigma^n$ be a prefix of $(\text{ab})^\omega$. Let $\sigma = (s_1, \ldots, s_k)$ be a deleting sequence for w such that there exists $j \geq 2$ with $s_{j-1} < s_j - 1$ and $s_j + 1 = s_{j+1}$. Then σ is equivalent $\sigma' = (s_1, \ldots, s_{j-1}, s_j - 1, s_{j+1} - 1, s_{j+2}, \ldots s_k)$, i.e., σ' is the sequence σ where both s_j and s_{j+1} were decreased by 1.*

Lemma 9. *Let $w \in \Sigma^n$ be a prefix of $(\text{ab})^\omega$. Let $\sigma = (s_1, \ldots, s_k)$ be a deleting sequence for w. Then there exists an integer $j \geq 0$ such that σ is equivalent to the* *deleting sequence* $(1, 2, \ldots, j, s'_{j+1}, \ldots, s'_k)$, *where* $s'_{j+1} > j+1$ *and* $s'_i > s'_{i-1}+1$, *for all* $j < i \leq k$. *Moreover,* $j \geq 1$ *if and only if* σ *contained two consecutive positions or* σ *started with* 1.

Lemma 10. *Let* $w \in \Sigma^n$ *be a prefix of* $(ab)^\omega$. *Let* $\sigma_1 = (1, 2, \ldots, j_1, s'_{j_1+1}, \ldots, s'_k)$, *where* $s'_{j_1+1} > j_1 + 1$ *and* $s'_i > s'_{i-1} + 1$, *for all* $j_1 < i \leq k$, *and* $\sigma_2 = (1, 2, \ldots, j_2, s''_{j_2+1}, \ldots, s''_k)$, *where* $s''_{j_2+1} > j_2 + 1$ *and* $s''_i > s''_{i-1} + 1$, *for all* $j_2 < i \leq k$. *If* $\sigma_1 \neq \sigma_2$ *then* σ_1 *and* σ_2 *are not equivalent (i.e.,* $u_{\sigma_1} \neq u_{\sigma_2}$).

Lemmas 8, 9, and 10 show that the representatives of the equivalence classes w.r.t. the equivalence relation between deleting sequences, introduced in Definition 7, are the sequences $(1, 2, \ldots, j, s'_{j+1}, \ldots, s'_k)$, where $s'_{j+1} > j + 1$ and $s'_i > s'_{i-1} + 1$, for all $j < i \leq k$. For a fixed $j \geq 1$, the number of such sequences is $\binom{(n-j-1)-(k-j)+1}{k-j} = \binom{n-k}{k-j}$. For $j = 0$, we have $\binom{(n-1)-k+1}{k} = \binom{n-k}{k}$ nonequivalent sequences (note that none starts with 1, as those were counted for $j = 1$ already). In total, we have, for a word w of length n, which is a prefix of $(ab)^\omega$, exactly $\sum_{j \in [k]_0} \binom{n-k}{k-j}$ nonequivalent deleting sequences of length k, so $\sum_{j \in [k]_0} \binom{n-k}{k-j}$ different scattered factors of length $n - k$. In the above formula, we assume that $\binom{a}{b} = 0$ when $a < b$.

Moreover, the distinct scattered factors of length $\ell = n - k$ of w can be obtained efficiently as follows. For j from 0 to ℓ, delete the first j letters of w. For all choices of $\ell - j$ positions in $w[j + 1..n]$, such that each two of these positions are not consecutive, delete the letters on the respective positions. The resulted word is a member of ScatFact$_\ell(w)$, and we never obtain the same word twice by this procedure. The next theorem follows from the above.

Theorem 11. *Let* w *be a word of length* n *which is a prefix of* $(ab)^\omega$. *Then* $|\text{ScatFact}_\ell(w)| = \sum_{j \in [n-\ell]_0} \binom{\ell}{n-\ell-j}$.

A straightforward consequence of the above theorem is that, if $\ell \leq n - \ell$ then $|\text{ScatFact}_\ell(w)| = 2^\ell$. With Theorem 11, we can now completely characterise the cardinality of the ℓ-spectra of the weakly-*c*-balanced word $(ab)^{k-c}a^c$ for $\ell \leq k$.

Theorem 12. *Let* $w = (ab)^{k-c}a^c$ *for* $k \in \mathbb{N}$, $c \in [k]_0$. *Then, for* $i \leq k - c$ *we have* $|\text{ScatFact}_i(w)| = 2^i$. *For* $k \geq i > k - c$ *we have* $|\text{ScatFact}_i(w)| = 1 + 2^{k-c} + \sum_{j \in [(i+c)-k-1]_0} |\text{ScatFact}_{i-j-1}((ab)^{k-c-1}a)|$.

As in the case of the scattered factors of prefixes of $(ab)^\omega$, we have a precise and efficient way to generate the scattered factors of $w = (ab)^{k-c}a^c$. For scattered factors of length $i \leq k-c$ of w, we just generate all possible words of length i. For greater i, on top of a^i, we generate separately the scattered factors of the form uba^j, for each $j \in [i-1]_0$. It is clear that, in such a word, $|u| = i - j - 1$, and if $j \geq c$ then u must be a scattered factor of $(ab)^{k-j-1}a$, while if $j < c$ then u must be a scattered factor of $(ab)^{k-c-1}a$. If $j \geq (i + c) - k$ then, by Theorem 11, u can take all 2^{i-j-1} possible values. For smaller values of j, we need to generate u of length $i - j - 1$ as a scattered factor of $(ab)^{k-c-1}a$, by the method described after Proposition 5.

Nevertheless, Theorems 11 and 12 are useful to see that in order to determine the cardinality of the sets of scattered factors of words consisting of alternating as and bs or, respectively, of $(ab)^{k-c}a^c$, it is not needed to generate these sets effectively.

4   Cardinalities of k-Spectra of Weakly-0-Balanced Words

In the last section a characterisation for the smallest and the largest k-spectra of words of a given length are presented (Theorem 2 and Proposition 5). In this section the part in between will be investigated for weakly-0-balanced words (i.e. words of length $2k$ with k occurrences of each letter). As before, we shall assume that $k \in \mathbb{N}_{\geq 3}$. In the particular case that $k = 3$, we have already proven that the k-spectrum with minimal cardinality has 4 elements and that the maximal cardinality is 8. Moreover as mentioned in Remark 3 a k-spectrum of cardinality 5 does not exist for weakly-0-balanced words of length $2k$. The question remains if k-spectra of cardinalities 6 and 7 exist, and if so, for which words.

Before showing that a k-spectrum of cardinality $2^k - 1$ for weakly-0-balanced words of length $2k$ also exists for all $k \in \mathbb{N}_{\geq 3}$, we prove that only scattered factors of the form $b^{i+1}a^{k-i-1}$ for $i \in [k-2]_0$ (up to renaming, reversal) can be "taken out" from the full set of possible scattered factors independently, without additionally requiring the removal of additional scattered factors as well. In particular, if a word of length k of another form is absent from the set of scattered factors of w, then $|\operatorname{ScatFact}_k(w)| < 2^k - 1$ follows.

Lemma 13. *If for $w \in \Sigma_{wzb}^{2k}$ there exists $u \notin \operatorname{ScatFact}_k(w)$ with $u \notin \{b^i a^{k-i} \mid i \in [k-1]\} \cup \{a^i b^{k-i} \mid i \in [k-1]\}$, then $|\operatorname{ScatFact}_k(w)| < 2^k - 1$.*

Proposition 14. *For $k \in \mathbb{N}_{\geq 3}$ and $w \in \Sigma_{wzb}^{2k}$, the set $\operatorname{ScatFact}_k(w)$ has $2^k - 1$ elements if and only if $w \in \{(ab)^i a^2 b^2 (ab)^{k-i-2} \mid i \in [k-2]_0\}$ (up to renaming and reversal). In particular $\operatorname{ScatFact}_k(w) = \Sigma^k \setminus \{b^{i+1}a^{k-i-1}\}$ holds for $w = (ab)^i a^2 b^2 (ab)^{k-i-2}$ with $i \in [k-2]_0$.*

By Proposition 14 we get that 7 is a possible cardinality of the set of scattered factors of length 3 of weakly-0-balanced words of length 6 and, moreover, that exactly the words $a^2 b^2 ab$ and $aba^2 b^2$ (and symmetric words obtained by reversal and renaming) have seven different scattered factors. The following theorem demonstrates that there always exists a weakly-0-balanced word w of length $2k$ such that $|\operatorname{ScatFact}_k(w)| = 2k$. Thus, for the case $k = 3$ also the question if six is a possible cardinality of $\operatorname{ScatFact}_3(w)$ can be answered positively.

Theorem 15. *The k-spectrum of a word $w \in \Sigma_{wzb}^{2k}$ has exactly $2k$ elements if and only if $w \in \{a^{k-1}bab^{k-1}, a^{k-1}b^k a\}$ holds (up to renaming and reversal). Moreover, there does not exist a weakly-0-balanced word $w \in \Sigma_{wzb}^{2k}$ with a k-spectrum of cardinality $2k - i$ for $i \in [k-2]$.*

By Proposition 14 and Theorem 15 the possible cardinalities of $\mathrm{ScatFact}_3(w)$ for weakly-0-balanced words w of length 6 are completely characterized. Theorem 15 determines the first gap in the set of cardinalities of $|\mathrm{ScatFact}_k(w)|$ for $w \in \Sigma_{wzb}^{2k}$: there does not exist a word $w \in \Sigma_{wzb}^{2k}$ with $|\mathrm{ScatFact}_k(w)| = k+i+1$ for $i \in [k-2]$ and $k \geq 3$, since all words that are not of the form $\mathsf{a}^k\mathsf{b}^k$, $\mathsf{b}^k\mathsf{a}^k$, $\mathsf{a}^{k-1}\mathsf{bab}^{k-1}$, or $\mathsf{a}^{k-1}\mathsf{b}^k\mathsf{a}$ have a scattered factor set of cardinality at least $2k+1$. As the size of this first gap is linear in k, it is clear that the larger k is, the more unlikely it is to find a k-spectrum of a small cardinality.

In the following we will prove that the cardinalities $2k+1$ up to $3k-4$ are not reachable, i.e. $3k-3$ is the thirst smallest cardinality after $k+1$ and $2k$ (witnessed by, e.g. $\mathsf{a}^{k-2}\mathsf{b}^k\mathsf{a}^2$).

Lemma 16. *For $i \in \left[\lfloor\frac{k}{2}\rfloor\right]$ and $j \in [k-1]$*

- $|\mathrm{ScatFact}_k(\mathsf{a}^{k-i}\mathsf{b}^k\mathsf{a}^i)| = k(i+1) - i^2 + 1$ *for $k \geq 4$,*
- $|\mathrm{ScatFact}_k(\mathsf{a}^{k-1}\mathsf{b}^2\mathsf{ab}^{k-2})| = 3k - 2$,
- $|\mathrm{ScatFact}_k(\mathsf{a}^{k-2}\mathsf{b}^j\mathsf{ab}^{k-j}\mathsf{a})| = k(2j+2) - 6j + 2$ *for $k \geq 5$, and*
- $|\mathrm{ScatFact}_k(\mathsf{a}^{k-2}\mathsf{b}^j\mathsf{a}^2\mathsf{b}^{k-j})| = k(2j+1) - 4j + 2$.

Notice that for $i \in \left[\lfloor\frac{k}{2}\rfloor\right]$ the sequence $(k(2i+1)-4i+2)_i$ is increasing and its minimum is $3k-2$ while for $i \in \left[\lfloor\frac{k}{2}\rfloor\right]$ the sequence $(k(2i+2)-6i+2)_i$ is increasing and its minimum is $4k-4$. The following lemma only gives lower bounds for specific forms of words, since, on the one hand, it proves to be sufficient for the Theorem 18 which describes the second gap, and, on the other hand, the proofs show that the formulas describing the exact number of scattered factors of a specific form are getting more and more complicated. It has to be shown that also words starting with i letters a, for $i \in [k-3]$, have a k-spectrum of greater (as lower is already excluded) cardinality. By Lemma 16 only words with another transition from a's to b's need to be considered, $(w = \mathsf{a}^{r_1}\mathsf{b}^{s_1}w_1\mathsf{a}^{r_1}\mathsf{b}^{s_2})$. W.l.o.g. we can assume s_1 to be maximal, such that w_1 starts with an a, and similarly, by maximality of r_2, ends with a b, thus only words of the form $\mathsf{a}^{r_1}\mathsf{b}^{s_1}\ldots\mathsf{a}^{r_n}\mathsf{b}^{s_n}$ have to be considered, and by Proposition 5, it is sufficient to investigate $n < k$.

Lemma 17.
- $|\mathrm{ScatFact}_k(\mathsf{a}^{k-2}\mathsf{b}^i\mathsf{ab}^j\mathsf{ab}^{k-i-j})| \geq 3k-3$ *for $i,j \in [k-2]$, $i+j \leq k-1$,*
- $|\mathrm{ScatFact}_k(\mathsf{a}^{k-2}\mathsf{b}^{s_1}\mathsf{a}^{r_1}\mathsf{b}^{s_2}\mathsf{a}^{r_2}\mathsf{b}^{s_3})| \geq 3k-4$ *for $s_1+s_2+s_3 = k$, $r_1+r_2 = 2, s_1 > 0$, $r_1, r_2, s_2, s_3 \geq 0$,*
- $|\mathrm{ScatFact}_k(\mathsf{a}^{r_1}\mathsf{b}^{s_1}\ldots\mathsf{a}^{r_n}\mathsf{b}^{s_n})| \geq 3k-3$ *for $r_1 \leq k-3$, $\sum_{i\in[n]} r_i = \sum_{i\in[n]} s_i = k$, and $r_i, s_i \geq 1$.*

By Lemmas 16 and 17 we are able to prove the following theorem, which shows the second gap in the set of cardinalities of $\mathrm{ScatFact}_k$ for words in Σ_{wzb}^{2k}.

Theorem 18. *For $k \geq 5$ there does not exist a word $w \in \Sigma_{wzb}^{2k}$ with k-spectrum of cardinality $2k+i$ for $i \in [k-4]$. In other words, i.e. between $2k+1$ and $3k-4$ is a cardinality-gap.*

Going further, we analyse the larger possible cardinalities of $\mathrm{ScatFact}_k$, trying to see what values are achievable (even if only asymptotically, in some cases).

Corollary 19. *All square numbers, greater or equal to four, occur as the cardinality of the k-spectrum of a word $w \in \Sigma_{wzb}^{2k}$; in particular $|\mathrm{ScatFact}_k(a^{\frac{k}{2}}b^k a^{\frac{k}{2}})| = \left(\frac{k}{2}+1\right)^2$ holds for k even.*

Inspired by the previous Corollary, we can show the following result concerning the asymptotic behaviour of the cardinality of $\mathrm{ScatFact}_k$ for words of length $2k$.

Proposition 20. *Let $i > 1$ be a fixed (constant) integer. Let $d = \lfloor \frac{k}{i} \rfloor$ and $r = k - di$, and $d' = \lfloor \frac{k}{i-1} \rfloor$ and $r' = k - d'(i-1)$. Then the following hold:*

- *the word $a^r b^r (a^d b^d)^i$ has $\Theta(k^{2i-1})$ scattered factors of length n;*
- *the word $a^r b^{r'} (a^d b^{d'})^{i-1} a^d$ has $\Theta(k^{2i-2})$ scattered factors of length n.*

Remark 21. Let i be an integer, and consider k another integer divisible by i. Consider the word $w_k = (a^{\frac{k}{i}} b^{\frac{k}{i}})^i$. The exact number of scattered factors of length k of w_k equals to the number $C\left(k, 2i, \frac{k}{i}\right)$ of weak $2i$-compositions of k, whose terms are bounded by $\frac{k}{i}$, i.e., the number of ways in which k can be written as a sum $\sum_{j \in [2i]} r_j$ where $r_j \in \left[\frac{k}{i}\right]_0$. From Proposition 20 we also get that this number is $\Theta(n^{2k-1})$, but we also have:

$$C\left(k, 2i, \frac{k}{i}\right) = \sum_{0 \le j < M} (-1)^j \binom{2i}{j} \binom{k + 2i - j(\frac{k}{i}+1) - 1}{2i - 1},$$

for $M = \frac{i(k+2i-1)}{k+i}$. It is known that there exists a constant $E > 0$ such that

$$C\left(k, 2i, \frac{k}{i}\right) \le E \cdot \sum_{0 \le j < M} (-1)^j \binom{2i}{j} \left(k + 2i - j\left(\frac{k}{i}+1\right) - 1\right)^{2i-1}.$$

The coefficient of k^{2i-1} in the right hand side of this inequality has to be positive. Consequently $\sum_{0 \le j < M} (-1)^j \binom{2i}{j}(i-j)^{2i-1} > 0$. This seems to be an interesting combinatorial inequality in itself.

One can also show as in Proposition 20 that the number of scattered factors of length k of w_k, which have, at their turn, $(ab)^i$ as a scattered factor, is $\Theta(k^{2i-1})$. This number also equals the number $C'\left(k, 2i, \frac{k}{i}\right)$ of $2i$-compositions of k whose terms are strictly positive integers upper bounded by $\frac{k}{i}$, i.e., the number of ways in which k can be written as a sum $\sum_{j \in [2i]} r_j$ where $r_j \in \left[\frac{k}{i}\right]$. Just as above, from this we get $\sum_{0 \le j < i} (-1)^j \binom{2i}{j}(i-j)^{2i-1} > 0$. Again, this inequality seems interesting to us.

We will end this analysis with the conjecture that, in contrast to the first gap, which always starts immediately after the first obtainable cardinality, the last gap ends earlier the larger k is. More precisely, if $w = a^2 b^2 (ab)^{k-3-i} ba(ab)^i$ for $k \in \mathbb{N}_{\ge 4}$, $i \in [k-2]_0$ then $|\mathrm{ScatFact}_k(w)| = 2^k - 2 - i$.

At the end of this section, we will briefly introduce θ-palindromes in this specific setting. Let $\theta : \Sigma^* \to \Sigma^*$ be an antimorphic involution, i.e. $\theta(uv) = \theta(v)\theta(u)$ and θ^2 is the identity on Σ^*. By $\Sigma = \{a, b\}$ only the identity and renaming are such mappings. The fixed points of θ are called θ-palindromes $(ab^3.\theta(b)^3\theta(a))$ and exactly the words where $w^R = \overline{w}$ holds. They were studied in different fields well (see e.g., [5,8]). A word $w \in \Sigma_{wzb}^{2k}$ is a θ-palindrome iff either $w \in \{aw'b, bw'a\}$ for some θ-palindrome $w' \in \Sigma_{wzb}^{2(k-1)}$ or additionally $w = a^{\frac{k}{2}}b^k a^{\frac{k}{2}}$ in the case that k is even. Two cardinality results for θ-palindromes are presented in Lemma 16 and Corollary 19. We believe that persuing the k-spectra of θ-palindromes may lead to a deeper insight of which cardinalities can be reached, but due to space restrictions we will only mention one conjecture here, which may already show that cardinalities are somehow propagating for θ-palindromes. Notice that this conjecture implies that indeed similar to the second gap here $4k - 4$ is always reached but that in contrast to the second gap, the third gap is not of the form $4k - 4 - i$ for $i \in [k - 4]$.

Conjecture 22. The k-spectrum of $w = ab^{k-1}a^{k-1}b$ has $4(k - 1)$ elements and moreover if $w' = w^R$ with a k-spectrum of cardinality $\ell \in \mathbb{N}_{\geq 12}$ then the scattered factor set of awb has cardinality $2\frac{1}{4}\ell - 5$.

5 Reconstructing Weakly-0-Balanced Words from Their k-Spectra

In the final section we consider the slightly different problem of reconstructing a word from its scattered factors, or more specifically in this case, k-spectra. More generally, we are interested in how much information about a (weakly-0-balanced) word w is contained in its scattered factors, and more precisely, which scattered factors are not necessary or useful for reconstructing the word w, or distinguishing it from others. Since w is a scattered factor of itself, it is trivial that the scattered factor of length $|w|$ is sufficient to uniquely reconstruct w. On the other hand, all words over $\{a, b\}^*$ containing both letters will have the same 1-spectrum. Thus we see that the length of the scattered factors of a word w plays a role in how much information about w they contain. This relationship is described more precisely by the following result of Dress and Erdös [3] along with the fact that (cf. e.g. Proposition 5) a word of length $2k$ is not uniquely determined by its scattered factors of length k.

Proposition 23 (Dress and Erdös [3]). *If* $\mathrm{ScatFact}_{k+1}(w) = \mathrm{ScatFact}_{k+1}(w')$ *holds for* $w, w' \in \Sigma^{\leq 2k}$ *then* $w = w'$ *follows.*

In the proof of Proposition 23, a pivotal role is played by scattered factors which contain many as and a few bs or vice-versa. The question arises as to whether this is due to the fact that these scattered factors contain inherently more information about the structure of the whole word than e.g., weakly-0-balanced ones. In the general case, the answer is, sometimes at least, yes: we cannot distinguish between e.g. two words in $\{a\}^*$ by their weakly-0-balanced scattered factors, as the only such factor is ε. The same problem arises for all words which have a sufficiently uneven ratio of as to bs.

However, if in addition we consider only weakly-0-balanced words, then the situation changes. We conjecture that in fact, for these words w, the weakly-0-balanced scattered factors are just as informative about the w as the unbalanced ones. More formally, we believe the following adaptation of Proposition 23 holds:

Conjecture 24. Let $k \in \mathbb{N}$. Let $k' = k+1$ for odd k, and $k' = k+2$ for even k. Let $w, w' \in \Sigma_{wzb}^{2k}$ such that $\mathrm{ScatFact}_{k'}(w) \cap \Sigma_{wzb}^{k'} = \mathrm{ScatFact}_{k'}(w') \cap \Sigma_{wzb}^{k'}$. Then $w = w'$.

While we do not resolve the conjecture, we give an example of a subclass of words for which it holds true, namely when there are at most two blocks of bs (and therefore by symmetry if there are at most two blocks of as).

Proposition 25. *Let $k \in \mathbb{N}$. If k is odd, then each word $w \in a^*b^*a^*b^*a^* \cap \Sigma_{wzb}^{2k}$ is uniquely determined by the set $\mathrm{ScatFact}_{k+1}(w) \cap \Sigma_{wzb}^{k+1}$. Similarly, if k is even, then each word $w \in a^*b^*a^*b^*a^* \cap \Sigma_{wzb}^{2k}$ is uniquely determined by the set $\mathrm{ScatFact}_{k+2}(w) \cap \Sigma_{wzb}^{k+2}$.*

The difficulty in proving Conjecture 24 seems to arise from the fact that, for different pairs of words $w, w' \in \Sigma_{wzb}$, the set of scattered factors which distinguish them, namely the symmetric difference of $\mathrm{ScatFact}_k(w) \cap \Sigma_{wzb}^k$ and $\mathrm{ScatFact}_k(w') \cap \Sigma_{wzb}^k$ (for appropriate k), varies considerably, unlike with the proof(s) of Proposition 23, where the set of distinguishing scattered factors is always made up words of the same form, regardless of the choice of w and w'. As an example, consider the words $w = ababab$, $w' = bababa$, and $w'' = ababba$. Then the symmetric difference of $\mathrm{ScatFact}_4(w) \cap \Sigma_{wzb}^4$ and $\mathrm{ScatFact}_4(w') \cap \Sigma_{wzb}^4$ is $\{aabb, bbaa\}$. On the other hand, considering $\mathrm{ScatFact}_4(w') \cap \Sigma_{wzb}^4$ and $\mathrm{ScatFact}_4(w'') \cap \Sigma_{wzb}^4$, the symmetric difference is $\{baab\}$.

6   Conclusions

We have considered properties of k-spectra of weakly-0-balanced words. In particular, in Sect. 3 we give several insights into the structure of the set of all k-spectra of weakly-0-balanced words of length $2k$ by considering for which numbers n there exists w such that the k-spectrum of w has cardinality n. In particular, we characterise the first two gaps in the possibilities for each k which are regular (in the sense that the first and second gaps are always from $k + 2$ to $2k - 1$ and $2k + 1$ to $3k - 4$ (inclusive). On the other hand, we see that the third gap is considerably less regular and thus resists a natural characterisation.

In Sect. 4, we consider the task of reconstructing weakly-0-balanced words from their k-spectra. We note that this is, in a sense, as hard as in the general case, however, we also conjecture that even if we consider only the scattered factors which are also weakly-0-balanced, then the situation remains the same, in the sense that it can be achieved for the same choices of k. Resolving this conjecture appears to require some new approach however since the techniques for the general case are not easily adapted.

As mentioned at the end of Sect. 3 some of the weakly-0-balanced words are θ-palindromes. Since the θ-palindromes of length $2k$ are constructible from the ones of length $2(k-1)$ (except for each even k exactly one θ-palindrome) we surmised that the structure and properties propagate. Moreover we expected that the knowledge of the word's second half helps in finding the cardinalities of the k-spectra. Nevertheless we were only able to get results for θ-palindromes in the same manner as for the other words, but we still believe that the structure of the θ-palindromes can reveal more insights with further work.

References

1. Berstel, J., Karhumäki, J.: Combinatorics on words - a tutorial. BEATCS: Bull. Eur. Assoc. Theor. Comput. Sci. **79** (2003)
2. Day, J.D., Fleischmann, P., Manea, F., Nowotka, D.: *k*-spectra of weakly-*c*-balanced words (2019). https://arxiv.org/abs/1904.09125
3. Dress, A.W.M., Erdös, P.: Reconstructing words from subwords in linear time. Ann. Comb. **8**(4), 457–462 (2004)
4. Elzinga, C.H., Rahmann, S., Wang, H.: Algorithms for subsequence combinatorics. Theor. Comput. Sci. **409**(3), 394–404 (2008)
5. Fazekas, S.Z., Manea, F., Mercas, R., Shikishima-Tsuji, K.: The pseudopalindromic completion of regular languages. Inf. Comput. **239**, 222–236 (2014)
6. Halfon, S., Schnoebelen, P., Zetzsche, G.: Decidability, complexity, and expressiveness of first-order logic over the subword ordering. In: Proceedings of LICS 2017, pp. 1–12 (2017)
7. Holub, Š., Saari, K.: On highly palindromic words. Discrete Appl. Math. **157**, 953–959 (2009)
8. Kari, L., Mahalingam, K.: Watson-Crick palindromes in DNA computing. Nat. Comput. **9**(2), 297–316 (2010)
9. Lothaire, M.: Combinatorics on Words. Cambridge University Press, Cambridge (1997)
10. Manuch, J.: Characterization of a word by its subwords. In: Developments in Language Theory, pp. 210–219. World Scientific (1999)
11. Mateescu, A., Salomaa, A., Yu, S.: Subword histories and Parikh matrices. J. Comput. Syst. Sci. **68**(1), 1–21 (2004)
12. Rozenberg, G., Salomaa, A. (eds.): Handbook of Formal Languages (3 volumes). Springer, Heidelberg (1997). https://doi.org/10.1007/978-3-642-59126-6
13. Salomaa, A.: Connections between subwords and certain matrix mappings. Theor. Comput. Sci. **340**(2), 188–203 (2005)
14. Zetzsche, G.: The complexity of downward closure comparisons. In: Proceedings of the ICALP 2016. LIPIcs, vol. 55, pp. 123:1–123:14 (2016)

Computing the k-binomial Complexity
of the Thue–Morse Word

Marie Lejeune$^{(\boxtimes)}$ (iD), Julien Leroy, and Michel Rigo (iD)

Department of Mathematics, University of Liège,
Allée de la Découverte 12 (B37), 4000 Liège, Belgium
{M.Lejeune,J.Leroy,M.Rigo}@uliege.be

Abstract. Two finite words are k-binomially equivalent whenever they share the same subwords, i.e., subsequences, of length at most k with the same multiplicities. This is a refinement of both abelian equivalence and the Simon congruence. The k-binomial complexity of an infinite word $\mathbf{x}$ maps the integer n to the number of classes in the quotient, by this k-binomial equivalence relation, of the set of factors of length n occurring in $\mathbf{x}$. This complexity measure has not been investigated very much. In this paper, we characterize the k-binomial complexity of the Thue–Morse word. The result is striking, compared to more familiar complexity functions. Although the Thue–Morse word is aperiodic, its k-binomial complexity eventually takes only two values. In this paper, we first express the number of occurrences of subwords appearing in iterates of the form $\Psi^\ell(w)$ for an arbitrary morphism Ψ. We also thoroughly describe the factors of the Thue–Morse word by introducing a relevant new equivalence relation.

1 Introduction

The Thue–Morse word $\mathbf{t} = 011010011001\cdots$ is ubiquitous in combinatorics on words [1,20,27]. It is an archetypal example of a 2-automatic sequence: it is the fixed point of the morphism $0 \mapsto 01$, $1 \mapsto 10$. See, for instance, [2]. Its most prominent property is that it avoids overlaps, i.e., it does not contain any factor of the form $auaua$ where u is a word and a a symbol. Consequently it also avoids cubes, i.e., words of the form uuu, and is aperiodic.

Various measures of complexity of infinite words have been considered in the literature. The most usual one is the *factor complexity* that one can, for instance, relate to the topological entropy of a symbolic dynamical system. The factor complexity of an infinite word $\mathbf{x}$ simply counts the number $p_{\mathbf{x}}(n) = \# \operatorname{Fac}_n(\mathbf{x})$ of factors of length n occurring in $\mathbf{x}$. One can also consider other measures such as abelian complexity or k-abelian complexity [10]. For instance, in the sixties, Erdős raised the question whether abelian squares can be avoided by an infinite word over an alphabet of size 4. In an attempt to generalize Parikh's theorem on context-free languages, k-abelian complexity counts the number of

The first author is supported by a FNRS fellowship.

P. Hofman and M. Skrzypczak (Eds.): DLT 2019, LNCS 11647, pp. 278–291, 2019.
https://doi.org/10.1007/978-3-030-24886-4_21

equivalence classes partitioning the set of factors of length n for the so-called k-abelian equivalence. Two finite words u and v are k-*abelian equivalent* if $|u|_x = |v|_x$, for all words x of length at most k, and where $|u|_x$ denotes the number of occurrences of x as a factor of u.

The celebrated theorem of Morse–Hedlund characterizes ultimately periodic words in terms of a bounded factor complexity function; for a reference, see [2,16] or [4, Sect. 4.3]. Hence, aperiodic words with the lowest factor complexity are exactly the Sturmian words characterized by $p_x(n) = n + 1$. It is also a well-known result of Cobham that a k-automatic sequence has factor complexity in $\mathcal{O}(n)$. The factor complexity of the Thue–Morse word is in $\Theta(n)$ and is recalled in Proposition 6.

For many complexity measures, Sturmian words have the lowest complexity among aperiodic words, and variations of the Morse–Hedlund theorem notably exist for k-abelian complexity [11].

Binomial coefficients of words have been extensively studied [15]: $\binom{u}{x}$ denotes the number of occurrences of x as a subword, i.e., a subsequence, of u. They have been successfully used in several applications: p-adic topology [3], non-commutative extension of Mahler's theorem on interpolation series [19], formal language theory [9], Parikh matrices, and a generalization of Sierpiński's triangle [14].

Binomial complexity of infinite words has been recently investigated [21,23]. The definition is parallel to that of k-abelian complexity. Two finite words u and v are k-*binomially equivalent* if $\binom{u}{x} = \binom{v}{x}$, for all words x of length at most k. This relation is a refinement of abelian equivalence and Simon's congruence. We thus take the quotient of the set of factors of length n by this new equivalence relation. For all $k \geq 2$, Sturmian words have k-binomial complexity that is the same as their factor complexity. However, the Thue–Morse word has bounded k-binomial complexity [23]. So we have a striking difference with the usual complexity measures. This phenomenon therefore has to be closely investigated. In this paper, we compute the exact value of the k-binomial complexity $b_{\mathbf{t},k}(n)$ of the Thue–Morse word $\mathbf{t}$. To achieve this goal, we first obtain general results computing the number of occurrences of a subword in the (iterated) image by a morphism. This discussion is not restricted to the Thue–Morse morphism.

This paper is organized as follows. In Sect. 2, we recall basic results about binomial coefficients, binomial equivalence and the Thue–Morse word. In Sect. 3, we give an expression to compute the coefficient $\binom{\Psi(w)}{u}$ for an arbitrary morphism Ψ in terms of binomial coefficients for the preimage w. To that end, we study factorizations of u of the form $u = x\Psi(u')y$.

In the second part of this paper, we specifically study the k-binomial complexity of the Thue–Morse word. For $k = 1$, the abelian complexity of $\mathbf{t}$ is well known and takes only the values 2 and 3. The case $k = 2$ is treated in Sect. 4. In the last three sections, we consider the general case $k \geq 3$. The precise statement of our main result is given in Theorem 5. The principal tool to get our result is a new equivalence relation discussed in Sect. 6. This relation is based on particular factorizations of factors occurring in the Thue–Morse word.

Due to space limitations for this 12-page version, we have omitted most of the technical difficulties but tried to convey the main ideas and concepts. The reader can find a comprehensive presentation in [13].

2   Basics

Let $A = \{0,1\}$. Let $\varphi : A^* \to A^*$ be the classical Thue–Morse morphism defined by $\varphi(0) = 01$ and $\varphi(1) = 10$. The *complement* of a word $u \in A^*$ is the image of u under the involutive morphism mapping 0 to 1 and 1 to 0. It is denoted by $\overline{u}$. The length of the word u is denoted by $|u|$.

2.1   Binomial Coefficients and Binomial Equivalence

The binomial coefficient $\binom{u}{v}$ of two finite words u and v is the number of times v occurs as a subsequence of u (meaning as a "scattered" subword). As an example, we consider two particular words over $\{0,1\}$ and

$$\binom{101001}{101} = 6 \ .$$

For more on these binomial coefficients, see, for instance, [15, Chap. 6]. In particular, $\binom{u}{\varepsilon} = 1$. In this paper, a *factor* of a word is made of consecutive letters. However this is not necessarily the case for a *subword* of a word.

Definition 1 (Binomial equivalence). *Let $k \in \mathbb{N}$ and u,v be two words over A. We let $A^{\leq k}$ denote the set of words of length at most k over A. We say that u and v are k-binomially equivalent if*

$$\binom{u}{x} = \binom{v}{x}, \ \forall x \in A^{\leq k} \ .$$

We simply write $u \sim_k v$ if u and v are k-binomially equivalent. The word u is obtained as a permutation of the letters in v if and only if $u \sim_1 v$. In that case, we say that u and v are abelian equivalent. *Note that, for all $k \geq 1$, if $u \sim_{k+1} v$, then $u \sim_k v$.*

Example 2. The four words 0101110, 0110101, 1001101 and 1010011 are 2-binomially equivalent. Let u be any of these four words. We have

$$\binom{u}{0} = 3, \ \binom{u}{1} = 4, \ \binom{u}{00} = 3, \ \binom{u}{01} = 7, \ \binom{u}{10} = 5, \ \binom{u}{11} = 6 \ .$$

For instance, the word 0001111 is abelian equivalent to 0101110 but these two words are not 2-binomially equivalent. To see this, simply compute the number of occurrences of the subword 10 in each.

Many classical questions in combinatorics on words can be considered in this binomial context [22,24]. Avoiding binomial squares and cubes is considered in [21]. The problem of testing whether two words are k-binomially equivalent or not is discussed in [7]. In particular, one can introduce the k-binomial complexity function.

Definition 3 (Binomial complexity). *Let* $\mathbf{x}$ *be an infinite word. The k-binomial complexity function of* $\mathbf{x}$ *is defined as*

$$b_{\mathbf{x},k} : \mathbb{N} \to \mathbb{N}, \ n \mapsto \#\left(\mathrm{Fac}_n(\mathbf{x})/\sim_k\right)$$

where $\mathrm{Fac}_n(\mathbf{x})$ *is the set of factors of length* n *occurring in* $\mathbf{x}$.

2.2 Context of This Paper

The Thue–Morse word denoted by $\mathbf{t}$ is the fixed point starting with 0 of the morphism φ. In [23, Thm. 13], it is shown that $\mathbf{t}$ has a bounded k-binomial complexity. Actually, this behavior occurs for all morphisms where images of letters are permutations of the same word.

Theorem 4 [23]. *Let* $k \geq 1$. *There exists* $C_k > 0$ *such that the k-binomial complexity of the Thue–Morse word satisfies* $b_{\mathbf{t},k}(n) \leq C_k$ *for all* $n \geq 0$.

Our contribution is the exact characterization of $b_{\mathbf{t},k}(n)$.

Theorem 5. *Let* k *be a positive integer. For all* $n \leq 2^k - 1$, *we have*

$$b_{\mathbf{t},k}(n) = p_{\mathbf{t}}(n).$$

For all $n \geq 2^k$, *we have*

$$b_{\mathbf{t},k}(n) = \begin{cases} 3 \cdot 2^k - 3, & \text{if } n \equiv 0 \pmod{2^k}; \\ 3 \cdot 2^k - 4, & \text{otherwise.} \end{cases}$$

Observe that $3 \cdot 2^k - 4$ is exactly the number of words of length $2^k - 1$ in $\mathbf{t}$, for $k \neq 2$. Indeed, the factor complexity of $\mathbf{t}$ is well known [4, Corollary 4.10.7].

Proposition 6 [4–6]. *The factor complexity* $p_{\mathbf{t}}$ *of the Thue–Morse word is given by* $p_{\mathbf{t}}(0) = 1$, $p_{\mathbf{t}}(1) = 2$, $p_{\mathbf{t}}(2) = 4$ *and for* $n \geq 3$,

$$p_{\mathbf{t}}(n) = \begin{cases} 4n - 2 \cdot 2^m - 4, & \text{if } 2 \cdot 2^m < n \leq 3 \cdot 2^m; \\ 2n + 4 \cdot 2^m - 2, & \text{if } 3 \cdot 2^m < n \leq 4 \cdot 2^m. \end{cases}$$

There are 2 factors of length $1 = 2^1 - 1$ and 6 factors of length $3 = 2^2 - 1$. The number of factors of $\mathbf{t}$ of length $2^k - 1$ for $k \geq 3$ is given by $2(2^k - 1) + 4 \cdot 2^{k-2} - 2 = 3 \cdot 2^k - 4$,

$$(p_{\mathbf{t}}(2^k - 1))_{k \geq 0} = 1, 2, 6, 20, 44, 92, 188, 380, 764, 1532, \ldots$$

which is exactly one of two values stated in our main result, Theorem 5.

3   Occurrences of Subwords in Images by φ

The aim of this section is to obtain an expression for coefficients of the form $\binom{\varphi(w)}{u}$. Even though we are mainly interested in the Thue–Morse word, our observations can be applied to any non-erasing morphism as summarized by Theorem 15.

A *multiset* is just a set where elements can be repeated with a (finite) integer multiplicity. If x belongs to a multiset M, its multiplicity is denoted by $m_M(x)$ or simply $m(x)$. If $x \notin M$, then $m_M(x) = 0$. If we enumerate the elements of a multiset, we adopt the convention to write multiplicities with indices. The *multiset sum* $M \uplus N$ of two multisets M, N is the union of the two multisets and the multiplicity of an element is equal to the sum of the respective multiplicities.

Let us start with an introductory example. We hope that this example will forge the intuition of the reader about the general scheme.

Example 7. We want to compute

$$\binom{\varphi(01100)}{u} \qquad \text{with } u = 011.$$

The word $w = \varphi(01100)$ belongs to $\{01, 10\}^*$. It can be factorized with consecutive blocks $b_1 b_2 \cdots b_5$ of length 2. To count the number of occurrences of the subword u in the image by φ of a word, two cases need to be taken into account:

- the three symbols of u appear in pairwise distinct 2-blocks of w (each 2-block contains both 0 and 1 exactly once), and there are

$$\binom{|w|/2}{|u|} = \binom{5}{3}$$

  such choices, or;
- the prefix 01 of u is one of the 2-blocks b_i of w and the last symbol of u appears in subsequent distinct 2-block b_j, $j > i$. Since $\varphi(0) = 01$, we have to count the number of occurrences of the subword $0z$, for all words z of length 1, in the preimage of w. There are

$$\sum_{z \in A} \binom{01100}{0z} = 4 + 1 = 5$$

  such choices.

The general scheme behind this computation is expressed by Theorem 12 given below. The reader can already feel that we need to take into account particular factorizations of u with respect to occurrences of a factor $\varphi(0)$ or $\varphi(1)$. The two cases discussed in Example 7 correspond to the following factorizations of u:

$$011, \quad \varphi(0)1.$$

We thus introduce the notion of a φ-factorization.

Definition 8 (φ-(factorization). *If a word $u \in A^*$ contains a factor* 01 *or* 10, *then it can be factorized as*

$$u = w_0\, \varphi(a_1)\, w_1 \cdots w_{k-1}\, \varphi(a_k)\, w_k \tag{1}$$

for some $k \geq 1$, $a_1, \ldots, a_k \in A$ and $w_0, \ldots, w_k \in A^*$ (some of these words are possibly empty). We call this factorization, a φ-factorization of u. It is coded by the k-tuple of positions where the $\varphi(a_i)$'s occurs:

$$\kappa = (|w_0|, |w_0\varphi(a_1)w_1|, |w_0\varphi(a_1)w_1\varphi(a_2)w_2|, \ldots, |w_0\varphi(a_1)w_1\varphi(a_2)w_2 \cdots w_{k-1}|).$$

The set of all the φ-factorizations of u is denoted by φ-$\mathrm{Fac}(u)$.

Since $|\varphi(a)| = 2$, for all $a \in A$, observe that if $(i_1, \ldots, i_k)$ codes a φ-factorization, then $i_{j+1} - i_j \geq 2$ for all j. Note that u starts with a prefix 01 or 10 if and only if there are φ-factorizations of u coded by tuples starting with 0.

We define a map f from A^* to the set of finite multisets of words over A^*. This map is defined as follows.

Definition 9. *If $u \in 0^* \cup 1^*$, then $f(u) = \emptyset$ (the meaning for this choice will be clear with Theorem 12). If u is not of this form, it contains a factor 01 or 10. With every φ-factorization $\kappa \in \varphi$-$\mathrm{Fac}(u)$ of u of the form (1)*

$$u = w_0\, \varphi(a_1)\, w_1 \cdots w_{k-1}\, \varphi(a_k)\, w_k$$

for some $k \geq 1$, $a_1, \ldots, a_k \in A$ and $w_0, \ldots, w_k \in A^*$, we define the language

$$\mathcal{L}(u, \kappa) := A^{|w_0|}\, a_1\, A^{|w_1|} \cdots A^{|w_{k-1}|} a_k A^{|w_k|}$$

of words of length $|u| - k$ (there are $2^{|u|-2k}$ of these words[1]). Such a language is considered as a multiset whose elements have multiplicities equal to 1. Now, $f(u)$ is defined as the multiset sum (i.e., we sum the multiplicities) of the above languages for all φ-factorizations of u, i.e.,

$$f(u) := \biguplus_{\kappa \in \varphi\text{-}\mathrm{Fac}(u)} \mathcal{L}(u, \kappa)\,.$$

Definition 10. *Now that f is defined over A^*, we can extend it to any finite multiset M of words over A. It is the multiset sum of the $f(v)$'s, for all $v \in M$, repeated with their multiplicities.*

Remark 11. If u does not belong to $0^* \cup 1^*$, then $f^{|u|-2}(u)$ contains only elements in $\{0, 1, 00, 01, 10, 11\}$ and $f^{|u|-1}(u)$ contains only elements in $\{0, 1\}$. For $n \geq |u|$, $f^n(u)$ is empty.

---

[1] We have all the words of length $|u| - k$ where in k positions the occurring symbol is given.

Recall that $f(u)$ is a multiset. Hence $m_{f(u)}(v)$ denotes the multiplicity of v as element of $f(u)$.

Theorem 12. *With the above notation, for all words u, w, we have*

$$\binom{\varphi(w)}{u} = \binom{|w|}{|u|} + \sum_{\substack{\kappa \in \varphi\text{-Fac}(u) \\ v \in \mathcal{L}(u, \kappa)}} \binom{w}{v} = \binom{|w|}{|u|} + \sum_{v \in f(u)} m_{f(u)}(v) \binom{w}{v} .$$

We can then establish the following result.

Corollary 13. *Let $k \geq 1$. For all words u, v, we have*

$$u \sim_k v \Rightarrow \varphi(u) \sim_{k+1} \varphi(v) .$$

In particular, $\varphi^k(0) \sim_k \varphi^k(1)$ for all $k \geq 1$.

Theorem 12 can be extended to iterates of φ.

Corollary 14. *With the above notation, for $\ell \geq 1$ and all words u, w, we have*

$$\binom{\varphi^\ell(w)}{u} = \sum_{i=0}^{\ell-1} \sum_{v \in f^i(u)} m_{f^i(u)}(v) \binom{|\varphi^{\ell-i-1}(w)|}{|v|} + \sum_{x \in f^\ell(u)} m_{f^\ell(u)}(x) \binom{w}{x} .$$

The reader should be convinced that the following general statement holds.

Theorem 15. *Let $\Psi : A^* \to B^*$ be a non-erasing morphism and $u \in B^+$, $w \in A^+$ be two words. We have*

$$\binom{\Psi(w)}{u} = \sum_{k=1}^{|u|} \sum_{\substack{u_1, \dots, u_k \in B^+ \\ u = u_1 \cdots u_k}} \sum_{a_1, \dots, a_k \in A} \binom{\Psi(a_1)}{u_1} \cdots \binom{\Psi(a_k)}{u_k} \binom{w}{a_1 \cdots a_k} .$$

The word u occurs as a subword of $\Psi(w)$ if and only if there exists $k \geq 1$ such that u can be factorized into $u_1 \cdots u_k$ where, for all i, u_i is a non-empty subword occurring in $\Psi(a_i)$ for some letter a_i and such that $a_1 \cdots a_k$ is a subword of w.

4   Computing $b_{t,2}(n)$

In this section we compute the value of $b_{t,2}(n)$. First of all, the next proposition ensures us that all the words we will consider in the proof of Theorem 17 really appear as factors of $\mathbf{t}$.

Proposition 16 (folklore). *Let $k, m \in \mathbb{N}$ and $a, b \in \{0, 1\}$. Let p_u be a suffix of $\varphi^k(a)$ and s_u be a prefix of $\varphi^k(b)$. There exists $z \in \{0, 1\}^m$ such that $p_u \varphi^k(z) s_u$ is a factor of $\mathbf{t}$.*

Using this result, we can compute the values of $b_{t,2}$.

Theorem 17 [12, Thm. 3.3.6]. *We have $b_{t,2}(0) = 1$, $b_{t,2}(1) = 2$, $b_{t,2}(2) = 4$, $b_{t,2}(3) = 6$ and for all $n \geq 4$,*

$$b_{t,2}(n) = \begin{cases} 9, & \text{if } n \equiv 0 \pmod 4; \\ 8, & \text{otherwise.} \end{cases}$$

Proof. Assume $n \geq 4$.

We have to consider four cases depending on the value of $\lambda \in \{0, 1, 2, 3\}$ such that $\lambda = n \bmod 4$. For every one of them, we want to compute

$$b_{t,2}(n) = \#\left\{ \left(\binom{u}{0}, \binom{u}{01} \right) \in \mathbb{N} \times \mathbb{N} : u \in \mathrm{Fac}_n(\mathbf{t}) \right\}.$$

Since $\mathbf{t}$ is the fixed point of the morphism φ, we know that every factor u of length n of $\mathbf{t}$ can be written $p_u \varphi^2(z) s_u$ for some $z \in A^*$ and p_u (resp., s_u) suffix (resp., prefix) of a word in $\{\varphi^2(0), \varphi^2(1)\}$. From the previous proposition, we also know that every word of that form occurs at least once in $\mathbf{t}$. Moreover, we have $|p_u| + |s_u| \in \{\lambda, \lambda + 4\}$ and, as a consequence, $|z| = \lfloor \frac{n}{4} \rfloor = \frac{n-\lambda}{4}$ or $|z| = \lfloor \frac{n}{4} \rfloor - 1$. Set $\ell = \frac{n-\lambda}{4}$.

Let us first consider the case $\lambda = 0$. We have

$$\mathrm{Fac}_n(\mathbf{t}) = \{\varphi^2(az), 0\varphi^2(z)011, 0\varphi^2(z)100, 1\varphi^2(z)011, 1\varphi^2(z)100,$$
$$01\varphi^2(z)01, 01\varphi^2(z)10, 10\varphi^2(z)01, 10\varphi^2(z)10,$$
$$110\varphi^2(z)0, 110\varphi^2(z)1, 001\varphi^2(z)0, 001\varphi^2(z)1 : z \in A^{\ell-1}, a \in A, az \in \mathrm{Fac}(\mathbf{t})\}.$$

Let us illustrate the computation of $\left(\binom{u}{0}, \binom{u}{01} \right)$ on $u = 0\varphi^2(z)011 \in \mathrm{Fac}_n(\mathbf{t})$. Firstly,

$$\binom{u}{0} = \binom{0}{0} + \binom{\varphi^2(z)}{0} + \binom{011}{0} = 2 + 2|z| = 2\ell$$

since $|z| = \ell - 1$. Similarly, we have

$$\binom{u}{01} = \binom{0}{01} + \binom{\varphi^2(z)}{01} + \binom{011}{01} + \binom{0}{0}\binom{\varphi^2(z)}{1} + \binom{0}{0}\binom{011}{1} + \binom{\varphi^2(z)}{0}\binom{011}{1}$$

$$= \binom{|\varphi(z)|}{2} + \binom{\varphi(z)}{0} + 2 + |\varphi(z)| + 2 + 2|\varphi(z)|$$

$$= |z|(2|z| - 1) + |z| + 6|z| + 4 = 2\ell^2 + 2\ell.$$

All the computations are summarized in the table below. We give the form of the factors and respective values for the pairs $\left(\binom{u}{0}, \binom{u}{01} \right)$.

Case	$\varphi^2(az)$ $01\varphi^2(z)10$ $10\varphi^2(z)01$	$0\varphi^2(z)011$ $001\varphi^2(z)1$	$1\varphi^2(z)100$ $110\varphi^2(z)0$	$0\varphi^2(z)100$	$001\varphi^2(z)0$
$\binom{u}{0}$	2ℓ	2ℓ	2ℓ	$2\ell + 1$	$2\ell + 1$
$\binom{u}{01}$	$2\ell^2$	$2\ell^2 + 2\ell$	$2\ell^2 - 2\ell$	$2\ell^2 - 1$	$2\ell^2$

Case	$1\varphi^2(z)011$	$110\varphi^2(z)1$	$01\varphi^2(z)01$	$10\varphi^2(z)10$	
$\binom{u}{0}$	$2\ell - 1$	$2\ell - 1$	2ℓ	2ℓ	
$\binom{u}{01}$	$2\ell^2$	$2\ell^2 + 1$	$2\ell^2 + 1$	$2\ell^2 - 1$	

This is thus clear that if $n \equiv 0 \pmod 4$, we have $b_{t,2}(n) = 9$.

The same type of computations can be carried out in cases where $\lambda \neq 0$, and give 8 equivalence classes. The obtained values can be found in [13].

5 How to Cut Factors of the Thue–Morse Word

Computing $b_{t,k}(n)$, for all $k \geq 3$, will require much more knowledge about the factors of t. This section is concerned about particular factorizations of factors occurring in t. Similar ideas first appeared in [25,26].

Since t is a fixed point of φ, it is very often convenient to view t as a concatenation of blocks belonging to $\{\varphi^k(0), \varphi^k(1)\}$. Hence, we first define a function bar_k that roughly plays the role of a ruler marking the positions where a new block of length 2^k occurs (these positions are called *cutting bars of order k*). For all $k \geq 1$, let us consider the function $\mathrm{bar}_k : \mathbb{N} \to \mathbb{N}$ defined by

$$\mathrm{bar}_k(n) = |\varphi^k(t_{[0,n)})| = n \cdot 2^k,$$

where $t_{[0,n)}$ is the prefix of length n of t.

Given a factor u of t, we are interested in the relative positions of $\mathrm{bar}_k(\mathbb{N})$ in u: we look at all the occurrences of u in t and see what configurations can be achieved, that is how an interval I such that $t_I = u$ can intersect $\mathrm{bar}_k(\mathbb{N})$.

Definition 18 (Cutting set). *For all $k \geq 1$, we define the set $\mathrm{Cut}_k(u)$ of non-empty sets of relative positions of cutting bars*

$$\mathrm{Cut}_k(u) := \left\{ \left([i, i + |u|] \cap \mathrm{bar}_k(\mathbb{N})\right) - i \mid i \in \mathbb{N}, u = t_{[i,i+|u|)} \right\}.$$

A cutting set of order k is an element of $\mathrm{Cut}_k(u)$. Observe that we consider the closed interval $[i, i + |u|]$ because we are also interested in knowing if the end of u coincide with a cutting bar.

Example 19. The word $u = 01001$ is the factor $t_{[3,8)}$ so the set $\{1, 3, 5\}$ which is equal to $([3, 8] \cap 2\mathbb{N}) - 3$ is a cutting set of order 1 of u. Observing that the factor 00 can only occur as a factor of $\varphi(10)$, one easily deduces that it is the unique cutting set of order 1 of u. On the opposite, we have $010 = t_{[3,6)} = t_{[10,13)}$, so that $\mathrm{Cut}_1(010)$ contains both $\{1, 3\}$ and $\{0, 2\}$.

Remark 20. Let u be a factor of t. Observe that, for all $\ell \geq 1$, $\mathrm{Cut}_\ell(u) \neq \emptyset$. It results from the following three observations.

Obviously, $\mathrm{bar}_k(\mathbb{N}) \subset \mathrm{bar}_{k-1}(\mathbb{N})$ and thus if $\mathrm{Cut}_k(u)$ is non-empty, then the same holds for $\mathrm{Cut}_{k-1}(u)$. Next notice that if $\mathrm{Cut}_k(u)$ contains a singleton, then $\mathrm{Cut}_{k+1}(u)$ contains a singleton. Finally, there exists a unique k such that $2^{k-1} \leq |u| \leq 2^k - 1$. There also exists i such that $u = t_{[i,i+|u|)}$. Simply notice that either $[i, i + |u|] \cap \mathrm{bar}_k(\mathbb{N})$ is a singleton or, $[i, i + |u|] \cap \mathrm{bar}_{k-1}(\mathbb{N})$ is a singleton.

Observe that for any word u and any set $C \in \mathrm{Cut}_k(u)$, there is a unique integer $r \in \{0, 1, \ldots, 2^k - 1\}$ such that $C \subset 2^k \mathbb{N} + r$.

Lemma 21. *Let k be a positive integer and u be a factor of $\mathbf{t}$. Let C be a set $\{i_1 < i_2 < \cdots < i_n\}$ in $\mathrm{Cut}_k(u)$. There is a unique factor v of $\mathbf{t}$ of length $n - 1$ such that $u = p\varphi^k(v)s$, with $|p| = i_1$. Furthermore, if $i_1 > 0$ (resp., $i_n < |u|$), there is a unique letter a such that p (resp., s) is a proper suffix (resp., prefix) of $\varphi^k(a)$.*

Definition 22. (Factorization of order k). *Let u be a factor of $\mathbf{t}$ and C a cutting set in $\mathrm{Cut}_k(u)$. By Lemma 21, we can associate with C a unique pair $(p, s) \in A^* \times A^*$ and a unique triple $(a, v, b) \in (A \cup \{\varepsilon\}) \times A^* \times (A \cup \{\varepsilon\})$ such that $u = p\varphi^k(v)s$, where either $a = p = \varepsilon$ (resp., $b = s = \varepsilon$), or $a \neq \varepsilon$ and p is a proper suffix of $\varphi^k(a)$ (resp., $b \neq \varepsilon$ and s is a proper prefix of $\varphi^k(b)$). In particular, we have $a = p = \varepsilon$ exactly when $\min(C) = 0$ and $b = s = \varepsilon$ exactly when $\max(C) = |u|$. The triple (a, v, b) is called the* desubstitution *of u associated with C and the pair (p, s) is called the* factorization *of u associated with C. If $C \in \mathrm{Cut}_k(u)$, then (a, v, b) and (p, s) are respectively* desubstitutions *and* factorizations *of order k.*

Pursuing the reasoning of Example 19, one could easily show that for any factor u of $\mathbf{t}$ of length at least 4, $\mathrm{Cut}_1(u)$ contains a single set. Furthermore, the substitution φ being primitive and $\mathbf{t}$ being aperiodic, Mossé's recognizability theorem ensures that the substitution φ^k is *bilaterally recognizable* [17,18] for all $k \geq 1$, i.e., any sufficiently long factor u of $\mathbf{t}$ can be uniquely desubstituted by φ^k (up to a prefix and a suffix of bounded length). In the case of the Thue–Morse substitution, we can make this result more precise. Similar results are considered in [8] where the term (maximal extensible) reading frames is used.

Lemma 23. *Let $k \geq 3$ be an integer and u be a factor of $\mathbf{t}$ of length at least $2^k - 1$. Then $\mathrm{Cut}_k(u)$ is a not a singleton if and only if u is a factor of $\varphi^{k-1}(010)$ or of $\varphi^{k-1}(101)$, in which case we have $\mathrm{Cut}_k(u) = \{C_1, C_2\}$ and $|\min C_1 - \min C_2| = 2^{k-1}$. In this case, let (p_1, s_1), (p_2, s_2) be the two factorizations of order k respectively associated with $C_1, C_2 \in \mathrm{Cut}_k(u)$. Without loss of generality, assume that $|p_1| < |p_2|$. Then, there exists $a \in A$ such that either*

$$|p_1| + |s_1| = |p_2| + |s_2| \text{ and } (p_2, \varphi^{k-1}(a)s_2) = (p_1\varphi^{k-1}(a), s_1)$$

or,

$$||p_1| + |s_1| - (|p_2| + |s_2|)| = 2^k \text{ and } (p_2, s_2) = (p_1\varphi^{k-1}(\bar{a}), \varphi^{k-1}(a)s_1).$$

Example 24. Let us consider $u = 101001011$. It is a factor of $\varphi^2(010)$. We have $\mathrm{Cut}_3(u) = \{\{2\}, \{6\}\}$, which means that $(p_1, s_1) = (10, 1001011)$ and $(p_2, s_2) = (101001, 011)$ are two factorisations of u of order 3. By taking $a = 1$, we have $(p_2, \varphi^2(a)s_2) = (101001, 1001011) = (p_1\varphi^2(a), s_1)$ as claimed in the previous lemma.

6 Types Associated with a Factor

Remark 25. All the following constructions rely on Lemma 23. Thus, in the remaining of this paper, we will always assume that $k \geq 3$.

Lemma 23 ensures us that whenever a word has two cutting sets, then their associated factorizations are strongly related. We will now show that whenever two factors u, v of the same length of $\mathbf{t}$ admit factorizations of order k that are similarly related, then these two words are k-binomially equivalent.

To this aim, we introduce an equivalence relation $\equiv_k$ on the set of pairs $(x, y) \in A^{<2^k} \times A^{<2^k}$. The core result of this section is given by Theorem 31 stating that two words are k-binomially equivalent if and only if their factorizations of order k are equivalent for this new relation $\equiv_k$. So, the computation of $b_{\mathbf{t},k}(n)$ amounts to determining the number of equivalence classes for $\equiv_k$ among the factorizations of order k for words in $\mathrm{Fac}_n(\mathbf{t})$.

Definition 26. *Two pairs (p_1, s_1) and (p_2, s_2) of $A^{<2^k} \times A^{<2^k}$ are equivalent for $\equiv_k$ whenever there exists $a \in A$ such that one of the following situations occurs:*

1. $|p_1| + |s_1| = |p_2| + |s_2|$ *and*
   (a) $(p_1, s_1) = (p_2, s_2)$;
   (b) $(p_1, \varphi^{k-1}(a)s_1) = (p_2\varphi^{k-1}(a), s_2)$;
   (c) $(p_2, \varphi^{k-1}(a)s_2) = (p_1\varphi^{k-1}(a), s_1)$;
   (d) $(p_1, s_1) = (s_2, p_2) = (\varphi^{k-1}(a), \varphi^{k-1}(\bar{a}))$;
2. $\left| |p_1| + |s_1| - (|p_2| + |s_2|) \right| = 2^k$ *and*
   (a) $(p_1, s_1) = (p_2\varphi^{k-1}(a), \varphi^{k-1}(\bar{a})s_2)$;
   (b) $(p_2, s_2) = (p_1\varphi^{k-1}(a), \varphi^{k-1}(\bar{a})s_1)$.

Remark 27. Note that if $(p_1, s_1) \equiv_k (p_2, s_2)$, then either $|p_1| = |p_2|$ or, $||p_1| - |p_2|| = 2^{k-1}$. So $(p_1, s_1) \equiv_k (p_2, s_2)$ implies that $|p_1| \equiv |p_2| \pmod{2^{k-1}}$.

The next result is a direct consequence of Lemma 23.

Corollary 28. *If a factor of $\mathbf{t}$ has two distinct factorizations of order k, then these two are equivalent for $\equiv_k$.*

Definition 29 (Type of order k). *Given a factor u of $\mathbf{t}$ of length at least $2^k - 1$, the type of order k of u is the equivalence class of a factorization of order k of u. We also let (p_u, s_u) denote the factorization of order k of u for which $|p_u|$ is minimal (we assume that k is understood from the context). Therefore, two words u and v have the same type of order k if and only if $(p_u, s_u) \equiv_k (p_v, s_v)$.*

Example 30. Continuing Example 24, the word u has two factorizations of order 3 that verify case 1.(c) in Definition 26. Thus, $(10, 1001011) \equiv_3 (101001, 011)$ and the type of order 3 of u is $\{(10, 1001011), (101001, 011)\}$.

Theorem 31. *Let u, v be factors of $\mathbf{t}$ of length $n \geq 2^k - 1$. We have*

$$u \sim_k v \Leftrightarrow (p_u, s_u) \equiv_k (p_v, s_v).$$

The proof that the condition is sufficient easily follows from Corollary 13 and [13, Lemma 31].

The proof that the condition is necessary is done in the extended version of this paper [13]. First, we consider the case of words u, v that do not have any non-empty common prefix or suffix and split the result into two lemmas: either $|p_u| \not\equiv |p_v| \pmod{2^{k-1}}$ or, $|p_u| \equiv |p_v| \pmod{2^{k-1}}$. We then add a lemma that permits us to deal with factors having some common prefix or suffix.

7 k-binomial Complexity of the Thue–Morse Word

The first results of this section deal with small factors.

Proposition 32. *Let u, v be two different factors of $\mathbf{t}$ of length $n \leq 2^k - 1$, which do not have any common prefix or suffix. We have $u \not\sim_k v$.*

Corollary 33. *Let $k \geq 3$. For all $n \leq 2^k - 1$, we have $b_{\mathbf{t},k}(n) = p_{\mathbf{t}}(n)$.*

Proof. Let us take two different factors u and v of the same length $n \leq 2^k - 1$. If u and v do not share any common prefix or suffix, $u \not\sim_k v$ by the previous proposition. Otherwise, there exist words x, y, u', v' such that $u = xu'y$ and $v = xv'y$, where u' and v' do not share any common prefix or suffix. We apply the previous proposition to u', v' and conclude because $u' \not\sim_k v'$ implies $u \not\sim_k v$ [13, Lemma 10]. ∎

Due to Theorem 31, the k-binomial complexity of $\mathbf{t}$ can be computed from

$$b_{\mathbf{t},k}(n) = \#\left(\mathrm{Fac}_n(\mathbf{t})/\sim_k\right) = \#\left(\{(p_u, s_u) : u \in \mathrm{Fac}_n(\mathbf{t})\}/\equiv_k\right).$$

The last theorem provides this quantity. The idea of the proof is just to enumerate all the possible factorizations and count them. The proof can be found in the extended version [13].

Theorem 34. *For all $k \geq 3$, $n \geq 2^k$, we have*

$$\#\left(\{(p_u, s_u) : u \in \mathrm{Fac}_n(\mathbf{t})\}/\equiv_k\right) = \begin{cases} 3 \cdot 2^k - 3, & \text{if } n \equiv 0 \pmod{2^k}; \\ 3 \cdot 2^k - 4, & \text{otherwise.} \end{cases}$$

As a consequence of Corollary 33, Theorems 31 and 34, we get the expected result stated in Theorem 5.

Acknowledgments. We would like to thank Jeffrey Shallit for his participation in the statement of the initial problem. A conjecture about $b_{\mathbf{t},k}(n)$ was made when he was visiting the last author.

References

1. Allouche, J.-P., Shallit, J.: The ubiquitous Prouhet-Thue-Morse sequence. In: Ding, C., Helleseth, T., Niederreiter, H. (eds.) Sequences and their Applications. Discrete Mathematics and Theoretical Computer Science, pp. 1–16. Springer, London (1999). https://doi.org/10.1007/978-1-4471-0551-0_1
2. Allouche, J.-P., Shallit, J.: Automatic Sequences. Theory, Applications, Generalizations. Cambridge University Press, Cambridge (2003)
3. Berstel, J., Crochemore, M., Pin, J.-E.: Thue-Morse sequence and p-adic topology for the free monoid. Discrete Math. **76**, 89–94 (1989)
4. Berthé, V., Rigo, M. (eds.): Combinatorics, Automata and Number Theory. Encyclopedia Mathematics and Its Application, vol. 135. Cambridge University Press, Cambridge (2010)
5. Brlek, S.: Enumeration of factors in the Thue-Morse word. Discrete Appl. Math. **24**, 83–96 (1989)
6. de Luca, A., Varricchio, S.: Some combinatorial properties of the Thue-Morse sequence and a problem in semigroups. Theor. Comput. Sci. **63**, 333–348 (1989)
7. Freydenberger, D.D., Gawrychowski, P., Karhumäki, J., Manea, F., Rytter, W.: Testing k-binomial equivalence. arXiv:1509.00622 (2015)
8. Greinecker, F.: On the 2-abelian complexity of the Thue-Morse word. Theor. Comput. Sci. **593**, 88–105 (2015)
9. Karandikar, P., Kufleitner, M., Schnoebelen, P.: On the index of Simon's congruence for piecewise testability. Inf. Process. Lett. **115**, 515–519 (2015)
10. Karhumäki, J., Saarela, A., Zamboni, L.Q.: On a generalization of abelian equivalence and complexity of infinite words. J. Combin. Theory Ser. A **120**, 2189–2206 (2013)
11. Karhumäki, J., Saarela, A., Zamboni, L.Q.: Variations of the Morse-Hedlund theorem for k-abelian equivalence. In: Shur, A.M., Volkov, M.V. (eds.) DLT 2014. LNCS, vol. 8633, pp. 203–214. Springer, Cham (2014). https://doi.org/10.1007/978-3-319-09698-8_18
12. Lejeune, M.: Au sujet de la complexité k-binomiale. Master thesis, University of Liège (2018). http://hdl.handle.net/2268.2/5007
13. Lejeune, M., Leroy, J., Rigo, M.: Computing the k-binomial complexity of the Thue-Morse word. arXiv:1812.07330, 34 p. (2018)
14. Leroy, J., Rigo, M., Stipulanti, M.: Generalized Pascal triangle for binomial coefficients of words. Adv. Appl. Math. **80**, 24–47 (2016)
15. Lothaire, M.: Combinatorics on Words. Cambridge Mathematical Library. Cambridge University Press, Cambridge (1997)
16. Morse, M., Hedlund, G.A.: Symbolic dynamics II. Sturmian trajectories. Am. J. Math. **62**, 1–42 (1940)
17. Mossé, B.: Puissances de mots et reconnaissabilité des points fixes d'une substitution. Theor. Comput. Sci. **99**, 327–334 (1992)
18. Mossé, B.: Reconnaissabilité des substitutions et complexité des suites automatiques. Bull. Soc. Math. France **124**, 329–346 (1996)
19. Pin, J.É., Silva, P.V.: A noncommutative extension of Mahler's theorem on interpolation series. Eur. J. Combin. **36**, 564–578 (2014)
20. Pytheas Fogg, N., et al.: Substitutions in Dynamics, Arithmetics and Combinatorics. Lecture Notes in Mathematics, vol. 1794. Springer, Heidelberg (2002). https://doi.org/10.1007/b13861

21. Rao, M., Rigo, M., Salimov, P.: Avoiding 2-binomial squares and cubes. Theor. Comput. Sci. **572**, 83–91 (2015)
22. Rigo, M.: Formal Languages, Automata and Numeration Systems 1, Introduction to Combinatorics on Words. Network and Telecommunications Series. ISTE-Wiley, London (2014)
23. Rigo, M., Salimov, P.: Another generalization of abelian equivalence: binomial complexity of infinite words. Theor. Comput. Sci. **601**, 47–57 (2015)
24. Rigo, M.: Relations on words. Indag. Math. (N.S.) **28**, 183–204 (2017)
25. Shur, A.M.: The structure of the set of cube-free words over a two-letter alphabet. Izv. Math. **64**, 847–871 (2000)
26. Shur, A.M.: Combinatorial complexity of rational languages. Diskretn. Anal. Issled. Oper. Ser. 1 **12**, 78–99 (2005). (Russian)
27. Thue, A.: Über die gegenseitige Lage gleicher Teile gewisser Zeichenreihen. Kra. Vidensk. Selsk. Skrifter. I. Mat. Nat. Kl. **10**, Christiana (1912)

Context-Free Word Problem Semigroups

Tara Brough[1], Alan J. Cain[1($\boxtimes$)], and Markus Pfeiffer[2]

[1] Centro de Matemática e Aplicações, Faculdade de Ciências e Tecnologia,
Universidade Nova de Lisboa, 2829-516 Caparica, Portugal
{t.brough,a.cain}@fct.unl.pt
[2] School of Computer Science, University of St Andrews, North Haugh, St Andrews,
Fife KY16 9SS, UK
markus.pfeiffer@st-andrews.ac.uk

Abstract. This paper studies the classes of semigoups and monoids with context-free and deterministic context-free word problem. First, some examples are exhibited to clarify the relationship between these classes and their connection with the notions of word-hyperbolicity and automaticity. Second, a study is made of whether these classes are closed under applying certain semigroup constructions, including direct products and free products, or under regressing from the results of such constructions to the original semigroup(s) or monoid(s).

1 Introduction

The deep connections between formal language theory and group theory are perhaps most clearly evidenced by the famous 1985 theorem of Muller and Schupp, which says that a group has context-free word problem if and only if it is virtually free [9,22]; indeed, virtually free groups have *deterministic* context-free word problem. Since then, many studies have analyzed the classes of groups with word problems in various families of formal languages. Herbst and Thomas characterized the groups with one-counter word problem [14, Theorem 5.1]. (For a later elementary proof of this result, see [17].) The first author of the present paper investigated groups whose word problem is an intersection of finitely many context-free languages [2,5]. Holt et al. studied the class of groups whose co-word problem is context-free [18] and Holt and Röver studied the class of groups whose co-word problem is indexed [19].

The word problem of a group is the language of words representing the identity over some set of generators and their inverses. Thus two words u and v are equal in a group G if and only if uV is in the word problem, where V is obtained from v by replacing each symbol by its inverse and reversing the word. A natural question is how to generalize this definition to semigroups. Duncan and Gilman [8, Definition 5.1] defined the word problem of a semigroup S with respect to a generating set A to be

$$\mathrm{WP}(S, A) = \{\, u \# v^{\mathrm{rev}} : u, v \in A^+, u =_S v \,\}, \tag{1}$$

© Springer Nature Switzerland AG 2019
P. Hofman and M. Skrzypczak (Eds.): DLT 2019, LNCS 11647, pp. 292–305, 2019.
https://doi.org/10.1007/978-3-030-24886-4_22

where v^{rev} is the reverse of v. This definition fits well with the group definition and is natural when considering word problems recognizable by automata equipped with a stack. It was used by Holt, Owens, and Thomas in their study of groups and semigroups with one-counter word problem [17], and by Hoffmann et al. in their study of semigroups with context-free word problem [15].

The main conclusions of Hoffmann et al.'s earlier study were the result that the class of semigroups with context-free word problem is closed under passing to finite Rees index subsemigroups and extensions [15, Theorem 1] and a characterization of completely simple semigroups with context-free word problem as Rees matrix semigroups over virtually free groups [15, Theorem 2].

This paper explores new directions in the study of the class of semigroups with context-free word problem, including monoids with context-free word problem, and also considers the classes of semigroups and monoids with deterministic context-free word problem. First, Sect. 3 exhibits some natural classes of semigroups and monoids that lie within and outside these classes; in particular Example 2 shows that having context-free and deterministic context-free word problem do not coincide for semigroups or monoids, unlike (as noted above) for groups. Section 4 discusses connections with the theories of word-hyperbolic and automatic semigroups: any semigroup or monoid with context-free word problem is word-hyperbolic, but there are non-automatic semigroups that have context-free word problem. The remainder of the core of the paper (Sects. 5–8) focuses on various constructions: direct products, free products, strong semilattices of semigroups, Rees matrix semigroups and Bruck–Reilly extensions. For each construction, the questions of interest are: (1) Are the classes of semigroups and monoids with context-free or deterministic context-free word problem closed under that construction? (2) If the result of applying such a construction lies in one of these classes, must the original semigroup(s) or monoids(s) lie in that same class? Finally, Sect. 10 lists some open problems.

2   Preliminaries

The *word problem* for a semigroup S is defined as (1) above. Similarly, the *word problem* for a monoid M with respect to a generating set A is the language

$$\text{WP}(M, A) = \big\{\, u \# v^{\text{rev}} : u, v \in A^*, u =_M v \,\big\}. \tag{2}$$

Proposition 1 ([15, Proposition 8]). *Let $\mathfrak{C}$ be a class of languages closed under inverse homomorphisms and intersection with regular languages. Then*

1. *If a semigroup or monoid has word problem in $\mathfrak{C}$ with respect to some generating set, then it has word problem in $\mathfrak{C}$ with respect to any generating set.*
2. *The class of semigroups (resp. monoids) with word problem in $\mathfrak{C}$ is closed under taking finitely generated subsemigroups (resp. submonoids).*

The preceding result applies in particular when $\mathfrak{C}$ is the class of context-free or deterministic context-free languages [12, 20].

If a semigroup (resp. monoid) has word problem in a class of languages $\mathfrak{C}$, it is said to be a $U(\mathfrak{C})$ semigroup (resp. monoid). We denote the classes of context-free and deterministic context-free languages by $\mathcal{CF}$ and $\mathcal{DCF}$ respectively. The 'U' notation is because (1) and (2) treat the word problem as an 'unfolded' relation rather than a 'two-tape' relation; see [4] for a systematic study.

3   Examples

We recall some less commonly-used terms from the theory of rewriting systems; see [1] for general background. A rewriting system $(A, \mathcal{R})$ is *monadic* if it is length-reducing and the right-hand side of each rewrite rule in $\mathcal{R}$ lies in $A \cup \{\varepsilon\}$. A monadic rewriting system $(A, \mathcal{R})$ is *regular* (respectively, *context-free*) if, for each $a \in A \cup \{\varepsilon\}$, the set of all left-hand sides of rewrite rules in $\mathcal{R}$ with right-hand side a is a regular (respectively, context-free) language.

Theorem 1 ([6, **Theorem 3.1**]). *Let* $(A, \mathcal{R})$ *be a confluent context-free monadic rewriting system. Then the monoid presented by* $\langle A \mid \mathcal{R} \rangle$ *is* $U(\mathcal{CF})$, *and a context-free grammar generating its word problem can be effectively constructed from context-free grammars describing* $\mathcal{R}$.

(The preceding result originally stated that a monoid satisfying the hypothesis was word-hyperbolic; however, the proof proceeds by constructing the word problem for the monoid. The 'effective construction' part follows easily by inspecting the construction in the proof.)

Example 1. This example shows that a $U(\mathcal{CF})$ monoid need not have a context-free cross section (that is, a language over some generating set containing a unique representative for every element).

Let $K = \{a^\alpha b^\alpha c^\alpha : \alpha \in \mathbb{N} \cup \{0\}\}$ and let $L = \{a, b, c\}^* - K$. It is well-known that K is not a context-free language but that L is a context-free language. Let $A = \{a, b, c, x, y, z\}$ and let $\mathcal{R} = \{(xwy, z) : w \in L\}$. Let M be the monoid presented by $\langle A \mid \mathcal{R} \rangle$. By Theorem 1, M is $U(\mathcal{CF})$. Suppose that M admits a context-free cross-section. Then M admits a context-free cross-section $J \subseteq A^*$. Let u be the unique word in J such that $u =_M z$, and let $J' = (J \setminus \{u\}) \cup \{z\}$; then J' is also a context-free cross-section of M. Let $H = J' \cap x\{a, b, c\}^* y$. Then H is context-free and comprises precisely the words xwy where $w \in K$, for if $w \in L$, then $xwy =_M z$, and the representative of z in J' is the word z itself. Hence, since the class of context-free languages is closed under right and left quotients with regular sets, $K = x \backslash H / y$ is context-free. This is a contradiction, and so M does not admit a context-free cross-section.

Example 2. This example shows that the class of $U(\mathcal{DCF})$ semigroups is properly contained in the class of $U(\mathcal{CF})$ semigroups.

Let K be the language of palindromes over $\{a, b\}$. It is well-known that K is context-free but not deterministic context-free. Let $A = \{a, b, x, y, z\}$ and let $\mathcal{R} = \{(xwy, z) : w \in L\}$. Let M be the monoid presented by $\langle A \mid \mathcal{R} \rangle$.

By Theorem 1, M is $U(\mathcal{CF})$. Suppose, with the aim of obtaining a contradiction, that M is $U(\mathcal{DCF})$. Then $\text{WP}(M, A)$ is deterministic context-free. Let $L = (\text{WP}(M, A) \cap A^* \# z)/\{\# z\} \cap \{a, b, x, y\}^*$; then L is the language of words over $\{a, b, x, y\}$ that are equal to z in M. Furthermore, L is deterministic context-free, since the class of deterministic context-free languages is closed under intersection with regular languages [20, Theorem 10.4] and right quotient by regular languages [20, Theorem 10.2].

Now, $K = x \backslash L/y$. The class of deterministic context-free languages is closed under left quotient by a singleton (since a deterministic pushdown automaton can simulate reading a fixed word before it starts reading input), and, as noted above, is closed under right quotient by regular languages. Hence K is deterministic context-free. This is a contradiction, and so M is not $U(\mathcal{DCF})$.

Example 3. An example of a monoid that is 'close' to being a free group but is not $U(\mathcal{CF})$ is the free inverse monoid of rank 1 and hence (by Proposition 1) of any finite rank. This follows from applying the pumping lemma to the intersection of the word problem and the regular language $x^*(x^{-1})^* x^* \# x^*$ (where x is the free generator); see [3, Theorem 1].

4 Relationship to Word-Hyperbolicity and Automaticity

Hyperbolic groups have become one of the most fruitful areas of group theory since their introduction by Gromov [13]. The concept of hyperbolicity can be generalized to semigroups and monoids in more than one way, but here we consider the linguistic definition that uses Gilman's characterization of hyperbolic groups using context-free languages [11]. A *word-hyperbolic structure* for a semigroup S is a pair $(L, M(L))$, where L is a regular language over an alphabet A representing a finite generating set for S such that L maps onto S, and where

$$M(L) = \{u \#_1 v \#_2 w^{\text{rev}} : u, v, w \in L \wedge uv =_S w\}$$

(where $\#_1$ and $\#_2$ are new symbols not in A) is context-free.

Theorem 2. *Every $U(\mathcal{CF})$ semigroup is word-hyperbolic.*

The proof is in effect the first paragraph of the proof of Theorem 1 as given in [6, Proof of Theorem 2].

All hyperbolic groups are automatic [10, Theorem 3.4.5], but word-hyperbolic semigroups may not even be *asynchronously* automatic [16, Example 7.7]. Even within the smaller class of $U(\mathcal{CF})$ semigroups, one can find semigroups that are not automatic:

Example 4. Let $A = \{a, b, c, d, z\}$, let $\mathcal{R} = \{(ab^\alpha c^\alpha d, z) : \alpha \in \mathbb{N}\}$. Let M be the monoid presented by $\langle A \mid \mathcal{R} \rangle$. Then M is $U(\mathcal{CF})$ by Theorem 1, but cannot be automatic [7, Corollary 5.5]. (In fact, it can be shown that M is not even asynchronously automatic.)

Given that $U(\mathcal{CF})$ groups are virtually free and thus automatic, and since the monoid in Example 4 is not cancellative, the following question is natural:

Question 1. Is a cancellative $U(\mathcal{CF})$ semigroup necessarily automatic?

5   Direct Products

A direct product of two finitely generated semigroups is not necessarily finitely generated. However, a direct product of two $U(\mathcal{CF})$ semigroups is not necessarily $U(\mathcal{CF})$, even if it is finitely generated: for example, the free monoid of rank 1 is $U(\mathcal{CF})$, but the direct product of two copies of this monoid is the free commutative monoid of rank 2, which is finitely generated but not $U(\mathcal{CF})$.

For a semigroup S, we say that S is *decomposable* if $S^2 = S$. We will show that for a direct product of two $U(\mathcal{CF})$ semigroups to be $U(\mathcal{CF})$, it is necessary and sufficient that one of the factors is finite and decomposable (decomposability being necessary to ensure finite generation). First we establish sufficiency.

Lemma 1. *The classes of $U(\mathcal{CF})$ and $U(\mathcal{DCF})$ semigroups are closed under taking direct product with a finite decomposable semigroup.*

Proof. Let S be a $U(\mathcal{CF})$ semigroup and T a finite decomposable semigroup. Then $S \times T$ is finitely generated [23, Theorem 8.2]. Let C be a finite generating set for $S \times T$ and let A and B be the projections of C onto S and T respectively. Then A and B are finite generating sets for S and T respectively. Thus there exists a pushdown automaton $\mathcal{A}$ recognising $\mathrm{WP}(S, A)$, which can be modified to give a pushdown automaton $\mathcal{A}'$ recognising $\mathrm{WP}(S \times T, A \times B)$, by processing the symbols from A as usual, while using the states to record the finite information required to check validity of the input on the second tape. Hence $S \times T$ is $U(\mathcal{CF})$. Moreover, if S is $U(\mathcal{DCF})$, then $\mathcal{A}$ can be taken to be deterministic, in which case $\mathcal{A}'$ is also deterministc, so $S \times T$ is $U(\mathcal{DCF})$. $\square$

Necessity arises from the following language-theoretic result, which encapsulates the idea that context-free languages cannot admit 'cross-dependencies'. For words w, w', we use the notation $w' \sqsubseteq w$ to mean that w' is a subword of w.

Lemma 2. *Let A and B be disjoint alphabets, and let ρ_A, ρ_B be equivalence relations on A^* and B^* respectively with infinitely many equivalence classes. Then the language $L(\rho_A, \rho_B) = \{u_1 v_1 u_2 v_2 : (u_1, u_2) \in \rho_A, (v_1, v_2) \in \rho_B\}$ is not context-free.*

Proof. Suppose that $L = L(\rho_A, \rho_B)$ is context-free, and let k be the pumping constant for L. Let $\mathcal{E}_A$ be the set of all equivalence classes of ρ_A that contain a word of length at most k, and define $\mathcal{E}_B$ similarly.

Let $w = u_1 v_1 u_2 v_2 \in L$ with $|v_1|, |u_2| > k$. Then we can write $w = pqrst$ where $|qrs| \leq k$, $|qs| \geq 1$ and $pq^i rs^i t \in L$ for all $i \in \mathbb{N}_0$. Due to the form of words in L, q and s must each be a subword of some u_i or v_i. Moreover, the lengths of u_2 and v_1 preclude the possibility that $q \sqsubseteq u_1$ and $s \sqsubseteq u_2$ or $p \sqsubseteq v_1$ and $q \sqsubseteq v_2$. Let $w' = prt = u_1' v_1' u_2' v_2'$. Then we have $u_i' = u_i$ for some $i \in \{1, 2\}$ and $v_j' = v_j$ for some $j \in \{1, 2\}$. Since $w' \in L$, this implies that the equivalence classes of the factors are unchanged between w and w'. By induction, we can repeat this process until we obtain a word $w^\flat = u_1^\flat v_1^\flat u_2^\flat v_2^\flat \in L$ with $|v_1^\flat| \leq k$ or $|u_2^\flat| \leq k$, where the $u_i^\flat$ are in the same ρ_A-equivalence class as the u_i and the $v_i^\flat$

are in the same ρ_B-equivalence class as the v_i. Hence our original word w had either $u_i \in C$ for some $C \in \mathcal{E}_A$ or $v_i \in D$ for some $D \in \mathcal{E}_B$. But $\mathcal{E}_A$ and $\mathcal{E}_B$ are both finite, and so L cannot contain all words of the form $u_1 v_1 u_2 v_2$ with $(u_1, u_2) \in \rho_A$ and $(v_1, v_2) \in \rho_B$. Hence L is not context-free.   □

The preceding lemma is immediately applicable only to monoids.

Lemma 3. *The direct product of two infinite monoids cannot be $U(\mathcal{CF})$.*

Proof. Let $S = \langle A \rangle$ and $T = \langle B \rangle$ be infinite monoids. Then the relations $\rho_A = \mathrm{WP}(S, A)$ and $\rho_B = \mathrm{WP}(T, B)$ both have infinitely many equivalence classes. Moreover, the language $L = \mathrm{WP}(S \times T, A \cup B) \cap A^* B^* \# A^* B^*$ has as a homomorphic image the language $L(\rho_A, \rho_B)$ defined in Lemma 2. Since the class of context-free languages is closed under homorphisms and intersection with regular sets, this implies that $S \times T$ is not $U(\mathcal{CF})$.

Thus if $S \times T$ is $U(\mathcal{CF})$, then at least one of S or T is finite.   □

In order to extend Lemma 3 to all semigroups, we first establish the following fact (which is clear for monoids, where direct factors are submonoids).

Lemma 4. *The class of $U(\mathcal{CF})$ semigroups is closed under taking direct factors.*

Proof. Assume that $S \times T$ is $U(\mathcal{CF})$. In particular, $S \times T$ is finitely generated. By [23, Theorem 2.1], S and T are finitely generated, and $S^2 = S$ and $T^2 = T$.

Let $C = \{c_1, \ldots, c_k\}$ be a finite generating set for T. Since $T^2 = T$, we can choose a factorization $c_i = c_{i\zeta} u_i$ for each $c_i \in C$. Construct a labelled digraph with vertex set C and an edge from c_i to $c_{i\zeta}$ labelled by u_i for each $c_i \in C$. Since this digraph is finite, it must contain a circuit. Fix some vertex c on that circuit and let w be the concatenation in reverse order of the labels on the edges around the circuit. Then $cw = c$.

Let A be a finite generating set for $S \times T$ and let B be a finite generating set for S. Then $X = A \cup (B \times \{c, w\})$ is a finite generating set for $S \times T$. Let R be the regular language $(B \times \{c\})(B \times \{w\})^* \# (B \times \{w\})^* (B \times \{c\})$. Let $L = \mathrm{WP}(S \times Y, X) \cap R$. Then

$$
\begin{aligned}
(b_1, c)(b_2, w) &\cdots (b_m, w) \#(b_n', w) \cdots (b_2', w)(b_1, c) \in L \\
\iff (b_1 b_2 \cdots b_m, cw^{m-1}) &=_{S \times T} (b_1' b_2' \cdots b_n', cw^{n-1}) \\
\iff (b_1 b_2 \cdots b_m, c) &=_{S \times T} (b_1' b_2' \cdots b_n', c) \\
\iff b_1 b_2 \cdots b_m &=_S b_1' b_2' \cdots b_n'.
\end{aligned}
\tag{3}
$$

Define a homomorphism

$$
\pi : \big((B \times \{c, w\}) \cup \{\#\}\big) \to (B \cup \{\#\}), \qquad (b, \_) \mapsto b, \quad \# \mapsto \#.
$$

Then (3) shows that $L\pi = \mathrm{WP}(S, B)$. Since the class of context-free languages is closed under homomorphism [20, Corollary to Theorem 6.2], S is a $U(\mathcal{CF})$ semigroup.   □

Theorem 3. *The direct product of two semigroups is $U(\mathcal{CF})$ if and only if it is finite or one of the factors is $U(\mathcal{CF})$ and the other factor is finite and decomposable.*

Proof. Sufficiency was already established in Lemma 1.

Conversely suppose that $S \times T$ is $U(\mathcal{CF})$. Let C be a finite generating set for $S \times T$ with the projection of C onto the first component being A and the projection onto the second component being B. By Lemma 4, S and T are both $U(\mathcal{CF})$. Let $A_1 = A \times \{1\}$, $B_1 = \{1\} \times B$, and $C_1 = A_1 \cup B_1 \cup C$. We will describe a pushdown automaton $\mathcal{P}$ recognising $\mathrm{WP}(S^1 \times T^1, C_1)$. This automaton is defined in terms of pushdown automata $\mathcal{A}$, $\mathcal{B}$ and $\mathcal{C}$, recognising $\mathrm{WP}(S, A)$, $\mathrm{WP}(T, B)$ and $\mathrm{WP}(S \times T, C)$ respectively.

On input $(x, y) \in C$, the automaton $\mathcal{P}$ behaves as a 'delayed' version of $\mathcal{C}$, storing the input symbol in the state and then (except in the start state, which has no stored symbol) simulating $\mathcal{C}$ on input of the current stored symbol. The automaton may guess at any point that the input is complete, and process the stored symbol from the current state as an ϵ-transition. In this case we move to a state with no stored symbol and accepting no further input, which is a final state if and only if it is a final state in $\mathcal{C}$. Thus on input in $(C \cup \{\#\})^*$, $\mathcal{P}$ behaves exactly like $\mathcal{C}$ but 'one step behind', and so the sublanguage of $(C \cup \{\#\})^*$ accepted by $\mathcal{P}$ is $\mathrm{WP}(S \times T, C)$.

In order to work with input from $A_1 \cup B_1$ we choose, for all $x, x' \in A$ and $y, y' \in B$, representatives $w_{x,x',y}$ and $w_{x,y,y'}$ in C for the elements (xx', y) and (x, yy') of $S \times T$.

Now, if the automaton $\mathcal{P}$ reads the symbol $(x', 1)$ in a state with stored symbol (x, y), it simulates reading all but the final symbol of $w_{x,x',y}$ in $\mathcal{C}$ from the current state, and stores the final symbol in the last state of this computation. Symmetrically, the same occurs when we replace $(x', 1)$ by $(1, y')$ and $w_{x,x',y}$ by $w_{x,y,y'}$. Thus on input $u \# v$ from $CC_1^* \# CC_1^*$, the automaton is able to simulate processing in $\mathcal{C}$ some $u' \# v'$ such that $u =_{S \times T} u'$ and $v =_{S \times T} v'$.

Finally, on input from A_1 or B_1 in the start state, the automaton guesses whether the remaining (non-$\#$) input will be in A_1^* resp. B_1^*. If it guesses yes, it moves to a copy of the appropriate automaton $\mathcal{A}$ resp. $\mathcal{B}$, treating input $(x, 1)$ as x and $(1, y)$ as y. Thus the sublanguage of $(A_1 \cup \{\#\})^*$ recognised by $\mathcal{P}$ is $\mathrm{WP}(S \times \{1\}, A_1)$, while the sublanguage of $(B_1 \cup \{\#\})^*$ recognised is $\mathrm{WP}(\{1\} \times T, B_1)$. If, on the other hand, the automaton guesses no, we describe what happens on input from A_1, the other case being symmetric. Supposing the input is $(x, 1)$, the automaton guesses which $y \in B$ will be read next, and stores this guess in the state, along with the symbol (x, y). States with a stored guess $y \in B$ operate as usual, except on input of the form (x, y). On such input, the automaton deletes the 'guess' y and otherwise operates as if the input were $(x, 1)$, since it already simulated reading y earlier. (If $x = 1$, then we simply delete the guess and otherwise do nothing.) The automaton must similarly make a guess on input from A_1 or B_1 in a state with stored symbol $\#$. Since $(x, 1)w(x', y) = (x, y)w(x', 1)$ for $w \in A_1^*$, the automaton $\mathcal{P}$ is now able to simulate reading a corresponding word in C^* for any input not in $(A_1 \cup \{\#\})^* \cup (B_1 \cup \{\#\})^*$.

Combined with the fact that $\mathcal{P}$ can also simulate the automata $\mathcal{A}$ and $\mathcal{B}$ on appropriate inputs, this establishes that $\mathcal{P}$ recognises $\mathrm{WP}(S^1 \times T^1, C_1)$.

Thus $S^1 \times T^1$ is $U(\mathcal{CF})$, and so by Lemma 3, without loss of generality we can assume T^1 is finite. Moreover, S^1 is $U(\mathcal{CF})$, and hence so is S, by Proposition 1.2. By [23, Theorem 8.1], if S is infinite then T must also be decomposable, since $S \times T$ is finitely generated. $\qquad\square$

6 Free Products

Theorem 4. *The class of $U(\mathcal{CF})$ semigroups is closed under taking semigroup free products and under taking free factors.*

Proof. Let S and T be $U(\mathcal{CF})$ semigroups. Let A_S and A_T be finite generating sets for S and T, respectively, and for $X \in \{S, T\}$, let $\mathcal{P}_X$ be a pushdown automaton recognizing $\mathrm{WP}(X, A_X)$ accepting by final state, Assume that in $\mathcal{P}_X$, the initial stack content is only a stack bottom symbol $\perp_X$, which is never never popped or pushed.

Construct a new pushdown automaton $\mathcal{Q}$ recognizing words over $A_S \cup A_T \cup \{\#\}$, functioning as follows. First, $\mathcal{Q}$ will recognize words in $(A_S \cup A_T)^+ \# (A_S \cup A_T)^+$; since this is a regular language, assume without loss that the input is in this form. When $\mathcal{Q}$ begins, it reads a symbol from A_X (for some $X \in \{S, T\}$). It pushes $\perp_X$ onto its stack and begins to simulate $\mathcal{P}_X$. Whenever it is simulating $\mathcal{P}_X$ and reads a symbol from A_Y, where $Y \neq X$, it pushes the current state of $\mathcal{P}_X$ onto the stack, then pushes $\perp_Y$ onto the stack and begins to simulate $\mathcal{P}_Y$. These alternating simulations of $\mathcal{P}_S$ and $\mathcal{P}_T$ continue until the $\#$ is encountered.

On reading the symbol $\#$, the automaton $\mathcal{Q}$ continues to simulate whichever $\mathcal{P}_X$ it was currently simulating. After this point, whenever it is simulating $\mathcal{P}_X$ (for some $X \in \{S, T\}$) and reads a symbol from A_Y, where $Y \neq X$, how it proceeds depends on whether the currently-simulated $\mathcal{P}_X$ is in an accept state:

- If it is in accept state, $\mathcal{Q}$ pops symbols from its stack until it encounters $\perp_X$, which it pops, then pops the state of $\mathcal{P}_Y$, restores the simulation of $\mathcal{P}_Y$ from this state (and with the stack contents down to the symbol $\perp_Y$), and simulates $\mathcal{P}_Y$ on reading $\#$ and then on reading the symbol just read by $\mathcal{Q}$. (If after popping $\perp_X$ the stack of $\mathcal{Q}$ is empty, it fails.)
- If it is not in an accept state, $\mathcal{Q}$ fails.

These alternating simulations of $\mathcal{P}_S$ and $\mathcal{P}_T$ continue until the end of the input unless $\mathcal{Q}$ fails before then. At this point $\mathcal{Q}$ accepts if the currently-simulated $\mathcal{P}_X$ is in an accept state, and if the stack only contains symbols from the stack alphabet B_X plus a single symbol $\perp_X$.

It follows from the above description that $\mathcal{Q}$ recognizes strings of the form

$$u_1 u_2 \cdots u_k \# v_k^{\mathrm{rev}} \cdots v_2^{\mathrm{rev}} v_1^{\mathrm{rev}}, \tag{4}$$

where $u_i \# v_i^{\mathrm{rev}} \in L(\mathcal{P}_{X(i)})$ and either $X(2j) = S$ and $X(2j+1) = T$, or else $X(2j) = T$ and $X(2j+1) = S$. Thus $\mathcal{Q}$ recognizes strings (4) such that

$$u_1 u_2 \cdots u_k =_{S*T} v_1 v_2 \cdots v_k,$$

and the u_i and v_i are either both in A_X^+ or both in A_Y^+ for alternating i. Thus Q recognizes $WP(S * T, A_X \cup A_Y)$.

The free factors of a finitely generated free product are themselves finitely generated, so closure under free factors follows from Proposition 1(2).   □

Notice that the strategy of the proof of Theorem 4 cannot be applied to show that the class of $U(\mathcal{DCF})$ semigroups is closed under taking free products. The problem is in the very last step: after the automaton has read its last input symbols from some A_X, it cannot deterministically check that the stack only contains symbols from the stack alphabet B_X plus a single symbol $\perp_X$. Therefore the following question remains open:

Question 2. Is the class of $U(\mathcal{DCF})$ semigroups closed under forming free products?

Theorem 5. *The class of $U(\mathcal{CF})$ monoids is closed under taking monoid free products and free factors.*

Proof (Sketch proof). It is easy to see that the construction of the Q from the proof of Theorem 4 can be adapted to the case of monoid free products. Using the notation from that proof, one observes that for $X \in \{S, T\}$ the language of words over A_X representing the identity of X is a context-free language K_X. Then one first modifies Q to accept $\#$ (that is, the empty word, followed by $\#$, followed by the empty word), then modifies Q so that it can non-deterministically read a string from either K_X at any point (including while reading another string from K_Y for $Y \in \{S, T\}$, so that such strings can be 'nested').   □

7 Strong Semilattices

We recall the definition of a strong semilattice of semigroups here, and refer the reader to [21, Sect. 4.1] for further background reading:

Let Y be a semilattice. Recall that the meet of $\alpha, \beta \in Y$ is denoted $\alpha \wedge \beta$. For each $\alpha \in Y$, let S_α be a semigroup. For $\alpha \geq \beta$, let $\phi_{\alpha,\beta} : S_\alpha \to S_\beta$ be a homomorphism such that

1. For each $\alpha \in Y$, the homomorphism $\phi_{\alpha,\alpha}$ is the identity mapping.
2. For all $\alpha, \beta, \gamma \in Y$ with $\alpha \geq \beta \geq \gamma$, $\phi_{\alpha,\beta}\phi_{\beta,\gamma} = \phi_{\alpha,\gamma}$.

The *strong semilattice of semigroups* $S = \mathcal{S}[Y; S_\alpha; \phi_{\alpha,\beta}]$ consists of the disjoint union $\bigcup_{\alpha \in Y} S_\alpha$ with the following multiplication: if $x \in S_\alpha$ and $y \in S_\beta$, then

$$xy = (x\phi_{\alpha,\alpha\wedge\beta})(y\phi_{\beta,\alpha\wedge\beta}).$$

Theorem 6. *Let $\mathfrak{C}$ be a class of languages closed under finite union, inverse gsm-mappings and intersection with regular languages (in particular, the class $\mathcal{CF}$). A strong semilattice of semigroups is $U(\mathfrak{C})$ if and only if it is finitely generated and all the semigroups in its semilattice are $U(\mathfrak{C})$.*

Proof. Let $S = \mathcal{S}[Y; S_\alpha; \phi_{\alpha,\beta}]$ be a strong semilattice of semigroups. If S is $U(\mathfrak{C})$, then it is finitely generated by some set A. It follows from the definition of a strong semilattice of semigroups that Y is generated by those $\alpha \in Y$ such that $A \cap S_\alpha \neq \emptyset$, and so is finite, and that each S_α is finitely generated by elements of the form $a\phi_{\beta,\alpha}$ where $a \in S_\beta$ and $\beta \geq \alpha$. Moreover, all the S_α are $U(\mathfrak{C})$, since they are finitely generated subsemigroups of S.

Conversely, suppose that Y is finite and each S_α is $U(\mathfrak{C})$. For each $\alpha \in Y$, let A_α be a finite generating set for S_α and $A'_\alpha = \bigcup_{\beta \geq \alpha} A_\alpha$. Let $A = \bigcup_{\alpha \in Y} A_\alpha$. Define homomorphisms $\phi_\alpha : (A'_\alpha)^* \to A^*_\alpha$ by $x \mapsto x\phi_{\beta,\alpha}$ for $x \in A_\beta$.

We can view $\mathrm{WP}(S, A)$ as the union of its restrictions to each S_α: that is, as the union of the languages $L_\alpha = \{u\#v^{\mathrm{rev}} \in \mathrm{WP}(S, A) : u, v \in S_\alpha\}$. In turn, each L_α can be expressed as $L'_\alpha \cap R_\alpha$, where $L'_\alpha = \{u\#v^{\mathrm{rev}} : u, v \in A^*, u\phi_\alpha =_{S_\alpha} v\phi_\alpha\}$ and $R_\alpha = \{u\#v^{\mathrm{rev}} : u, v \in A^*, u, v \in S_\alpha\}$. Note that $u\#v^{\mathrm{rev}} \in L'_\alpha$ implies $u, v \in S_\beta$ for some $\beta \geq \alpha$, since otherwise ϕ_α is not defined. We have $L'_\alpha, R_\alpha \subseteq (A'_\alpha)^*$ for all $\alpha \in Y$.

Defining $R'_\alpha = \{w \in (A'_\alpha)^* : w \in S_\alpha\}$, we have $R_\alpha = R'_\alpha \# R'_\alpha$ (since membership of w in S_α depends only on the content of w). The language R'_α is recognised by a finite automaton consisting of the semilattice Y with an adjoined top element $\top$ as the start state, and final state α. The transition function is given by the meet operation: $(\top, x) \mapsto \gamma$ and $(\beta, x) \mapsto \beta \wedge \gamma$ for $x \in A_\gamma$. A word w is accepted by this automaton if and only if the meet of all γ such that w contains a symbol in A_γ is α. Thus R'_α is regular, and hence so is R_α, as a concatenation of regular languages.

Now choose a homomorphism $\psi_\alpha : (A'_\alpha)^* \to A^*_\alpha$ defined by $x \mapsto w_x$ such that $w_x =_S x\phi_\alpha$. Let $W = \{w_x : w \in A^*_\alpha\}$ and $M = \mathrm{WP}(S_\alpha, A_\alpha) \cap W^*$. Then $M \in \mathfrak{C}$, and L'_α is the inverse image of M under the gsm-mapping from $(A'_\alpha)^* \# (A'_\alpha)^*$ to $(A_\alpha)^* \# (A_\alpha)^*$ that preserves $\#$ and maps all symbols in x before the $\#$ to $x\psi_\alpha$ and all symbols x after the $\#$ to $(x\psi_\alpha)^{\mathrm{rev}}$. Since $\mathfrak{C}$ is closed under inverse gsm-mappings, L'_α is thus in $\mathfrak{C}$. In turn, L_α is in $\mathfrak{C}$, hence so is $\mathrm{WP}(S, A)$, as the union of the finitely many L_α. $\qquad\square$

The class $\mathcal{DCF}$ is not closed under finite union [20, Theorem 10.5(b)]. We conjecture that a finitely generated strong semilattice of $U(\mathcal{DCF})$ semigroups need not be $U(\mathcal{DCF})$. Let $Y = \{\alpha, \beta\}$ be a two-element semilattice with $\alpha > \beta$. Let S_α be the free group generated by $\{x, y\}$ and let S_β be $\mathbb{Z}$ (under $+$). Define $\phi_{\alpha,\beta}$ to be the homomorphism extending $x \mapsto 1$, $y \mapsto -1$. Both S_α and S_β are virtually free groups and so $U(\mathcal{DCF})$, but the word problem of $\mathcal{S}[Y; \{S_\alpha, S_\beta\}; \phi_{\alpha,\beta}]$ does not appear to be deterministic context-free, for checking equality in S_α seems to require computing reduced words on the stack, while checking equality in $\mathbb{Z}$ seems to require using the stack as a counter, and there is no way to know in advance which is required.

8   Rees Matrix Semigroups

Let us recall the definition of a Rees matrix semigroup. Let S be a semigroup, let I and Λ be abstract index sets, and let $P \in \mathrm{Mat}_{\Lambda \times I}(S)$ (that is, P is a $\Lambda \times I$

matrix with entries from S). Denote the (λ, i)-th entry of P by $p_{\lambda i}$. The *Rees matrix semigroup* over S with sandwich matrix P, denoted $\mathcal{M}[S; I, \Lambda; P]$, is the set $I \times S \times \Lambda$ with multiplication defined by

$$(i, x, \lambda)(j, y, \mu) = (i, x p_{\lambda j} y, \mu).$$

This construction is important because it arises in the classification of completely simple semigroups as Rees matrix semigroups over groups; see [21, Sect. 3.2–3.3].

Hoffmann et al. showed that a completely simple semigroup is $U(\mathcal{CF})$ if and only if it is isomorphic to a Rees matrix semigroup over a finitely generated virtually free group [15, Theorem 2]; their proof depends on virtually free groups having *deterministic* context-free word problem. The following theorem generalizes Hoffmann et al.'s characterization to Rees matrix semigroups over arbitrary semigroups. See [12, 20] for background on inverse gsm-mappings.

Theorem 7. *Let $\mathfrak{C}$ be a class of languages closed under inverse gsm-mappings and intersection with regular languages (in particular, $\mathcal{CF}$ or $\mathcal{DCF}$). Then a finitely generated Rees matrix semigroup over a semigroup S is $U(\mathfrak{C})$ if and only if S is $U(\mathfrak{C})$.*

Proof. Let $M = \mathcal{M}[S; I, \Lambda; P]$ be a Rees matrix semigroup and let $\mathfrak{C}$ be as in the statement of the theorem. If M is $U(\mathfrak{C})$, then it must be finitely generated, hence S is also finitely generated and thus $U(\mathfrak{C})$.

Conversely, suppose that S is $U(\mathfrak{C})$ and M is finitely generated by $B \subseteq I \times S \times \Lambda$, and let A be the projection of B onto S. For each $i \in I$ and $\lambda \in \Lambda$, choose a word $w_{\lambda i} \in A^*$ representing $p_{\lambda i}$. Let W be the (finite) set of all the $w_{\lambda i}$. Let $L = \mathrm{WP}(S, A) \cap (AW)^* A \# A (WA)^*$, which is in $\mathfrak{C}$, as the intersection of a language in $\mathfrak{C}$ with a regular language. We will define a gsm-mapping Φ such that $\mathrm{WP}(M, B)$ is the inverse image of L under Φ.

First, define a gsm-mapping $\phi : B^* \to A^*$ by

$$(i_1, x_1, \lambda_1) \ldots (i_m, x_m, \lambda_m) \mapsto x_1 w_{\lambda_1 i_2} x_2 \ldots w_{\lambda_{m-1} i_m} x_m.$$

Then for $w = (i_1, x_1, \lambda_1) \ldots (i_m, x_m, \lambda_m)$ we have $w =_M (i(w), w\phi, \lambda(w))$, where $i(w) := i_1$ and $\lambda(w) := \lambda_m$.

Now extend ϕ to a gsm-mapping $\Phi : (B \cup \{\#\})^* \to (A \cup \{\#\})^*$ as follows: For $u, v \in B^*$ and $w \in (B \cup \{\#\})^*$, let $(u \# v^{\mathrm{rev}})\Phi = u\phi \# (v\phi)^{\mathrm{rev}} c$, where $c = \varepsilon$ if $i(u) = i(v)$ and $\lambda(u) = \lambda(v)$, and $c = \#$ otherwise. (Since I and Λ are finite, the computation of c can be done by storing $i(u)$ and $\lambda(u)$ in the state and then checking against $\lambda(v)$ and $i(v)$.) Let $(u \# v^{\mathrm{rev}} \# w)\Phi = u\phi \# (v\phi)^{\mathrm{rev}} \#$ (achieved by storing in the state whether $\#$ has already been seen).

The preimage of L in $(B \cup \{\#\})^*$ under Φ consists of all words of the form $u \# v^{\mathrm{rev}}$ with $u, v \in B^*$ such that $i(u) = i(v)$, $\lambda(u) = \lambda(v)$ and $u\phi \# (v\phi)^{\mathrm{rev}} \in \mathrm{WP}(S, A)$. But this is exactly all $u \# v^{\mathrm{rev}}$ such that $u =_M v$, so $L\Phi^{-1} = \mathrm{WP}(M, B)$. Hence M is $U(\mathfrak{C})$, since its word problem is obtained from a language in $\mathfrak{C}$ by an inverse gsm-mapping. $\square$

The fact that every completely regular semigroup is isomorphic to a semilattice (not necessarily strong) of completely simple semigroups [21, Theorem 4.1.3] raises the following question:

Question 3. Which completely regular semigroups are $U(\mathcal{CF})$?

9   Bruck–Reilly Extensions

Let M be a monoid with presentation $\langle A \mid \mathcal{R} \rangle$ and $\phi : M \to M$ an endomorphism. The *Bruck–Reilly extension* $\mathrm{BR}(M, \phi)$ of M by ϕ is the monoid with presentation $\langle A, b, c \mid \mathcal{R}, bc = 1, ba = (a\phi)b, ac = c(a\phi) \quad (a \in A) \rangle$. This is an analogue for monoids of the notion of HNN-extensions for groups.

If ϕ is the identity endomorphism, then $\mathrm{BR}(M, \phi)$ is isomorphic to the direct product of M with the bicyclic monoid generated by $\{b, c\}$. Thus by Lemma 3 the class of $U(\mathcal{CF})$ semigroups is not closed under Bruck–Reilly extensions. However, we can establish a necessary and sufficient condition for $\mathrm{BR}(M, \phi)$ to be $U(\mathcal{CF})$, though we omit the proof here.

Theorem 8. *Let M be a monoid and $\phi : M \to M$ an endomorphism. Then $\mathrm{BR}(M, \phi)$ is $U(\mathcal{CF})$ if and only if M is $U(\mathcal{CF})$ and $\mathrm{im}\phi^n$ is finite for some n.*

10   Further Open Problems

Question 4. Does every cancellative $U(\mathcal{CF})$ semigroup have deterministic context-free word problem?

Question 5. Is it possible to characterize the commutative (respectively, cancellative, inverse) $U(\mathcal{CF})$ semigroups?

The previous two questions are motivated by the group case, since the classes of $U(\mathcal{CF})$ and $U(\mathcal{DCF})$ groups coincide and are precisely the virtually free groups. In particular, the abelian $U(\mathcal{CF})$ groups are thus either finite or of the form $\mathbb{Z} \times F$, where F is finite and abelian.

Question 6. Does there exist an infinite periodic $U(\mathcal{CF})$ semigroup?

Acknowledgements. The first author was supported by the FCT (Fundação para a Ciência e a Tecnologia/Portuguese Foundation for Science and Technology) fellowship SFRH/BPD/121469/2016 and by the FCT project UID/Multi/04621/2013.

The second author was supported by the 'Investigador FCT' fellowship IF/01622/2013/CP1161/CT0001.

For the first and second authors, this work was partially supported by FCT projects UID/MAT/00297/2019 (Centro de Matemática e Aplicações), PTDC/MHC-FIL/2583/2014 and PTDC/MAT-PUR/31174/2017.

This work was started during a visit by the third author to the Universidade Nova de Lisboa, which was supported by the exploratory project IF/01622/2013/CP1161/CT0001 attached to the second author's research fellowship.

References

1. Book, R.V., Otto, F.: String Rewriting Systems. Texts and Monographs in Computer Science. Springer, New York (1993). https://doi.org/10.1007/978-1-4613-9771-7
2. Brough, T.: Groups with poly-context-free word problem. Groups Complex. Cryptol. **6**(1), 9–29 (2014). https://doi.org/10.1515/gcc-2014-0002
3. Brough, T.: Word problem languages for free inverse monoids. In: Konstantinidis, S., Pighizzini, G. (eds.) DCFS 2018. LNCS, vol. 10952, pp. 24–36. Springer, Cham (2018). https://doi.org/10.1007/978-3-319-94631-3_3
4. Brough, T., Cain, A.J.: A language hierarchy of binary relations (2018)
5. Brough, T.R.: Groups with poly-context-free word problem. Ph.D. thesis, University of Warwick (2010). https://wrap.warwick.ac.uk/35716/
6. Cain, A.J., Maltcev, V.: Context-free rewriting systems and word-hyperbolic structures with uniqueness. Int. J. Algebra Comput. **22**(7) (2012). https://doi.org/10.1142/S0218196712500610
7. Campbell, C.M., Robertson, E.F., Ruškuc, N., Thomas, R.M.: Automatic semigroups. Theor. Comput. Sci. **250**(1–2), 365–391 (2001). https://doi.org/10.1016/S0304-3975(99)00151-6
8. Duncan, A., Gilman, R.H.: Word hyperbolic semigroups. Math. Proc. Camb. Philos. Soc. **136**(3), 513–524 (1999). https://doi.org/10.1017/S0305004103007497
9. Dunwoody, M.J.: The accessibility of finitely presented groups. Invent. Math. **81**(3), 449–457 (1985). https://doi.org/10.1007/BF01388581
10. Epstein, D.B.A., Cannon, J.W., Holt, D.F., Levy, S.V.F., Paterson, M.S., Thurston, W.P.: Word Processing in Groups. Jones & Bartlett, Boston (1992)
11. Gilman, R.H.: On the definition of word hyperbolic groups. Math. Z. **242**(3), 529–541 (2002). https://doi.org/10.1007/s002090100356
12. Ginsburg, S., Greibach, S.: Deterministic context free languages. Inf. Control **9**(6), 620–648 (1966). https://doi.org/10.1016/S0019-9958(66)80019-0
13. Gromov, M.: Hyperbolic groups. In: Gersten, S.M. (ed.) Essays in Group Theory. Mathematical Sciences Research Institute Publications, vol. 8, pp. 75–263. Springer, New York (1987). https://doi.org/10.1007/978-1-4613-9586-7_3
14. Herbst, T., Thomas, R.M.: Group presentations, formal languages and characterizations of one-counter groups. Theor. Comput. Sci. **112**(2), 187–213 (1993). https://doi.org/10.1016/0304-3975(93)90018-O
15. Hoffmann, M., Holt, D.F., Owens, M.D., Thomas, R.M.: Semigroups with a context-free word problem. In: Yen, H.-C., Ibarra, O.H. (eds.) DLT 2012. LNCS, vol. 7410, pp. 97–108. Springer, Heidelberg (2012). https://doi.org/10.1007/978-3-642-31653-1_10
16. Hoffmann, M., Kuske, D., Otto, F., Thomas, R.M.: Some relatives of automatic and hyperbolic groups. In: Gomes, G.M.S., Pin, J.É., Silva, P.V. (eds.) Semigroups, Algorithms, Automata and Languages, pp. 379–406. World Scientific, River Edge (2002). https://doi.org/10.1142/9789812776884_0016
17. Holt, D.F., Owens, M.D., Thomas, R.M.: Groups and semigroups with a one-counter word problem. J. Aust. Math. Soc. **85**(02), 197 (2008). https://doi.org/10.1017/S1446788708000864
18. Holt, D.F., Rees, S., Röver, C.E., Thomas, R.M.: Groups with context-free co-word problem. J. London Math. Soc. **71**(3), 643–657 (1999). https://doi.org/10.1112/S002461070500654X

19. Holt, D.F., Röver, C.E.: Groups with indexed co-word problem. Int. J. Algebra Comput. **16**(5), 985–1014 (2006). https://doi.org/10.1142/S0218196706003359
20. Hopcroft, J.E., Ullman, J.D.: Introduction to Automata Theory, Languages, and Computation, 1st edn. Addison-Wesley, Reading (1979)
21. Howie, J.M.: Fundamentals of Semigroup Theory. London Mathematical Society Monographs: New Series, vol. 12. Clarendon Press, Oxford University Press, New York (1995)
22. Muller, D.E., Schupp, P.E.: Groups, the theory of ends, and context-free languages. J. Comput. Syst. Sci. **26**(3), 295–310 (1983). https://doi.org/10.1016/0022-0000(83)90003-X
23. Robertson, E.F., Ruškuc, N., Wiegold, J.: Generators and relations of direct products of semigroups. Trans. Am. Math. Soc. **350**(07), 2665–2686 (1998). https://doi.org/10.1090/S0002-9947-98-02074-1

Analysis of Symbol Statistics in Bicomponent Rational Models

M. Goldwurm[1(⊠)], J. Lin[2], and M. Vignati[1]

[1] Dipartimento di Matematica, Università degli Studi di Milano, Milan, Italy
massimiliano.goldwurm@unimi.it
[2] Department of Mathematics, Khalifa University, Abu Dhabi, United Arab Emirates

Abstract. We study the local limit distribution of sequences of random variables representing the number of occurrences of a symbol in words of length n in a regular language, generated at random according to a rational stochastic model. We present an analysis of the main local limits when the finite state automaton defining the stochastic model consists of two primitive components. Our results include an evaluation of the convergence rate, which in the various cases is of an order slightly slower than $O(n^{-1/2})$.

1 Introduction

This work continues the analysis developed in [3,7,10] on the limit distribution of the number of symbol occurrences in words of given length, chosen at random in regular languages. More precisely, we consider sequences of random variables $\{Y_n\}$, where each Y_n is the number of occurrences of a symbol a in a word w of length n, generated at random in a *rational stochastic model*. Such a model can be formally defined by a finite state automaton with real positive weights on transitions. In this setting the probability of generating a word w is proportional to the weight the automaton associates with w; thus, the language recognized by the automaton is the family of all words having non-null probability to be generated. This model is quite general, it includes as special cases the traditional Bernoullian and Markovian sources [13,14] and contains the random generation of words of length n in any regular language under uniform distribution.

The properties of $\{Y_n\}$ are of particular interest for the analysis of regular patterns occurring in words generated by Markovian models [3,13,14] and for the asymptotic estimate of the coefficients of rational series in commutative variables [3,4]. They are also related to the study of the descriptional complexity of languages and computational models [5] and to the analysis of the values of additive functions defined on regular languages [11]. Clearly, the asymptotic behaviour of $\{Y_n\}$ depends on the properties of the finite state automaton $\mathcal{A}$ defining the stochastic model. It is known that if $\mathcal{A}$ has a primitive transition matrix then Y_n has a Gaussian limit distribution [3,13] and, under a suitable aperiodicity condition, it also satisfies a local limit theorem [3]. The limit distribution of Y_n in the global sense is known also when the transition matrix of $\mathcal{A}$

© Springer Nature Switzerland AG 2019
P. Hofman and M. Skrzypczak (Eds.): DLT 2019, LNCS 11647, pp. 306–318, 2019.
https://doi.org/10.1007/978-3-030-24886-4_23

consists of two primitive components [7] and a first (non-Gaussian) local limit theorem in a particular bicomponent case is presented in [10].

Here we improve these results presenting an analysis of the local limits of $\{Y_n\}$ when the transition matrix of $\mathcal{A}$ consists of two primitive components equipped with some transition from the first to the second component. At the cost of adding suitable aperiodicity conditions, we prove that the main convergences in distribution obtained in [7] also hold true in the local sense. Moreover, we evaluate the rates of convergence to our limits both in the primitive case and in all bicomponent cases (a tight convergence rate is a natural goal in these contexts [12]). Our results are obtained by applying the Saddle Point Method [8, Chapter VII] and, as our limit densities often are not normal, proofs can be regarded as an application of this tool in non-Gaussian cases[1].

In this context it is crucial to observe that a local limit theorem does not follow immediately from a traditional convergence in distribution (which occurs for instance in the usual central limit theorems), since single probabilities are differences of values of the corresponding distribution functions, and hence they may not be detected by a standard analysis of convergence in law. Usually, in order to prove a local limit theorem from a convergence in distribution, some additional regularity or aperiodicity conditions are necessary; standard counterexamples show that such conditions cannot be avoided [4,9].

The material we present is organized as follows. In Sect. 2 we define the problem, recalling the notions of convergence in distribution and local limit law. In Sect. 3 we revise the primitive case stating a local limit theorem for our statistics Y_n with a convergence rate of the order $O(n^{-1/2})$. In Sect. 4 we study the behaviour of Y_n in (communicating) bicomponent models: first we show a Gaussian local limit property when there is a dominant component, yielding a convergence rate analogous to the primitive model. Then, in Subsect. 4.1, we consider the equipotent bicomponent case, occurring when the main eigenvalues of the two components coincide; in this case the results depend on the values of four constants: β_1, γ_1 and β_2, γ_2, representing the leading terms of mean value and variance of our statistics associated to the first and the second component, respectively. When $\beta_1 \neq \beta_2$ we strengthen the result on local limit towards a uniform density obtained in [10] by showing a convergence rate "almost" of the order $O(n^{-1/2} \log^{3/2} n)$. If $\beta_1 = \beta_2$ but $\gamma_1 \neq \gamma_2$, then the local limit density turns out to be a suitable mixture of Gaussian densities, with a convergence rate "almost" of the order $O(n^{-1/2} \log^2 n)$. When $\beta_1 = \beta_2$ and $\gamma_1 = \gamma_2$ we obtain again a Gaussian local limit with convergence rate $O(n^{-1/2})$. Finally, these results are summarized in the last section, where we discuss possible future investigations.

2   Problem Setting

Given the binary alphabet $\{a, b\}$, for every word $w \in \{a, b\}^*$ we denote by $|w|$ the length of w and by $|w|_a$ the number of occurrences of a in w. For each $n \in \mathbb{N}$,

---

[1] However, due to space constraints, all proofs in the present work are omitted.

we also represent by $\{a,b\}^n$ the set $\{w \in \{a,b\}^* : |w| = n\}$. Here a *formal series* in the non-commutative variables a, b is a function $r : \{a,b\}^* \to \mathbb{R}_+$, where $\mathbb{R}_+ = \{x \in \mathbb{R} \mid x \geq 0\}$, and for every $w \in \{a,b\}^*$ we denote by (r, w) the value of r at w. Such a series r is called *rational* if for some integer $m > 0$ there is a monoid morphism $\mu : \{a,b\}^* \to \mathbb{R}_+^{m \times m}$ and two arrays $\xi, \eta \in \mathbb{R}_+^m$, such that $(r, w) = \xi' \mu(w) \eta$, for every $w \in \{a,b\}^*$ [2,15]. In this case, as the morphism μ is generated by matrices $A = \mu(a)$ and $B = \mu(b)$, we say that the 4-tuple (ξ, A, B, η) is a *linear representation* of r of size m. Clearly, such a 4-tuple can be considered as a finite state automaton over the alphabet $\{a, b\}$, with transitions (as well as initial and final states) weighted by positive real values. Throughout this work we assume that the set $\{w \in \{a,b\}^n : (r,w) > 0\}$ is not empty for every $n \in \mathbb{N}_+$ (so that $\xi \neq 0 \neq \eta$), and that A and B are not null matrices, i.e. $A \neq [0] \neq B$. Then we can consider the probability measure Pr over the set $\{a,b\}^n$ given by

$$\Pr(w) = \frac{(r,w)}{\sum_{x \in \{a,b\}^n}(r,x)} = \frac{\xi'\mu(w)\eta}{\xi'(A+B)^n\eta} \qquad \forall \, w \in \{a,b\}^n$$

Note that, if r is the characteristic series of a language $L \subseteq \{a,b\}^*$ then Pr is the uniform probability function over the set $L \cap \{a,b\}^n$. Thus we can define the random variable (r.v. for short) $Y_n = |w|_a$, where w is chosen at random in $\{a,b\}^n$ with probability $\Pr(w)$. As $A \neq [0] \neq B$, Y_n is not a degenerate r.v.. It is clear that, for every $k \in \{0, 1, \ldots, n\}$,

$$p_n(k) := \Pr(Y_n = k) = \frac{\sum_{|w|=n, |w|_a = k}(r,w)}{\sum_{w \in \{a,b\}^n}(r,w)}$$

Since r is rational also the previous probability can be expressed by using its linear representation. It turns out that

$$p_n(k) = \frac{[x^k]\xi'(Ax+B)^n\eta}{\xi'(A+B)^n\eta} \qquad \forall \, k \in \{0,1,\ldots,n\} \tag{1}$$

For sake of brevity we say that Y_n is *defined* by the linear representation (ξ, A, B, η). The distribution of Y_n can be represented by the map $h_n(z)$ and the characteristic function $\Psi_n(t)$, given respectively by

$$h_n(z) = \xi'(Ae^z + B)^n\eta \qquad \forall \, z \in \mathbb{C} \tag{2}$$

$$\Psi_n(t) = \sum_{k=0}^{n} p_n(k)e^{itk} = \frac{\xi'(Ae^{it}+B)^n\eta}{\xi'(A+B)^n\eta} = \frac{h_n(it)}{h_n(0)} \qquad \forall \, t \in \mathbb{R} \tag{3}$$

In particular mean value and variance of Y_n are determined by

$$\mathrm{E}(Y_n) = \frac{h_n'(0)}{h_n(0)}, \quad \mathrm{Var}(Y_n) = \frac{h_n''(0)}{h_n(0)} - \left(\frac{h_n'(0)}{h_n(0)}\right)^2 \tag{4}$$

Our general goal is to study the limit distribution of $\{Y_n\}$ as n grows to $+\infty$ and in particular its possible local limit law.

We recall that a sequence of r.v.'s $\{X_n\}$ *converges in distribution* (or in law) to a random variable X of distribution function F if $\lim_{n\to+\infty} \Pr(X_n \le x) = F(x)$, for every $x \in \mathbb{R}$ of continuity for F. The central limit theorems yield classical examples of convergence in distribution to a Gaussian random variable.

Instead, the local limit laws establish the convergence of single probabilities to a density function (see for instance [1,8,9]). More precisely, consider a sequence of r.v.'s $\{X_n\}$ such that each X_n takes value in $\{0, 1, \ldots, n\}$. We say that $\{X_n\}$ *satisfies a local limit law* of Gaussian type if there are two real sequences $\{a_n\}$, $\{s_n\}$, satisfying $a_n \sim \mathrm{E}(X_n)$, $s_n^2 \sim \mathrm{Var}(X_n)$ and $s_n > 0$ for all n, such that for some real $\epsilon_n \to 0$, the relation

$$\left| s_n \Pr(X_n = k) - \frac{e^{-\left(\frac{k-a_n}{s_n}\right)^2/2}}{\sqrt{2\pi}} \right| \le \epsilon_n \tag{5}$$

holds uniformly for every $k \in \{0, 1, \ldots, n\}$ and every $n \in \mathbb{N}$ large enough. Here, ϵ_n yields the *convergence rate* (or the speed) of the law. A well-known example of such a property is given by the de Moivre-Laplace local limit theorem, which concerns sequences of binomial r.v.'s [9].

Similar definitions can be given for other (non-Gaussian) types of local limit laws. In this case the Gaussian density $e^{-x^2/2}/\sqrt{2\pi}$ appearing in (5) is replaced by some density function $f(x)$; clearly, if $f(x)$ is not continuous at some points, the uniformity of k must be adapted to the specific case.

3   Primitive Models

A relevant case occurs when $M = A + B$ is primitive, i.e. $M^k > 0$ for some $k \in \mathbb{N}$ [16]. In this case it is known that Y_n has a Gaussian limit distribution and satisfies a local limit property [3,13]. Here we improve this result, showing a convergence rate $O(n^{-1/2})$, and revisit some material appearing in [3,4] that is useful in the following sections.

Since M is primitive, by Perron-Frobenius Theorem, it admits a real eigenvalue $\lambda > 0$ greater than the modulus of any other eigenvalue. Thus, we can consider the function $u = u(z)$ implicitly defined by the equation

$$\mathrm{Det}(Iu - Ae^z - B) = 0$$

such that $u(0) = \lambda$. It turns out that, in a neighbourhood of $z = 0$, $u(z)$ is analytic, is a simple root of the characteristic polynomial of $Ae^z + B$ and $|u(z)|$ is strictly greater than the modulus of all other eigenvalues of $Ae^z + B$. Moreover, a precise relationship between $u(z)$ and function $h(z)$, defined in (2), is proved in [3] stating that there are two positive constants c, ρ and a function $r(z)$ analytic and non-null at $z = 0$, such that

$$h_n(z) = r(z)\, u(z)^n + O(\rho^n) \qquad \forall z \in \mathbb{C} : |z| \le c \tag{6}$$

where $\rho < |u(z)|$ and in particular $\rho < \lambda$.

Mean value and variance of Y_n can be estimated from relations (4) and (6). In turns out [3] that the constants

$$\beta = \frac{u'(0)}{\lambda} \quad \text{and} \quad \gamma = \frac{u''(0)}{\lambda} - \left(\frac{u'(0)}{\lambda}\right)^2 \tag{7}$$

are strictly positive and satisfy the relations

$$E(Y_n) = \beta n + O(1) \quad \text{and} \quad \text{Var}(Y_n) = \gamma n + O(1)$$

Other properties concern function $y(t) = u(it)/\lambda$, defined for real t in a neighbourhood of 0. In particular, there exists a constant $c > 0$, for which relation (6) holds true, satisfying the following relations [3]:

$$|y(t)| = 1 - \frac{\gamma}{2}t^2 + O(t^4), \ \arg y(t) = \beta t + O(t^3), \ |y(t)| \le e^{-\frac{\gamma}{4}t^2} \qquad \forall \ |t| \le c \ (8)$$

The behaviour of $y(t)$ can be estimated precisely when t tends to 0. For any q such that $1/3 < q < 1/2$ it can be proved [3] that

$$y(t)^n = e^{-\frac{\gamma}{2}t^2 n + i\beta t n}(1 + O(t^3)n) \qquad \text{for } |t| \le n^{-q} \tag{9}$$

The previous properties can be used to prove a local limit theorem for $\{Y_n\}$ when M is primitive, with a convergence rate $O(n^{-1/2})$. The result, stated in Theorem 1 below, holds under a further assumption, introduced to avoid periodicity phenomena. To state this condition properly, consider the transition graph of the finite state automaton defined by matrices A and B, i.e. the directed graph G with vertex set $\{1, 2, \ldots, m\}$ such that, for every $i, j \in \{1, 2, \ldots, m\}$, G has an edge from i to j labelled by a letter a (b, respectively) whenever $A_{ij} > 0$ ($B_{ij} > 0$, resp.). Also denote by d the GCD of the differences in the number of occurrences of a in the (labels of) cycles of equal length of G. Here and in the sequel we say that the pair (A, B) is *aperiodic* if $d = 1$. Such a property is often verified; for instance it holds true whenever $A_{ij} > 0$ and $B_{ij} > 0$ for two (possibly equal) indices i, j.

Theorem 1. *Let $\{Y_n\}$ be defined by a linear representation (ξ, A, B, η) such that $M = A + B$ is primitive, $A \ne [0] \ne B$ and (A, B) is aperiodic. Moreover, let β and γ be defined by equalities (7). Then, as n tends to $+\infty$, the relation*

$$\left| \sqrt{n} Pr(Y_n = k) - \frac{e^{-\frac{(k-\beta n)^2}{2\gamma n}}}{\sqrt{2\pi\gamma}} \right| = O\left(n^{-1/2}\right) \tag{10}$$

holds true uniformly for every $k \in \{0, 1, \ldots, n\}$.

4   Bicomponent Models

In this section we study the behaviour of $\{Y_n\}_{n \in \mathbb{N}}$ defined by a linear representation (ξ, A, B, η) of size m, such that the matrix $M = A + B$ consists of two irreducible components. Formally, there are two linear representations, $(\xi_1, A_1, B_1, \eta_1)$ and $(\xi_2, A_2, B_2, \eta_2)$, of size m_1 and m_2 respectively, where $m = m_1 + m_2$, such that:

(1) for some $A_0, B_0 \in \mathbb{R}_+^{m_1 \times m_2}$ we have

$$\xi' = (\xi_1', \xi_2'), \quad A = \begin{pmatrix} A_1 & A_0 \\ 0 & A_2 \end{pmatrix}, \quad B = \begin{pmatrix} B_1 & B_0 \\ 0 & B_2 \end{pmatrix}, \quad \eta = \begin{pmatrix} \eta_1 \\ \eta_2 \end{pmatrix} \quad (11)$$

(2) $M_1 = A_1 + B_1$ and $M_2 = A_2 + B_2$ are irreducible matrices and we denote by λ_1 and λ_2 the corresponding Perron-Frobenius eigenvalues;
(3) $\xi_1 \neq 0 \neq \eta_2$ and matrix $M_0 = A_0 + B_0$ is different from $[0]$.

Note that condition (2) is weaker than a primitivity hypothesis for M_1 and M_2. Condition (3) assures that there is communication from the first to the second component and hence the main term of the probability function of Y_n also depends on the convolution of their behaviours.

Assuming these hypotheses the limit properties of $\{Y_n\}$ first depend on whether $\lambda_1 \neq \lambda_2$ or $\lambda_1 = \lambda_2$. In the first case there is a dominant component, corresponding to the maximum between λ_1 and λ_2, which determines the asymptotic behaviour of $\{Y_n\}$. In the second case the two components are equipotent and they both contribute to the limit behaviour of $\{Y_n\}$. In both cases the corresponding characteristic function has some common properties.

For $j = 1, 2$, let us define $h_n^{(j)}(z)$, $u_j(z)$, $y_j(t)$, β_j, and γ_j, respectively, as the values $h_n(z)$, $u(z)$, $y(t)$, β, γ referred to component j. We also define $H(x, y)$ as the matrix-valued function given by

$$H(x, y) = \sum_{n=0}^{+\infty} (Ax + B)^n y^n = \begin{bmatrix} H^{(1)}(x, y) & G(x, y) \\ 0 & H^{(2)}(x, y) \end{bmatrix}, \quad \text{where}$$

$$H^{(1)}(x, y) = \frac{\mathrm{Adj}\,(I - (A_1 x + B_1)y)}{\mathrm{Det}\,(I - (A_1 x + B_1)y)}, H^{(2)}(x, y) = \frac{\mathrm{Adj}\,(I - (A_2 x + B_2)y)}{\mathrm{Det}\,(I - (A_2 x + B_2)y)}, \quad (12)$$

$$G(x, y) = H^{(1)}(x, y)\,(A_0 x + B_0)y\,H^{(2)}(x, y)\,.$$

Thus, the generating function of $\{h_n(z)\}_n$ satisfies the following identities

$$\sum_{n=0}^{\infty} h_n(z)y^n = \xi' H(e^z, y)\eta = \xi_1' H^{(1)}(e^z, y)\eta_1 + \xi_1' G(e^z, y)\eta_2 + \xi_2' H^{(2)}(e^z, y)\eta_2 \quad (13)$$

Hence, setting $g_n(z) = [y^n]\xi_1' G(e^z, y)\eta_2$, we obtain

$$h_n(z) = h_n^{(1)}(z) + g_n(z) + h_n^{(2)}(z) \quad (14)$$

to be used in the analysis of the characteristic function $\Psi_n(it)$ given by (3).

The dominant case is similar to the primitive one. Assume that $\lambda_1 > \lambda_2$, M_1 is aperiodic (and hence primitive) and $A_1 \neq [0] \neq B_1$. For sake of brevity, we say that $\{Y_n\}$ is defined in a *dominant bicomponent model* with $\lambda_1 > \lambda_2$. In this case we have $0 < \beta_1 < 1$, $0 < \gamma_1$, and it is known that $\frac{Y_n - \beta_1 n}{\sqrt{\gamma_1 n}}$ converges in distribution to a normal r.v. of mean value 0 and variance 1 [7]. Moreover, one can prove the following result:

Theorem 2. *Let $\{Y_n\}$ be defined in a dominant bicomponent model with $\lambda_1 > \lambda_2$ and assume (A_1, B_1) aperiodic. Then, as n tends to $+\infty$, the relation*

$$\left| \sqrt{n} Pr(Y_n = k) - \frac{e^{-\frac{(k - \beta_1 n)^2}{2\gamma_1 n}}}{\sqrt{2\pi\gamma_1}} \right| = O\left(n^{-1/2}\right)$$

holds true uniformly for every $k \in \{0, 1, \ldots, n\}$.

4.1 Equipotent Case

Now, let us assume that $\lambda_1 = \lambda_2 = \lambda$, both matrices M_1 and M_2 are aperiodic (and hence primitive) and $A_j \neq [0] \neq B_j$ for $j = 1, 2$. Under these hypotheses we say that $\{Y_n\}$ is defined in an *equipotent bicomponent model*. In this case the limit distribution of $\{Y_n\}$ depends on the parameters β_1, β_2, γ_1, γ_2, defined as in (7), which now satisfy conditions $0 < \beta_j < 1$ and $0 < \gamma_j$, for both $j = 1, 2$. Before studying the different cases, we recall some properties presented in [7] that are useful in our context.

Observe that both $h_n^{(1)}(z)$ and $h_n^{(2)}(z)$ satisfy relation (6). Moreover, from relations (12) and an analysis of function $\xi_1' G(e^z, y)\eta_2$, for some $c > 0$ it can be shown that

$$g_n(z) = s(z) \sum_{j=0}^{n-1} u_1(z)^j u_2(z)^{n-1-j} + O(\rho^n) \qquad \forall z \in \mathbb{C} : |z| \le c \qquad (15)$$

where $s(z)$ is an analytic and non-null function for $|z| \le c$, and $\rho < \max\{|u_1(z)|, |u_2(z)|\}$. Therefore, by equality (14) we obtain

$$h_n(z) = s(z) \sum_{j=0}^{n-1} u_1(z)^j u_2(z)^{n-1-j} + O(u_1(z)^n) + O(u_2(z)^n) \quad \forall z \in \mathbb{C} : |z| \le c$$

$$(16)$$

This relation has two consequences. First, since $u_1(0) = \lambda = u_2(0)$, it implies

$$h_n(0) = s(0)n\lambda^{n-1}(1 + O(1/n)) \qquad (s(0) \neq 0) \qquad (17)$$

Second, if $u_1(z) \neq u_2(z)$ for some $z \in \mathbb{C}$ satisfying $0 < |z| \le c$, then one gets

$$h_n(z) = s(z)\frac{u_1(z)^n - u_2(z)^n}{u_1(z) - u_2(z)} + O(u_1(z)^n) + O(u_2(z)^n) \qquad (18)$$

Finally, in the equipotent bicomponent models the aperiodicity condition consists of requiring that both pairs (A_1, B_1) and (A_2, B_2) are aperiodic. Under this hypothesis, the following property holds true.

Proposition 3. *Let $\{Y_n\}$ be defined in an equipotent bicomponent model and let both pairs (A_1, B_1) and (A_2, B_2) be aperiodic. Then, for every $c \in (0, \pi)$ there exists $\varepsilon \in (0, 1)$ such that $|\Psi_n(t)| = O(\varepsilon^n)$ for all $t \in \mathbb{R}$ satisfying $c \le |t| \le \pi$.*

4.1.1 Local Limit with Different β's

In this subsection we assume an equipotent bicomponent model with $\beta_1 \neq \beta_2$. In this case it is known that $\{Y_n/n\}$ converges in distribution to a uniform r.v. [7]. Here we state a local limit theorem with a speed of convergence of an order arbitrarily slower than $O(n^{-1/2}(\log n)^{3/2})$, thus improving a recent result presented in [10]. To this end, in view of Proposition 3, we study the characteristic function $\Psi_n(t)$ for $|t| \leq c$, where $c \in (0, \pi)$ is a constant satisfying relation (16). Recall that in such a set both functions $y_1(t) = u_1(it)/\lambda$ and $y_2(t) = u_2(it)/\lambda$ satisfy relations (8), and hence for every real t such that $|t| \leq c$, we have

$$y_1(t) = 1 + i\beta_1 t + O(t^2) , \qquad y_2(t) = 1 + i\beta_2 t + O(t^2) \tag{19}$$

$$|y_1(t)| \leq e^{-\frac{\gamma_1}{4}t^2} , \qquad |y_2(t)| \leq e^{-\frac{\gamma_2}{4}t^2} \tag{20}$$

Moreover, since in the present case (18) holds true for z near 0, using the previous relations, for a suitable $c \in (0, \pi)$ and every $t \in \mathbb{R}$ such that $0 < |t| \leq c$, we obtain

$$\Psi_n(t) = \frac{h_n(it)}{h_n(0)} = \frac{1 + O(t)}{1 + O(1/n)} \left(\frac{y_1(t)^n - y_2(t)^n}{i\,(\beta_1 - \beta_2)\,tn} \right) + \sum_{j=1,2} O\left(\frac{y_j(t)^n}{n} \right) \tag{21}$$

Now, for such a constant c, let us split $[-c, c]$ into sets S_n and V_n, given by

$$S_n = \left\{ t \in \mathbb{R} : |t| \leq \sqrt{\frac{\log n}{n}}\, \tau_n^{1/3} \right\}, \quad V_n = \left\{ t \in \mathbb{R} : \sqrt{\frac{\log n}{n}}\, \tau_n^{1/3} < |t| \leq c \right\} \tag{22}$$

where $\{\tau_n\} \subset \mathbb{R}_+$ is any sequence such that $\tau_n \to +\infty$ and $\tau_n = o(\log \log n)$ (i.e. τ_n tends to $+\infty$ with an arbitrarily slow order of growth). The behaviour of $\Psi_n(t)$ in these sets is given by the following two propositions, where we assume an equipotent bicomponent model with $\beta_1 \neq \beta_2$.

Proposition 4. *For some $a > 0$ one has $|\Psi_n(t)| = o\left(n^{-a\tau_n^{2/3}} \right)$ for all $t \in V_n$.*

In order to evaluate $\Psi_n(t)$ for $t \in S_n$, let us define

$$K_n(t) = \frac{e^{-\frac{\gamma_1}{2}t^2 n + i\beta_1 tn} - e^{-\frac{\gamma_2}{2}t^2 n + i\beta_2 tn}}{i(\beta_1 - \beta_2)tn} \tag{23}$$

and consider relation (21). Since for $t \in S_n$ one has $nO(t^3) = o(1)$, relation (9) applies to both $y_1(t)$ and $y_2(t)$ yielding

$$y_j(t)^n = e^{-\frac{\gamma_j}{2}t^2 n + i\beta_j tn}(1 + nO(t^3)) \qquad \forall\, t \in S_n, \quad j = 1, 2$$

Replacing these values in (21), after some computation one gets

$$\Psi_n(t) = \left[1 + O(t) + nO(t^3) + O(1/n) \right] K_n(t) + O(1/n) \qquad \forall\, t \in S_n \tag{24}$$

Proposition 5. *Defining S_n and $K_n(t)$ as in (22) and (23), we have*

$$\left| \int_{S_n} (\Psi_n(t) - K_n(t)) \, dt \right| = O\left(\left(\frac{\log n}{n} \right)^{3/2} \tau_n \right)$$

Now, we are able to state the local limit in the present case. Set $b_1 = \min\{\beta_1, \beta_2\}$, $b_2 = \max\{\beta_1, \beta_2\}$ and denote by $f_U(x)$ the density function of a uniform r.v. U in the interval $[b_1, b_2]$, that is

$$f_U(x) = \frac{1}{b_2 - b_1} \chi_{[b_1, b_2]}(x) \qquad \forall x \in \mathbb{R}$$

where χ_I denotes the indicator function of the interval $I \subset \mathbb{R}$. Then we have

Theorem 6. *Let $\{Y_n\}_{n \in \mathbb{N}}$ be defined in an equipotent bicomponent model with $\beta_1 \neq \beta_2$ and assume aperiodic both pairs (A_1, B_1) and (A_2, B_2). Then, for n tending to $+\infty$, the r.v. Y_n satisfies the relation*

$$|n \, Pr(Y_n = k) - f_U(x)| = O\left(\frac{(\log n)^{3/2} \tau_n}{\sqrt{n}} \right) \tag{25}$$

for every real sequence $\{\tau_n\}$ satisfying $\tau_n \to +\infty$, $\tau_n = o(\log \log n)$ and for every integer $k = k(n)$, provided that $k/n \to x$ for a constant x such that $\beta_1 \neq x \neq \beta_2$.

As an example, consider the rational stochastic model defined by the weighted finite automaton of Fig. 1, where each transition is labelled by an alphabet symbol and a weight, together with the arrays $\xi = (1, 0, 0, 0)$ and $\eta = (0, 0, 1, 1)$. Such an automaton recognizes the set of all words $w \in \{a, b, c\}^*$ of the form $w = xcy$, such that $x, y \in \{a, b\}^*$ and the strings aa and bb do not occur in x and y, respectively. Clearly this is a bicomponent model, with both pairs (A_1, B_1) and (A_2, B_2) aperiodic. Moreover $M_1 = M_2$, while $A_1 \neq A_2$. Hence the two components are equipotent and $\beta_1 \neq \beta_2$. This means that Y_n/n converges in distribution to a uniform r.v. of extremes β_1, β_2, and Y_n satisfies Theorem 6. Note that simple changes may modifies the limit distribution: for instance, setting to 3 the weight of transition $2 \xrightarrow{b} 1$ makes dominant the first component, implying a Gaussian local limit law (Theorem 2).

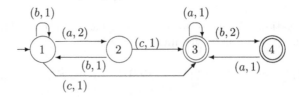

Fig. 1. Weighted finite automaton defining an equipotent bicomponent model ($\lambda_1 = \lambda_2 = 2$) with $1/3 = \beta_1 \neq \beta_2 = 2/3$.

4.1.2   Local Limit with Equal β's and Different γ's

In this section we present a local limit theorem for $\{Y_n\}$ defined in an equipotent bicomponent model with $\beta_1 = \beta_2$ and $\gamma_1 \neq \gamma_2$. In this case, setting $\beta = \beta_1 = \beta_2$ and $\gamma = \frac{\gamma_1 + \gamma_2}{2}$, it is known [7] that $\frac{Y_n - \beta n}{\sqrt{\gamma n}}$ weakly converges to a random variable T whose distribution is a mixture of Gaussian laws of mean 0 and variance uniformly distributed over the interval of extremes $\frac{\gamma_1}{\gamma}$ and $\frac{\gamma_2}{\gamma}$.

Formally, the density function of T is given by

$$f_T(x) = \frac{\gamma}{\gamma_2 - \gamma_1} \int_{\frac{\gamma_1}{\gamma}}^{\frac{\gamma_2}{\gamma}} \frac{e^{-\frac{x^2}{2s}}}{\sqrt{2\pi s}} \, ds \qquad \forall \, x \in \mathbb{R} \tag{26}$$

In passing, we observe that, for each $x \in \mathbb{R}$, $f_T(x)$ may be regarded as the mean value of the "heat kernel" $K(x,t) = (4\pi t)^{-1/2} e^{\frac{-x^2}{4t}}$ at point x in the time interval of extremes $\gamma_1/(2\gamma)$ and $\gamma_2/(2\gamma)$ [6].

Note that $E(T) = 0$ and $\text{Var}(T) = 1$, while its characteristic function is

$$\Phi_T(t) = \int_{-\infty}^{+\infty} f_T(x) e^{itx} dx = 2\gamma \, \frac{e^{-\frac{\gamma_1}{2\gamma}t^2} - e^{-\frac{\gamma_2}{2\gamma}t^2}}{(\gamma_2 - \gamma_1) t^2} \tag{27}$$

Then, $f_T(x)$ can be expressed in the form

$$f_T(x) = \frac{1}{2\pi} \int_{-\infty}^{+\infty} \Phi_T(t) e^{-itx} dt = \frac{1}{2\pi} \int_{-\infty}^{+\infty} 2\gamma \, \frac{e^{-\frac{\gamma_1}{2\gamma}t^2} - e^{-\frac{\gamma_2}{2\gamma}t^2}}{(\gamma_2 - \gamma_1) t^2} e^{-itx} dt$$

Our goal is to present a local limit property for $\{Y_n\}$ (suitably scaled) toward the r.v. T, with a speed of convergence of an order arbitrarily slower than $O\left(\frac{\log^2 n}{\sqrt{n}}\right)$.

Also in this case we assume aperiodic both pairs (A_1, B_1) and (A_2, B_2), which implies Proposition 3. As in the previous section, $c \in (0, \pi)$ is a constant for which relation (16) holds true; as a consequence, both functions $y_1(t)$ and $y_2(t)$ satisfy relations (8), which now can be refined in the following form:

$$y_j(t) = \frac{u_j(it)}{\lambda} = 1 + i\beta t - \frac{\gamma_j + \beta^2}{2} t^2 + O(t^3), \qquad \forall \, x \in \mathbb{R} : |t| \leq c, \, j = 1, 2$$

Applying these values in (18), which is valid also in the present case for z near to 0, and using (17), for some $c \in (0, \pi)$ and every $t \in \mathbb{R}$ such that $0 < |t| \leq c$, we obtain

$$\Psi_n(t) = \frac{h_n(it)}{h_n(0)} = 2 \, \frac{1 + O(t)}{n + O(1)} \, \frac{y_1(t)^n - y_2(t)^n}{(\gamma_2 - \gamma_1) t^2 + O(t^3)} + \sum_{j=1,2} O\left(\frac{y_j(t)^n}{n}\right) \tag{28}$$

Now, for such a constant c, split the interval $[-c, c]$ into sets S_n and V_n given by

$$S_n = \left\{ t \in \mathbb{R} : |t| \leq \sqrt{\frac{\log n}{n}} \, \tau_n^{1/4} \right\}, \quad V_n = \left\{ t \in \mathbb{R} : \sqrt{\frac{\log n}{n}} \, \tau_n^{1/4} < |t| \leq c \right\} \tag{29}$$

where τ_n is defined as in (22). The behaviour of $\Psi_n(t)$ in these sets is described by the propositions below where we assume an equipotent bicomponent model with $\beta_1 = \beta_2 = \beta$ and $\gamma_1 \neq \gamma_2$.

Proposition 7. *For some $a > 0$ we have $|\Psi_n(t)| = o\left(n^{-a\tau_n^{1/2}}\right)$ for every $t \in V_n$.*

For sake of brevity, we define

$$K_n(t) = 2\,\frac{e^{-\frac{\gamma_1}{2}t^2 n} - e^{-\frac{\gamma_2}{2}t^2 n}}{(\gamma_2 - \gamma_1)t^2 n}\,e^{i\beta t n}, \qquad \forall\, t \in \mathbb{R} \tag{30}$$

It is easy to see that $|K_n(t)| \leq 2 \displaystyle\sum_{j=1,2} \left(\frac{1 - e^{-\frac{\gamma_j}{2}t^2 n}}{|\gamma_2 - \gamma_1|t^2 n}\right)$ for every $t \in \mathbb{R}$. A simple study of these expressions shows that both addends take their maximum value at $t = 0$, where they have a removable singularity, and such values are independent of n. As a consequence we can state that $|K_n(t)| \leq \frac{\gamma_1 + \gamma_2}{|\gamma_2 - \gamma_1|}$, for every $n \in \mathbb{N}_+$ and every $t \in S_n$.

Proposition 8. *Defining S_n and $K_n(t)$ by (29) and (30), respectively, we have*

$$\int_{S_n} |\Psi_n(t) - K_n(t)|\, dt = O\left(\frac{(\log n)^2\, \tau_n}{n}\right)$$

Now we can state the local limit theorem in the present case:

Theorem 9. *Let $\{Y_n\}_{n \in \mathbb{N}}$ be defined in an equipotent bicomponent model with $\beta_1 = \beta_2 = \beta$, $\gamma_1 \neq \gamma_2$, assume aperiodic pairs (A_1, B_1) and (A_2, B_2) and set $\gamma = (\gamma_1 + \gamma_2)/2$. Then, for n tending to $+\infty$, Y_n satisfies the relation*

$$\left| \sqrt{\gamma n}\, Pr(Y_n = k) - f_T\left(\frac{k - \beta n}{\sqrt{\gamma n}}\right) \right| = O\left(\frac{(\log n)^2\, \tau_n}{\sqrt{n}}\right) \tag{31}$$

uniformly for $k \in \{0, 1, \ldots, n\}$, where f_T is defined in (26) and $\{\tau_n\} \subset \mathbb{R}_+$ is any sequence such that $\tau_n \to +\infty$ and $\tau_n = o(\log\log n)$.

4.1.3 Local Limit with Equal β's and Equal γ's

In this section we study the local limit properties of $\{Y_n\}$ assuming an equipotent bicomponent model with $\beta_1 = \beta_2 = \beta$ and $\gamma_1 = \gamma_2 = \gamma$. In this case, it is known [7] that $\frac{Y_n - \beta n}{\sqrt{\gamma n}}$ converges in distribution to a Gaussian random variable of mean 0 and variance 1. Here we prove that a Gaussian local limit property holds true with a convergence rate of the order $O(n^{-1/2})$, assuming aperiodic both pairs (A_1, B_1) and (A_2, B_2).

Again we assume $c \in (0, \pi)$ is a constant for which equality (16) holds true, so that both functions $y_1(t)$ and $y_2(t)$ satisfy relations (8) and (9), which we now restate in the following form for sake of clearness:

$$|y_j(t)| \leq e^{-\frac{7}{4}t^2} \qquad \forall\, t \in \mathbb{R}\, :\, |t| \leq c, \qquad j = 1, 2 \tag{32}$$

$$y_j(t)^n = e^{-\frac{7}{2}t^2 n + i\beta t n}(1 + nO(t^3)) \qquad \forall\, t \in \mathbb{R}\, :\, |t| \leq n^{-q}, \qquad j = 1, 2 \tag{33}$$

where q is an arbitrary value such that $1/3 < q < 1/2$.

The following propositions yield properties of the characteristic function $\Psi_n(t)$ respectively for $|t| \leq n^{-q}$ and $n^{-q} < |t| \leq c$.

Proposition 10. *For every $q \in (1/3, 1/2)$, we have*

$$|\Psi_n(t)| = O\left(e^{-\frac{7}{4}n^{1-2q}}\right) \qquad \forall\, t \in \mathbb{R} \;:\; n^{-q} < |t| \leq c$$

Proposition 11. *For every $q \in (1/3, 1/2)$, we have*

$$\int_{|t|\leq n^{-q}} \left| \Psi_n(t) - e^{-\frac{7}{2}t^2 n + i\beta t n} \right| dt \;=\; O(n^{-1})$$

Then, our last result follows:

Theorem 12. *Let $\{Y_n\}_{n\in\mathbb{N}}$ be defined in an equipotent bicomponent model with $\beta_1 = \beta_2 = \beta$ and $\gamma_1 = \gamma_2 = \gamma$, and assume aperiodic both pairs (A_1, B_1) and (A_2, B_2). Then, for n tending to $+\infty$ the relation*

$$\left| \sqrt{n} Pr(Y_n = k) - \frac{e^{-\frac{(k-\beta n)^2}{2\gamma n}}}{\sqrt{2\pi\gamma}} \right| \;=\; O\left(n^{-1/2}\right)$$

holds true uniformly for every $k \in \{0, 1, \ldots, n\}$.

5 Conclusions

The analysis of the symbol statistics Y_n's presented in this work concerns the cases when the rational stochastic model consists of one or two primitive components. Our results are summarized in Table 1, which refers to the previous literature for already known properties.

Table 1. Symbols $N_{0,1}$, U_{β_1,β_2} and T denote respectively a Gaussian, uniform and T-type local limit, T being defined in Sect. 4.1.2. Also, τ_n is defined in Theorem 6

	Primitive models	Bicomponent models			
		Dominant	Equipotent		
			$\beta_1 \neq \beta_2$	$\beta_1 = \beta_2$ $\gamma_1 \neq \gamma_2$	$\beta_1 = \beta_2$ $\gamma_1 = \gamma_2$
Local limit distribution	$N_{0,1}$ (see [3])	$N_{0,1}$	U_{β_1,β_2} (see [10])	T	$N_{0,1}$
Convergence rate	$O(n^{-1/2})$	$O(n^{-1/2})$	$O\left(\frac{\tau_n \log^{3/2} n}{\sqrt{n}}\right)$	$O\left(\frac{\tau_n \log^2 n}{\sqrt{n}}\right)$	$O(n^{-1/2})$

Natural extensions of these results concern rational models with more than two primitive components having equal dominant eigenvalue and, possibly, the evaluation of neglected terms in the asymptotic expressions. Also in the case of bicomponent models our analysis is not complete as it does not include the non-communicating cases ($M_0 = [0]$) nor the degenerate cases (when, for a dominant component $i \in \{1, 2\}$, either $A_i = 0$ or $B_i = 0$). In these cases rather different limit distributions are obtained [7, Sect. 8], due to the diverse type of generating functions appearing therein. Even if these situations are somehow particular, they are representative of typical regular languages, and hence they seem to be natural subjects for future investigations.

References

1. Bender, E.A.: Central and local limit theorems applied to asymptotic enumeration. J. Comb. Theory **15**, 91–111 (1973)
2. Berstel, J., Reutenauer, C.: Rational Series and Their Languages. Springer, Heidelberg (1988)
3. Bertoni, A., Choffrut, C., Goldwurm, M., Lonati, V.: On the number of occurrences of a symbol in words of regular languages. Theoret. Comput. Sci. **302**, 431–456 (2003)
4. Bertoni, A., Choffrut, C., Goldwurm, M., Lonati, V.: Local limit properties for pattern statistics and rational models. Theory Comput. Syst. **39**, 209–235 (2006)
5. Broda, S., Machiavelo, A., Moreira, N., Reis, R.: A hitchhiker's guide to descriptional complexity through analytic combinatorics. Theoret. Comput. Sci. **528**, 85–100 (2014)
6. Cannon, J.R.: The One-Dimensional Heat Equation. Encyclopedia of Mathematics and its Applications, vol. 23. Addison-Wesley Publishing Company, Boston (1984)
7. de Falco, D., Goldwurm, M., Lonati, V.: Frequency of symbol occurrences in bicomponent stochastic models. Theoret. Comput. Sci. **327**(3), 269–300 (2004)
8. Flajolet, P., Sedgewick, R.: Analytic Combinatorics. Cambridge University Press, Cambridge (2009)
9. Gnedenko, B.V.: Theory of Probability. Gordon and Breach Science Publishers, Amsterdam (1997)
10. Goldwurm, M., Lin, J., Vignati, M.: A local limit property for pattern statistics in bicomponent stochastic models. In: Konstantinidis, S., Pighizzini, G. (eds.) DCFS 2018. LNCS, vol. 10952, pp. 114–125. Springer, Cham (2018). https://doi.org/10.1007/978-3-319-94631-3_10
11. Grabner, P., Rigo, M.: Distribution of additive functions with respect to numeration systems on regular languages. Theory Comput. Syst. **40**, 205–223 (2007)
12. Hwang, H.-K.: On convergence rates in the central limit theorem for combinatorial structures. Europ. J. Comb. **19**, 329–343 (1998)
13. Nicodeme, P., Salvy, B., Flajolet, P.: Motif statistics. Theoret. Comput. Sci. **287**(2), 593–617 (2002)
14. Régnier, M., Szpankowski, W.: On pattern frequency occurrences in a Markovian sequence. Algorithmica **22**(4), 621–649 (1998)
15. Salomaa, A., Soittola, M.: Automata-Theoretic Aspects of Formal Power Series. Springer, New York (1978). https://doi.org/10.1007/978-1-4612-6264-0
16. Seneta, E.: Non-negative Matrices and Markov Chains. Springer, New York (1981). https://doi.org/10.1007/0-387-32792-4

Author Index

Printed in the United States
By Bookmasters